The EU Crowdfunding Regulation

OXFORD EU FINANCIAL REGULATION SERIES

The Oxford EU Financial Regulation Series provides rigorous analysis of all aspects of EU Financial Regulation and covers the regulation of banks, capital markets, insurance undertakings, asset managers, payment institutions, and financial infrastructures. The aim of the series is to provide high-quality dissection of and comment on EU Regulations and Directives, and the EU financial regulation framework as a whole. Titles in the series consider the elements of both theory and practice necessary for proper understanding, analysing the legal framework in the context of its practical, political, and economic background, and offering a sound basis for interpretation.

Series Editors:
DANNY BUSCH

Professor of Financial Law and founding Director of the Institute for Financial Law,
Radboud University Nijmegen;
Research Fellow of Harris Manchester College and Fellow of the Commercial Law Centre,
University of Oxford;
Visiting Professor at Università Cattolica del Sacro Cuore di Milano;
Visiting Professor at Università degli Studi di Genova;
Visiting Professor at Université de Nice Côte d'Azur;
Member of the Dutch Banking Disciplinary Committee (Tuchtcommissie Banken);
Member of the Appeal Committee of the Dutch Complaint Institute Financial Services
(Klachteninstituut Financiële Dienstverlening or KiFiD).

GUIDO FERRARINI

Emeritus Professor of Business Law, University of Genoa;
Visiting Professor, Radboud University Nijmegen;
Founder and fellow of the European Corporate Governance Institute (ECGI), Brussels;
Former member of the Board of Trustees, International Accounting
Standards Committee (IASC), London.

Previous volumes published in the series:
Prospectus Regulation and Prospectus Liability, Edited by Danny Busch, Guido Ferrarini,
and Jan Paul Franx, March 2020, 9780198846529
European Banking Union, Second Edition, Edited by
Danny Busch and Guido Ferrarini, March 2020, 9780198827511
Governance of Financial Institutions, Edited by
Danny Busch, Guido Ferrarini, and Gerard van Solinge, January 2019, 9780198799979
Capital Markets Union, Edited by Danny Busch, Emilios Avgouleas,
and Guido Ferrarini, March 2018, 9780198813392
Regulation of the EU Financial Markets—MiFID II and MiFIR, Edited by
Danny Busch and Guido Ferrarini, January 2017, 9780198767671
European Banking Union, First Edition, Edited by Danny Busch and
Guido Ferrarini, July 2015, 9780198727309
Alternative Investment Funds in Europe—Law and Practice, Edited by
Lodewijk van Setten and Danny Busch, May 2014, 9780199657728

The EU Crowdfunding Regulation

Edited by

PIETRO ORTOLANI

AND

MARIJE LOUISSE

OXFORD

UNIVERSITY PRESS

OXFORD
UNIVERSITY PRESS

Great Clarendon Street, Oxford, OX2 6DP,
United Kingdom

Oxford University Press is a department of the University of Oxford.
It furthers the University's objective of excellence in research, scholarship,
and education by publishing worldwide. Oxford is a registered trade mark of
Oxford University Press in the UK and in certain other countries

First Edition published in 2021

Impression: 1

Published in the United States of America by Oxford University Press
198 Madison Avenue, New York, NY 10016, United States of America

British Library Cataloguing in Publication Data
Data available

Library of Congress Control Number: 2021946722

ISBN 978–0–19–285639–5

DOI: 10.1093/law/9780192856395.001.0001

Printed and bound by
CPI Group (UK) Ltd, Croydon, CR0 4YY

Series Editors' Preface

Crowdfunding platforms act as intermediaries between investors and businesses, making it easier for investors to identify projects they want to invest in. In the EU Crowdfunding Regulation, crowdfunding platforms are referred to as 'crowdfunding service providers'.

Generally speaking, investing through crowdfunding can be done in two ways: by granting loans (loan-based crowdfunding) or by participating in the capital of a business (equity-based crowdfunding). Crowdfunding seems to be an interesting additional or even alternative source of financing for SMEs, especially start-ups. European SMEs are still far too dependent on bank loans, and it would therefore be a good thing if they could gain easier access to the capital markets. But whether that is feasible remains to be seen. Crowdfunding will sometimes provide easier access and thus perhaps be a more realistic option than recourse to the traditional capital markets. In any event, it is becoming an increasingly important source of funding for start-ups. The EU Crowdfunding Regulation is intended to make it easier for crowdfunding platforms to operate throughout the EU and applies from 10 November 2021.

It was originally intended that the European Securities and Markets Authority (ESMA) should become the authorizing authority and should also directly supervise the crowdfunding service provider. Moreover, the initial Commission proposal provided for the crowdfunding service provider to have the choice between applying the national crowdfunding rules (if any) and the application of the European regime. In the former case, the crowdfunding service provider had nothing to do with European rules and the authorization and supervision was at most the responsibility of a local supervisor, in any event not of ESMA. The disadvantage of this option was that the service provider was then only allowed to operate within its own national borders. If the service provider opted for the European regime, the authorization granted by ESMA would enable it to operate throughout the EU/EEA.

The final text reads differently. Once a party comes within the scope of the EU Crowdfunding Regulation, that regime applies. The scope for a provider to operate within its own country's borders on the basis of local rules (if any) has therefore been dropped. Moreover, responsibility for authorization and supervision was given not to ESMA but simply to the competent national supervisors. Once a party has been granted authorization, it can operate throughout the EU/EEA. The local authorization therefore functions as a European passport. Crowdfunding services should be provided only by legal persons established in the Union. The question of whether it would be desirable to allow entities established in third countries to obtain authorization as a crowdfunding service provider under the EU Crowdfunding Regulation will be taken into account in a future evaluation report.

The competent supervisor will be able to grant the authorization only if various requirements are met. A crowdfunding service provider must meet certain prudential requirements, its management must be assessed for suitability and reputation and it must have established, for example, a procedure for handling customer complaints. Naturally, these requirements also apply on a continuous basis. What also apply on a continuous basis are conduct-of-business rules, i.e. rules that prescribe how the service provider must treat its customers. First, the service provider must always act honestly, fairly, and professionally in the best interests of the client. This general obligation of loyalty is partly defined in more detail in specific conduct-of-business rules. These include rules about the provision of information so that clients and prospects can make an informed and balanced decision on the basis of the information provided about granting a loan or investing in securities through the crowdfunding service provider. The service provider must also comply with know-your-client rules in relation to non-experienced investors. It must therefore not only *provide* information but also *gather* it.

These authorization requirements and conduct-of-business rules thus resemble but are certainly not identical to the rules that providers of investment services (such as portfolio management, advice, and execution-only services) must comply with under the MiFID II rules. Quite apart from all kinds of other differences, there is a periodic obligation under the EU Crowdfunding Regulation in relation to inexperienced investors to simulate the potential losses in order to give them a better understanding of the investment risks they run, and there is a statutory reflection period of four days.

This edited volume provides an in-depth and timely analysis and discussion of various aspects of the EU Crowdfunding Regulation, also in relation to private law aspects and Brexit.

The Series Editors are pleased to include the work in the Oxford EU Financial Regulation Series.

Danny Busch
Nijmegen, the Netherlands
Guido Ferrarini
Genoa, Italy

Summary Contents

Contents

PART I SKETCHING A LEGAL TAXONOMY OF CROWDFUNDING

PART III   REGULATING THE CROWDFUNDING SERVICE PROVIDERS UNDER THE CROWDFUNDING REGULATION

7. Authorization and Supervision of Crowdfunding Service Providers
Marije Louisse and Adam Pasaribu

8. Organizational and Operational Requirements for
    Crowdfunding Service Providers
    Kitty Lieverse and Wendy Pronk

PART IV THE POSITION OF PROJECT OWNERS UNDER THE
CROWDFUNDING REGULATION AND BEYOND

9. The Regulatory Position and Obligations of Project Owners
    Jonneke van Poelgeest and Marije Louisse

PART V PROTECTING THE CROWD UNDER THE
CROWDFUNDING REGULATION AND BEYOND

PART VI MANAGING, PREVENTING, AND RESOLVING
CROWDFUNDING-RELATED DISPUTES

List of Contributors

Margarita Amaxopoulou is Visiting Lecturer and PhD in Law Candidate, Kings College London, London, UK.

Tomas Arons is Professor of Financial Law and Collective Redress at Utrecht University and Legal Counsel at VEB, The Hague, the Netherlands.

Raffaele Battaglini is Founding Partner, Futura Law Firm, Turin, Italy.

Christopher A Cotropia is Dennis I. Belcher Professor of Law & Director, Intellectual Property Institute, University of Richmond School of Law, Richmond, VA, USA.

Davide Davico is General Counsel, Ersel, Turin, Italy.

Mateja Durovic is Reader in Law and Co-Director of the Centre for Technology, Ethics, Law and Society, Kings College London, London, UK.

Martin Ebers is Associate Professor of IT Law at University of Tartu, Tartu, Estonia, and President of RAILS (Robotics & AI Law Society), Berlin, Germany.

Sam Gaunt is a Fundraiser at the European Legal Support Center, Amsterdam, the Netherlands.

Catalina Goanta is Assistant Professor in Private Law, Maastricht University, Maastricht, the Netherlands.

Anne Hakvoort is a Lawyer and Partner at FG Lawyers, Amsterdam, the Netherlands, and Fellow at the International Center for Financial law & Governance, affiliated to the Erasmus School of Law of the Erasmus University Rotterdam, Rotterdam, the Netherlands.

Petja Ivanova is Assistant, University of Zurich, Zurich, Switzerland.

Joseph Lee is Reader in Law, University of Manchester, Manchester, UK.

Kitty Lieverse is member of the Banking & Finance practice group at Loyens & Loeff, Amsterdam, the Netherlands; Professor of Financial Supervision Law at Radboud University, Nijmegen, the Netherlands.

Andrea Longo is a Doctoral Candidate at the University of Milan Bicocca, Milan, Italy.

Marije Louisse is Senior Legal Counsel at De Nederlandsche Bank NV, Amsterdam, the Netherlands; Fellow at the Financial Law Centre of the Radboud University, Nijmegen, the Netherlands; and member of the Associate Researchers Group of the European Banking Institute, Frankfurt, Germany.

Eugenia Macchiavello is Lecturer in Banking Law, University of Genoa, Genoa, Italy.

Gerard McMeel QC is professor of Commercial and Financial Law, University of Reading, London, UK.

Pietro Ortolani is Professor of Digital Conflict Resolution, Radboud University, Nijmegen, the Netherlands.

Adam Pasaribu is a Senior Legal Counsel at De Nederlandsche Bank NV, Amsterdam, the Netherlands, and Fellow at the International Center for Financial law & Governance of the Erasmus University Rotterdam, Rotterdam, the Netherlands.

Jonneke van Poelgeest is a Lawyer at Trivvy, Amsterdam, the Netherlands.

Wendy Pronk is a member of the Banking & Finance practice group at Loyens & Loeff, Amsterdam, the Netherlands.

Benedikt M Quarch is a Co-founder and Managing Director of the RightNow Group, an international LegalTech company based in Düsseldorf and Berlin, and graduated with a PhD in the European Regulation of Crowdlending in 2019 from EBS Law School, Wiesbaden, Germany.

List of Abbreviations and Terms

All references to legal acts are to the most recent—amended—version, where applicable.

ADR	Alternative Dispute Resolution
AIF	Alternative Investment Fund
AIFMD	Alternative Investment Fund Managers Directive (Directive 2011/61/EU of the European Parliament and of the Council of 8 June 2011 on Alternative Investment Fund Managers)
ALF	Alternative Litigation Financing
AML	Anti-Money Laundering
AON	All-Or-Nothing
B2B	Business-to-Business
B2C	Business-to-Consumer
BA	Business Angel
CCD	Consumer Credit Directive (Directive 2008/48/EC of the European Parliament and of the Council of 23 April 2008 on credit agreements for consumers)
CESR	Committee of European Securities Regulators
CGFS	Committee on the Global Financial System
CMU	Capital Markets Union
COBS	Investment Conduct of Business Sourcebook (UK)
Collective Redress Directive	Directive (EU) 2020/1828 of the European Parliament and of the Council of 25 November 2020 on representative actions for the protection of the collective interests of consumers
Commission	European Commission
Commission Proposal	Proposal for a European Commission Crowdfunding Regulation, COM(2018)113
CRD IV	Capital Requirements Directive IV (Directive 2013/36/EU of the European Parliament and of the Council of 26 June 2013 on access to the activity of credit institutions and the prudential supervision of credit institutions and investment firms)
CRD V	Capital Requirements Directive V (Directive (EU) 2019/878 of the European Parliament and of the Council of 20 May 2019 amending Directive 2013/36/EU as regards exempted entities, financial holding companies, mixed financial holding companies, remuneration, supervisory measures and powers, and capital conservation measures)
Crowdfunding Directive	Directive (EU) 2020/1504 of the European Parliament and of the Council of 7 October 2020
Crowdfunding Investments	Transferable securities and admitted instruments for crowdfunding purposes as defined in points (m) and (n) of Article 2(1) of the Crowdfunding Regulation
Crowdfunding Regulation	Regulation (EU) 2020/1503 of the European Parliament and of the Council of 7 October 2020 on European crowdfunding service providers for business

CRR	Capital Requirements Regulation (Regulation (EU) No 575/2013 of the European Parliament and of the Council of 26 June 2013 on prudential requirements for credit institutions and investment firms)
CRR II	Capital Requirements Regulation II (Regulation (EU) 2019/876 of the European Parliament and of the Council of 20 May 2019 amending Regulation (EU) No 575/2013 as regards the leverage ratio, the net stable funding ratio, requirements for own funds and eligible liabilities, counterparty credit risk, market risk, exposures to central counterparties, exposures to collective investment undertakings, large exposures, reporting and disclosure requirements, and Regulation (EU) No 648/2012)
CSP	Crowdfunding Service Provider
CSRD Proposal	Proposal for a Corporate Sustainability Reporting Directive, COM/2021/189 final
CFT	Combatting the Financing of Terrorism
DFP	Digital Finance Package
Distance Marketing Directive	Directive 2002/65/EC of the European Parliament and of the Council of 23 September 2002 concerning the distance marketing of consumer financial services
DLT	Distributed Ledger Technology
DMA Proposal	Proposal for a Regulation on contestable and fair markets in the digital sector (Digital Markets Act), COM/2020/842 final
DORA Proposal	Proposal for a Regulation on digital operational resilience for the financial sector and amending Regulations (EC) No 1060/2009, (EU) No 648/2012, (EU) No 600/2014 and (EU) No 909/2014, COM/2020/595 final
DSA Proposal	Proposal for a Regulation on a Single Market for Digital Services (Digital Services Act) and amending Directive 2000/31/EC, COM/2020/825 final
EBA	European Banking Authority
ECB	European Central Bank
ECI	European Citizens' Initiative
ECJ	European Court of Justice
ECON	Committee on Economic and Monetary Affairs
ECSP	European Crowdfunding Service Provider
EEA	European Economic Area
EEA Agreement	Agreement on the European Economic Area (OJ No L 1, 3.1.1994, p. 3)
EIOPA	European Insurance and Occupational Pensions Authority
ELI	European Law Institute
ELTIF	European Long-Term Investments Funds
ELTIF Regulation	European Long-Term Investment Funds Regulation (Regulation (EU) 2015/760 of the European Parliament and of the Council of 29 April 2015 on European long-term investment funds)
EMI Directive	Electronic Money Institutions Directive (Directive 2009/110/EC of the European Parliament and of the Council of 16 September 2009 on the taking up, pursuit and prudential supervision of the business of electronic money institutions)

EMT	E-Money Token
ESA	European Supervisory Authority
ESAP	European Single Access Point
ESMA	European Securities and Markets Authority
ESMA Regulation	Regulation (EU) No 1095/2010 of the European Parliament and of the Council of 24 November 2010 establishing a European Supervisory Authority (European Securities and Markets Authority)
ETO	Equity Token Offering
EU or Union	European Union
EuSEF Regulation	European Social Entrepreneurship Funds Regulation (Regulation (EU) No 346/2013 of the European Parliament and of the Council of 17 April 2013 on European social entrepreneurship funds)
EuVECA	European Venture Capital Funds Regulation (Regulation (EU) No 345/2013 of the European Parliament and of the Council of 17 April 2013 on European venture capital funds)
FinTech	Financial Technology
Fourth AML Directive	Fourth Anti-Money Laundering Directive (Directive (EU) 2015/849 of the European Parliament and of the Council of 20 May 2015 on the prevention of the use of the financial system for the purposes of money laundering or terrorist financing)
FSB	Financial Stability Board
FSDS Directive	Financial Services Distance Selling Directive (Directive 2002/65/EC of the European Parliament and of the Council of 23 September 2002 concerning the distance marketing of consumer financial services)
GC	General Court or, where relevant, its predecessor, the Court of First Instance
HLFCMU	High Level Forum on the Capital Markets Union
HNWI	High Net Worth Individual
IBC	Investment-Based Crowdfunding
ICCO	Initial Convertible Coin Offering
ICO	Initial Coin Offering
ICS Directive	Investor-Compensation Schemes Directive (Directive 97/9/EC of the European Parliament and of the Council of 3 March 1997 on investor-compensation schemes)
IEO	Initial Exchange Offering
IFD or Investment Firm Directive	Directive (EU) 2019/2034 of the European Parliament and of the Council of 27 November 2019 on the prudential supervision of investment firms
IFR or Investment Firm Regulation	Regulation (EU) 2019/2033 of the European Parliament and of the Council of 27 November 2019 on the prudential requirements of investment firms
ILO	Initial Liquidity Offerings
Impact Assessment	European Commission Staff Working Document, 'Impact Assessment Accompanying the document Proposal for a Regulation of the European Parliament and of the Council on European Crowdfunding Service Providers (ECSP) for Business

	and Proposal for a Directive of the European Parliament and of the Council amending Directive 2014/65/EU on markets in financial instruments', SWD(2018) 56 final—2018/048 (COD), 18
IP	Intellectual Property
IPO	Initial Public Offering
ITO	Initial Token Offering
ITS	Implementing Technical Standards
ITU	Intent-To-Use
KIA	Keep-It-All
KID	Key Information Document
KIIS	Key Investment Information Sheet
KYC	Know Your Customer
LBC	Lending-Based Crowdfunding
LP	Liquidity Provider
MCD	Mortgage Credit Directive (Directive 2014/17/EU of the European Parliament and of the Council of 4 February 2014 on credit agreements for consumers relating to residential immovable property)
Member State	A member state of the European Union or, where applicable, a participating state in the European Economic Area
MiCA Regulation Proposal or MiCA Proposal	Proposal for a Regulation on Markets in Crypto-assets, and amending Directive (EU) 2019/1937, COM/2020/593 final
MiFID I	Markets in Financial Instruments Directive I (Directive 2004/39/EC of the European Parliament and of the Council of 21 April 2004 on markets in financial instruments)
MiFID II	Markets in Financial Instruments Directive II (Directive 2014/65/EU of the European Parliament and of the Council of 15 May 2014 on markets in financial instruments)
MiFID II Delegated Regulation	Commission Delegated Regulation (EU) 2017/565 of 25 April 2016 supplementing Directive 2014/65/EU of the European Parliament and of the Council as regards organizational requirements and operating conditions for investment firms and defined terms for the purposes of that Directive
MiFIR	Markets in Financial Instruments Regulation (Regulation (EU) No 600/2014 of the European Parliament and of the Council of 15 May 2014 on markets in financial instruments)
MSC	Member State Court
MTF	Multilateral Trading Facility
NFRD	Non-Financial Reporting Directive (Directive 2014/95/EU of the European Parliament and of the Council of 22 October 2014 amending Directive 2013/34/EU as regards disclosure of non-financial and diversity information by certain large undertakings and groups)
NGO	Non-Governmental Organization
OTC	Over The Counter
OTF	Organized Trading Facility

P2B Regulation	Platform-to-Business Regulation (Regulation (EU) 2019/1150 of the European Parliament and of the Council of 20 June 2019 on promoting fairness and transparency for business users of online intermediation services)
P2P	Peer-to-Peer
PE	Private Equity
PEPP Regulation	Pan-European Personal Pension Product Regulation (Regulation (EU) 2019/1238 of the European Parliament and of the Council of 20 June 2019 on a pan-European Personal Pension Product)
PRIIPs Regulation	Packaged Retail and Insurance-based Investment Products Regulation (Regulation (EU) No 1286/2014 of the European Parliament and of the Council of 26 November 2014 on key information documents for packaged retail and insurance-based investment products)
Prospectus Regulation	Regulation (EU) 2017/1129 of the European Parliament and of the Council of 14 June 2017 on the prospectus to be published when securities are offered to the public or admitted to trading on a regulated market
PSD 2	Payment Services Directive 2 (Directive (EU) 2015/2366 of the European Parliament and of the Council of 25 November 2015 on payment services in the internal market)
RBC	Reward-Based Crowdfunding
RTS	Regulatory Technical Standards
SLAPP	Strategic Lawsuits Against Public Participation
SME	Small- and Medium-sized Enterprise
SPV	Special Purpose Vehicle
STO	Security Token Offering
TEU	Treaty on European Union
TFEU	Treaty on the Functioning of the European Union
TPLF	Third-Party Litigation Funding
UCITS Directive	Undertaking for the Collective Investment in Transferable Securities Directive (Directive 2009/65/EC of the European Parliament and of the Council of 13 July 2009 on the coordination of laws, regulations, and administrative provisions relating to undertakings for collective investment in transferable securities)
UCPD	Unfair Commercial Practices Directive (Directive 2005/29/EC of the European Parliament and of the Council of 11 May 2005 concerning unfair business-to-consumer commercial practices in the internal market)
UCTD	Unfair Contract Terms Directive (Council Directive 93/13/EEC of 5 April 1993 on unfair terms in consumer contracts)
UK	United Kingdom
US	United States
UTO	Utility Token Offering
VC	Venture Capital
Whistle-blower Directive	Directive (EU) 2019/1937 of the European Parliament and of the Council of 23 October 2019 on the protection of persons who report breaches of Union law

PART I
SKETCHING A LEGAL TAXONOMY OF CROWDFUNDING

1

Introduction: Keep Calm and Continue Crowdfunding

Pietro Ortolani and Marije Louisse

I. The Road to an EU Crowdfunding Regulation

With the adoption of Regulation 2020/1503 (hereinafter, the 'Crowdfunding Regulation'), **1.01** the European Union (EU) aims at levelling the playing field for crowdfunding services, providing legal certainty, and facilitating access to capital for companies (especially in the start-up phase). The main goal of this book is to provide the reader with an in-depth analysis of this new instrument, answering the main legal questions that the Crowdfunding

Regulation raises, and assessing its impact on legal practice. This introduction will set the scene, presenting the contents of the book and placing them into context.

1.02   The remainder of this section will briefly describe the rise of crowdfunding, sketching a taxonomy of the phenomenon, and elaborating on its different varieties. Section II, then, will offer a succinct comparative overview of the national regimes existing before the entry into force of the Crowdfunding Regulation. The four legal systems discussed in this section (Germany, the Netherlands, Italy, and France) have been chosen because of the existence of a specific crowdfunding regime, and because of their relevance as a source of 'regulatory inspiration' for the Crowdfunding Regulation. Law in the United Kingdom (UK), instead, will be discussed separately in Chapters 3 and 4. Against this background, section III will briefly outline the process leading to the adoption of the Crowdfunding Regulation. Finally, section IV will provide an overview of the book, describing the contents of each chapter, and their relevance in relation to the Crowdfunding Regulation.

II. The Rise of Crowdfunding

1.03   Over the past ten years, technology has reshaped economic relationships on a global scale. One of the most notable developments in this respect is the rise of crowdfunding, which increasingly allows a wide range of ventures to receive funding through a variety of Internet-based financing channels rather than through the traditional vehicles of corporate finance.[1] Digital globalization has enabled a vast crowd of non-professional investors (alongside professional ones) to contribute capital to various entities. In the wake of the restrictive lending policies following the 2007–2008 financial crisis, the possibility to receive financing has attracted numerous small and medium-sized enterprises (SMEs). For start-up companies, crowdfunding has established itself as a particularly attractive financing technique, allowing young entrepreneurs to raise capital without—solely—relying on private equity investors (such as venture capitalists or business angels) and without borrowing from their social circle. From this point of view, crowdfunding can certainly have positive social effects, enhancing entrepreneur diversity.

1.04   Recipients of crowdfunding include not only SMEs and start-up companies, but also individuals and charities. In just a few years, crowdfunding has demonstrated its enormous potential, enabling peer-to-peer financing and facilitating access to capital for projects that would otherwise not be able to obtain the funds they need.[2] The available statistical evidence confirms the crucial relevance of the phenomenon: as of December 2019, the volume of crowdfunding has reached USD17.2 billion in the United States (US) alone.[3] The crowdfunding transaction value in Europe (excluding the United Kingdom) was a little over USD1 billion in 2018, and has been growing since then.[4]

---

[1] A Parhankangas, C Mason, and H Landström, 'Crowdfunding: An Introduction' in H Landström, A Parhankangas, and C Mason (eds), *Handbook of Research on Crowdfunding* (Elgar 2019) 1.

[2] A Schwartz, 'Inclusive Crowdfunding' (2016) 4 Utah Law Review 661.

[3] <https://www.statista.com/topics/1283/crowdfunding/> accessed 4 May 2021.

[4] <https://www.statista.com/statistics/412487/europe-alternative-finance-transactions-crowdfunding/> accessed 4 May 2021.

From a legal point of view, crowdfunding constitutes a Pandora's box of under-explored prob-   **1.05**
lems but also a challenging opportunity for legal modernization. It is first of all necessary to
characterize the phenomenon in legal terms, identifying the fields of law which are relevant for
those involved in crowdfunding, and the extent to which the rules can be applied to this form
of non-traditional financing. Against this background, new normative questions can be formulated: what regulatory approaches exist, and how should national and international authorities
choose among them?

These questions have recently come to the fore in the EU, leading to the adoption of the   **1.06**
Crowdfunding Regulation. With the Regulation, the EU attempts to provide a solution, striking
a balance between the enhancement of access to capital for project owners, and the protection
of the crowd of non-professional investors. Before delving into the details of this new instrument, however, it is useful to distinguish among different varieties of crowdfunding, understanding the different purposes that crowdfunding can serve.

III. Varieties of Crowdfunding

Different forms of peer-to-peer and peer-to-business financing tend to be conflated under the   **1.07**
'crowdfunding' label. The legal framework applicable to the phenomenon, however, may vary
significantly, depending on the type of venture that is being funded, and the rights acquired by
those who make a financial contribution.[5] In this respect, it is possible to draw a useful, basic
distinction among four different 'families' of crowdfunding:[6]

- In **investment-based crowdfunding**, the funders acquire a certain form of control or
  ownership over the entity they fund[7] or they acquire debt instruments, such as notes, issued by this entity.[8]
- In **loan-based crowdfunding**, the funding mechanism resembles a loan, and the funders
  expect repayment with a certain interest rate, at a later stage in time.
- In **reward-based crowdfunding**, the crowd provides funds in exchange for a 'reward' to be
  received in the future. By way of example, an entrepreneur may advertise a product that is
  currently at the prototype stage, not yet available on the retail market. As a reward for their
  financial commitment, the funders will receive the product, once the entrepreneur completes its development.[9]
- In **charity crowdfunding**, the funders donate money, without expecting any reward,
  but often on the basis of the expectation that the funded entity will use the money to

---

[5] SN Demper and ML Louisse, *Crowdfunding: Een Juridische Verkenning* (Ars Aequi 2019).
[6] D Cumming and S Johan, *Crowdfunding: Fundamental Cases, Facts, and Insights* (Elsevier 2020) 3.
[7] D Ibrahim, 'Equity Crowdfunding: A Market for Lemons?' (2015–2016) 100 Minnesota Law Review 561.
[8] As investment-based models have advanced, more diversified applications have emerged, such as real estate
and property-based crowdfunding, with investors able to acquire ownership of a property asset via the purchase
of property shares: R Shneor, 'Crowdfunding Models, Strategies, and Choices Between Them' in K Wenzlaff and
others (eds), *Crowdfunding in Europe: Between Fragmentation and Harmonization* (Springer 2020) 26.
[9] J Biemans, 'Reward-Based Crowdfunding and EU Consumer Rights' (2020) 28(1) European Review of Private
Law 51.

undertake specific charitable and/or public interest-driven activities, such as public interest litigation.[10]

1.08   These different families of crowdfunding typically correspond to different reasons for action on the part of the funders. The crowd of funders is not necessarily motivated by the prospect of an economic payoff: in some cases, those who contribute to the crowdfunding wish to participate in certain social or political processes, or to act as patrons for certain causes.[11] From this point of view, the recent COVID-19 pandemic is emblematic: many SMEs resorted to crowdfunding as a way to maintain liquidity and weather the hardship that the virus outbreak brought about, for example in the form of forced closures or limited working capacities. The numerous 'support your locals' campaigns currently being conducted in both Europe and the United States are best understood as a form of consumer patronage and social participation.[12]

1.09   The aforementioned variety of incentives and reasons for action is important from a legal perspective because many branches of law presuppose a certain homogeneity of expectation on the parts of those who make a financial contribution: securities law, for instance, normally proceeds on the assumption that those who purchase securities expect some form of economic return or benefit. Crowdfunding, however, casts doubt on this type of assumption, and forces lawyers to problematize the applicability of different bodies of law, depending on the nature and characteristics that crowdfunding can have.[13] In light of this, an in-depth analysis of the new Crowdfunding Regulation is interesting not only for lawyers but also for a wider audience of practitioners who increasingly encounter crowdfunding in its different forms.

IV. Crowdfunding Vehicles and Techniques: The Role of Platforms

1.10   A further layer of complexity concerns the variety of vehicles and techniques that can be used to carry out crowdfunding and the different legal consequences that each of them entails. Over the past ten years, a number of online platforms have established themselves as key players in the crowdfunding world. Not only can these platforms contribute to the success or failure of a campaign, by determining its visibility, in addition, they streamline payments, enabling the flow of funds from the crowd to the recipients. From this point of view, any legal analysis of crowdfunding necessarily intersects with the recent debates (especially

---

[10]   See Chapter 11 in this volume; see also J Tomlison, 'Crowdfunding Public Interest Judicial Reviews: A Risky New Resource and the Case for a Practical Ethics' (2019) 1 Public Law 166; R Perry, 'Crowdfunding Civil Justice' (2018) 59 Boston College Law Review 1358.

[11]   R Weinstein, 'Crowdfunding in the U.S. and Abroad: What to Expect When You're Expecting' (2013) 46 Cornell International Law Journal 427.

[12]   S Hong and J Ryu, 'Crowdfunding Public Projects: Collaborative Governance for Achieving Citizen Co-Funding of Public Goods' (2019) 36(1) Government Information Quarterly 145; A Schwartz, 'The Nonfinancial Returns of Crowdfunding' (2014–2015) 34 Review of Banking and Financial Law 565.

[13]   M Massi and others, 'Turning Crowds into Patrons: Democratizing Fundraising in the Arts and culture' in W Byrnes and A Brkić (eds), *The Routledge Companion to Arts Management* (Routledge 2020).

at the European level) concerning the regulation of platforms and the need to overhaul European private law, to account for the new reality of the platform economy.[14]

V. National Regulation of Crowdfunding

This section presents four case studies: Germany, the Netherlands, France, and Italy. The choice of the case studies was based on two criteria: market volumes and peculiarity of regulatory framework. From the first point of view, after Brexit, the EU Member States with the largest total market volumes are France, Germany, and the Netherlands.[15] From the second point of view, Italy was the first EU Member State to introduce a specific framework, which only applies to investment-based crowdfunding.   **1.11**

The case studies as presented in this section describe the regulatory regimes prior to the introduction of the Crowdfunding Regulation, as further discussed in section III. Naturally, the Crowdfunding Regulation has an impact on these regulatory regimes as it introduces a new European authorization regime that partly replaces and supplements the national regimes. At the time of writing this chapter, the national regimes were still in the process of being updated.[16] Comparing how these jurisdictions have tackled the rise of crowdfunding, however, helps to understand the most relevant regulatory choices that lawmakers are faced with, and how the solutions adopted at the national level have inspired the Crowdfunding Regulation. As already mentioned, UK law is discussed separately, in Chapters 3 and 4.   **1.12**

It can be deduced from the case studies that the Member States adopted different approaches towards crowdfunding. Germany and the Netherlands have no specific crowdfunding regime, albeit the Netherlands introduced a tailored dispensation regime for crowdfunding service providers (CSPs). Italy introduced an *ad hoc* regulatory framework, but only for investment-based crowdfunding. Meanwhile, France introduced a new regulatory regime, covering both investment- and loan-based crowdfunding. Project owners are generally not subject to an authorization requirement in all four jurisdictions, but they must be aware of prospectus requirements, unless an exemption applies. All four jurisdictions introduced specific exemptions from the prospectus requirement for crowdfunding projects, though   **1.13**

---

[14] See eg the European Law Institute Model Rules on Online Platforms <https://www.europeanlawinstitute. eu/projects-publications/completed-projects-old/online-platforms/> accessed 8 July 2020; P Alexiadis and A de Streel (2020) 'Designing an EU Intervention Standard for Digital Platforms' EUI Working Papers RSCAS 2020/ 14; C Busch, 'Self-regulation and Regulatory Intermediation in the Platform Economy' in A Cantero Gamito and HW Micklitz, *The Role of the EU in Transnational Legal Ordering: Standards, Contracts and Codes* (Elgar 2019) 115; I Graef, 'Differentiated Treatment in Platform-to-Business Relations: EU Competition Law and Economic Dependence' (2019) 38 Yearbook of European Law 448; M Kenney, D Bearson, and J Zysman (2019) 'The Platform Economy Matures: Pervasive Power, Private Regulation, and Dependent Entrepreneurs' Berkeley Roundtable on the International Economy Working Paper 2019-11; C Busch and others, 'The Rise of the Platform Economy: A New Challenge for EU Consumer Law?' (2016) 5(1) Journal of European Consumer and Market Law 3.

[15] European Commission Staff Working Document, 'Impact Assessment Accompanying the document Proposal for a Regulation of the European Parliament and of the Council on European Crowdfunding Service Providers (ECSP) for Business and Proposal for a Directive of the European Parliament and of the Council amending Directive 2014/65/EU on markets in financial instruments', SWD(2018) 56 final—2018/048 (COD), 18.

[16] In Germany a draft proposal has been published that shall regulate the licensing procedure and the liability of CSPs in Germany, <https://www.afm.nl/nl-nl/professionals/doelgroepen/crowdfundingplatformen/vergunn ing-vereisten/eu-verordening> accessed 6 May 2021. In the Netherlands, the Authority for the Financial Markets (AFM) has published guidance on its website <https://www.afm.nl/nl-nl/professionals/doelgroepen/crowdfundin gplatformen/vergunning-vereisten/eu-verordening> accessed 6 May 2021.

the conditions thereof differ per jurisdiction. Lastly, the protection of the crowd is an attention point in each jurisdiction. In Germany, such protection is basically arranged for in the general bodies of law covering investor protection, such as the implementation of the Consumer Credit Directive (hereinafter, CCD) and Distance Marketing Directive. In the Netherlands, Italy, and France, specific provisions have been introduced covering retail investor protection in crowdfunding. As will be described in Part V of this Book, protecting the crowd is a pivotal element of the Crowdfunding Regulation.

VI.   Germany

1. Scope of the German Crowdfunding Regime

1.14   There is no specific law that regulates crowdfunding in Germany.[17] A few exemptions have been introduced to relax primary market disclosure obligations in securities laws for crowdfunding activities.[18] The intermediation of donation and reward-based crowdfunding does not constitute an activity that can come under the regimes of prudential banking and capital market regulation, as long as platforms avoid attracting repayable funds from the public. However, crowdinvesting and crowdlending may entail authorization requirements, depending on the business model of the CSP.[19] Since granting unconditionally repayable loans is subject to a licencing obligation as a credit institution in Germany, as of today crowdlending in Germany is typically offered as 'unreal crowdlending'. In this context crowdlending refers to the brokering of a loan over an internet services platform between a customer (the borrower) and a credit institution (the lender) which holds authorization pursuant to section 32(1) of the German Banking Act (*Kreditwesengesetz*, hereinafter KWG).[20] The loan receivables are then assigned from the credit institution to investors via the crowdfunding platform. In crowdinvesting, the financier either participates in the future profits of the financed project or receives shares or debt instruments, if the investment involves securities.[21]

2. Regulatory Framework for Crowdfunding Platforms in Germany

1.15   Since there is no specific crowdfunding regime in Germany, authorization requirements can only flow from the general bodies of law that regulate the financial sector.[22] For the operation of a *crowdinvesting* CSP, the following authorization requirements may be of relevance. First, pursuant to the German Banking Act (KWG), an authorization requirement applies, when the CSP performs deposit business and/or lending business.[23] This is the case, for example, if it has the funds (with which the financiers wish to finance projects

---

[17] We would like to thank Alireza Siadat, and Till Christopher Otto, lawyers at Annerton Rechtsanwaltsgesellschaft mbH, for their valuable input.
[18] T Tröger (2017) Regulation of crowdfunding in Germany, SAFE Working Paper, No 199, 11.
[19] ibid 13.
[20] BaFin, 'Crowdlending' <http://www.bafin.de> accessed 17 April 2021.
[21] BaFin, 'Crowdinvesting' <http://www.bafin.de> accessed 17 April 2021.
[22] Tröger (n 18) 12–13.
[23] See section 32(1) sentence 1 of the KWG.

via the platform) paid by potential financiers before the conclusion of specific contracts. In addition, the German Payment Services Supervision Act (*Zahlungsdiensteaufsichts gesetz*, hereinafter ZAG) applies when the crowdinvesting CSP receives money from investors and transfers it to the equity investment providers (however, the requirement for a ZAG licence is exempted, once the lender holds a deposit and loan business authorization (eg credit institution authorization)). It is then performing money-remittance business.[24] Furthermore, the German Investment Code (*Kapitalanlagegesetzbuch*, hereinafter KAGB) may be applicable if one of the parties involved is an investment fund. Crowdinvesting CSPs, however, generally do not collect capital from investors for their own purposes. Instead, they merely bring together investors and the project or undertaking which is to be financed. For this reason, such platforms are not usually considered investment funds within the meaning of the KAGB.[25] Moreover, through the Retail Investor Protection Act (*Kleinanlegerschutzgesetz*), as implemented in, for example, the German Capital Investment Act (*Vermögensanlagengesetz*, hereinafter VermAnlG) and Securities Prospectus Act (*Wertpapierprospektgesetz*, hereinafter WpPG), other authorization and documentation requirements may arise for the CSP, if it brokers or places financial instruments. Certain exemptions may be available.[26]

Authorization pursuant to the KWG is required for the operation of a *crowdlending* CSP, **1.16** if it conducts banking business or provides financial services in Germany commercially or on a scale which requires commercially organized business operations. Authorization requirements pursuant to the ZAG may come into play, if payment services are provided. However, when the activity of the CSP is limited to (a) brokering a loan agreement between a borrower and a credit institution and (b) brokering the conclusion of agreements on the purchase of receivables between the credit institution and several investors, no banking or payment services are provided and no authorization requirement applies under the KWG or ZAG.[27]

Lastly, crowdinvesting and crowdlending CSPs may be confronted with other obligations, **1.17** for example arising from the German Securities Trading Act (*Wertpapierhandelsgesetz*, hereinafter WpHG).[28]

3. Position of the Project Owner in Germany

Project owners are typically not subject to any authorization requirement. The project **1.18** owner that offers capital investments may however be subject to a prospectus requirement pursuant to the VermAnlG, unless an exemption applies. Section 2a of the VermAnlG contains a specific exemption for crowdfunding. This states that there is no obligation to

---

[24] Pursuant to section 1(2) no 6 of the ZAG.
[25] BaFin, 'Crowdinvesting' (n 21).
[26] ibid. See also Tröger (n 18) 14–16.
[27] BaFin, 'Crowdlending' (n 20). See also Tröger (n 18) 13–14. If the crowdlending CSP acts under the authorization/documentation exemption under eg Art 2a VermAnlG, it requires an authorization as intermediary of financial instruments under the German Securities Institutions Act (*Wertpapierinstitutsgesetz*, hereinafter WpIG) or authorization under commercial law pursuant to section 34c or section 34f of the German Industrial Code (*Gewerbeordnung*, hereinafter GewO).
[28] BaFin, 'Crowdinvesting' (n 21).

publish a prospectus for the capital investments offered, if they are brokered via a CSP and the selling price of all capital investments of the same issuer offered by an offeror does not exceed EUR 6 million.[29] In addition, when a project owner offers securities, the prospectus requirements of the WpPG may apply, unless an exemption applies.[30] There is no specific exemption for crowdfunding.

4. Protection of the Crowd in Germany

1.19   First of all, the crowd is protected through general information and transparency requirements. In case of *crowdlending*, the bank that cooperates with the platform has to fulfil the extensive disclosure obligations stipulated for consumer loans as prescribed in European law. The platform itself incurs a duty to disclose information on the specifics of its involvement and the remuneration received for it.[31] In the case of *crowdinvesting*, the CSP has, according to general standards, an obligation to provide all information material fully and correctly for the investment decision it possesses. Furthermore, it has to verify the plausibility of the information the project owner supplies. In addition, the prospectus requirements apply as described in the previous paragraph.

1.20   Secondly, protection beyond general contract law flows from the provisions on standard terms and on consumer credit. While the law on standard terms requires that platforms make all respective contractual terms readily available before the contract is concluded, the law on consumer credit provides for a withdrawal right in a cooling-off period post contracting. Moreover, with regard to crowdinvesting, contributors benefit from a specific regime aimed at protecting their freewill.[32]

VII. The Netherlands

1. Scope of the Dutch Crowdfunding Regime

1.21   Although there is no specific law that regulates crowdfunding in the Netherlands, the general laws that regulate financial sector parties have been amended to cater for crowdfunding. The aim was to, on the one hand, avoid that general laws and regulations hinder the development of crowdfunding, and, on the other hand, protect the interests of the project owners and the crowd.[33] Investment-based and loan-based crowdfunding may trigger supervision by the Netherlands Authority for the Financial Markets (the AFM) or the Dutch Central Bank (DCB). The other forms of crowdfunding, reward-based and charity crowdfunding, generally do not trigger the applicability of Dutch financial laws and regulations.

---

[29] BaFin, 'Crowdinvesting' (n 21); see also BaFin, 'Crowdlending' (n 20).
[30] BaFin, 'Crowdinvesting' (n 21).
[31] Tröger (n 18) 17.
[32] ibid 21.
[33] Dutch Official Gazette (2016) 98, p 11.

2. Regulatory Framework for Crowdfunding Platforms in the Netherlands

CSPs in the Netherlands are generally active on the basis of a so-called dispensation inter- **1.22** mediary in repayable funds.[34] This is a dispensation granted by the AFM from the prohibition to provide intermediary services in the attraction of repayable funds from the public.[35] This prohibition is applicable when a CSP intermediates in loans between the crowd[36] and project owners that are not consumers.[37] When the project owners qualify as consumers, the CSP has to obtain a licence as an offeror of consumer credit.[38] In order to obtain the dispensation, the CSP has to meet certain conditions, *inter alia*, in relation to the integrity and fit and properness of its (daily) policy-makers and the soundness of its business operations. In addition, the AFM imposes certain conditions to the dispensation. These conditions should be seen in the light of the objective to protect the crowd and are therefore further discussed in subsection IV.4. CSPs should also be aware of the fact that they may provide payment services. An authorization requirement is however only triggered when these services are provided as a separate activity. The DCB has issued an interpretation on its website that clarifies when CSPs are considered to provide payment services as a separate activity.[39] According to this interpretation, CSPs will generally not require an authorization as a payment services provider. Only a handful of CSPs in the Netherlands have obtained a Markets in Financial Instruments Directive II (MiFID II) authorization for the receipt and transmission of orders in financial instruments, placement activities, investment advice, or individual portfolio management.[40] These services may come into play when the CSP is involved in investment-based crowdfunding. A CSP may also be confronted with the authorization requirement for managing an alternative investment fund (AIF) or an Undertaking for the Collective Investment in Transferable Securities (UCITS).

3. Position of the Project Owner in the Netherlands

Project owners should be aware of certain regulatory obligations, depending on the way **1.23** they fund their projects through crowdfunding. When project owners make use of loan-based crowdfunding (or issue debt instruments), they may be faced with the prohibition to attract repayable funds from the public. Since 1 April 2016, a special exemption from this prohibition has been included in Dutch law for project owners that attract repayable funds from the public.[41] This exemption can be used in relation to 'crowd loans'

---

[34] This will change as a result of the introduction of the Crowdfunding Regulation. See ML Louisse, 'Crowdfunding' in D Busch, CWM Lieverse, and JWPM van der Velden, *Leerboek Financieel Recht* (Ars Aequi 2021).

[35] Art 4(3) of the Dutch Act on Financial Supervision (*Wet op het financieel toezicht*, hereinafter AFS).

[36] That is, 'the public'. The term 'public' is not further defined in banking regulation. This results in a degree of variation between the Member States as to the interpretation thereof. For the Netherlands, reference is made to the explanation by the DCB: DCB, 'Definitie bank' <http://www.dnb.nl> accessed 17 April 2021.

[37] As defined in Art 1(1) of the AFS.

[38] Art 2(60) of the AFS.

[39] DCB, 'Reikwijdte betaaldienstverlening—niet op zichzelf staande betaaltransacties' <http://www.dnb.nl> accessed 17 April 2021.

[40] See the public 'Register Crowdfundingplatformen' that is kept by the AFM, <http://www.afm.nl> accessed 17 April 2021.

[41] SN Demper and ML Louisse, *Crowdfunding: Een Juridische Verkenning* (Ars Aequi 2019) 23–24.

(*publieksleningen*). Certain conditions have to be met. For example, the crowd loans should be attracted through a CSP that has obtained a 'dispensation intermediary repayable funds' and the total amount of repayable funds that is attracted per crowdfunding may not exceed EUR 2.5 million over a period of twelve months. In case of investment-based crowdfunding, project owners should be aware of the prospectus requirements. However, most of them may be able to make use of the Dutch exemption for the offers of securities within the European Economic Area (EEA) of which the total amount does not exceed EUR 5 million over a period of 12 months. The use of this exemption requires prior notification to the AFM and the provision of an information document prior to the offer.[42]

4. Protection of the Crowd in the Netherlands

1.24   The protection of the crowd is a driving factor behind the alterations that have been made to the general Dutch laws and regulations that cover financial sector parties. As a result, the 'dispensation intermediary repayable funds' can only be obtained after certain conditions have been met. In addition, the AFM imposes certain conditions to the dispensation that provide further protection for retail investors. These conditions include, *inter alia*, investment limitations and the requirement for retail investors to conduct an investment test prior to investment in a crowdfunding project and the requirement for the CSP to advise retail investors that their investments should not exceed 10% of their assets and that they should spread their investments over multiple projects. In addition, the CSP should have a policy for assessing loan applications and risk classification thereof. Lastly, the CSP should comply with certain transparency requirements.[43]

1.25   As discussed in subsection VII.2, CSPs in the Netherlands generally conduct their activities on the basis of the aforementioned dispensation, but some of them have obtained an authorization as the offeror of consumer credit or a MiFID II authorization. In case the CSP offers consumer credit, the protection of the crowd is regulated by the Dutch implementation of the CCD (or the Mortgage Credit Directive, MCD), in addition to some specific Dutch regulations in respect of consumer credit. Lastly, when the CSP has obtained a MiFID II authorization, the protection of the investors derives from MiFID II. It is noteworthy in that respect that the inducement ban that the Netherlands introduced for the provision of investment services to retail clients is not applicable to CSPs with a MiFID II authorization when they receive and transmit orders from retail clients in securities issued by project owners.[44]

---

[42] ibid 24–27. Art 5:5(1) AFS and Art 53(2) of the Dutch Exemption Regulation AFS (*Vrijstellingsregeling Wft*).
[43] ibid 29–32, 36–41. Arts 2a, 2b, and 2c Dutch Decree on Supervision of Conduct of Financial Undertakings AFS (Besluit *Gedragstoezicht financiële ondernemingen Wft*).
[44] Art 168a(2) lit. (f) Dutch Decree on Supervision of Conduct of Financial Undertakings AFS (*Besluit Gedragstoezicht financiële ondernemingen Wft*).

VIII. France

1. Scope of the French Crowdfunding Regime

In 2014, France introduced a new regulatory regime, covering both investment- and loan-based crowdfunding. To this end, two different types of CSP are regulated in the Monetary and Financial Code: advisors in participative investment (*conseiller en investissement participatif*, hereinafter CIP), and participative finance intermediaries (*intermédiaire en financement participative*, hereinafter IFP). CIPs manage investment-based crowdfunding platforms, through which investors can retrieve offers concerning the subscription of certain types of shares or equity participations, and/or certain debt instruments.[45] IFPs, conversely, manage loan-based crowdfunding platforms, where project owners seek financing from non-professional lenders. The two qualifications of CIP and IFP cannot be cumulated by the same legal person.   **1.26**

The French system allows CIPs to operate in a MiFID-exempt regime.[46] As a consequence, the services provided by CIPs are necessarily limited, as described below, unless the investment-based crowdfunding platform is operated by a 'regular' authorized investment service provider (which needs no further authorization to that end). Along similar lines, the services that IFPs can provide are also limited so as not to encroach on the activities that are exclusively reserved for credit institutions, investment firms, payment service providers, portfolio managers, and other authorized service providers.   **1.27**

CIPs and IFPs are placed under the supervision of two different authorities: the Financial Markets Authority (*Autorité des marchés financiers*, hereinafter AMF) and the Prudential Supervision and Resolution Authority (*Autorité de contrôle prudentiel et de résolution*, hereinafter ACPR).   **1.28**

2. Regulatory Framework for Crowdfunding Platforms in France

While CIPs and IFPs are subject to two separate regimes, many features of the regulatory framework are comparable. Both CIPs and IFPs must be legal persons, and both are subject to a registration requirement. French law requires both CIPs and IFPs to be insured, in order to protect the crowd adequately. Furthermore, French law requires that the managers of both CIPs and IFPs meet certain honourability requirements and demonstrate their professional capabilities through certain qualifications and credentials (*inter alia*, a national diploma on the relevant topics, or past professional experience in the fields of banking and finance). In addition, it is mandatory that CIPs must become members of a professional   **1.29**

---

[45] C Kleiner, 'La regulation juridique du *crowdfunding*' in K Boele-Woelki, D Fernandez Arroyo, and A Senegacnik (eds), *General Reports of the XXth General Congress of the International Academy of Comparative Law—Rapports généraux du XXème Congrès général de l'Académie internationale de droit compare* (Springer 2021) 323, 332.

[46] The regime applicable to CIPs is, in any event, largely inspired by that applicable to financial investment advisors: S Cieply and A-L Le Nadant, 'Le *crowdfunding*: modèle alternatif de financement ou généralisation du modèle de marché pour les start-up et les PME?' (2016) 2 Revue d'Économie Financière 255, 262.

association, which sets forth a code of conduct for its members. The supervision of CIPs, hence, is carried out by the AMF together with the relevant professional association.

1.30   MiFID-exempt CIPs cannot receive or hold funds or financial instruments on behalf of third parties. French law described CIPs as professional providers of investment advice, concerning offers of equity and debt instruments.[47] The management of an equity-based crowdfunding platform, hence, is qualified as the provision of professional advice through electronic means. Furthermore, CIPs are allowed to provide advice to enterprises on matters such as capital structure, industrial strategy, and mergers and acquisitions.

1.31   Along similar lines, French law also limits the activities of IFPs, which mainly fall within two categories. First of all, IFPs publish on their portals offers aimed at non-professional lenders, concerning the extension of loans in favour of certain enterprises. Secondly, IFPs provide model contracts, which lenders and borrowers use, to regulate the terms of the loan agreement.[48]

3. Position of the Project Owner in France

1.32   As far as investment-based crowdfunding is concerned, French law sets a maximum threshold for total consideration at EUR 2.5 million. Consequently, project owners are exempted from prospectus obligations.[49] As for loan-based crowdfunding, a maximum of EUR 1 million per project may be borrowed, and the duration of the loan cannot exceed seven years.

1.33   While project owners are not required to obtain a specific authorization, they do have certain information duties, both in investment- and loan-based crowdfunding. In the case of investment-based crowdfunding, CIPs provide advice to non-professional investors (as outlined in the following section), on the basis of (*inter alia*) the information transmitted by the project owners, which must be truthful and accurate. Along similar lines, IFPs analyse and select projects, on the basis of the information provided by the project owners. By resorting to crowdfunding, hence, project owners undertake certain obligations to provide accurate and exhaustive information. In investment-based crowdfunding, this information is comparable in content to the essential elements that would be included in a prospectus;[50] this, in turn, will enable CSPs to perform their tasks and discharge their information obligations *vis-à-vis* potential investors.

4. Protection of the Crowd in France

1.34   As already mentioned, in investment-based crowdfunding, the service provided by CIPs to the crowd is qualified in terms of investment advice, which must be provided honestly,

---

[47]   Art L547-1(1) of the French Monetary and Financial Code.
[48]   Art R548-6 of the French Monetary and Financial Code.
[49]   Art L411-2 of the French monetary and Financial Code.
[50]   P-H Conac, 'Entrée en vigueur du nouveau régime français du financement participatif (*crowdfunding*)' (2015) 1 Revue des sociétés 60.

without bias, and professionally, in the interest of the client.[51] CIPs, therefore, must adapt their offer for each client, and must not propose offers which are not in the client's interest. For this reason, when users visit a crowdfunding platform, they cannot directly access the area of the website where the offers are listed. To the contrary, users must register themselves and answer some questions which aim at evaluating each user's knowledge and experience in the field of investment with reference to a specific type of instrument, the user's financial situation, and her investment goals, so as to adapt the offer to the user's individual situation. If a user does not provide such information, the offer cannot be considered as 'adapted' to the individual user. Furthermore, the user must be warned about the risks arising out of crowdfunding investments, including the risk of a total loss.[52] If CIPs provide the aforementioned advice, they must also receive information from their clients concerning their ability to bear losses, and their risk tolerance, so as to present the clients with suitable instruments.[53]

CIPs must provide information about the offers and the terms of the investment transparently. Such an information duty encompasses not only the information provided by each project owner (concerning *inter alia* the nature of the project, the risks arising therefrom, and the level of participation of the project owner's managers) but also the rights deriving from the financial instrument, the exit conditions for investors, the fees to be paid by the investors, and the right to obtain information as to the services offered by the CIP to the project owner and the fees levied.   **1.35**

In the field of loan-based crowdfunding, the goal of protecting the crowd is pursued, first of all, through the imposition of a relatively low maximum threshold for individual contribution: in the case of loans with interest, each individual lender can extend a maximum loan of EUR 2,000 per project.[54] In this case, the IFP must also ensure that the interest rate does not exceed the usury threshold.[55] For loans without interest, the maximum loan threshold is heightened to EUR 5,000 per lender per project.[56]   **1.36**

Within the limits of their activities, IFPs must act in an 'honest, fair, transparent and professional' manner.[57] In this context, IFPs have first of all some duties of transparency concerning themselves: users must be provided with comprehensible information as to the identity of the IFP, its governance, and its yearly activities.[58] In addition, IFPs must disclose information on the eligibility conditions and the criteria for the analysis of selection of projects and project owners, and the rate of default in the past 36 months.[59] For each offer, the IFP must publish information as to the project, its financing plan, and the project owner.[60] Before the conclusion of the loan agreement, the IFP must point out the key aspects of the agreement to the parties, and warn the lender as to the risk arising out of crowdfunding lending (such as the risk of default).[61]   **1.37**

---

[51] Art L547-9(1) of the French Monetary and Financial Code.
[52] Art L547-9(6) of the French Monetary and Financial Code.
[53] ibid.
[54] Art D548-1 of the French Monetary and Financial Code.
[55] ibid.
[56] ibid.
[57] Art L548-6 of the French Monetary and Financial Code.
[58] ibid.
[59] Art R548-5 of the French Monetary and Financial Code.
[60] ibid.
[61] Art R548-7 of the French Monetary and Financial Code.

1.38   As an additional measure to protect the crowd of lenders, IFPs must offer a tool on their portals through which the lenders can evaluate their capacity to extend credit, in relation to their financial situation.[62]

IX.   Italy

1.   Scope of the Italian Crowdfunding Regime

1.39   Italy has introduced an *ad hoc* legislative framework for certain types of crowdfunding. The regime, which was only applicable to specific categories of investment-based crowdfunding, has progressively been extended over time to different types of equity investments. In 2019, the regime has also become applicable to certain types of debt instruments that, however, are only available to professional investors. Conversely, loan-based crowdfunding is not subject to an *ad hoc* regulatory framework in Italy.[63]

2.   Regulatory Framework for Crowdfunding Platforms in Italy

1.40   Under Italian law, crowdfunding portals can only be managed by authorized service providers, which must be registered in a special register at Consob, the Italian Companies and Exchange Commission. Two categories of providers can register: first, registration is possible for banks, investment firms, intermediation firms, and other subjects that have already been authorized to provide investment services. Those entities must notify Consob before opening a portal, but they do not need any further authorization. Secondly, crowdfunding platforms can be managed by other service providers, set up specifically to that end. While the first category of service providers is subject to MiFID, the second category is exempted from it. Originally, Italian law relied on Article 3 MiFID, which allowed EU Member States (under certain conditions) not to apply the Directive to parties receiving and transmitting orders. Subsequently, MiFID II introduced further requirements in relation to the exemption regime of Article 3, and the Italian law-maker has amended the legal framework accordingly.

1.41   In order to be registered, MiFID-exempt CSPs must meet certain requirements: they must be a company seated or established in Italy, whose motive is the provision of crowdfunding services. Furthermore, Consob sets forth honourability requirements for those who control the company and those who administer, direct, and manage it, and professionality requirements for the latter category of subject. In addition, CSPs must be insured, so as to guarantee adequate investor protection.

1.42   While Italian law does not contain a definition of crowdfunding services, the legal framework repeatedly qualifies those services as the reception and transmission of orders to specific authorized subjects. This (rather restrictive) characterization of the activities carried

---

[62]   ibid.
[63]   E Macchiavello, 'La problematica regolazione del lending-based crowdfunding in Italia' (2018) 1 Banca borsa e titoli di credito 65.

out by CPSs is meant to meet the exemption requirements currently enshrined in Article 3 MiFID II. In practice, this characterization can prove problematic. While such a limited scope is justified in theory for MiFID exemption purposes, such an approach does not fully reflect the range of services typically offered through crowdfunding platforms. CSPs, for instance, routinely select project owners and offer various forms of administrative support, such as the drafting of standard contract forms to be used by project owners and investors.

3. Position of the Project Owner in Italy

The Italian framework imposes a maximum threshold for total consideration for each **1.43** crowdfunding offer: according to Article 100-*ter* of the Italian consolidated statute on finance, crowdfunding offers concerning instruments issued by SMEs must not exceed the threshold set by Consob for prospectus exemption. Such a threshold, initially set at EUR 5 million, has been heightened to EUR 8 million in November 2018.[64]

Project owners are not subject to any authorization requirement; however, they have certain **1.44** duties to cooperate with the platform, so as to provide potential investors with sufficient information. More specifically, the project owner must provide the CSP with the information listed by Consob in Annex 3 to its Regulation. When presenting the information on the platform, the CSP must highlight that the information is not subject to approval by Consob, and the project owner is the only party responsible for the completeness and truthfulness of the information. Consob, hence, merely streamlines the contents of the project owner's communications, which must include information on the business plan, the identity of the company's administrators and their *curriculum vitae*, the description of the offered financial instruments, the risks of the offer, and the general terms and conditions of the offer, among other items. It has been argued that the extensiveness of the information provided by the project owner (which is not very different from the information required in the context of an initial public offering (IPO)) may result in an information overload for non-professional investors.[65]

4. Protection of the Crowd in Italy

The goal of protecting the crowd of investors is pursued, first of all, through general infor- **1.45** mation and transparency requirements. More specifically, the CSP must publish detailed information on itself and its activities. Furthermore, the CSP must publish the information provided by the project owner concerning each project, as already mentioned. In addition, the CSP must provide investors with more general investment information, concerning *inter alia* the risk of a total loss, the particular risks arising out of investments in start-up companies, and the particular regulatory regime applicable to this type of company.

---

[64] Consob has thus made use of the exemption possibility enshrined in Art 3(2) of Regulation 2017/1129 (Prospectus Regulation), so as to facilitate access to capital for SMEs.
[65] E Macchiavello, 'La travagliata evoluzione normativa dell'equity crowdfunding in Italia, il nuovo regolamento Consob e la prospettiva di regolazione del crowdfunding a livello europeo: una disciplina destinata a breve vita?' (2018) 1 Rivista di Diritto Bancario 133, 158.

1.46   As far as non-professional investors are concerned, their protection is enhanced by an additional obligation for CSPs: platforms must not allow non-professional investors to access the section of the portal where crowdfunding offers can be accepted, unless the following conditions are met:

> (1)   The user must have received the so-called investor education information, provided by Consob, and the aforementioned warnings as to the risks and specificities of this type of investment;
>
> (2)   The user must have provided information as to her knowledge and experience, so as to understand the basic features and risks entailed by the offered financial instruments;
>
> (3)   The user must have declared that she is able to bear the total loss of the investment financially.

1.47   The Italian crowdfunding regime does not impose any maximum thresholds for investments by a single investor. This choice has attracted criticism; according to Macchiavello, for instance, the imposition of such limits would have allowed the Italian law-maker to justify a 'lighter' and more permissive regulatory regime, thus potentially enhancing the overall attractiveness of crowdfunding.[66] Instead of imposing limits to individual investments, the Italian law-maker has introduced a different type of threshold: pursuant to Article 24(2) of the Consob regulation, when the offer concerns shares or equity participations in companies, at least 5%[67] of the offered instruments must be subscribed by professional investors, banks, start-up incubators, or business angels. The mandatory involvement of professional investors aims at protecting the non-professional ones, ensuring *inter alia* a control on the correctness of the price.

1.48   When a non-professional investor places an order, a test must be performed, to assess whether the investment is appropriate, in light of the client's level of experience and knowledge, as resulting from the information provided by the client when accessing the section of the portal where the crowdfunding offers are listed. CSPs have the possibility to perform such test directly, or have the test provided by the entity executing the order. If the CSP performs the test directly, this has consequences on the CSP's insurance requirements.[68]

1.49   After accepting a crowdfunding offer, non-professional investors have a right of cancellation, within a period of seven days. Furthermore, an investor can withdraw her acceptance if, at a moment in time after the investor has accepted but before the crowdfunding offer is closed, or the financial instruments have been delivered, new relevant facts occur, or the provision of incorrect information on the portal has been detected. This right of withdrawal must also be exercised within a period of seven days. Investors must be adequately informed about the existence of these rights.

1.50   A further layer of investor protection concerns the scenario where, after the conclusion of the crowdfunding offer, a change of control occurs, or the founder exits the company. For

---

[66]   ibid 162.

[67]   This threshold is lowered to 3% if the project owner's balance sheets are certified: see Art 24(2-*ter*) of the Consob regulation.

[68]   Namely, the overall coverage must be EUR1 million per year, instead of EUR 500,000: see Art 7*bis*(1)(b) of the Consob regulation.

a start-up company, such developments can have a decisive impact on the company's prospects of future success, which are typically linked to the person of the founder, and to the
identity of those who control the start-up company. As a result, non-professional investors
must be granted the right to either withdraw from the company, or 'tag along' and sell their
participation, under the same conditions as those under which the control of the company
was transferred. On pain of inadmissibility, the CSP must ensure that the project owner's
statutes or articles of incorporation grant such rights to non-professional investors, for a
period of no less than three years.

CSPs can also facilitate the secondary trading of instruments originally offered on their   **1.51**
portals. To this end, the portal can include a separate bulletin board, where investors can express their interest to sell or buy those instruments. The CSP, however, must limit its involvement to the communication (in confidential form) of the data of the interested investors.

X. The Introduction of the Crowdfunding Regulation

Until recently, in Europe there was no common set of rules applicable to crowdfunding. As   **1.52**
the previous section summarizes with reference to four legal systems, each Member State
had its own regulatory framework, and significant differences existed among the various
national approaches.[69] This lack of harmonization hindered the scaling up of crowdfunding
services across the internal market, and created significant uncertainty, increasing the costs
associated with compliance, and with the provision of crowdfunding services. As a result,
the level of protection of non-professional investors remained uneven across the EU, and
the ambiguity of the regulatory framework significantly constrained the development of a
single European crowdfunding market.[70]

In recent times, however, the EU has recognized the importance of crowdfunding, and   **1.53**
taken steps to introduce a new Regulation, which constitutes the main focus of this book.
More specifically, in 2018, the European Commission presented its proposal for the
Crowdfunding Regulation.[71] The Crowdfunding Regulation was finally approved—in
amended form—on 5 October 2020,[72] and is applicable as of 10 November 2021. The introduction of a uniform set of rules on crowdfunding services can significantly benefit the
industry, facilitating the flow of capital[73] (especially towards start-up companies) in the

---

[69] G Dushnitsky and others, 'Crowdfunding in Europe: Determinants of Platform Creation across Countries'
(2016) 58(2) California Management Review 44.

[70] D Busch, V Colaert, and G Helleringer, 'An "Assist Your Customer" Obligation for the Financial Sector?' in
V Colaert, D Busch, and T Incalza, *European Financial Regulation: Levelling the Cross-Sectoral Playing Field* (Hart
2019) 343, 347.

[71] COM(2018) 113 final, 2018/0048 (COD), Proposal for a Regulation of the European Parliament and
of the Council on European Crowdfunding Service Providers (ECSP) for Business (Text with EEA relevance),
{SWD(2018) 56 final}—{SWD(2018) 57 final}.

[72] Regulation (EU) 2020/1503 of the European Parliament and of the Council of 7 October 2020 on European
crowdfunding service providers for business, and amending Regulation (EU) 2017/1129 and Directive (EU) 2019/
1937, OJ L 347, 20.10.2020, p 1–49.

[73] The available empirical evidence confirms that the introduction of crowdfunding-specific legislation appears
to increase the volume of crowdfunding: P Raghavendra Rau, 'Law, Trust and the Development of Crowdfunding'
(2020) available at <https://papers.ssrn.com/sol3/papers.cfm?abstract_id = 2989056&download = yes >; D
Cumming and S Johan, 'Demand-Driven Securities Regulation: Evidence from Crowdfunding' (2013) 15(4)
Venture Capital 361.

Digital Single Market and pursuing Capital Markets Union goals.[74] The introduction of an authorization that allows CSPs to offer their services across the EU, besides the creation of clear and uniform criteria as to the information that should be provided by project owners and platforms, as well as harmonized organizational and operational requirements for CSPs, are the guiding criteria for this new European instrument.[75]

1.54   Given the ambition of this new Regulation, numerous questions unavoidably arise. How can the different national approaches that currently exist be successfully approximated and merged into a coherent, workable Regulation? And what balance does this new instrument strike between the protection of non-professional investors, on the one hand, and a broad access to finance, on the other hand? In addition, questions arise as to the scope of application of the Regulation, which focuses exclusively on certain types of platform-based crowdfunding (and, in particular, debt and equity crowdfunding), while not applying to blockchain-based crowdfunding,[76] nor to crowdfunding services that are provided to project owners that are consumers.[77] To what extent, then, will the Regulation bring about a harmonized and consistent regulatory framework for crowdfunding in Europe? This book will address these questions.

XI. Overview of the Book

1. Part I: Sketching a Legal Taxonomy of Crowdfunding

1.55   Part I sketches a legal taxonomy of crowdfunding. After this general introduction, Chapter 2 scrutinizes the broader EU law context within which the new Crowdfunding Regulation

---

[74] E Macchiavello, 'Financial-Return Crowdfunding and Regulatory Approaches in the Shadow Banking, Fintech and Collaborative Finance Era' (2017) 14(4) European Company and Financial Law Review 662.

[75] E Macchiavello, '"What to Expect When You Are Expecting"' a European Crowdfunding Regulation: The Current "Bermuda Triangle" and Future Scenarios for Marketplace Lending and Investing in Europe' (2019) European Banking Institute Working Paper Series, no 55.

[76] See Chapter 6 in this volume. On these gaps in the Regulation see E Macchiavello, 'The European Crowdfunding Service Providers Regulation and the Future of Marketplace Lending and Investing in Europe: The "Crowdfunding Nature" Dilemma' (2021) 32(3) European Business Law Review 557–608. In the blockchain ecosystem, it is standard practice for start-up companies to finance themselves through Initial Coin Offerings (ICOs), Initial Token Offerings (ITOs), Initial Exchange Offerings (IEOs), or other similar techniques. Typically, the start-up company makes an offer to the public, concerning the sale of digital assets (often referred to as 'tokens') whose circulation is recorded through a distributed ledger technology (DLT). Subsequently, the crowd is allowed to purchase the tokens, typically paying with a cryptocurrency (such as Ethereum or Bitcoin). Importantly, ICOs/ITOs/ IEOs are currently shrouded by regulatory uncertainty, and it is unclear whether and to what extent securities laws should apply to them. From the regulatory point of view, this model of crowdfunding raises different issues, as compared to the platform-based one: regulators must assess on a case-by-case basis the nature of the activities undertaken by the token issuer, the legal qualification of the tokens and other digital assets received by the investors, and the subsequent, delicate issues of compliance with capital market laws. Despite such regulatory uncertainties, ICOs/ITOs/IEOs have proved to be an attractive financing strategy not only for start-up companies but also for well-established actors of the digital economy: the instant messaging service Telegram, for instance, raised USD1.7 billion with an ICO. This trend, in turn, has triggered stern regulatory reactions. In October 2019, for instance, the US Securities and Exchange Commission (SEC) obtained a restraining order from a US court, aimed at halting the Telegram ICO for an alleged violation of securities law. In the EU, besides the publication of several warnings for virtual currencies, the European Banking Authority and the European Authority for the Securities and Markets published reports to the European Commission with advice on crypto-assets. At the end of 2019, the European Commission consulted on the establishment of a European framework for markets in crypto-assets.

[77] Crowdfunding is for example used for the issuance of mortgages to consumers. This type of crowdfunding is not covered by the proposal. See RM Garcia-Teruel, 'A Legal Approach to Real Estate Crowdfunding Platforms' (2019) 3 Computer Law & Security Review 281–94.

fits. In her contribution, Eugenia Macchiavello provides an overview of how the Regulation interacts with the existing instruments of EU law (eg the aforementioned MiFID II, the Payment Services Directive (PSD2), the Alternative Investment Fund Managers Directive (AIFMD), and the proposed Regulation on Markets in Crypto-Assets). This overview helps highlight the main regulatory challenges associated with crowdfunding, which will be discussed in the rest of the book.

2. Part II: Defining and Assessing the Scope of the Crowdfunding Regulation

Part II scrutinizes the Regulation's scope of application. This is particularly important both **1.56** in light of Brexit, and because certain forms of crowdfunding fall outside of the Regulation's scope of application *ratione materiae*, as already mentioned. Chapter 3, by Petja Ivanova, clarifies the scope of application of the Regulation, and discusses the impact of Brexit on the application of the crowdfunding legal framework and the further development of the crowdfunding market, from a European perspective. In turn, in Chapter 4, Gerard McMeel tackles the impact of Brexit on the development and application of the Crowdfunding Regulation summarizing the main features of the UK legal framework applicable to crowdfunding, and assessing the enduring relevance of that framework, in the wake of the Withdrawal Agreement.

In Chapter 5, Martin Ebers and Benedikt Quarch chart the interactions and the 'boundaries' **1.57** between the Crowdfunding Regulation and European Consumer Law. These questions are particularly relevant, not only because some forms of crowdfunding fall outside of the scope of the Regulation (eg when the project owner herself is a consumer) but also because EU Consumer Law may meaningfully complement the provisions of the Crowdfunding Regulation, protecting the 'crowd', in cases where the Regulation is applicable.[78]

Finally, Chapter 6 assesses the scope of application of the Regulation *ratione materiae*, with **1.58** reference to the rapidly evolving world of blockchain-based crowdfunding techniques, such as ICOs, ITOs, and IEOs. In their contribution, Raffaele Battaglini and Davide Davico investigate whether the choice to exclude ICOs/ITOs/IEOs from the scope of the Crowdfunding Regulation was correct. The chapter will carry out a comparison between the Regulation and the future possible regulation of crypto-assets in the EU, with particular reference to the proposed Markets in Crypto-Assets (MiCA) Regulation, and the Distributed Ledger Technology Pilot Regime.

3. Part III: Regulating the Crowdfunding Service Providers Under the Crowdfunding Regulation

Part III of the book zooms in on the regulatory position of CSPs, operating as match-makers **1.59** between investors and project owners. In Chapter 7, Marije Louisse and Adam Pasaribu

---

[78] J Armour and L Enriques, 'The Promise and Perils of Crowdfunding: Between Corporate Finance and Consumer Contracts' (2018) 81(1) Modern Law Review 51.

discuss provisions of the Crowdfunding Regulation governing the new authorization for CSPs to provide crowdfunding services in the EU. This chapter elaborates on the crowdfunding services that may be provided and the scope of the authorization, the authorization process, and the cross-border provision of crowdfunding services. In addition, it discusses the supervision by the competent authorities, including the exercise of supervisory powers and powers to impose sanctions, and the obligations of the crowdfunding service provides towards competent authorities. Lastly, it also assesses how the authorization for crowdfunding service providers contributes towards market access for crowdfunding service providers under other EU and national law instruments.

1.60   In Chapter 8, Kitty Lieverse and Wendy Pronk analyse the organizationa– operational requirements for CSPs under the Crowdfunding Regulation. CSPs should comply with certain requirements designed to ensure that projects on their platforms are selected in a professional, fair, and transparent way, and that crowdfunding services are provided in the same manner. In addition, the chapter discusses the governance arrangements that CSPs should have in place to ensure their effective and prudent management, including the prevention of conflicts of interest. Lastly, it assesses the prudential requirements that are applicable in order to protect clients against operational risks and the rules in respect of outsourcing.

4. Part IV: The Position of Project Owners Under the Crowdfunding Regulation and Beyond

1.61   Part IV focuses on the position of project owners. The circumstance that a project owner has received funding from a crowd of investors, rather than through traditional channels of corporate finance, is far from irrelevant, in terms of its regulatory position and compliance duties. Project owners, for instance, play an important role in ensuring the information transparency towards the investors, for example through the key investment information sheet. In Chapter 9, Jonneke van Poelgeest and Marije Louisse tackle the position of project owners under the Crowdfunding Regulation. The Regulation requires Member States to ensure that project owners can pursue lending-based crowdfunding without any specific authorization. This, however, does not mean that project owners have no regulatory obligations at all. The chapter starts with an introduction to the position of project owners, and the CSPs' obligations towards project owners, including the obligations to perform due diligence and credit risk assessment. Subsequently, the chapter assesses the obligations of project owners, including the (lack of an) authorization requirement, the provision of information, and the cooperation with CSPs. Lastly, the chapter discusses whether project owners require some form of protection, and whether that is a missing piece of the Crowdfunding Regulation.

1.62   In Chapter 10, Chris Cotropia enlarges the perspective, considering some intellectual property (IP) issues that are not directly covered by the Crowdfunding Regulation but are of great practical relevance for project owners pursuing a crowdfunding campaign. When attempting to raise funds through crowdfunding, project owners provide information as to their plans, strategies, and business model. This often happens at a time when project owners are still in the start-up phase. In this delicate moment, IP rights can play a twofold rule. On the one hand, the crowd may be more inclined to invest in a project that is patented or patent-pending. From this point of view, IP rights can act as a sort of quality trustmark for crowdfunded projects. On the other hand, however, the disclosure of information at such an early stage entails the risk that the innovative aspects of the proposed business venture will be emulated by 'copycats', piggybacking on the project owner's efforts. Far from being merely theoretical, this risk has already been reported in practice; therefore, it is useful to investigate the phenomenon in its complexity. The chapter provides an overview of this problem and presents empirical data to estimate its relevance.

Finally, in Chapter 11, Sam Gaunt and Andrea Longo present their first-hand experience of   **1.63** project owners, successfully using charity crowdfunding to finance strategic litigation. By focusing on a form of crowdfunding which is excluded from the scope of the Regulation, this chapter will offer the chance to assess whether a comparable regulatory regime should be extended beyond the boundaries of investment-based and loan-based crowdfunding, and what the consequences would be for those who make use of crowdfunding in the non-profit sector.

5. Part V: Protecting the Crowd Under the Crowdfunding Regulation and Beyond

Part V discusses the protection of the crowd. Once again, the main focus lies on the provi-   **1.64** sions of the Crowdfunding Regulation, with reference to investor protection. At the same time, the book also enlarges the perspective, considering the position of the crowd in those forms of crowdfunding that are not covered by the Regulation. In Chapter 12, Joseph Lee discusses the different levels of investor protection safeguards that apply distinguishing between sophisticated and non-sophisticated investors. The chapter describes the transparency and information requirements under the Crowdfunding regulation, including the default rate disclosure and the key investment information sheet for crowdfunding offers and at platform level. It furthermore discusses the entry knowledge test, the simulation of the ability to bear losses, and the pre-contractual reflection period.

Chapter 13, by Anne Hakvoort, discusses the introduction by the Regulation of the possi-   **1.65** bility for investors to advertise on a bulletin board their interest in buying or selling loans, transferable securities, or other instruments. It describes the obligations of the crowdfunding service providers when allowing the advertisement of interests on such a bulletin board. It furthermore assesses the interlinkage with the obligations under MiFID II in respect of internal matching systems which execute client orders on a multilateral basis. It also looks into the qualification of a crowdfunding investment as transferable security or loan and the consequences thereof for secondary trading.

In Chapter 14, Catalina Goanta, Pietro Ortolani, and Marije Louisse discuss marketing   **1.66** communications. The regulation of online crowdfunding advertisement is particularly challenging, for two interrelated reasons. First, it plays a key role in the protection of weaker parties (such as non-professional investors), both at the national and EU level. Second, this phenomenon highlights the rising regulatory role of web platforms (such as social media networks) which enable and moderate advertisement. The chapter analyses these challenges, and the relevance of Articles 27 and 28 of the Crowdfunding Regulation.

1.67   In Chapter 15, Mateja Durovic and Margarita Amaxopoulou discuss the EU legal framework applicable to reward-based crowdfunding, and the consumer protection mechanisms
enshrined therein. While being excluded from the scope of the Crowdfunding Regulation,
reward-based crowdfunding falls within the scope of application of EU Consumer Law.
The EU consumer acquis is currently being reviewed and modernized, with a view to the
creation of a Digital Single Market. The chapter scrutinizes to what extent the current instruments of EU Consumer Law are adequate to deal with the rising phenomenon of
reward-based crowdfunding, and how they could be modernized.

6.   Part VI: Managing, Preventing, and Resolving Crowdfunding-Related Disputes

1.68   Part VI is dedicated to the management, prevention, and resolution of disputes between investors, project owners, and crowdfunding service providers. Given the growing relevance
of the phenomenon, an increase in the number of disputes relating to crowdfunding is not
entirely avoidable. For this reason, it is desirable to elaborate a framework facilitating an effective and reliable resolution of these disputes. To this end, in Chapter 16, Pietro Ortolani
discusses the allocation of court jurisdiction in the EU, for crowdfunding-related litigation.
Importantly, the Crowdfunding Regulation allows the cross-border provision of crowdfunding services but does not include any heads of jurisdiction for civil disputes arising out
of such provision of services. In the absence of any relevant rules in the new Regulation,
the allocation of jurisdiction among Member State courts is regulated by the Brussels I*bis*
Regulation. However, the recent case law of the European Court of Justice casts significant
doubts as to whether the Brussels regime is indeed adequate to deal with this type of cases,
also in light of the multiplication of available fora it potentially entails. The chapter applies
the existing rules of EU civil procedure to the phenomenon of crowdfunding, scrutinizing
which national courts may be competent to hear disputes arising out of services and investments covered by the Crowdfunding Regulation.

1.69   In Chapter 17, Tomas Arons explores the use of class action procedures, to resolve
crowdfunding-related disputes. In principle, this type of dispute seems to be suitable for
class action schemes, for example aggregating the claims of a multitude of investors against
a project owner, or a service provider. Yet, the availability of this sort of procedures varies
largely among European legal systems. This chapter will discuss class actions as a method
for the resolution of crowdfunding-related disputes, also in light of the new EU Directive on
collective redress.

2

The Crowdfunding Regulation in the Context of the Capital Markets Union

Eugenia Macchiavello

I. Putting the Crowdfunding Regulation in Context: Capital Markets Union and Recent Challenges

The Crowdfunding Regulation was proposed by the Commission in March 2018 as part of **2.01** the Fintech Action Plan (recently renamed Digital Finance Strategy), within the broader and pre-existing Capital Markets Union (CMU) Action Plan (September 2015),[1] and eventually adopted in October 2020 as Regulation No 1503/2020.[2]

---

[1] Commission, 'Action Plan on Building a Capital Markets Union' COM(2015) 468 final; Commission, 'FinTech Action Plan: For a More Competitive and Innovative European Financial Sector' (8 March 2018) COM/2018/0109 final; Commission, 'A Digital Finance Strategy for the EU' (Communication) COM(2020) 591 final. Cut-off date for all electronic resources: 30 March 2021.

[2] Please also refer to my previous contributions on the Crowdfunding Regulation: E Macchiavello, 'The European Crowdfunding Service Providers Regulation and the Future of Marketplace Lending and Investing in Europe: The "Crowdfunding Nature" Dilemma' (2021) 32(3) European Business Law Review 557; E Macchiavello and A Sciarrone Alibrandi, 'Marketplace Lending as a New Form of Capital Raising in the Internal Market: True Disintermediation or Re-intermediation?' European Company and Financial law Review 2021, special issue 'Digital Finance in Europe: Law, Regulation, Governance' (forthcoming, available in the pre-print version at <https://ssrn.com/abstract=3903292>); E Macchiavello, '"What to Expect When You Are Expecting" a European Crowdfunding Regulation: The Current "Bermuda Triangle" and Future Scenarios for Marketplace Lending and Investing in Europe' (20 August 2019), EBI Working Paper Series No 55/2019 <https://ssrn.com/abstract = 3493 688>. Recently on the Crowdfunding Regulation: SN Hooghiemstra, 'The European Crowdfunding Regulation—Towards Harmonization of (Equity- and Lending-Based) Crowdfunding in Europe?' (22 August 2020) <https://ssrn.com/abstract = 3679142>; M Hobza and A Vondráčková, 'The New Financial Crowdfunding Regulation and Its Implications for Investment Services under MiFID II (6 November 2020), Charles University in Prague Faculty of Law Research Paper No 2020/III/2, <https://ssrn.com/abstract = 3725997>; K Wenzlaff and others, 'Crowdfunding in Europe: Between Fragmentation and Harmonization' in R Shneor, L Zhao, and B-T Flåten (eds) *Advances in Crowdfunding* (Palgrave Macmillan 2020).

2.02   In particular, the CMU Action Plan, among other objectives,[3] aims at improving European companies' access to capital markets and diversifying their funding sources. Particular attention is reserved for small and medium-sized enterprises (SMEs),[4] the backbone of the European economy[5] and so far mainly dependent on bank loans,[6] therefore considered less resilient to shocks.[7] Although last year's data about SMEs' access to finance have been promising,[8] SMEs have suffered after the financial crisis from the credit crunch and lack of availability of other external sources of financing (especially equity),[9] a situation which they might face again due to the COVID-19 pandemic and once the public funds for business support are exhausted.[10]

2.03   SMEs traditionally face several obstacles to access external financing because of the inevitable opaqueness of their business and the consequent information asymmetry problem, compared to large firms. For instance, investors can count on a limited track record and less publicly available and standardized information. Furthermore, they face higher costs to obtain this information. Banks, instead, partially overcome this problem through their traditional information advantage related to relationship banking,[11] but tend to rely also on the presence of collaterals (often non-existent in case of innovative firms). Furthermore, the expenses incurred in accessing funding (eg administrative and compliance costs, advisory fees; in case of public markets, underwriting and listing fees) are fixed and therefore relatively higher for SMEs which, moreover, face certain specific legal obstacles (eg national

---

[3] The following CMU's objectives are the most relevant in connection with companies' (in particular, SME) financing: 'financing for innovation, start-ups and non-listed companies'; 'Making it easier for companies to enter and raise capital on public market'; 'leveraging banking capacity to support the wider economy'. See European Commission, 'Addressing Information Barriers in SME Funding Market in the Context of the Capital Markets Union' SWD (2017) 229 final.

[4] According to Art 2(1)(f) Prospectus Regulation (PR), SMEs are: (a) companies meeting at least two of the following criteria: (i) average number of employees of less than 250; (ii) total balance sheet not exceeding EUR 43 million; (iii) annual turnover not exceeding EUR 50 million (see Commission Recommendation of 6 May 2003, No 2003/361/EC); (b) companies with an average market capitalization of less than EUR 200 million (SMEs under Art 4(1)(13) MiFID II).

[5] In 2018, SMEs accounted for 99.8% of all European (EU-28) non-financial enterprises (of which 93% micro-enterprises) and generated 56.4% of value added and 66.6% of employment: K Hope and others, *Annual Report on European SMEs 2018/2019* (European Commission 2019) 11.

[6] European Central Bank, 'Survey on the Access to Finance of Enterprises—SAFE—in the Euro Area' (April–September 2019) 18 (all SAFE survey Reports available at <http://www.ecb.europa.eu/pub/pub/stats/html/index.en.html?skey = survey%20access>).

[7] About CMU's attempt to limit EU companies' over-dependence on bank loans and move towards a more market-based economy (taking inspiration from the US), under the assumption of improving the ability to recover from shocks (despite the mixed results of the economic studies): N Moloney, 'Capital Markets Union: "Ever Closer Union" for the EU Financial System' (2016) European Law Review 41(3) 307; A Werner, M Torben Menk, and F Neitzert, 'The European Capital Markets Union and its Impact on Future SME Financing' in A Moritz and others (eds), *Contemporary Developments in Entrepreneurial Finance* (Springer 2020) 32; D Busch, 'A Capital Markets Union for a Divided Europe' (2017) Journal of Financial Regulation 3(2) 262. Particularly critical about CMU's goals and the premise that less bank lending and more market-based financing would benefit the sector, D Pesendorfer, *Financial Markets (Dis)Integration in a Post-Brexit EU. Towards a More Resilient Financial System in Europe* (Palgrave 2020) chapter 5.

[8] ECB, 'Survey on the Access to Finance of Enterprises in the Euro Area—April to September 2019' (November 2019) 25–26.

[9] N Moloney, 'The Legacy Effects of the Financial Crisis on Regulatory Design in the EU' in E Ferran and others (eds), *The Regulatory Aftermath of the Global Financial Crisis* (CUP 2012) 177ff.

[10] About the first sign of the worsening situation concerning SMEs access to finance after some positive years after the financial crisis: ECB, 'Survey on the Access to Finance of Enterprises in the Euro Area—April to September 2020' (November 2020) 25ff.

[11] D Diamond, 'Financial Intermediation and Delegated Monitoring' (1984) Review of Economic Studies 51(3) 393.

limits to public offers and share transferability, in the case of private limited companies).[12] The same SMEs might not be interested in accessing capital markets because of the risk of losing control over their business and disclosing, also to competitors, relevant corporate and business information, as well as because of a lack of corporate finance skills.[13]

The CMU, therefore, has planned several actions to increase SMEs access to funding and in particular to capital markets, with differentiated measures based on companies' different sizes (micro, small, medium, large) and development stages (eg start-up, seed, fast growing, established, etc) and consequent distinct financing needs (from business angels and venture capital to public markets).[14] At the same time, the CMU aims to increase retail and institutional investors' participation in capital markets, restoring confidence after the financial crisis through product comparability, increased investor choice, and protection (see also the Pan-European Personal Pension Products-PEPPs Regulation No 2019/1238). However, other actions try to incentivize continuous bank support to SMEs, such as the adjustments to the Simple, Transparent, and Standardized (STS) securitization framework, prudential treatment of the same (Regulations No 2402 and 2401/2017) and covered bonds (see also section II). **2.04**

Against this backdrop, financial-return crowdfunding (FRC) has been regarded as a particularly interesting funding tool for SMEs, filling a relevant gap in the existing market of financing. In particular, start-up (especially innovative and fast-growing ones) and micro or small companies can use investment-based crowdfunding (IBC) as a bridge from the typical first stage of financing (friends, family, and fools—FFF) to business angels (BA), venture capital (VC), or even certain small established firms, towards private equity (PE) and public capital markets. Lending-based crowdfunding (LBC) would fill a short-term funding and debt-securities financing gap for micro and young SMEs, and substitute for the expensive but commonly used bank overdrafts/credit card loans.[15] **2.05**

The availability of alternative finance becomes even more urgent in times of crises, like the current pandemic turmoil, because of the inevitable credit crunch (with banks progressively concerned with risky exposures) and the context of extreme uncertainty which pushes both retail investors and BA/VCs towards safer and later-stage investments.[16] Although the **2.06**

---

[12] About SMEs' financing obstacles: P Schammo, 'Market Building and the Capital Markets Union: Addressing Information Barriers in the SME Funding Market' (2017) 2 European Company and Finance Law Review 271; R Banerjee, 'SMEs, Financial Constraints and Growth' BIS Working Papers 475/2014 <https://www.bis.org/publ/work475.pdf>; M Pagano, F Panetta, and L Zingales, 'Why Do Companies Go Public? An Empirical Analysis' (1998) 53(1) Journal of Finance 27; G Ferrarini and A Ottolia, 'Corporate Disclosure as a Transaction Cost: The Case of SMEs' (2013) 9 European Review of Contract Law 363, 370.

[13] Werner and others (n 7) 51; Schammo (n 12) 281–83.

[14] For example, review of Prospectus Regulation and MiFID II/MiFIR SME Growth Markets: see subsection II.4.

[15] Commission, 'Impact Assessment Accompanying the Document Proposal for a Regulation ... on European Crowdfunding Service Providers (ECSP) for Business' (8 March 2018) 6, 13ff. See also Y Pierrakis and L Collins, 'Crowdfunding: A New Innovative Model of Providing Funding to Projects and Businesses' (2013) 5–6 <https://papers.ssrn.com/sol3/papers.cfm?abstract_id = 2395226>; J Jagtiani and C Lemieux, 'Do Fintech Lenders Penetrate Areas that are Underserved by Traditional Banks?' (2018) 100 Journal of Economics and Business 43; C De Roure, L Pelizzon, and AV Thakor, 'P2P Lenders Versus Banks: Creak Skimming or Bottom Fishing?', SAFE Working Paper No 206/2019 <http://hdl.handle.net/10419/203316>.

[16] N Lee, H Sameen, and M Cowling, 'Access to Finance for Innovative SMEs Since the Financial Crisis' (2015) 44(2) Research Policy 370. Specifically on the effect of COVID-19 on financial markets: R Brown, A Rocha, and M Cowling, 'Financing Entrepreneurship in Times of Crisis: Exploring the Impact of COVID-19 on the Market for Entrepreneurial finance in the United Kingdom' (2020) 38(5) International Small Business Journal 380; S Papadamou and others, 'Direct and Indirect Effects of COVID-19 Pandemic on Implied Stock Market

crowdfunding market has also been significantly hit by the pandemic crisis, it has shown a certain resilience (especially as regards tech-based companies) despite the lack of targeted public support, also because of its characteristics as a fast, affordable, digital, and distant tool, and the platforms' ability to implement targeted measures (eg more stringent selection criteria, active search of new investors, moratoria, donations, fee waiver).[17]

2.07   The Crowdfunding Regulation aims to create a single crowdfunding market, improving firms' financing while protecting investors and ensuring a level-playing field for different operators. This is in line with other actions included in the Fintech Action Plan, whose main objectives are creating or adapting legal frameworks to encourage innovative business models in the financial sector, without endangering investors and customers, and reinforcing cyber-security. Therefore, the Crowdfunding Regulation shares with most CMU actions the difficult task of balancing the goal, on the one hand, of expanding SMEs access to finance through simplification and, on the other, of ensuring investor protection and maintaining stability (sections II–IV).

2.08   The briefly described CMU plan has remained central (despite political obstacles to certain proposals, and the change in the Commission's Presidency), and it has been inserted, together with digitalization, among the 2019–24 priorities. The 2017 CMU Mid-Term Review[18] and subsequent updates[19] (including the 2020 New CMU Action plan)[20] as well as the recent Capital Markets Recovery Package[21] have in fact put forth most of the already announced initiatives, but they have also reviewed certain measures[22] and added others[23] to respond to new challenges, such as Brexit, climate change, Big Tech's entrance in financial services, financial scandals, and the pandemic crisis (section III).

2.09   This chapter will analyse FRC in comparison with traditional forms of finance and other alternative funding methods touched upon by the CMU Plan, as well as identify the related main legal issues raised by the Crowdfunding Regulation (section II), which will be

---

Volatility: Evidence from Panel Data Analysis' MPRA 100020/2020 <https://mpra.ub.uni-muenchen.de/100020/1/MPRA_paper_100020.pdf>.

[17] About the impact of the pandemic and related restrictive measures but generally sector's and platforms' ability to adequately react: European Crowdfunding Network (ECN), 'Early Impact of CoVid19 on the European Crowdfunding Sector' (April 2020) <https://eurocrowd.org/wp-content/blogs.dir/sites/85/2020/04/ECN_CoVid19_Survey_20200414.pdf>; F Battaglia, F Busato, and M Manganiello, 'Equity Crowdfunding: Brave Market or Safe Haven for the Crowd During the COVID-19 Crisis?' (1 July 2020) <https://ssrn.com/abstract = 3666021>; T Ziegler and others, 'The Global Covid-19 FinTech. Market Rapid Assessment Study' (December 2020) 87–88, <http://www.jbs.cam.ac.uk/wp-content/uploads/2020/12/2020-ccaf-global-covid-fintech-market-rapid-assessment-study.pdf> (capital raising platforms recorded an increase in volumes and number of operations as well as in the number of new issuers, while digital lending platforms presented negative figures as regards the first two categories).

[18] Commission, 'Mid-Term Review of the Capital Markets Union Action Plan' (Communication) COM/2017/0292 final and Accompanying Staff Working Document SWD/2017/0224 final.

[19] Commission, 'Capital Markets Union: Progress on Building a Single Market for Capital for a Strong Economic and Monetary Union' (Communication) (15 March 2019) COM(2019) 136 final.

[20] Commission, 'A Capital Markets Union for People and Businesses—New Action Plan' (Communication) (24 September 2020) COM(2020) 590 final (hereinafter, New CMU Action Plan); High Level Forum on the Capital Markets Union (HLFCMU), 'A New Vision for Europe's Capital Markets—Final Report' (June 2020).

[21] Commission, 'EU Capital Markets Recovery Package' (24 July 2020) SWD(2020) 120 final.

[22] For example, in the areas of the Prospectus Regulation, securitizations, ELTIF, PEPP, etc: see subsequent sections.

[23] For example, ESAs Review, prudential requirements for investment firms, bank referral, sustainability considerations.

discussed in further details in other chapters. Finally, it will assess the coherence of the resulting overall framework (section IV).

II. Distinctive Features of Crowdfunding and Other Funding Options

1. FRC and Its Characteristics—General Aspects

Because of its peer-to-peer and digital based nature, as well as variety of business models **2.10** (Chapter 1), crowdfunding has puzzled regulators worldwide. In this respect, the most challenging form is FRC, which is the only one covered by the Crowdfunding Regulation[24] (see Chapters 11 and 15). FRC has received different legal qualifications/responses worldwide, ranging from the application of existing financial regulation (eg banking, lending, payment services, or investment services law), to dedicated regimes (Chapter 1), to prohibition, or, on the contrary, absolute freedom. Such significant differences are the consequence of the variety of national interpretations with regard to fundamental terms included in EU financial directives and regulations (such as investment products, financial instruments, and investment services), national discretion/exemptions in these instruments, and the lack of EU harmonization in certain relevant areas (such as company law and lending regulation).[25]

One of the original features of FRC (at least supposedly) is the elimination of traditional **2.11** financial intermediaries and the creation of marketplaces for the direct interaction of firms and investors/lenders ('disintermediation'), with digital platforms only offering basic checks, communication channels, filter mechanisms, and post-transaction assistance (eg coordination and updates). This allows for the reduction of costs associated with the long chains of intermediaries.[26] On the other hand, disintermediation also brings about significant effects by removing the important function performed by traditional intermediaries in containing information asymmetries.

---

[24] Donation- and reward-based crowdfunding, lacking any financial-return perspective, cannot be reconnected to the general CMU framework and its goal of deepening EU capital markets. However, the Commission has recommended the application to them of consumer laws and the AML/CT regime: Commission, 'Impact Assessment' (n 15) 33. About these two forms of crowdfunding, see Chapters 11 and 15.

[25] For a detailed analysis of the main legal issues, also from a comparative point of view (in addition to contributions in footnote 2): E Macchiavello, 'Peer-to-peer Lending and the "Democratization" of Credit Markets: Another Financial Innovation Puzzling Regulator' (2015) 21(3) Columbia Journal of European Law 521; E Macchiavello, 'Financial-return Crowdfunding and Regulatory Approaches in the Shadow Banking, Fintech and Collaborative Finance Era' (2017) 14(4) European Company and Financial Law Review 662; G Ferrarini and others, 'Investment-based Crowdfunding: Is MiFID II Enough?' in D Busch and G Ferrarini (eds), *Regulation of EU Financial Markets: MiFID II* (OUP 2017); E Macchiavello, 'Disintermediation in Fund-raising Marketplace Investing Platforms and EU Financial Regulation' in I Chiu and G Deipenbrock (eds), *Routledge Handbook on Financial Technology and Law* (Routledge 2021) 295; M Klaes and others, 'Identifying Market and Regulatory Obstacles to Crossborder Development of Crowdfunding in the EU–Final Report' (December 2017) <https://ec.eur opa.eu/info/sites/info/files/171216-crowdfunding-report_en.pdf>; D Zetzsche and C Preiner, 'Cross-Border Crowdfunding—Towards a Single Crowdfunding Market for Europe (2018) 19 European Business Organization Law Review 217; O Havrylchyk (2018) 'Regulatory Framework for the Loan-Based Crowdfunding Platforms' OECD Economics Department Working Papers No 1513/2018; D Ahern (1 March 2018) 'Regulatory Arbitrage in a FinTech World: Devising an Optimal EU Regulatory Response to Crowdlending' EBI Working Paper 24/2018 <https://ssrn.com/abstract = 3163728>.

[26] For instance, BAs financing absorbs in various fees 40–45%of capital raised by issuers, IPOs 7%(more if SMEs), while crowdfunding only 4–5%: D Cumming and S Johan, *Crowdfunding. Fundamental Cases, Facts, and Insights* (Academic Press 2019) 5.

2.12   Therefore, investors seem to rely on various and unusual types of 'soft' information (eg candidates' picture, education, social network coverage, retention rates, speed of early investments by other users, size of investments from family and friends, patents) instead of typical financial documentation. This raises the risk of irrational and herding behaviours. Studies, however, seem to attest positive results concerning the investors' ability to choose among the available options ('rational herding').[27] The sector has also developed alternative and market-based methods to reduce information asymmetries or, more generally, contain risks in crowdfunding markets, such as risk-based categories of borrowers determined by the platform, lending groups with a leader tasked with conducting due diligence, co-investing with business angels or the platform itself, feedbacks and forums, contingent funds, and investment limits to force diversification. Certain platforms provide users also with ratings/rankings, often based on innovative and algorithmic-based evaluation systems, again relying on soft information data about utility bills, spending, log hours, etc. Some have also partially or fully implemented auto-investment systems, or even portfolio management of loans with guaranteed returns. Under the first model, platforms automatically match investor preferences (in terms of risk, maturity, industry, etc) and borrowers' characteristics, based on a deeper due diligence performed by the platform on the latter. Under the second model (widespread in the UK, China, and US), the platform more actively manages crowd investments, to attain a determined return.[28] Investors' reliance on platforms' due diligence and even portfolio management obviously raises even more doubts on a true 'disintermediation', suggesting instead a 're-intermediation', with platforms performing old and new intermediary functions.[29]

2.13   The Crowdfunding Regulation has taken a strict approach on this matter, not only excluding certain 'indirect' models and disregarding alternative risk-mitigation mechanisms but also imposing stringent organizational and conduct requirements on platforms offering pricing/credit scoring and portfolio management of loans, even when not offering a guaranteed return (see subsection II.4 and Chapter 8).[30]

2.14   FRC also offers to firms, especially SMEs, a cheaper and faster process, thanks to technology, lighter regulation, and cost minimization,[31] while testing/giving visibility to their

---

[27]   Among many: A Agrawal, C Catalini, and A Goldfarb (2013) 'Some Simple Economics of Crowdfunding' NBER Working Paper 19133/2013, 22ff, <https://www.nber.org/papers/w19133>; Cumming and Johan (n 26) chapter 2, 10; G Ahlers and others, 'Signaling in Equity Crowdfunding' (2015) 39(4) Entrepreneurship Theory and Practice 955; S Vismara, 'Equity Retention and Social Network Theory in Equity Crowdfunding' (2016) 46(4) Small Business Economics 579; M Nitani, A Riding, and B He, 'On Equity Crowdfunding: Investor Rationality and Success Factors' (2019) 21(2/3) Venture Capital 243; Battaglia and others (n 17).

[28]   About the prediction of a shift towards re-intermediation in P2P lending markets because of increased institutional investors' involvement and consequent improved screening by platforms to attract non-sophisticated investors (showing therefore a more passive attitude) as well as in response to liquidity shocks: B Vallée and Y Zeng, 'Marketplace Lending: A New Banking Paradigm?' (2019) 32(5) Review of Financial Studies 1939, 1946; J Franks, N Serrano-Velarde, and O Sussman, 'Marketplace Lending, Information Aggregation, and Liquidity' (16 March 2020), ECGI-Finance Working Paper No 678/2020 <https://ssrn.com/abstract = 2869945>.

[29]   About different models/services: A Rossi and S Vismara, 'What Do Crowdfunding Platforms Do? A Comparison Between Investment-Based Platforms in Europe (2018) 8 Eurasian Business Review 93; T Ziegler and R Shneor, 'Lending Crowdfunding: Principles and Market Development' in Shneor and others (n 2) 63. On the FRC platform's dilemma see also contributions in footnotes 2 and 25; I H-Y Chiu, 'Fintech and Disruptive Business Models in Financial Products, Intermediation and Markets-Policy Implications for Financial Regulators' (2016) 21(1) Journal of Technology Law & Policy 55, 86–87.

[30]   In this regard: Macchiavello, 'European' (n 2) 597; Macchiavello and Sciarrone Alibrandi (n 2).

[31]   LBC platforms' operating costs are minimized through technology (eg automated systems), off-balance sheet loans, lack of transformation and maturity risk and, consequently, also disregard of banking regulation: C

products and leveraging investments from other sources. Compared to both initial public offerings (IPOs) and bank lending, FRC seems also to convey a more democratic distribution of funds across economic categories of borrowers/issuers, territories, gender, and minorities, but evidence is not always conclusive.[32] Furthermore, entrepreneurs might be able to maintain the control over the activity and more autonomy, in contrast to typical IPOs, VC, and PE operations (subsections II.3–II.4) but also in respect to certain lending operations. The offering of debt-based, hybrid, or non-equity opportunities (eg subordinated/participating loans, deals recognizing only a participation to profits, etc) through crowdfunding platforms might in fact reach this goal, although the legal qualification of such instruments might be subject to discussion at national level and within the Crowdfunding Regulation (see Chapter 13).[33]

From an investors' perspective, crowdfunding (especially reward-based crowdfunding but also partially IBC) appears to respond to expectations of non-financial returns (eg engagement, sense of community, and ideals sharing),[34] resilience, and diversification, but might also raise doubts about risk.[35] Compared again to more classical forms of funding, crowdfunding lacks typical protections (eg deposit guarantee schemes, authority's checks on the information document) but it should, consequently, also create lower expectations and lower systemic risk. The Crowdfunding Regulation requires crowdfunding service providers (CSPs) to disclose this aspect to investors and, in case they operate a contingent fund, to describe its functioning clearly and update clients about its performance, as well as to warn investors about the related risks (eg lack of repayment/pay-out). However, the Crowdfunding Regulation also imposes general prudential requirements for operational risk (as for investment firms under the recent Investment Firm Directive/Investment Firm Regulation (IFD/IFR) package, but capital requirements are lower under the Crowdfunding Regulation) and specific organizational requirements when operating contingent funds (see Chapter 8). **2.15**

The following subsections will provide a closer look at FRC compared to other funding options, discussing the main legal issues and regulatory evolution in the framework of the CMU. **2.16**

Serrano-Cinca, B Gutierrez-Nieto, and L López-Palacios, 'Determinants of Default in P2P Lending' (2015) 10(10) PLoS One 1, 3.

[32] A Schwartz, 'Crowdfunding Issuers in the United States' (2020) 61 Journal of Law & Policy 155. But see D Cumming, M Meoli, and S Vismara, 'Does Equity Crowdfunding Democratize Entrepreneurial Finance?' (2019) Small Business Economics (rejecting the hypothesis that EBC increases female entrepreneurs' opportunities).

[33] For instance, the definition in Art 2(1)b of 'loan' as an 'unconditional obligation to repay' seems to exclude certain subordinated loans from the Crowdfunding Regulation's scope: Macchiavello 'European' (n 2) 566.

[34] A Schwienbacher and B Larralde, 'Crowdfunding of Small Entrepreneurial Ventures' in D Cumming (ed), *The Oxford Handbook of Entrepreneurial Finance* (OUP 2012) 369, 373ff; D Popescul and others, 'Psychological Determinants of Investor Motivation in Social Media-Based Crowdfunding Projects: A Systematic Review' (2020) 11 Frontiers in Psychology 1. About reward-based crowdfunding, see Chapter 15.

[35] See D Blaseg, D Cumming, and M Koetter, 'Equity Crowdfunding: High-Quality or Low-Quality Entrepreneurs? (2020) Entrepreneurship Theory and Practice 1 (crowdfunding would attract riskier SMEs because strong SMEs tend to access other forms of financing); X Walthoff-Borm, T Vanacker, and V Collewaert, 'Equity Crowdfunding, Shareholder Structures, and Firm Performance' (2018) 26 Corporate Governance: An International Review 314 (firms recurring to crowdfunding present higher risk of failure but also of higher chances of getting a patent); A Signori and S Vismara, 'Does Success Bring Success? The Post-offering Lives of Equity-crowdfunded Firms' (2018) 50 Journal of Corporate Finance 575 (firms' risk of failure is lower in crowdfunding when investments are backed by qualified investors); see also X Walthoff-Borm, A Schwienbacher, and T Vanacker, 'Equity Crowdfunding. First Resort or Last Resort?' (2018) 33(4) Journal of Business Ventures 513.

2. Banking, Lending, and Payment Services

2.17   Banks (traditionally and according to the EU legal definition in Article 4(1)1 CRR) accept repayable funds from the public to grant loans for their own account. In doing so, banks perform a fundamental economic function, funding valuable activities through underused economic resources, and also ensuring money and liquidity creation and maturity transformation. This contributes to justifying the existence of strict banking regulation, especially in terms of prudential regulation/supervision.[36]

2.18   LBC platforms, in principle, do not engage in banking, given that they do not acquire the ownership of the funds received from crowd-lenders, and they do not provide loans for their own account. Loans, under the basic model, are in fact provided directly by crowdlenders to crowdborrowers chosen by the former, with platforms only facilitating such transaction through the creation of an information system.[37] Nonetheless, in certain countries, LBC platforms have been regarded as abusively conducting banking activities, because of wide national definitions of the latter. Sometimes, those definitions cover lending-only services, even when provided by natural persons acting outside a business activity (eg Germany or France, until recent reforms), or reception of repayable funds even when not conducted in a professional/regular way (eg Italy and Belgium). Therefore, in these countries, even the mere facilitation by the platform of such activities (in violation of the banking monopoly) would be illegal. The Crowdfunding Regulation explicitly distinguishes crowdfunding from banking. The Crowdfunding Service Providers (CSPs) authorization is sufficient to provide crowdfunding services within a Member State and across borders within the EU,[38] and CSPs are not required to hold a banking licence (unless they want to provide services not covered by the Crowdfunding Regulation such as reception of repayable funds). Furthermore, the Crowdfunding Regulation also obliges Member States to refrain from requiring crowdborrowers and crowdlenders to hold or apply for a banking licence, or for an individual exemption or dispensation, as well as from applying banking laws to them, unless they are authorized as credit institutions (Article 1(3) and recital 9; see Chapter 9).[39]

2.19   In any event, putting lenders in contact with potential borrowers would be better classified as a broker-like service, which is not regulated at EU level (and often not even at national level; see, however, the dispensation required of crowdfunding platforms in this regard in the Netherlands, discussed in Chapter 1), at least when the lender is not a professional

---

[36] About (traditional and new) rationales of banking regulation: M Duwatripont and J Tirole, *The Prudential Regulation of Banks* (MIT Press 1993); R Cranston and others, *Principles of Banking Law* (OUP 2017); J Armour and others, *Principles of Financial Regulation* (OUP 2016).

[37] Distinguishing LBC from banking activity: Committee on the Global Financial System (CGFS)–Financial Stability Board (FSB), *FinTech Credit. Market Structure, Business Models and Financial Stability Implications* (BIS 2017) 31; S Claessens and others, 'Fintech Credit Markets Around the World: Size, Drivers and Policy Issues' (2018) 32 Business Information Systems Quarterly Review; O Havrylchyk and M Verdier, 'The Financial Intermediation Role of the P2P Lending Platforms' (2018) 60(1) Comparative Economic Studies 115; T Balyuk and S Davydenko, 'Reintermediation in FinTech: Evidence from Online Lending', Michael J Brennan Irish Finance Working Paper No 18-17/2019, 38, <https://ssrn.com/abstract = 3189236>; Vallée and Zeng (n 28); AV Thakor, 'Fintech and Banking: What Do We Know?' (2020) 41 Journal of Financial Intermediation 1.

[38] For instance, in the Netherlands, a dispensation from the authorization to attract repayable funds from the public is currently required (see Chapter 1), but this requirement should disappear.

[39] The Bank of Italy, in order to exclude the violation by crowd-borrowers of the rules governing the acceptance of repayable funds from the public and the banking monopoly, requires evidence of private negotiations between the parties and investment limits (see Macchiavello, 'Financial-return crowdfunding', n 25, 684): such requirements should be in principle eliminated in implementing the Crowdfunding Regulation.

lender and the borrower is not a consumer. However, business models entailing instant investors' redemption rights and forms of portfolio management of loans, with the platform performing all due diligence checks and deciding (discretionally or through algorithms) where to invest, might move crowdlending close to banking,[40] unless the credit risk remains the investor's. Nevertheless, FRC differs from banking because of the lack of banking regulation-related aspects (eg absence of fund protection), limited permissible activities (in the absence of other separate authorizations), products, and, often, even access to official national databases about defaults and creditworthiness (credit bureaux). The aforementioned features, thus, seem to move crowdfunding closer to investment portfolio management, or other investment services/schemes.

The fact that the platform is not a direct lender has often excluded the applicability of (national) lending laws. In particular, since the lender is another individual, and not a professional, even in case of consumer-borrowers, the Directive 2008/48/EC (CCD) has not found application to peer-to-peer lending in many countries (due to the absence of a consumer loan, a condition for its application), potentially leaving consumer crowd-borrowers unprotected, and convincing the EU to review the directive also in this regard (the review is still ongoing). However, Member States have been allowed to expand or interpret the CCD differently, leading to different national approaches as regards the application of consumer credit protection to peer-to-peer (P2P) loans to consumers (or even small companies, eg in the UK). On the contrary, the Commission has excluded consumer LBC from the Crowdfunding Regulation's scope, considering the area already covered by the CCD. A possible additional reason for the exclusion of P2P loans was the lack of connection with a CMU perspective, and the delicate nature of this type of loans (hardly compatible with the Crowdfunding Regulation's view of borrowers as issuers). Nonetheless, taking into consideration its market coverage and the inability of the CCD or other consumer instruments (see Chapter 5) to respond to all risks (eg investor/lender protection from frauds), such a decision might appear questionable.[41]   **2.20**

However, as already mentioned, certain platforms have adopted a business model that entails co-lending by the platform (with its own funds) along with crowdborrowers in order to align the platform's and investors' interests. This model, although once again different from banking, would require compliance with national rules on lending, which are not harmonized at EU level yet. The Crowdfunding Regulation, instead, prohibits CSPs to engage in balance-sheet lending (unless they have a separate authorization as banks) or to have any other financial participation in the offers (potentially even in the form of success fees), so as to maintain their role as 'neutral' intermediaries (Chapter 7).[42]   **2.21**

Since LBC platforms do not bear the underlying credit risk, an 'originate-to-distribute' risk (as with subprime loans/securitizations during the financial crisis) might arise, as well as agency costs and doubts about the effective diligence in selecting borrowers (especially in   **2.22**

---

[40] Havrylchyk and Verdier (n 37).
[41] See, also more generally about the CCD scope and Member States' approaches: Macchiavello 'European' (n 2) 565–66; Macchiavello, 'Financial-return' (n 25) 696; Macchiavello and Sciarrone Alibrandi (n 2). About the application of the CCD, MCD, and EU consumer law, see in this book Chapter 5.
[42] Macchiavello 'European' (n 2) 583–84; Macchiavello and Sciarrone Alibrandi (n 2).

case of volume-based fees).[43] In any case, studies seem to attest that crowdfunding platforms have increased the level of diligence over time, due to several factors, such as competition and reputation capital (also linked to repetitive lenders), performance-based fees (reducing agency problems related to volume-based fees), and willingness to attract retail investors (who demand reduced informational asymmetries).[44] Despite this evidence (which may change due to new market factors), in addition to a general duty of diligence towards clients, the Crowdfunding Regulation prefers to impose on LBC platforms the requirement to adopt appropriate systems and controls to assess the risks of the loans they intermediate (but not investment-based products). Additional, detailed, and differentiated requirements in terms of credit risk assessment and management are set in case of scoring/pricing services and portfolio management of loans (see Chapter 9). This is not surprising, considering the recent trend to also impose requirements on banks (which bear credit risk), with respect to creditworthiness assessment, loan origination, and monitoring.[45] These requirements are justified by stability concerns (also related to the non-performing loans problem) but also by borrower protection. By contrast, the Crowdfunding Regulation does not focus much on (SMEs) borrower protection (except for fairness and disclosure) but imposes detailed disclosure about creditworthiness or selection systems (so far opaque also for industrial secrecy concerns),[46] and complaint handling procedures to the advantage of both borrowers and investors (see Chapter 8). This approach is consistent with the fact that the Regulation regards crowdborrowers as issuers. Nonetheless, such detailed organizational requirements, in the LBC context, run the risk of limiting innovation and financial inclusion, and pushing crowdfunding closer to traditional financial services.[47]

2.23   Being an alternative form of financing potentially benefiting otherwise unserved customers, crowdfunding could be in theory associated with microcredit, that is, the provision of small loans (generally up to EUR 25,000 and with short maturity) to small and micro-entrepreneurs or disadvantaged consumers, together with accompanying services (such as business support or financial education). One of the first LBC platforms in the US has been Kiva, facilitating interest-free loans provided by Western users to microfinance providers (and, indirectly, to micro-entrepreneurs) in developing countries.[48] Nonetheless, the two

---

[43] P Giudici and B Hadji Misheva, 'P2P Lending Scoring Models: Do They Predict Default?' (2018) 2 Journal of Digital Banking 353; P Giudici, B Hadji-Misheva, and A Spelta, 'Network Based Scoring Models to Improve Credit Risk Management in Peer to Peer Lending Platforms' (2019) Frontiers of Artificial Intelligence.

[44] Balyuk and Davydenko (n 37). On the different type and weight of reputational incentives for banks and non-bank lenders: R Thakor and R Merton, 'Trust in Lending', NBER Working Paper No 24778/2018, <http://www.nber.org/papers/w24778> (version updated September 2019 at <http://www.researchgate.net/publication/326473894_Trust_in_Lending>); Thakor (n 37).

[45] The first stricter requirements for banks in this sense have been introduced only for FinTech banks by the European Central Bank 'Guide to Assessments of Fintech Credit Institution Licence Applications' (March 2018) but the recent EBA guidelines on loan origination and monitoring (20 May 2020) have set detailed requirements (best practices) in terms of internal governance for credit granting and monitoring, loan origination procedures based on the type of borrowers, pricing, collateral valuation, and monitoring framework (still on a 'comply-or-explain' basis). Stricter responsible lending requirements are set for residential consumer loans in the Mortgage Credit Directive 2014/17 (and, partially, also CCD).

[46] CGFS-FSB (n 37) 11–12; Ziegler and Shneor (n 2) 77–79.

[47] See more extensively on all these issues, Macchiavello 'European' (n 2) 581–82, 595–99; Macchiavello and Sciarrone Alibrandi (n 2).

[48] A Kallio and L Vuola, 'History of Crowdfunding in the Context of Ever-Changing Modern Financial Markets' in Shneor and others (n 2) 221; H Kraemer-Eis and F Lang, 'Access to Funds: How Could CMU Support SME Financing?' (2017) 86(1) Quarterly Journal of Economics Research 96, 100–01; E Mollick, 'Swept Away by the Crowd? Crowdfunding, Venture Capital, and the Selection of Entrepreneurs' (25 March 2013) 9 <https://ssrn.com/abstract = 2239204>. About microcredit and microfinance regulation in Europe and the interaction with

phenomena, although both constituting funding opportunities for small and micro enter-prises and low-income consumers, present relevant differences: microcredit institutions provide loans at their own risk to individual entrepreneurs and disadvantaged people, on the basis of a very labour-intensive and relationship-based business model in close con-nection with local social services and not-for-profit organizations, and are therefore hardly financially sustainable. Moreover, microcredit has not received a harmonized regulation in Europe, being regulated differently in different Member States, and it remains a local/na-tional activity.

At any rate, in order to manage the transfer of money from crowd-lenders to crowd-bor-rowers and/or their relative payment accounts, the platform would need an authorization as payment service providers under the Payment Services Directive II (PSD II), unless it falls within an exemption, or an authorized provider would need to step in. In this way, client money would be protected from platforms' misappropriation or failure, despite the lack of traditional safeguards (such as deposit protection), since the funds, under PSD II, must be separated from the providers' funds and deposited at a bank, thus being indirectly protected by a deposit guarantee scheme. Certain countries have even indicated the payment service (or e-money) provider authorization as the one recommended for LBC platforms (eg Italy, Poland, Czech Republic, Denmark, Sweden). Such an authorization, however, would not cover much more complex services which are typical of CSPs (eg project owner selection, matching, pricing, information channelling, etc). Under the Crowdfunding Regulation, au-thorized CSPs are subject to a comprehensive regime tailored to the specific crowdfunding services they offer, but they can also offer payment services, either indirectly through a third party, or directly, after having obtained a separate PSD II authorization (Article 10(4) and recital 29). Anti-money laundering checks required under Directive (EU) 2015/849 (AMLD) will be performed by the PSD provider (the CSP itself, the partner used for funds transfers, or the external PSD provider), hence reducing the platform's compliance burden when not providing payment services directly (Chapter 8).[49]

2.24

3. Business Angels, Venture Capital, and Private Equity Funds

Evaluating a start-up or high-growth company requires entrepreneurial skills and technical expertise. For this reason, as already mentioned, crowdfunding investees are often served

2.25

crowdfunding, please see E Macchiavello, *Microfinance and Financial Inclusion. The Challenge of Regulating Alternative Forms of Finance* (Routledge 2018).

[49] The recently issued 'EBA Guidelines on ML/TF risk factors (revised)' (1 March 2021; EBA/GL/2021/02) sound ambiguous in this regard since they contain an entire section (guideline 17) dedicated to CSPs, as they were *per se* subject to AML/CT know-your-customer obligations. However, considering Art 10 Crowdfunding Regulation, Art 45(2) under p (entrusting the Commission with the task of assessing in a future report whether to list AML/CT obligations directly to CSPs) and the discussions during trilateral negotiations, guideline 17 should be referred to CSPs already covered by AML/CT Directive being, for instance, a PSD provider, an agent of PSD provider, a bank, an investment firm, etc, and should find application in addition to other guidelines (eg guide-lines 9, 11, 15) and justified by the need to address additional risks, specific to crowdfunding services, not ad-dressed in other sections of the same EBA guidelines. See also guidelines 17.10–17.13 (the latter also specifying that crowdfunding providers authorized under national crowdfunding laws—ie not covered by the Crowdfunding Regulation—and subject to national law implementing AML/CT Directive, should also follow such EBA guide-lines for consistent and harmonized AML/CT application and supervision).

by BAs, VCs, and PE funds. These three 'traditional' forms of finance actually differ among themselves. BAs tend to be individual qualified investors and invest at an early stage (representing the first step after FFF), locally and across different industries, while VCs and PE (generally funds where institutional investors and high net worth individuals—HNWIs— invest) focus primarily on later-stage, technological, and high-growth companies.[50]

2.26 Nonetheless, while BAs, VCs, and PE are 'intrusive' investors with investments of relevant size in few companies (located in few countries), customized contracts and preferential terms,[51] FRC appears more 'democratic' and might allow entrepreneurs (including small ones) to retain control over their business activity,[52] and have a large and distributed investor base.[53] On the other hand, BAs and VCs ensure a high level of business, technical, and strategic support,[54] as well as more secrecy (about intellectual property (IP) issues, see Chapter 10). Moreover, on the investors' side, exit from IBC is more difficult, due to the lack of IPOs and liquid markets (see also Chapter 13).[55]

2.27 However, the most challenging—but also characteristic—aspect of crowdfunding is allowing retail investors to operate without the traditional safeguards in a very risky environment (seed and start-up companies) typically accessible only to experienced investors.[56] In fact, the European Venture Capital Funds Regulation (EuVECA, together with European Social Entrepreneurship Funds Regulation (EuSEF)) sets a minimum ticket size of EUR 100,000, to ensure that only professional/institutional investors and HNWIs can access such a market. Even the EuVECA review (Regulation No 2017/1991), within the CMU Action, has left this limit untouched, despite initial proposals, and cross-border venture capital investments in unlisted medium-size innovative enterprises are incentivized in other ways, that is through the extension of the scope of admissible managers (even larger alternative investment funds (AIFs), improving economies of scale), and admissible firms[57]

---

[50] OECD, *Financing High-Growth Firms: The Role of Angel Investors* (OECD 2011) 10, 21, 28; C Mason and R Harrison, 'Business Angel Investment Activity in the Financial Crisis: UK evidence and Policy Implications' (2015) 33(1) Environment and Planning C: Government and Policy 43.

[51] While BA generally invest in common shares, VC use various forms of corporate mechanisms to monitor and, in case, assume control (staged investments, preferred stock, convertible shares, tag-/drag-along clauses, etc): P Gompers and others, 'How Do Venture Capitalists Make Decisions?', NBER Working Paper No 22587/ 2016; E Pederzini and A Toniolo, 'SMEs' Equity Financing: Does Corporate Law Matter?' (2020) 17(6) European Company Law (2020) 216.

[52] This, however, depends on the type of instrument—equity stock versus non-voting shares or profit-participation rights—and the coordination role played by the platform.

[53] Mollick (n 48) 10; Commission 'SWD' (n 18) 26–27; L Hornuf and A Schwienbacher, 'Crowdinvesting: Angel Investing for the Masses?' in H Landström and C Mason (eds), *Handbook of Research on Business Angels* (Elgar 2016) 381.

[54] See D Gordon Smith, 'Team Production in Venture Capital Investing' (1999) 24 Journal of Corporate Law 949; J Abor, *Entrepreneurial Finance for MSMEs* (Palgrave 2017). About VC dynamics: P Gompers and J Lerner, *The Venture Capital Cycle* (MIT Press 1999); S Kaplan and P Strömberg, 'Financial Contracting Theory Meets the Real World: An Empirical Analysis of Venture Capital Contracts (2003) 70(2) Review of Financial Studies 281. See also P Giudici and P Agstner, 'Startups and Company Law: The Competitive Pressure of Delaware on Italy (and Europe?)', ECGI Law Working Paper No 471/2019 <https://ssrn.com/abstract = 3433366>; M D'Ambrosio and G Gianfrate, 'Crowdfunding and Venture Capital: Substitutes or Complements?' (2016) 20(1) Journal of Political Economy 7.

[55] Hornuf and Schwienbacher (n 53).

[56] J Armour and L Enriques, 'The Promise and Perils of Crowdfunding: Between Corporate Finance and Consumer Contracts' (2018) 81(1) Modern Law Review 51.

[57] Admissible firms have been extended to unlisted firms with no more than 499 employees and SMEs admitted to SME growth markets (other than regulated financial institutions). Other revisions pertain to initial minimum capital requirement (EUR 50,000) and own funds requirement (one eighth of the preceding year fixed overheads, with additional own funds for AUM above EUR 250 million).

(to further allow diversification). By contrast, the European Long-Term Investments Funds (ELTIF) Regulation sets a lower threshold (EUR 10,000) so as to foster long-term investments in non-financial unlisted companies of certain industries (eg infrastructure, energy, transport) even from retail investors. Such a lower threshold, however, is counterbalanced *inter alia* by diversification requirements, investment threshold, limits on leverage and derivatives, and short-selling ban.

Among the risk-mitigation practices developed by the crowdfunding market (eg diversi-   **2.28** fication, platform's rating, 'signalling', performance-based fees: see subsections II.1–II.2), the possibility to co-invest with BAs or other sophisticated investors is worth mentioning. This way, retail investors can leverage the knowledge of more experienced investors, and these can in turn leverage the funds from a large number of investors, with a possible paradigm shift in the BA/VC market. However, more generally, the increased participation of institutional investors in the crowdfunding sector ('institutionalization'), especially in the LBC segment,[58] might put non-sophisticated investors at a disadvantage. this is particularly true when transparency and fair conditions are not ensured, so that non-sophisticated investors are left with 'lemons', while institutional investors 'cherry-pick'. The Crowdfunding Regulation limits the risks for retail investors through a system of investor protection based on clear and nontechnical information (eg the Key Investment Information Sheet or KIIS) and, for non-sophisticated investors, several warnings (but no maximum absolute investment limit), entry-knowledge test, simulation of losses test, and withdrawal rights (Chapter 12). By contrast, the Crowdfunding Regulation does not address the 'institutionalization' risk, save for requiring equal terms among investors.[59]

4. IPOs, Investment Services, and Collective Investment Schemes

FRC is an open call for funds from people needing financing to the public with an invest-   **2.29** ment perspective; it is facilitated, in reaching investors and structuring the operation, by a platform. When involving transferable securities, therefore, the similarities with IPOs and investment services are evident, despite the 'disintermediation' narratives. Consequently, the principles of technology neutrality and 'same activity same rules' require these activities to be regulated in the same way (eg prospectus to be published under the Prospectus Regulation (PR); authorization and requirements/duties in Markets in Financial Instruments Directive II (MiFID II)/Markets in Financial Instruments Regulation (MiFIR)), ensuring a level playing field, unless relevant differences justify a differentiated treatment.

FRC has certain peculiarities that might meet this last condition. In particular, LBC loans   **2.30** are not generally considered transferable securities (at least unless freely negotiable) and

---

[58] In 2018, European platforms with more than one-third of their volumes funded through institutional investors represented 55% of P2P Business Lending, 38% of P2P Property Lending, 60% of debt-based securities, and 70% of invoice trading (versus only 18% of P2P Consumer lending and 16% of equity-based and real estate crowdfunding), with peaks in Italy, Benelux, and Germany: T Ziegler and others, 'The Global Alternative Finance Market Benchmarking Report' (2020) 86–88, <www.jbs.cam.ac.uk/fileadmin/user_upload/research/centres/alternative-finance/downloads/2020-04-22-ccaf-globalalternative-finance-market-benchmarking-report.pdf>.

[59] Further details in Macchiavello 'European' (n 2) 599; Macchiavello, Sciarrone (n 2).

might be requested not only by a company but also by an individual (even a consumer), although complex LBC models echo certain investment services or funds (see subsection II.2).

2.31   Furthermore, IBC may involve products other than transferable securities, also depending on the interpretations and conditions for 'negotiability' set by each Member State, and small-ticket investments as well as small private limited companies as issuers (instead of mature ones going public with a relevant track record after a VC exit). In light of this, IBC can serve SMEs which would otherwise be excluded from capital markets (see section I, subsection II.1). The CMU has tried to reduce the costs of SMEs in accessing public markets through simplifications in the prospectus[60] and secondary issuance documents, as well as through the creation of SME Growth Markets (a label for multilateral trading facilities (MTFs) dedicated to SMEs). However, these measures have not proved to be very successful.[61]

2.32   Although the Crowdfunding Regulation aims to facilitate access to capital for SMEs, it does not restrict the category of possible investees on the basis of size, leaving eligibility choices to CSPs. It limits, though, to EUR 5 million in total consideration the maximum amount of all exempted offers presented by the same issuer/borrower in 12 months (a compromise between the PR EUR 1 million mandatory exemption, and the EUR 8 million voluntary exemption). As a consequence, the interest of large firms to resort to such a financing channel is possibly limited but not excluded. In this respect, the originally proposed EUR 1 million threshold would have been oriented more towards SMEs but would have also appeared too low for certain types of start-ups in capital-intensive industries (eg the renewable energy sector).[62]

2.33   Moreover, IBC aims, in principle, to substitute investment intermediation with alternative methods for risk and asymmetric information reduction (see subsection II.1). In light of this, it might be difficult to identify the traditional structures of IPOs/distribution (eg underwriting syndicate) and related investment services. In fact, Member States have adopted divergent approaches in identifying whether CSPs offer investment services and, if they do, which ones. Depending on the business models, the CSP may provide only certain parts of specific MiFID II services, and/or single aspects of several investment services. In light of the peculiar nature of these services, some Member States have applied the available exemptions (eg the exemption from prospectus obligations—ranging nationally from EUR

---

[60] The EU Growth Prospectus is available to SMEs and mid-cap companies with certain characteristics (with securities traded or to be traded on a SME growth market and market capitalization below EUR 500 million; or with no securities traded on an MTF and average number of employees up to 499, provided that the total consideration for the offering does not exceed EUR 20 million in twelve months) (Art 15 PR). About the PR, D Busch, G Ferrarini, and JP Franx (eds), *Prospectus Regulation and Prospectus Liability* (OUP 2020); specifically about EU Growth Prospectus: A Perrone, '"Light" Disclosure Regimes: The EU Growth Prospectus' in ibid chapter 10; B de Tong and T Arons, 'Modernizing the Prospectus Directive' in D Busch, E Avgouleas, and G Ferrarini (eds), *Capital Markets Union in Europe* (OUP 2018) 238.

[61] SMEs Growth Markets aimed to facilitate SMEs access to recognized trading venues while reducing the risk of adverse selection for investors and improving market liquidity and venture capital exit but the concrete choices about admission to trading criteria and disclosure to investors and periodic reporting have been delegated to the same SMEs Growth Markets within Member States' regulatory framework to preserve local needs, with consequent only partial and anyway locally-differentiated realization of the above-mentioned goals: A Perrone, 'Small and Medium Enterprises Growth Markets' in Busch and others (eds), *Capital Markets Union* (n 60) 253.

[62] Macchiavello, 'European' (n 2) 568–69; E Macchiavello and M Siri, 'Sustainable Finance and Fintech: Can Technology Contribute to Achieving Environmental Goals? A Preliminary Assessment of 'Green FinTech', EBI Working Paper 71/2020 <https://ssrn.com/abstract = 3672989>.

1 million to EUR 8 million[63]—and Article 3(1) of MiFID II), while others have introduced special national regimes (as described in Chapter 1).[64] Furthermore, crowdfunding investment decisions appear rooted both in financial and non-financial motivations, and are often based on alternative information provided also through video and graphic pitches, pictures, captivating narratives, and other communication tools, instead of traditional financial documents (see subsection II.1).[65] Finally, if measures to respond to 'institutionalization' are in place (subsection II.3), IBC should ensure more equal terms for retail investors, since it transcends the private/public offering dichotomy of IPOs.

The Crowdfunding Regulation has taken a stand on most of these issues: it has in principle assimilated the regime of business LBC and IBC, and defined the latter's activities as MiFID II placing without guarantee in combination with reception and transmission of orders, although exempted from both MiFID II and Prospectus requirements, and subject to a special regime. Therefore, LBC and IBC are regarded as 'peculiar', but close to investment services. As a consequence, they are subject to similar, but simplified rules (stricter and more detailed in case of loan facilitation and more complex LBC models). In addition to organizational requirements and prudential safeguards, CSPs should abide by general conduct rules and disclosure requirements, including the provision of a KIIS with the most important financial information and risks (substituting, in case, the Packaged Retail Investment And Insurance-Based Products-Key Information Document (PRIIPs-KID)).[66] CSPs are allowed to provide additional information (Recital 52), potentially recognizing a role for alternative/non-financial information. However, the provision of this additional information may entail complex consequences (eg consistency with the KIIS, information overload, and liability issues). Investor protection is reinforced in case of non-sophisticated investors, a new residual category within the category of retail investors, consisting of investors without particular experience or economic/financial resources (or, in any case, those not asking to be treated as 'sophisticated' despite presenting certain characteristics). Such 'reinforced' protection—to balance investor protection and compliance costs—consists of warnings, 'second thoughts' withdrawal rights, entry knowledge, and simulation of losses tests (distant relatives of the appropriateness/suitability tests),[67] while product governance measures are absent (Chapter 12). Different models (eg entailing investment advice, operation of investment funds, etc) remain subject to traditional financial regulation (MiFID II, the Alternative Investment Fund Managers Directive (AIFMD), etc), with little space left for special national regimes (Chapter 7). Separate authorizations are also necessary for the

2.34

---

[63] As of 23 October 2020, eleven countries have a EUR 8 million general threshold, nine a EUR 5 million one, and eight between EUR 1 million and EUR 3 million, while some countries have introduced special crowdfunding thresholds. See ESMA, 'National Thresholds Below Which the Obligation to Publish a Prospectus Does Not Apply' <https://www.esma.europa.eu/sites/default/files/library/esma31-62-1193_prospectus_thresholds.pdf>.

[64] See for further discussion and references, in addition to Chapter 1, Macchiavello 'Disintermediation' (n 25) 300; 'European' (n 2) 571, 598; 'Financial-return' (n 25) 701–02.

[65] Battaglia and others (n 17).

[66] The KIIS is prepared by project owners but checked by ECSPs for completeness, clarity, and correctness (concept not clarified yet), except in the case of portfolio management of loans where the KIIS is prepared by the ECSP. See, also the recently issued Crowdfunding Regulation regulatory and technical standards, touching upon several aspects, including the KIIS: ESMA, 'Consultation Paper—Draft technical standards under the ECSP Regulation' (26 February 2021).

[67] Macchiavello 'European' (n 2) 592; D Busch, V Colaert, and G Helleringer, 'An "Assist-Your-Customer Obligation" for the Financial Sector?' in V Colaert, D Busch, and T Incalza (eds), *Levelling the Cross-Sectoral Playing Field* (Hart 2019) 345, 363. See also recently: ESMA, 'Consultation Paper Draft technical standards under the ECSP Regulation' (26 February 2021) ESMA/35-36-2201, 23ff.

provision of other regulated services such as payment services, custody services pertaining to financial instruments, operation of multilateral exchanges (except 'passive' bulletin boards, allowing users to advertise their selling/buying interests pertaining to previously subscribed crowdfunding products with the objective of concluding the transaction outside of the platform), as discussed in Chapter 13.

2.35   Collective investment schemes or special purpose vehicle (SPV) structures, while not wide-spread in the crowdfunding sector (although the former might even materialize in presence of contingent funds),[68] have been used both in IBC and LBC to reduce coordination and governance problems within the investee. In addition, these models can facilitate subsequent investment rounds and private-public partnership, generally entailing the application of AIFMD (since liquidity requirements under the Undertaking for the Collective Investment in Transferable Securities (UCITS) Directive can hardly be met in a crowdfunding context). The Crowdfunding Regulation, conceiving crowdfunding as a form of direct investment, explicitly excludes such models from its scope, save only for the use of SPVs allowing crowdinvestors to invest in one illiquid and indivisible asset (otherwise not accessible), and therefore likely to refer to large equity or real estate investments.[69] Nonetheless, collective crowdfunding investments in loans might be facilitated by the implementation of the current proposal (presented, again, within the CMU) for the harmonization of the regime for direct lending by credit funds.[70] This instrument would overcome the current situation of national fragmentation under the AIFMD as regards requirements for direct lending and retail distribution.[71] The reform is expected to favour mostly loan-based investments by large institutional investors in bigger mid-caps and large firms, but it could be beneficial for crowdfunding as well.[72]

5. ICOs and Other Blockchain-based Offerings

2.36   An Initial Coin Offering (ICO) or, more recently, Initial Token Offering (ITO) is a form of funding consisting in the offering to the public of tokens, which are electronic assets representing a value, or the right to access a service/product, or to participate to certain decisions and profits (depending on its 'prevalent' payment, utility, or investment nature). Tokens circulate on a blockchain (eg Ethereum), and can be exchanged via crypto-exchanges (see Chapter 6).[73] These have been regarded as an evolution of crowdfunding, especially in light of the similarities between utility tokens offerings and reward-based crowdfunding.[74] In

---

[68] FCA, 'Call for Input to the Post-Implementation Review of the FCA's Crowdfunding Rules' (2016) 13–14, available at <http://www.fca.org.uk/publication/call-for-input/call-input-crowdfunding-rules.pdf>.

[69] See also ESMA 'Questions and Answers on the European Crowdfunding Service Providers for Business Regulation' (25 February 2021) 7, Answer 2.

[70] Commission, 'Assessing the Application and the Scope of Directive 2011/61/EU ... on Alternative Investment Fund Managers' (10 June 2020), SWD(2020) 110 final, 29.

[71] ESMA, 'Key Principles for a European Framework on Loan Origination by Funds' (Opinion) (11 April 2016), ESMA/2016/596.

[72] Kraemer-Eis and Lang (n 48) 101–02.

[73] Extensively about ICOs, STOs, IEOs, etc (and related references), see Chapter 6.

[74] R Amsden and D Schweizer, 'Are Blockchain Crowdsales the New "Gold Rush"? Success Determinants of Initial Coin Offerings' (16 April 2018) <https://ssrn.com/abstract = 3163849>; S Howell, M Niessner, and D Yermack (3 September 2019) 'Initial Coin Offerings: Financing Growth with Cryptocurrency Token Sales' ECGI-Finance Working Paper No 564/2018 <https://ssrn.com/abstract = 3201259>; OECD, 'Initial Coin Offerings (ICOs) for SME Financing' (2019) 26 <www.oecd.org/finance/initial-coin-offerings-for-sme-financing.htm>.

addition, ICOs/ITOs and crowdfunding have certain features in common, such as the creation of a community around a project (and the leveraging of network effects), disintermediation (with lower costs and level of bureaucracy but hidden expenses),[75] and seed and early-stage companies as target investees.[76]

However, the two forms of funding present several differences, in addition to the ones stemming from the different technical means. The blockchain enables decentralization at the infrastructure level, and therefore with regard to transaction registration.[77] Furthermore, ICOs/ITOs seem to be used mainly by technological firms (specifically, blockchain-based products/services),[78] at an earlier stage (when not even a prototype has been developed), and to ensure a higher level of control retention by the entrepreneur, liquidity (tokens are tradeable by design but not all of them are eventually listed on crypto-exchanges), investor anonymity, and global reach.[79] The selection and pricing appear challenging not only compared to IPOs but also to FRC, since no intermediary or platform with reputational risk conducts due diligence or preliminary screening, and scarce information is provided through 'white papers' on a voluntary basis.[80] In response to these issues, rating platforms and Initial Exchange Offerings (IEOs) have been developed. In the latter case, crypto-exchanges select and sponsor offerings, with a role closer to promoters or underwriters than crowdfunding platforms. In addition, Security Token Offerings (STOs) have arisen. In this case, the offered securities are tokenized, and therefore issued, stored, and exchanged on a blockchain.[81] While the regulation applicable to ICOs/ITOs is discussed and varies among countries, also depending on the type of token, STOs should be in principle subject to the bulk of financial regulation (eg Prospectus Regulation/MiFID II). Nevertheless, issues might emerge in connection with the legal treatment of smart contracts and blockchain technologies in general (eg legal value, compatibility with existing laws, etc), especially in case of decentralized structures.

2.37

Certain crowdfunding platforms have started organizing security-tokens offerings and automated/decentralized offerings (eg STOKR, Conda) and markets (eg RealMarket), adding further complexity.[82] The Crowdfunding Regulation excludes ICOs/ITOs from its scope, and remains silent about STOs. The current proposals in the area of crypto-assets within the above-mentioned Digital Finance Strategy (such as the proposed Markets in Crypto-Assets (MiCA) Regulation, and the pilot regime for distributed ledger technology

2.38

---

[75] Among hidden costs: fees for technical and legal support, and new services such as pricing indexes, rating platforms, and wallet providers.

[76] A Schwienbacher, 'Equity Crowdfunding: Anything to Celebrate?' (2019) 21(1) Venture Capital 65, 71.

[77] Presenting crowdfunding and ICOs as different forms and levels of decentralized finance: FSB, 'Decentralised Financial Technologies. Report on Financial Stability, Regulatory and Governance Implications' (6 June 2019), available at <http://www.fsb.org/wp-content/uploads/P060619.pdf>. About forms of power concentration in the blockchain governance (eg mining and coding): A Walch, 'Deconstructing "Decentralization": Exploring the Core Claim of Crypto Systems' in C Brummer (ed), *Crypto Assets: Legal and Monetary Perspectives* (OUP 2019).

[78] E Ackermann, C Bock, and R Bürger, 'Democratising Entrepreneurial Finance: The Impact of Crowdfunding and Initial Coin Offerings (ICOs)' in Moritz (n 7) 285.

[79] OECD (n 74) 27–29; D Boreiko, G Ferrarini, and P Giudici, 'Blockchain Startups and Prospectus Regulation' (2019) 20 European Business Organization Law Review 665.

[80] Ackermann (n 78).

[81] See also Commission, 'An SME Strategy for a sustainable and digital Europe' (Communication) (10 March 2020) COM(2020) 103 final, 15 (with measures to encourage bond-tokens offering by SMEs).

[82] See also Macchiavello, 'Disintermediation' (n 25).

(DLT) based markets)[83] do not seem to provide clear answers with respect to token-based crowdfunding offers either. The gap will have to be filled through interpretative efforts and regulatory adaptations, as discussed extensively in Chapter 6.

III. Recent Evolution of the CMU and Implications for the Crowdfunding Regulation

2.39   Since its first design, the CMU has been facing several challenges potentially mining its base, from Brexit to the COVID-19 pandemic and climate change. Nonetheless, the New CMU Action Plan[84] has shown adaptability to such new priorities.

2.40   For instance, the CMU Action Plan focuses on the integration of sustainability factors in corporate and investment decisions, through the design of investment taxonomies, financial operators' duties, and supervisory action.[85] However, the Crowdfunding Regulation postpones to 2023 the decision about special measures to promote sustainable projects (Article 45(2)(s)), despite the presence of specialized 'green' crowdfunding platforms that can channel funds to sustainable businesses. This lack of attention for sustainability can result in a number of potential frictions and problems. For instance, compliance costs may rise, on the top of existing environmental, social, and governance (ESG) analysis costs. Furthermore, the limited maximum offering threshold may conflict with the generally large initial investments required in the green energy field, and the aforementioned limitations to the use of SPV structures are not consistent with the frequent use of public-private partnerships in the 'green' sector. Explanations might be found in the need to wait for a more stable sustainable finance legal framework (still continuously evolving at a fast pace), and the potential additional costs on platforms for ESG assessment of companies. Similar issues arise with respect to the MiCA Proposal: despite the diffuse use and positive implications of tokens for sustainable finance and for the presale of green energy, the MiCA proposal might treat them as (lightly regulated) utility tokens, or even (strictly regulated) asset-referenced tokens.[86]

2.41   The COVID-19 pandemic has only reinforced the CMU's foundation and objectives. In fact, the CMU is regarded as a way to ensure long-term sustainability and stable funding

---

[83] Proposal for a Regulation ... on Markets in Crypto-assets, and amending Directive (EU) 2019/1937 COM/2020/593 final; Proposal for a Regulation ... a pilot regime for market infrastructures based on distributed ledger technology COM/2020/594 final. For a first comment: DA Zetzsche and others, 'The Markets in Crypto-Assets Regulation (MICA) and the EU Digital Finance Strategy (5 November 2020), EBI Working Paper No 77, <https://ssrn.com/abstract = 3725395>. See also Chapter 6.

[84] Commission (n 20) 4ff.

[85] Commission, 'Action Plan: Financing Sustainable Growth' (8 March 2018) COM/2018/097 final; Commission, 'Consultation on the Renewed Sustainable Finance Strategy' (8 April 2020). See also more recently, Commission, 'EU Taxonomy, Corporate Sustainability Reporting, Sustainability Preferences and Fiduciary Duties: Directing finance towards the European Green Deal' (Communication) COM/2021/188 final. About the same: D Busch, G Ferrarini, and A van den Hurk, 'The European Commission's Sustainable Finance Action Plan' (9 October 2018), <https://ssrn.com/abstract = 3263690>; D Busch, G Ferrarini, and S Grünewald (eds), *Sustainable Finance in Europe. Corporate Governance, Financial Stability and Financial Markets* (Palgrave 2021). D Busch, 'Sustainable Finance Disclosure in the EU Financial Sector' (13 July 2020), EBI Working Paper 70/2020 <https://ssrn.com/abstract = 3650407>; M Siri and S Zhu, 'Will the EU Commission Successfully Integrate Sustainability Risks and Factors in the Investor Protection Regime? A Research Agenda' (2019) 11(22) Sustainability 6292.

[86] About all these issues, see Macchiavello and Siri (n 62).

for EU firms after the extraordinary public support and bank lending efforts in response to the immediate real economic needs. These goals should also be pursued through further reforms in the area of ELTIF (reviewing eligible assets, initial investment limit, tax incentives) and incentives in terms of prudential treatment of banks' long-term equity investments in SMEs.[87] Other actions advanced within the New CMU and Recovery Strategy (2020/21) keep trying to expand firms' access to markets while protecting investors (in the same vein as the Crowdfunding Regulation). These objectives are pursued not only through further (temporary/COVID-19-related) simplifications in informative documents[88] and adjustments to securitization rules,[89] but also through potentially more far-reaching measures, such as the elimination of certain regulatory/administrative over-burdens in listing and MiFID II rules,[90] and the creation of a European single access point (ESAP) to reduce investors' information costs.[91] This would consist of a platform accessible by various stakeholders, and containing certain companies' financial and sustainability-related information in a standardized and machine-readable format. A similar EU-wide database about post-trade equity and equity-like financial instruments prices and volumes has also been proposed.[92] Although it is still under discussion which companies and information should be covered by the ESAP, the inclusion of Crowdfunding Regulation disclosures is unlikely.[93] Instead, the role of LBC platforms may be reinforced by the concurrent proposal to impose on banks, when denying a loan, a duty not only to provide the reasons but also to refer the applicants to alternative credit providers.[94]

---

[87] Commission (n 20) 9.

[88] About the recent 'EU Recovery Prospectus', a temporary measure introduced by the CMU Recovery Package (consisting in a short Prospectus of 30 pages for secondary markets' shares with simplified disclosure rules and accompanied by a short summary) to facilitate companies, with already shares admitted on a regulated market or SME Growth Market, in quickly raising capital and meeting their urgent financing needs: Commission, 'Proposal for a Regulation ... amending Regulation (EU) 2017/1129 as regards the EU Recovery prospectus ... to help the recovery from the COVID19 pandemic' (24 July 2020) COM(2020) 281 final; C Gortsos and ME Terzi, 'The Prospectus Regulation (Regulation (EU) 2017/1129) and the Recent Proposal for an EU Recovery Prospectus: Elements of Continuity and Change with the Past and the Way Forward', EBI Working Paper 79/2020 <https://ssrn.com/abstract = 3742863>.

[89] The Proposal (within the Capital Markets Recovery Package) extends the harmonized and simplified framework to certain on-balance sheet synthetic securitizations (using guarantees to relieve banks' balance sheet instead of a true sale) and to securitizations with NPLs as underlying assets (implying 'active' servicing): Commission, 'Proposal for a Regulation ... amending Regulation (EU) 2017/2402 laying down a general framework for securitisation ... to help the recovery from the COVID-19 pandemic' (24 July 2020) COM(2020) 282 final. The EU Coronavirus Banking Package has also anticipated the CRR II extension of the SME supporting factor's discount (Regulation 2020/873 of 24 June 2020 amending Regulations (EU) No 575/2013 and (EU) 2019/876 as regards certain adjustments in response to the COVID-19 pandemic).

[90] Commission (n 20) 7–8.

[91] More recently: Commission, 'Targeted Consultation Document—Establishment of a European Single Access Point (ESAP) for Financial and Non-Financial Information Publicly Disclosed by Companies' (21 January 2021). See also the interlinked European Strategy for Data (19 February 2020, COM(2020) 66 final).

[92] Commission (n 20) 7, 13–14; HLFCMU (n 20) 12, 30.

[93] ESMA excludes the imposition under the Crowdfunding Regulation of machine-readable format requirements to limit implementation costs: ESMA (n 67) 34. More generally, ESAP will at most cover companies already subject to existing disclosure requirements (eg Transparency Directive, Market Abuse Regulation, Accounting Directive, etc), therefore excluding unlisted SMEs. About the exclusion of unlisted SMEs also from the linked Non-financial reporting Directive (NFRD), recently renamed Corporate Sustainability Reporting Directive (CSRD), see Commission, 'Questions and Answers: Corporate Sustainability Reporting Directive proposal' (21 April 2021) and 'Proposal for a Directive ... amending Directive 2013/34/EU, Directive 2004/109/EC, Directive 2006/43/EC and Regulation (EU) No 537/2014, as regards corporate sustainability reporting' and 'EU Taxonomy' (n 85).

[94] Commission (n 20) 9. A similar referral duty was implemented in the UK through the 2015 Small Business, Enterprise and Employment Bill ('Bank Referral Scheme').

2.42   Digital finance (including ICOs/STOs) has been regarded as contributing to solving the pandemic crisis, lowering costs, and enabling long-distance provision of services. Certain proposals within the Digital Finance Strategy might impact FRC as well. For instance, the open-finance proposal, planning to extend PSD II-open-banking to other financial services (investments, insurance, etc), might also benefit FRC platforms, even incentivizing them to diversify and expand their offering. Similarly, Regulatory Technology/Supervisory Technology (RegTech/SupTech)[95] measures and the EU-wide interoperable digital identities project should help simplify certain CSP duties (eg identification/certification of sophistication, entry knowledge test). Moreover, the Digital Operational Resilience (DORA) proposal[96] will fill a relevant gap of the Crowdfunding Regulation, designing a cross-sectoral regime for cybersecurity, applicable not only to banks, investment firms, and payment service providers but also explicitly to crowdfunding platforms.

2.43   On the contrary, certain other initiatives appear less coordinated. Big tech's entrance in financial services (including lending) is not accounted for in the Crowdfunding Regulation.[97] which does not even mention the Platform-to-Business (P2B) Regulation.[98] Future actions in this area within the Digital Finance Strategy and aiming at realizing the principle 'same activity, same risks, same rules' might ensure better coordination. However, the Digital Markets Act (DMA) and Digital Services Act (DSA) proposals of December 2020, conceived for all online platforms (including social media, Internet access providers, marketplaces, cloud services) that act as intermediaries/gatekeepers, and with special duties for large platforms (such as algorithmic transparency and risk management obligations), never refer to the Crowdfunding Regulation.

2.44   The persistence of obstacles to cross-border investments[99] and a recent (also FinTech-related) financial scandal (the *Wirecard* case)[100] have given the Commission the opportunity to bring back to the table the proposal to complete the CMU with a single market supervision beyond existing experiments,[101] after the failure of previous attempts, also downsizing ESMA's role within the Crowdfunding Regulation framework (Chapter 7).[102] This might also affect future reviews of the Crowdfunding Regulation. However, even in the absence of such a reform, the Crowdfunding Regulation's current passport and highly harmonized supervisory powers improve the crowdfunding market integration, at the expenses of

---

[95] About RegTech, see V Colaert, 'RegTech as a Response to Regulatory Expansion in the Financial Sector' (June 2018) <https://ssrn.com/abstract = 2677116>; D Arner and others, 'Fintech and Regtech: Enabling Innovation While Preserving Financial Stability' (2017) 18(3) Georgetown Journal of International Affairs 47; L Enriques, 'Financial Supervisors and Regtech: Four Roles and Four Challenges' (2017) Revue Trimestrielle de Droit Financier 53.

[96] Proposal for a Regulation on digital operational resilience for the financial sector ... COM/2020/595 final.

[97] See J Ehrentraud, D Garcia Ocampo, and C Quevedo Vega, *Regulating Fintech Financing: Digital Banks and Fintech Platforms* (BIS 2020); FSB, *FinTech and Market Structure in Financial Services: Market Developments and Potential Financial Stability Implications* (14 February 2019) <www.fsb.org/wp-content/uploads/P140219.pdf>; J Frost and others, 'BigTech and the Changing Structure of Financial Intermediation', BIS Working Papers No 779/2020, <https://www.bis.org/publ/work779.htm>.

[98] Regulation (EU) 2019/1150 on promoting fairness and transparency for business users of online intermediation services.

[99] K Lannoo and A Thomadakis, *Rebranding Capital Markets Union: A Market Finance Action Plan* (CEPS-ECMI 2019) 42–43.

[100] See the studies promoted by the European Parliament-ECON and summarized and downloadable from <http://www.europarl.europa.eu/RegData/etudes/BRIE/2020/651345/IPOL_BRI(2020)651345_EN.pdf>.

[101] Commission, 'Mid-term' (n 18) 10–11; Commission (n 20) 14.

[102] Macchiavello, 'What to' (n 2).

small local platforms which, after a transitional period, will not be allowed to request an exemption (unlike low-volumes payment/e-money providers, investment brokers/advisers pursuant Article 3(1) MiFID II). On the other hand, certain aspects (exclusions, nationally based rules for civil liability, marketing, and transfers, etc.) might partially impair market integration (Chapters 16 and 17 on jurisdiction and dispute settlement).[103]

Finally, despite the long Brexit negotiations, the December 2020 deal has not clarified the legal treatment of all financial services, so that the relevant rules are set forth by uncertain and expensive service-by-service solutions (also considering the limited and differentiated scope of the equivalence principle), or separate treaties.[104] Considering the relative size of the British crowdfunding market (the biggest in Europe), the lack of a third country regime in the Crowdfunding Regulation, as well as the difficult qualification of FRC services, constitute a relevant issue in the crowdfunding sector (Chapter 4).[105]   **2.45**

IV. Conclusions

The Crowdfunding Regulation seems to fit perfectly within the CMU project, complementing other traditional or innovative funding sources and related CMU reforms (eg growth prospectus and markets, ESAP, ELTIF). However, it shares with these instruments the difficult task of striking a balance between firms' and financial services providers' costs and investor protection. For instance, simplifications in the prospectus and secondary issuance documents for SMEs, as well as measures to incentivize securitizations, contribute to reducing SMEs' compliance costs, but might shift on investors the risk of picking 'lemons' (despite being accompanied by a retail investor-friendly key information summary). This risk is particularly concrete, considering that the SMEs market is more opaque and riskier, therefore requiring in principle more disclosure and protection, not less.[106]   **2.46**

The trend characterizing EU financial regulation, especially after the financial crisis, has been to curtail retail investors' access to the riskiest and most complex investments, through product governance, high initial investment ticket (see EuVECA, despite the recent review), national product intervention measures for complex products, and reliance on investment advice/portfolio management services (and the related suitability test).[107]   **2.47**

---

[103] Macchiavello and Sciarrone Alibrandi (n 2).

[104] About Brexit and financial services, see J Deslandes, 'Third Country Equivalence in EU Banking and Financial Regulation (August 2019), <https://www.europarl.europa.eu/RegData/etudes/IDAN/2018/614495/IPOL_IDA(2018)614495_EN.pdf>; K Alexander, 'The UK's Third-Country Status Following Brexit: Post-Brexit Models, Third-Country Equivalence and Switzerland' in K Alexander and others (eds), *Brexit and Financial Services. Law and Policy* (Hart 2018) 115–54; M Lehmann and DA Zetzsche, 'How Does It Feel to Be a Third Country? The Consequences of Brexit for Financial Market Law' (15 April 2018) <https://ssrn.com/abstract = 3155355>.

[105] See also Macchiavello, 'European' (n 2) 579–80.

[106] For criticism towards simplifications in disclosure by SMEs as in the recent Prospectus Regulation: MB Fox, 'Initial Public Offerings in the CMU. A US Perspective' in Busch and others, 'Capital Markets' (n 60) 268, 296–98; Moloney (n 9) 179; L Enriques, 'EU Prospectus Regulation: Some Out-of-the-Box Thinking' (2017) 4 Revista Lex Mercatoria 39.

[107] About the risk of excessive restriction in product availability to retail investors: V Colaert, 'Building Blocks of Investor Protection: All-embracing Regulation Tightens its Grip' (2017) 6(6) Journal of European Consumer and Market Law 229, 241.

2.48   In the Crowdfunding Regulation, a compromise is reached through a simplified regime (for both project owners and platforms) for limited activities/products (types and total size), simple and synthetic information documents for investors focused on risks and key terms (substituting, not complementing, the prospectus), coupled with general conduct duties and reinforced measures for non-sophisticated investors (eg warnings, tests, withdrawal rights). A renewed interest for key-information documents (following the KID's model of PRIIPs Regulation, which echoes the 2009 UCITS-KIID), so as to reduce information overload and other behavioural biases and improve comparability, is also recognizable in the new seven-page prospectus summary, Pan-European Personal Pension Product-Key Information Document, European Long-term Investment Funds-Key Information Document (PEPPs-KID, ELTIFs-KID) (when marketed to retail investors) and similar announced changes to MiFID II. However, the new CMU seems also to rely on improved financial education and further simplifications in case of 'sophisticated' retail investors (action 8), taking inspiration from the category created by the Crowdfunding Regulation (which however does not differentiate information duties based on the type of investor),[108] while reinforcing financial advisors' professional requirements and inducements rules.

2.49   Nonetheless, from other points of view, the Crowdfunding Regulation fails to achieve co-ordination with other pieces of EU financial regulation, and thus to ensure a higher level of coherence in the overall legal framework (a feature still missing from a cross-sectoral perspective).[109] Indeed, the Crowdfunding Regulation contains requirements for LBC (in terms of creditworthiness assessment, scoring/pricing, portfolio management of loans), which appear stricter or anyway more detailed than the corresponding ones for credit funds, and management of investment portfolios.[110]

2.50   Moreover, coordination is still lacking in relation to sustainable finance, or actions in the area of responsible lending and regulation of online platforms. It might be too soon to assess the implications deriving from other initiatives within the Digital Finance Strategy (ICOs/STOs, open-finance, DORA, etc) but these seem overall potentially positive.

---

[108] Macchiavello, 'European' (n 2) 587–88.

[109] Colaert and others (n 67).

[110] Macchiavello and Sciarrone (n 2). The Commission, in its Report on the application of the Crowfunding Regulation, will evaluate 'the impact of this Regulation in relation to other relevant Union law, including Directive 97/9/EC, Directive 2011/61/EU of the European Parliament and of the Council, Directive 2014/65/EU and Regulation (EU) 2017/1129' (Article 45 (2) under a).

PART II
DEFINING AND ASSESSING THE SCOPE OF THE CROWDFUNDING REGULATION

3

The Scope of the Crowdfunding Regulation and the Impact of Brexit

Petja Ivanova

I. Introduction

In 2016, the Commission still assumed that, in light of the predominantly local nature **3.01** of crowdfunding, there was no strong case for Union-wide policy intervention.[1] Over time, however, the need to regulate the provision of crowdfunding services at Union level emerged as a response to the steadily developing and growing crowdfunding sector that had led to different national regimes throughout the EU and to a subsequent legislative fragmentation. As an essential component in the development of the Capital Markets Union (CMU)[2] and the first step in implementing the Commission's FinTech Action Plan[3], the Crowdfunding Regulation, for the first time, sets out directly applicable uniform requirements for the provision of crowdfunding services, and restates harmonized standards for investor protection. At the same time, the Crowdfunding Directive[4] amends the Markets in Financial Instruments Directive II (MiFID II) by excluding the application of the latter to

---

[1] EC, Commission Staff Working Document—Crowdfunding in the EU Capital Markets Union (3 May 2016) SWD(2016) 154 final, 31.

[2] cf, for example, EC Press release, Capital Markets Union and Fintech: Commission welcomes political agreement to boost crowdfunding in the EU (19 December 2019).

[3] EC, FinTech Action Plan: For a more competitive and innovative European financial sector (8 March 2018) COM(2018) 109 final.

[4] The Member States had to implement the Crowdfunding Directive by 10 May 2021 and shall apply the respective domestic law parallel to the requirements set out in the Crowdfunding Regulation from 10 November 2021, see Art 2(1) Crowdfunding Directive.

crowdfunding service providers (CSPs) covered by the Crowdfunding Regulation (see sub-section II.3.A.para 3.10).

3.02 Against this backdrop, the Crowdfunding Regulation claims an entirely new and unique regu-latory stance towards European CSPs. Yet, its provisions either remain inapplicable to particular forms of crowdfunding or result in an interdependence with other existing EU instruments. In order to assess whether the Crowdfunding Regulation will bring about benefits for small- and medium-sized enterprises (SMEs) (and particularly for start-ups and scale-ups), and in order to evaluate possible obstacles, it is indispensable to analyse the personal, material, and geo-graphic scope of the Regulation (see subsections II.3.A and II.3.B). In addition, it is essential to consider the subject matters excluded from the scope of the Regulation (see subsection II.4). Furthermore, in light of the withdrawal of the UK from the EU, it is necessary to scrutinize the effects of Brexit on the application of the new European crowdfunding regime (see section III). Finally, since the UK does make up the largest part of the crowdfunding market in Europe,[5] and it has inspired the European crowdfunding legal framework, the impact of Brexit, also on the further development of the crowdfunding market, should be taken into account.

II. The Scope of the Crowdfunding Regulation

1. General Overview and Objectives

3.03 Given the lack of specific EU rules on the provision of crowdfunding services, several Member States had adopted domestic crowdfunding frameworks or *ad hoc* rules,[6] focusing

---

[5] In 2015, 81% of the overall European crowdfunding market volume, though shrinking to 73% in 2016 and 68% in 2017, see T Ziegler and others, 'Shifting Paradigms—The 4th European Alternative Finance Benchmarking Report' (Cambridge Centre for Alternative Finance 2019) 13, 16, 22, <https://www.jbs.cam.ac.uk/wp-cont ent/uploads/2020/08/2019-05-4th-european-alternative-finance-benchmarking-industry-report-shifting-paradigms.pdf> accessed 14 September 2021; see also European Crowdfunding Network (ECN), Country Crowdfunding Factsheet—United Kingdom (June 2018) 4, <https://eurocrowd.org/wp-content/blogs.dir/sites/85/2018/06/CF_FactSheet_UK_June2018.pdf> accessed 23 May 2021. By worldwide comparison too, the UK pro-vides at third place, together with the US at second and China at first place, for most of the crowdfunding-related transactions, cf T Ziegler and others, 'Global Alternative Finance Benchmarking Report' (Cambridge Centre for Alternative Finance, April 2020) 6, 24 <https://papers.ssrn.com/sol3/papers.cfm?abstract_id=3771509> accessed 14 September 2021; T Ziegler, R Shneor, and BZ Zhang, 'The Global Status of the Crowdfunding Industry' in R Shneor, L, Zhao, and B-T Flåten (eds), *Advances in Crowdfunding—Research and Practice* (Palgrave Macmillan 2020) 47 et seq.

[6] For an overview of crowdfunding regulatory frameworks in selected Member States, see EC, Commission Staff Working Document, 'Impact Assessment—Accompanying the document Proposal for a Regulation of the European Parliament and of the Council on European Crowdfunding Service Providers (ECSP) for Business and Proposal for a Directive of the European Parliament and of the Council amending Directive 2014/65/EU on markets in financial instruments' (8 March 2018) SWD(2018) 56 final, Annex 4. While some bespoke crowd-funding regimes (eg in Germany) focused on investment limits and disclosure requirements, others (eg in the UK, France, Spain, and Portugal) subjected crowdfunding intermediation to lighter requirements than banks and investment firms, see G Ferrarini and E Macchiavello, 'FinTech and Alternative Finance in the CMU' in D Busch, E Avgouleas, and G Ferrarini (eds), *Capital Markets Union in Europe* (OUP 2018) 10.31 and n 52; D Chervyakov and J Rocholl, 'How to make crowdfunding work in Europe', Bruegel Policy Contribution, Issue No 6 (March 2019) 11, <https://www.bruegel.org/2019/03/how-to-make-crowdfunding-work-in-europe/?utm_content=buffer99b2a&utm_medium=social&utm_source=twitter.com&utm_campaign=buffer+(bruegel)> accessed 14 September 2021. On a global scale, a forerunner in designing a legal framework tailored to crowdfunding were the US with the Jumpstart Our Business Startups Act, Pub L. No 112–106, 126 Stat. 306 (2012) (JOBS Act) adopted in 2012. Pursuant to its Title III the SEC adopted the 'Regulation Crowdfunding' that came into force in May 2016, see SEC, 'Crowdfunding: Final Rule' (2015) 80 Federal Register71388 (17 CFR Parts 200, 226, 232, 239, 240, 249, 269, and 274).

on investment- and loan-based crowdfunding activities.[7] The national crowdfunding regulations diverged substantively, depending on the characteristics and needs of local markets and investors.[8] Consequently, the individual national rules showed shortcomings with regard to the provision of crowdfunding services in a cross-border context. The regulatory differences in the design and implementation of the domestic crowdfunding frameworks with respect to the scope of admissible crowdfunding activities, authorization requirements, and the conditions of running crowdfunding platforms impeded the passporting of platform business models across the EU and directly affected the internal crowdfunding market.[9] Not surprisingly, crowdfunding could primarily expand at domestic level, with very little cross-border activity of EU-based CSPs.[10]

Against this background, in March 2018, the Commission proposed the EU crowdfunding **3.04** regime, consisting of a regulation and a directive, as part of a package of measures to strengthen the CMU and to further its overarching goals of supporting a more sustainable financial integration and private investments for the benefit of job creation and economic growth.[11] The Commission acknowledged that, due to structural information asymmetries, access to finance remains difficult for innovative SMEs, start-ups, and other unlisted firms throughout the EU, particularly when they move from a start-up into the expansion phase. Over-reliance on short-term unsecured bank lending is often expensive and bank lending volumes to SMEs and start-ups were seriously affected by the 2008 financial crisis, thus contributing to start-ups' failures.[12] In light of this, crowdfunding is considered an important alternative to unsecured bank lending for SMEs, helping to match investors with SME business projects in need of funding.[13] Therefore, the European crowdfunding rules embracing investment- and loan-based crowdfunding aim to facilitate the scaling up of crowdfunding services across the internal market, make the allocation of resources more efficient and assets more diverse, and counteract systemic risk by supplying investors with the necessary information on crowdfunding and the underlying risks.[14] After some extensive revisions of the originally suggested crowdfunding regime, the European Parliament and the Council adopted the Crowdfunding Regulation and the Crowdfunding Directive on 7 October 2020.

---

[7] cf Chervyakov and Rocholl (n 6) 8. On lending- and investment-based crowdfunding, see below, subsection II.3.B.paras 3.13 et seq. Unlike crowdlending that, as such, hardly fell under existing EU legislation (on the potential applicability of EU law at that time, see EBA, Opinion on lending-based crowdfunding, EBA/Op/2015/03 (26 February 2015) 24 et seq), investment-based crowdfunding services could at least be subsumed under MiFID II as far as they met the respective requirements (on the applicability of MiFID II before and after the adoption of the EU crowdfunding regime, see subsection II.3.A.para 3.10). However, where investment services offered through a crowdfunding platform did not fall under MiFID II, only national regulations (either a regime specifically conceived for crowdfunding, new *ad hoc* rules or already existing and adjusted banking and financial regulation) could come into play. See, on national approaches, Ferrarini and Macchiavello (n 6) 10.22 et seq for crowdlending, 10.38 et seq for crowdinvesting.

[8] Recital 5; cf E Macchiavello, 'The European Crowdfunding Service Providers Regulation: The Future of Marketplace Lending and Investing in Europe and the 'Crowdfunding Nature' Dilemma' (2021) 32 European Business Law Review 557, 559, and 561.

[9] See Recitals 5 and 6; cf Chervyakov and Rocholl (n 6) 8.

[10] See EC (n 6) 18.

[11] See EC, Proposal for a Regulation of the European Parliament and of the Council on European Crowdfunding Service Providers (ECSP) for Business (8 March 2018) COM(2018) 113 final, 1.

[12] This is all the more the case in Member States with less developed capital markets and banking systems.

[13] EC (n 11) 1.

[14] EC (n 11) 2; Recital 1 Crowdfunding Directive and Recital 3.

3.05 In line with the specific regulatory process in financial services in the EU, as introduced with the Lamfalussy report, the Crowdfunding Regulation, together with the Crowdfunding Directive, constitute the Level 1 basic laws. Subsequently, at Level 2, regulatory technical standards (RTS) and implementing technical standards (ITS) developed by the European Banking Authority (EBA) and the European Securities and Markets Authority (ESMA) and adopted by the Commission ensure consistency in applying the Crowdfunding Regulation.[15] At Level 3, the adoption and implementation of Level 1 and Level 2 are guided by EBA and ESMA.

2. From an Optional to a Mandatory Regime

3.06 As far as the provision of crowdfunding services is covered by the Crowdfunding Regulation (see subsection II.3.B), the pan-European regime replaces domestic crowdfunding rules that have been previously in force.[16] Initially, the Commission had suggested an optional regime that would not have affected national bespoke crowdfunding frameworks or existing authorizations, including those under MiFID II, the Payment Services Directive 2 (PSD 2), or the Alternative Investment Fund Managers Directive (AIFMD). According to this original proposal, the Regulation should have offered CSPs the possibility to apply for an EU label, enabling them to expand their operations throughout the Union under certain conditions.[17] On the one hand, such an optional regime would have eased cross-border crowdfunding activities while possibly eliminating regulatory hurdles for CSPs existing in national laws and stimulating crowdfunding businesses to apply for an EU label, as well as promoting regulatory competition.[18] On the other hand, such an opt-in solution would have caused legal uncertainty as to the rules applicable to crowdfunding businesses and investors. Considering the disadvantages of an only optional EU crowdfunding legal framework, the Crowdfunding Regulation followed the position of the Council[19] by introducing a mandatory EU crowdfunding regime with obligatory authorization requirements and a transitional period (on the latter, see subsection II.6.A).

---

[15] See, for RTS, Arts 6(7), 7(5), 8(7), 12(16), 19(7), 20(3), 21(8), 23(16), and 31(8) and Recitals 70, 71 Crowdfunding Regulation. With regard to ITS, see Arts 16(3), 28(5), 31(9), 32(4) and Recital 72 Crowdfunding Regulation. At the time of writing this chapter, the final RTS and ITS were not available yet. However, a proposal for draft RTS and ITS open for comments has been published, see ESMA, Consultation Paper—Draft technical standards under the ECSP Regulation, ESMA/35-36-2201 (26 February 2021), <https://www.esma.europa.eu/sites/default/files/library/esma35-36-2201_cp_-_ecspr_technical_standards.pdf> accessed 14 September 2021.

[16] For instance, in France, the 'Conseillers en investissements participatifs' in Art L547-1 and the 'Intermédiaire en financement participatif' in Arts L548-2 et seq Code monétaire et financier. On the French crowdfunding framework, C Kleiner, 'Lights and Shadows of Crowdfunding à la Française' (2019) 27 Zeitschrift für Europäisches Privatrecht 756.

[17] See EC (n 11) 2 and Recital 14. For a critical assessment of the Proposal, eg M Will and B Quarch, 'Der Kommissionsvorschlag einer EU-Crowdfunding-Verordnung—Eine kritische Analyse' (2018) 32 Wertpapiermitteilungen 1481.

[18] Macchiavello (n 8) 563.

[19] Council of the European Union, Proposal for a Regulation of the European Parliament and of the Council on European Crowdfunding Service Providers (ECSP) for Business and amending Regulation (EU) No 2017/1129—Mandate for negotiations with the European Parliament = Compromise proposal (24 June 2019) 10557/19, Recitals 44a–44c.

3. Scope and Limits of Application

Article 1[20] sets out the scope of the Crowdfunding Regulation, including exceptions to its **3.07** applicability. According to Article 1(1), the uniform requirements of the Crowdfunding Regulation apply to CSPs, including their organization, authorization, and supervision[21] and the operation of crowdfunding platforms (scope *ratione personae*), and to the provision of crowdfunding services,[22] including transparency and marketing communications (scope *ratione materiae*). On the personal and material scope of application, see hereafter subsections II.3.A and II.3.B. Article 1(2), in turn, excludes particular subject matters from the scope of application (see subsection II.4). Article 1(3) identifies the cases in which no authorization as credit institution is required for offering crowdfunding services (see, subsection II.5).

In order to analyse the scope of the Crowdfunding Regulation, one should, first, under- **3.08** stand the meaning of the terms 'crowdfunding services', 'crowdfunding service providers', and 'crowdfunding platform', as defined in Article 2(1).

A. Scope *ratione personae*
Crowdfunding Service Providers
As set forth in Article 2(1)(e), a crowdfunding service provider is a legal person that **3.09** provides crowdfunding services (on the term 'crowdfunding services', see subsection II.3.B.paras 3.13 et seq). Compared to credit institutions, being traditional intermediaries, a CSP acts as an intermediary that offers crowdfunding services through an online platform, the crowdfunding platform.[23] As defined in Article 2(1)(d),[24] the crowdfunding platform is 'a publicly accessible internet-based information system operated or managed by the crowdfunding service provider'. Pursuant to Article 3(1), crowdfunding services under the Regulation should be offered by legal persons 'established in the Union[25] and that have been authorised as crowdfunding service providers [with the competent authority of their home Member State][26] in accordance with Article

---

[20] References to Articles and Recitals without indication of the respective act are to the Crowdfunding Regulation.

[21] The organizational and operational requirements of CSPs are laid down in Arts 4–11, the specifications with regard to authorization and supervision in Arts 12–17.

[22] As part of the provision of crowdfunding services, three actors must be distinguished (see Recital 2). First, the crowdfunding service provider. Second, the project owner, who, according to Art 2(1)(h), is 'any natural or legal person [seeking] funding through a crowdfunding platform'. Thereby, the business activity or activities that the project owner wants to finance constitute the crowdfunding project as defined in Art 2(1)(l). Third, the investor, who, pursuant to Art 2(1)(i), is 'any natural or legal person [granting] loans or [acquiring] transferable securities or admitted instruments for crowdfunding purposes [through a crowdfunding platform]'. The Crowdfunding Regulation differentiates between a 'sophisticated investor' in Art 2(1)(j) and a 'non-sophisticated investor' in Art 2(1)(k). The 'client' comprises 'any prospective or actual investor or project owner' to whom a crowdfunding service provider provides, or intends to provide, crowdfunding services' (see Art 2(1)(g)).

[23] Recitals 2 and 26. J Klein and M Nathmann, 'Die EU-weite Regulierung des Crowdfunding-Markts—Vorstellung und Analyse des Vorschlags der EU-Kommission' (2019) 21 BetriebsBerater 1158, 1159 classify the crowdfunding platform as the intermediary. The platform, however, is not the intermediate body itself, but rather the medium that facilitates the operation of services.

[24] See also Recital 12.

[25] For the purpose of effective supervision of CSPs, Recital 31, further, underlines that 'only legal persons having an *effective and stable establishment* (emphasis by the author) in the EU, including the necessary resources, should be able to apply for authorisation as crowdfunding service providers under the [Crowdfunding Regulation]'.

[26] Insertion added by the author. In contrast, the Commission's Proposal, originally, had drawn upon an authorization with ESMA, see EC (n 11) Art 10.

12'[27]. The personal scope, thus, includes limitations to the application of the crowdfunding rules also in territorial terms, since CSPs must be established in the EU. On third-country CSPs, see subsection II.3.A.para 3.11.

Recourse to MiFID II

3.10 Before the adoption of the Crowdfunding Regulation, providers of investment-based crowdfunding services, in principle, were subject to the authorization requirement under MiFID II which applies to persons providing investment services or performing investment activities as defined in Article 4(1)(2) MiFID II in conjunction with Section A of Annex I to MiFID II. Insofar as crowdinvesting services could be qualified as investment services and activities, their providers had to obtain an authorization in accordance with Article 5 et seq MiFID II,[28] unless the respective home Member State had chosen not to apply the MiFID II regime to crowdfunding in accordance with the conditions set out in Article 3(1) MiFID II.[29] Through the Crowdfunding Directive, the EU aims at avoiding the application of the strict conditions for authorization under MiFID II in the context of the provision of crowdfunding services and, thus, enabling less stringent requirements without running the risk of multiple authorizations for the same activity.[30] Therefore, Article 1 Crowdfunding Directive explicitly excludes CSPs from the scope of application of MiFID II by adding point (p) to the list of exemptions in Article 2(1) MiFID II.[31] Hence, MiFID II does not apply to CSPs as defined in Article 2(1)(e). However, where a person does not meet the requirements for being classified as a CSP under the Crowdfunding Regulation, an authorization under MiFID II might still be necessary. On the relation and the interplay of the Crowdfunding Regulation with MiFID II, see Chapter 7.

Treatment of Third-Country Firms

3.11 Since, according to Article 3(1), only CSPs established in the Union can apply for authorization under the Crowdfunding Regulation, third-country providers of crowdfunding services fall outside the personal scope of application of the Crowdfunding Regulation.[32] The Committee on Economic and Monetary Affairs (ECON) of the European Parliament had initially[33] advocated applying the rules on crowdfunding to third-country providers too, on two conditions: (a) that they were authorized by the authorities of a third country whose domestic legal framework and supervisory practice are equivalent to those of the EU, and (b) that they registered with ESMA.[34] However, the European

---

[27] The application for authorization required in Art 12(1) shall contain the elements listed in Art 12(2), as well as follow the requirements and arrangements set by ESMA in its RTS (see Art 12(16)(a)).

[28] See, at that time in relation to the applicability of the old version of MiFID, ESMA, Opinion Investment-based crowdfunding, ESMA/2014/1378 (18 December 2014) 14 et seq.

[29] In which case, the activities of those persons should be authorized and regulated at national level.

[30] Recital 3 Crowdfunding Directive. Originally, since the crowdfunding regime was first intended to be an optional one (see subsection II.2), different authorizations for the same activity should be avoided by excluding from the scope of the Crowdfunding Regulation crowdfunding services provided by persons that have been authorized under MiFID II or in accordance with national law, see EC (n 11) Recital 9.

[31] On the amendment of MiFID II, see EC, Proposal for a Directive of the European Parliament and of the Council amending Directive 2014/65/EU on markets in financial instruments (8 March 2018) COM(2018) 99 final, 2018/0047 (COD) 1–4; see, further, Macchiavello (n 8) 575 et seq discussing whether the MiFID II exemption affects the level-playing field.

[32] On the treatment of UK-based CSPs, see subsection III.2.

[33] In contrast to the Commission's Proposal, EC (n 11) Art 4.

[34] ECON, Draft Report on the proposal for a regulation of the European Parliament and of the Council on European Crowdfunding Service Providers (ECSP) for Business (10 August 2018) 2018/0048(COD) 22.

Parliament[35] as well as the Council[36] declared themselves in favour of excluding third countries from the personal scope of the European crowdfunding regime. Furthermore, according to the Commission's assessment, only a limited impact would arise from the application of the Crowdfunding Regulation on providers established in third countries.[37] Hence, the Crowdfunding Regulation does not regulate CSPs originating from non-EU countries. Yet, in view of the interconnectedness of the financial sector regarding different areas of financial services, including alternative financing through crowdfunding, the exclusion of third-country providers from the scope of application of the Crowdfunding Regulation might be questioned.[38] In order to ensure the functioning of cross-border financial flows, also in connection with countries outside the EU, and the effectiveness of transnational operations of crowdfunding platforms bringing together project owners and investors from different EU and non-EU countries, CSPs from third countries should not be disregarded. However, it is positive that the EU has not 'jumped the gun' by hastily drawing up third-country rules within the Crowdfunding Regulation. Article 45(1) engages the Commission, before 10 November 2023, to present a report to the European Parliament and the Council on the application of the Crowdfunding Regulation in the areas listed in Article 45(2)(a)–(z), where appropriate accompanied by a legislative proposal. Pursuant to Article 45(2)(q), the Commission's report shall assess to what extent entities established in third countries should be granted an authorization as CSPs under the Crowdfunding Regulation. For completeness' sake, in the absence of a third country regime in the Crowdfunding Regulation, Member States have the possibility to adopt a national regime dealing with the access for non-EU CSPs to their home market.

B. Scope *ratione materiae*

Pursuant to Article 1(1), the material scope of application of the Crowdfunding Regulation encompasses the provision of crowdfunding services in the EU. **3.12**

Crowdfunding services

Article 2(1)(a) defines crowdfunding services as 'the matching of business funding interests of investors and project owners through the use of a crowdfunding platform'. The matching comprises two types of crowdfunding activities, both of which ensure financial returns on the investments in the respective crowdfunding project. The first field of crowdfunding activities covers 'the facilitation of granting of loans' (see Article 2(1)(a) point (i)), and is known as loan-based crowdfunding or crowdlending.[39] The second area of activities relates **3.13**

---

[35] European Parliament, 'Position of the European Parliament adopted at first reading on 27 March 2019 with a view to the adoption of Regulation (EU) 2019/... of the European Parliament and of the Council on European Crowdfunding Service Providers (ECSP) for Business' (27 March 2019) EP-PE_TC1-COD(2018)0048, Art 4(1), <https://www.europarl.europa.eu/doceo/document/TC1-COD-2018-0048_EN.pdf> accessed 14 September 2021.

[36] Council of the European Union (n 19) Art 4(1).

[37] See EC (n 6) 56.

[38] Especially if considering that more and more business investors get involved in crowdfunding, and that the crowdfunding markets of many third countries grow quickly. In Switzerland, for instance, notwithstanding a decline in the number of crowdfunding campaigns in 2019, the overall market volume has grown, see A Dietrich and S Amrein, 'Crowdfunding Monitor Schweiz 2020' (Hochschule Luzern 2020)9 et seq, <https://blog.hslu.ch/retail banking/crowdfunding/> accessed 14 September 2021.

[39] In loan-based crowdfunding, a large number of lenders finance a particular crowdfunding project and receive interest payments in return: Ferrarini and Macchiavello (n 6) 10.08; G Gabison, 'Understanding Crowdfunding and its Regulations. How Can Crowdfunding help ICT Innovation?', EC Joint Research Centre Science and Policy Report (2015) 10; Will and Quarch (n 17) 1481, 1482. On the different types of crowdlending, see eg Ivanova,

to 'the placing, without a firm commitment basis (as referred to in point (7) of Section A of Annex I to MiFID II), of transferable securities and admitted instruments for crowdfunding purposes issued by project owners or a special purpose vehicle, and the reception and transmission of client orders (as referred to in point (1) of that Section) in relation to those transferable securities and admitted instruments for crowdfunding purposes' (see Article 2(1) (a) point (ii)). According to this definition, the Crowdfunding Regulation, thus, covers investment-based crowdfunding too, also known as crowdinvesting.[40] The Crowdfunding Regulation, by contrast, does not extend to donation-based and reward-based crowdfunding as these alternative methods of financing do not involve financial products with particular financial returns.[41]

3.14   As far as loan-based crowdfunding is concerned, the Regulation does not further explicitly differentiate various business models.[42] Yet, Recital 11 specifies that the facilitation of granting of loans includes presenting crowdfunding offers to clients and pricing or assessing the credit risk of crowdfunding projects or project owners. The business models, hence, should be such as to enable 'a loan agreement between one or more investors and one or more project owners to be concluded through a crowdfunding platform'. Loans included within the scope of the Crowdfunding Regulation 'should be loans with unconditional obligations to repay an agreed amount of money to the investor'.[43] However, the Crowdfunding Regulation restricts the application of loan-based crowdfunding services to business loans (see subsection II.4.A).

3.15   As regards investment-based crowdfunding services under the Crowdfunding Regulation, their provision covers placement activities and the reception and transmission of orders (as defined in MiFID II) in respect of 'transferable securities' and 'admitted instruments for crowdfunding purposes'.

3.16   Pursuant to Article 2(1)(m), the term 'transferable securities' follows the definition in Article 4(1)(44) MiFID II. Accordingly, transferable securities are 'those classes of securities that are negotiable on the capital market, except for instruments of payment'. Transferable

---

'Cross-border regulation and fintech: are transnational cooperation agreements the right way to go?' (2019) 24 Uniform Law Review 367, 373.

[40] In comparison to the narrower term of equity-based crowdfunding, investment-based crowdfunding includes more types of investment than only equity, see Chervyakov and Rocholl (n 6) 8, n 8; Macchiavello (n 8) 558; for a general definition, see Ivanova (n 39) 372. About the risks of equity-based crowdfunding, see, at large, J Armour and L Enriques, 'The Promise and Perils of Crowdfunding: BetweenCorporate Finance and Consumer Contracts' (2018) 81 The Modern Law Review 51, 58 et seq.

[41] Nor do they deal with information asymmetries caused by financial products, see EC (n 11) 2; EC (n 6) 33.

[42] As part of their crowdlending activities, under strict, *inter alia*, disclosure requirements, CSPs are permitted to offer individual portfolio management of loans (see Art 3(4) subpara (2) and Art 6, also ESMA (n 15) Annex I, 84 et seq). Pursuant to Art 2(1)(c), a crowdfunding service provider who offers 'individual portfolio management of loans' '[allocates] a pre-determined amount of funds of an investor, which is an original lender, to one or multiple crowdfunding projects on its crowdfunding platform in accordance with an individual mandate given by the investor on a discretionary investor-by-investor basis'. Thereby business models using automated processes (so-called auto-investing) are considered individual portfolio management of loans too (see Recital 20).

[43] See Recital 11 that, further, explains that lending-based crowdfunding platforms only facilitate the conclusion by investors and the project owner of loan agreements without the crowdfunding service provider at any moment acting as a creditor of the project owner. For lack of unconditional repayability, subordinated loans are excluded from the material scope of application, see T Riethmüller, '§ 22: Crowdfunding und Crowdinvesting— Praktische Anwendungsfälle' in F Möslein and S Omlor (eds), *FinTech Handbuch* (2nd edn, CH Beck 2019) para 185 and, also there, M Renner, '§23: Theoretische und dogmatische Grundlagen' para 71.

securities include (a) 'shares in companies, other securities equivalent to shares in companies, partnerships or other entities and depositary receipts in respect of shares'; (b) 'bonds or other forms of securitised debt and depositary receipts in respect of such securities'; and (c) 'any other securities giving the right to acquire or sell any such transferable securities or giving rise to a cash settlement determined by reference to transferable securities, currencies, interest rates or yields, commodities or other indices or measures'. Transferability functions as a safeguard for investors who should be able to exit their investment, since this allows them to dispose of their interest on the capital markets.[44] Although the reference to the MiFID II definition of transferable securities seems to be helpful at first sight, it also brings about some difficulties since, domestically, the approaches to identify 'transferable securities' vary among Member States.[45] The same applies to the definition of 'placement without a firm commitment' and 'reception and transmission of client orders'.[46]

Pursuant to Article 2(1)(n), 'admitted instruments for crowdfunding purposes' comprise **3.17** 'shares of a private limited liability company that are not subject to restrictions that would effectively prevent them from being transferred, including restrictions to the way in which those shares are offered or advertised to the public'. The reason for including shares of certain private limited liability companies incorporated under the domestic law of Member States in the scope of the Crowdfunding Regulation is that they are also freely transferable on the capital markets.[47] However, if some Member States regulate the transferability of admitted instruments for crowdfunding purposes in national laws requiring, for instance, authentication by a notary, the Crowdfunding Regulation should apply without prejudice to these domestic laws governing the transfer of such instruments.[48] The inclusion of 'admitted instruments' in the material scope of application of the Crowdfunding Regulation therefore positively contributes to eliminating some of the differences among Member States in respect of the explanation of 'transferability'. Yet, uncertainties in respect of the identification of 'admitted instruments' and the transferability requirements under national laws will remain.[49]

Finally, there are further definitional issues with regard to the activities covered by the **3.18** term 'crowdfunding service' within the meaning of Article 2(1)(a). For instance, CSPs are allowed to use filtering tools on their crowdfunding platform that, however, should not be classified as investment advice in the meaning of Article 4(1)(4) MiFID II, as long as those tools provide information to clients neutrally and do not constitute a recommendation.[50] Besides, since the Crowdfunding Regulation aims at facilitating direct investment without reliance on financial intermediaries that are already covered by other stricter EU regulations, CSPs under the Crowdfunding Regulation are not allowed to offer individual or collective asset management services—as these services are being governed by different EU instruments, such as the AIFMD, MiFID II, and the Undertakings for the Collective

---

[44] Recital 13; see already Council of the European Union (n 19) Recital 11; cf also, EC (n 6) 35.

[45] Macchiavello (n 8) 566.

[46] See, with this critique, ibid 570 et seq and, discussing the different opinions about and proposals on permissible crowdfunding activities, ibid 571 et seq.

[47] See Recital 13.

[48] See Recital 14. Consequently, CSPs will have to make sure which measures and procedures need to be complied with in order such assets to be transferable under national law, cf Macchiavello (n 8) 567.

[49] Not least because of the discretion of national authorities in classifying 'admitted instruments', see ibid.

[50] See Recital 21 laying down objective criteria on which the operation of such filtering tools should be based.

Investment in Transferable Securities (UCITS) Directive.[51] Therefore, the interposition of any legal structures between the crowdfunding project and investors, including so-called special purpose vehicles (SPVs),[52] should be subject to strict regulations and permitted for the provision of crowdfunding services according to Article 3(6) only where enabling an investor to acquire an interest in an illiquid or indivisible asset, through issuance of transferable securities by a SPV.[53]

Blockchain-Based Crowdfunding

3.19   Initial coin offerings (ICOs) cannot be considered crowdfunding services[54] under the Crowdfunding Regulation. The Crowdfunding Regulation does not apply to ICOs on the ground that, even if ICOs can potentially fund SMEs and innovative start-ups and scale-ups, their characteristics differ significantly from crowdfunding services.[55] About the exclusion of blockchain-based crowdfunding from the scope of the Crowdfunding Regulation see Chapter 6.

4. Statutory Exemptions

3.20   Article 1(2) lists three exemptions from the scope of the Crowdfunding Regulation that limit the application of the European crowdfunding regime.

A. Article 1(2)(a)—Consumer Lending

3.21   As already indicated by the official name of the Regulation 'on European crowdfunding service providers for business' and emphasized by Article 2(1)(a) that puts 'business funding interests' at the core of crowdfunding services, the Crowdfunding Regulation only applies to entrepreneurial crowdfunding. According to Article 1(2)(a), the Regulation does not apply to the provision of crowdfunding services to project owners that are consumers, as defined in Article 3(a) of the Consumer Credit Directive (CCD). Hence, crowdlending under the Crowdfunding Regulation covers only lending to businesses (known as peer-to-peer business lending or just peer-to-business, P2B) and not to consumers (known as peer-to-peer consumer lending or just P2P) aiming for alternative access to finance through an online platform.[56] Although consumer lending does not fall within the scope of the Crowdfunding

---

[51] Recitals 19 and 22. However, pursuant to Art 12(13), CSPs authorized under the Crowdfunding Regulation may engage in asset management activities too, if receiving a separate authorization in accordance with the relevant Union or national law applicable to these activities.

[52] SPV simplify terms' negotiations, support financing deals, reduce collective action problems and provide investors with the same rights as non-crowdfunding investors and with an easy exit option, see ECN, Support for—and Proposed Improvements to—the European Commission Proposal for a Regulation on European Crowdfunding Service Providers (ECSP) for business (3 July 2018) 47, <https://www.crowd-funding.cloud/public/dps/dwl_file/ECSP-teoria/C-20180319-ECN-reaction-to-ECSP-regulation_final.pdf> accessed 14 September 2021.

[53] Recital 22 sentence 2. The use of SPVs for the provision of crowdfunding services falls under 'other services and activities', see ESMA (n 15) Annex I, 85. See also Chapter 9, subsection II.5.A.

[54] On the similarities and differences between ICOs and crowdfunding services, eg Dietrich and Amrein (n 38) 5 et seq.

[55] Recital 15.

[56] See also Recital 8. Whilst the crowdfunding regime strives to promote the protection of non-professional investors (see Recital 7), it excludes non-professional lending from its scope. This can be questioned, inasmuch as P2P consumer lending resembles P2P business lending more than equity-based crowdfunding: Karsten Wenzlaff and others, 'Crowdfunding in Europe: Between Fragmentation and Harmonization' in (n 5) 384.

Regulation, consumer-related cases are, at least partly, covered by existing EU legislation. If a consumer, for instance, receives a loan for personal consumption, this activity would generally fall within the scope of the CCD; if a consumer is granted credit to purchase an immovable property, that activity is regulated by the Mortgage Credit Directive (MCD).[57] However, the CCD and the MCD apply to credit agreements[58] between consumers and professional creditors,[59] while the case of consumers seeking funding from non-professional creditors, viz. from lenders that are also consumers, is not subjected to these directives. The application of the CCD and the MCD has been extended to P2P scenarios by some Member States when implementing the directives, but there are still domestic regimes that do not regulate P2P cases.[60] Considering the exemption of consumer lending from the Crowdfunding Regulation and the inconsistencies with regard to other instruments potentially relevant in consumer cases, the question arises as to whether P2P lending is adequately regulated at EU level, and whether it should have been included in the Crowdfunding Regulation too. On the role of EU Consumer Law in relation to the Crowdfunding Regulation, see Chapter 5.

B Article 1(2)(b)—Related Services

The Crowdfunding Regulation does not apply to other services related to crowdfunding **3.22** that are provided in accordance with national law. Since the Crowdfunding Regulation does not contain a definition or at least a non-exhaustive list of possible related activities the performance of which would remain governed by domestic law, there is vast room for interpretation and inclusion of countless related services. Such related activities may comprise, in particular, payment services (instruments of payment are not covered by the term 'transferable securities' according to the Crowdfunding Regulation, see subsection II.3.B.para 3.16) and investment services (as covered by the Member States' rules implementing MiFID II). One could also think of certain intermediary services, for example in respect of electronic money or payment accounts, or particular accounting services.[61] In practice, this might not only be a source of legal uncertainty for project owners and investors as to what set of rules would apply to which activities exercised by the CSP. Moreover, there is a risk of abuse. The latter is conceivable, for instance, where a crowdfunding service provider offers other related services under the guise of crowdfunding services within the meaning of Article 2(1)(a) while, in fact, this activity would, according to Article 1(2)(d), not be covered by the Crowdfunding Regulation. On the side of the CSP, this could happen for reasons of aiming at benefitting from the new crowdfunding regime instead of having the related

---

[57] See EC (n 11) 2.

[58] See Art 2(1) CCD in connection with Art 3(c) CCD and Art 3 MCD in connection with Art 4(3) MCD. On the gap in the protection of consumers where a consumer finances a certain project not by entering into a credit agreement but by choosing another type of financing, see F Möslein and Ch Rennig, '§ 21: 'Anleger- und Verbraucherschutz bei Crowdfunding-Finanzierungen' in (n 43) para 21.

[59] See Art 3(b) CCD and Art 4(2) MCD. The non-applicability of neither the CCD and the MCD nor the Crowdfunding Regulation where consumers address non-professional lenders is a further gap in the protection of the former, see ibid.

[60] As for the CCD, Macchiavello (n 8) 565 and n 27 with a list of examples of different national approaches to transposing the scope of the CCD.

[61] At this stage, ESMA (n 15) Annex I, 85 et seq, has proposed to consider the following 'other services and activities': asset safekeeping, payment services, the use of SPV for the provision of crowdfunding services, the application of credit scores to crowdfunding projects, the suggestion of the price and/or the interest rate of crowdfunding offers, operating a bulletin board and establishing and operating contingency funds. On applying credit scores to crowdfunding projects and pricing of offers, see Recital 41 and Art 19(6).

services subjected to separate, potentially stricter, domestic laws (requiring, for instance, additional authorizations).

C. Article 1(2)(c)—Total Consideration of Offers

3.23 The third exemption, as provided in Article 1(2)(c), entails that the Crowdfunding Regulation is inapplicable to crowdfunding offers with an overall consideration of more than EUR 5 million over a period of twelve months.[62] While the Commission's Proposal, in its Article 2(2)(d), referred to a maximum consideration of only EUR 1 million per crowdfunding offer in twelve months with regard to a particular crowdfunding project,[63] the ECON[64] and the European Parliament[65] advocated for an exemption of crowdfunding offers with a consideration of up to EUR 8 million. The Council likewise favoured the same high threshold.[66] These two thresholds had different points of reference. The limit of EUR 1 million determined by the Commission built upon the threshold set out in the Prospectus Regulation for the mandatory drawing up and approval of a prospectus above that minimum threshold.[67] The threshold of EUR 8 million, conversely, conformed to the maximum up to which Member States are entitled to exempt offers of securities to the public from the obligation to publish a prospectus in accordance with Article 3(2)(b) Prospectus Regulation.[68] The amount of EUR 8 million was also inspired by the fact that, in the wake of adopting the Prospectus Regulation, numerous domestic crowdfunding regimes had introduced higher thresholds.[69] In an attempt to avoid excessively low[70] or high thresholds, the final choice for a threshold of EUR 5 million[71] (following the threshold used by most Member States to exempt offers of securities to the public from the obligation to publish a prospectus)[72] tries to balance out investor protection and the promotion of SMEs.

3.24 In addition, since the characteristics of a crowdfunding offer and the information needs of investors are dealt with in the key investment information sheet (KIIS),[73] crowdfunding offers covered by the Crowdfunding Regulation are *expressis verbis* exempted from the

---

[62] Art 49 enables a temporary derogation from the threshold of EUR 5 million that is further discussed below at subsection II.6.B.

[63] EC (n 11) 20.

[64] ECON, Report on the proposal for a regulation of the European Parliament and of the Council on European Crowdfunding Service Providers (ECSP) for Business (9 November 2018) A8-0364/2018, Art 2(2)(d).

[65] European Parliament (n 35) Art 2(2)(d).

[66] Council of the European Union (n 19) Art 1(2)(d). The difference, compared to the Parliament's Position, being that Member States should be able to determine lower thresholds for crowdfunding offers and to prohibit the raising of capital for crowdfunding projects for amounts exceeding that domestic threshold.

[67] cf Recital 12 in EC (n 11) 14.

[68] See ECON (n 64) Recital 12 and European Parliament (n 35) 4; Council of the European Union (n 19) Recital 8a.

[69] Macchiavello (n 8) 568 et seq, n 42 with examples of different national thresholds as exceptions to the obligation to publish a prospectus.

[70] See ECN (n 52) 4, *inter alia*, criticizing that cross-border crowdfunding would be at risk since providers of platforms willing to grow in scale would rather operate domestically; consenting, T Riethmüller, '§ 10: Crowdfunding and Crowdinvesting—Praktische Anwendungsfragen' in (n 43) (CH Beck 2019) para 139.

[71] In the US, § 227.100(a)(1) and (2) JOBS Act (n 6) contains an exemption for small offers up to USD 1 million. For a comparison of the approaches in the US and the UK, see Armour and Enriques (n 40) 65 et seq.

[72] Recital 16 highlights that setting up a threshold for the total consideration of offers serves the effective protection of investors; see already Recital 12 in EC (n 11) 14.

[73] Art 23(1) requires CSPs to inform investors by making available a KIIS in accordance with Art 23(2)–(16) in order to ensure high level transparency vis-à-vis prospective investors. See also Recitals 50, 51.

obligation to publish a prospectus as required by Article 3(1) Prospectus Regulation.[74] Article 46 amends the Prospectus Regulation by adding Article 1(2)(k) to the list of exceptions from the Prospectus Regulation. On this exemption, see, in further detail, Chapter 9.

5. Article 1(3)—Relation to CRD IV

In general, for the purpose of avoiding regulatory arbitrage and ensuring their effective supervision, CSPs, in line with Article 9 of the Capital Requirements Directive (CRD IV), should not be allowed to take deposits or other repayable funds from the public, unless they are also authorized as a credit institution in accordance with Article 8 CRD IV.[75] Yet, Article 1(3)(a) and (b) prohibits Member States from applying national requirements implementing Article 9(1) CRD IV and obliges them to ensure that national law does not require an authorization as credit institution or any other individual authorization, exemption, or dispensation in connection with the provision of crowdfunding services in the following two situations:[76] **3.25**

  (a) for 'project owners that in respect of loans facilitated by the crowdfunding service provider accept funds from investors', and
  (b) for 'investors grant loans to project owners facilitated by the crowdfunding service provider'.[77]

By not applying the CRD IV provisions to CSPs, when providing services in respect of lending-based crowdfunding, the operation of start-ups and SMEs is kept away from greater authorization hurdles and, thus, the funding and the activity of such businesses is further promoted. See, in more detail, Chapter 7. **3.26**

6. Application *ratione temporis*

A. Period of Transition
The Crowdfunding Regulation applies from 10 November 2021 (see Article 51). From that moment on, it replaces national provisions that have been in place hitherto (in some domestic regimes, see Chapter 1). Considering this, for the purpose of legal certainty, Article 48 prescribes a transitional period in which CSPs can adapt their activities (so far governed by national law) to the new set of rules, and apply for authorization under the new regime.[78] Article 48(1) ensures that CSPs continue to offer their services, insofar as these are included in the scope of the Crowdfunding Regulation, in accordance with the applicable national **3.27**

---

[74] See Recital 67 following Recital 12a of the proposal by the European Parliament (n 35) 4 et seq to explicitly exclude offers under the Crowdfunding Regulation from the scope of application of the Prospectus Regulation and accordingly amend the latter.

[75] Recital 9 sentence 1.

[76] See also Recital 9 sentence 2.

[77] The facilitation of granting loans in connection with a crowdfunding project (and, thus, under the Crowdfunding Regulation) is to be distinguished from the activity of credit institutions that grant credits for their own account and take deposits or other repayable funds from the public, see Recital 11 sentence 4.

[78] See also Recital 76.

law until 10 November 2022, or alternatively (and depending on whether it is sooner) until the respective crowdfunding service provider is granted an authorization according to Article 12. In order to ease the transitional period, pursuant to Article 48(2), Member States are allowed to have simplified authorization procedures for CSPs that, at the time of entry into force of the Crowdfunding Regulation, are authorized under domestic law. These procedures, though, must be consistent with the requirements of Article 12 (on the authorization and supervision of CSPs see, in detail, Chapter 7). If a CSP has failed to obtain authorization in accordance with Article 12 by 10 November 2022, no new crowdfunding offers should be issued after that date, and the calls for funding should be closed by then.[79] Article 48(3) guarantees an extension of the transition period by twelve more months, until 10 November 2023, insofar as the Commission, after having made an assessment in consultation with ESMA on the application of the Crowdfunding Regulation to providers that offer crowdfunding services only nationally, makes use of the competence to adopt a delegated act in accordance with Article 44.

B. Temporary Derogation

3.28 Where, in a Member State, the threshold of total consideration for the publication of a prospectus in accordance with the Prospectus Regulation has been set below EUR 5 million, Article 49 allows for a non-renewable derogation from the maximum admissible amount of total consideration of crowdfunding offers set out in Article 1(2)(c). In that Member State, the Crowdfunding Regulation applies only to crowdfunding offers with a total consideration up to the relevant lower threshold for a period of twenty-four months, starting from 10 November 2021. The rationale behind the derogation mainly bears on two considerations.[80] First, the regime under the Crowdfunding Regulation and the requirements for offers of securities to the public in the Prospectus Regulation intersect with regard to a threshold of EUR 5 million. This overlap might increase the regulatory arbitrage as well as disrupt the access to finance and the development of capital markets in certain domestic capital markets. Second, those Member States who have implemented the Prospectus Regulation by introducing a threshold below EUR 5 million should be able to make sufficient effort to adjust their national law and ensure the application of the single threshold under the Crowdfunding Regulation.

7. Assessment of the Scope

3.29 The design of the scope of the Crowdfunding Regulation is pivotal for achieving a homogenous regulatory environment for the operation of crowdfunding services. Since convergence in crowdfunding regulation cannot be reached by relying on best practices in the Member States,[81] the Crowdfunding Regulation introduces a first-time harmonized legal framework covering two crowdfunding sectors at once: crowdlending and crowdinvesting.[82] While the Commission's proposal had built upon a regulatory regime

---

[79] Recital 77, further, stipulating that existing contracts, nevertheless, can continue being executed in accordance with the applicable domestic law after 10 November 2022.

[80] See Recital 17.

[81] cf Chervyakov and Rocholl (n 6) 12.

[82] Since donation-based and reward-based crowdfunding are not covered by the Crowdfunding Regulation, the existing consumer laws still apply to both models, while the application of the rules on anti-money laundering and

applying almost equally to both forms of crowdfunding, irrespective of their considerably differing risk profiles, diverse markets, and different rules applicable to each type,[83] the adopted Crowdfunding Regulation introduces some stricter and more detailed rules with respect to loan-based crowdfunding.[84]

Providers of investment-based and loan-based crowdfunding services established and op-   **3.30** erating in the Union can now rely on directly applicable uniform rules on crowdfunding, rather than being confronted with different domestic legal regimes. Particularly with regard to the provision of investment-based crowdfunding services, the new EU crowdfunding framework consisting of the Crowdfunding Regulation and the Crowdfunding Directive provides, to some notable extent, regulatory clarity. Regulatory fragmentation mostly used to relate to investment-based crowdfunding and, at this point, MiFID II and the requirements under the Prospectus Regulation were meant to ensure appropriate rules but turned out to be unsuitable for these business models.[85] Therefore, it is all the more important that the Crowdfunding Regulation covers crowdinvesting. However, the remaining prospect of applying MiFID II, insofar as CSPs do not meet the requirements for authorization under the Crowdfunding Regulation, is likely to hamper the desirable level of regulatory convergence. Moreover, considering the different national approaches in determining the activities under MiFID II, the fact that several provisions of the Crowdfunding Regulation refer to MiFID II in order to define the crowdfunding activities within the meaning of 'crowdfunding service' further impedes harmonization.

As regards loan-based crowdfunding, the exemption of consumer lending is question-   **3.31** able. The inconsistencies with regard to overlapping instruments, such as CCD and MCD, have adverse effects for consumers seeking funding through alternative financing. Where Member States do not apply the requirements under CCD and MCD to P2P lending, for instance, consumers willing to raise money through crowdfunding will have to rely on differing domestic rules. Therefore, and since P2P lending resembles P2B lending, it might have been more suitable to also integrate consumer loans in the scope of application, in order to rectify the existing loophole.

Lastly, the exemption of related services from the scope of the Crowdfunding Regulation   **3.32** according to Article 1(2)(b) will most likely hinder the cross-border effectiveness of the provision of crowdfunding services, by generating legal uncertainty and leading to risk of abuse. By contrast, the threshold of EUR 5 million for offers to be exempted from the application of the Crowdfunding Regulation as well as the non-application of CRD IV provisions according to Article 1(3) will most likely promote the crowdfunding business of SMEs.

On another note, it seems reasonable that rules on the treatment of third-country CSPs   **3.33** have been left aside at this stage. However, depending on the further development of the

---

terrorism financing under domestic legislations and supervisory arrangements to donation-based crowdfunding remains less clear, see EC (n 6) 33. See also Wenzlaff and others (n 56) 381, 382.

[83] See Macchiavello (n 8) 580 et seq with pros and cons of applying the same rules to crowdlending and crowdinvesting; Wenzlaff and others (n 56) justify the originally proposed same treatment with the difficulty to distinguish some debt and equity instruments from one another.
[84] Macchiavello (n 8) 581. These include the individual portfolio management of loans (see above, n 42 and on the inspiration by UK law, subsection III.1).
[85] Wenzlaff and others (n 56) 382.

crowdfunding market after the Crowdfunding Regulation has entered into force, provisions on third-country providers should be introduced. One possibility would be to add a clause ensuring an equivalence decision by the Commission, subject to certain conditions. Another possibility for enabling third-country service providers to offer services in the Union might be to insert additional rules on cross-border cooperation of the competent authorities in the Crowdfunding Regulation,[86] or to sign and ratify bilateral or multilateral treaties[87] on the access to and the operation on the crowdfunding market for third-country CSPs. Yet, since financial regulation at the global level is mainly governed by soft law instruments, the adoption of international standards and principles on cross-border crowdfunding seems to be a more likely approach in the foreseeable future.

3.34   All in all, the Crowdfunding Regulation certainly contributes to avoiding further regulatory fragmentation and segmentation of the crowdfunding market in the Union. Compliance and legal costs for SMEs are now reduced, and authorization hurdles removed. Thus, despite the obstacles still existing and within the limits of the Crowdfunding Regulation, cross-border operations of CSPs throughout the Union are significantly facilitated. Hopefully, European CSPs will scale their activities and augment cross-border flows. It remains to be seen whether alternative funding through crowdfunding platforms will increase throughout the EU.

III. The UK and the EU Crowdfunding Regulation

1. The Role of the UK in the Development of the EU Crowdfunding Regulation

3.35   As a European pioneer committing itself to building a strong sector for crowdfunding services by having established the first P2P lending platform (Zopa) in 2005, the UK has had a decisive impact on the rise of crowdfunding activities in the Union and pushed regulatory progress in the field.[88] In the run-up to the adoption of the EU crowdfunding regime, the withdrawal of the UK from the EU has encouraged the Union to become more attractive for UK-based crowdfunding firms by facilitating the passporting of crowdfunding activities while, at the same time, causing uncertainty, thus slowing down the regulatory development in the EU.[89] In any event, despite Brexit, the UK's efficient regulatory approach to crowdfunding, based on long-term practical experience, can certainly be seen as a source of inspiration for other jurisdictions as well as for the design of the EU crowdfunding regime.[90] An example in this respect is the optional exemption in UK law under the Prospectus

---

[86]   Arts 31–38 relate to the cooperation between competent Member States' authorities in the meaning of Art 2(1)(r).

[87]   While transnational FinTech cooperation agreements primarily aiming at promoting innovative businesses already exist (see thereon Ivanova (n 39)), treaties about the access and activity of third-country CSPs, especially at multilateral level, are, at least in the near future, rather unimaginable.

[88]   cf Ziegler, Shneor, and Zheng Zhang, in (n 5) 54.

[89]   See Macchiavello (n 8) 561 et seq.

[90]   cf Armour and Enriques (n 40) 64 with regard to the relevance of the regulation of equity-based crowdfunding in the UK. On the mainly MiFID-oriented regulatory approach in the UK, see G Ferrarini and E Macchiavello, 'Investment-Based Crowdfunding' in D Busch and G Ferrarini (eds), *Regulation of the EU Financial Markets—MiFID II and MiFIR* (OUP 2017) 23.20.

Regulation for securities offerings by a single firm over a period of twelve months, formerly set at an amount of less than EUR 5 million.[91] This exception has, at least, reasserted the decision to raise to EUR 5 million the limit for excluding offers from the scope of application of the Crowdfunding Regulation (see subsection II.4.C). Furthermore, although the UK had initially adopted separate regimes for loan-based and investment-based crowdfunding, it later gradually aligned its rules.[92] This process of aligning the regulation of loan-based crowdfunding to the rules of investment-based crowdfunding was particularly driven by the need to strengthen investor protection in relation to loan-based activities.[93] The UK therefore introduced stricter requirements for crowdlending services regarding governance and risk management, where crowdfunding platforms set the price of loan agreements and generate a target rate of investment return. In addition, the UK set a limit for investors at 10% of their net investible assets in P2P agreements and established an appropriateness assessment similar to the one applying to investment-based CSPs.[94] Against this background, it is not surprising that the EU has addressed crowdinvesting and crowdlending in one instrument, rather than adopting two different legal frameworks for each type of crowdfunding activity. The introduction of stricter requirements for loan-based activities in the UK has also acted as a source of inspiration for the Crowdfunding Regulation. Examples are the entry knowledge test in Article 21[95] (required for CSPs before giving prospective non-sophisticated investors full access to investing in crowdfunding projects on their platform),[96] the investment limit at 10%[97] and the requirements for credit risk assessment in case of pricing the credit risk of loans[98], as well as for the assessment of risk and risk management and financial modelling in case of individual portfolio management of loans[99].

2. Brexit and Its Consequences for the Application of the EU Crowdfunding Regulation

CSPs established in the UK are, as things stand at present, treated as third-country providers   **3.36**
and do not therefore fall under the new European crowdfunding regime. The Crowdfunding Regulation does not contain an equivalence clause with regard to third-country firms (see subsection II.3.A.para 3.11), so that no legal basis exists for the Commission to deem a third country's crowdfunding regulatory regime equivalent to the EU framework, and to allow

---

[91] FSMA, section 86(1)(e) that, as amended, now takes up the higher general threshold of the Prospectus Regulation of EUR 8 million.

[92] Macchiavello (n 8) 581, n 81.

[93] See ECN (n 5) 6 and Financial Conduct Authority (FCA), Loan-based ('peer-to-peer') and investment-based crowdfunding platforms: Feedback on our post-implementation review and proposed changes to the regulatory framework, CP 18/20 (July 2018) 1.27 et seq <https://www.fca.org.uk/publication/consultation/cp18-20.pdf> accessed 14 September 2021.

[94] FCA, Loan-based ('peer-to-peer') and investment-based crowdfunding platforms: Feedback to CP18/20 and final rules, PS19/14 (June 2019) 2.3 et seq, 2.12 et seq, 2.18 et seq, <https://www.fca.org.uk/publication/policy/ps19-14.pdf> accessed 14 September 2021.

[95] See also Recitals 43, 44.

[96] The UK is one of very few jurisdictions requiring an appropriateness test also for lending-based crowdfunding, see Macchiavello (n 8) 592, n 107.

[97] See Art 23(6)(c).

[98] See Arts 4(4), 19(6) and (7). On the differences between the EU and UK regimes, the former being stricter and less flexible, Macchiavello (n 8) 596, n 124.

[99] See Arts 4(2), 6(1), (2), and (5)–(7).

third-country providers authorized in their home country to be active in the Union on that basis. Consequently, CSPs established in the UK, if willing to operate on the EU market, will not be able to benefit from the new crowdfunding regime. A UK-based CSP can be considered active on the EU market when offering crowdfunding services towards Union-based project owners and/or vis-à-vis an investing crowd based in the EU.

3.37   Therefore, if UK-based CSPs want to access the EU crowdfunding market, they have limited options. Currently, CSPs from the UK would be able to become active on the market in the Union under the Crowdfunding Regulation only if they have an effective and stable establishment, viz. an independent subsidiary, in the EU,[100] and an authorization with the responsible authority in the respective Member State in accordance with Article 12. Insofar as UK firms conducting investment-based crowdfunding do not establish an EU subsidiary, they may offer investment services and perform investment activities on the EU crowd-funding market under the third-country regimes of MiFID II (Articles 39–43 MiFID II) and MiFIR (Articles 46–49 MiFIR).[101] By contrast, the provision of crowdlending services by UK-based CSPs in the EU market is likely to be far more complex, in the absence of a third-country regime in the Crowdfunding Regulation.

3.   Brexit and Its Implications for the Development of the Crowdfunding Market

3.38   Brexit will most probably lead to a significant shrinking of the overall volume of the crowd-funding market in the Union, taking into account that the UK makes up a large share of the total EU crowdfunding market.[102] In order to avoid any abrupt interruption of crowd-funding service provision after the departure of the UK from the EU, third-country rules had been taken into consideration as a possible way to ensure the functioning of the crowdfunding market.[103] Due to the current lack of such provisions in the Crowdfunding Regulation, however, a downsizing of the EU crowdfunding market is most probably to be expected.

3.39   Likewise, EU CSPs will not be able to offer their services to UK-based investors and project owners without complying with authorization and disclosure requirements, as well as con-duct of business rules under UK law. Since the UK is no longer a Member State, EU CSPs authorized under MiFID II will not be able to exercise passport rights to the UK.[104] EU-based providers of investment- and loan-based crowdfunding services that want to offer services falling under the definition of 'regulated activity' according to section 22 of the Financial Services and Markets Act (FSMA) to investors and/or project owners in the UK will be obliged to obtain authorization with the FCA pursuant to section 19 FSMA.[105]

---

[100]   Recital 31.
[101]   On the access of third-country investment firms to the EU market under MiFID II and MiFIR, see, in-depth, D Busch and M Louisse, 'MiFID II/MiFIR's Regime for Third-Country Firms' in (n 90) 10.01 et seq.
[102]   Chervyakov and Rocholl (n 6) 4.
[103]   See EC (n 6) 56.
[104]   Prior to Brexit, this was still the case, see ECN (n 5) 9 on the regulatory barriers for inbound activities.
[105]   cf ECN (n 5) 8, 9.

If providers of investment-based crowdfunding services established in the EU want to ad-   **3.40**
dress UK-based companies seeking to raise finance through issuing securities, the latter will
have to either fulfil the prospectus requirement under UK law or claim an exemption from
disclosure. Otherwise, offering transferable securities to the public without making available an approved prospectus would be a criminal offence.[106] The current UK legal framework is described in Chapter 4.

Considering the aforementioned obstacles, EU-based CSPs will be more likely to expand   **3.41**
their activities in multiple EU Member States rather than provide services in the UK. Yet,
depending on the business opportunities of the UK crowdfunding market, operating in
both, the UK and the EU, might still remain an attractive option.

---

[106] See the prohibition in section 85(1) FSMA.

4

Crowdfunding and UK Law

Gerard McMeel QC

I. Introduction

The UK prides itself as a leading international financial centre and a hub for financial tech- **4.01**
nology (FinTech). Innovations in financial technology offer the promise of a revolution in
financial intermediation, providing opportunities for 'crowdfunded' finance and investment for small and medium-sized businesses, and credit for individuals, which traditional
banks would probably not have offered. In traditional banking law and theory it was the
function of banks to act as 'financial reservoir',[1] bringing together those with surplus resources (savers and depositors) and those in need of credit (borrowers and mortgagors),
but such financial intermediation can no longer be seen as a unique privilege of banks.[2]
Platforms and their associated algorithms can now perform that function. Financial innovations, however, have not sprung into being in an environment where there is no existing legal and regulatory matrix. The regulation of crowdfunding in the UK starts from
the premise that where the activities of peer-to-peer (P2P) loan-based or investment-based
platforms fall within the existing perimeter of financial regulation, they are regulated as
such. In the words of Mark Carney, then Governor of the Bank of England: 'Just because

---

[1] *Commissioners of the Savings Banks of Victoria v Permewan, Wright & Co Ltd* (1914) 19 CLR 457, 470–71
(HCA: Issacs J).
[2] See V Bavoso, 'Financial Intermediation in the Age of FinTech: P2P Lending and the reinvention of Banking'
(2021) Oxford Journal of Legal Studies (forthcoming).

something is new doesn't mean it should be treated any differently.'[3] To the extent that investment-based platforms are engaged in established regulated activities such as arranging or advising on investments, they are subject to the established high-level principles (PRIN) and the investment conduct of business sourcebook (COBS). Where loan-based platforms are engaged in consumer credit business, they are subject to what remains of the Consumer Credit Act 1974 and the FCA's consumer credit rules (CONC). In addition, there are bespoke rules introduced to ensure an appropriate degree of regulation and consumer protection in this arena. Speaking in January 2017 Mark Carney, then Governor of the Bank of England observed:

> peer-to-peer ('P2P') lending has grown rapidly in recent years from a small base. In the UK, P2P lending now represents about 14% of new lending to SMEs. Estimates suggest that more than half of these credits were unlikely to have been provided by existing banks.

He recorded that in 2015 loans originated by P2P lenders in the UK were £40 billion. With that background, both conduct issues and anti-money laundering/counter-terrorist (AML/CT) financing concerns needed to be addressed by financial regulators. He continued:

> Conduct regulators—such as the UK's Financial Conduct Authority ('FCA')—have taken an early lead in seeking to ensure that standards for financial advice and services offered are upheld, and the integrity of the financial system is protected.[4]

Mr Carney also referenced the FCA's 'regulatory sandbox' which permits businesses to test innovative products and services in a live environment with proportionate regulatory requirements, which provides a learning experience for both those businesses and their regulators.[5] The UK government and regulators remain vocal in their support and facilitation of financial innovation.[6]

4.02   This chapter discusses the regulation of crowdfunding in the UK, being one of the leading jurisdictions for the development of the crowdfunding market. It starts with a brief note on Brexit (section II), followed by an overview of the legislative framework and regulatory regime in the UK for crowdfunding (section III). Section IV discusses the authorization and supervision of crowdfunding platforms in the UK. Section V discusses the protection of the crowd and project owners in the UK. Section VI concludes.

II. A Note on Brexit

4.03   As is well-known, following a national referendum on 23 June 2016, the UK voted to leave the EU, having been a member of it and its predecessors since 1 January 1973, under the European Communities Act 1972. This was implemented by the European Union

---

[3] M Carney, 'Building the Infrastructure to Realise FinTech's Promise' (International FinTech Conference 2017, Old Billingsgate, 12 April 2017) <https://www.bankofengland.co.uk/speech/2017/building-the-infrastructure-to-realise-fintechs-promise>.

[4] M Carney, 'The Promise of FinTech—Something New under the Sun?' (Deutsche Bundesbank G20 conference on 'Digitising finance, financial inclusion and financial literacy', Wiesbaden, 25 January 2017) <https://www.bankofengland.co.uk/speech/2017/the-promise-of-fintech-something-new-under-the-sun>.

[5] <https://www.fca.org.uk/firms/innovate-innovation-hub>.

[6] See the *Kalifa Review of UK FinTech* (February 2021) <https://www.gov.uk/government/publications/the-kalifa-review-of-uk-fintech>.

(Withdrawal) Act 2018, which repealed the European Communities Act 1972 on 'exit day', which eventually took place on 31 January 2020.[7] The UK and EU negotiated a revised Withdrawal Agreement in October 2019,[8] which was implemented by the European Union (Withdrawal Agreement) Act 2020. This included provision for an 'implementation period' which expired on 31 December 2020.[9] Much of the UK's detailed financial services law and regulation was constituted by directly applicable EU measures or the national implementation of EU directives, and this has very largely remained the case since exit day and the expiry of the implementation period. Section 2 of the European Union (Withdrawal) Act 2018 retained EU-derived primary and secondary legislation. Section 3(1) provided that directly applicable EU law which was operative before withdrawal became part of domestic UK law as 'retained EU law' at the end of the implementation period. By section 6 UK courts are 'not bound by any principles laid down, or any decisions made' by the ECJ, and can no longer refer matters to that court on or after the implementation period completion day. Section 1A, inserted by the European Union (Withdrawal Agreement) Act 2020, gave continuing effect to EU law until the end of the 'implementation period' on 31 December 2020. So EU measures, such as the Markets in Financial Instruments Directive II (MiFID II), continue to provide the substance of UK law and regulation post-Brexit. It also follows that the Crowdfunding Regulation[10] is an EU measure that is not directly applicable in the UK in consequence of the timing of its withdrawal from the EU. The impact of Brexit on the development of crowdfunding as an alternative funding means and market access for CSPs after Brexit (both to the UK and the EU) is discussed in Chapter 3.

III. The Legislative Framework and Regulatory Regime for Crowdfunding in the UK

Financial services in the UK are governed by the Financial Services and Markets Act 2000 **4.04** (FSMA). The Act provides only the framework, with a large part of the substance of the reforms left to secondary legislation. These encompass such crucial matters as what constitute regulated activities, or which firms require statutory authorization. FSMA is at heart a licencing statute providing that those who engage in financial services by way of business in the UK must be authorized under Part 4A of the Act. The development of the UK's regime for crowdfunding initially took place through extension of FSMA, after which the FCA took care of further professionalization of the regime (see subsection III.3). The applicable legislative framework for financial services in general, and crowdfunding in particular, in the UK resembles a wedding cake. The top tier consists of the FSMA. The middle tier comprises hundreds of separate pieces of secondary legislation, including such significant measures

---

[7] Section 1, European Union (Withdrawal) Act 2018. Subsequent measures, principally the European Union (Withdrawal) Act 2019, the European Union (Withdrawal) (No 2) Act 2019 and the European Union (Withdrawal) Act 2018 (Exit Day) (Amendment) (No 3) Regulations 2019, SI 2019/1423 postponed 'exit day' to 31 January 2020.

[8] HM Government, Agreement on the withdrawal of the United Kingdom of Great Britain and Northern Ireland from the European Union and the European Atomic Energy Community (19 October 2019) <https://assets.publishing.service.gov.uk/government/uploads/system/uploads/attachment_data/file/840655/Agreement_on_the_withdrawal_of_the_United_Kingdom_of_Great_Britain_and_Northern_Ireland_from_the_European_Union_and_the_European_Atomic_Energy_Community.pdf>.

[9] European Union (Withdrawal Agreement) Act 2020, section 39(1); European Union (Withdrawal) Act 2018, section 1A(6).

[10] Regulation (EU) 2020/1503.

as the Financial Services and Markets Act 2000 (Regulated Activities) Order 2001, SI 2001/ 544 (the RAO), and the Financial Services and Markets Act 2000 (Financial Promotion) Order 2005, SI 2005/1529 (see subsection III.3). The bottom and largest tier comprises the FCA Handbook made pursuant to the rule-making powers in the FSMA, and implementing much of the detail of financial services law and regulation, much of which is based on EU measures (see subsection III.4).

4.05   FSMA established a single safety-net compensation scheme to provide a form of statutory insurance for investors, and customers where financial institutions fail. Part XV of FSMA created the scheme, known as the Financial Services Compensation Scheme (FSCS).[11] FMSA also established a single ombudsman system as an alternative to dispute resolution before the courts, not only for retail consumers but also for smaller businesses. Part XVI of FSMA created the scheme, known as the Financial Ombudsman Service (FOS). Eligible complainants are able to bring claims in respect of crowdfunding providers before the FOS (see subsection III.5).

1. The Development of the UK's Regulation of Crowdfunding

4.06   To the extent that investment-based or loan-based crowdfunding platforms fell within existing regulated activities such as arranging investments or credit broking, they already fell within the regulatory perimeter created by FSMA and the RAO. The applicable conduct of business rules for investment-based crowdfunding were based on the revised MiFID II,[12] and its predecessor, and are discussed further below in section V.1. The first specific measures of UK regulation addressed to crowdfunding were introduced when the FSMA[13] was initially extended by an amendment to the RAO in 2014 to include operating an electronic system in relation to lending.[14] This took place at the same time that the responsibility for consumer credit regulation was moved from the now defunct Office of Fair Trading to the FCA (see subsection III.1). Prior to 1 April 2014 there was a regulatory split between the FCA (and its predecessor, the Financial Services Authority) which regulated most financial services, including deposit-taking by banks, and lending and credit activities which were within the remit of the Office of Fair Trading, and regulated by the Consumer Credit Act 1974, and delegated legislation made under that Act. After 1 April 2014 the FCA assumed responsibility for consumer credit activities as well, pursuant to an untidy set of provisions under both FSMA and a heavily amended and eviscerated Consumer Credit Act 1974.[15]

---

[11]   For detailed discussion, see section F of Ch 19, FSMA.

[12]   Directive 2014/65/EU, implemented in the UK from 3 January 2018.

[13]   The FSMA is a UK enactment encompassing the three jurisdictions of England and Wales, Scotland, and Northern Ireland (FSMA, section 430(1). See also FSA Act 2012, section 121).

[14]   Financial Services and Markets Act 2000 (Regulated Activities) (Amendment) (No 2) Order 2013, SI 2013/ 1881, introducing new regulated activity of operating an electronic system in relation to lending (as Art 36H of the RAO).

[15]   For the consultation, see HM Treasury and the Department for Business, Innovation and Skills, 'A New Approach to Financial Regulation: Consultation on Reforming the Consumer Credit Regime' (December 2010). See also FSA 13/07, 'High level proposals for an FCA regime for consumer credit' (March 2013); FCA CP 13/10, 'Detailed Proposals for the FCA Regime for Consumer Credit' (October 2013) and FCA PS 14/3, 'Detailed Rules for the FCA Regime for Consumer Credit—Including Feedback on FCA QCP 13/18' (February 2014).

The background to the two phases of the FCA's review of measures applicable to crowd-   **4.07**
funding and proposed reforms are to be found in the following regulatory consultation papers and policy statements:

(1) Financial Conduct Authority, *The FCA's regulatory approach to crowdfunding and similar activities* (October 2013) (CP13/13);

(2) Financial Conduct Authority, *The FCA's regulatory approach to crowdfunding over the internet, and the promotion of non-readily realisable securities by other media* (March 2014) (PS14/4);

(3) Financial Conduct Authority, *Loan-based ('peer-to-peer') and investment-based crowdfunding platforms: Feedback on our post-implementation review and proposed changes to the regulatory framework*, Consultation Paper CP18/20 (July 2018) (CP18/20);

(4) Financial Conduct Authority, *Loan-based ('peer-to-peer') and investment-based crowdfunding platforms: Feedback to CP 18/20 and final rules*, Policy Statement PS19/14 (June 2019) (PS19/14).

In 2016, the FCA commenced a post-implementation review (PIR) of its crowdfunding regime, investigating the market for crowdfunding in the UK and how its initial regulatory measures (as discussed in CP13/13 and PS14/4) were working in practice. The latter two documents (CP18/20 and PS19/14) provide details of the findings of the PIR, and how the FCA proposed to act on its conclusions. The PIR identified a number of poor business practices, particularly on the loan-based side, which might translate into consumer detriment, in respect of disclosure of information, charging structures, pricing and quality, disorderly failure, and record-keeping.[16] It therefore proposed a revised rules-based approach to loan-based crowdfunding to include:

(1) More explicit governance arrangements and systems controls to support advertised outcomes, credit risk assessment, and fair valuation practices;

(2) Strengthening the regime for orderly winding down of platforms where they fail;

(3) Applying marketing restrictions to debt-based platforms to protect less sophisticated and experienced investors;

(4) Introducing a requirement that platforms assess investors' knowledge and experience of products where no advice had been received;

(5) Providing for minimum information for disclosure to would-be investors;

(6) Applying its mortgage conduct of business rules to platforms offering home finance products.[17]

The reforms resulted in substantial amendments to the FCA Handbook, including a whole new sub-chapter into COBS entitled 'Operating an electronic system in relation to lending' in COBS 18.12, discussed further below in section V.1.

---

[16] CP18/20, paras 1.17–1.21. In respect of the investment-based crowdfunding regime, which is largely based on EU measures, the FCA concluded that it was appropriate. CP18/20, paras 1.25–1.26.

[17] PS19/14, para 1.14.

2. The Regulated Activities Order

4.08   The Financial Services and Markets Act 2000 (Regulated Activities) Order 2001 (RAO) fleshes out section 22 of, and Schedule 2 to, FSMA. It specifies those activities which, if carried on by way of business, will be regulated.[18] Firms undertaking any one or more of these regulated activities must be authorized by the FCA under Part 4A or FSMA or else be committing a criminal offence under sections 19 and 23 of FSMA. RAO is concerned with doing (verbs) in respect of things, usually contracts, services, property, or products of some description (nouns).[19] Reversing the order of RAO, it is easier to consider the specified investments first, and then the activities specified in relation to them.

3. The Specified Investments in the RAO

4.09   Part III of RAO lists the specified investments.[20] RAO now provides the detailed statutory definitions of each of these 'investments'. The word investment is used in a much wider sense than its usual economic meaning and embraces a wide range of financial contracts. The *specified investments* potentially applicable to crowdfunding platforms include:

- shares in companies or stock in share capital;[21]
- instruments creating or acknowledging indebtedness, such as debentures, debenture stock, loan stock, bonds, and certificates of deposit;[22]
- certificates representing securities;[23]
- units in a collective investment scheme;[24]
- rights under a regulated mortgage contract;[25]
- rights under a credit agreement;[26]
- rights under a consumer hire agreement;[27]
- rights to or in investments.[28]

4. Regulated Activities under the RAO

4.10   RAO specifies the kinds of activities and investments which, if carried on by way of business, will be regulated under FSMA.[29] The *specified activities* potentially applicable to crowdfunding platforms include:[30]

---

[18]   See also the Financial Services and Markets Act 2000 (Carrying on Regulated Activities by Way of Business) Order 2001, SI 2001/1177.
[19]   See generally PERG, 2.5–2.7.
[20]   See PERG 2.6.
[21]   RAO, Art 76.
[22]   RAO, Art 77.
[23]   RAO, Art 80.
[24]   RAO, Art 81.
[25]   RAO, Art 88.
[26]   RAO, Art 88.
[27]   RAO, Art 88E.
[28]   RAO, Art 89.
[29]   See PERG 2.7–2.11.
[30]   RAO, Art 4(1).

- dealing in (by buying, selling, subscribing, or underwriting) securities and derivatives[31] as principal;[32]
- dealing in (by buying, selling, subscribing, or underwriting) securities or relevant investments[33] as agent;[34]
- arranging deals for another person as principal or as agent in securities or relevant investments;[35]
- credit broking;[36]
- operating an electronic system in relation to lending;[37]
- advising on investments, including the merits of buying, selling, subscribing for, or underwriting 'a particular investment' which is a security or a relevant investment, or exercising rights in respect of such investments;[38]
- entering into regulated credit agreements as lender;[39]
- entering into regulated consumer hire agreements as owner.[40]

5. FCA Rules and Guidance

The FCA's Handbook of Rules and Guidance is in practice one of the most significant   **4.11**
sources of information on financial services regulation in the UK. The FCA's Handbook is
the repository of the fruits of the broad powers conferred on the FCA by Part 9A of FSMA
(as amended) to make rules and issue guidance. The principal components of the FCA
Handbook relevant to crowdfunding are:

High Level Standards:

- Principles for Businesses (PRIN);
- Senior Management Arrangements, Systems, and Controls (SYSC).[41]

Business Standards:

- Conduct of Business Sourcebook (COBS);
- Mortgages and Home Finance: Conduct of Business (MCOB);
- Client Assets (CASS).

Specialist sourcebooks:

- Consumer credit sourcebook (CONC)

---

[31] Contractually based investments other than those under RAO, Arts 87 and 89. For 'securities' and 'contractually based investments' see RAO, Art 3.
[32] RAO, Art 14.
[33] The 'relevant investments' are defined in RAO, Art 3. For 'securities' see RAO, Art 3.
[34] RAO, Art 21.
[35] RAO, Art 25.
[36] RAO, Art 36A.
[37] RAO, Art 36H.
[38] RAO, Art 53.
[39] RAO, Art 60B; as from 1 April 2014.
[40] RAO, Art 60N; as from 1 April 2014.
[41] See SYSC 4.1.1R and SYSC 4.1.8A R and following; CP18/20, paras 5.5–5.22.

Each paragraph of the FCA Handbook has an explicitly designated 'regulatory status' identified by single letters of the alphabet. There are three principal species of provision: rules; evidential provisions; and guidance. The letter 'R' indicates a *general rule*.[42] Rules generally impose binding obligations upon authorized persons. Breach of such rules exposes a firm to the possibility of enforcement action by the FCA,[43] and may expose it to a private claim for damages.[44] The letter 'E' signifies an *evidential provision*.[45] Such rules have two functions, depending on their express terms. Either failure to comply with an evidential rule may be relied on as 'tending to establish contravention' of the main rule,[46] or compliance with such provisions may be relied on as 'tending to demonstrate compliance' with the main rule.[47] The letter 'G' indicates *guidance*.[48] Such provisions lack both the binding nature of general rules and the indicative status of evidential provisions. Given the potential disciplinary and private law consequences of breaking a 'rule', such a provision has the greatest practical importance. In addition, there is a sub-species of rule termed a 'high level principle'. High level principles are rules of a greater degree of generality than ordinary rules. They may be the basis for disciplinary action but are not of themselves the basis for private law claims. The most important are the FCA *Principles for Businesses* (the FCA Principles or PRIN).[49] The FCA Principles include amongst others:

(1) *Integrity*. A firm must conduct its business with integrity.

(2) *Skill, care, and diligence*. A firm must conduct its business with due skill, care, and diligence.

(3) *Management and control*. A firm must take reasonable care to organize and control its affairs responsibly and effectively, with adequate risk management systems.

...

(6) *Customers' interests*. A firm must pay due regard to the interests of its customers and treat them fairly.

(7) *Communications with clients*. A firm must pay due regard to the information needs of its clients, and communicate information to them in a way which is clear, fair, and not misleading.

(8) *Conflicts of interest*. A firm must manage conflicts of interest fairly, both between itself and its customers, and between one customer and another client.

6. Rights under the FSCS and the FOS

4.12   As stated above, Part XV of FSMA created the FSCS. Strikingly, the UK has not extended this safety-net compensation scheme for insolvent regulated firms under the Financial Services

---

[42] Made principally under FSMA, sections 137A.

[43] FSMA, sections 205–206.

[44] FSMA, section 138D(2)–(4), as substituted by FSA 2012, section 24(1). This significant provision conferring a right of action on private persons was previously contained in FSMA, section 150 as originally enacted.

[45] FSMA 2000, section 138C.

[46] FSMA 2000, section 138C(2)(a).

[47] FSMA 2000, section 137C(2)(b).

[48] FSMA 2000, section 139A.

[49] PRIN 2.1.1R.

Compensation Scheme to customers of P2P lenders.[50] However, the scheme does apply to investment-based crowdfunding. In contrast, all customers of both loan-based and investment-based crowdfunding platforms are eligible complainants before the FOS and are able to bring claims in respect of the activities of authorized crowdfunding providers. The FOS provides a quick, free, and informal alternative to dispute resolution in the courts.[51] In practice, it is the most significant dispute resolution mechanism in UK retail financial services. Strikingly, whilst the FOS generally follows the applicable laws, regulations, and rules, it is entitled to adjudicate on what it considers fair and reasonable in all the circumstances.[52]

IV. Authorization and Supervision of Crowdfunding Platforms

The FSMA was heavily amended in 2012[53] to introduce a 'twin peaks' structure for the regulatory agencies, being the FCA and the Prudential Regulation Authority (PRA), replacing the former single regulator, the Financial Services Authority (FSA). The PRA, which is now part of the Bank of England, the UK's central bank, and is concerned with the prudential regulation of systemically important firms, such as banks, insurers, and certain larger investment firms, is likely to be of no direct relevance to most crowdfunding platforms. For crowdfunding, the FCA is the most relevant supervisory authority, being responsible for both the conduct of business regulation of all financial firms as well as the prudential supervision of most firms not considered to be systemically significant. The FCA became responsible for conduct of business regulation for both retail and wholesale firms under FSMA from 1 April 2013. A year later the FCA was also given responsibility for consumer credit regulation. In 2013, its predecessor had regulated some 26,000 firms under FSMA and the Office of Fair Trading had been responsible for some 99,000 firms as the licencing body under the Consumer Credit Act 1974 (CCA). There was an overlap of some 16,000 firms. The transfer of responsibility took place on 1 April 2014. The FCA's new powers embraced 'product intervention' powers which would permit it to impose requirements on financial products, or even to ban them,[54] and improvements to the powers to deal with misleading financial promotions.[55] **4.13**

As stated above, FSMA is at its core a licencing statute. Its purpose is to require those undertaking regulated financial services in the UK to seek authorization either from the FCA or for systemically important firms both the PRA and FCA. However, FSMA itself contains no definitive legislative statement of the activities or investments with which it is concerned. Part II of FSMA creates the 'general prohibition'. Only an authorized person or an exempt person may carry on, or may purport to carry on, a regulated activity in the UK.[56] The exempt firms regime will not be relevant to crowdfunding platforms. Accordingly, to carry on **4.14**

---

[50] PS14/4, paras 3.2–3.5. See the proposal in FCA CP13/13, paras 3.6–3.8. In the second phase see CP18/20, para 2.12, although the position is being kept under review.
[51] FSMA section 225(1).
[52] FSMA, section 228(2).
[53] By the Financial Services Act 2012.
[54] FSMA, sections 137D and 137E.
[55] FSMA, sections 137R and 137S.
[56] FSMA, section 19.

business lawfully, platforms need to seek authorization under Part 4A of FSMA by making an application to the FCA.[57] In order to do so a firm will have to comply with the threshold conditions for authorization. These include requirements as to appropriate resources; location of offices; being capable of being effectively supervised; being a fit and proper person; and providing a suitable business model.[58]

4.15   Once authorized, the firm is subject to oversight by FCA supervisors, and to the detailed regulation of the FCA Handbook. As already mentioned, this includes the Principles for Businesses, and the need to comply on an ongoing basis with the threshold conditions, including appropriate financial resources.[59] Important provisions specifically targeted at crowdfunding platforms include the need for debt-based firms to have in place 'living wills', that is arrangements to administer loans in the event of the failure of the platform under SYSC 4.1.8A R–SYSC 4.1.8E.

V. Protection of the Crowd and Project Owners

4.16   This section describes in outline the principal conduct of business measures for crowdfunding platforms. Section V.1 discusses the MiFID based regime which applies to investment-based platforms. Section IV.2 discusses the bespoke regime for debt-based crowdfunding introduced in 2019. Section IV.3 introduces the rules for the protection of borrowers in debt-based crowdfunding derived from the CCA and CONC.

1. Protection of the Crowd in Equity Crowdfunding

4.17   Crowdinvesting firms and platforms are required to be authorized by the FCA because they are engaged in financial promotions and arranging deals in investments, or because they are engaged in activities in relation to collective investment schemes.[60] This means that the conduct of business rules in COBS apply. When initially responding to investment-based crowdfunding, the FCA decided to restrict direct offer financial promotions to certain categories of investors who were better able to assess or handle the risks. It also decided to apply the appropriateness standards of MiFID to all crowdfunding firms, whether they fell within MiFID or not.[61]

4.18   However the UK also implemented in full the exemption under the EU's Prospectus Directive for offerings of less than EUR 5 million by a single firm in a twelve-month period. With the transition from the Prospectus Directive to the Prospectus Regulation, the UK took the opportunity to increase the public offer threshold below which a prospectus does not need to published to EUR 8 million from 20 July 2018.[62]

---

[57] FSMA, section 55A.
[58] FSMA, section 55B and schedule 6, Part 1B. See also FCA Handbook: COND.
[59] The COND component of the FCA Handbook.
[60] PS14/4, para 1.7. See also CP13/13, paras 2.7–2.11.
[61] PS14/4, paras 1.14 to 1.16 and chapter 4.
[62] FSMA section 86(1)(e) as amended by Financial Services and Markets Act 2000 (Prospectus and Markets in Financial Instruments) Regulations 2019, SI 2018/786, reg 2(2); FCA, Changes to align the FCA Handbook with the EU Prospectus Regulation (January 2019) (CP19/6), para 3.3. See D Busch, G Ferrarini, and J Franx (eds), *Prospectus Regulation and Prospectus Liability* (Oxford University Press 2020), para 26.27.

The conduct of business rules in COBS reflect MiFID II.[63] These include, first the client's **4.19** best interests rule, requiring that a firm must act 'honestly, fairly and professionally in ac- cordance with the best interests of its client'.[64] Unlike FCA Principle 6 (treating customers fairly), this rule will be actionable by private persons in accordance with section 138D of FSMA. Secondly, the fair, clear, and not misleading rule provides that a 'firm must ensure that a communication or financial promotion is fair, clear and not misleading'.[65]

The restriction on direct offer financial promotions of what were defined as 'non-readily **4.20** realisable securities' was introduced in COBS 4.7.7R–COBS 4.7.10R. COBS 4.7.7R in its current form provides:

(1) Unless permitted by *COBS 4.7.8 R*, a *firm* must not *communicate* or *approve* a *direct- offer financial promotion* relating to a *non-readily realisable security* a *P2P agreement* or a *P2P portfolio* to or for *communication* to a *retail client* without the conditions in (2) and (3) being satisfied.

(2) The first condition is that the *retail client* recipient of the *direct-offer financial promo- tion* is one of the following:
   (a) certified as a 'high net worth investor' in accordance with *COBS 4.7.9 R*;
   (b) certified as a 'sophisticated investor' in accordance with *COBS 4.7.9 R*;
   (c) self-certified as a 'sophisticated investor' in accordance with *COBS 4.7.9 R*; or
   (d) certified as a 'restricted investor' in accordance with *COBS 4.7.10 R*.

(3) The second condition is that the *firm* itself or:
   (a) the *person* who will *arrange* or *deal* in relation to the *non-readily realisable se- curity*; or
   (b) the *person* who will facilitate the *retail client* becoming a *lender* under a *P2P agreement* or a *P2P portfolio*,
      will comply with the *rules* on appropriateness (see *COBS 10* and *COBS 10A*) or equivalent requirements for any application or order that the *firm* or *person* is aware, or ought reasonably to be aware, is in response to the *direct offer financial promotion*.

Thirdly, where investment advice is proffered, the suitability rule applies.[66] Fourthly, the standard of 'appropriateness' applies to non-advised services. The rules are contained in COBS 10. Whereas previously UK regulation drew a sharp line between those transactions (advisory and discretionary portfolio management) where a suitability regime applied and 'execution only' transactions, MiFID/MiFID II recognized a distinct 'appropriateness' standard.[67] For those transactions which fall within the scope of the rule, the firm must ask the (potential) client to provide information regarding his/her knowledge and experience in the investment field relevant to the specific type of product or service offered, so as to enable the investment firm to assess whether the investment service or product envisaged is appropriate for the (potential) client. If the firm concludes the investment is not appro- priate, it must warn the (potential) client, although this can be in a standardized format. Where the (potential) client elects to provide no information or inadequate information,

---

[63] Directive 2014/65/EU, implemented in the UK from 3 January 2018.
[64] COBS 2.1.1R. MiFID II, Art 24(1).
[65] COBS 4.2.1R. MiFID II, Art 24(3) and Art 30(1).
[66] COBS 9A.2.1R. MiFID II, Art 25(2).
[67] MiFID II Art 25(3).

the firm must warn him that they are unable to judge the appropriateness of the service or product for him, albeit in a standardized format.[68]

2. Protection of the Crowd in Loan-based Crowdfunding

4.21   The FCA in its consultations refer to those lending money on loan-based platforms as 'investors' rather than lenders and considers the risks analogous to those for other regulated investments. The consequence from the platforms' perspective is the need to have regard to two distinct components of the FCA Handbook. First, the protection for borrowers in CONC. Secondly, the protection for lenders/investors in COBS.

4.22   When operating a loan-based crowdfunding platform became a regulated activity in April 2014, the FCA decided to apply both the FCA Principles and core Handbook provisions to the sector, including conduct of business rules, financial promotions, client money rules, and dispute resolution rules (including access to the FOS).[69]

4.23   As to investment risks, the FCA determined that existing guidance as to disclosure[70] should be upgraded to mandatory rules.[71] Detailed provisions were proposed for platforms that employed contingency funds.[72]

4.24   When the FCA revisited the loan-based crowdfunding guidance in 2018, it proposed new measures including marketing restrictions analogous to those for investment-based crowdfunding.[73] The proposal to impose marketing restrictions to protect less sophisticated and experienced investors was done by analogy with the rules of non-readily realizable investments already in place for investment-based platforms.[74] This was done by amendments to COBS 4.7.7R (as quoted above) to extend its application to credit business. As to disclosure, whilst debt-based crowdfunding was already subject to the fair, clear, and not misleading rule, it was considered appropriate to require debt-based platforms to provide a much more detailed description of their role.[75]

4.25   In addition to the new marketing restrictions it was decided that where no advice was given to a retail client, the platform must comply with the appropriateness rules in COBS 10 before the client can invest.[76] This was done by amending COBS 10.1.2R to bring debt-based crowdfunding within its scope, and by the introduction in December 2019 of specific guidance for appropriateness in respect of crowdfunding. The new guidance is to be found in COBS 10.2.9G, which provides:

>   (1)   When determining whether a *client* has the necessary knowledge to understand the risks involved in relation to a *P2P agreement* or a *P2P portfolio*, a *firm* should

---

[68]   COBS 10.2 and 10.3.
[69]   PS14/4, paras 1.11–1.13 and chapter 3.
[70]   Formerly COBS 14.3.7A G(1)–(10).
[71]   CP18/20, paras 5.74–5.78.
[72]   CP18/20, paras 5.87–5.91; PS09/14, paras 2.54–2.56.
[73]   CP18/20, paras 5.43–5.51.
[74]   PS19/14, paras 2.18–2.22.
[75]   CP18/20, paras 5.65– 5.69; PS09/14, paras 2.36–2.40.
[76]   PS19/14, paras 2.22–2.28.

consider asking the *client* multiple-choice questions that avoid binary (yes/no) answers and cover, at least, the following matters:

(a)   the nature of the *client's* contractual relationships with the borrower and the *firm*;
(b)   the *client's* exposure to the credit risk of the borrower;
(c)   that all capital invested in a *P2P agreement* or *P2P portfolio* is at risk;
(d)   that *P2P agreements* or *P2P portfolios* are not covered by *FSCS*;
(e)   that returns may vary over time;
(f)   that entering into a *P2P agreement* or investing in a *P2P portfolio* is not comparable to depositing money in a savings account;
(g)   the characteristics of any:
    (i)   security interest, insurance or guarantee taken in relation to the *P2P agreements* or *P2P portfolio*; or
    (ii)   risk diversification facilitated by the *firm*; or
    (iii)   *contingency fund* offered by the *firm*; or
    (iv)   any other risk mitigation measure adopted by the *firm*;
(h)   that any of the measures in (g) adopted by the *firm* cannot guarantee that the *client* will not suffer a loss in relation to the capital invested;
(i)   that where a *firm* has not adopted any risk mitigation measures (such as those in (g)), the extent of any capital losses is likely to be greater than if risk mitigation measures were adopted by the *firm*;
(j)   illiquidity in the context of a *P2P agreement* or *P2P portfolio*, including the risk that the lender may be unable to exit a *P2P agreement* before maturity even where the *firm* operates a secondary market;
(k)   the role of the *firm* and the scope of its services, including what the *firm* does and does not do on behalf of lenders; and
(l)   the risks to the management and administration of a *P2P agreement* or *P2P portfolio* in the event of the *firm's* becoming insolvent or otherwise failing.

Whilst at the time of the consultation in 2018 no UK P2P platform was engaged in home finance, it was proposed to subject such activity to elements of the MCOB.[77]

The most significant change is the introduction of a whole new sub-chapter into COBS entitled 'Operating an electronic system in relation to lending' in COBS 18.12. This includes detailed rules on credit risk assessments (COBS 18.12.5R–COBS 18.12.10R), pricing, allocation, and portfolio composition (COBS 18.12.11R–COBS 18.12.17R).   **4.26**

As to disclosure of information, COBS 18.12.24R provides: **4.27**

A *firm* must provide to a lender a description of its role in facilitating *P2P agreements*. That description must include:

(1)   the nature and extent of due diligence the *firm* undertakes in respect of borrowers;
(2)   a description of how loan risk is assessed, including a description of the criteria that must be met by the borrower before the *firm* considers the borrower eligible for a *P2P agreement*;

---

[77]   CP18/20, chapter 7; PS19/14, chapter 4. These changes were introduced on 4 June 2019.

(3) whether the *firm* will play a role in determining the *price* of a *P2P agreement* and, if so, what role;

(4) where lenders do not have the choice to enter into specific *P2P agreements*, what role the *firm* will play in selecting *P2P agreements* for the lender;

(5) where a *firm* offers a *P2P portfolio* to lenders, what role it will play in assembling or managing that *P2P portfolio*;

(6) an explanation of the *firm's* procedure for dealing with a loan in late payment or default;

(7) an explanation of how any tax liability for lenders arising from investment in *P2P agreements* will be calculated;

(8) whether the *firm* will play a role in facilitating a secondary market in *P2P agreements* and, if so, what role, including:

    (a) the procedure for a lender to access their money before the term of the *P2P agreement* has expired and the risk to their investment of doing so; and

    (b) whether the *firm* displays *P2P agreements* that lenders wish to exit and that other lenders may choose to enter into; or

    (c) whether the *firm* decides if the *P2P agreement* should be transferred to another lender without involving either lender in that decision.

COBS 18.12.25R requires a firm to confirm to the lender that there is no recourse to the FSCS.

4.28   Separate information rules apply where the lender selects the agreements: COBS 18.12.26R and COBS 18.12.27R. Further rules provide for information concerning platform failure (COBS 1.12.12R), ongoing disclosure (COBS 1.12.31R), and for risk warnings about contingency funds (COBS 1.12.23R–COBS 18.12.38R).

3. Protection of the Borrower in Loan-based Crowdfunding

4.29   As stated above, the borrower in debt-based crowdfunding is entitled to the standard UK domestic consumer credit protections, based in part on the EU Consumer Credit Directive,[78] including under the CCA 1974 (the unfair relationships regime under sections 140A–140D) and CONC, including requirements to assess would-be borrowers' creditworthiness and affordability.[79]

VI. Conclusion

4.30   Overall the regime for crowdfunding in the UK is intended to facilitate business of this type, whilst ensuring that the usual protections for investors and debtors in orthodox financial services apply equally to functionally equivalent crowdfunded activities. The UK regime owes debts to earlier EU legislation, principally MiFID II for investment-based activity, and the Consumer Credit Directive for debt-based activity. However, given the UK's withdrawal from the EU, it represents a distinct regime unaffected by the Crowdfunding Regulation.

---

[78]   Directive 2008/48/EC.
[79]   CP18/20, para 1.57.

5

EU Consumer Law and the Boundaries
of the Crowdfunding Regulation

*Martin Ebers and Benedikt M Quarch**

I. Introduction

One of the main goals of the Crowdfunding Regulation[1] is the protection of non-profes- **5.01**
sional investors. In a similar vein, EU Consumer Law strives to achieve a high level of consumer protection in the EU Digital Single Market.[2] This chapter delineates the 'boundaries'
of the Crowdfunding Regulation and its potential interactions with EU Consumer Law. The
interplay between these legal regimes is particularly relevant to this discussion not only
because some forms of crowdfunding fall outside of the scope of the Regulation (eg when
the project owner is a consumer) but also because EU Consumer Law may meaningfully

---

* This work was supported by Estonian Research Council grant no PRG124.
[1] Regulation (EU) 2020/1503 of the European Parliament and of the Council of 7 October 2020 on European
crowdfunding service providers for business, and amending Regulation (EU) 2017/1129 and Directive (EU) 2019/
1937 [2020] OJ L347/1.
[2] On the development of EU Consumer law cf M Ebers, *Rechte, Rechtsbehelfe und Sanktionen im
Unionsprivatrecht* (Mohr Siebeck 2016) 737ff; G Howells and T Wilhelmsson, *EC Consumer Law* (Routledge 1997)
9ff; J Stuyck, 'European Consumer Law After the Treaty of Amsterdam: Consumer Policy in or beyond the Internal
Market?' (2000) 37 Common Market Law Review 367–400 at 377ff; S Weatherill, *EU Consumer Law and Policy*
(2nd edn, Elgar 2005) 1ff.

complement the provisions of the Crowdfunding Regulation in cases where the latter applies.

5.02 In crowdfunding, consumers can be involved in two ways. On the one hand, consumers can act as borrowers of capital, or, in the wording of Article 2(h) Crowdfunding Regulation, as 'project owners'. On the other hand, consumers can be investors (Article 2(i) Crowdfunding Regulation). Accordingly, this chapter is structured as follows: section II gives an overview of the crowdfunding market, its business models and the various ways in which consumers can be involved in crowdfunding. We address the extent to which the Crowdfunding Regulation and EU Consumer law apply to the field of financial services when consumers act as project owners in section III or investors in section IV. Thereafter, we analyse whether general EU consumer law can protect consumers as project owners or investors in crowdfunding situations in section V. The concluding section, section VI, summarizes the results and gives an outlook on further legislative activities at the European level.

II. The Consumer in the Crowdfunding Market

5.03 'Banking is necessary, banks are not', claimed software entrepreneur Bill Gates several years ago, alluding to one of the most important developments of the twenty-first century: digital disruption.[3] Until recently, it seemed self-evident that the financial market was largely shaped by banks. However, digitalization has now led to a fundamental change in that an increasing number of purely digital businesses are processing financial market transactions without traditional credit institutions.[4]

1. Business Models in the Crowdfunding Market

5.04 Economically speaking, the most significant phenomenon in this context is so-called crowdlending.[5] Crowdlending is a subset of crowdfunding, which originated in the early 2000s.

5.05 In crowdfunding, an Internet platform directly brings together capital seekers and capital providers. The capital providers then jointly invest smaller amounts in a specific project of the capital seeker,[6] who uses the 'crowd' mediated via an Internet platform[7] to finance its project through many individual smaller amounts.[8] Currently, four types of crowdfunding

---

[3] <https://techwireasia.com/2019/11/fintech-companies-prove-gates-point-banking-is-necessary-banks-are-not/> accessed 18 September 2021.

[4] BM Quarch, *Die Europäische Regulierung des Crowdlendings* (Mohr Siebeck 2020) 57ff.

[5] T Ziegler and others, 'Shifting Paradigms, The 4th European Alternative Finance Benchmarking Report' (2019) University of Cambridge Centre for Alternative Finance 31 <https://papers.ssrn.com/sol3/papers.cfm?abstract_id = 3772260> accessed 3 March 2021.

[6] T Polke, *Crowdlending oder Disintermediation in der Fremdkapitalvergabe* (Duncker Humblot 2017) 23ff.

[7] J Schedensack, *Crowdinvesting* (Duncker Humblot 2018) 63.

[8] European Commission, 'Crowdfunding Explained' 7 <https://ec.europa.eu/growth/tools-databases/crowdfunding-guide/what-is/explained_en> accessed 18 September 2021; C Blecher and S Fink, 'Wie funktioniert Kapitalbeschaffung über das Internet?' (2017) 70 Die Wirtschaftsprüfung 938; G Lebouef and A Schwienbacher, 'Crowdfunding as a New Financing Tool' in D Cumming and L Hornuf (eds), *The Economics of Crowdfunding* (Springer 2018) 11, 15ff; M Will and BM Quarch, 'Der Kommissionsvorschlag einer EU-CrowdfundingVerordnung' [2018] Wertpapiermitteilungen 1481, 1482.

can be distinguished, which exemplify how such models can lie at the intersection of the platform economy and the 'sharing economy'.[9] In reward-based crowdfunding, the investor receives a 'creative' reward on its funds, such as the very product it has helped to finance.[10] In equity-based crowdfunding, the investor participates in a (start-up)[11] company with equity capital.[12] In charity crowdfunding, only donations are collected, and no counter-performance is offered. Finally, and most importantly, in crowdlending or loan-based crowdfunding,[13] an Internet platform brings together capital seekers and investors—very much in the spirit of Bill Gates' comment—without an intermediary bank. Investors grant the borrower a conventional loan, which must then be repaid with interest over time.[14]

The crowdlending market has grown steadily in recent years. In Europe, crowdlending had a total volume of around EUR 2 billion in 2017.[15] This may still be small compared to fig-ures in the traditional banking sector. However, the annual growth rates of 50–150% show that crowdlending has already gained a respectable place in financial markets. As such, the following analysis will primarily focus on crowdlending *pars pro toto* for the crowdfunding market in general.   **5.06**

There are two main models on the market:[16] direct and indirect crowdlending.[17] While direct crowdlending corresponds to the basic idea described above, indirect crowdlending, which is mainly present in Germany, involves a bank that grants the loan to the borrower and the financial resources for this come from investors. Investors buy their loan repayment claims from the bank (also called a 'fronting bank') and thus finance the loan. This seem-ingly absurd situation is based on the fact that investors in direct crowdlending, if acting for commercial purposes, are still required[18] to have a licence for lending under German law according to sections 32(1) and 1(1) no 2 of the German Banking Act (*Kreditwesengesetz*, hereinafter KWG),[19] which they generally do not have.   **5.07**

In addition to these two models predominant in Europe, securities-based crowdlending is also present in the market.[20] In this case, the investor neither grants a loan directly nor acquires loan repayment claims from a bank. Rather, the investor purchases notes[21] from   **5.08**

---

[9] Monopolies Commission, *XXI Main Report* (2016) 424.

[10] L Klöhn and L Hornuf, 'Crowdinvesting in Deutschland' (2012) 24 Zeitschrift für Bankrecht und Bankwirtschaft 237, 242ff.

[11] E Ries, *The Lean Startup* (Crown Business 2011) 15ff.

[12] Schedensack (n 7) 54ff.

[13] CR Everett (2014) 'Origins and Development of Credit-Based Crowdfunding' Graziadio Working Paper Series Paper 7, 1ff <https://papers.ssrn.com/sol3/papers.cfm?abstract_id = 2442897> accessed 18 September 2021.

[14] Quarch (n 4) 65ff; Schedensack (n 7) 60; T Aschenbeck and T Drefke, 'Crowdfunding' in U Klebeck and G Dobrauz-Saldapenna (eds), *Rechtshandbuch Digitale Finanzdienstleistungen* (CH Beck 2018) 101ff.

[15] Ziegler, 'Shifting Paradigms' (n 5) 31ff.

[16] Quarch (n 4) 65ff.

[17] In German the different models are called 'unechtes' and 'echtes' Crowdlending, cf Quarch (n 4) 65ff.

[18] Art 1(3) CR will partially change this; cf subsection III.5.B.

[19] M Renner, '"Banking Without Banks"? Rechtliche Rahmenbedingungen des Peer-to-Peer Lending' (2014) 26 Zeitschrift für Bankrecht und Bankwirtschaft 261, 265ff; SScholz-Fröhling, 'FinTechs und die bankaufsichtsrechtlichen Lizenzpflichten' [2017] Zeitschrift für Bank und Kapitalmarktrecht 133, 136; J Veith, 'Crowdlending—Anforderungen an die rechtskonforme Umsetzung der darlehensweisen Schwarmfinanzierung' [2016] Zeitschrift für Bank- und Kapitalmarktrecht 184, 186; Polke (n 6) 106; BJ Hartmann, 'Digitale Ökonomie am Beispiel der Fintechs' [2017] Zeitschrift für Bank- und Kapitalmarktrecht 321, 324.

[20] M Renner, '§ 11: Kreditfinanzierung (Crowdlending), Theoretische und dogmatische Grundlagen' in F Möslein and S Omlor (eds), *FinTech-Handbuch* (CH Beck 2019) paras 12ff; LM Siering, '§ 12: Kreditfinanzierung (Crowdlending), Praktische Anwendungsfragen' in F Möslein and S Omlor (eds), *FinTech-Handbuch* (CH Beck 2019) para 29; on current figures Ziegler, 'Shifting Paradigms' (n 5) 31ff.

[21] Borrower Payment Contingent Notes, ie debt instruments that depend on the payments of the borrower.

an issuer through the platform operator.[22] The issuer uses the proceeds from this purchase to acquire loan repayment claims from a partner bank of the platform operator, which has previously granted a loan to the loan seeker.[23] The investors, who are therefore noteholders, will only receive payments on their notes if and to the extent that the issuer receives payments from the borrower.[24]

2. The Consumer in the Crowdfunding Market

5.09   Consumers may be involved on both sides of the crowdfunding transaction, that is, both as capital providers (investors) and capital recipients (project owners).

A.   Consumers as Investors

5.10   Crowdlending, as a facet of the 'sharing economy', is characterized by the basic idea that many individual retail investors jointly finance a loan. In the recent past, however, other investors have also become aware of the possibility of crowdfunding. In the US, for example, 80% of all loans brokered via the leading crowdlending platforms are now[25] financed by institutional investors, that is, hedge funds, insurance companies, or even banks.[26] This trend is also evident among European platforms.[27] According to 2016 statistics, 45% of consumer crowdfunding loans and 29% of business crowdfunding loans in Europe are now provided by institutional investors.[28]

---

[22] In other chapters of this book, equity- and securities-based crowdfunding are discussed jointly as 'investment-based crowdfunding'. For the purposes of this chapter, however, this further distinction is necessary. cf S Berger and B Skiera, 'Elektronische Kreditmarktplätze: Funktionsweise, Gestaltung und Erkenntnisstand bei dieser Form des "Peer-to-Peer Lending"' (2012) 45 Credit and Capital Markets 289, 296.

[23] Summary of the Prospectus of *CrossLend Securities SA*, point B 25 <https://documents.crosslend.com/de/investor/prospectus-summary.pdf> accessed 18 September 2021.

[24] Summary of the prospectus of *CrossLend Securities SA*, point B 28 <https://documents.crosslend.com/de/investor/prospectus-summary.pdf> accessed 18 September 2021; cf Renner, '§ 11: Kreditfinanzierung (Crowdlending)' (n 20) paras 12ff.

[25] M Heimann, 'The Evolving Nature of P2P Lending Marketplaces' (TechCrunch, 24 January 2016) <https://techcrunch.com/2016/01/24/the-evolving-nature-of-p2p-lending-marketplaces/?guccounter = 1&guce_referrer = aHR0cHM6Ly93d3cuZ29vZ2xlLmNvbS8&guce_referrer_sig = AQAAAMqOHd6mRxXRsyg1d8q2A EgdbsmDDN9K-iQGFz_NW0cyL0gMjoawTUNWShWItUJGb-2hN9LEvE3HnRxsHnZ5PrLdOHd_Z7uvwjg QSgEP4vjm03V3kY-iuLF7EFNi6e3Ow2rhK_JuSbISRMmQ0Yxt7R7iz_OdCQ1uVMPoJht-UtAa> accessed 18 September 2021.

[26] P Tasca and L Pelizzon, 'Klassifikation von Crowdfunding und P2P-Krediten im Finanzsystem' in O Gajda and others (eds), *Jahrbuch Crowdfunding 2015* (Slingshot Return 2015) 16, 18; A Cortese, 'Loans That Avoid Banks? Maybe Not' *New York Times* (New York, 3 May 2014) <www.nytimes.com/2014/05/04/business/loans-that-avoid-banks-maybe-not.html> accessed 18 September 2021; T Granier and N Chapier-Granier, 'Nadège, L'encadrement du crowdlending en droit français' [2015] Revue luxembourgeoise de bancassurfinance 68, 69; K Judge, 'The Future of Direct Finance: The Diverging Paths of Peer-to-Peer Lending and Kickstarter' (2015) 50 Wake Forest Law Review 101, 112; A McQuinn and others, 'Policy Principles for Fintech' (2016) Information Technology and Innovation Foundation 21 <www2.itif.org/2016-policy-principles-fintech.pdf> accessed 18 September 2021; Adam Morse, 'Peer-to-Peer Crowdfunding: Information and the potential disruption in consumer lending' (2015) NBER Working Paper No 20899, 8 <www.nber.org/papers/w20899> accessed 18 September 2021; JM González-Páramo, 'Financial Innovation in the digital age: Challenges for regulation and supervision' (2017) 32 Banco de España—Revista de Estabilidad Financiera, 23 <https://repositorio.bde.es/bitstream/123456789/11292/1/REF_Mayo2017.pdf> accessed 18 September 2021.

[27] G Dorfleitner and L Hornuf, 'FinTech-Markt in Deutschland' (2016) Abschlussbericht Bundesministerium der Finanzen 72 <www.bundesfinanzministerium.de/Content/DE/Standardartikel/Themen/Internationales_Finanzmarkt/2016-11-21-Gutachten.html> accessed 18 September 2021; European Commission, 'Crowdfunding in the EU Capital Markets Union' SWD(2016) 154 final, 13.

[28] T Ziegler and others, 'Expanding Horizons—The 3rd European Alternative Finance Industry Report' (2017) University of Cambridge Centre for Alternative Finance 38 <www.jbs.cam.ac.uk/faculty-research/centres/alternative-finance/publications/expanding-horizons/#.YEC6Oy1XZQI> accessed 18 September 2021; with

Accordingly, McQuinn, Guo, and Castro point out that '[p]eer-to-peer lending plat- **5.11**
forms ... provide a platform that connects individuals and businesses with *institutional
investors*.[29] Although this statement does not apply in all cases, because private investors
continue to play a role,[30] it rightly highlights how the crowdlending market has changed
strategically.

B. Consumers as Project Owners

On the other hand are the borrowers (project owners). These can also be private individ- **5.12**
uals—a case referred to as 'consumer lending'—or companies[31] ('business lending'[32]).[33] In
terms of statistics, in 2017, financing amounting to EUR 1.3 billion was brokered to private individuals and EUR 466.6 million to businesses across Europe via crowdlending.[34]
Most platforms address either one or the other target group.[35] However, the vast majority of
crowdfunding is aimed at consumers.

3. The Consumer under EU Law

Over the past thirty-five years, the EU has enacted a vast number of directives and regu- **5.13**
lations in an effort to protect the consumer, who is commonly defined as a natural person
acting for purposes which are outside his or her business, commercial, or trade activity.[36]

A characteristic feature of (European) consumer law is that the consumer is protected in **5.14**
a standardized manner. Any natural person can be a consumer, regardless of his or her intellectual or economic status. The only decisive factor is whether this person is acting for
private purposes.

---

slightly different figures from 2017: Ziegler, 'Shifting Paradigms' (n 5) 41ff; Will and Quarch (n 8) 1482. This
is overlooked by G Dorfleitner and others, '§ 2: Allgemeiner Marktüberblick' in F Möslein and S Omlor (eds),
FinTech-Handbuch (CH Beck 2019) para 43.

[29] McQuinn (n 26) 21; emphasis by authors.
[30] On the fact that in the UK about one third of all loans are granted by institutional investors: A Milne and
P Parboteeah (2016) 'The Business Models and Economics of Peer-to-Peer Lending' European Credit Research
Institute Research Report No 17, 7 <www.ceps.eu/ceps-publications/business-models-and-economics-peer-peer-
lending/> accessed 18 September 2021; cf also González-Páramo (n 26) 23.
[31] O Johnen and DJ Goebel (2010) 'Peer-to-Peer-Kredite: Eine empirische Überprüfung der Signaling-Wirkung
auf die Kreditvergabe' HHU Discussion Paper on Economics, Financing and Taxation 4/2010, 9 <http://www.
vwlmoneco.hhu.de/fileadmin/redaktion/Oeffentliche_Medien/Fakultaeten/Wirtschaftswissenschaftliche_Fakult
aet/Fachgebiet_VWL/Discussionpaper0410.pdf> accessed 18 September 2021.
[32] For a detailed market analysis for Germany, see M Kolbecher and A Alscher, 'Ist Deutschlands Mittelstand
bereit für FinTech und Online-Kredite?' (2018) 30 Zeitschrift für Bankrecht und Bankwirtschaft 43; for *Funding
Circle*, see Oxford Economics, 'The Big Business of Small Businesses' (2019) <http://www.fundingcircle.com/uk/
impact> accessed 18 September 2021.
[33] McQuinn (n 26) 21; C Savarese, 'Crowdfunding and P2P Lending: which Opportunities for Microfinance'
[2015] EMN Magazine 8; E Macchiavello, 'Peer-to-Peer Lending and the "Democratization" of Credit
Markets: Another Financial Innovation Puzzling Regulators' (2015) 21 Columbia Journal of EU Law 521, 522; Will
and Quarch (n 8) 1482.
[34] Ziegler, 'Shifting Paradigms' (n 5) 31.
[35] cf Kim Wales, *Peer-to-Peer Lending and Equity Crowdfunding* (Praeger 2017) 78ff.
[36] For an overview of the various definitions of 'consumer' in EU directives and the respective case law, cf Martin
Ebers in H Schulte-Nölke, C Twigg-Flesner, and M Ebers, *EC Consumer Law Compendium. The Consumer Acquis
and its Transposition in the Member States* (Sellier European Law Publishers 2008) 453ff.

5.15   In order to determine whether a person qualifies as a consumer, as the European Court of Justice (ECJ) has already clarified in *Benincasa*,[37] 'reference must be made to the position of the person concerned in a particular contract, having regard to the nature and aim of that contract, and not to the subjective situation of the person concerned'. Accordingly, consumer protection does not depend on the specific circumstances but rather on whether the person in question acts for private purposes. The underlying idea is that the consumer is in 'a weak position vis-à-vis the seller or supplier, as regards both his bargaining power and his level of knowledge'.[38]

4. The Consumer in Crowdfunding

5.16   In crowdfunding, consumers can, as stated, be involved in two ways: as borrowers of capital (project owners, Article 2(h) Crowdfunding Regulation) or as investors (Article 2(i) Crowdfunding Regulation). Accordingly, the following section focuses on whether the Crowdfunding Regulation and EU consumer law in the area of financial services applies to consumers as project owners in crowdlending (section III). Thereafter, we examine the applicability of EU law in the field of financial services when consumers act as investors (section IV). Finally, we address the question of whether other EU Consumer Law Directives not specifically tailored to financial services can help protect consumers in crowdfunding (section V).

III. Protection of Consumers as Project Owners

1. Crowdfunding Regulation 2020/1503

A. Exclusion of Consumers from the Scope, Article 1(2)(a) Crowdfunding
   Regulation

5.17   If we first look at consumers in their role as 'project owners', that is, borrowers of capital, it quickly becomes clear that the Crowdfunding Regulation is not applicable. Article 1(2) (a) Crowdfunding Regulation explicitly states that the Regulation does not apply to crowdfunding services provided to a consumer according to Article 3(a) Consumer Credit Directive (CCD) 2008/48.[39] Hence, consumer crowdfunding is explicitly exempt from harmonization sought by the new Crowdfunding Regulation. This exception, which was already present in the European Commission's first draft for the crowdfunding regulation, was justified through the following arguments.

5.18   First, the new Regulation is primarily intended to complete the capital markets union (Recital (3) Crowdfunding Regulation). Since the main goal of the capital markets union is to provide new funding sources for businesses, the Regulation recognizes as project owners

[37] Case C-269/95 *Francesco Benincasa v Dentalkit Srl* EU:C:1997:337, [1997] ECR I-3767, para 16.
[38] cf (in the context of the Unfair Contract Terms Directive 93/13) Case C-137/08 *VB Pénzügyi Lízing Zrt. v Ferenc Schneider* ECLI:EU:C:2010:659, [2010] ECR I-0847, para 46; Ebers (n 36) 753.
[39] European Parliament and Council Directive 2008/48/EC of 23 April 2008 on credit agreements for consumers and repealing Council Directive 87/102/EEC [2008] OJ L133/66.

only persons who act for business purposes. Recital (8) Crowdfunding Regulation high-lights in this regard:

> By addressing the obstacles to the functioning of the internal market in crowdfunding services, this Regulation aims to foster cross-border funding of businesses. Crowdfunding services in relation to lending to consumers, as defined in point (a) of Art. 3 of Directive 2008/48/EC of the European Parliament and of the Council, should therefore not fall within the scope of this Regulation.

In other words, consumer crowdfunding has been excluded because the Regulation is in-tended to promote the cross-border flow of corporate finance capital.

Second, the European Commission holds that a harmonization of consumer crowdlending **5.19** is unnecessary because most transactions take place only locally and not cross-border.[40] Third, the Commission considers consumer crowdlending to be economically trivial since only small credit volumes are typically granted.[41] Fourth and finally, it deems add-itional consumer protection rules to be unnecessary because loans brokered via consumer-lending platforms would fall under the scope of the CCD and the Mortgage Credit Directive (MCD)[42] in any case.[43]

B. Arguments Against the Exception

A closer look at these four arguments reveals none of them to be wholly convincing. **5.20** Sounder arguments support the claim that consumer crowdfunding should be harmonized at the European level.

First of all, as was already mentioned, the majority of all financing brokered via crowd- **5.21** funding is aimed at consumers. In 2017, the market volume of consumer crowdlending, as the most economically relevant form of crowdfunding, amounted to EUR 1.3 billion in continental Europe and thus to 41% of the entire financial technology (FinTech) market, while only EUR 466 million (14%) was brokered to businesses.[44] Accordingly, the European Parliament's Committee on the Internal Market and Consumer Protection specifically em-phasized the importance of regulating consumer-directed crowdfunding.[45] By leaving out

---

[40] European Commission, 'Impact Assessment accompanying the document Proposal for a Regulation of the European Parliament and of the Council on European Crowdfunding Service Providers (ECSP) for Business and Proposal for a Directive of the European Parliament and of the Council amending Directive 2014/65/EU on mar-kets in financial instruments' SWD(2018) 56 final, 32; see also Quarch (n 4) 439ff.

[41] European Commission, SWD(2018) 56 final, 32.

[42] European Parliament and Council Directive 2014/17/EU of 4 February 2014 on credit agreements for con-sumers relating to residential immovable property and amending Directives 2008/48/EC and 2013/36/EU and Regulation (EU) No 1093/2010 [2014] OJ L60/34; cf Commission, SWD(2018) 56 final, 112ff.

[43] European Commission, 'Proposal for a Regulation of the European Parliament and of the Council on European Crowdfunding Service Providers (ECSP) for Business' COM(2018) 113 final, 2; European Commission, SWD(2018) 56 final, 32.

[44] Ziegler, 'Shifting Paradigms' (n 5) 29; Ziegler, 'Expanding Horizons' (n 28) 28; strongly arguing that crowdlending is primarily suitable for consumer borrowers: BJ Hartmann, 'Crowdlending and Fintechs in Germany' (2017) 6 Journal of European Consumer and Market Law 245, 249; Aschenbeck and Drefke (n 14) 104; T Aschenbeck and T Drefke, 'EU-Crowdfunding-VO als (Teil-)Lösung der Regulierung von ICO—eine vertane Chance?' [2019] Recht der Finanzinstrumente 12, 15; cf Quarch (n 4) 440ff.

[45] European Parliament, 'Report on FinTech: the influence of technology on the future of the financial sector (2016/2243(INI))' A8-0176/2017, 25 para 7.

the entire consumer crowdfunding market, the Regulation fails to achieve a comprehensive harmonization of crowdfunding in Europe[46] promoting the free movement of capital.

5.22   In addition, the cross-border flow of capital in consumer crowdlending is significantly greater than in business crowdlending. Current studies reveal that about 84% of all consumer crowdlending is cross-border in terms of total market volume.[47] In this vein, the study 'Expanding Horizons' by the University of Cambridge even concludes that 'P2P [peer-to-peer] consumer lending emerges as the most cross-border dependent model'.[48] In business crowdlending, on the other hand, cross-border financing was only 3% in 2016. It is therefore hardly sustainable for the European Commission to dismiss consumer crowdlending as a local matter;[49] such a classification is better suited to business crowdlending.[50] The Commission rightly emphasizes that consumer crowdlending regularly yields lower individual financing volumes. In 2016, for example, the average amount financed for consumers was EUR 6,382 while businesses borrowed an average of EUR 111,633.[51] It remains unclear, however, why this lower amount of individual financing should speak against regulation, when the total financing amount as well as the cross-border capital flow—and thus the significance for the functioning of the financial and internal market as a whole—are much greater in the consumer sector than in the corporate sector.[52] Finally, for the European Commission to assume that consumer crowdlending is generally subject to the CCD is in any case doubtful, as will be shown in subsection III.2.

5.23   Taken together, the exception of Article 1(2)(a) Crowdfunding Regulation prevents a comprehensive harmonization of investor protection rules for all cases in which a consumer is a crowdfunding borrower.[53] Such a harmonization strategy can hardly be reconciled with the obligation of the EU under primary law to ensure the protection of consumers' economic interests pursuant to Article 169 Treaty on the Functioning of the European Union (TFEU),[54] and in particular those of borrowers ('project owners').[55]

C. Summary

5.24   We do not find the European Commission's arguments for excluding consumer crowdfunding from the Crowdfunding Regulation's scope to be convincing. It is particularly worthy of criticism that the largest market segment fails to achieve a comprehensive level of harmonization. Moreover, it remains unclear how to deal with platforms offering

---

[46] cf European Commission, 'FinTech Action plan: For a more competitive and innovative European financial sector' (Communication) COM(2018) 109 final, 6.

[47] Ziegler, 'Shifting Paradigms' (n 5) 50.

[48] Ziegler, 'Expanding Horizons' (n 28) 46; Ziegler, 'Shifting Paradigms' (n 5) 50.

[49] Ziegler, 'Expanding Horizons' (n 28) 46: 7% of inflow funding and 3% of outflow funding; in 2017 the figures increased but still did not reach the level of consumer crowdlending, cf Ziegler, 'Shifting Paradigms' (n 5) 49ff.

[50] Aschenbeck and Drefke (n 14) 129.

[51] Ziegler, 'Expanding Horizons' (n 28) 35.

[52] Ziegler, 'Shifting Paradigms' (n 5) 50.

[53] cf BEUC, 'European Commission's legislative proposal on crowdfunding—missed opportunity!' (2018) 5 <http://www.beuc.eu/publications/beuc-x-2018-075_regulation_on_european_crowdfunding.pdf> accessed 18 September 2021.

[54] cf Deutscher Bundesrat, 'Vorschlag für eine Verordnung des Europäischen Parlaments und des Rates über Europäische Crowdfunding-Dienstleister für Unternehmen' BR-Drs 69/18, 1ff.

[55] cf F Möslein and S Omlor, 'Die europäische Agenda für innovative Finanztechnologien (FinTech)' [2018] Zeitschrift für Bank- und Kapitalmarktrecht 236, 240; F Möslein, 'Innovative Finanztechnologien (FinTechs) im künftigen Europäischen Recht' (2019) 59 Juristische Schulung 294, 297; Quarch (n 4) 442.

crowdfunding to both consumers and businesses. In view of this, it can hardly be expected that the Crowdfunding Regulation—as Recital (7) suggests—will lead to a 'facilitation' of crowdfunding services.

D. Legal Consequences of the Inapplicability of the Crowdfunding Regulation

The consequence of this legal situation is that crowdfunding directed at consumers will continue to be regulated primarily by national law and only to a certain extent by general EU consumer law, as will be shown below.   **5.25**

A closer look at the situation in Member States reveals a 'patchwork of [27] different laws'.[56] France, for example, has created an independent regulatory regime.[57] With the *intermédiaire en financement participatif*, the French *code monétaire et financier* imposes strict requirements on the granting of permissions for and the operation of crowdlending businesses.[58] The law focuses solely on the intermediary role of the platform operator and even prohibits activities beyond it, such as automated portfolio management. By contrast, the Dutch regulation of crowdfunding is much broader. The Dutch '*voorschriften*' are provisions specifically coined for crowdfunding, leaving platforms considerable self-regulatory leeway in their implementation.[59]   **5.26**

However, Recital (6) Crowdfunding Regulation highlights that the legislator wanted to prevent exactly this chaos: **5.27**

> The differences between the existing national rules are such that they obstruct the cross-border provision of crowdfunding services and thus have a direct effect on the functioning of the internal market in such services.

Unfortunately, the Crowdfunding Regulation fails to achieve this goal for consumer crowdfunding.

2. Consumer Credit Directive 2008/48

Since the Crowdfunding Regulation does not apply to situations in which consumers act as project owners, the following paragraphs analyse whether other EU consumer law Directives in the field of financial services could protect consumers as project owners in crowdfunding.   **5.28**

The most important European Directive in this regard is the CCD.   **5.29**

According to Article 2(1) CCD, the Directive applies to credit agreements between consumers and creditors. A creditor is a natural or legal person that grants or promises to grant credit in the exercise of its trade, business, or profession;[60] a consumer is a natural person   **5.30**

---

[56] Commission, 'Better regulation for better results—An EU agenda' (Communication) COM(2015) 215 final, 2; overview of EU law that may apply to crowdfunding see Quarch (n 4) 272ff.

[57] B Clasen, 'Crowdfunding in Frankreich' [2015] Recht der internationalen Wirtschaft 344; Quarch (n 4) 277ff.

[58] Enacted in *ordonnance 2014-559 du 30 mai 2014 relative au financement participatif*.

[59] In detail Quarch (n 4) 309ff.

[60] Art 3(b) Directive 2008/48.

who, upon entering into the loan, acts for a purpose outside his or her trade, business, or profession.[61]

5.31   In consumer crowdlending, borrowers can be regarded as 'consumers' according to this definition.[62] Moreover, credit agreements in the form of crowdlending can be regarded as loans. What is not so clear, however, is the question of whether the other party in consumer crowdlending can be regarded as a 'creditor' within the meaning of Article 3(b) CCD.[63] In this respect, we must distinguish between the various crowdlending models.[64]

A. Indirect Crowdlending

5.32   In the case of indirect crowdlending, which is widespread mainly in Germany, the loan is *de jure* not granted by individual investors but rather through an intermediary bank. Such a bank is normally a legal person that grants credit in the exercise of its trade, business or profession and thus qualifies as a creditor. The loan agreement concluded between the bank and the consumer-borrower is therefore a credit agreement within the meaning of Article 3(c) CCD.[65]

5.33   This has two consequences. First, the bank must comply with certain information requirements under CCD. Second, the platform through which the respective loan agreement is concluded must be classified as a credit intermediary pursuant to Article 3(f) CCD. Accordingly, platforms must comply as credit intermediaries with the obligations of Articles 21 and 5(1)(1) CCD,[66] which especially constitute certain information requirements (eg about the fees charged).

B. Direct Crowdlending

5.34   Whether the CCD also applies to direct crowdlending, in which loan agreements are concluded directly between the borrower and investors, is less clear. The decisive question is who qualifies as a creditor.

5.35   At first glance, the respective investors might be considered creditors according to Article 3(b) CCD. For this to be the case, they would have to grant the credit in the exercise of their trade, business, or profession. Having said this, a distinction must again be made between two forms of the direct crowdlending model.

---

[61]   Art 3(a) Directive 2008/48.

[62]   Hartmann, 'Digitale Ökonomie am Beispiel der Fintechs' (n 19) 325; Renner, ' "Banking Without Banks"?' (n 19) 268ff; Renner, '§ 11: Kreditfinanzierung (Crowdlending) '(n 20) para 71; Ziegler, 'Shifting Paradigms' (n 5) 31 (figures from 2017): 41% of the total FinTech market is consumer crowdlending; Ziegler, 'Expanding Horizons' (n 28) 28 (2016 figures): 33.8% of the total FinTech market is consumer crowdlending.

[63]   EBA, 'Opinion of the European Banking Authority on lending-based crowdfunding' (2015) EBA/Op/2015/ 03, 31 <http://www.eba.europa.eu/sites/default/documents/files/documents/10180/983359/f6106173-dc94- 4d22-ade8-d40fce724580/EBA-Op-2015-03%20%28EBA%20Opinion%20on%20lending%20based%20Crowd funding%29.pdf?retry = 1> accessed 18 September 2021.

[64]   Committee on Petitions of the European Parliament, 'Notice to Members, Petition 0599/2013 by Christian Lichtenauer (German), on direct loan operations' (2014) 2 <http://www.europarl.europa.eu/doceo/document/ PETI-CM-532656_EN.pdf?redirect> accessed 18 September 2021.

[65]   JH Kunz, 'Online-basiertes individuelles Portfolio-Management' in P Bräutigam and D Rücker (eds), *E-Commerce—Rechtshandbuch* (CH Beck 2017) 924; C Meller-Hannich, 'Zu eigenen rechtlichen Aspekten der "Share-Economy"' [2014] Zeitschrift für Wirtschafts- und Bankrecht 2337, 2344; Moritz Renner and Jan Böhle, 'Crowdlending in der Fallbearbeitung' (2019) 59 Juristische Schulung 316, 318.

[66]   P Rott, 'Die neue Verbraucherkredit-Richtlinie 2008/48/EG und ihre Auswirkungen auf das deutsche Recht' [2008] Zeitschrift für Wirtschafts- und Bankrecht 1104, 1113.

As described above, a large number of loans granted via crowdlending are granted by in-   **5.36**
stitutional investors. In granting such loans, these investors act for purposes relating to
their commercial activities. If institutional investors are involved in the granting of loans to
consumer borrowers, we do have a credit agreement pursuant to Article 3(c) CCD and the
Directive applies.[67]

However, the situation differs if the loans are granted by private investors. As far as can be   **5.37**
seen, these investors regularly invest solely for private financial investment purposes and
thus not in the exercise of their commercial and professional activities.[68] Accordingly, they
are not creditors within the meaning of Article 3(b) CCD.[69] Consequently, the Directive
does not apply to private investors as creditors.[70]

As a result, credit agreements in direct crowdlending are *prima facie* only subject to the   **5.38**
CCD if the lenders are institutional investors.[71]

C. Platform as Creditor?

However, the CCD could still apply in the case of the sole participation of private investors,   **5.39**
if and to the extent that the platform itself is classified as a lender. This consideration may
seem surprising at first glance,[72] as we explained previously that the loan agreement in
direct crowdlending is concluded directly between the borrower (consumer) and the private investors, without the platform becoming a party to the contract. Still, the decisive role
of the platform operator as the interface of all interactions reflects a need to classify the platform as a creditor within the meaning of the CCD.

Comparable situations

Comparable issues have already come to light in other sectors of the economy. For example,   **5.40**
in 2016 the ECJ ruled in *Wathelet* that a platform acting as an intermediary on behalf of a
private individual who has not duly informed the consumer of the fact that the owner of
the goods sold is a private individual has to be considered a 'seller' within the meaning of
the Consumer Sales Directive 1999/44.[73] Specifically, the ECJ derived this result from the
idea that liability under the Consumer Sales Directive 1999/44 'must be capable of being

---

[67] Veith (n 19) 192ff; ESMA, 'Opinion Investment-based crowdfunding' (2014) ESMA/2014/1378, 39 <www.
esma.europa.eu/sites/default/files/library/2015/11/2014-1378_opinion_on_investment-based_crowdfunding.
pdf> accessed 18 September 2021.

[68] Renner, '"Banking Without Banks"?' (n 19) 269; Renner, '§ 11: Kreditfinanzierung (Crowdlending) (n
20) para 73; F Möslein and C Rennig, '§ 9: Anleger- und Verbraucherschutz bei Crowdfunding-Finanzierungen' in
F Möslein and S Omlor (eds), *FinTech-Handbuch* (CH Beck 2019) para 29; cf also A Lordt and C Rennig, 'FinTech
in der zivilrechtlichen Klausur' (2019) 59 Juristische Schulung 311, 312.

[69] Renner and Böhle (n 65) 318.

[70] cf C Busch and others, 'The Rise of the Platform Economy: A New Challenge for EU Consumer Law?' (2016)
5 Journal of European Consumer and Market Law 3, 6; ESMA/2014/1378, 39; Granier and Chapier-Granier (n
27) 71; Renner, '"Banking Without Banks"?' (n 19) 269.

[71] On this problem in general also Busch (n 70) 4; K Tonner, 'Verbraucherschutz in der Plattform-Ökonomie'
[2017] Verbraucher und Recht 161; Quarch (n 4) 249ff.

[72] In a different context, a similar idea can be found in Commission, 'A European agenda for the collaborative economy' (Communication) COM(2016) 356 final, 6; Tonner (n 71) 162 takes up this; cf A Engert, 'Digitale
Plattformen' (2018) 218 Archiv für die civilistische Praxis 304, 315ff with reference to the distinction between tour
operator and intermediary in the case law of the German Supreme Court. Lordt and Rennig (n 69) 312 omit this
idea; Renner (n 20) para 74, however, hints at it.

[73] Parliament and Council Directive 1999/44/EC of 25 May 1999 on certain aspects of the sale of consumer
goods and associated guarantees [1999] OJ L171/12; Case C-149/15 *Sabrina Wathelet v Garage Bietheres & Fils
SPRL* [2017] OJ C006/15.

imposed on an intermediary that, by addressing the consumer, creates a likelihood of confusion in the mind of the latter, leading it to believe in its capacity as owner of the goods sold'.[74]

5.41   The decisions on *Uber Spain*,[75] *Uber France*,[76] and *AirBnB Ireland*,[77] in which the ECJ dealt with the application of the E-Commerce Directive 2000/31 to intermediary services, are in line with this. The underlying idea of a broad interpretation is that the new platforms play an integral role in the transaction mediated by it by taking over (almost) all essential functions.[78]

Referral to the ECJ

5.42   Similar questions were also submitted to the ECJ for crowdfunding. In 2015, the Finnish Supreme Court, *Korkein oikeus*,[79] referred the following question to the ECJ:[80]

Is Art. 3(b) of Directive 2008/48/EC on credit agreements for consumers and repealing Council Directive 87/102/EEC to be interpreted as meaning that an undertaking which promotes the sale of so-called peer-to-peer credit to consumers on the internet and exercises vis-à-vis the consumer the right of determination to which a creditor is normally entitled in relation to the terms of credit, the granting of credit and the recovery of credit, even though the credit funds are voted by private individuals who remain anonymous and remain separate from the undertaking's own assets, is also to be regarded as a creditor?

The case was preceded by a dispute that had been fought through all instances of the Finnish courts and concerned the applicability of the interest rate cap provided for in the Finnish Consumer Protection Act to the business model of the crowdlending provider *TrustBuddy*. The precondition for the application of the Finnish Consumer Protection Act in this respect is that a consumer credit agreement is concluded within the meaning of the CCD.[81] Since the *Korkein oikeus* also came to the conclusion that, in the case of the sole participation of private investors within the framework of the direct crowdlending model, no credit agreement within the meaning of Article 3(c) of Directive 2008/48 exists, the Finnish Court submitted this question to the ECJ.

5.43   However, the ECJ never decided the case due to the insolvency of the provider *TrustBuddy*.[82]

---

[74]   Case C-149/15 *Sabrina Wathelet v Garage Bietheres & Fils SPRL* [2017] OJ C006/15.
[75]   Case C-434/15 *Asociación Profesional Elite Taxi v Uber Systems Spain SL* [2018] OJ C072/02; Case C-320/16 *Uber France SAS* [2018] OJ C200/05.
[76]   Case C-320/16 *Uber France SAS* [2018] OJ C200/05.
[77]   Case C-390/18 *Airbnb Ireland* EU:C:2019:1112.
[78]   cf P Hacker, 'UberPop, UberBlack, and the Regulation of Digital Platforms after the Asociación Profesional Elite Taxi Judgment of the CJEU' (2018) 14 European Review of Contract Law 80–96.
[79]   Korkein Oikeus, Päätös Diaarinro 1 (19), S2015/29 v 23 June 2015, No 1281—*TrustBuddy AB v Lauri Pihlajaniemi*.
[80]   Case C-311/15 *TrustBuddy AB v Lauri Pihlajaniemi* [2016] OJ C038/59; see also M Williams, 'Peer-to-peer lending in the Netherlands' [2016] 5 Journal of European Consumer and Market Law 188, 189; C Wendehorst, 'Platform Intermediary Services and Duties under the E-Commerce Directive and the Consumer Rights Directive' (2016) 5 Journal of European Consumer and Market Law 30, 32; Busch (n 70) 6; C Busch and V Mak, 'Peer-to-peer lending in the European Union' (2016) 5 Journal of European Consumer and Market Law 181; Quarch (n 4) 252ff.
[81]   Korkein Oikeus, Päätös Diaarinro 1 (19), S2015/29 v 23 June 2015, No 1281—*TrustBuddy AB v Lauri Pihlajaniemi*, paras 39ff.
[82]   Discontinued by order C-311/15 *TrustBuddy AB v Lauri Pihlajaniemi* [2016] OJ C038/59.

General observations

First of all, it must be emphasized once again that the relevant loan agreements are in any   **5.44**
case concluded between the private investors and the consumer-borrowers. Hence, a classification of the platform as a creditor within the meaning of the CCD 2008/48 would not
change the general contractual obligations under contract law. The question posed by the
Korkein oikeus is rather relevant for the question of whether platforms must observe the
pre-contractual information duties of Articles 5 and 10 CCD when loans are granted solely
by private investors.[83]

Arguments against classifying the platform as a lender

The contractual situation just described speaks against not only classifying the platform as   **5.45**
a creditor but also the fact that the loan proceeds are provided solely by private investors.
According to the wording of Article 3(b) CCD, the creditor is the one who 'grants' or 'promises to grant' the loan. Other language versions similarly speak of '*gewähren*' or '*zu gewähren*
verspricht' (German), '*consent*' or '*s'engage à consentir un credit*' (French) and '*verleent*' or
'*toezegt*' (Dutch). This similarity of wording in different authoritative versions of the directive underlines that, according to Article 3(b) CCD, what matters is who grants the credit.
Since platform operators—who are not party to the loan agreement—neither promise to
grant a loan nor fulfil the credit claim in any way, it must be assumed in this respect that they
cannot be classified as creditors.

A systematic argument might additionally speak against classifying platforms as cred-   **5.46**
itors: Since the CCD explicitly regulates credit intermediaries in Article 3(f), the EU legislator has created a role that, at least at first glance, aptly covers crowdlending platform
operators. Therefore, it could be argued that the lack of applicability of the credit intermediary provisions cannot be circumvented in the absence of a suitable creditor (Article
22(3) CCD 2008/48) by simply upgrading the actual intermediary to a creditor.

Arguments for classifying the platform as a lender

In the same breath, the legislative purpose of the CCD argues precisely for such a   **5.47**
classification.

First of all, the essential aspects of the loan agreement—especially the contractual terms,   **5.48**
interest, volume, costs, and the like—are not determined by the investors as creditors but
by the platform operator within the framework of a financing proposal. The provider pre-
pares this proposal after submission of the loan application and, after the borrower's consent, makes it the sole basis of the loan project in which the investors invest.[84] Although
the contracts are concluded between the investors and the borrower, it is only the platform
operator who usually appears to the outside world, especially in the performance phase of
the contract. In this respect, the platform operator handles all communications between the

---

[83] cf also Ministerie van Financien (Netherlands), 'Consultatiedocument—Juridisch kader crowdfundingplatformen onderhandse leningen' (2016) 9 <http://www.internetconsultatie.nl/crowdfunding> accessed 18
September 2021.

[84] Korkein Oikeus, Päätös Diaarinro 1 (19), S2015/29 v 23 June 2015, No 1281—*TrustBuddy AB v Lauri
Pihlajaniemi*, para 47 formulates this as follows (translated): 'Moreover, essential aspects of lending, such as the
amount of loans to be granted, the interest rate, the loan costs, the length of the loan period and the possibility
of extending the loan period, are all established by TrustBuddy AB on the basis of the conditions.'; see European
Commission, SWD(2016) 154 final, 27.

parties and monitors compliance with ongoing payment obligations. Usually, the platform does not even disclose the names of the borrowers.[85] Hence, the platform operator plays *the* central role in all crowdlending transactions. In fact, this role is not limited to that of an intermediary but, in light of the other services provided by the platform operator, goes far beyond that, which is why the platform operator can also be described as *the* economic 'bottleneck'.

5.49   The provider's central function is even more striking in the case of automated forms of investment that are now widespread in the market. In this context, the algorithm programmed by the platform operator alone decides in which loan project the respective investor invests his money.[86] In the case of a regular loan, the lender usually assumes all the tasks described above: it determines the conditions under which the loan is granted, it communicates with the borrower, and it monitors the performance of the contract. In particular, it is usually the lender alone who decides which loans are financed. The fact that all of this is done by the platform operator in the context of crowdlending suggests that the platform operator should be classified as a creditor within the meaning of Article 3(b) CCD—entirely in line with the aforementioned *Wathelet* decision of the ECJ.

5.50   Moreover, Recital (8) CCD 2008/48 underlines that the aim of the Directive is to create a 'sufficient degree of consumer protection' and 'optimum conditions' for borrowers. In light of the overarching principle of the *effet utile* and the principle of effective legal protection prescribed by EU law,[87] the scope of application of the CCD has to be interpreted broadly as well so that practically effective consumer protection can be guaranteed in as many cases as possible.[88]

As a result, it must be stated that an interpretation of Article 3(b) CCD based on the *effet utile* of EU law and the intentions of the legislator shows that the platform operators, in the context of direct crowdlending, are to be regarded as creditors within the meaning of the Directive in the case of sole investment by private investors. The question of the *Korkein oikeus* should therefore have been answered with a 'yes'.

D.   Result

5.51   The CCD applies to all examined crowdlending models, if and to the extent that the borrowers are consumers.[89] The concrete consequence of this is that sufficient information must be provided by the platform in the form of the so-called Standard European Consumer Credit Information form before the conclusion of the loan agreement, in accordance with Article 5 CCD. In addition, the creditworthiness of the borrower must be checked by the platform before the conclusion of the credit agreement in accordance with Article 8 CCD. Thus, any rating carried out by the crowdlending platform operators is in principle

---

[85]   This was the case in K Oikeus, Päätös Diaarinro 1 (19), S2015/29 v 23 June 2015, No 1281—*TrustBuddy AB v Lauri Pihlajaniemi*, para 50.

[86]   See also in this direction Korkein Oikeus, Päätös Diaarinro 1 (19), S2015/29 v 23 June 2015, No 1281—*TrustBuddy AB v Lauri Pihlajaniemi*, para 45.

[87]   cf Art 4(3) subparas 2–3 and Art 19(1) subpara 2 TEU; Art 47(1) European Charta on Fundamental Rights. Thereto, Ebers (n 37) 249–326; J Lindholm, *State Procedure and Union Rights. A Comparison of the European Union and the United States* (Författaren och Iustus Förlag AB 2007).

[88]   Case C-499/13 *Marian Macikowski v Dyrektor Izby Skarbowej w Gdańsku* [2015] OJ C171/04.

[89]   Quarch (n 4) 253ff; different opinion see EBA/Op/2015/03, 31ff.

mandatory for consumer credit agreements. Nevertheless, there are no further specifications on the type and scope of the creditworthiness check, and thus no attempt to ensure the trustworthiness of the information used. Finally, according to Article 10(1) CCD, the credit agreement itself must be drawn up on paper or on a durable medium, and must contain the essential information set out in Article 10(2) of the CCD in a 'clear and concise manner'. Article 14 CCD also grants the consumer a right of withdrawal within fourteen days of the conclusion of the contract. This may be surprising, since the platform is, as said, not a party to the credit agreement under contract law.[90] Nevertheless, this rule follows from the broad application of the Directive to the specific case examined here.

E. General Perspective on Crowdfunding Based on the Results

As we have seen, crowdlending is characterized by a trilateral network of relationships be-   **5.52**
tween investors, borrowers, and the platform. By contrast, in traditional bank financing, only the capital seeker and the capital provider regularly face each other and conclude a contract bilaterally. The CCD is obviously only geared toward the classic bilateral relationship between borrower and lender. Nevertheless, we develop the teleologically based interpretation here that the platform operator is to be regarded as the creditor. From the borrower's point of view, this conclusion seems to be quite evident. *Tonner* summarizes this as follows:

> For the customer, the name of the platform is nevertheless in the foreground. The service itself is provided by economic nobodies who contract with the customer.[91]

The central importance of the platforms is also evident in the mentioned insolvency of *TrustBuddy*: here, investors were only able to enforce their repayment claims in protracted legal disputes because regularly only the platform operators have the necessary information for debt collection. A normative representation of this almost overpowering position of the platform operator as the central interface of all crowdlending transactions is unfortunately missing *expressis verbis* in the CCD and could only be reached through interpretation. Nonetheless, there will only be legal certainty when the legislator acts or when the ECJ answers the above-mentioned question. In the meantime, despite the interpretation we have developed, a significant protection gap remains for consumer-borrowers who contract with private investors.

3. Mortgage Credit Directive 2014/17

In addition to the CCD 2008/48, the MCD 2014/17 could also apply in the context of crowd-   **5.53**
funding when consumers act as project owners.

A. Personal Scope of the Directive

According to Article 4 No 3 MCD, credit agreements are agreements in which a creditor   **5.54**
grants or promises to grant to a consumer a credit defined in Article 3(1) of the Directive, in particular in the form of a loan. Similar to the CCD, the parties involved are defined as consumers (borrowers, Article 4 No 1 of the MCD) and creditors (Article 4 No 2 of the MCD).

---

[90] See para 5.44.
[91] Tonner (n 71) 161.

Regarding these definitions, we can refer to our previous analysis of the CCD, in that project owners acting for private purposes can be regarded as consumers and platforms as creditors if the investors act privately.[92]

B. Substantive Scope of the Directive

5.55   However, according to Article 3(1), the MCD only applies to credit agreements secured either by a mortgage or a comparable security customarily used in a Member State for residential immovable property, or by a right relating to residential immovable property (lit. a) or to credit agreements intended for the acquisition or maintenance of property rights in land or in an existing or planned building (lit. b). As crowdfunding typically does not involve a mortgage, the only provision which could apply is Article 3(1)(b) MCD. However, this provision requires that the credit agreement is expressly *intended* for the acquisition of real property.[93] In crowdlending, though, the creditor usually does not know the specific purpose for which the borrower wants to use the loan. Most platforms do not even offer the possibility for the project owner to indicate as purpose the acquisition of real estate.[94]

5.56   By contrast, the situation is different for so-called real estate platforms which broker loans solely for the purchase of real estate.[95] Although these platforms are not (yet) significant in practice, they are becoming increasingly important.[96] Examples include the UK provider *Landbay*[97] and the Estonian platform operator *EstateGuru*.[98] In the case of real estate platforms, there is no doubt that Article 3(1)(b) MCD can be applied.

C. Result

5.57   In crowdlending, the MCD applies only in exceptional cases: either if the borrower and the lender agree that the purpose of the loan is real estate financing or if the loan is brokered via a platform specialized solely in real estate financing.

This can lead to two different situations. If investors are acting for purposes relating to their trade, business, or profession, the platform does not 'need' to be qualified as creditor and, thus, acts as credit intermediary according to Article 4(5) MCD. While Articles 13–16 MCD also contain information requirements comparable to those of the CCD, the information requirements tailored to credit intermediaries pursuant to Article 15 of the MCD go beyond the requirements of Article 21 of the CCD. The central regulation of credit

---

[92]   See paras 5.39 et seq.

[93]   cf EBA/Op/2015/03, 25.

[94]   An exception is the crowdlending provider CrossLend, which allows [parties] to set the purpose of use to 'real estate purchase' on its website. For more information, see <https://de.crosslend.com/geld-leihen/#> accessed 18 September 2021.

[95]   J Wunschel and A Gaßner, 'Crowdfunding—Echte Alternative für Immobilienfinanzierungen?' [2015] Zeitschrift für Immobilienrecht 853.

[96]   B Engels and M Voigtländer, 'Digitalisierung und Immobilienfinanzierung—Potenziale und Perspektiven' [2017] Gutachten des Instituts der deutschen Wirtschaft Köln 13, 16, 19ff <http://www.iwkoeln.de/fileadmin/publikationen/2017/368788/Gutachten_Digitalisierung_und_Immobilienfinanzierung.pdf> accessed 18 September 2021; EBA/Op/2015/03, 26.

[97]   3.1 of the GTCs of Landbay <https://landbay.co.uk/terms-and-conditions> accessed 18 September 2021: 'The Landbay P2P Portfolio Service is a loan management service which enables you to lend to Landbay borrowers via the Landbay platform. The money you provide will be used by Landbay borrowers *to finance the acquisition of buy-to-let properties*'.

[98]   <https://estateguru.co/faq/faq> accessed 18 September 2021; K Barghoorn and L Wrobbel, *Investieren in P2P Kredite* (3rd edn, CreateSpace 2016) 70ff.

intermediaries is then to be found in Article 29 et seq. of the Directive: Article 29(1) provides for a licencing requirement for all credit intermediaries within the meaning of Article 4(5) MCD. Prerequisites for this are, for example, professional liability insurance and good conduct on the part of the management bodies. Credit intermediaries licenced on this basis must be entered in an intermediary register with the national competent authority.

If investors act privately, the platform, as already outlined for the CCD, qualifies as creditor. **5.58** The resulting information obligations have already been pointed out. In addition, Article 7(1) MCD provides for duties of conduct for both creditors and credit intermediaries. According to this, the persons concerned must always act 'honestly, fairly, transparently and professionally'. In addition, Article 7(2) and (3) MCD emphasize that the remuneration policy of the persons acting is also subject to these principles of good conduct. It is also worth noting that Article 9 of the MCD requires staff to have appropriate, up-to-date knowledge of credit agreements.

4. Financial Services Distance Selling Directive 2002/65

Finally, the Financial Services Distance Selling (FSDS) Directive 2002/65[99] could also apply **5.59** to crowdlending.

A. Scope of Application

According to Article 1(1), the FSDS only applies to distance contracts in relation to finan- **5.60** cial services. According to Article 2(a), a distance contract is any contract concluded between a supplier and a consumer concerning financial services which is concluded within the framework of a distribution or service system of the supplier organized for distance sales, where the supplier exclusively uses one or more means of distance communication for the conclusion of the contract. Financial services in this sense are any banking services as well as any services in connection with the granting of credit, insurance, pensions for individuals, investment, or payment, according to Article 2(b) of the FSDS. Crowdlending contracts clearly fall under the notion of financial services. Such contracts are also frequently concluded at a distance.

Additionally, the FSDS requires that the parties involved are, on the one hand, consumers **5.61** and, on the other, so-called providers, which, according to the FSDS, cover any natural or legal person, public or private, who, in the course of its trade, business, or profession, provides services under distance contracts, Article 2(c) Directive 2002/65.

In the case of professional investors, there is no doubt that this lender qualifies as a pro- **5.62** vider according to the FSDS. In the case of private investors, however, the Directive can only be applied to platforms if one assumes—in accordance with the above analysis—that platforms are to be classified as suppliers due to their dominant position in the contractual framework.[100]

---

[99] European Parliament and Council Directive 2002/65/EC of 23 September 2002 concerning the distance marketing of consumer financial services and amending Council Directive 90/619/EEC and Directives 97/7/EC and 98/27/EC [2002] OJ L271/16.

[100] See paras 5.39 et seq.

B. Consequences

5.63   As a consequence, the consumer must be provided, by either the professional investor or the platform (if investors act privately), with detailed information on the respective contract according to Articles 3 and 5 FSDS. Furthermore, according to Article 6 of the FSDS, the consumer has a right of withdrawal for fourteen days after conclusion of the contract—similar to Article 22 Crowdfunding Regulation.

5. Protection under National Law

A. Applicability of National Law in Case Consumers are Project Owners

5.64   According to Article 48(1) Crowdfunding Regulation, national law will be replaced by the Crowdfunding Regulation as of 10 November 2022 at the latest. However, this does not apply to crowdfunding that falls outside the scope of the Crowdfunding Regulation—that is, specifically in the case where consumers are project owners. In such a case, national law continues to apply—influenced by the Union law requirements of the various directives we just analysed.

B. Absurd Consequences: Taking Germany as an Example

5.65   The consequences of the applicability of national law can be illustrated through the example of German law. Since consumer crowdlending is not covered by the Crowdfunding Regulation, investors still need a licence pursuant to §§ 1(1) no 2, 32 KWG, which they generally do not have. For this reason, transactions are conducted via banks, which technically act as lenders.

5.66   Although Member States shall ensure, according to Article 1(3) Crowdfunding Regulation, that national law does not require an authorization as credit institution or any other individual authorization for crowdfunding, such an authorization is still necessary under national (German) law in the case of consumer crowdlending, because the Regulation does not apply here.

5.67   Consequently, a platform that mediates crowdfunding to both consumers and companies must mediate the contracts with consumers in Germany via an intermediary bank—as a 'regulatory artifact'[101]—whereas it can arrange transactions with companies directly between project owners and investors.

5.68   This example alone nicely demonstrates the limited harmonizing effect of the Crowdfunding Regulation, which intends to 'facilitate' crowdfunding (Recital 7). Obviously, there is an urgent need for legislative action.

---

[101] F Allen and AM Santomero, 'The Theory of financial Intermediation' (2001) 25 Journal of Banking & Finance 279.

IV. Protection of Consumers as Investors

Consumers can participate in crowdfunding not only as project owners but also as in- **5.69**
vestors. Accordingly, the following sections analyse the extent to which consumers are protected in this constellation.

1. Crowdfunding Regulation 2020/1503

According to Recital (7), investor protection is one of the central aims of the Crowdfunding **5.70**
Regulation. To this end, Chapter IV (Article 19 et seq) Crowdfunding Regulation provides
for a number of protective provisions, which can be summarized as follows.

First of all, Article 19(1) Crowdfunding Regulation stipulates that all information provided **5.71**
by crowdfunding service providers (CSPs) to their clients must be 'fair, clear and not misleading'. In addition, CSPs must provide investors with a Key Investment Information Sheet
(KIIS), which is defined in more detail in Article 23 Crowdfunding Regulation. The KIIS,
which consists of a maximum of six A4 pages (Article 23(7) Crowdfunding Regulation),[102]
should give the investor all necessary information in order to ensure an informed investment decision and prevent adverse selection.

Article 23(6), in connection with Annex I to the Crowdfunding Regulation, contains a de- **5.72**
tailed list of information that the KIIS must contain. This includes, in particular, information about the borrower, the conditions of the borrowing, possible risk factors, as well as
information on fees and legal remedies. In addition, the KIIS must contain risk warnings
according to Article 23(6)(b)(c) Crowdfunding Regulation. Particularly important, and
convincing in terms of content, is the warning pursuant to Article 23(6)(c) Crowdfunding
Regulation that investments in crowdfunding projects are associated with risks. According
to Article 23(7) Crowdfunding Regulation, the KIIS must also be 'fair, clear and not misleading'. Particularly noteworthy in this regard is that platform operators are not only required to check the completeness and clarity of the information sheet but must also verify
the correctness of the information contained in the KIIS (Article 23(11) Crowdfunding
Regulation). The latter obligation in particular strengthens the trustworthiness of the information provided by the KIIS. Finally, it should be highlighted that according to Article
23(9) Crowdfunding Regulation, liability for the KIIS must be regulated by national law.

The other provisions of the Regulation also contribute to establishing a comprehensive **5.73**
regulatory framework to strengthen investor protection in the crowdfunding sector. For
example, Article 5 Crowdfunding Regulation requires service providers to conduct a minimum level of due diligence in relation to project owners. If crowdfunding companies
provide asset safekeeping services and payment services, they must also comply with the information duties regulated in Article 10 Crowdfunding Regulation. In addition, Chapter III
Crowdfunding Regulation harmonizes the procedures and requirements for authorization

---

[102] In Quarch (n 4) 520, the author had called for a limitation to one page; Benedikt M Quarch, *Die Europäische
Neuregelung des Crowdfundings* [2021] Zeitschrift für das Recht der digitalen Wirtschaft 59ff.

and supervision of CSPs by authorities of the Member State where the service provider is established.

2. MiFID II Directive 2014/65

5.74   Beyond the Crowdfunding Regulation, EU law provides for a number of other investor protection rules that could also apply to crowdfunding.

5.75   These include above all the MiFID II Directive 2014/65,[103] which was recently amended by Directive 2020/1504[104] in order to take into account the new Crowdfunding Regulation.

A. New Exception in Article 2(1)(p) MiFID II for Crowdfunding under Crowdfunding Regulation

5.76   Article 2(1)(p) MiFID II explicitly states that CSPs as defined in Article 2(1)(e) Crowdfunding Regulation are excluded from the scope of the MiFID II. The rationale behind this provision is that the Crowdfunding Regulation should take precedence over MiFID II as a *lex specialis*. Recital (3) of Directive 2020/1504 emphasizes in this respect that legal persons authorized as CSPs under the Crowdfunding Regulation should be excluded from the scope of the MiFID II in order to provide legal certainty and to avoid a situation where the same activity is subject to multiple authorizations within the Union.

5.77   Accordingly, the MiFID II could only apply to crowdfunding which is not covered by the Crowdfunding Regulation. The most important exception in this regard is laid down in Article 1(2)(a) Crowdfunding Regulation for crowdfunding directed to project owners as consumers.[105] Additionally, Article 1(c) Crowdfunding Regulation also exempts crowdfunding transactions from the Crowdfunding Regulation which have a total funding volume of more than EUR 5 million per year.

5.78   For these two areas, we will now examine whether MiFID II applies.

B. Crowdfunding Platforms as Investment Firms

5.79   The MiFID only applies if crowdlending platform operators can be considered as investment firms within the meaning of MiFID II. According to Article 4(1) No 1 MiFID II, an investment firm is a legal entity that provides investment services on a professional basis in the course of its ordinary or business activities.[106] Pursuant to Article 4(1) No 2 MiFID II, investment services are services listed in Annex I section A which relate to one of the financial instruments listed in Annex I section C.

---

[103] Directive 2014/65/EU of the European Parliament and of the Council of 15 May 2014 on markets in financial instruments and amending Directive 2002/92/EC and Directive 2011/61/EU [2014] OJ L173/349.

[104] Directive 2020/1504 of the European Parliament and of the Council of 7 October 2020 amending Directive 2014/65/EU on markets in financial instruments [2020] OJ L347/50.

[105] See paras 5.17 et seq.

[106] N Moloney, *EU Securities and Financial Markets Regulation* (3rd edn, OUP 2014) 343; P Pfisterer, *Die neuen Regelungen der MiFID II zum Anlegerschutz* (Springer 2016) 10ff; P Jung and E Bischof, *Europäisches Finanzmarktrecht* (Nomos 2015) 66; ESMA/2014/1378, 14; G Ferrarini, 'Investment-based Crowdfunding: Policy Issues and Regulatory Responses' in M Casper and others (eds), *Festschrift für Johannes Köndgen* (RWS Verlag 2016) 190.

Loans as financial instruments (transferable securities)?
In view of this regulatory system, the applicability of the MiFID II therefore depends first **5.80**
of all on whether the loans brokered via crowdlending platforms are financial instruments
within the meaning of Article 4(1) No 15 in conjunction with Annex I section C MiFID
II.[107] This includes above all transferable securities (No 1).

According to Article 4(1) No 44 MiFID II, 'transferable securities' within the meaning **5.81**
of No 1 Annex I section C are those classes of securities that are negotiable on the capital market, such as shares (lit. a) and bonds (lit. b).[108] Accordingly, four criteria must be
present for a financial product to qualify as a financial instrument within the meaning of
No 1 Annex I section C MiFID II: first, the financial product in question must (a) be a security[109] (b) which can be allocated to a class of securities. Second, the security must (c) be
transferable[110]and (d) be capable of being traded on the capital market.[111]

Direct and indirect crowdlending
Although a loan can be transferred after individual examination, crowdlending loans are **5.82**
not suitable for large-scale trading on the capital market, which is characterized by the increased marketability of the products that is detached from an individual examination.[112]
Accordingly, traditional crowdlending loans lack tradability on the capital market required
for their characterization as a financial instrument within the meaning of No 1 Annex I
section C MiFID II. Thus, they are not transferable securities within the meaning of Article
4(1) No 44 in conjunction with No 1 Annex I section C MiFID II.[113]

Securities-based model
The securities-based model of crowdlending is somewhat different. The term chosen here **5.83**
for this crowdlending system already implies a relevance of No 1 Annex I section C MiFID
II. The issued borrower payment contingent notes are a case of Article 4(1) No 44 lit. b Var. 1
MiFID II, and thus a financial instrument within the meaning of the Directive.

Result
As a result, MiFID II can only apply to the securities-based model of crowdlending, which **5.84**
is not yet widely used in Europe so far. Even in this case, however, MiFID II only applies
if the respective crowdfunding service provider does not fall under the Crowdfunding
Regulation, Article 2(1)(p) MiFID II.

---

[107] SN Hooghiemstra and K de Buyere, 'The Perfect Regulation of Crowdfunding' in D Brüntje and O Gajda (eds), *Crowdfunding in Europe* (Springer 2016) 145.

[108] Moloney (n 106) 344.

[109] On the concept of a security M Lehmann, *Finanzinstrumente* (Mohr Siebeck 2009) 11ff.

[110] H-D Assmann, '§ 2: Begriffsbestimmung' in H-D Assmann, UH Schneider, and PO Mülbert (eds), *WpHG* (7th edn, Otto Schmidt 2019) para 10.

[111] ibid, paras 6ff.

[112] G Ferrarini, 'Regulating FinTech: Crowdfunding and Beyond' (2017) Fintech and Banking. Friends or Foes? 129 <http://european-economy.eu/wp-content/uploads/2018/01/EE_2.2017-2.pdf> accessed 18 September 2021; Renner (n 20) para 44; Quarch (n 4), 155ff.

[113] Ferrarini, 'Investment-based Crowdfunding' (n 106) 191 comes to the same conclusion: 'The absence of a financial instrument bars loan-based crowdfunding from qualifying as an investment service'; European Commission, SWD(2016) 154 final, 30; EBA/Op/2015/03, which rejects the applicability of MiFID; T Aschenbeck-Florange and A Dlouhy (2015) 'Review of Crowdfunding Regulation & Market Developments for RES project fi-nancing in the EU' 325 <https://eurocrowd.org/wp-content/blogs.dir/sites/85/2016/09/CrowdFundRES-Crowd funding-RES-Regulation-in-EU.pdf> accessed 18 September 2021.

C. Consequences

5.85 If MiFID II applies to crowdfunding platforms, various investor protection rules take effect. MiFID II aims to establish a comprehensive regulatory regime in order to ensure high quality of execution of investor transactions orders, and to uphold the integrity and overall efficiency of the financial system.[114] To this end, the Directive provides for a licencing requirement[115] including conduct of business rules.[116] These include the requirement to avoid conflicts of interest and the obligation to act honestly, fairly, and professionally in accordance with the best interests of the client.[117]

5.86 If MiFiD II does not apply, because the Crowdfunding Regulation take prevalence, CSPs must, on the other hand, inform their clients of the non-application of MiFID II in accordance with Article 19(2) Crowdfunding Regulation.

3. Prospectus Regulation 2017/1129

5.87 Additional investor-protective obligations may also result from the Prospectus Regulation 2017/1129.[118]

A. Scope of Application

5.88 In the crowdfunding market, the Prospectus Regulation 2017/1129 applies only insofar as crowdfunding is related to the public offering of securities.[119] Since the term 'securities' is defined in the Prospectus Regulation in the same way as in MiFiD II (Article 2(a) Prospectus Regulation), the following can be briefly summarized for crowdfunding.[120]

Conventional models

5.89 As already shown, credit claims in both direct and indirect crowdlending are not transferable securities within the meaning of Article 4(1) No 44 MiFID II. For this reason alone, the Prospectus Regulation 2017/1129 does not apply to the most widespread crowdlending models in Europe.[121]

Securities-based model

5.90 In the securities-based crowdlending model, however, investors do not invest directly in credit claims but in borrower payment contingent notes, which are to be classified as transferable securities pursuant to Article 4(1) No 44 MiFID II, and thus as securities within the

---

[114] Recital (13) MiFiD II 2014/65.

[115] Art 5 MiFID II 2014/65.

[116] Pfisterer (n 106) 9ff; Macchiavello (n 33) 566ff.

[117] Art 24(1) MiFID II 2014/65. A similar provision can be found in Art 19 Insurance Intermediation Directive (IDD) 2016/97; European Parliament and Council Directive (EU) 2016/97 of 20 January 2016 on insurance distribution (recast) [2016] OJ L26/19. cf M Ebers, 'Commentary on § 1a VVG' in H-P Schwintowski, C Brömmelmeyer, and M Ebers (eds), *Praxiskommentar zum VVG* (4th edn, Verlag Versicherungswirtschaft 2021).

[118] European Parliament and Council Regulation (EU) 2017/1129 of 14 June 2017 on the prospectus to be published when securities are offered to the public or admitted to trading on a regulated market, and repealing Directive 2003/71/EC [2017] OJ L168/12 (Prospectus Regulation).

[119] Art 5 Reg 2017/1129/EU; Art 3 Dir 2003/71; see Quarch (n 4) 225ff.

[120] See paras 5.80 et seq.

[121] ESMA/2014/1378, 13; Macchiavello (n 33) 564ff; European Commission, SWD(2016) 154 final, 22.

meaning of Article 2(a) Prospectus Regulation 2017/1129, which are offered to the public in accordance with Article 6(1) Prospectus Regulation 2017/1129.

It is thus clear that according to Article 5(1) Prospectus Regulation, a prospectus must be **5.91** prepared, published, and approved by the competent supervisory authority prior to the public offering of a debt security in this form.[122] Since crowdlending debt securities are non-equity securities within the meaning of Article 2(c) Prospectus Regulation 2017/1129, a base prospectus pursuant to Article 8 Prospectus Regulation 2017/1129 may also be drawn up at the issuer's discretion.

B. Exceptions
Some exceptions could be relevant, as outlined below.   **5.92**

Article 1(3) Prospectus Regulation 2017/1129
According to Article 1(3) Prospectus Regulation 2017/1129, the Regulation does not apply **5.93** to public offers of securities with a total consideration in the EU of less than EUR 1 million, which shall be calculated over a period of twelve months.

Until the adoption of the Prospectus Regulation 2017/1129, an EU limit of EUR 100,000 **5.94** applied. In order to[123] exempt investments by means of crowdfunding platforms from the prospectus requirement throughout the Union,[124] Article 1(3) Prospectus Regulation 2017/1129 generally raised the limit to EUR 1 million.[125] The Member States are not permitted to set lower thresholds, only higher ones, as outlined in Article 1(3)(2) Prospectus Regulation 2017/1129.[126]

According to the prevailing view, the decisive factor for the applicability of Article 1(3) **5.95** Prospectus Regulation 2017/1129 is that the debt securities relating to a loan project usually do not exceed EUR 1 million in one year throughout the Union.[127] As far as can be seen, it can be assumed that this is generally the case: according to current statistics, the average crowdfunding size does not exceed EUR 1 million in any sub-segment of the market.[128]

Article 1(4)(k) Prospectus Regulation 2017/1129
Article 46 Crowdfunding Regulation added a new Article 1(4)(k) to the Prospectus **5.96** Regulation. According to this provision, the Regulation does not apply to an offer of securities to the public from a crowdfunding service provider authorized under the

---

[122] Renner, '§ 11: Kreditfinanzierung (Crowdlending)' (n 20) para 45 for German law.
[123] cf European Commission, 'Proposal for a Regulation of the European Parliament and of the Council on the prospectus to be published when securities are offered to the public or admitted to trading' COM(2015) 583 final, 15; cf European Commission, SWD(2016) 154 final, 23.
[124] In many cases, platforms broker loans of more than EUR 100,000 but less than EUR 1 million.
[125] cf European Commission, COM(2015) 583 final, 15; cf European Commission, SWD(2016) 154 final, 23; European Crowdfunding Network, 'Crowdfunding is a vital source of financing for European high-tech and digital businesses' (2016) 2 <https://eurocrowd.org/wp-content/blogs.dir/sites/85/2016/12/ECN-position-paper-on-the-Prospectus-Directive-2016.pdf> accessed 18 September 2021; K de Buysere and others, 'A Framework for European Crowdfunding' (2012) 28 <http://eurocrowd.org/wp-content/blogs.dir/sites/85/2013/06/FRAMEW ORK_EU_CROWDFUNDING.pdf> accessed 18 September 2021.
[126] Critically Schedensack (n 7) 508.
[127] Anna Heidelbach, '§ 3 WpPG' in E Schwark and D Zimmer (eds), *Kapitalmarktrechts-Kommentar* (5th edn, CH Beck 2020) para 21; Y Schnorbus, '§ 3 WpPG' in C Berrar and others (eds), *Frankfurter Kommentar WpPG und EU-ProspektVO* (2nd edn, dfv and R&W 2017) para 34.
[128] Ziegler, 'Expanding Horizons' (n 28) 35.

Crowdfunding Regulation, provided that it does not exceed the threshold laid down in Article 1(2)(c) Crowdfunding Regulation.

Article 1(2)(c) Crowdfunding Regulation

5.97   Insofar as the Prospectus Regulation applies to crowdfunding, issuances generally remain prospectus-free pursuant to Article 1(3), 1(4)(k) Prospectus Regulation 2017/1129. It is noteworthy that the Crowdfunding Regulation itself stipulates an exception from a total financing volume of EUR 5 million (Article 1(2)(c) Crowdfunding Regulation). The legislator justifies this in Recital (16) Crowdfunding Regulation with the fact that this limit was set by most Member States in application of Regulation 2017/1129. At the same time, Article 49 Crowdfunding Regulation allows a deviation from the EUR 5 million limit for the period until 10 November 2023. According to this, the Crowdfunding Regulation only applies up to the total financing volume under national law, which may be increased in the application of Article 1(3) Prospectus Regulation 2017/1129, if it remains below EUR 5 million. If, for example, Member State A sets the exemption limit according to Article 1(3) Prospectus Regulation 2017/1129 at EUR 2 million, then the Crowdfunding Regulation applies until 10 November 2023 only up to this limit and not for financing with higher volumes.

C. Result

5.98   The complex legal rules can be summarized as follows:

- The Prospectus Regulation 2017/1129 can only apply to securities-based crowdfunding, as defined at the beginning of this chapter. However, even in this case, the Regulation does not apply if the total financing volume is below the limit of Article 1(2)(c) Crowdfunding Regulation, whereby this limit per se is EUR 5 million; until 10 November 2023, however, it can also be below this, but not below EUR 1 million (Article 1(3) Prospectus Regulation 2017/1129), cf Article 46 Crowdfunding Regulation, Article 1(4)(k) Prospectus Regulation.
- The Crowdfunding Regulation does not apply if the total financing volume is above EUR 5 million (Article 1(2)(c) Crowdfunding Regulation); unless by 10 November 2023 the national threshold for the Prospectus Regulation is between EUR 1 million and EUR 5 million, in which case the Crowdfunding Regulation applies up to this value and not beyond. In this case, Prospectus Regulation 2017/1129 applies.

Hence, for the vast majority of crowdfunding investments, the requirements of the Prospectus Regulation do not play a role, in view of the consistently smaller financing amounts.[129] This is quite welcome, as the effort involved in preparing a comprehensive prospectus for each individual crowdfunding project would be—as the European Commission[130] has emphasized—simply too great.

---

[129] ibid.
[130] European Commission, COM(2015) 583 final, 15; see also European Commission, SWD(2016) 154 final, 23.

4. PRIIPs Regulation 1286/2014

The PRIIPs Regulation 1286/2014[131] is closely related to the Prospectus Regulation described above.[132] It aims to enable investors to make an informed investment decision, in a similar way to the Prospectus Regulation, which generally applies in parallel (cf Article 3(1) PRIIPs Regulation 1286/2014).[133]   **5.99**

Article 5 Packaged Retail Investment and Insurance-based Products (PRIIP) Regulation stipulates that before retail investors are offered so-called PRIIPs (cf Article 4 No 3 lit. a PRIIPs Regulation), a Key Information Document[134] on the respective investment product must be prepared and published.[135] This key information document must contain the essential information about the investment product in a comprehensible form[136] and on a maximum of three A4 pages (Article 6(4) PRIIPs Regulation).   **5.100**

A. Scope of Application
The relevant question is therefore what qualifies as a so-called PRIIP. According to Article 4 No 3 PRIIPs Regulation, PRIIPs is an acronym for packaged investment products for retail investors (alternative 1) and insurance investment products (alternative 2). Since crowdlending is obviously not about insurance, only the first alternative can be relevant. This in turn is referred to as PRIP and is, according to Article 4 No 1 PRIIPs Regulation, an investment, including instruments issued by securitization special purpose vehicles within the meaning of Article 4(1)(an) AIFM Directive 2011/61, for which, irrespective of the legal form of the investment, the amount to be repaid to the retail investor is subject to fluctuations due to the dependence on reference values or on the performance of one or more assets that are not acquired directly by a retail investor.[137] Pursuant to Article 4 No 4(a) PRIIPs Regulation, the producer of the PRIP is the legal entity that launches the respective financial product; pursuant to Article 4 No 5 PRIIPs Regulation, the seller is the person who offers or concludes a PRIP contract with a retail investor.[138] Depending on the structure of the contractual relationship, the crowdlending platform could be both producer and seller.   **5.101**

---

[131] European Parliament and Council Regulation (EU) 1286/2014 of 26 November 2014 on key information documents for packaged retail and insurance-based investment products (PRIIPs) [2014] OJ L352/1 (PRIIPs Regulation).

[132] ibid. In more detail, eg C Luttermann, 'Kapitalmarktrechtliche Information bei Finanzprodukten (PRIIP), Privatautonomie (Vertragskonzept) und Vermögensordnung' (2015) 36 Zeitschrift für Wirtschaftsrecht 805ff; Moloney (n 106) 778, 821ff, at 824 on the complicated legislative history. The Regulation is supplemented by Guidelines: Commission, 'Guidelines on the application of Regulation (EU) No 1286/2014 of the European Parliament and of the Council on key information documents for packaged retail and insurance-based investment products (PRIIPs)' (Communication) [2017] OJ C218/11; Quarch (n 4) 232ff.

[133] Recital (15) PRIIPs Regulation 1286/2014; R Jordans, 'Zum aktuellen Stand der Finanzmarktnovellierung in Deutschland' [2017] Zeitschrift für Bank- und Kapitalmarktrecht 273, 276; Luttermann (n 132) 805ff.

[134] European Commission, 'Guidelines on the application of Regulation (EU) No 1286/2014 of the European Parliament and of the Council on key information documents for packaged retail and insurance-based investment products (PRIIPs)' (Communication) [2017] OJ C218/11, para 1; J Seitz, A Juhnke, and S Seibold, 'PIBs, KIIDs und nun KIDs—Vorschlag der Europäischen Kommission für eine Verordnung über Basisinformationsblätter für Anlageprodukte im Rahmen der PRIPs-Initiative' [2013] Zeitschrift für Bank- und Kapitalmarktrecht 1.

[135] R Litten, 'PRIIPs: Anforderungen an Basisinformationsblätter' [2016] Der Betrieb 1679, II.

[136] Luttermann (n 132) 807ff; Jordans (n 133) 276; T Möllers, 'Europäische Gesetzgebungslehre 2.0: Die dynamische Rechtsharmonisierung im Kapitalmarktrecht am Beispiel von MiFID II und PRIIP' [2016] Zeitschrift für Europäisches Privatrecht 325, 335; Seitz, Juhnke, and Seibold (n 134) 6; Litten (n 135) II 4.

[137] In this respect too narrow for a combination of assets: Möllers (n 136) 335.

[138] Seitz, Juhnke, and Seibold (n 134) 4ff; Litten (n 135) II 3; *Handbuch des EU-Wirtschaftsrechts*, para 214 (issue 51 October 2020).

5.102   In sum, it is necessary to examine whether crowdlending investments are PRIPs.[139]

Conventional models

5.103   In conventional crowdlending models, investors acquire direct loan repayment claims against the borrowers. Thus, investors directly hold the underlying assets, so that there is no packaged investment product (PRIP). This applies regardless of whether the claims are first acquired by a bank or directly by investors.

Securities-based models

5.104   In the securities-based model, by contrast, the investor purchases a debt security that is dependent on the borrower's repayments made on a loan agreement not entered into with the investor. Here, the investor buys an investment product that is linked to an asset not held directly by the investor, namely the loan agreement. Therefore, debt securities issued under the securities-based model are PRIPs if and to the extent that they are intended for non-professional investors (cf Article 4 No 6 PRIIPs Regulation), which is still common in the market. Since platform operators offer the purchase of the bonds to the investors, they must be regarded as PRIP sellers pursuant to Article 4 No 5 PRIIPs Regulation, whereas the manufacturer is the issuer.

B. Consequences

5.105   Accordingly, in the securities-based model, it would be necessary to prepare a Key Information Sheet. However, Article 23(15) Crowdfunding Regulation provides that the KIIS according to the Crowdfunding Regulation is considered a KIIS within the meaning of the PRIIPs Regulation. In other words, the EU legislator has recognized the interplay of its various legislative measures and led to a sensible result.

5.106   However, the same does not apply to securities-based crowdlending, which is directed at consumers as project owners. Since the Crowdfunding Regulation does not apply to this form of crowdlending, it is still subject to the PRIIPs Regulation alone.

5. Investor Compensation Schemes Directive 97/9

5.107   The Investor Compensation Schemes Directive 97/9 stipulates that, in order to protect investor confidence, investor compensation schemes must be set up in all Member States,[140] which according to Article 2(2) of Directive 97/9, ensure coverage in any case if an investment firm is not able to meet its obligations towards investor clients.[141] According to Article 1 No 1, first indent of the Directive, investment firms are defined with reference to Directive 93/22 (one of the predecessor directives of today's MiFID II).[142] Nowadays, the definition of an investment firm in Article 4(1) No 1 MiFID II is relevant.[143]

---

[139] Luttermann (n 132) 806.
[140] cf Moloney (n 106) 836.
[141] Recital 4 of Directive 97/9; very apt in this respect is Moloney (n 106) 835: '*ex-post*, last-resort safety net for investors when investment firms fail', emphasis in original.
[142] See recitals 1 and 2 of Directive 2014/65/EU.
[143] Instead of all ESMA/2014/1378, 20; Moloney (n 106) 837ff.

Accordingly, Directive 97/9 only applies to securities-based crowdlending if MiFID II ap-   **5.108**
plies, which, as discussed, is rarely the case. CSPs must inform their clients of the non-application of Directive 97/9 in accordance with Article 19(2) Crowdfunding Regulation.

6. Protection under National Law

Insofar as the Crowdfunding Regulation applies, national law is no longer applicable, pur-   **5.109**
suant to Article 48 Crowdfunding Regulation. If and to the extent that the Crowdfunding
Regulation does not apply, national investor protection rules can still apply. An example
of this is the Netherlands where, for example, an investor test, as provided for in Article 21
Crowdfunding Regulation, is also prescribed.[144]

V. General Consumer Protection Laws and Crowdfunding

The preceding considerations have focused primarily on the applicability of regulations and   **5.110**
directives adopted by the EU in the area of financial services. Finally, we will take a brief look
at other, more general consumer protection Directives that could apply to crowdfunding.

1. Unfair Commercial Practices Directive 2005/29

A very general regulation of EU consumer law is the Unfair Commercial Practices Directive   **5.111**
(UCPD) 2005/29,[145] which aims to establish European-wide safeguards against unfair commercial practices which contravene the requirements of professional diligence, mislead
consumers, or expose them to aggressive commercial practices.

Article 6 and Article 7 of the UCPD, which prohibit misleading actions and omissions, are   **5.112**
particularly important. As explained earlier, business models of crowdfunding vary widely
and are sometimes complex. In particular, the involvement of the bank in indirect crowdfunding, which will continue to be represented on the market in certain situations as described above, can easily confuse and mislead consumers. It is therefore indispensable that
CSPs explain their business models and contractual structures in a transparent and comprehensive way in order to rule out any misleading effects from the outset. This applies in
particular to situations in which the Crowdfunding Regulation does not apply, as Article 19
Crowdfunding Regulation already provides for comprehensive information obligations on
the part of the crowdfunding service provider.

---

[144] Autoriteit Financiële Markten, 'Nieuwsbrief Crowdfunding' (10 December 2015) <http://afm.m13.mailp
lus.nl/archief/mailing-488439.html> accessed 18 September 2021; cf Johannes de Jong and Coen Barneveld
Binkhuysen (2017) 'Netherlands' in European Crowdfunding Network, 'Review of Crowdfunding Regulation
2017', 453, <https://eurocrowd.org/wp-content/blogs.dir/sites/85/2017/10/ECN_Review_of_Crowdfunding_
Regulation_2017.pdf> accessed 18 September 2021.
[145] European Parliament and Council Directive 2005/29/EC of 11 May 2005 concerning unfair business-to-consumer commercial practices in the internal market and amending Council Directive 84/450/EEC, Directives 97/7/
EC, 98/27/EC and 2002/65/EC of the European Parliament and of the Council and Regulation (EC) No 2006/2004
of the European Parliament and of the Council [2005] OJ L149/22 (Unfair Commercial Practices Directive).

2. Digital Content and Services Directive 2020/770

5.113   The recently adopted Digital Content and Services Directive 2019/770[146] is an important instrument for the governance of the Digital Single Market. However, according to Article 3(5)(e), the Directive does not apply to financial services as defined in the FSDS Directive 2002/65. As crowdfunding is such a financial service, Directive 2019/770 is not applicable.

3. Unfair Contract Terms Directive 93/13

5.114   The Unfair Contract Terms Directive 93/13,[147] on the other hand, is applicable to all financial services. However, the Directive does not have any significant harmonizing effect, since the ECJ has consistently held that the court will not decide whether a non-negotiated contractual term is unfair according to Article 3(1) of the Directive. According to settled case law,[148] the ECJ is only willing to interpret in an abstract way the concept of 'unfair term' used in Article 3(1) of the Directive, and to the criteria which the national court may or must apply when examining a contractual term in the light of the provisions of the directive, whereas it is for the national court to determine, in the light of those criteria, whether a particular contractual term is actually unfair in the circumstances of the case.

VI. Summary

5.115   In the preceding analysis, we discussed how consumers are protected in crowdfunding when they act either as borrowers of capital (project owners) or as lenders of capital (investors). The analysis shows that the Crowdfunding Regulation has not led to the harmonization of consumer crowdlending. Rather, there are still considerable gaps in the protection of consumers, which can be summarized as follows:

- Article 1(2)(a) Crowdfunding Regulation excludes crowdlending aimed at consumer-borrowers. The arguments for excluding consumers as project owners from the Crowdfunding Regulation's scope are not convincing.[149] Since crowdlending aimed at consumers is the largest and most economically important area of crowdfunding, the Crowdfunding Regulation fails to facilitate crowdfunding services in the EU.
- As long as consumer-borrowers are excluded from the Crowdfunding Regulation's scope, they can only be protected to a limited extent under existing EU consumer law directives and fragmented national laws.
- The CCD 2008/48 applies, according to its wording, only to credit agreements between consumers and professional investors. By contrast, the Directive does not seem

---

[146] European Parliament and Council Directive 2019/770 of 20 May 2019 on certain aspects concerning contracts for the supply of digital content and digital services [2019] OJ L136/1.

[147] Council Directive 93/13/EEC of 5 April 1993 on unfair terms in consumer contracts [1993] OJ L95/29.

[148] Case C-237/02 *Freiburger Kommunalbauten GmbH Baugesellschaft & Co. KG v Ludger Hofstetter and Ulrike Hofstetter* [2004] ECR I-3403, para 19; Case C-243/08 *Pannon GSM Zrt v Erzsébet Sustikné Győrfi* [2009] ECR I-4713, para 37; Case C-415/11 *Mohamed Aziz v Caixa d'Estalvis de Catalunya, Tarragona i Manresa (Catalunyacaixa)* EU:C:2013:164.

[149] cf paras 5.20 et seq.

to be applicable if loans are granted by private investors. This is also true for the FSDS Directive 2002/65: here too, it seems that consumer-borrowers are usually not protected when they contract with private investors.

- This shortcoming in consumer protection could be remedied by considering platforms as 'creditors' or 'suppliers' with the meaning of the Directives. Indeed, our analysis shows that many arguments as well as ECJ case law speak in favour of assuming a liability of platforms, if the essential aspects of the loan agreement are not determined by the investor but—as is common in crowdfunding—by the platform itself.[150] In the same vein, the European Law Institute (ELI) proposed in its Model Rules on Online Platforms that platform operators should be liable vis-à-vis customers if the customer can reasonably rely on the platform operator having a predominant influence over the supplier.[151]

- Whether the ECJ will follow this approach in crowdfunding is nevertheless doubtful. Accordingly, there is currently considerable legal uncertainty as to how consumers can be protected as project owners under EU or national laws when they enter into contracts with private investors.

- The legal situation is different, however, when the consumer acts as an investor in crowdfunding. In this scenario, the Crowdfunding Regulation provides for a balanced system of consumer-investor protection rules, which is supplemented under certain conditions by additional EU directives and regulations.[152]

Accordingly, the overall result of our analysis is ambivalent. Whereas the Crowdfunding Regulation protects consumers to a large extent when they act as investors in crowdfunding, it provides insufficient protection for consumers as project owners who conclude contracts with private investors. One solution could be to revise the recently adopted Crowdfunding Regulation and delete the exception provided for in Article 1(2)(a) Crowdfunding Regulation.[153]

Beyond this, however, a fundamental paradigm shift appears to be necessary. The preceding **5.116** analysis pinpoints the fundamental problem that many EU Directives and Regulations in the field of financial services and consumer law still do not sufficiently consider the specific nature of the platform economy, which creates a triangular structure that is based on relations between (a) the platform and the supplier, (b) the platform and the consumer, and (c) the supplier and the consumer.[154] Although many platforms have a predominant influence over the contracts concluded between a supplier and a consumer, the existing EU law does not provide clear rules on the platform's position within contractual relations, and what legal consequences follow from the platform's engagement in the process of concluding or even performing contracts between customers and suppliers.[155]

---

[150] cf paras 5.39 et seq.

[151] European Law Institute (2019) 'Art. 19 Model Rules on Online Platforms' <https://www.europeanlawin stitute.eu/fileadmin/user_upload/p_eli/General_Assembly/2019/2019_Conference_Materials/Model_Rules_ on_Online_Intermediary_Platforms/ELI_Model_Rules_on_Online_Platforms_Instrument.pdf> accessed 18 September 2021.

[152] cf 5.69 et seq.

[153] With a detailed proposal Quarch (n 4) 479ff.

[154] See C Wendehorst, 'Platform Intermediary Services and Duties under the E-Commerce Directive and the Consumer Rights Directive' (2016) 5 Journal of European Consumer and Market Law 30–33; Busch (n 70) 3–4.

[155] A Wiewiórowska-Domagalska (2017) 'Briefing for the European Parliament on "Online-Platforms: How to Adapt Regulatory Framework to the Digital Age?"', PE 607.323, 6, <http://www.europarl.europa.eu/RegData/etu des/BRIE/2017/607323/IPOL_BRI(2017)607323_EN.pdf> accessed 18 September 2021.

5.117 What is necessary, therefore, is a paradigm shift towards a more platform-orientated regulation. The European legislator should take into account not only the relationship between the contracting parties, but also the position of platforms in the contractual structure.[156] With such a platform-oriented harmonization, the EU could make an important contribution to ensuring that a functioning internal market also emerges—as intended by the Crowdfunding Regulation[157]—for crowdfunding services.

---

[156] First steps towards a more platform-oriented regulation are already visible at European level. cf in particular the P2B Regulation 2019/1150 on promoting fairness and transparency for business users of online intermediation services [2019] OJ L186/57. Additionally, the European Commission presented two proposals in December 2020: first, the proposal for a Digital Services Act, which aims to introduce mechanisms for removing illegal content, possibilities for users to challenge platforms' content moderation decisions and transparency measures for online platforms (European Commission, 'Proposal for a Regulation on a Single Market For Digital Services [Digital Services Act] and amending Directive 2000/31/EC' COM[2020] 825 final); and second, the proposal for a Digital Markets Act, which aims to ensure that large online platforms (so called gatekeepers) behave in a fair way vis-à-vis business users who depend on them (European Commission, 'Proposal for a Regulation on contestable and fair markets in the digital sector [Digital Markets Act]' COM[2020] 842 final).

[157] cf Recitals (6)–(8) CR.

6

Is the Crowdfunding Regulation Future-Proof?

Forms of Blockchain-based Crowdfunding Falling Outside of the Scope of the Regulation

Raffaele Battaglini and Davide Davico

I. The Problem of Token and Cryptocurrency Classification

The Crowdfunding Regulation does not apply to tokens and other blockchain-based techniques that project owners can use to finance themselves. On the one hand, the gap may partially be closed in the future by the proposed Regulation on Markets in Crypto-Assets, which falls outside of the scope of this book. On the other hand, however, it is important to investigate whether the choice to exclude crypto-assets from the scope of the Crowdfunding Regulation was correct. This chapter addresses the issue, describing the regulatory framework applicable to cryptocurrencies and tokens, and assessing the exclusion of these instruments from the scope of the Regulation. **6.01**

Cryptocurrencies pose two questions that seem far from being resolved: their definition and their legal nature. While the purpose of this chapter is not to provide definitive answers **6.02** to these two issues, it is nevertheless appropriate to present the considerations underlying them.

6.03   The term 'cryptocurrency' refers to the concept of money, which is misleading or at least reductive. Depending on their functions and technological peculiarities, cryptocurrencies may differ significantly from one to another, which necessarily affects their legal nature. Indeed, there are numerous definitions and legal analyses, often conflicting or inconsistent, offered by scholars as well as national and supranational institutions.

6.04   With Directive (EU) 2015/849 (known as the Fourth Anti-Money Laundering Directive), as amended by Directive (EU) 2018/843 (known as the Fifth Anti-Money Laundering Directive) and its subsequent transposition in the EU Member States, a definition has been introduced into the European landscape, reading as follows: 'virtual currencies means a digital representation of value that is not issued or guaranteed by a central bank or a public authority, is not necessarily attached to a legally established currency and does not possess a legal status of currency or money, but is accepted by natural or legal persons as a means of exchange and which can be transferred, stored and traded electronically'.[1]

6.05   Within the EU, the European Banking Authority (EBA), in its opinion of 4 July 2014, defined 'virtual currencies' as 'a digital representation of value not issued by a central authority and freely accepted by the market as a medium of exchange'.[2]

6.06   The Court of Justice of the European Union (ECJ), in its judgment of 22 October 2015 in Case C-264/14,[3] stated that bitcoin, the first cryptocurrency based on blockchain technology created in 2009, is a 'virtual currency', where the term *currency* is to be understood as money in the economic sense and not currency as legal tender in a State.[4]

6.07   According to the Bank of Italy, virtual currencies have both exchange and investment purposes.[5]

6.08   German institutions have put forward conflicting opinions. The Ministry of Finance defined bitcoins as 'private money' and excluded that it could be electronic money or foreign currency. Similarly, the Berlin Court of Appeal, on 25 September 2018,[6] ruled out bitcoins as a financial instrument. Of a different opinion is the Financial Markets Authority, BaFin, according to which tokens can be financial instruments or capital investments.[7]

---

[1]   Art 3 n (18) of the Council Directive (EU) 2015/849 on the prevention of the use of the financial system for the purposes of money laundering or terrorist financing, amending Regulation (EU) No 648/2012 of the European Parliament and of the Council, and repealing Directive 2005/60/EC of the European Parliament and of the Council and Commission Directive 2006/70/EC OJ L141/73.

[2]   European Bank Authority, *Opinion on virtual currencies* (4 July 2014) <https://eba.europa.eu/documents/10180/657547/EBA-Op-2014-08 + Opinion+on + Virtual+Currencies.pdf> accessed 21 March 2021.

[3]   Case C-264/14, *Skatteverket v David Hedqvist*, ECLI:EU:C:2015:718.

[4]   ML Perugini, *Distributed ledger technologies e sistemi di Blockchain: digital currency, smart contract e altre applicazioni* (Key Editore 2018).

[5]   Banca d'Italia, *Avvertenze sull'utilizzo delle cosiddette 'valute virtuali'* (30 January 2015) <https://www.bancaditalia.it/compiti/vigilanza/avvisi-pub/avvertenza-valute-virtuali/index.html> accessed 21 March 2021.

[6]   Case no: (4) 161 Ss 28/18 (35/18).

[7]   Bundesanstalt für Finanzdienstleistungsaufsicht, *Advisory letter* no WA 11-QB 4100-2017/0010 <https://www.iosco.org/library/ico-statements/Germany%20-%20BaFin%20-%20Advisory%20Letter%20on%20the%20%20Classification%20of%20Tokens%20as%20Financial%20Instruments.pdf> accessed 21 March 2021.

In any case, the above definitions are not sufficient to define the highly heterogeneous **6.09** phenomenon of cryptocurrencies. Indeed, this confusing scenario also includes tokens, a cryptocurrency that, thanks to a programmable layer, is susceptible to further sub-categories that, in some cases, have nothing to do with money, coins, and currencies. As a matter of fact, it is common practice to distinguish tokens into three categories, based on their functions as follows:

- payment token (cryptocurrency or coin): a token created to be used as a payment in-strument accepted by a community (broad or small), such as, for example, bitcoin, monero, and litecoin;
- utility token: a token required to access a platform or to use the services offered by a platform (eg ether and filecoin);
- investment tokens (security tokens): tokens that are equivalent to financial or invest-ment instruments in that they represent equity or assets (eg neufund).

This tripartition, however, is not always accepted by public authorities and governments, which have proposed adapted versions or applied entirely different criteria. For this reason, the following section will provide an overview of the different taxonomies that have been sketched by European institutions and national courts.

II. Token Classification within the European Union

The question as to how tokens should be classified has been answered in different ways **6.10** within the EU. This section summarizes the classifications that have been put forth at the European level and in some select jurisdictions. More specifically, attention will be devoted to those legal systems where the question of token classification has been addressed by courts, or other national authorities.

1. EBA and ESMA

At institutional level, both EBA[8] and the European Securities and Markets Authority **6.11** (ESMA)[9] provided advice to the European Commission by adopting the term '*crypto-assets*', and introducing further subcategories, based on the abovementioned common prac-tice. In particular, EBA has proposed the following tripartition of crypto-assets:

- payment/exchange/currency tokens (also virtual currency or cryptocurrency): tokens that do not grant rights to the holders and are used as a means of exchange, investment, or store of value;
- investment tokens: tokens granting rights such as ownership or profit sharing;

---

[8] European Bank Authority, *Report with advice for the European Commission on crypto-assets* (9 January 2019) <https://eba.europa.eu/documents/10180/2545547/EBA + Report+on + crypto+assets.pd f> accessed 21 March 2021.
[9] European Securities and Markets Authority, *Advice Initial Coin Offering and Crypto-Assets* (9 January 2019) <https://www.esma.europa.eu/sites/default/files/library/esma50-157-1391_crypto_advice.pdf> accessed 21 March 2021.

- utility tokens: tokens allowing access to a specific product or service usually provided using blockchain technology and not accepted as a means of payment for other purposes.

Along similar lines, ESMA has formulated the following tripartite classification:

- payment-type crypto-asset: a token to be used as a payment instrument for goods and services outside the ecosystem in which it was issued;
- utility-type crypto-asset: tokens that have an additional utility with respect to being a means of payment for goods and services outside the ecosystem in which they were issued;
- investment-type crypto-asset: tokens with characteristics of financial instruments.

2. Italy

6.12 In Italy, case law offered several definitions of cryptocurrency. The Court of Verona, with a decision dated 24 January 2017 no 195, established that bitcoins are financial instruments.[10] According to the Court of Brescia,[11] cryptocurrencies and tokens are highly heterogeneous and, therefore, the analysis of the legal nature of the token should be conducted on a case-by-case basis. In the second instance, the Court of Appeal of Brescia[12] pointed out that cryptocurrencies are always equivalent to currency. The Court of Florence,[13] ruling on the bankruptcy of Bitgrail S.r.l. (the first Italian cryptocurrencies exchange), stated that cryptocurrencies fall within the general category of goods referred to in Article 810 of the Italian Civil Code, as they are things subject to rights. As a consequence, the Court of Florence suggests assessing the actual legal nature of cryptocurrencies on a case-by-case basis.

6.13 Authors from the Bank of Italy, on the basis of the mentioned advice of EBA and ESMA, subdivided crypto-assets (which they call distributed ledger technology (DLT) digital tokens) into a sophisticated taxonomy:[14]

- DT1—virtual currencies: tokens with no embedded rights or liabilities;
- DT2—digital coins or payment tokens: tokens with a fixed-value monetary function which are subdivided into (a) *stablecoins* if issued by a private entity with a fixed value ratio with respect to a legal tender deposited with a third entity; (b) central bank digital currencies if issued by a central bank; (c) non-convertible tokens, if their purpose is to facilitate the exchange of goods and services in a closed circuit (excluding exchange for money);
- DT3—security/asset tokens: dematerialized tradable securities with embedded rights usually issued in token offerings;

---

[10] Court of Verona, second civil division, decision 24 January 2017 no 195.
[11] Court of Brescia, companies division, decree 18 July 2018, Seven Business S.r.l.
[12] Court of Appeal of Brescia, first division, decree 24 October 2018, Seven Business S.r.l.
[13] Court of Florence, bankruptcy division, decision 21 January 2019 n 18, Bitgrail S.r.l.
[14] A Caponera and C Gola, *Questioni di Economia e Finanza: aspetti economici e regolamentari delle cripto-attività* (Issue 484, March 2019) <https://www.bancaditalia.it/pubblicazioni/qef/2019-0484/QEF_484_19.pdf> accessed 21 March 2021.

- DT4—utility tokens/consumer tokens: non-tradable tokens granting access rights to a platform.

3. Lithuania

The Ministry of Finance of Lithuania, in its guidelines dated 8 June 2018,[15] analyses the **6.14** rights conferred by tokens and thus identifies two macro-categories:

- tokens that do not carry voting or participation rights;
- tokens granting voting or participation rights.

The first category is divided into three sub-categories: payment tokens, utility tokens, and donations.

The second category is divided into five sub-categories in the light of the actual rights they **6.15** grant as follows:

- tokens representing equity participations;
- crowdfunding projects;
- token constituting financial instruments other than equity participations;
- secondary token exchange markets;
- collective investment schemes.

Then, with a press release dated 21 October 2019,[16] the Bank of Lithuania divulged the document *Guidelines on Security Token Offering* (STO) as one of the first market regulators in the world to issue guidelines on STOs.

Such Guidelines provide also definitions of tokens as follows: **6.16**

- payment-type tokens: they serve as a means of exchange or payment for goods or services (eg bitcoin);
- utility-type tokens: they provide rights such as the ability to access or buy services/products (eg lympo);
- investment-type tokens: they meet the definition of transferable securities or other financial instruments, like a share or a debt instrument.

4. Malta

On 4 July 2018, Malta passed the Virtual Financial Assets Act which describes two categories **6.17** of tokens. The first is called a 'virtual token', that is, a token whose use is limited to the purchase of goods and services on the issuing platform or on a limited network of platforms

---

[15] Ministry of Finance, *ICO Guidelines* (8 June 2018) <https://finmin.lrv.lt/uploads/finmin/documents/files/ICO%20Guidelines%20Lithuania.pdf> accessed 21 March 2021.
[16] Bank of Lithuania, *Guidelines on Security Token Offering* (17 March 2019), <https://www.lb.lt/en/news/bank-of-lithuania-provides-recommendations-on-raising-capital-through-stos#:~:text = The%20Bank%20of%20Lithuania%20has,aim%20at%20higher%20investor%20protection.&text = Businesses%20are%20interested%20in%20this,an%20alternative%20to%20bank%20lending> accessed 28 March 2021.

(expressly excluding exchanges). In other words, it would be a utility token that is not listed on exchanges. The second category, by contrast, is named 'virtual financial asset', defined as a digital representation of value used as a medium of exchange, unit of account, or reserve that is not an electronic money, financial instrument, or virtual token. In essence, it is a payment token or usage token without the limitations seen for virtual tokens.

III. Token Classification outside the European Union

6.18   This section completes the overview of token classifications, describing the distinctions that have been made by certain institutions and courts outside of the EU. Once again, the criterion for the selection of these jurisdictions is the fact that the question of token classification has been explicitly addressed by the competent national authorities.

1. Switzerland

6.19   The Swiss Financial Markets Supervisory Authority, FINMA, with its Guidelines dated 16 February 2018, identified the following three categories of tokens based on their functions:[17]

- payment tokens: pure cryptocurrencies generated for use as a payment instrument, currency, or value transfer;
- utility tokens: tokens intended for the use of a service on a blockchain infrastructure;
- asset tokens: tokens representing securities such as shares, bonds, financial instruments, and profit participation.

However, the Guidelines are nuanced enough to allow other criteria for categorizing tokens.

6.20   First, the token sale strategy can be relied upon as a criterion, leading to the following further tripartition of tokens:

- immediate generation: tokens generated at the very moment of fundraising, even if on a pre-existing blockchain;
- pre-financing: the initial coin offering (ICO) participant signs a contract that gives it the right to receive tokens in the future;
- pre-sale: the ICO participant receives a temporary token that grants the right to obtain the definitive token in the future.

Therefore, applying both the above categorizations, it is possible to identify the following types of tokens under the FINMA Guidelines:

- payment tokens;
- utility tokens;
- hybrid tokens (utility tokens with payment or investment functions);

---

[17] Financial Market Supervisory Authority, *Guidelines for enquiries regarding the regulatory framework for initial coin offerings* (ICOs) (16 February 2018) <https://www.finma.ch/en/~/media/finma/dokumente/dokumentencenter/myfinma/1bewilligung/fintech/wegleitung-ico.pdf?la = en> accessed 21 March 2021.

- investment tokens (which include tokens issued prior to the implementation of the service, pre-financing contracts, and temporary pre-sale tokens).

2. San Marino

The Republic of San Marino[18] introduced the concept of Initial Token Offering (ITO) by giving legal recognition to two categories of tokens: utility tokens and investment tokens. Utility tokens are considered vouchers for the purchase of goods or services of the issuing institution and may only be issued if such goods or services are already available on the market. The regulations expressly exclude tokens that may have monetary or speculative characteristics or confer voting or participation rights. Investment tokens, by contrast, represent share capital, equity instruments, or debt securities of the issuer.   **6.21**

3. United Kingdom

With its 2019 policy statement,[19] the Financial Conduct Authority put forth the general notion of 'crypto-assets', encompassing all types of tokens. Within this general category, the following types of tokens can be distinguished: **6.22**

- security token: a token that is an investment excluding e-money tokens;
- e-money token: a token that meets the definition of e-money;
- unregulated token: a token that does not grant rights or provide obligations as above.

4. Liechtenstein

In 2019, the Liechtenstein Parliament unanimously passed the so-called Liechtenstein Blockchain Act[20] which aims at providing investor protection, transparency, and anti-money laundering measures. On the basis of the principle according to which a token is a representation of a right, this Act introduces the 'token container model' so that the token is just a technological layer and its legal nature is established according to the rights it contains.   **6.23**

5. Singapore

With the Payment Services Act (PSA) approved on 14 January 2019, Singapore defined the term 'digital payment token' as a digital representation of value that: **6.24**

- is expressed as a unit;
- is not denominated in any currency and is not pegged by its issuer to any currency;

---

[18] Delegated Decree 23 May 2019 no 86 approved by Captains Regent of the Most Serene Republic of San Marino.

[19] Financial Conduct Authority, *Guidance on Cryptoassets Feedback and Final Guidance top CP 19/3* (July 2019) <https://www.fca.org.uk/publication/policy/ps19-22.pdf> accessed 21 March 2021.

[20] Tokens and TT Service Providers Law approved by the Liechtenstein Parliament on 3 October 2019.

- is, or is intended to be, a medium of exchange accepted by the public, or a section of the public, as payment for goods or services or for the discharge of a debt;
- can be transferred, stored, or traded electronically; and
- satisfies such other characteristics as the Monetary Authority of Singapore may prescribe.

Bitcoin and ether have been recognized as digital payment tokens.

IV. Definitions of Token Offerings

6.25 Tokens can be offered to the public through a range of different techniques. In order to understand how blockchain-based crowdfunding works in practice (and how it is regulated), it is therefore necessary to distinguish among different types of offering, which are linked to the concept of token.

6.26 The most well-known term in this respect is Initial Coin Offerings (ICOs), which refers to operations to raise capital, where a certain amount of a new token is generated specifically for the funded business project and offered in exchange for a certain amount of cryptocurrency or legal tender. The European Commission has broadly defined ICOs as a 'new way of raising money using what are called "coins" or "tokens"'.[21]

6.27 After a huge uptake in 2017 and the first half of 2018, ICOs have slowed down significantly, and new updated and revised versions of this mode of capital raising are taking their place with associated new terminologies strictly related to the wide range of categories and definitions of tokens. By analysing the current market trends and practice, a more granular terminology seems to emerge where different, narrower definitions (which may reflect the features of the issued tokens or the way in which the offering is conducted) are deployed, substituting the general label of 'ICO'. Thus, 'Token Generation Event' (TGE), and 'Initial Token Offering' (ITO) are generic terms replacing ICO. They adopt the word 'token' instead of 'coin' because the latter is usually linked to payment tokens, while 'token' has a broader meaning.

6.28 Expressions such as 'Utility Token Offering' (UTO), 'Security Token Offering' (STO), 'Equity Token Offering' (ETO), and 'Initial Convertible Coin Offering' (ICCO) focus on the typology of the issued tokens and clarify the subject matter of the offering to the public. This taxonomy, hence, is closely connected to the distinctions drawn in the previous sections of the chapter: UTOs are ICOs concerning only utility tokens; STOs are issuances of investment tokens; an ETO is an STO involving investment tokens representing the equity of the issuing company; an ICCO is the issuance of tokens which are convertible into shares of the issuing company.

---

[21] European Commission, *Communication from the Commission to the European Parliament, the Council, the European Central Bank, the European Economic and Social Committee and the Committee of the Regions, FinTech Action plan: For a more competitive and innovative European financial sector* (8 March 2018) COM(2018) 109 final <https://ec.europa.eu/transparency/regdoc/rep/1/2018/EN/COM-2018-109-F1-EN-MAIN-PART-1.PDF> accessed 30 March 2021.

In other instances, the distinction among different sorts of ICOs focuses on the way in   **6.29**
which the tokens are issued. This is the case with 'Initial Exchange Offerings' (IEOs) and
'Initial Liquidity Offerings' (ILOs). In particular, through IEOs, the issuer offers the token
through the launch platform of an existing cryptocurrency exchange. The pros of this specific type of offering include an already available potential market of purchasers of the token
(represented by the users of the exchange itself), the marketing activities conducted by the
exchange, and compliance with anti-money laundering (AML) and know your customer
(KYC) procedures managed by the exchange. Usually, exchanges request the issuer to provide a legal opinion ensuring that the token to be issued is not a security.

ILOs are the most recent way to conduct ICOs, revolving around decentralized exchanges,   **6.30**
automated market makers and smart contracts. Let us assume that a user holds two tokens,
called A Token and B Token. Such a user may deposit in a smart contract both tokens in
a certain ratio which, in turn, determines the initial purchase price of each token: this
smart contract is called 'liquidity pool' and represents a new market for that pair of tokens
while the user would be considered the first so-called liquidity provider of that pair.
Further liquidity providers may send additional A Tokens and B Tokens to the liquidity
pool, increasing the supply of both. From this moment, any third user may purchase either A Tokens or B Tokens from the liquidity pool by paying with the other token; on each
transaction a fee is applied by the smart contract itself. Also, with each transaction, a price
adjustment is applied according to a deterministic pricing algorithm embedded into the
smart contract managing the liquidity pool which is called automatic market maker. Each
liquidity provider receives a third type of token, called a Liquidity Provider (LP) token, in
proportion to the liquidity supplied. The LP tokens grant their holders the right to get back
the A Tokens and B Tokens provided as liquidity, plus a percentage of the fees applied to
transactions in proportion to the LP tokens held; the LP tokens are destroyed (in blockchain
terminology: they are 'burnt') when this withdraw is performed. Thus, a liquidity pool is a
smart contract that locks tokens to ensure liquidity for those tokens on a decentralized exchange. Liquidity pools replace the traditional order book model used by centralized crypto
exchanges.

In other words, an ILO requires, first of all, the setting-up of a liquidity pool related to a pair   **6.31**
of tokens. Such a pair is made of the newly issued token and a well-established one which,
usually is the ether, the native cryptocurrency of the Ethereum blockchain.

V. Laws and Guidelines on Token Offerings

Similarly to what has been described with reference to cryptocurrencies in sections II and   **6.32**
III above, several national regulators have issued rules and guidelines on different types of
token offerings. In this section, we briefly highlight the first and most publicly discussed
laws and guidelines issued by regulators.

1. Switzerland

6.33   The aforementioned 2018 FINMA Guidelines[22] establish that, according to the category of token to be issued, the issuing entity has to comply with specific legislation. For instance, if the token sale includes the obligation to return previously invested capital to an investor, possibly with a certain amount of interest on the capital invested, the combination of borrowing and repaying will be regarded as banking activity and will require the relevant licences. If the funds collected with the ICO are managed by third parties, these are collective investments subject to the relevant legislation. In addition, issuances of payment tokens are subject to anti-money laundering legislation.

2. Malta

6.34   The Virtual Financial Assets (VFA) Act regulates the Initial VFA Offering, a method of raising funds whereby an issuer issues VFAs and offers them in exchange for funds. A VFA Offering needs to be conducted with the support of a so-called VFA Agent, a person registered with the competent authority. The offering must be described in a white paper, whose structure and content are provided under the First Schedule of the VFA Act and should include the details of the issuer and of the directors, a description of the project from a business and technical point of view, a description of the VFA from an economic and technical point of view, and the challenges, risks and mitigating measures.

3. Republic of San Marino

6.35   The aforementioned Delegated Decree no 86/2019[23] regulates ITOs in the form of both utility and security tokens. In both cases, the issuing companies are required to be registered in a dedicated registry kept by the local authority, and to divulge a white paper describing the project and the offering. ITOs regarding investment tokens shall provide further and detailed information such as list of shareholders, list of participated entities, and the CVs of directors.

4. Lithuania

6.36   The aforementioned Bank of Lithuania 2019 Guidelines on STOs[24] include crowdfunding platforms in their scope and apply only to 'investment-type' tokens and hybrids thereof. The regulatory status of STOs depends on the design and scope of the relevant token and should be analysed in light of EU and national laws. In light of the technological neutrality principle, investment-type tokens should be treated as equivalent to financial instruments and regulated as such on a case-by-case basis. STOs are considered to be offers of securities to

---

[22] See n 17.
[23] See n 18.
[24] See n 16.

the public as defined in the Prospectus Regulation. Smart contracts managing the issuance of the token should be subject to audit by a third party expert.

5. Singapore

The Monetary Authority of Singapore drafted 'A Guide to Digital Token Offering', last up-   **6.37**
dated on 26 May 2020.[25] The document offers guidance on the application of the relevant laws in relation to offerings in Singapore, regarding digital tokens which may be qualified as capital markets products. Therefore, on a case-by-case basis, the laws on each type of capital markets product will apply.

VI. The EU Digital Finance Package

On 24 September 2020, the European Commission (hereinafter the 'Commission') adopted   **6.38**
the so-called Digital Finance Package[26] (DFP), a comprehensive set of legislative proposals aimed at providing the FinTech sector with a dedicated regulatory framework. The DFP adoption followed a broad public consultation which brought the Commission to cover the most significant trends in the digital finance ecosystem in its proposals. Namely, the DFP contains (a) a communication outlining the EU digital finance strategy; (b) a proposal for a regulation on market in crypto-assets (hereinafter the 'Proposal' or the 'MICA Regulation');[27] (c) a proposal on a pilot regime for market infrastructures based on distributed ledger technology; and (d) a proposal for an EU regulatory framework on digital operational resilience.[28]

The Commission's approach to the digital finance field moves from the clear perception of   **6.39**
the opportunities arising from the digital transformation of the financial sector. According to the Commission, not only must such a crucial change in the financial playground be seen as a potential boost to the European economic recovery (also by unlocking new ways to access funding channels by EU companies) but it can also help the financial inclusion of people currently unable to access financial services.

The Commission recognizes the paramount importance of modernizing the EU regulatory   **6.40**
framework in order to facilitate the digital transformation of the financial system. At the same time, the Commission sees the regulation of digital finance field as an opportunity to prevent the systemic risks associated with such a paramount change to the existing paradigms in the financial sector. From this point of view, the regulatory framework needs to

---

[25] The Monetary Authority of Singapore, *A Guide to Digital Token Offering* (26 May 2020 version) <https://www.mas.gov.sg/-/media/MAS/Sectors/Guidance/Guide-to-Digital-Token-Offerings-26-May-2020.pdf> accessed 28 March 2021.

[26] The Digital Finance Package <https://ec.europa.eu/info/publications/200924-digital-finance-proposals_en> accessed 29 March 2021.

[27] Proposal for a Regulation of the European Parliament and the Council on Markets in Crypto-assets, and amending Directive (EU) 2019/1937 dated 24 September 2020 <https://eur-lex.europa.eu/legal-content/EN/TXT/?uri=CELEX%3A52020PC0593> accessed 16 April 2021.

[28] Furthermore, the DFP includes, for harmonization purposes of the current regulatory framework, a proposal for a EU Directive amending Directives 2006/43/EC, 2009/65/EC, 2009/138/EU, 2011/61/EU, EU/2013/36, 2014/65/EU, (EU) 2015/2366, and EU/2016/2341.

evolve to meet the new challenges to EU financial stability, consumer protection, market integrity, fair competition, cyber security, and, finally, to the safeguard of the level playing field between existing financial institutions and new market participants.

6.41   The Proposal can be divided into three main sections:

- the first section (Titles II, III, and IV) deals with the offer and marketing of crypto-assets;
- the second section (Title V) provides a set of rules addressed to the providers of crypto-asset services;
- the third section (Titles VI and VII) is dedicated to the prevention of market manipulation actions and to the relationship between central and local authorities when supervising the offering and marketing of crypto-assets.

The following paragraphs provide a short taxonomy of the MICA Regulation based on the version available on the Commission website at the time when this chapter was drafted and focus on the scope of application of the Proposal in light of the existing financial regulatory framework. In this respect, it has to be noted that on 19 February 2021, the European Central Bank (ECB) released an opinion on the Commission's proposal suggesting several amendments which, while this chapter was drafted, were still under scrutiny by the Commission.[29]

6.42   Such an analysis will be conducted having in mind the current evolution of the EU financial regulatory framework, which has been recently extended in scope, encompassing forms of alternative finance for start-ups and small and medium-sized enterprises (SMEs) through the Crowdfunding Regulation. A question arises about the existence of a potential overlapping between the MICA Regulation and the Crowdfunding Regulation, with respect to the 'market share' represented by enterprises potentially interested in both crowdfunding forms of financing and in crypto-assets offerings or, on the contrary, about the existence of areas potentially still unregulated.

VII. The Scope of the MICA Regulation

6.43   Pursuant to Article 2, paragraph 1, the MICA Regulation applies to issuers of 'crypto-assets' as well as to providers of services in 'crypto-assets' operating in the territory of the EU. In order to assess the practical applicability of the MICA Regulation to financial intermediaries or, in general, to providers of services connected with the 'crypto-asset ecosystem', it is therefore crucial to assess how the Proposal defines a crypto-asset is in the Proposal meaning.

6.44   First of all, the Proposal excludes the following assets from the definition of crypto-asset:

- financial instruments as defined in Article 4(1), point (15), of Directive 2014/65/EU;

---

[29] European Central Bank, Opinion of the European Central Bank of 19 February 2021 on a proposal for a regulation on Markets in Crypto-assets, and amending Directive (EU) 201/1937 (CON/2021/4) <https://www.ecb.eur opa.eu/pub/pdf/other/en_con_2021_4_f_sign~ae64135b95.pdf> accessed 16 April 2021.

- electronic money as defined in Article 2, point (2), of Directive 2009/110/EC, except where they qualify as electronic money tokens under this Regulation;
- deposits as defined in Article 2(1), point (3), of Directive 2014/49/EU of the European Parliament and of the Council;
- structured deposits as defined in Article 4(1), point (43), of Directive 2014/65/EU;
- securitization as defined in Article 2, point (1), of Regulation (EU) 2017/2402 of the European Parliament and of the Council.

Based on such provision, a first conclusion can be reached about the exclusion from the scope of the MICA Regulation of investment-type tokens which have to be characterized as financial instrument subject to the Markets in Financial Instruments II (MiFID II) Directive. Therefore, the MICA Regulation is not aimed at covering the market area represented by STOs and ETOs in all those cases where the investment-like or equity-like nature of the offered tokens is clear. Such a conclusion seems unavoidable, given the crystal-clear wording used by the aforementioned Article 2, despite the fact that the 'Legislative Financial Statement' attached to the Proposal identifies, among the specific objectives of the MICA Regulation, the growth of 'the sources of funding for companies through increased Initial Coin Offerings and Securities Token Offerings'.[30]

As already mentioned, ICOs are excluded from the scope of the Crowdfunding Regulation which states in Recital 15 that 'whilst initial coin offerings have the potential to fund SMEs, innovative start-ups and scale-ups, and can accelerate technology transfer, their characteristics differ considerably from crowdfunding services regulated under this Regulation'. **6.45**

The Commission has therefore adhered to the suggestions provided by ESMA with the aforementioned 2019 advice on initial coin offerings and crypto-assets.[31] On that occasion ESMA observed that those crypto-assets which do not qualify as MiFID financial instruments (or as electronic money) are likely to fall outside the existing EU financial services rules, in which case investors will not benefit from the safeguards that these rules provide, and invited the EU policy-makers to consider the opportunity to set up a bespoke regime for those crypto-assets. **6.46**

Indeed, it is a matter of fact that due to their features and their inner mechanics, the majority of crypto-assets are not subject to the current financial regulatory framework and can therefore potentially raise, among others, challenges in terms of investor protection, market integrity, and financial stability. **6.47**

In such a *de facto* scenario, the Commission's aim is to provide a full coverage to the subject matter by removing, through the proposal of a pilot regime for market infrastructures based on DLT, any regulatory obstacle to the development of DLT market infrastructures for crypto-assets that qualify as financial instruments under MiFID II on one hand and by setting out a bespoke regulatory regime for the crypto-asset not qualifying as financial instruments under MiFID II through the MICA Regulation on the other hand.[32] **6.48**

---

[30] See p 145, para 1.4.2 of the Proposal.
[31] See n 9.
[32] P Carrière, 'Crypto-assets: le proposte di regolamentazione della Commissione UE. Opportunità e sfide per il mercato italiano' (*Diritto Bancario*, 5 October 2020) <https://www.dirittobancario.it/approfondimenti/fintech/crypto-assets-le-proposte-di-regolamentazione-della-commissione-ue-opportunita-e-sfide-il-mercato-italia> accessed 3 April 2021.

6.49   Having in mind the main aforementioned categories of crypto-asset, the MICA Regulation proposes to regulate the offering of utility tokens and monetary (or payment-like) tokens, whilst security (or investment-type) tokens, as suggested by ESMA, remain regulated by the existing financial regulatory framework. However, it must be noted that the MICA Regulation, similarly to Crowdfunding Regulation, makes reference to several definitions and principles provided by the regulatory framework addressing the issuance and offering of financial instruments. Clear examples of that are the exemption provisions relating to the requirements to publish a white paper before offering a crypto-asset, which resemble the provisions of Regulation (EU) 2017/1129 (the so-called Prospectus Regulation). Along similar lines, the list of 'crypto-asset services' of the MICA Regulation replicate the investment services known by the existing regulatory framework.[33]

6.50   Of course, as observed by the ECB in its opinion, more clarity on these aspects would help to draw a precise line of distinction between utility and monetary tokens on one side and security tokens on the other. This is particularly true when considering that the main challenge faced by the crypto ecosystem in order to definitely flourish within the EU is the ability of the token issuers to qualify precisely their offer within the regulatory framework so as to avoid any uncertainty vis-à-vis the potential investors about the legal regime applicable to the offered crypto-assets. In this respect, Article 7 of the Proposal provides for a specific obligation of crypto-asset issuers to explain by means of the white paper accompanying the issuance why the relevant crypto-asset is not to be considered a financial instrument or another instrument outside the MICA Regulation scope. After the notification of the white paper, the local competent authority will have the power to suspend or prohibit the offering whenever doubts should arise about the qualification of the relevant crypto-asset.

6.51   After having defined what crypto-assets fall out of its scope of application, the MICA Regulation tries to set forth a definition of 'crypto-asset' which is, according to Article 3, paragraph 1, a 'digital representation of value or rights which may be transferred or stored electronically, using distributed ledger technology or similar technology'. Maybe inevitably, the definition sounds more technical than legal, not dissimilarly by the definition provided by the Fifth AML Directive in 2018[34] mentioned in Paragraph 6.04 above. An extra effort is then required of practitioners to provide the crypto ecosystem with a taxonomy based on the economic rationale behind a token's issuance.

6.52   If the distinction between utility/monetary tokens and security tokens is not immediate, the relationship between monetary tokens subject to the MICA Regulation and electronic money as defined by Directive 2009/110/EC can be even more confusing at a first sight. Indeed, both instruments have a payment function but what makes the difference is the technology underlying the issuance and circulation of monetary tokens based on the usage of distributed ledger technology, whilst electronic money (in the wording of Article 2 of Directive 2009/110/EC) is 'electronically, including magnetically, stored monetary value as represented by a claim on the issuer to a magnetically storage of value'. Therefore, a crypto-asset falls within the scope of the MICA Regulation if it is a digital representation of value

---

[33]   See n 29.
[34]   See n 1.

or rights that can be transferred or held electronically using DLT but which does not qualify as a financial instrument, electronic money, deposit, structured deposit, or securitization.

Finally, an important remark has to be made about the exclusion from the scope of the **6.53** MICA Regulation of cryptocurrencies such as bitcoin, whose issuer cannot be identified, due to their technological infrastructure.[35] Inevitably, such an exclusion (which depends on the issuer-based approach typical of the existing financial regulatory framework) leaves room for a very wide unregulated area; in light of the current increasingly significant growth of such crypto-currencies, some doubt about this approach can legitimately be raised.

Article 4(2) of the Proposal provides for the exemptions from the publication of a white **6.54** paper, where the crypto-asset is the result of a mining activity or is automatically attributed to the subjects that are responsible for supporting a DLT network infrastructure by holding a copy of the distributed ledger and validating the transactions. Due to the notoriety and the increasingly importance in the financial system of bitcoin and several other cryptocurrencies, such a legislative choice can at a first sight appear bewildering; however, on closer scrutiny, the public offering of a crypto-asset with the aforementioned characteristics will not be attributable to corporate entities or physical persons and therefore the set of rules provided for by the Proposal would not have an addressee.

VIII. Categories of Crypto-assets Falling into the MICA Regulation Scope

The Proposal lays down a separate framework in respect of three distinct categories of **6.55** crypto-assets falling into the MICA Regulation scope:

- 'other crypto-assets';
- e-money tokens (EMTs);
- asset-referenced tokens (ARTs).

In terms of crypto-asset taxonomy, the category of the 'other crypto-asset' encompasses in first instance the so-called utility tokens; the Proposal describes such tokens as crypto-assets issued for the purpose of providing digital access to a good or service, available on a DLT network and which are accepted by the issuer.

ART are defined as crypto-assets that keep their value stable by referring to the value of legal **6.56** tender currencies, baskets of assets, other crypto-assets, or a combination of these. Such a definition recalls the so-called stablecoins which are cryptocurrencies based on algorithms aimed to link the token value to the value of fiat currencies or other assets usually traded on regulated markets such as shares or bonds.

EMTs are crypto-assets meant to be deemed as medium of exchange for the purchase of **6.57** goods or services which are also purported to maintain a stable value by referring to the

---

[35] R Lener, 'Cripto-attività: prime riflessioni sulla proposta della commissione europea. Nasce una nuova disciplina dei servizi finanziari "crittografati"?' (*Diritto Bancario*, 9 October 2020) <https://www.dirittobancario.it/approfondimenti/fintech/cripto-attivita-prime-riflessioni-sulla-proposta-della-commissione-europea-nasce-una-nuova-disciplina> accessed 2 April 2021.

value of a fiat currency. Based on the last-mentioned feature EMT, similarly to ART, can therefore be classified as a particular type of stablecoin whose value is however exclusively linked to a legal tender currency.

6.58   In light of the above, it must be concluded that, as stressed by the ECB in its opinion on the MICA Regulation, both ARTs and EMTs have a monetary substitution dimension; the difference between the two categories is the specific function of money which each token purports to firstly realize: store of value for ARTs, and medium of exchange for EMTs. Having in mind the variety of crypto-assets issued at the global level, the practical meaning of such a categorization does not appear so immediate, but possibly the existence of a bespoke regulation setting out such a precise tokens taxonomy could push the crypto ecosystem towards a standardization of the tokens issuance, with an undeniable improvement in terms of investor protection and market transparency.

6.59   The regime of the three categories of crypto-asset responds to the perception by the Commission that offerings concerning both ARTs and EMTs call for stricter regulation, in comparison with the offering of utility tokens. In particular, in light of the widespread concern that ARTs could become a 'competitor' of legal tender currencies, the relevant bespoke regime provides for an authorization proceeding involving not only the local competent authority but also ESMA, EBA, and the ECB, and the possibility of prohibiting an offer if this could threaten financial stability or the principles of monetary sovereignty.

IX.   Requirements to be Fulfilled by Crypto-asset Issuers under the MICA Regulation

1.   The Crucial Role of the 'White Paper'

6.60   The requirements to be met in order to offer crypto-assets to the public in the EU are very close to those provided for by the Prospectus Regulation in respect of initial public offerings (IPOs) and consists according to the MICA Regulation in drafting a white paper, which has to be notified to the competent authorities and published on the issuer's website.

6.61   With a clear reference to the information schemes relating to initial public offers under the existing regulatory framework, crypto-assets offerings must be accompanied by the publication of a prospectus-like document referred to as the 'white paper', in accordance with the crypto-market jargon. The white paper's purpose is a crystal-clear explanation to potential investors as to the objectives of the fund-raising initiative, as well as the business project underlying this. The contents of the document are listed in detail by Articles 5, 17, and 46 of the Proposal.

6.62   Without any doubt, there are certain analogies between the MICA Regulation and the Crowdfunding Regulation, with respect to the area of information obligation to be provided by issuers and service providers in order to ensure investor protection principles. Indeed, the Crowdfunding Regulation provisions on the subject matter descend from the information measures set out by the MiFID Directive and are mainly based on the information to be provided through the service providers' website and the so-called key information sheet (KIS) which, to some extent, resembles in its structure the corresponding information documents provided for with respect to the offering of financial instruments to the public.

The white paper must mandatorily include, *inter alia*, the following: **6.63**

- information regarding the governance of issuer as well as of third parties involved in the offering;
- a detailed description of the custody arrangements;
- detailed information on the nature and enforceability of rights.

The white paper must be very clear with respect to the description of the business project and the specific features of the crypto-activities offered, including the number of crypto-assets to be issued and the relevant issue price. A specific set of information must be dedicated to the underlying technology on the token issuance and offering is based.

In order to ensure the effectiveness of the white paper in reaching its investor protection   **6.64** purposes, the document needs to contain a summary which shall in brief and nontechnical language providing 'key information about the offer to the public of the asset referenced tokens or about the intended admission of asset-referenced tokens to trading on a trading platform for crypto-assets, and in particular about the essential elements of the asset-referenced tokens concerned'.

The Proposal attaches great importance to the accuracy of the information published in the   **6.65** white paper. Article 14 provides for liability of the issuer in the event of the publication of untrue, unclear, or misleading information within the white paper or in any amendments thereto; further to the issuer liability, the Proposal sets out a joint responsibility of its management body with express exclusion of any form of limitation of liability applicable.

The white paper must contain a 'clear and unambiguous statement' about the following   **6.66** circumstances:

- the crypto-assets may lose their value in part or in full;
- the crypto-assets may not always be transferable;
- the crypto-assets may not be liquid;
- where the offer to the public concerns utility tokens, such utility tokens may not be exchangeable against the good or service promised in the white paper.

Paradoxically, as observed,[36] while the Proposal refers to the effective use of utility tokens for the purchase of good or services, the inclusion of such a circumstance among the typical risk factor relating to these crypto-assets could weaken the position of the investors seeking protection in court for breach of the utility tokens issuers' duties and obligations.

From a more formal point of view, the white paper must always be dated and drawn up in at   **6.67** least one of the official languages of the issuer's Member State of origin or, in the words of the Proposal (Articles 5 and 17), 'in a language generally known in the sphere of international

---

[36] R Lener, '*Cripto-attività: prime riflessioni sulla proposta della commissione europea. Nasce una nuova disciplina dei servizi finanziari "crittografati"?*', published on "Diritto Bancario", 9 October 2020 <https://www.dirittobancario.it/approfondimenti/fintech/cripto-attivita-prime-riflessioni-sulla-proposta-della-commissione-europea-nasce-una-nuova-disciplina> accessed 16 April 2021.

finance'. Additionally, the white paper must be made available in machine-readable formats, based on technological standards that will be released by ESMA.

6.68   The white paper may be subject to amendment when significant new circumstances potentially affect the features of the offering; such amendments have to be promptly communicated to the public as well as notified to the competent authorities.

2. The 'Other Crypto-assets' Regime

6.69   With respect to the category of 'other-crypto assets', the white paper is not subject to any prior control by the competent authorities and, according to Article 5(3) of the Proposal, an express mention of such circumstance within the document is required.

6.70   An exemption from the obligation of publishing the whitepaper is granted pursuant to Article 4(2) of the Proposal in the event that:

- the crypto-assets are offered to the public free of charge;
- the crypto-assets are the result of a mining activity;
- the crypto-assets cannot be exchanged with other crypto-assets;
- with a reference to the capital markets regulation, when the crypto-assets are offered to fewer than 150 natural or legal persons, the total consideration of the offer does not exceed EUR 1 million over a twelve-month period, or the offer is addressed exclusively to qualified investors and can subsequently held only by qualified investors.

Pursuant to Article 8 of the MICA Regulation, once at least twenty days from the notification to the competent authority have passed, the white paper has to be published on the issuer's website before the beginning of the offer and it must remain easily accessible and available for the entire duration of the offer.

6.71   A question arises whether a verification or preliminary investigation to be conducted by the local competent authority with regard to technological reliability profile of the infrastructure adopted by the issuer would be suggestable. Indeed, the current crypto eco-system and, more in general, the DLT protocols appear to be quite far from a technological standardization and this circumstance could determine significant differences in terms of security levels guaranteed to subscribers and transaction recordings. This could raise, in turn, technological risks which can be hardly recognized by investors in crypto-assets without a report by a third-party expert.

3. The ART Regime

6.72   With respect to ART offerings, the white paper has not only to be notified to the competent authority but needs also to be expressly authorized pursuant to Article 15 of the Proposal; furthermore, the amount of information to be provided by the white paper is significantly more extensive than the one for 'other crypto-assets' and EMTs.

Pursuant to Article 15 of the Proposal, ART offerings do not need to be authorized if the **6.73** outstanding amount of ARTs do not exceed EUR 5 million over a twelve-month period or if the offer is solely addressed to 'qualified investors'.[37]

Also to be mentioned is the provision laid down by Article 16 of the MICA Regulation, ac- **6.74** cording to which the issuers must procure a legal opinion stating that the relevant tokens do not qualify as financial instruments, electronic money, deposits, or structured deposits.

The authorization procedure is quite articulated and provides for a twenty-day term for the **6.75** competent authority to communicate the completeness of the information received and a further three-month period starting from such communication for the issuance of a first draft of the authorization which needs to be notified to EBA, ESMA, and the ECB.

The three European authorities will be required to issue, within the following three months, **6.76** a non-binding opinion addressed to the local competent authority which will then decide whether to grant the authorization.

Prudential rules very similar to those of regulated financial intermediaries are laid down by **6.77** the Proposal with respect to own-funds requirements, discipline of the acquisition and orderly wind-down of issuers of ARTs.

Finally, specific additional obligations for issuers of '*significant asset-referenced tokens*' are **6.78** provided for by Article 41 of the Proposal, in order to further limit the risks arising from ART offers entailed by quantitative elements such as an extended customer base and a considerable overall value of the offer.

4. The EMT Regime

Compared to the discipline of ART offerings, the EMT framework appears slightly less **6.79** stringent; of course, such a different approach is not only due to the different nature of the relevant crypto-assets but also depends on the circumstance that pursuant to Article 43 of the Proposal the EMT issuers can solely be an authorized credit institution or an authorized 'electronic money institution'. Indeed, EMTs are to be considered in all respects the tokenized version of electronic money, as defined by Directive 2009/110/EC.

As provided for with respect to ARTs, according to Article 43 (2) of the MICA Regulation, **6.80** EMT offerings can be exempted by filing for authorization if (a) EMTs are marketed, distributed, and held by 'qualified investors' only, or (b) the average outstanding of the relevant tokens do not exceed EUR 5 million over a period of twelve months.

The authorization exemption does not, however, exempt from the publication of a white **6.81** paper which, in this case, must simply be notified to the competent authority. From a different standpoint, such an exemption regime also implies that the offering of EMTs the overall consideration of which is below the aforementioned threshold is not limited to regulated credit institution or electronic money institutions.

---

[37] Pursuant to Art 3(20) of the Proposal, 'qualified investors' means 'qualified investors' as defined in Art 2, point (e), of Regulation (EU) 2017/1129.

6.82   Interestingly, the MICA Regulation derogates from Article 11 of Directive 2009/110/EC, providing according to Article 44 that holders of EMTs shall always be provided with a claim for the return of the amount paid in legal tender currency on the issuer of such EMTs. A further feature differentiating EMTs from e-money under Directive 2009/110/EC is the prohibition for the issuers to grant interest or any other benefit related to the length of time during which a holder of EMTs holds such EMTs.

X. Authorization and Obligations of Crypto-asset Service Providers

6.83   The authorization package for crypto-asset service providers is established in Title V of the MICA Regulation, which is divided in four chapters. Chapter 1 of Title V (Articles 53–58) lays down the procedure to obtain the authorization. First of all, only legal persons within the EU may obtain the authorization to act as a crypto-asset service provider. Furthermore, the authorization specifies the actual services that can be carried out by the authorized provider and is valid throughout the entire EU.

6.84   The authorization is requested to the competent authority of the European Member State where the legal person's registered office is located, providing the information listed in Article 54(2) of the MICA Regulation. The assessment procedure before the competent authority lasts three months. It is worth mentioning that, according to Article 55(5), the authorization may be refused in any of the following cases:

- the management body of the applicant poses a threat to its effective, sound and prudent management and business continuity, and to the adequate consideration of the interest of its clients and the integrity of the market;
- the applicant fails to meet or is likely to fail to meet any requirements of Title V of the MICA Regulation.

ESMA keeps a publicly available register of all authorized crypto-asset service providers. Article 56 lists the rights granted to competent authorities to withdraw an authorization.

6.85   Chapter 2 of Title V defines the obligations for crypto-asset service providers. Such obligations are quite familiar in the financial sector and include the following:

- to act honestly, fairly, and professionally in the best interest of clients;
- to provide fair, clear, and not misleading information to clients;
- to warn clients of risks associated with crypto-assets;
- to have in place prudential safeguards in terms of funds and insurance policies;
- to maintain organizational requirements such as reputable management bodies, skilled personnel, business continuity policies, and internal control mechanisms;
- to safeguard the ownership rights of their clients on crypto-asset and funds held on their behalf;
- to establish a complaint handling procedure;
- to keep procedures and rules to avoid, identify, and manage conflict of interests;
- to set out rules on outsourcing in order to avoid additional operational risks.

Chapter 3 of Title V regulates obligations dedicated to seven specific crypto-asset services. With reference to crypto-asset service providers authorized for the custody of crypto-assets on behalf of third parties, the agreement governing the services should include a description of the adopted security systems. Also, such service providers are required to keep a register of all positions and movements for each client, to adopt a custody policy, and to segregate holdings on behalf of their clients from their own holdings. Finally, the service providers are liable for loss of crypto-assets in the event of malfunctions or hacks, up to the market value of the crypto-assets lost.

Crypto-asset service providers authorized for the operation of a trading platform for crypto-assets are required to set out operating rules for the trading platform, which should include the following: **6.86**

- procedures and rules to admit crypto-assets to the trading platform;
- types of crypto-assets excluded from trading;
- policies, procedures, and fees for the admission to the trading platform;
- requirements to ensure fair and orderly trading;
- liquidity thresholds and periodic disclosure requirements;
- conditions under which trading of crypto-assets can be suspended.

Additionally, such service providers are required to assess the quality of the crypto-asset to be traded on the platform. The quality assessment should take into consideration the experience, track record, and reputation of the issuer and its development team.

It is worth pointing out that, according to Article 68(1), 'crypto-assets which have inbuilt anonymisation function are not admissible for trading unless the holders of the crypto-assets and their transaction history can be identified by the crypto-asset service providers that are authorised for the operation of a trading platform for crypto-assets or by competent authorities'. **6.87**

In addition, crypto-asset service providers authorized for the operation of a trading platform for crypto-assets are required to ensure that the platform has sufficient capacity to sustain severe market stress and is able to reject orders that exceed predetermined volume and price thresholds or are clearly erroneous. Also, prices, volumes, and time of transactions are public. **6.88**

The third service concerns the exchange of crypto-assets against fiat currency or other crypto-assets. The relevant service providers are required to publish a firm price of the crypto-assets or a method for determining the price of the crypto-assets they propose for exchange. **6.89**

Article 70 regulates the execution of orders for crypto-assets on behalf of third parties. In this case, the provider is required to **6.90**

> take all necessary steps to obtain, when executing orders, the best possible result for their clients taking into account the best execution factors of price, costs, speed, likelihood of execution and settlement, size, nature or any other consideration relevant to the execution of the order, unless the crypto-asset service provider concerned executes orders for crypto-assets following specific instructions given by its clients.

6.91   The placing of crypto-assets is the fifth service specifically regulated by the MICA Regulation. It is provided that the following information be communicated to the issuer:

- type of placement considered;
- transaction fees;
- timing, process, and price for the proposed operation;
- information about the targeted purchasers.

Crypto-asset service providers authorized for the reception and transmission of orders on behalf of third parties are required to 'establish and implement procedures and arrangements which provide for the prompt and proper transmission of client's orders for execution on a trading platform for crypto-assets or to another crypto-asset service provider'. The crypto-asset service provider may not gain monetary or non-monetary benefits from the recipient.

6.92   The last service taken into consideration is advice on crypto-assets. First of all, service providers in this field assess the compatibility of the crypto-assets with the needs of the clients. Then, service providers ensure that natural persons giving advice possess the necessary knowledge and experience.

6.93   Finally, Chapter 4 of Title V sets out the rules on acquisition of crypto-assets service providers. According to Article 74(1) and (2), the procedure applies in the event of:

- acquisition of a qualifying holding in a crypto-asset service provider or increase of a qualifying holding in a crypto-asset service provider 'so that the proportion of the voting rights or of the capital held would reach or exceed 10%, 20%, 30% or 50% or so that the crypto-asset service provider would become' the subsidiary of the acquirer.
- dispose of a qualifying holding in a crypto-asset service provider 'so that the proportion of the voting rights or of the capital held would fall below 10%, 20%, 30% or 50% or so that the crypto-asset service provider would cease to be' the vendor's subsidiary.

The transaction may be completed only if the competent authority grants its approval after an assessment which takes into consideration:

- the reputation and financial soundness of the acquirer;
- the reputation and experience of any person who will direct the business of the crypto-asset service provider as a result of the intended acquisition or disposal;
- whether there are reasonable grounds to suspect that money laundering or terrorist financing is being or has been committed or attempted, or that the intended acquisition could increase the risk thereof.

6.94   ESMA, in cooperation with the EBA, will develop draft regulatory technical standards to establish an exhaustive list of information that is necessary to carry out the assessment, which should be completed within sixty working days.

XI. Will a Financial Regulatory Framework (Inclusive of the Crowdfunding Regulation and the MICA Regulation) be effectively omni-comprehensive?

The Commission, as emerges from the statements contained both in the Crowdfunding **6.95** Regulation and in the MICA Proposal, has a clear view about the necessity to implement an EU financial regulation framework, in order to avoid the systemic risk arising from the new forms of financing based on new technologies on one hand, and to favour, coherently with the general pursuit of the economic growth of the EU area, the flourish of such market developments on the other hand. The adoption of bespoke regimes is seen by the Commission as the most efficient way to reach such goals within the EU legislative action. However, due to the fast day-by-day evolution of financing schemes based on the use of technology, especially DLT, issues arise about the effective capacity of the regulatory framework set out by the Commission to encompass the entire subject matter. In an attempt to provide an answer to such underlying question, an effort to look at the entire financial regulatory framework as an 'ensemble' is required.

As previously mentioned, the MICA Regulation excludes from its scope the offers of tokens **6.96** that can be qualified as financial instruments pursuant to MiFID II, and the Crowdfunding Regulation states that ICOs differ considerably from crowdfunding services. The circumstance that ICOs of security tokens are not encompassed in the scope of application of either the MICA Regulation or the Crowdfunding Regulation may lead to the conclusion that a significant unregulated area still exists. However, in light of the whole financial regulatory framework, this conclusion does not appear to be accurate. As a matter of fact:

- offerings to the public of private limited liability companies' shares for a maximum consideration of EUR 5 million are regulated by the Crowdfunding Regulation;
- offerings to the public private of limited liability companies' shares for a consideration higher than EUR 5 million are regulated by Prospectus Regulation and with respect to the rules pertaining investment services by MiFID II rules;
- offerings to the public of crypto-assets as defined by the MICA Regulation will be (once the Regulation will be adopted) subject to the relevant set of rules;
- offerings to the public of crypto-assets qualifying as financial instruments, based on the 2019 ESMA advice and the MICA, are subject to Prospectus Regulation and, with respect to the rules pertaining investment services, to MiFID II.

Therefore, the overall architecture seems clear and may be summarized, taking into account the terminologies adopted in previous paragraphs, as follows:

- the Crowdfunding Regulation expressly excludes ICOs, and regulates offerings of transferable securities and shares up to EUR 5 million for the traditional venture capital sector;
- the Prospectus Regulation and MiFID II, in relation to which the DFP has already proposed amendments for consistency purposes, would cover STOs and ETOs, because those would be issuances of actual financial instruments (security and investment tokens) according to the financial traditional regulatory framework;
- the MICA Regulation would cover ITOs relating to payment tokens and utility tokens.

In this perspective, the inclusion of ICOs in the Crowdfunding Regulation would probably, in the Commission's view, have brought confusion within the system. However, what the financial regulatory framework still does not seem to be able to address adequately is the result of the most radical technological evolution in the blockchain sphere. In particular, the current framework does not consider the whole set of tokens whose issuance is based on decentralized finance technologies like the ILOs discussed in paragraphs 6.29, 6.30, and 6.31, decentralized exchanges, and stablecoins managed by rebase algorithms. More in general, any computerized processes which are not in any way linked to identifiable legal or natural persons fall outside of the aforementioned regulatory framework. This will probably be the main challenge that all global regulators will have to face in the coming years, if they intend to pursue both the growing economic interests associated with this evolution of the financial eco-system, and investor protection.

6.97   In conclusion, the MICA Regulation and the Crowdfunding Regulation are undoubtedly capable of bringing the EU financial regulatory framework closer to the recent technology-based financing forms as an important channel for the matching of capital demand and offer; however, the EU financial regulatory framework cannot probably still be deemed fully 'future-proof' because the ever-evolving blockchain world, and especially the decentralized finance movement, is already a fact, but is definitely far from being adequately regulated.

PART III
REGULATING THE CROWDFUNDING SERVICE PROVIDERS UNDER THE CROWDFUNDING REGULATION

7

Authorization and Supervision of Crowdfunding Service Providers

Marije Louisse and Adam Pasaribu

I. Introduction

With the Crowdfunding Regulation, a new authorization for crowdfunding service providers (CSPs) to provide crowdfunding services in the EU is introduced. Several Member States have already introduced bespoke regimes on crowdfunding. Those regimes are tailored to the characteristics and needs of local markets and investors. As a result, the existing national rules diverge across the EU as regards the conditions of operation of crowdfunding platforms, the scope of permitted activities, and the authorization requirements. The differences between the existing national rules are such that they obstruct the cross-border provision of crowdfunding services and thus have a direct effect on the functioning of the internal market in such services. The Crowdfunding Regulation aims to address these obstacles by introducing an authorization that can be used to provide crowdfunding services in the whole EU.   **7.01**

This chapter elaborates on the crowdfunding services that may be provided, the authorization process, and the cross-border provision of crowdfunding services (section II). In addition, it discusses the supervision by the competent authorities, including the exercise of investigatory and supervisory powers and powers to impose sanctions, and the obligations   **7.02** of the crowdfunding service provides towards competent authorities (section III). Where relevant, sections II and III make a comparison with the Markets in Financial Instruments Directive II (MiFID II), in order to assess whether the Crowdfunding Regulation indeed provides for a more proportional regime as advocated by the Commission.[1] In section IV, we assess how the authorization for CSPs interferes with market access under other EU and national law instruments. Section V concludes.

II. The Authorization of Crowdfunding Service Providers

1. Competent Authorities

7.03   When the Commission proposed the Crowdfunding Regulation, it was intended that the European Securities and Markets Authority (ESMA) would be the competent authority for authorization. The Commission believed that granting supervisory competences to ESMA allowed for a more efficient and centrally managed authorization and oversight, generating economies of scale. Such a central supervisory regime was deemed to be beneficial to the market participants in terms of greater transparency, investor protection, and market efficiency.[2] However, the European Parliament thought differently.[3] As a result, the Member States have to designate the competent authorities responsible for carrying out the functions and duties provided for in the Crowdfunding Regulation.[4] Where Member States designate more than one competent authority, they have to determine their respective tasks and designate one of them as a single point of contact for cross-border administrative cooperation between competent authorities, as well as with ESMA.[5] CSPs provide their services under the supervision of the competent authorities that granted authorization.[6] As a result of the change from ESMA to the national authorities being the competent authorities, the designation of the competent authorities is very similar to MiFID II.[7]

7.04   The Commission expected that ESMA would be in charge of authorizing and supervising twenty-five CSPs in the first full year of implementation.[8] This was, however, still based on the presumption that the Crowdfunding Regulation would not be applicable to crowdfunding services that are provided by natural or legal persons in accordance with national law.[9] In other words, the presumption that the regime under the Crowdfunding Regulation

---

[1] European Commission Staff Working Document, 'Impact Assessment Accompanying the document Proposal for a Regulation of the European Parliament and of the Council on European Crowdfunding Service Providers (ECSP) for Business and Proposal for a Directive of the European Parliament and of the Council amending Directive 2014/65/EU on markets in financial instruments', SWD(2018) 56 final 2018/048 (COD), 29, 31, 49.

[2] Recital 41 Commission Proposal.

[3] Report on the proposal for a regulation of the European Parliament and of the Council on European Crowdfunding Service Providers (ECSP) for Business (COM(2018)0113—C8-0103/2018—2018/0048(COD)) Committee on Economic and Monetary Affairs Rapporteur: Ashley Fox. See also E Macchiavello, 'FinTech Regulation from a Cross-Sectoral Perspective' in V Colaert, D Busch, and T Incalza, *European Financial Regulation: Levelling the Cross-Sectoral Playing Field* (Hart 2019) 83–84.

[4] Art 29(1) Crowdfunding Regulation.

[5] Art 29(2) Crowdfunding Regulation.

[6] Art 15(1) Crowdfunding Regulation. See Chapter 8 on the ongoing obligations of CSPS after having obtained an authorization.

[7] See CV Gortsos, 'Public Enforcement of MiFID II' in D Busch and G Ferrarini, *Regulation of the EU Financial Markets, MiFID II and MiFIR* (OUP 2017) 534–35.

[8] Commission Proposal, pp 8, 61.

[9] See Art 2(2)(c) Commission Proposal.

would coexist with national ones, while the entity of a CSP could only hold one licence at a time (ie either a European Crowdfunding Service Providers (ECSP) licence, national, or MiFID).[10] The idea of a complementary service-based solution was however not embraced by the European Parliament and the Council. As a result, CSPs that want to provide crowd-funding services in scope of the Crowdfunding Regulation need to obtain an authorization under the Crowdfunding Regulation. We therefore expect the number of CSPs that will be authorized and supervised on the basis of the Crowdfunding Regulation to be significantly higher than twenty-five.

2. Definition of Crowdfunding Services and Scope of Authorization

The authorization of crowdfunding services providers is restricted to 'crowdfunding serv- **7.05** ices'. These are defined in Article 2(1)(a) of the Crowdfunding Regulation as the matching of business funding interests of investors and project owners through the use of a crowd-funding platform and which consists of any of the following activities: (a) the facilitation of granting of loans (crowdlending services), and (b) the placing without a firm commitment basis, as referred to in point (7) of section A of Annex I to MiFID II, of transferable secur-ities and admitted instruments for crowdfunding purposes issued by project owners or a special purpose vehicle (SPV), and the reception and transmission of client orders, as re-ferred to in point (1) of that section, in relation to those transferable securities and admitted instruments for crowdfunding purposes (crowdinvesting services).[11] Taking into account that the crowdfunding services comprise both crowdlending and crowdinvesting services, the authorization under the Crowdfunding Regulation may be used both for investment-based crowdfunding and lending-based crowdfunding.[12]

Article 1(2) of the Crowdfunding Regulation restricts the scope of the Crowdfunding **7.06** Regulation by stipulating that the Crowdfunding Regulation does not apply to:

(1) Crowdfunding services that are provided to project owners that are consumers, as defined in point (a) of Article 3 of the CCD;
(2) other services related to crowdfunding services and that are provided in accordance with national law;
(3) crowdfunding offers with a consideration of more than EUR5 million which are to be calculated over a period of twelve months as the sum of: (a) the total consider-ation of offers of transferable securities and admitted instruments for crowdfunding purposes as defined in points (m) and (n) of Article 2(1) of the Crowdfunding Regulation and amounts raised by means of loans through a crowdfunding platform by a particular project owner; and (b) the total consideration of offers to the public of transferable securities made by the project owner referred to in point (i) in its

---

[10] This is Option 4, as described in the Impact Assessment.
[11] See Chapter 3 for an elaborate discussion of the definition of crowdfunding services.
[12] The definition of crowdfunding services was fairly different in the Commission's proposal for the Crowdfunding Regulation. See also E Macchiavello, 'FinTech Regulation from a Cross-Sectoral Perspective' in V Colaert, D Busch, and T Incalza, *European Financial Regulation: Levelling the Cross-Sectoral Playing Field* (Hart 2019) 83–84.

capacity as an offeror pursuant to the exemption under Article 1(3), or Article 3(2), of the Prospectus Regulation.

7.07 As a result, the authorization of a CSP only allows it to provide crowdfunding services to project owners that are not consumers and for crowdfunding offers with a consideration that does not exceed EUR 5 million. In case a CSP wants to provide other services[13] and/or to project owners that are consumers and/or for crowdfunding offers with a consideration that exceeds EUR 5 million other authorization requirements may apply. Yet, in Article 1(3) of the Crowdfunding Regulation, it is noted that, unless a CSP is authorized as a credit institution in accordance with Article 8 of CRD, Member States shall not apply national requirements implementing Article 9(1) of that directive and shall ensure that national law does not require an authorization as a credit institution or any other individual authorization, exemption, or dispensation in connection with the provision of crowdfunding services in the following situations:

(1) for project owners that in respect of loans facilitated by the CSP accept funds from investors; or

(2) for investors that grant loans to project owners facilitated by the CSP.

We understand this provision to relate only to crowdlending services and not to crowdinvesting services. As a result, it is our understanding that only CSPs that provide crowdlending services may not be subjected by Member States to any other authorization requirements than the authorization requirement under the Crowdfunding Regulation. This means that CSPs that provide crowdinvesting services may be subjected to other authorization requirements. See also section IV.4.

7.08 The competent authorities that grant an authorization under the Crowdfunding Regulation have to ensure that such authorization specifies the crowdfunding services which the CSP is authorized to provide. A CSP seeking authorization to extend its business to additional crowdfunding services not foreseen at the time of the authorization has to submit a request for extension of its authorization to the competent authorities that granted the CSP its authorization.[14]

A. Other Activities

7.09 Although the authorization of a CSP is limited to crowdfunding services in scope of the Crowdfunding Regulation, the Crowdfunding Regulation actually also includes some requirements in respect of the performance of other activities by CSPs. It can be derived from the annex to the draft regulatory technical standards (RTS) from ESMA on the authorization process,[15] as published on 26 February 2021, that such other activities may include

---

[13] Recital 38 of the Crowdfunding Regulation states that in order to provide a broad range of services to their clients, a CSP authorized under the Crowdfunding Regulation should be allowed to engage in activities other than the provision of crowdfunding services covered by an authorization under this regulation. See also Art 12(13) Crowdfunding Regulation. These other activities may, for example, include investment services or payment services. These services should then be provided in accordance with the relevant applicable EU or national law. See also section IV in that respect.

[14] Art 13 Crowdfunding Regulation.

[15] ESMA, Consultation Paper Draft technical standards under the ECSP Regulation, ESMA/35-36-2201, 26 February 2021, Annex VI Draft RTS pursuant to Article 12(16) of the ECSPR (hereinafter referred to as the draft RTS on the authorization process).

asset safekeeping, payment services, use of SPVs for the provision of crowdfunding services, application of credit scores to crowdfunding projects, suggestion of the price and/or the interest rate of crowdfunding offers, operating a bulletin board, and establishing and operating contingency funds. As the requirements for these other activities are not authorization requirements, they are not covered in this chapter, but they are discussed in other chapters of this book:

- Article 10 sets requirements when CSPs provide asset safekeeping services or payment services.[16] As these services typically involve an authorization under MiFID II or the Payment Services Directive (PSD) 2, it is our understanding that these requirements apply as a 'top-up' of the requirements under said directives. See further Chapter 8.
- Article 3(6) deals with the situation in which a SPV is used. See also Chapter 9.
- Article 19(6) imposes additional (investor protection) requirements on CSPs that apply credit scores to crowdfunding projects or suggest the pricing of crowdfunding offers on their crowdfunding platform. See Chapter 12.
- Operating a bulletin board is covered by Article 25. See Chapter 13.
- Establishing and operating contingency funds is covered by Article 6(5) and (6). See Chapter 8.
- Article 6 includes requirements when a CSP offers individual portfolio management of loans. This is the allocation by the CSP of a predetermined amount of funds of an investor, which is an original lender, to one or multiple crowdfunding projects on its crowdfunding platform in accordance with an individual mandate given by the investor on a discretionary investor-by-investor basis.[17] This service does not qualify as a crowdfunding service, but when provided by a CSP, it should adhere to the requirements set in that respect in Article 6 of the Crowdfunding Regulation. See also Chapter 8.

3. Authorization Process

Only legal persons that have an effective and stable establishment in the EU, including the necessary resources, are able to apply for authorization as CSPs under the Crowdfunding Regulation.[18] This means that undertakings which are not legal persons and natural persons cannot obtain an authorization as a CSP.[19] A legal person who intends to provide crowdfunding services has to apply to the competent authority of the Member State where it is established for authorization as a CSP.[20] Under MiFID II, the authorization requirement only applies where the provision of investment services and/or performance of investment activities takes place *as a regular occupation or business on a professional basis.*[21] The Crowdfunding Regulation does not contain such a condition for the authorization

7.10

---

[16] See also Art 25(4) Crowdfunding Regulation.
[17] Art 2(1) point (c) Crowdfunding Regulation.
[18] Art 3(1) Crowdfunding Regulation.
[19] Art 4(1)(1) MiFID II allows Member States to include in the definition of investment firms undertakings which are not legal persons and even natural persons, provided that the conditions set out in Art 4(1)(1) MiFID II are met.
[20] Art 12(1) Crowdfunding Regulation.
[21] Art 5(1) Crowdfunding Regulation.

requirement to apply. The practical relevance thereof may be in the moment that the authorization requirement is triggered. This may be as soon as the CSP provides one crowdfunding service.

A. Authorization Requirements

7.11   The application for the authorization has to include the name, Internet address and physical address, legal form, and articles of association of the CSP. In addition, a programme of operations and a description of the CSP's governance arrangements, internal control mechanisms, systems, resources and procedures for the control and safeguarding of the data processing systems, operational risks, prudential safeguards (including proof that these are met), business continuity plan, internal rules for preventing certain persons affiliated with the CSP from engaging as project owners in crowdfunding services offered by the prospective CSP, outsourcing arrangements, complaint handling procedures, and procedures in relation to investment limits for non-sophisticated investors have to be included. Also, the identity of the natural persons responsible for the management of the CSP and proof that such persons are of good repute and possess sufficient knowledge, skills, and experience to manage the prospective CSP[22] have to be provided. Lastly, the prospective CSP has to confirm whether it intends to provide payment services itself or through a third party.[23]

7.12   Article 2 of the draft RTS on the authorization process of ESMA establishes that an applicant seeking authorization as a CSP in accordance with Article 12 of the Crowdfunding Regulation has to submit to the competent authority its application by filling in the template set out in the Annex of the draft RTS. In order for competent authorities to fulfil their obligations and be able to analyse the files received by legal persons who intend to provide crowdfunding services, the Annex to the draft RTS further specifies the information listed in Article 12(2) of the Crowdfunding Regulation that has to be provided by applicants for purposes of being authorized as a CSP. Interestingly, the Annex also requires CSPs to include in their application proof of good repute of shareholders who directly or indirectly hold 20% or more of the share capital or voting rights in the CSP. This requirement cannot be derived as such from the Crowdfunding Regulation, although Article 12(3)(a) Crowdfunding Regulation mentions those shareholders.

7.13   Under MiFID II, the authorization requirements are actually quite similar. Commission Delegated Regulation (EU) 2017/1943 sets out in detail what information and documents need to be provided in the application for a MiFID II authorization. Although this may be a bit more extensive than provided in the Annex to the draft RTS on the authorization process under the Crowdfunding Regulation (eg in respect of the information that needs to be provided about the members of the management board), there are quite some similarities. It remains therefore to be seen whether the application process under the Crowdfunding Regulation will indeed be considered less arduous compared to the MiFID II application process.

---

[22]   As further detailed in Art 12(3) Crowdfunding Regulation.
[23]   Art 12(2) Crowdfunding Regulation.

B. Timeline of the Application Process

With regard to the timeline of the application process, Article 3 of the draft RTS specifies   **7.14**
that the competent authority in principle needs to send an acknowledgment of receipt of
the application within ten working days from the day of receipt of the application. The competent authority has to assess within twenty-five working days of receipt of the application
assess whether the application is complete. Where the competent authority requires the applicant to provide missing information, the deadline for the completion of the assessment
shall be suspended from the date of request for information until the date of receipt of such
information.[24] Where an application remains incomplete after the deadline given by the
competent authority to complete the application, the application may be refused. Where an
application is complete, the competent authority has to notify the prospective CSP immediately. The competent authority has to adopt a fully reasoned decision granting or refusing
to grant authorization as a CSP within three months from the date of receipt of a complete
application. If there are any changes to the information provided in the application for authorization, the applicant needs to inform the competent authority without undue delay. If
the changes are material, the application shall be treated as a new application.[25]

In the Commission Proposal, when ESMA was still the competent authority, these time-   **7.15**
lines were considerably shorter. According to the proposal, ESMA would have had to assess within twenty working days whether the application is complete. In addition, it would
have had to adopt a fully reasoned decision on the application within two months.[26] The
timelines in the final Crowdfunding Regulation are however, compared to MiFID II, still
relatively short. Under MiFID II, competent authorities have six months after submission
of the complete application to inform the application whether or not authorization will be
granted.[27] Taking into account that the information and documents that need to be provided in the application under the Crowdfunding Regulation are quite similar to the information and documents that need to be provided under MiFID II, this process may turn
out to be arduous for the competent authorities responsible for handling the authorization
applications under the Crowdfunding Regulation.

C. Assessment Process

In its assessment, the competent authority assesses whether the prospective CSP com-   **7.16**
plies with the requirements set out in the Crowdfunding Regulation. The assessment shall
take into account the nature, scale, and complexity of the crowdfunding services that the
prospective CSP intends to provide. Article 12(8) of the Crowdfunding Regulation states
that the competent authority may refuse authorization if there are objective and demonstrable grounds for believing that the management body of the prospective CSP could pose
a threat to its effective, sound, and prudent management and business continuity, and to
the adequate consideration of the interest of its clients and the integrity of the market. We
understand this to be a separate ground for refusal besides not complying with the (other)
requirements set out in the Crowdfunding Regulation. For example, if the prospective CSP

---

[24] Art 4 draft RTS.
[25] Art 5 draft RTS.
[26] Art 10(6) Commission Proposal.
[27] Art 7(3) MiFID II.

has not sufficient own funds to comply with the prudential requirements, or an adequate in-surance policy, this could also be a ground for refusal of the authorization.

7.17   When a competent authority decides to grant an authorization, it needs to inform ESMA thereof. ESMA may request information from the competent authority in order to ensure that the competent authorities of the Member States grant authorizations in a consistent manner.[28] In certain cases, the competent authority needs to consult the competent au-thority of another Member States before adopting a decision granting or refusing to grant authorization. This is the case, when the prospective CSP is the subsidiary of (the parent undertaking of), or controlled by the same natural or legal person who controls, a CSP au-thorized in another Member State.[29]

7.18   Lastly, the Crowdfunding Regulation provides for a 'light' authorization process when a CSP is already authorized pursuant to one of the directives mentioned in Article 12(14) of the Crowdfunding Regulation or when a CSP simultaneously applies for an authorization under PSD 2. See further section IV.

4. Withdrawal of Authorization

7.19   The competent authority that has granted the authorization also has the power to with-draw the authorization in the situations set out in the Crowdfunding Regulation. These situations are that the CSP has not used its authorization within eighteen months of the date of granting the authorization, has expressly renounced its authorization, has not provided crowdfunding services for nine successive months and is also no longer involved in the ad-ministration of existing contracts that are the result of initial matching of business funding interests through the use of its crowdfunding platform, has obtained its authorization by irregular means, including making false statements in its application for authorization, no longer meets the conditions under which the authorization was granted, or has seriously infringed the Crowdfunding Regulation.[30] In addition, competent authorities should also have the power to withdraw an authorization under the Crowdfunding Regulation when-ever a CSP, or a third party acting on its behalf, has lost its authorization allowing for the provision of payment services under PSD II or investment services under MiFID II, or whenever a CSP that is also a payment service provider, or its managers, employees, or a third party acting on its behalf, has infringed national law implementing the Fourth Anti-money Laundering (AML) Directive.[31] CSPs are, as such, not in scope of the Fourth AML Directive.[32] The withdrawal grounds included in the Crowdfunding Regulation are com-parable to the ones included in MiFID II provided that under MiFID II the authorization

---

[28]   Art 12(9) Crowdfunding Regulation.
[29]   Art. 12(7) Crowdfunding Regulation.
[30]   Art 17(1) Crowdfunding Regulation.
[31]   See also Recital 32 Crowdfunding Regulation.
[32]   See also Chapter 8. This may however change in the future. Recital 32 of the Crowdfunding Regulation states that with a view to further ensuring market integrity by preventing risks of money laundering and terrorist fi-nancing, and taking into account the amount of funds that can be raised by a crowdfunding offer in accordance with this Regulation, the Commission should assess the necessity and proportionality of subjecting CSPs to obli-gations to comply with national law implementing the Fourth AML Directive in respect of money laundering or terrorist financing and of adding such CSPs to the list of obliged entities for the purposes of that directive.

can be withdrawn when the investment firm does not make use of its authorization within twelve months or has not provided investment services or performed investment activities for the preceding six months.[33]

The competent authority that is designated as the single point of contact (see subsection **7.20** II.1) needs to notify ESMA and the competent authorities of the other Member States in which the CSP provides crowdfunding services without undue delay of the withdrawal. Before making a decision to withdraw the authorization, the competent authority needs to consult the competent authorities of other Member States in the same situations as required before making a decision to grant the authorization (see subsection II.3).[34]

5. Cross-border Provision of Crowdfunding Services

Article 18 of the Crowdfunding Regulation contains the notification procedure that CSPs **7.21** need to follow when they want to provide crowdfunding services in other Member States (the so-called EU passport). In order to obtain that EU passport, the CSP should submit its application to the competent authority designated as the single point of contact (see subsection II.1) by the Member State where authorization was granted. The application should include the following information: a list of Member States where the CSP intends to provide crowdfunding services; the identity of the natural and legal persons responsible for the provision of such services in these Member States; the starting date of the intended provision of the services; and a list of any other activities conducted by the CSP not covered by the Crowdfunding Regulation. It is our understanding that these other activities, such as payment services or investment services, are not covered by the EU passport provided under the Crowdfunding Regulation. It would therefore be necessary to check whether an EU passport could be obtained under the relevant EU acts for these activities. If these activities are not covered by an EU act that includes a EU passport, for example the Consumer Credit Directive (CCD), it will not be possible to conduct these activities on a cross-border basis.

After receipt of the application, the competent authority needs to communicate the infor- **7.22** mation of such application to the competent authorities of the Member States in which the CSP intends to provide crowdfunding services and to ESMA within ten working days. The competent authority will inform the CSP of this communication without delay. The crowdfunding service provider may start to provide crowdfunding services on the basis of the EU passport from the date of the receipt of such communication by the competent authority or at the latest fifteen calendar days after submitting the information for the application.[35]

Recital 31 of the Crowdfunding Regulation stipulates that Member States are not allowed to **7.23** impose additional requirements on those CSPs that are authorized under the Crowdfunding Regulation in order to enable CSPs to operate cross-border without facing divergent rules and thereby to facilitate the funding of projects across the EU by investors from different Member States. Although Article 18 of the Crowdfunding Regulation does not reiterate this, it is our understanding that it is meant that the EU passport enables CSPs to provide

---

[33] Art 8(a) MiFID II.
[34] Art 17(3) Crowdfunding Regulation.
[35] Art 18(2)-(4) Crowdfunding Regulation.

crowdfunding services on a cross-border basis without being faced with additional requirements in other Member States. Otherwise, the main objective of the Crowdfunding
Regulation, for example breaking down the barriers that obstruct cross-border provision of
crowdfunding services, would be hindered.[36]

7.24 Lastly, Member States may not require CSPs that provide crowdfunding service on a cross-
border basis to have a physical presence in the territory of a Member State other than the
Member State in which those CSPs are authorized.[37]

7.25 The Crowdfunding Regulation does not contain a third-country regime. As a result,
Member States have the possibility to adopt a national regime allowing access of third
country CSPs to their jurisdiction. Such third country CSPs cannot obtain authorization
under the Crowdfunding Regulation and can therefore also not obtain an EU passport.[38]

6. Register of Crowdfunding Service Providers

7.26 To facilitate transparency for investors as regards the provision of crowdfunding services,
ESMA keeps a public and up-to-date register of all CSPs authorized in accordance with the
Crowdfunding Regulation on its website.[39] That register includes information on all operating crowdfunding platforms in the EU, including information on the crowdfunding services for which the CSP is authorized, a list of Member States in which the CSP has notified
its intention to provide crowdfunding services, any other services provided by the CSP not
covered by the Crowdfunding Regulation (see section IV) and any penalties imposed on
the CSP or its manager.[40] In respect of the latter, ESMA is dependent on the national competent authorities providing this information, as they are the authorities imposing such
penalties (see subsection III.6 on the cooperation between ESMA and the national competent authorities). Also, information on the withdrawal of an authorization is included in the
register by ESMA.[41]

III. Supervision by the Competent Authorities

1. Obligations of Crowdfunding Service Providers towards
Competent Authorities

7.27 CSPs need, at all times, meet the conditions for their authorization.[42] They have to notify
the relevant competent authority of any material changes to the conditions for authorization without undue delay and provide, upon request, the information needed to assess their
compliance with the Crowdfunding Regulation.[43] In addition, CSPs have to provide a list of

[36] See Recitals 6–8 and 30 Crowdfunding Regulation.
[37] Art 12(12) Crowdfunding Regulation.
[38] See also Chapter 3.
[39] Art 14 Crowdfunding Regulation.
[40] Art 39 Crowdfunding Regulation.
[41] Art 17(2) Crowdfunding Regulation.
[42] Art 12(11) Crowdfunding Regulation. See also Chapter 8.
[43] Art 15(2) Crowdfunding Regulation.

projects funded through their crowdfunding platforms to the competent authority, specifying for each project: the project owner and the amount raised, the instruments issued and
aggregated information about the investors, and invested amount broken down by fiscal
residency of the investors, distinguishing between sophisticated and non-sophisticated investors.[44] This list should be provided annually and on a confidential basis. The competent
authorities need to provide this information to ESMA in anonymized format, which, in
its turn, develops and publishes aggregated annual statistics relating to the crowdfunding
market in the EU on its website. On 26 February 2021, ESMA published draft implementing
technical standards (ITS) specifying data standards and formats, templates and procedures
for reporting information on projects funded through crowdfunding platforms.[45] It can be
derived from these draft ITS that CSPs need to provide the information in relation to each
calendar year by the end of February of the following calendar year.

In addition, the relevant competent authority assesses the compliance with the obligations   **7.28**
provided for in the Crowdfunding Regulation. The frequency and depth of that assessment
should be determined having regard to the nature, scale, and complexity of the CSP. For
the purpose of that assessment, the competent authority may subject the CSP to an on-site
inspection.[46]

2. Investigatory and Supervisory Powers

In order to fulfil their duties under the Crowdfunding Regulation, the competent author-   **7.29**
ities need to have certain investigatory and supervisory powers in accordance with national
law. The investigatory powers should at least include the power (a) to require CSPs and
third parties designated to perform functions in relation to the provision of crowdfunding
services, and the natural or legal persons that control them or are controlled by them, to
provide information and documents; (b) to require auditors and managers of the CSPs,
and of third parties designated to perform functions in relation to the provision of crowdfunding services, to provide information; and (c) to carry out on-site inspections or investigations at sites other than the private residences of natural persons, and for that purpose
to enter premises in order to access documents and other data in any form, where a reasonable suspicion exists that documents and other data related to the subject matter of the
inspection or investigation may be relevant to prove an infringement of the Crowdfunding
Regulation.[47] Compared to the investigatory powers under MiFID II, it is interesting that
the Crowdfunding Regulation does not mention the power to require existing recordings of
telephone conversations or electronic communications or other data traffic records held by
a CSP,[48] despite the fact that the Crowdfunding Regulation provides for several recording
obligations for CSPs to facilitate transparency and to ensure proper documentation of communications with clients.[49] Also, the power to summon and question a person with a view

---

[44] Art 16(1) Crowdfunding Regulation.
[45] ESMA, Consultation Paper Draft technical standards under the ECSP Regulation, ESMA/35-36-2201, 26
February 2021, Annex X Draft ITS pursuant to Art 16(3) of the ECSPR.
[46] Art 15(3) Crowdfunding Regulation.
[47] Art 30(1) Crowdfunding Regulation.
[48] Art 69(2)(d) MiFID II.
[49] Recital 56 Crowdfunding Regulation. See Arts 4(4)(g), 6(3), 7(3), 22(4), and 26 Crowdfunding Regulation.
See also Recital 144 MiFID II in that respect, which states that access to recordings constitutes crucial, and

to obtaining information is not included.[50] The fact that the Crowdfunding Regulation does not include these powers does not mean that Member States cannot decide to grant more powers to their competent authorities. The Crowdfunding Regulation provides for minimum harmonization in that respect. The same applies for the supervisory powers.

7.30   The supervisory powers should at least include the power (a) to suspend a crowdfunding offer for a maximum of ten consecutive working days on any single occasion where there are reasonable grounds for suspecting that this Crowdfunding Regulation has been infringed; (b) to prohibit or suspend marketing communications, or to require a CSP or a third party designated to perform functions in relation to the provision of crowdfunding services to cease or suspend marketing communications, for a maximum of ten consecutive working days on any single occasion where there are reasonable grounds for believing that the Crowdfunding Regulation has been infringed; (c) to prohibit a crowdfunding offer where they find that the Crowdfunding Regulation has been infringed or where there are reasonable grounds for suspecting that it would be infringed; (d) to suspend, or to require a CSP to suspend, the provision of crowdfunding services for a maximum of ten consecutive working days on any single occasion where there are reasonable grounds for believing that the Crowdfunding Regulation has been infringed; (e) to prohibit the provision of crowdfunding services where they find that the Crowdfunding Regulation has been infringed; (f) to make public the fact that a CSP or a third party designated to perform functions in relation to the provision of crowdfunding services is failing to comply with its obligations; (g) to disclose, or to require a CSP or a third party designated to perform functions in relation to the provision of crowdfunding services to disclose, all material information which may have an effect on the provision of the crowdfunding service in order to ensure investor protection or the smooth operation of the market; (h) to suspend, or to require a CSP or a third party designated to perform functions in relation to the provision of crowdfunding services to suspend, the provision of crowdfunding services where the competent authorities consider that the CSP's situation is such that the provision of the crowdfunding service would be detrimental to investors' interests; and (i) to transfer existing contracts to another CSP in cases where a CSP's authorization is withdrawn because it has not provided crowdfunding services for nine successive months and is also no longer involved in the administration of existing contracts that are the result of initial matching of business funding interests through the use of its crowdfunding platform, subject to the agreement of the clients and the receiving CSP.[51] The supervisory powers in the Crowdfunding Regulation focus on the prohibition or suspension of services and the power to disclose information. Although they are tailored to crowdfunding services, they are more or less comparable to the supervisory powers in MiFID II.[52]

---

sometimes the only, evidence to, *inter alia*, detect and prove the existence of market abuse and to verify compliance by firms with investor protection (Gortsos (n 7) 539).

[50]   See Art 69(2)(b) MiFID II.

[51]   Art 30(2) Crowdfunding Regulation. The CSP to which the existing contracts are transferred must be authorized to provide crowdfunding services in the same Member State where the original CSP was authorized (Art 30(4) Crowdfunding Regulation).

[52]   Art 69(2) MiFID II.

3. Powers to Impose Sanctions

In addition to the supervisory and investigatory powers, competent authorities need to   **7.31**
have[53] the power to impose administrative penalties and take appropriate other administrative measures in accordance with national law in respect of infringements of certain Articles of the Crowdfunding Regulation and the failure to cooperate or comply in an investigation or with an inspection or request to provide information or documents.[54] The powers should include at least the power to impose (a) a public statement indicating the natural or legal person responsible for, and the nature of, the infringement; (b) an order requiring the natural or legal person to cease the conduct constituting the infringement and to desist from a repetition of that conduct; (c) a ban preventing any member of the management body of the legal person responsible for the infringement, or any other natural person held responsible for the infringement, from exercising management functions in CSPs; (d) maximum administrative fines of at least twice the amount of the benefit derived from the infringement where that benefit can be determined, even if it exceeds the maximum amounts set out in point (e); (e) in the case of a legal person, maximum administrative fines of at least EUR 500,000 or of up to 5% of the total annual turnover of that legal person according to the last available financial statements approved by the management body; and (f) in the case of a natural person, maximum administrative fines of at least EUR 500,000.[55] Member States may provide for additional penalties or measures and for higher levels of administrative fines than those provided for in the Crowdfunding Regulation, in respect of both natural and legal persons responsible for the infringement.[56]

The powers to impose sanctions, as mentioned above, are fairly comparable to the powers   **7.32**
included in MiFID II. The maximum administrative fines that can be imposed in case of violation of MiFID II are however much higher, at EUR 5 million or (in the case of a legal person) up to 10% of the total annual turnover.[57]

4. Publication of Decisions

Competent authorities have to publish the following decisions on their website: (a) a deci-   **7.33**
sion imposing administrative penalties or other administrative measures for infringement of the Crowdfunding Regulation; (b) where the decision to impose a penalty or measure is subject to appeal before the relevant judicial or other authorities, such information and any subsequent information on the outcome of such appeal; and (c) any decision annulling a previous decision to impose a penalty or a measure. Any publication has to remain on the website for a period of at least five years after its publication.[58]

---

[53] Unless the relevant Member State decided to subject the infringements to criminal penalties under national law (Art 39(1) para 2 Crowdfunding Regulation).
[54] Art 39(1) Crowdfunding Regulation.
[55] Art 39(2) Crowdfunding Regulation.
[56] Art 39(3) Crowdfunding Regulation.
[57] Art 70(6) MiFID II.
[58] Art 42(1), (3), and (4) Crowdfunding Regulation. Personal data contained in the publication should be kept only for the period which is necessary in accordance with the applicable data protection rules (Art 42(4) Crowdfunding Regulation).

7.34   The decision to impose administrative penalties or other administrative measures has to be published immediately after the natural or legal person subject to that decision has been informed of that decision. Where the decision is subject to appeal, such information also has to be published immediately on the website.[59]

7.35   The publication of the decision to impose administrative penalties or other administrative measures has to include at least information on the type and nature of the infringement and the identity of the natural or legal persons responsible. Where the publication of the identity is considered by the competent authority to be disproportionate, following a case-by-case assessment, or where such publication would jeopardize an ongoing investigation, competent authorities may defer the publication, publish the decision on an anonymous basis, or not publish the decision where the other options are considered to be insufficient to ensure the proportionality of the publication with regard to measures which are deemed to be of a minor nature.[60]

7.36   This publication regime is similar to the publication regime included in MiFID II, the only difference being that under MiFID II competent authorities may decide not to publish a decision if deferring the publication or publishing the decision on an anonymous basis would put the stability of the financial markets in jeopardy.[61]

5. Safeguards when Exercising Powers

7.37   Any supervisory measures adopted and any administrative penalty or other administrative measure to be imposed should be proportionate, duly justified, and taken in accordance with the safeguards set out in Article 40 of the Crowdfunding Regulation.[62] In addition, any decision taken under the Crowdfunding Regulation should be properly reasoned and subject to the right of appeal before a tribunal. The right of appeal before a tribunal should also apply where, in respect of an application for authorization which provides all the information required, no decision is taken within six months of its submission.[63] These safeguards are similar to the safeguards included in MiFID II.[64] This Directive, however, imposes on Member States that they shall provide that certain bodies may also take action before the courts or competent authorities in the interests of consumers and in accordance with national law.[65] It could have benefited the consumer-investors, if such a provision was included in the Crowdfunding Regulation.

---

[59] Art 42(1) and (3) Crowdfunding Regulation.
[60] Art 42(2) Crowdfunding Regulation.
[61] Art 71(1) MiFID II.
[62] Art 30(2) para 2 Crowdfunding Regulation. Art 40(1) and (2) Crowdfunding Regulation.
[63] Art 41 Crowdfunding Regulation.
[64] Art 72(2) and 74 MiFID II.
[65] Art 74(2) MiFID II.

6. Cooperation

A. Cooperation between Competent Authorities

The competent authorities have to cooperate with each other for the purposes of the   **7.38**
Crowdfunding Regulation. They have to exchange information without undue delay and
cooperate in investigation, supervision, and enforcement activities. Where Member States
have chosen to lay down criminal penalties for an infringement of the Crowdfunding
Regulation, they have to ensure that appropriate measures are in place so that competent
authorities have all the necessary powers to liaise with judicial, prosecuting, or criminal
justice authorities within their jurisdiction to receive specific information related to criminal investigations or proceedings commenced for infringements of the Crowdfunding
Regulation and to provide the same information to other competent authorities as well as
to ESMA. A competent authority may refuse to act on a request for information or a request
to cooperate with an investigation only in any of the following circumstances: (a) where
complying with the request is likely to adversely affect its own investigation, enforcement
activities or a criminal investigation; (b) where judicial proceedings have already been initiated in respect of the same actions and against the same natural or legal persons before the
authorities of the Member State addressed; or (c) where a final judgment has already been
delivered in relation to such natural or legal persons for the same actions in the Member
State addressed.[66]

Where a CSP provides crowdfunding services on a cross-border basis, the competent au-   **7.39**
thority of the Member State in which such services are provided on a cross-border basis
(the competent authority of the host Member State) should notify the competent authority
which granted the authorization (the competent authority of the home Member State) and
ESMA when it has clear and demonstrable grounds for believing that irregularities have
been committed by the CSP or by third parties designated to perform functions in relation
to the provision of crowdfunding services or that the CSP or third parties have infringed
their obligations under the Crowdfunding Regulation. Where such infringement persists,
despite measures taken by the competent authority of the home Member State, the competent authority of the host Member State can, after having informed the competent authority
of the home Member State and ESMA, take all appropriate measures in order to protect
investors (so-called precautionary measures). When this leads to a dispute between the
competent authorities involved, the matter may be brought to the attention of ESMA who
can then act in accordance with the powers conferred on it under Article 19 of the ESMA
Regulation.[67]

B. Cooperation between Competent Authorities and ESMA

The competent authorities also have to cooperate closely with ESMA for the purposes   **7.40**
of the Crowdfunding Regulation. They shall exchange information in order to carry out
their duties.[68] In addition to this general cooperation requirement, competent authorities
are required to provide ESMA on an annual basis with aggregate information regarding

---

[66] Art 31 Crowdfunding Regulation.
[67] Art 37 Crowdfunding Regulation.
[68] Art 32 Crowdfunding Regulation.

all administrative penalties and other administrative measures. In addition, they have to provide ESMA annually with anonymized and aggregated data regarding all criminal investigations undertaken and criminal penalties imposed. Administrative penalties, other administrative measures, or criminal penalties that have been disclosed to the public, should be simultaneously reported to ESMA. Competent authorities also need to inform ESMA of all administrative penalties or other administrative measures imposed but not published, including any appeal in relation thereto and the outcome thereof. Member States have to ensure that competent authorities receive information and the final judgment in relation to any criminal penalty imposed and submit it to ESMA. This Authority maintains a central database of penalties and administrative measures communicated to it solely for the purposes of exchanging information between competent authorities. That database is only accessible to ESMA, EBA, and the competent authorities and is updated on the basis of the information provided by the competent authorities.[69] As discussed in section II.6, the publicly available register of CSPs also includes information on the penalties imposed on them.

C. Cooperation with Other Authorities

7.41   Lastly, where a CSP engages in activities other than those covered by its CSP authorization, the competent authorities shall cooperate with the authorities responsible for the oversight of such other activities as provided for in the relevant Union or national law.[70]

7. Complaint Handling

7.42   Competent authorities need to have procedures which allow clients and other interested parties, including consumer associations, to submit complaints to the competent authorities with regard to CSPs' alleged infringements of the Crowdfunding Regulation. In all cases, complaints should be accepted in written or electronic form and in an official language of the Member State in which the complaint is submitted or in a language accepted by the competent authorities of that Member State.[71] On 26 February 2021, ESMA published draft RTS specifying the requirements, standard formats, and procedures for complaint handling by CSPs.[72] These draft RTS do not contain any further requirements in respect of complaint handling by competent authorities.

7.43   The Crowdfunding Regulation is also included in Part I.B of the Annex to the Whistleblower Directive.[73] This means that the common minimum standards under this directive apply for the protection of persons reporting breaches of the Crowdfunding Regulation, both internally (within the CSP) and externally (to the competent authority).

---

[69] Art 43 Crowdfunding Regulation.
[70] Art 33 Crowdfunding Regulation. See on the cooperation arrangements under MiFID II: Gortsos (n 7) 551–63.
[71] Art 38 Crowdfunding Regulation.
[72] ESMA, Consultation Paper Draft technical standards under the ECSP Regulation, ESMA/35-36-2201, 26 February 2021, Annex III Draft RTS pursuant to Article 7(5) of the ECSPR.
[73] Art 47 Crowdfunding Regulation. See Art 50 Crowdfunding Regulation in respect of the transposition of the amendment of the Whistle-blower Directive.

IV. Other Activities by Crowdfunding Service Providers

Article 12(13) of the Crowdfunding Regulation explicitly states that CSPs authorized under   **7.44**
the Crowdfunding Regulation may also engage in activities other than those covered by
the CSP authorization in accordance with the relevant applicable EU or national law.[74]
The Crowdfunding Regulation remains silent on the nature of such 'other activities'. It is
not clear whether these are the same as those mentioned in the Annex to the draft RTS
from ESMA on the authorization process, as mentioned in section II.2. In this section, we
therefore discuss the potential applicable EU law to other activities that may be provided by
CSPs, also taking into account the opinions of EBA and ESMA.[75]

1. Investment Services

As indicated in section II.2, the scope of the Crowdfunding Regulation includes   **7.45**
crowdinvesting services. To some extent, the provision of such services may also qualify as
the provision of one or more investment services to third parties or the performance of one
or more investment activities on a professional basis, within the meaning of MiFID II, for
which, in principle, an authorization under MiFID II is required. This necessitates the need
to look at the interplay between the Crowdfunding Regulation and MiFID II.

A. Exemption of MiFID II?
CSPs falling under the scope of the Crowdfunding Regulation are exempt from the applica-   **7.46**
tion of MiFID II.[76] However, should a CSP provide investment services which do not qualify
as crowdfunding services within the meaning of Article 2((1))(a) of the Crowdfunding
Regulation, authorization under MiFID II still is required. The possibility of the need to seek
authorization under MiFID II is also explicitly worded in Recital 35 of the Crowdfunding
Regulation, which reads: 'It should be possible for entities that have been authorised under
… [MiFID II] … and that intend to provide crowdfunding services, to hold an authorisation
both under [that Directive] and under this Regulation. '[77]

It should be noted that where an entity authorized pursuant to MiFID II prior to the ap-   **7.47**
plication of the Crowdfunding Regulation applies for authorization as a CSP under the
Crowdfunding Regulation, the competent authority shall not require that entity to provide
information or documents which it has already submitted when applying for authorization

---

[74] See also E Macchiavello, 'FinTech Regulation from a Cross-Sectoral Perspective' in V Colaert, D Busch, and T Incalza, *European Financial Regulation: Levelling the Cross-Sectoral Playing Field* (Hart 2019) 69–70.

[75] EBA, Opinion on Lending-Based Crowdfunding, EBA/Op/2015/03, 26 February 2015 and ESMA, Opinion on Investment-Based Crowdfunding, ESMA/2014/1378, 18 December 2014. In these opinions, EBA and ESMA discuss the potentially applicable EU-level regulatory regimes for lending-based crowdfunding and investment-based crowdfunding, respectively. EBA mentions the applicability of PSD (currently PSD 2).

[76] The Crowdfunding Directive adds an exemption to Art 2(1) MiFID II which exempts the application of MiFID II to 'crowdfunding service providers as defined in point (e) of Article 2(1) of Regulation (EU) 2020/1503 of the European Parliament and of the Council'. A reference to the Crowdfunding Directive is made in Recital 75 Crowdfunding Regulation, which states that the date of application of the Crowdfunding Regulation should be deferred to align it with the date of application of the national rules transposing the Crowdfunding Directive.

[77] It is also addressed in Art 12(13) Crowdfunding Regulation. This paragraph reads: 'Crowdfunding service providers authorized under this Regulation may also engage in activities other than those covered by the authorization referred to in this Article in accordance with the relevant applicable Union or national law.'

pursuant to MiFID II, provided that such information or documents remain up-to-date and are accessible to the competent authority.[78]

B. Investment Services and Activities

7.48   Under MiFID II, an investment firm is any legal person whose regular occupation or business is the provision of one or more investment services to third parties and/or the performance of one or more investment activities on a professional basis.[79] Investment services and activities comprise the following services:

- the reception and transmission of orders in relation to one or more financial instruments;
- the execution of orders on behalf of clients;
- dealing on own account;
- portfolio management;
- investment advice;
- underwriting of financial instruments and/or placing of financial instruments on a firm commitment basis;
- placing of financial instruments without a firm commitment basis;
- the operation of a multilateral trading facility; and
- the operation of an organized trading facility,

in as far as these services and activities relate to financial instruments as specified in section C of Annex I of MiFID II.[80] Such financial instruments include, amongst others, transferable securities and units in collective investment undertakings.

7.49   Next we look into the relation of the abovementioned investment services and activities on the one hand and the two crowdfunding services, (a) the facilitation of granting loans and (b) placing without a firm commitment basis, regulated in the Crowdfunding Regulation on the other.

C. The Facilitation of Granting Loans

7.50   As indicated above in section II.2, the facilitation of granting of loans is one of the crowdfunding services in scope of the Crowdfunding Regulation. The regulation, however, does not contain a definition of this service. According to Recital 11, this service consist of services as presenting crowdfunding offers to clients and pricing or assessing the credit risk of crowdfunding projects or project owners. Under the Crowdfunding Regulation, a 'loan' means an agreement whereby an investor makes available to a project owner an agreed amount of money for an agreed period of time and whereby the project owner assumes an unconditional obligation to repay that amount to the investor, together with the accrued interest, in accordance with the instalment payment schedule.[81] The elements 'agreed period of time', 'agreed amount of money', 'unconditional obligation to repay that amount', 'accrued interest', and 'instalment payment schedule' in the definition of 'loan' bear similarities to the concept of certain 'transferable securities'[82] within the meaning of MiFID

---

[78]   Art 12(14) Crowdfunding Regulation.
[79]   Art 4(1)(1) MiFID II.
[80]   Art 4(1)(2) MiFID II.
[81]   Art 2(1)(b) Crowdfunding Regulation.
[82]   Art 4(1)(44) MiFID II.

II,[83] particularly when one looks at the investment service 'portfolio management'. Under MiFID II, 'portfolio management' means managing portfolios in accordance with mandates given by clients on a discretionary client-by-client basis where such portfolios include one or more financial instruments.[84] This type of service should not be confused with business models using automated processes whereby funds are automatically allocated by the CSP to crowdfunding projects in accordance with parameters and risk indicators predetermined by the investor, so called auto-investing.[85] The latter services are considered to be individual portfolio management of loans instead of management one or more financial instruments, and fall within the scope of the definition of a crowdfunding service.[86] Here, a reference has to be made to Recital 19 of the Crowdfunding Relation, which states that the authorization obtained under the Crowdfunding Regulation should not grant CSPs the right to provide individual or collective asset management services. In order to provide *individual* asset management services, a CSP would, in principle, need to obtain authorization under MiFID II, whereas in order to provide *collective* asset management services, a CSP would, in principle, need to seek authorization or registration under the Alternative Investment Fund Managers and Undertaking for the Collective Investment in Transferable Securities (AIFMD/UCITS) Directives. The latter is discussed below in section IV.2.

D. Placing without a Firm Commitment Basis

As indicated above in section II.2, the second of the crowdfunding services is the placing without a firm commitment basis, as referred to in point (7) of section A of Annex I to MiFID II, of transferable securities and admitted instruments for crowdfunding purposes issued by project owners or a SPV, and the reception and transmission of client orders, as referred to in point (1) of that section, in relation to those transferable securities and admitted instruments for crowdfunding purposes. For the provision of these services, a CSP does not have to seek additional authorization under MiFID II.

7.51

E. The Reception and Transmission of Orders in Relation to One or More Financial Instruments and Executing Orders on Behalf of Clients

A CSP may perform the investment service 'the reception and transmission of orders in relation to one or more financial instruments' if he is both receiving and transmitting orders.[87] Should the CSP act as an agent for a client or commit a client to a transaction, he will do more than merely receiving and transmitting orders and will need to need to consider whether he provides the investment service of 'executing orders on behalf of clients'.[88]

7.52

F. Investment Advice

On the basis of Article 3(4) CSPs may propose to individual investors specific crowdfunding projects that correspond to one or more specific parameters or risk indicators chosen by the investor. The risk indicators can include the type or sector of business activity or a credit

7.53

---

[83] Compare ELM van Kranenburg and DAJM Melchers, *De toekomstige Europese Verordening voor Crowdfundingdienstverleners (Deel II)* (Tijdschrift voor Financieel Recht 2020-12) 9.

[84] Art 4(1)(8) MiFID II.

[85] See Recital 20 Crowdfunding Regulation.

[86] Art (1)(1)(i)(a) Crowdfunding Regulation.

[87] SN Hooghiemstra, *The European Crowdfunding Regulation—towards harmonization of (Equity- and Lending-based) Crowdfunding in Europe?*, <https://ssrn.com/abstract = 3679142> accessed on 3 June 2021.

[88] ibid.

rating, which have been communicated in advance to the CSP by the investor.[89] It is worth wondering whether such proposals constitute 'investment advice' within the meaning of MiFID II. This might depend on whether the crowdfunding proposal is to be seen as a 'personal recommendation'.

7.54 In this respect, it is worth noting that according to Recital 21 of the Crowdfunding Regulation:

> the existence of filtering tools on a crowdfunding platform under this Regulation should not be regarded as investment advice under Directive 2014/65/EU as long as those tools provide information to clients in a neutral manner that does not constitute a recommendation. Such tools should include those that display results based on criteria relating to purely objective product features. Objective product features in the context of a crowdfunding platform could be pre-defined project criteria such as the economic sector, the instrument used and the interest rate, or the risk category where sufficient information regarding the calculation method is disclosed. Similarly, key financial figures calculated without any scope for discretion should also be considered to be objective criteria.

G. The Operation of a Multilateral Trading Facility or an Organized Trading Facility

7.55 CSPs may operate a bulletin board on which they allow their clients to advertise interest in buying and selling loans, transferable securities, or admitted instruments for crowdfunding purposes that were originally offered on their crowdfunding platforms.[90] The bulletin board should not be used to bring together buying and selling interests by means of the CSP's protocols or internal operating procedures in a way that results in a contract.[91] If, however, it does bring together buying and selling interest in a way that results in a contract, it will possibly be deemed to be an internal matching system which executes client orders on a multilateral basis, for which, if in relation to transferable securities, the CSP will need a separate authorization as an investment firm in accordance with Article 5 of MiFID II, or as a regulated market in accordance with Article 44 of that Directive.[92]

7.56 It is worth noting that CSPs that do not hold such an authorization in relation to transferable securities are required to inform investors clearly that they do not accept the reception of orders for the purposes of buying or selling contracts in relation to investments originally made on the crowdfunding platform, that any buying and selling activity on their crowdfunding platform is at the investor's discretion and responsibility, and that they do not operate a trading venue in accordance with MiFID II.[93]

2. Managing an AIF or UCITS

7.57 Under the Crowdfunding Regulation, a 'project owner' means any natural or legal person who seeks funding through a crowdfunding platform.[94] The definition of 'project owner'

---

[89] See Recital 19 Crowdfunding Regulation.
[90] Art 25(1) Crowdfunding Regulation. See also Chapter 13.
[91] Art 25(2) Crowdfunding Regulation.
[92] Compare Recital 55 Crowdfunding Regulation.
[93] ibid.
[94] Art 2(1)(h) Crowdfunding Regulation.

allows for an entity to accept funds from investors, but this definition does not set limits on what to do with the funds obtained. As a result thereof, an Alternative Investment Fund (AIF) or an Undertaking for the Collective Investment in Transferable Securities (UCITS) could qualify as a project owner, if the accepted funds concerned are obtained through crowdfunding (within the meaning of the Crowdfunding Regulation).[95]

In principle, managers of an AIF or UCITS require a registration or licence under the   **7.58** AIFMD or the UCITS Directive. As noted in section II.2, Article 1(3) of the Crowdfunding Regulation only relates to loan-based crowdfunding. As a result, this article does not cover the situation in which an AIF or UCITS qualifies as project owner. This qualifies as investment-based crowdfunding, since the AIF or UCITS attracts funding by means of offering units, participation rights, or shares to the crowd.

3. Payment Services

An authorization to provide crowdfunding services under the Crowdfunding Regulation   **7.59** does not equate to an authorization to also provide payment services. Only payment service providers are permitted to provide payment services within the meaning of the PSD 2. Recital 29 of the Crowdfunding Regulation therefore clarifies that, where a CSP provides such payment services in connection with its crowdfunding services, it also needs to be a payment service provider as defined in PSD 2. That requirement is without prejudice to entities authorized under MiFID II that carry out an activity referred to in Article 3 of PSD 2 and that are also subject to the notification requirement set out in Article 37 of PSD 2. In order to enable proper supervision of such activities, the CSP should inform the competent authorities whether it intends to provide payment services itself with the appropriate authorization or whether such services will be outsourced to an authorized third party.

Where a CSP does not provide payment services in relation to the crowdfunding services,   **7.60** either itself or through a third party, such a CSP shall put in place and maintain arrangements to ensure that project owners accept funding of crowdfunding projects, or any other payment, only by means of a payment service provider in accordance with PSD 2.[96]

Where a CSP also seeks to apply for an authorization to provide payment services solely in   **7.61** connection with the provision of crowdfunding services, and to the extent that the competent authorities are also responsible for the authorization under PSD 2, the competent authorities shall require that the information and documents to be submitted under each application are submitted only once.[97] It should be noted that in some Member States, the competent authority that grants authorization to payment institutions may not be the same as the competent authority that will grant authorization under the Crowdfunding Regulation.

---

[95] See also Chapter 9.
[96] Art 10(5) Crowdfunding Regulation.
[97] Art 12(15) Crowdfunding Regulation.

4. Market Access under National Regimes

A. Transitional Period

7.62   The rules set out in the Crowdfunding Regulation will replace national rules insofar as these national rules concern crowdfunding services which are now within the scope of the Crowdfunding Regulation. Recital 76 calls for transitional arrangements allowing persons providing such crowdfunding services in accordance with national law preceding the Crowdfunding Regulation to adapt their business activities to this regulation and to have sufficient time to apply for an authorization under the Crowdfunding Regulation. The transitional period should last until 10 November 2022 or until such a person is granted an authorization under the Crowdfunding Regulation.[98]

B. Intermediary in Respect of Repayable Funds

7.63   In some Member States, it is currently prohibited to act as an intermediary in respect of repayable funds. For instance, in the Netherlands, a dispensation from the said prohibition is, at the moment, required to act as an intermediary in respect to repayable funds. The granting of such dispensation will, however, not be allowed once the abovementioned transitional period of Crowdfunding Regulation ends, insofar such a dispensation will cover crowdfunding services within the meaning of the Crowdfunding Regulation. Persons who have been issued such a dispensation will need to obtain authorization under the Crowdfunding Regulation in order to provide crowdfunding services on a continuing basis.

C. Consumer Credit

7.64   As indicated above in section II.2, the Crowdfunding Regulation does not apply to crowdfunding services that are provided to project owners that are consumers, as defined in point (a) of Article 3 of the CCD. A consumer in that sense is a natural person who, in transactions covered by the CCD, is acting for purposes which are outside his trade, business or profession. As a consequence, a CSP seeking to provide services that are provided to project owners that are consumers, is likely to need to seek authorization for the offering of consumer credit.[99]

V. Conclusion

7.65   In this chapter, we discussed the authorization and supervision of CSPs. Where relevant, we made a comparison with MiFID II to assess whether the regime under the Crowdfunding Regulation is indeed more proportional to the business of CSPs, as advocated by the Commission. Our findings are that the authorization and supervision framework in the Crowdfunding Regulation is clearly inspired by MiFID II. In general, it is quite comparable. Where it was first proposed by the Commission that ESMA would be the competent authority, this was not accepted by the European Parliament and the Council. As a result, the Member States have to designate the national authorities responsible for authorization and supervision under the Crowdfunding Regulation. The authorization requirements under

---

[98]   Art 48(1) Crowdfunding Regulation.
[99]   See also Chapter 5.

the Crowdfunding Regulation are actually quite similar to those under MiFID II, while the competent authorities under the Crowdfunding Regulation have considerably less time to assess an application. In addition, the powers that the competent authorities should at least have under the Crowdfunding Regulation are similar to the powers mentioned in MiFID II, provided that the maximum amounts for the administrative fines are much higher in MiFID II. Proportionality seems therefore only to be accomplished with regard to some aspects of the authorization and supervision framework, while others are still quite comparable to MIFID II. Lastly, CSPs should be aware of the fact that they may be subject to other authorization requirements, whether under EU law or national law, when they conduct 'other activities'.

8

Organizational and Operational Requirements for Crowdfunding Service Providers

Kitty Lieverse and Wendy Pronk

I. Introduction

The Crowdfunding Regulation subjects an authorized crowdfunding service provider **8.01** (CSP) to a number of organizational and operational requirements. These requirements differ, depending on the services provided by the CSP. The generic description of crowdfunding services entails the matching of business funding interests of project owners and investors.[1] In addition, the CSP may provide individual portfolio management services in respect of investment in loans.[2] Insofar as the CSP will provide asset safekeeping services and payment services, this is subject to additional authorization and requirements.[3]

First of all, a CSP has to meet requirements in relation to the effective and prudent manage- **8.02** ment of its business. This includes the requirement for the management board to have policies and procedures in place that provide for the segregation of duties, business continuity, and the prevention of conflicts of interest.[4] Further, management is required to establish and oversee systems and controls to assess the risks of loans intermediated on the platform.[5] Additional requirements are posed when the CSP determines the price of a crowdfunding offer.[6] The requirements that are posed to complaints handling are detailed in Article 7 of

---

[1] Art 2(1)(a) of the Crowdfunding Regulation.
[2] Art 6 of the Crowdfunding Regulation.
[3] Art 10 of the Crowdfunding Regulation.
[4] Art 4(1) of the Crowdfunding Regulation.
[5] Art 4(2) of the Crowdfunding Regulation.
[6] Art 4(4) of the Crowdfunding Regulation. These requirements are discussed in Chapter 9.

the Crowdfunding Regulation. In Article 8 of the Crowdfunding Regulation, detailed provisions on the prevention, management, and disclosure of conflicts of interest are posed. These requirements in relation to the effective and prudent management and on complaints handling and conflicts of interest are discussed in paragraph II of this chapter.

8.03   CSPs are also subject to requirements in relation to the provision of the crowdfunding services. These requirements are discussed in paragraph III of this chapter. In short, these requirements entail the following. CSPs must act honestly, fairly, and professionally and in accordance with the interests of their clients.[7] CSPs may not receive or provide any fee, discount, or non-monetary benefit for routing orders of investors to a particular crowdfunding offering on their platform or to a particular crowdfunding offering on a crowdfunding platform of a third party.[8] CSPs must also meet certain due diligence requirements with regard to project owners. This entails a check whether a project owner does not have a criminal record and is not established in a high-risk third country or a non-cooperative jurisdiction.[9]

8.04   In paragraph IV of this chapter, the prudential requirements are discussed. In order to protect clients from operational risks, CSPs have to meet prudential requirements. In short, they must either hold a minimum equity of EUR 25,000 or a quarter of the fixed costs (whichever amount is higher), or take out an insurance policy, or a combination thereof. These requirements do not apply to CSPs which are already subject to prudential requirements, such as a bank or investment firm.[10]

8.05   Lastly, CSPs will have to meet certain rules in respect of outsourcing. These requirements are discussed in paragraph V of this chapter.[11]

8.06   In this chapter, securities and admitted instruments for crowdfunding purposes[12] are collectively referred to as securities.

II. Governance Arrangements and Operational Requirements

1. Effective and Prudent Management

8.07   For CSPs, ensuring an effective system of governance is essential for the proper management of risk and for preventing any conflict of interest. CSPs should therefore have in place governance arrangements that ensure their effective and prudent management.[13] In this respect, an important role is played by the management body of the CSP. On the basis of Article 4(1) of the Crowdfunding Regulation, the management body of the CSP will have to establish and implement adequate policies and procedures to ensure effective and prudent management, including the segregation of duties, business continuity, and the prevention

---

[7] Art 3(2) and Art 2(1)(g) of the Crowdfunding Regulation.
[8] Art 3(3) of the Crowdfunding Regulation.
[9] Art 5(2) of the Crowdfunding Regulation.
[10] Art 11 of the Crowdfunding Regulation.
[11] Art 9 of the Crowdfunding Regulation.
[12] Art 2(1)(n) Crowdfunding Regulation. These instruments typically also qualify as securities, reference is made to Art 2(2) and (3) Crowdfunding Regulation.
[13] Recital (23) of the Crowdfunding Regulation.

of conflicts of interest,[14] in a manner that promotes the integrity of the market and the interests of its clients. The general concept of segregation of duties is that certain functions, such as risk management and the operational functions, are not combined in the same person but divided over the management body of the CSP. In this respect, we note that there is no requirement with regard to the minimum number of persons the management body of the CSP should comprise. However, in order to obtain a licence, proof has to be provided that the management board as a whole possesses sufficient knowledge, skills, and experience to manage the CSP and that the natural persons involved can commit sufficient time to the performance of their duties.[15] As a result of this requirement, depending on the size of the business, it may be required that the management board consists of more than one person. This will then also facilitate an appropriate segregation of duties.

As part of the effective and prudent management, the management body of a CSP shall establish, and oversee the implementation of, appropriate systems and controls to assess the risks related to the *loans* intermediated on the crowdfunding platform.[16] There is no similar requirement specifically linked to securities that are placed with investors via the crowdfunding platform. The required risk assessment systems for loans that have to be in place are linked to the transparency requirements of Articles 19 and 23 of the Crowdfunding Regulation: investors can only be properly informed of risks associated with an investment in loans if such risks have been identified.   **8.08**

Where the crowdfunding platform determines the price of a crowdfunding offer, specific requirements apply on the basis of Article 4(4) of the Crowdfunding Regulation. This is applicable to both loans intermediated via the platform and securities that are placed with investors via the platform. The obligations of the CSP in this respect entail, amongst others, to undertake a reasonable assessment of the credit risk of a crowdfunding project or the project owner before the offer is made via the platform, to ensure that the price is fair and appropriate, and to have a risk-management framework in place to achieve compliance with these and other obligations in relation to determining the price of the crowdfunding offer. This requirement is linked to the due diligence requirements of Article 5, as discussed in paragraph III.2.   **8.09**

The individual portfolio management of loans is viewed as a more complex business model for a CSP. In addition to the detailed requirements that are posed in Article 6, there is also a more generic requirement posed in Article 4(2), second paragraph that requires the CSP to ensure that it has in place adequate systems and controls for the management of risk and financial modelling for that provision of services.   **8.10**

When applying for its licence, the CSP has to provide its business continuity plan to the national competent supervisor.[17] In addition to a description of the operational risks of its business, the CSP should also describe how it meets the prudential safeguards of Article 11.[18] Once the licence is in place, the management body of a CSP is under the obligation to   **8.11**

---

[14] The prevention of conflicts of interest is further described in Art 8 of the Crowdfunding Regulation and discussed in paragraph II.3 of this chapter.

[15] Art 12(2)(l) and (3)(b) of the Crowdfunding Regulation.

[16] Art 4(2), first paragraph of the Crowdfunding Regulation.

[17] Art 12(2)(j) of the Crowdfunding Regulation.

[18] Art 12(2)(g) and (i) of the Crowdfunding Regulation. The prudential requirements are further described in paragraph IV of this chapter.

review, at least once every two years, taking into account the nature, scale, and complexity of the crowdfunding services provided, the adequacy of the prudential safeguards[19] and the business continuity plan.[20]

2. Complaints Handling

8.12 Article 7 of the Crowdfunding Regulation provides for complaints handling requirements for CSPs. These requirements relate to the complaints handling procedure a CSP should have in place, the format for filing complaints, and the investigation to be performed by the CSP and the responses to complaints of its clients. On the basis of Article 7(5) of the Crowdfunding Regulation, the European Securities and Markets Authority (ESMA) is required to develop regulatory technical standards (RTS) to specify the requirements, standard formats, and procedures for complaints handling by CSPs.[21]

8.13 First of all, the CSP should have a complaints handling procedure for the prompt, fair, and consistent handling of complaints received from clients.[22] The complaints handling procedure should be in writing and include clear and accurate information. Article 1 of the draft RTS specifies the minimum information which should be included therein, such as the conditions for admissibility of the complaint and which process will be followed when handling complaints. The CSP has to publish the procedure in an easily accessible manner on its website and the procedure should be made available in the official language(s) of the Member State(s) in which the CSP is active.[23]

8.14 Article 7(2) of the Crowdfunding Regulation prescribes that clients should be able to file complaints against CSPs free of charge. For purposes of lodging a complaint, the client can make use of a standard template. The draft RTS provide for such template.[24] Complainants can file a complaint by filling out the standard format in one of the official languages of the Member State where the CSP offers its services or another language which has been agreed upon between the client and the CSP, provided such language is a customary language in international finance or accepted by the Member State where the CSP is authorized.

8.15 In communicating with complainants, the CSP shall use clear, plain language. Any communication shall be made available by electronic means, however, complainants have the right to request communicating on paper form instead.[25]

8.16 Once the complainant has lodged a complaint, the CSP shall acknowledge receipt of such complaint and confirm whether the complaint is admissible within ten working days of its receipt. The acknowledgement of receipt will include the identity and contact details of the complainant and the indicative timeframe within which a decision on the complaint will

---

[19] As referred to in point (h) of Art 12(2) and as set out in Art 11 of the Crowdfunding Regulation.
[20] As referred to in point (j) of Art 12(2).
[21] The draft RTS were published on 26 February 2021.
[22] Art 7(1) of the Crowdfunding Regulation and Art 1 draft RTS.
[23] Art 7(1) of the Crowdfunding Regulation and Art 1(4) draft RTS.
[24] Art 7(3) of the Crowdfunding Regulation and Art 2 draft RTS.
[25] Art 6 draft RTS.

be provided to the complainant. In case a complaint is considered as inadmissible, the CSP shall provide the complainant with a motivated decision.[26]

CSPs are under the obligation to handle all complaints in a timely and fair manner and **8.17** communicate the outcome within a reasonable period of time to the complainant. The time frame within which a decision on the complaint will be notified to the complainant should be included in the procedure of the CSP.[27] It is not further specified in the Crowdfunding Regulation and the draft RTS what such a reasonable time frame is. It is however specified in the draft RTS that the CSP shall, without *undue delay*, assess whether the complaint is clear and complete and that the CSP shall *promptly* request any additional information necessary for the proper handling of the complaint. In addition, the CSP will keep the complainant duly informed about the further handling of the complaint and will reply to reasonable information requests from the complainant without any undue delay.[28] If, in exceptional circumstances, the CSP cannot provide a decision on a complaint within the indicated time frame, it shall inform the complainant of the reasons for such delay and inform when the complainant is expected to receive the decision.

Once the CSP has reached a decision regarding a complaint, it will communicate the deci- **8.18** sion to the complainant as soon as possible. The decision will include all points raised in the complaint and will state the reasons for the decision taken by the CSP. The decision should be consistent with any previous decision taken by the CSP in respect of a similar complaint, unless the CSP can justify why a different approach is chosen.[29] We note that such a requirement in respect of the content of the decision regarding a complaint is unprecedented in EU legislation for other types of financial institutions, such as investment firms. If the final decision does not or only partially upholds the complaint, the CSP will inform the complainant on the possibility to file a complaint with the competent authority on the basis of Article 38 of the Crowdfunding Regulation or to take civil actions.[30]

Lastly, the CSP shall keep a record of all complaints received and the measures taken on the **8.19** basis of the investigation of such complaints.[31]

3. Conflicts of Interest

When providing crowdfunding services, conflicts of interest may arise. In order to prevent **8.20** and manage such conflicts of interest, Article 8 of the Crowdfunding Regulation sets out a conflicts of interest regime for CSPs. On the basis of Article 8(7) of the Crowdfunding Regulation, ESMA is required to develop draft RTS in respect of the internal rules to prevent conflicts of interest and the appropriate steps to be taken to identify, manage, and disclose conflicts of interest.[32]

---

[26] Art 3 and 1(2)(f) of the draft RTS.
[27] Art 7(4) of the Crowdfunding Regulation and Art 1(2)(f) draft RTS.
[28] Art 4 draft RTS.
[29] Art 5 draft RTS.
[30] Art 5(4) draft RTS.
[31] Art 7(3) of the Crowdfunding Regulation.
[32] The draft RTS were published on 26 February 2021.

8.21   To start, CSPs shall establish and maintain an effective internal procedure for the prevention of conflicts of interest. This should be proportionate to the nature, scale, and complexity of the crowdfunding platform.[33] Where the CSP is part of a group, any conflicts of interest arising from the structure and business activities of other members of the group shall be taken into account as well.[34]

8.22   In order to prevent certain conflicts of interest, the Crowdfunding Regulation provides for a number of specific rules. First of all, CSPs are not allowed to have any participation in any crowdfunding offer on their crowdfunding platforms.[35] Secondly, CSPs shall not accept project owners, which are (a) their shareholders holding 20% or more share capital or voting rights, (b) their managers or employers, and (c) any natural or legal person linked to those shareholders, managers or employees by means of control (as defined in point (35)(b) of Article 4(10) of MiFID II).[36] The aforementioned persons may be accepted as *investors* in crowdfunding projects. Crowdfunding platforms shall fully disclose this on their websites and ensure that such investments are made under the same conditions as those of other investors. This entails that there is no preferential treatment or privileged access to information on the crowdfunding projects that are involved.[37] The draft RTS of ESMA further specify how this should be ensured in practice, for instance by having an effective procedure to prevent or control the exchange of information with such an investor.[38]

8.23   In addition to having these internal rules, CSPs will need to take steps to ensure that the risks of damage to client interests will be prevented or, where this is not possible, appropriately managed. Such steps will need to be taken in respect of conflicts of interest between the CSPs themselves, their shareholders, managers, employees, and any natural or legal persons linked to them by control, and their clients, or between one client and another client.[39] The draft RTS prescribe minimum criteria for the CSP to take into account for purposes of identifying any conflicts of interest. First of all, these criteria include the circumstance that the CSP, its shareholders, managers, or employees is or are likely to make a financial gain, or avoid a financial loss, at the expense of the client. In addition, a conflict of interest may exist where the CSP, its shareholders, managers, or employees or any persons linked to them (a) have a personal interest which is different from the clients' interest or (b) have a financial or other incentive to favour the interest of another client or group of clients over the interest of the client.[40]

8.24   CSPs will have to disclose the general nature and source of any identified conflicts of interest and take steps to mitigate these conflicts of interest.[41] The disclosure will have to be made on a prominent place at the website of the CSP. In addition, the information has to be disclosed to clients on a durable medium, unless no conflicts of interest have been identified. This disclosure will need to be made in due time to enable the clients to take an informed

---

[33] Art 1(1) draft RTS.
[34] Art 1(2) draft RTS.
[35] Art 8(1) of the Crowdfunding Regulation.
[36] Art 8(2) of the Crowdfunding Regulation.
[37] Art 8(2) of the Crowdfunding Regulation.
[38] Art 1(5) draft RTS.
[39] Art 8(4) of the Crowdfunding Regulation.
[40] Art 2(2) draft RTS.
[41] Art 8(4) and (5) of the Crowdfunding Regulation.

decision with regard to the service in the context of which the conflicts of interest arises. The disclosure should include a description of the conflicts of interests and related risks for the clients, as well as of the steps taken to mitigate those risks. The description should be sufficiently detailed in order to ensure that clients are properly informed before taking their decision as regards the provision of the relevant crowdfunding services.[42]

III. Provision of Crowdfunding Services

1. General Duty of Care

Based on Article 3(2) of the Crowdfunding Regulation, CSPs shall act honestly, fairly, and professionally in accordance with the best interests of their clients.[43] As a reminder, the clients include parties on either side of the investment in securities or in the loan, namely both the project owners and the investors.[44] The position of the CSP as the platform that matches the business funding interests of investors on the one hand and project owners on the other hand, implies that a CSP has to serve the best interests of counterparties. By nature, their best interests may not necessarily be fully aligned.[45]   **8.25**

A similar duty of care is imposed on investment firms,[46] which are required when providing investment services to act honestly, fairly, and professionally in accordance with the best interests of their clients.[47] For an investment firm, a 'client' means any natural or legal person to whom an investment firm provides investment or ancillary services.[48] As a further comparison, managers of alternative investment funds (AIFs) are expected to act in the best interests of the AIFs or the investors of the AIFs they manage and the integrity of the market and to treat the investors fairly.[49] Compared to a CSP, the position of an investment firm or manager of an AIF is slightly less complicated though, as they typically do not have to serve the best interest of opposing parties to the same transaction.   **8.26**

This intermediary position of the CSP in our view defines the 'best interests' of clients that need to be served in the sense that both the project owners and the investors have to anticipate that a CSP by nature also has to serve the best interests of the other side. This implies that they may not expect that the CSP only acts in their best interest. This balancing act that the CSP has to perform underlines the importance of compliance with the provisions on conflicts of interest[50] and transparency.[51] In addition, the specific provisions that   **8.27**

---

[42] Art 3 draft RTS.

[43] Reference is made to Recital (18) to the Crowdfunding Regulation: in order to maintain a high standard of investor protection, to reduce the risks associated with crowdfunding and to ensure fair treatment of all clients, CSPs should have in place a policy designed to ensure that projects on their platforms are selected in a professional, fair and transparent way, and that crowdfunding services are provided in the same manner. The reference to acting in the best interests of the clients is not reflected in this Recital.

[44] Art 2(1)(g) of the Crowdfunding Regulation.

[45] The general duty of care is also discussed in Chapter 9.

[46] Art 24(1) MiFID II.

[47] And in doing so, they have to comply with and comply, in particular, with Art 24 and Art 25 of MIFID II.

[48] Art 2(1)(g) MiFID II.

[49] Art 12(1)(b) and (f) AIFMD.

[50] Art 8 of the Crowdfunding Regulation.

[51] Chapter IV of the Crowdfunding Regulation.

the CSP needs to comply with when conducting its services (such as the required level of due diligence it needs to observe in respect of the selecting of projects as discussed in the next paragraph) further define the general duty of care as set forth in Article 3(2) of the Crowdfunding Regulation.

2. Due Diligence Requirements

8.28   Based on Recital (18), a certain level of due diligence is required by the CSP in respect of the selection of projects, to maintain a high standard of investor protection and to reduce the risks associated with crowdfunding. Recital (18) stipulates that CSPs should have *a policy* in place that is designed to ensure that projects on their platforms are selected in a professional, fair and transparent way. The provisions of the Crowdfunding Regulation itself however do not state in so many words that there should be a policy in place that describes the due diligence process and the level of quality that is maintained. However, based on the generic reference in Article 12(2)(e) of the Crowdfunding Regulation to a description of the governance arrangements to ensure compliance with the Regulation, it makes sense to record in a policy document how the due diligence process takes places and how the required minimum level of quality of the projects that are selected for the platform is ensured.

8.29   This is further defined by Article 5(1) of the Crowdfunding Regulation which requires the CSP to undertake at least a minimum level of due diligence in respect of project owners that propose their projects to be funded through the crowdfunding platform of the CSP. Article 5(2) of the Crowdfunding Regulation sets the minimum level of due diligence to include obtaining all the following evidence: (a) that the project owner has no criminal record in respect of infringements of national rules in fields of commercial law, insolvency law, financial services law, anti-money laundering (AML) law, fraud law, or professional liability obligations; and (b) that the project owner is not established in a non-cooperative jurisdiction, as recognized by the relevant Union policy, or in a high-risk third country pursuant to Article 9(2) of the Fourth AML Directive.

8.30   Item (b) can be established quite easily by the CSP by determining the country of establishment of the project owner and checking this against the lists as referred to. Item (a) in our view provides for more challenges. Criminal records are typically not publicly accessible for private parties, such as a CSP. Some countries of establishment may allow a project owner himself to obtain an extract from the criminal record to substantiate that there are no listings in such records. In the absence of such access, the CSP may have to rely on a self-certification by the project owner for the absence of a criminal record, potentially combined with other sources, such as a check in insolvency registers, the sanctions lists, and a bad-press check.

8.31   As a further comment to the minimum level of due diligence that is required we note that the CSP as such is not required to conduct a customer due diligence in accordance with the Fourth AML Directive, as the CSP has not been labelled as an institution (known as an 'obliged entity') under this directive.[52] However, the European Banking Authority (EBA) has recognized the risks related with the services of a crowdfunding platform and has included

---

[52] See Art 17(1), final subparagraph, for a reference to compliance with the Fourth AML Directive in the event that the CSP is also a payment service provider. Also, in Recital (32) it is noted that the European Commission

a sectoral guideline for regulated crowdfunding platforms in which specific risk factors for crowdfunding platforms are described in the revised Money Laundering/Terrorism Financing (ML/TF) Risk Factor Guidelines.[53] The sectoral guideline will have to be applied by crowdfunding platforms which are subjected to national AML and Combatting the Financing of Terrorism (CTF) laws and by CSPs that are authorized as a payment institution under PSD 2 or as an investment firm under MiFID II. That being said, a CSP which is not subjected to AML/CTF legislation may derive some inspiration from this directive and the ML/TF Risk Factor Guidelines to determine the appropriate level of due diligence and, for example, include a check on the ultimate beneficial owner (UBO) of the project owner and the risk profile of the business of the project owner. Depending on the specific circumstances of a project owner, the minimum level of due diligence as set out in Article 5(2) of the Crowdfunding Regulation may not be sufficient to meet the duty of care as set forth in Article 3(2) of the Crowdfunding Regulation.

3. Individual Crowdfunding Offer

The generic description of crowdfunding services (the matching of business funding interests of project owners and investors) implies that such services may be limited to arranging an offer of projects via the platform and the self-selection of any such projects by an investor through the system of the platform. The services to an individual investor, however, may also be extended to include proposing crowdfunding projects to such individual investors based on one or more specific parameters or risk indicators, such as the type or sector of business activity or a credit rating, which have been communicated in advance to the CSP by the investor.[54] This is reflected in Article 3(4), first paragraph of the Crowdfunding Regulation. In that case, where the investor wishes to make an investment in the suggested crowdfunding projects, the investor shall review and expressly take an investment decision in relation to each individual crowdfunding offer. This implies that services by the CSP are still limited in scope. These services include that the CSP will make a selection and a proposal to the investor. The investment decision lies, however, solely with the investor. This concerns both a potential investment in loans and in securities via the platform. As an alternative or in addition to individual crowdfunding offers, it is possible for a CSP to make use of filtering tools on its platform. The existence of such filtering tool is not regarded as investment advice within the meaning of MiFID II as long as such a tool provides information in a neutral manner, displays results based on criteria relating to purely objective product

8.32

---

should assess the necessity and proportionality of subjecting CSPs to obligations to comply with national law implementing the Fourth AML Directive and of adding such CSPs to the list of obliged entities for the purposes of that directive. The AML/CFT package published by the European Commission on 20 July 2021 with four legislative proposals does *not* add CSPs within the scope of the Crowdfunding Regulation to the list of obliged entities under the AML legislation, as (according to the European Commission) the Crowdfunding Regulation already contains sufficient safeguards for CSPs falling under its scope. CSPs falling outside the scope of the Crowdfunding Regulation are added to the list of obliged entities.

[53] Guidelines on customer due diligence and the factors credit and financial institutions should consider when assessing the money laundering and terrorist financing risk associated with individual business relationships and occasional transactions ('The ML/TF Risk Factors Guidelines') under Arts 17 and 18(4) of Directive (EU) 2015/849, EBA/GL/2021/02, 1 March 2021.

[54] Recital (19) to the Crowdfunding Regulation.

features, and does not constitute a recommendation.[55] A further extension of the services to an investor is made if the CSP is charged with the individual portfolio management of loans. This is discussed in the next paragraph.

4. Individual Portfolio Management of Loans

8.33   This service as may be provided by a CSP only relates to investments in loans. It does not extend to investments in securities. This is confirmed by Recital (19): the authorization obtained under the Crowdfunding Regulation does not grant CSPs the right to provide individual asset management services. This refers to discretionary asset management services (in respect of financial instruments) as regulated under MiFID II. Recital (19) also confirms that a CSP may not conduct collective asset management (ie act as a manager of certain loans or securities for a group of investors which would imply a fund like structure).[56] So, the service described here relates to asset management services for a single investor and (only) in respect of loans as an asset class. This individual portfolio management of loans is subject to a number of requirements. These include the items listed in Article 3(4), second paragraph, and (5), Article 4(2) second paragraph, Article 6, Article 22(7), and Article 24 of the Crowdfunding Regulation. In this paragraph, we only discuss Article 3(4), second paragraph, and (5), and Article 6.

8.34   Individual portfolio management of loans includes a best execution obligation in accordance with the parameters agreed with the investor. Article 3(4), second paragraph states that individual portfolio management of loans has to be performed in adherence to the parameters provided by the investors. The CSP must take all necessary steps to obtain the best possible result for these investors. The decision-making process for executing the received discretionary mandate must be disclosed by the CSP to the investor who provided the mandate.

8.35   Recital (20) clarifies that business models using automated processes whereby funds are *automatically* allocated by the CSP to crowdfunding projects in accordance with parameters and risk indicators predetermined by the investor, so called auto-investing, should be considered individual portfolio management of loans. This implies that the CSP is responsible for effecting that its automated processes ensure adherence to the parameters as set by the investor.

8.36   In the event of individual portfolio management of loans, the investment in the loan requires an investment decision by the CSP, acting on behalf of the investor. In this case, by way of derogation from the first subparagraph of Article 3(4), CSPs may exercise discretion on behalf of their investors within the agreed parameters without requiring investors to review and take an investment decision in relation to each individual crowdfunding offer.[57]

---

[55] Recital (21) to the Crowdfunding Regulation. Objective product features in the context of a crowdfunding platform could be predefined project criteria such as the economic sector, the instrument used, the interest rate, or the risk category where sufficient information regarding the calculation method is disclosed and key financial figures calculated without any scope for discretion.

[56] As is regulated under the AIFMD and the UCITS Directive.

[57] Art 3(5) of the Crowdfunding Regulation.

Further details in the requirements that are posed to a mandate for individual portfolio   **8.37**
management of loans and the performance thereof, are set by Article 6. As a starting point,
the mandate must be properly recorded.[58] The mandate must also specify the parameters
for providing the service.[59] The mandate must include at least two of the following criteria
that every loan in the portfolio will have to comply with: (a) the minimum and maximum
interest rate payable under any loan facilitated for the investor; (b) the minimum and maximum maturity date of any loan facilitated for the investor; (c) the range and distribution of
any risk categories applicable to the loans; and (d) if an annual target rate of return on investment is offered, the likelihood that the selected loans will enable the investor to achieve
the target rate with reasonable certainty.[60] The CSP that is charged with such a mandate
has to be able to conduct the mandate in accordance with the parameters as set. This is
specified in Article 6(2), which requires the CSP to have in place robust internal processes
and methodologies and use appropriate data to ensure such compliance. The CSP may use
its own data or data sourced from third parties. This would seem to be relatively straightforward for item (a) and (b) as listed above (on the ranges of interest rates and maturity).
However, properly determining risk categories and ensuring proper asset management in
relation to an annual target rate of return, if these items are included in the mandate (item
(c) and (d)), would seem to add complexity to the mandate. This is confirmed by the stipu-
lation in Article 6(2) that the CSP is charged with the assessment of: (a) the credit risk of
individual crowdfunding projects selected for the investor's portfolio; (b) the credit risk at
the investor's portfolio level; and (c) the credit risk of the project owners selected for the
investor's portfolio by verifying the prospect of the project owners meeting their obligations
under the loan. This assessment must take place on the basis of sound and well-defined criteria and taking into account all the relevant factors that may have unfavourable effects on
the performance of the loans. The method used for the assessments referred to in points (a),
(b), and (c) above must be disclosed to the investor. RTS must be developed to specify the
elements, including the format, that are to be included in this description of the method.[61]

Once the mandate is in place, the CSP is subject to transparency obligations vis-à-vis the   **8.38**
investor on the composition of the portfolio of loans and its performance. This information
must be provided on a continuous basis and upon the request of an investor, via electronic
means. The details of the portfolio report are set out in Article 6(4).[62] RTS are to be developed to specify this information.[63]

---

[58] Art 6(3) of the Crowdfunding Regulation.
[59] Art 6(1) of the Crowdfunding Regulation.
[60] Art 6(1) of the Crowdfunding Regulation.
[61] Art 6(7) of the Crowdfunding Regulation. Drafts must be submitted by EBA to the Commission by 10 November 2021.
[62] This report includes *inter alia* (a) the list of individual loans of which a portfolio is composed; (b) the weighted average annual interest rate on loans in a portfolio; (c) the distribution of loans according to risk category, in percentage and absolute numbers; (d) for every loan of which a portfolio is composed, key information, including at least an interest rate or other compensation to the investor, maturity date, risk category, schedule for the repayment of the principal, and payment of interest, compliance of the project owner with that instalment payment schedule; (e) for every loan of which a portfolio is composed, risk mitigation measures including collateral providers or guarantors or other types of guarantees; (f) any default on credit agreements by the project owner within the past five years; (g) any fees paid in respect of the loan by the investor, the CSP or the project owner; (h) information on the valuation of the loan, if the CSP has carried out a valuation of the loan.
[63] Art 6(7) of the Crowdfunding Regulation. Drafts must be submitted by EBA to the Commission by 10 November 2021.

8.39   As a starting point, an investor who invests in loans via an individual portfolio mandate is not covered by any protection against the credit risk of a project owner, unless the investor would seek such protection separately, for example by concluding credit insurance against the insolvency risk of project owner. Further, the investor is not protected against insolvency of the CSP and any discontinuity of its services as portfolio manager, but for the protection that would result from the equity held by the CSP in accordance with Article 11. In addition hereto, the CSP has the option, but not the obligation, to provide some protection to investors that have provided an individual mandate for the management of loans by establishing and operating a *contingency fund*. If such a contingency fund is established, it triggers transparency requirements. Investors must receive a risk warning.[64] They must also be informed on the policy of the contingency fund, including the discretion of the contingency fund operator to pay out from the fund.[65] Further, the investors must be informed on a quarterly basis about the size of the contingency fund compared to the total amounts outstanding on loans relevant to the contingency fund and the ratio between payments made out of the contingency fund to the total amounts outstanding on loans relevant to the contingency fund.[66]

8.40   There is no further specification in the Crowdfunding Regulation of the operations of such optional contingency funds. There is also no specification as to whether any pay out from the contingency fund should be linked to the credit risks of the investments (ie a default of the project owner) or, generally, more to the continuity of the CSP (ie a default of the CSP). The latter would seem to be the more logical link[67] but this is not specified yet. The RTS to be developed will however specify the policies, procedures, and organizational arrangements that CSPs are to have in place as regards any contingency funds they might offer as referred to in Article 6(5) and (6).[68]

5. Provision of Asset Safekeeping Services and Payment Services

8.41   The authorization as a CSP entitles it to conduct the crowdfunding services as defined.[69] This includes the provision of investment services (otherwise regulated via MiFID II) to the extent that the crowdfunding services also qualify as such. Other services *in connection with* crowdfunding services, however, are not covered by the authorization under the Crowdfunding Regulation.[70] This includes asset safekeeping services and payment services. If these are provided additional authorization and other requirements apply, as set forth in Article 10 of the Crowdfunding Regulation.

---

[64] Specifying: 'The contingency fund we offer does not give you a right to a payment so it may happen that you do not receive a pay-out even if you suffer loss. The contingency fund operator has absolute discretion as to the amount that may be paid, including making no payment at all. Therefore, investors should not rely on possible pay-outs from the contingency fund when considering whether or how much to invest.'

[65] Art 6(5) of the Crowdfunding Regulation.

[66] Art 6(6) of the Crowdfunding Regulation.

[67] Art 6(5) of the Crowdfunding Regulation refers to the activity of the CSP.

[68] Art 6(7) of the Crowdfunding Regulation. Drafts must be submitted by EBA to the Commission by 10 November 2021.

[69] Art 2(1)(a) of the Crowdfunding Regulation.

[70] Art 1(2), under (b) of the Crowdfunding Regulation.

As a starting point, the transparency requirements of Article 10(1) apply. It should be made **8.42** clear to the clients *inter alia* whether the asset safekeeping and/or payment services are provided by the CSP or by a third party.

The safekeeping of transferable securities or admitted instruments for crowdfunding purposes which can be registered in a financial instruments account or which can be physically delivered to the custodian should be safe-kept by a qualified custodian, which is authorized in accordance with Capital Requirements Directive (CRD) IV[71] or MiFID II.[72] This entails that the CSP may only offer this service if it holds an additional licence as a bank or an investment firm. It is noteworthy that investor compensation scheme protection[73] does not apply to the safekeeping of securities acquired through the crowdfunding platform. This is based on the fact that the safekeeping of assets connected with crowdfunding services provided by an investment firm that is also authorized pursuant to MiFID II does not involve the provision of investment services within the meaning of point (2) of Article 4(1) of that Directive.[74]

Depending on the type of assets to be safe-kept, assets are either to be held in custody, as is **8.43** the case with transferable securities which can be registered in a financial instruments account or which can be physically delivered, or to be subject to ownership verification and record-keeping. Safekeeping of transferable securities or admitted instruments for crowdfunding purposes that in accordance with national law are only registered with the project owner or its agent, such as investments in non-listed companies, or are held on an individually segregated account that a client could open directly with a central securities depository, is considered equivalent to asset safekeeping by qualified custodians.[75]

Since only payment service providers are permitted to provide payment services as defined **8.44** in PSD 2, an authorization to provide crowdfunding services does not equate to an authorization also to provide payment services. This means that if a CSP provides such payment services in connection with its crowdfunding services, it also needs to be a payment service provider as defined in PSD 2. Where CSPs carry out payment transactions related to transferable securities and admitted instruments for crowdfunding purposes, they have to deposit the funds either with a central bank; or with a licenced credit institution.[76]

IV. Prudential Requirements for Crowdfunding Service Providers

CSPs are subject to prudential requirements, on the basis of Article 11 of the Crowdfunding **8.45** Regulation. This is based on the analysis that clients are exposed to operational risks in relation to CSPs and should be protected against such risks.[77] The clients that are to be protected

---

[71] Directive (EU) 2013/36/EU.
[72] Recital (28), Art 10(3) of the Crowdfunding Regulation.
[73] In accordance with the ICS Directive.
[74] This is reflected in Recital (49). This should be made transparent to non-sophisticated investors in the key investment information sheet.
[75] Recital (28).
[76] Art 10(2) of the Crowdfunding Regulation.
[77] Recital (24) to the Crowdfunding Regulation.

include both the investors and the project owners.[78] In order to further discuss and evaluate the prudential requirements that are posed to CSPs, below we will first consider the risk profile of the CSP in view of the services it provides to both investors and project owners. We will then describe the prudential regime and discuss whether the prudential regime that applies to CSPs adequately captures these risks.

8.46   The prudential requirements that are posed by the Crowdfunding Regulation to cater for the risks connected to the business of a CSP, basically entail that the CSP must maintain own funds that are at least equal to the higher of (a) EUR 25 000 and (b) one-quarter of the fixed overheads of the preceding year, reviewed annually, which are to include the cost of servicing loans for three months where the CSP also facilitates the granting of loans.[79] If there is no full preceding year, the CSP may use forward-looking business estimates in calculating the fixed overheads, provided that it starts using historical data as soon as these becomes available.[80]

8.47   The fixed overheads must be calculated as follows.[81] The starting point would be the total expenses after distribution of profits to shareholders in the most recently audited annual financial statements.[82] From this amount, the following variable items may be deducted: (a) staff bonuses and other remuneration, to the extent that they depend on a net profit of the CSP in the relevant year; (b) employees', directors', and partners' shares in profits; (c) other appropriations of profits and other variable remuneration, to the extent that they are fully discretionary; (d) shared commission and fees payable which are directly related to commission and fees receivable, which are included within total revenue, and where the payment of the commission and fees payable is contingent upon the actual receipt of the commission and fees receivable; and (e) non-recurring expenses from non-ordinary activities.[83] If the CSP is exposed to fixed costs that are charged by a third party, these should be included in the calculation.[84]

8.48   Instead of maintaining own funds,[85] the CSP may opt for an insurance policy covering the territories of the Union where crowdfunding offers are actively marketed, or a comparable guarantee, or a combination of both.[86] The insurance policy, in order to qualify as an alternative to the own funds, is subject to the conditions posed in Article 11(6) of the Crowdfunding Regulation.[87]

---

[78]   Art 2(1)(g) of the Crowdfunding Regulation.

[79]   Art 11(1) of the Crowdfunding Regulation.

[80]   Art 11(5) of the Crowdfunding Regulation.

[81]   The proposed system resembles that of Commission Delegated Regulation (EU) 2015/488 of 4 September 2014 amending Delegated Regulation (EU) No 241/2014 as regards own funds requirements for firms based on fixed overheads.

[82]   Or, where audited statements are not available, in annual financial statements validated by national supervisors, Art 11(9) of the Crowdfunding Regulation.

[83]   Art 11(8) of the Crowdfunding Regulation.

[84]   Art 11(9) of the Crowdfunding Regulation.

[85]   These should consist of ordinary shares, namely: Common Equity Tier 1 items as referred to in Arts 26–30 of Regulation (EU) No 575/2013 (CRR) after the deductions in full, pursuant to Art 36 CRR, without the application of threshold exemptions pursuant to Arts 46 and 48 CRR, Art 11(2) of the Crowdfunding Regulation.

[86]   This is an alternative that is also offered by Art 9 AIFMD.

[87]   These include that the policy has an initial term of no less than one year; the notice period for its cancellation is at least ninety days; it is taken out from an undertaking authorized to provide insurance, in accordance with Union law or national law; and it is provided by a third-party entity. Further, the insurance policy must include coverage against the risk of: loss of documents; misrepresentations or misleading statements made; acts, errors or omissions resulting in a breach of: legal and regulatory obligations; duty of skill and care towards clients;

If the CSP is also licenced as a bank or an investment firm, it is not subject to any *additional*   **8.49**
prudential requirements.[88] The same reasoning applies to the CSPs that are also subject to
the supervision as a e-money institution or a payment service provider.[89]

The 'fixed overhead requirement' described above basically aims to ensure that if oper-   **8.50**
ational risks materialize and the CSP faces potential insolvency as a result thereof, there
is a three-month survival period.[90] This should enable the clients to transfer their need for
services to another service provider during this three-month period rather than to keep the
CSP 'alive' for the long term. This prudential system can also be found in Article 11(1) and
Article 13 Investment Firm Regulation (IFR) (the new prudential regime for investment
firms).

On the adequacy of this prudential system, we note the following. The function of the CSP   **8.51**
is to act as the matching platform for the business funding interests of investors and project
owners.[91] Crowdfunding services may consist of two types of activities: (a) the facilitation
of granting of loans and (b) the receipt and transmission of orders in securities and the placing thereof.[92] But for the fact that loans technically do not qualify as securities, the type of
services that the CSP would provide in relation to all these instruments would seem very
comparable to those of an investment firm that is involved both at the side of the issuer/
borrower (project owner) and of the investor/lender (investor). The services to the project
owner, regardless of whether or not the funding that is required takes the form of a loan or
securities, consist of the assistance in finding a lender/investor, and ensuring the placement
of the loan/securities with the investors, and the receipt of the funds corresponding thereto
by the project owner. The services to the investor/lender basically consist of effecting that the
loan/investment is made. These services are comparable to investment services as provided
by investment firms, more specifically the investment services as listed in Part A, under
(1) and (7) to MiFID II. In addition, the CSP may provide individual portfolio management
of loans.[93] This service can be compared somewhat to portfolio management as listed in
Part A, under (4) of MiFID II.[94] Finally, a CSP may provide, subject to certain conditions,
asset safekeeping services and payment services.[95] For the provision of payment services, an
authorization as payment service provider in accordance with PSD 2 is required. This directive contains prudential requirements to cater for the risks connected to the provision of
payment services. For asset safe keeping services that relate to securities a licence as a bank

---

obligations of confidentiality; failure to establish, implement, and maintain appropriate procedures to prevent
conflicts of interest; losses arising from business disruption, system failures or process management; and where
applicable to the business model, gross negligence in carrying out asset valuation or credit pricing, and scoring.

[88] Art 11(3) of the Crowdfunding Regulation, with reference to the applicability of the prudential regimes of
CRR (Title III of Part Three) and the IFR: Regulation (EU) 2019/2033 of the European Parliament and of the
Council.
[89] Art 11(4) refers to institutions which are subject to Arts 4 and 5 of the EMI Directive or Arts 7–9 of PSD II.
[90] This is a 'gone-concern' approach, rather than a 'going-concern' approach. This approach is also used
in Art 95 CRR. See section 3.2.4 of EPM Joosen and ML Louisse, 'Een nieuw prudentieel regime voor
beleggingsondernemingen (I)', Tijdschrift voor financieel recht, nr 3, maart 2018, for a discussion on the going-
concern nature of the fixed overhead requirement for investment firms.
[91] Art 2(1)(a) of the Crowdfunding Regulation.
[92] Art 2(1)(a)(i) and (ii) of the Crowdfunding Regulation, without any guarantee.
[93] Art 2(1)(c) of the Crowdfunding Regulation.
[94] Art 3(4) and (5) of the Crowdfunding Regulation, Article 6 of the Crowdfunding Regulation.
[95] Art 10 of the Crowdfunding Regulation.

or investment firm is required.[96] This, however, does not apply to any safekeeping services in relation to loans that do not qualify as securities. Banks and investment firms involved in the safekeeping of financial instruments need to adhere to prudential requirements under Capital Requirements Regulation (CRR)/CRD IV or IFR/ Investment Firm Directive (IFD) (as applicable).

8.52   The services described above (notably the crowdfunding services and the individual portfolio management of loans) entail financial risks for clients if these are not properly performed. Part of these risks is 'compensated' by posing organizational and operational requirements and safeguards, such as the prevention of conflict of interests[97] and due diligence requirements.[98] However, despite these safeguards and requirements, errors may be made, exposing a client to operational risks, for example, if an order is overlooked or not executed in time. This results in a liability risk for the CSP.

8.53   The safekeeping of assets constitutes a somewhat different risk profile. As set out above, this is particularly relevant in relation to the safekeeping of loans,[99] which is not covered by Article 10(3) of the Crowdfunding Regulation. As there is no further regulation on the safekeeping of loans whatsoever, we assume that the Crowdfunding Regulation does not anticipate any safekeeping of loans and is based on the assumption that these loans are always held directly in the name of the investor in his own books and not by the CSP for the benefit of the investor. We will proceed on the basis of the same assumption, otherwise the prudential regime as discussed above would be inadequate in view of the specific risks associated with the safekeeping of loans that requires an effective system of asset segregation (both from a legal and administrative perspective). The safekeeping of loans would lead to a significant increase of the risk profile of the CSP.

8.54   In view of the type of risks that are connected to the business of a crowdfunding service provided which are basically operational in nature, in a similar manner as is the case for investment firms that provide comparable services,[100] it is understandable that a comparable prudential system has been selected to cater for these risks. Notably, the revisions and update to this system as is introduced by the IFR and which introduce quantitative indicators (ie the K-factors) as an additional safeguard have not been included.[101] In view of the limitations to the business of CSPs,[102] this can be considered a correct approach from a proportionality perspective.

---

[96] Art 10(3) of the Crowdfunding Regulation. This system differs from that of investment firms where safekeeping services qualify as ancillary services that on a stand-alone basis do not trigger a licence requirement.

[97] Art 4(1) of the Crowdfunding Regulation, Art 8 of the Crowdfunding Regulation.

[98] Art 5 of the Crowdfunding Regulation.

[99] Further, the safekeeping of loans may entail that the CSP attracts, acquires, or holds repayable funds which may be contrary to the prohibition of Art 9 of CRD IV.

[100] See N Moloney, *EU Securities and Financial Markets Regulation* (3rd edn, OUP 2014) 320 et seq.

[101] Art 13 IFR.

[102] Art 1(2) under c of the Crowdfunding Regulation.

V. Rules in Respect of Outsourcing

CSPs are allowed to entrust *any* operational function, in whole or in part, to a third party. **8.55**
Outsourcing is considered to be in the interest of the efficient and smooth provision of
crowdfunding services. However, such outsourcing may not impair the quality of CSPs' internal controls or the effective supervision of the CSPs. In addition, CSPs remain fully responsible for compliance with the provisions of the Crowdfunding Regulation with respect
to the outsourced activities.[103] Below, we will further discuss the regulation of outsourcing
by the CSP.

To start, the Crowdfunding Regulation does not pose restrictions to the scope of any **8.56**
outsourcing.[104] All operational functions may be outsourced. The reference to *operational
functions* in our view entails that any policy making decisions cannot be outsourced.
Although there is no limitation to the scope of outsourcing of operational functions, the
CSP must at all times maintain sufficient substance to be able to supervise and control the
outsourced activities.[105] This entails that the staff of the CSP must contain sufficient resources and expertise to conduct oversight of the outsourced activities.

Further, the CSP must take all reasonable steps to avoid additional operational risk.[106] The **8.57**
reference to 'reasonable steps' includes that there is room for a proportional and risk-based
compliance with this provision. Typically, the measures that are required will include that
the outsourcing is based on a written agreement with the delegate and that this arrangement will provide for control and audit possibilities, for the CSP, and also access rights for
its supervisor. This serves to ensure that the ability of the competent authority to monitor
the CSPs' compliance with the Crowdfunding Regulation is not impaired.[107] To ensure that
the outsourcing of operational functions does not impair the quality of the CSPs' internal
control,[108] the CSP should in our view maintain sufficient internal resources to conduct this
function.

Based on Article 9(3) of the Crowdfunding Regulation CSPs remain fully responsible for **8.58**
compliance with the provisions of the Crowdfunding Regulation with respect to any outsourced activities. This entails in our view that both vis-à-vis the competent supervisor and
vis-à-vis the clients, the CSP cannot refer to the poor performance of any delegate. If the
delegate fails to properly perform an outsourced task, the CSP should step in and reassume
this task.

To conclude, the regulation of the outsourcing entails a quite liberal approach which enables **8.59**
the CSP to apply full outsourcing of all operational functions. However, at the same time the
CSP must maintain sufficient staffing to be able to conduct the required oversight and assume the regulatory responsibility for all its business, including any outsourced functions.

---

[103] This starting point is set out in Recital (27) to the Crowdfunding Regulation.
[104] Contrary to, eg, outsourcing by a manager under the AIFMD which may not become a letter box entity and
should always conduct the activities as listed in Annex I under (1) in accordance with the provisions of Art 20.
[105] Art 9(2) of the Crowdfunding Regulation.
[106] Art 9(1) of the Crowdfunding Regulation.
[107] Art 9(3) of the Crowdfunding Regulation.
[108] As is required by Art 9(3) of the Crowdfunding Regulation.

VI. Conclusion

8.60 In this chapter, the organizational and operational requirements for CSPs have been discussed. These requirements are in follow-up to the authorization requirements that the CSPs have to meet in order to obtain market access. Once this access is obtained, the ongoing organizational and operational requirements aim to ensure the effective and prudent management of the CSP and that certain conflicts of interest are prevented and others are properly managed and disclosed. Further, complaints handling and outsourcing are regulated. To protect clients against the operational risks of its business, a CSP is subject to prudential requirements to ensure a continuity of business of at least three months.

PART IV

THE POSITION OF PROJECT OWNERS UNDER THE CROWDFUNDING REGULATION AND BEYOND

9

The Regulatory Position and
Obligations of Project Owners

Jonneke van Poelgeest and Marije Louisse

I. Introduction

Raising funds and/or issuing financial instruments through a crowdfunding platform can **9.01** be interesting for many different reasons. For example, the target audience can be broad, and (potential) investors can be reached that have no connection with the person/company obtaining the funds. Crowdfunding can also enable companies to obtain funds when there are no other, more traditional ways to obtain these funds. Crowdfunding can be a useful tool for start-up companies, indicating whether the intended offer of products or services might be valuable. More mature companies can also use crowdfunding to obtain funds and/ or or to create a support base for the (intended) products or services. Crowdfunding is for example often used as a tool to create a support base in relation to sustainability projects with an impact on the (direct) living environment. Crowdfunding can also be used as a marketing tool.[1]

9.02   As a result, natural and legal persons raising funds through a crowdfunding platform (hereinafter, project owners) come in many different sizes and shapes.[2] They do share, however, certain regulatory obligations when raising funds. In this chapter, we solely focus on the position of the project owner, and more specifically on the situation where the project owner obtains funds through a crowdfunding platform that is regulated by the Crowdfunding Regulation.[3] Where relevant, the Netherlands is used as a case study. Some details about Dutch law and other illustrative examples are provided in indented paragraphs.

9.03   This chapter starts with an introduction of the project owner (section II) and continues with the obligations of the crowdfunding service provider in respect of project owners (section III). Section IV subsequently discusses the (lack of an) authorization requirement for project owners under the Crowdfunding Regulation. Section V assesses the regulatory obligations of project owners under the Crowdfunding Regulation and discusses the concurrence with obligations arising from other EU directives and regulations. Lastly, section VI raises the issue whether project owners also require some form of protection, similar to investors, and whether this is a missing piece of the Crowdfunding Regulation. Section VII concludes.

II. Meet the Project Owner

9.04   A project owner is defined in the Crowdfunding Regulation as a natural or legal person who seeks funding through a 'crowdfunding platform'. A crowdfunding platform is a publicly accessible Internet-based information system operated or managed by a crowdfunding service provider.[4] Taking into account the scope of the Crowdfunding Regulation, a project owner, within the meaning of the Crowdfunding Regulation, is a (legal) person acting in the course of its business or profession that seeks funding through investment or loan-based crowdfunding, by issuing transferable securities or other admitted instruments for crowdfunding purposes or attracting loans with a consideration of EUR 5 million or less, using a crowdfunding service provider that is licenced on the basis of the Crowdfunding Regulation and to whom the project owner is not related. Below, we further discuss these different characteristics of project owners.

---

[1] Reference is also made to Recital 4 of the Crowdfunding Regulation. See also J Viotta da Cruz, 'Beyond financing: crowdfunding as an informational mechanism' (2018) Journal of Business Venturing 2.
[2] See also M Gray and B Zhang, 'Crowdfunding: Understanding Diversity' in R Martin and J Pollard, *Handbook on the Geographies of Money and Finance* (Elgar 2018) 603–05.
[3] For more information about the Crowdfunding Regulation and its impact in the Netherlands reference is also made to J Baukema, 'Regulering crowdfunding: nationale ontwikkelingen en ontwerp ECSP Verordening' (2018) 11 Tijdschrift voor financieel recht 517–26 and to ELM Kranenburg and DAJM Melchers, 'De toekomstige Europese Verordening voor Crowdfundingdienstverleners (Deel I)' (2020) 11 Tijdschrift voor financieel recht 1–7 and SN Demper and ML Louisse, *Crowdfunding—een juridische verkenning* (Ars Aequi 2019).
[4] Art 2(1) under (d) Crowdfunding Regulation.

1. (Legal) Person Acting in the Course of Its Business or Profession

A project owner, within the meaning of the Crowdfunding Regulation, is by definition **9.05**
a (legal) person acting in the course of its business or profession. The Crowdfunding
Regulation does not apply to the provision of crowdfunding services in relation to consumers[5] attracting consumer loans via a (crowdfunding) platform. Therefore, these crowdfunding services and the regulatory position of project owners qualifying as consumers
are still regulated by means of national rules and regulations of the EU Member States
(including national laws implementing the Consumer Credit Directive/Mortgage Credit
Directive (CCD/MCD)), as illustrated in Chapter 5.[6]

> Pursuant to Dutch rules and regulations, a license is required to offer a loan to consumers.
> Therefore, a crowdfunding service provider would need an additional, national license
> to be able to facilitate the granting of loans to project owners that qualify as consumers
> through its crowdfunding platform in the Netherlands.[7]

2. Funding through Investment or Loan-based Crowdfunding

Donation and reward-based crowdfunding via a crowdfunding platform does not fall **9.06**
within the scope of the Crowdfunding Regulation. The European Commission considered
that the inclusion of those business models would be disproportionate as they do not deal
with financial products and the information asymmetries that these products create.[8] This
means that project owners that are looking at attracting funds through donation or by
granting perks, such as advanced versions of a product, are not bound by the framework
set out in the Crowdfunding Regulation. This is without prejudice to national regimes that
may apply.

> In the Netherlands, crowdfunding in the form of donation is not a regulated activity, be-
> sides the application of general consumer laws which is supervised by the Netherlands
> Authority for Consumers and Markets, because the project owners do not have an obli-
> gation to repay the donation.[9] This is not without controversy. For example, the crowd-
> funding website Dream or Donate went offline after having received donations from
> thousands of people. The website claimed to be hacked and eventually reached a settlement
> with the sponsors.[10] See also Chapter 11 on crowdfunding through donation.

---

[5] As defined in Art 3 under (a) CDD (Art 1(2) under (a) and Recital 8 Crowdfunding Regulation). In accordance with this definition, a consumer is a natural person who is acting for purposes which are outside his trade,
business, or profession. See also Chapter 5.

[6] See also COM(2018) 113 final, 2018/0048 (COD), Proposal for a Regulation of the European Parliament and
of the Council on European Crowdfunding Service Providers (ECSP) for Business (Text with EEA relevance),
{SWD(2018) 56 final}—{SWD(2018) 57 final}, 2.

[7] In the Netherlands, this licence obligation is included in Article 2:60 of the Dutch Act on Financial
Supervision (AFS, *Wet op het financieel toezicht*). Reference is made to JM van Poelgeest, *Kredietverstrekking aan
consumenten* (Kluwer 2020).

[8] Commission Proposal (n 5) 2.

[9] Minister of Economic Affairs and Climate, Answers to questions of SP-fraction on costs of crowdfunding, 4
February 2019. AFM, Wanneer heeft u een vergunning nodig voor crowdfunding? <http://www.afm.nl> accessed
27 April 2020. If the payments flow is processed via the platform, it is however possible that a licence is required to
provide payment services.

[10] NOS, 'Gedupeerden donatiewebsite Dream or Donate hebben hun geld terug', 3 December 2019. RTL Nieuws,
'Oprichter donatiesite Dream or Donate vrijuit: mogelijke oplichting niet verder onderzocht', 24 November

3. Attraction of Loans or Issuance of Transferable Securities or Other Admitted Instruments for Crowdfunding Purposes

9.07   A project owner, within the meaning of the Crowdfunding Regulation, can seek funds by attracting loans or issuing transferable securities or other admitted instruments for crowdfunding purposes.[11] This means that if instruments are issued by a project owner through a (crowdfunding) platform, other than transferable securities or other admitted instruments for crowdfunding purposes (such as utility tokens that do not qualify as transferable securities), the project owner does not fall within the scope of the Crowdfunding Regulation. It is intended that an offer of crypto-assets will be covered by the proposed 'Markets in Crypto-Assets Regulation', as illustrated in Chapter 6.[12] Importantly, if funds are attracted through loans, the loan agreement should be concluded by and between the project owner and the investors directly. The Crowdfunding Regulation does not support crowdfunding structures whereby the service provider itself provides the loan to the project owner (on its own behalf) which seems to exclude crowdfunding structures with an assignment of (part of) the claims arising from the loan.[13]

4. Crowdfunding Offers with a Maximum Amount of EUR 5 Million

9.08   A project owner, within the meaning of the Crowdfunding Regulation, is limited in the amount of funds that it can attract. Crowdfunding offers within the scope of the Crowdfunding Regulation are in principle limited to EUR 5 million (calculated over a period of twelve months).[14] This is discussed further in subsection V.3.A.

5. Shareholders, Managers, and Employees Cannot Act as Project Owners

9.09   Crowdfunding service providers (CSPs) may not accept as project owners their own shareholders, holding 20% or more of share capital or voting rights. The same prohibition applies to the providers' managers and employees, and any natural or legal person closely linked to

---

2020. M Schoutens, 'Hoe kunnen we leren van het Dream or Donate debacle?' Vakblad fondsenwerving, 30 September 2019.

[11] See Chapter 3 for an explanation of these terms.

[12] Proposal for a regulation of the European parliament and of the council on Markets in crypto-assets, amending directive (EU) 2019/1937, COM (2020) 593 final. The definition of crypto assets is broad and covers all kinds of crypto assets not qualifying as financial instruments. Reference is also made to SW van de Ven, 'Van Mifid naar MiCa: een juridisch raamwerk voor crypto asset service providers' (2020) 12 Tijdschrift voor financieel recht 593–98. See also Chapter 6.

[13] Recital 11 Crowdfunding Regulation. The crowdfunding service provider should only facilitate the conclusion by investors and project owners of loan agreements without the crowdfunding service provider at any moment acting as a creditor of the project owner.

[14] Art 1(2) under (c) (and Recital 16 and 17) Crowdfunding Regulation. In an earlier proposal for the regulation, this was an amount of EUR 1 million. Art 49 Crowdfunding Regulation provides for a temporary derogation, which is further discussed in section V.3.A.

those shareholders, managers, or employees by control.[15] This prohibition applies in order to avoid conflicts of interest.

A. Use of Special Purpose Vehicles

The Crowdfunding Regulation pays specific attention to the situation in which legal struc-   **9.10** tures, including special purpose vehicles (SPVs), interpose between the project owner and investors. According to Recital 22 of the Crowdfunding Regulation, this should be strictly regulated and permitted only where it is justified by enabling an investor to acquire an interest in, for example, an illiquid or indivisible asset through issuance of transferable securities by an SPV. Such an SPV would issue transferable securities or other admitted instruments for crowdfunding purposes to the investors. An SPV is defined as an entity created solely for, or which solely serves the purpose of, a securitization within the meaning of point (2) of Article 1 of Regulation (EU) No 1075/2013 of the European Central Bank (ECB).[16] Article 3(6) of the Crowdfunding Regulation provides that where an SPV is used for the provision of crowdfunding services, only *one* illiquid or indivisible asset shall be offered through such an SPV. That requirement shall apply on a look-through basis to the underlying illiquid or indivisible asset held by financial or legal structures fully or partially owned or controlled by SPV. The decision to take exposure to that underlying asset shall exclusively lie with investors.[17]

On 25 February 2021, the European Securities and Market Authority (ESMA) published   **9.11** its first Q&A on the Crowdfunding Regulation, which exclusively covers the use of SPVs.[18] The Q&A clarifies that the Crowdfunding Regulation does not envisage the possibility of loan-based crowdfunding offers made via an SPV. It also underlines that the SPV can only give exposure to one underlying asset, which should be either illiquid or indivisible. An asset should be deemed to be illiquid when it cannot be turned into cash swiftly. Indications are that there is no organized market for assets of that type, sales for that type of assets usually take place over the counter, there is no readily available value for assets of that type or reaching an agreement on a selling price with a potential buyer encompasses significant costs and takes from a few weeks to a few months. An asset should be deemed to be indivisible when it cannot be easily or swiftly divided into smaller, more moderately priced components for the purpose of its partial or total sale to investors or when such division in smaller components is not economically rational, notably because it prevents the asset from serving its core economical purpose. Factors that are relevant in that respect are the legal structure, nature, and core economical purpose.

The ability to use an SPV for crowdfunding purposes is of special relevance to real estate   **9.12** crowdfunding.[19] In that case, the SPV is created to enable investors to obtain ownership

---

[15] Recital 26 and Art 8 Crowdfunding Regulation.

[16] Art 4(1) under q Crowdfunding Regulation.

[17] On 2 November 2020, the US Securities and Exchange Commission (SEC) approved an amendment of the Security Act of 1933 that allows the use of SPVs to invest in deals under the Regulation Crowdfunding, also known as Title III of the JOBS act.

[18] ESMA, Q&A on the European crowdfunding service providers for business Regulation, 25 February 2021, ESMA35-42-1088.

[19] See on the development of real estate crowdfunding T Ziegler and others, *Expanding Horizons: The 3rd European Alternative Finance Industry Report* (Cambridge Centre for Alternative Finance 2017). See also M-L Matthiesen and BI Steininger (2017) Finanzinnovation: Crowdfunding für die Immobilienwirtschaft, Real Estate Finance Working Paper No 2017-01.

of a property by purchasing shares of a single property or a portfolio of properties through an SPV.[20]

III. Obligations of Crowdfunding Service Providers in Relation to Project Owners

1. Duty of Care

9.13 Both investors and project owners qualify as clients of CSPs.[21] These CSPs enter into contractual arrangements not only with the investors but also with the project owners.[22] This implies a certain duty of care towards project owners, although this has not been extensively substantiated in the Crowdfunding Regulation. In general, CSPs need to act honestly, fairly, and professionally in accordance with the best interests of project owners.[23]

The duty of care of crowdfunding service providers hence resembles the duty of care in MiFID II, which requires investment firms to act honestly, fairly and professionally in accordance with the best interests of its clients.[24] From a Dutch perspective, this is interesting, because most crowdfunding platforms in the Netherlands currently operate on the basis of a dispensation (granted by the Netherlands Authority for the Financial Markets, or AFM) from the prohibition to act as an intermediary in attracting repayable funds from the public, or on the basis of an authorization as a financial service provider. Only a few operate as an investment firm. In the Netherlands, a general duty of care for financial service providers was introduced in the Dutch Act on Financial Supervision (AFS) in 2014. In respect of this duty of care, a distinction is made between financial service providers that provide advice, and those that do not provide advice. For the former, the obligation applies to act in the interest of the consumer or beneficiary.[25] For the latter, the obligation applies to take the justified interests of the consumer or beneficiary in consideration. The duty of care for financial service providers that do not provide advice is considered lighter than the duty of care for financial service providers that do provide advice. It is interesting in that respect that the Crowdfunding Regulation requires crowdfunding service providers, that explicitly do not provide advice to their clients, to act in accordance with the best interests of project owners. It remains to be seen in practice whether this leads to a different interpretation of the duty of care of crowdfunding service providers towards their clients in the Netherlands.

---

[20] M Gray and B Zhang, 'Crowdfunding: Understanding Diversity' in R Martin and J Pollard, *Handbook on the Geographies of Money and Finance* (Elgar 2018) 590.

[21] Art 2(1) under (g) Crowdfunding Regulation.

[22] They need to maintain such agreements for at least five years (Art 26 Crowdfunding Regulation). Competent authorities can transfer existing contracts to another crowdfunding service provider in cases where a crowdfunding service provider's authorization is withdrawn, subject to the agreement of the clients and the receiving crowdfunding service provider (Art 30(2) under (i) Crowdfunding Regulation).

[23] Art 3(2) Crowdfunding Regulation. See also Art 4(1) Crowdfunding Regulation.

[24] Art 24(1) MiFID II. See also V Colaert and M Peeters, 'Is there a Case for a Cross-Sectoral Duty of Care for the Financial Sector?' in V Colaert, D Busch, and T Incalza, *European Financial Regulation: Levelling the Cross-Sectoral Playing Field* (Hart 2019) 324.

[25] As discussed in section II, a project owner, within the meaning of the Crowdfunding Regulation, cannot be a consumer.

In addition, the complaints handling procedures should cover complaints from project owners.[26] Furthermore, policies on conflicts of interests should not only cover conflicts of interest between the crowdfunding service provider and its clients but also between one client and another client. This could therefore also include conflicts among multiple project owners, or conflicts between project owners and investors.

> In accordance with Recital 26 of the Crowdfunding Regulation, crowdfunding service providers should operate as neutral intermediaries between clients on their crowdfunding platform. Questions arise as to the interplay between such a neutral role, and the obligation to act in the best interests of the clients. Another question is how a crowdfunding service provider can act both in the best interests of the project owner and the investor. Although they do have some shared interests, for example, making the crowdfunding project into a success, their interests may also be opposite, for example in relation to risk and reward. It seems therefore that situations may arise where the crowdfunding service provider cannot, at the same time, act in the best interests of the project owner and the investor. The Crowdfunding Regulation does not provide any guidance in that respect, other than the conflicts of interest rules.

CSPs also have certain information obligations towards project owners, for example, in **9.14** relation to the risks, costs, and charges related to the crowdfunding services that are provided.[27] Specific obligations apply when asset safekeeping service or payment services are provided,[28] or when CSPs operate a bulletin board.[29] Finally, when taking out an insurance policy to comply with the applicable prudential requirements, this policy should cover acts, errors, or omissions resulting in a breach of duty of skill and care towards project owners.[30]

2. Remuneration

CSPs are not allowed to pay or accept any remuneration, discount, or non-monetary benefit **9.15** for routing investors' orders to a particular crowdfunding offer made on their crowdfunding platform, or to a particular crowdfunding offer made on a third-party crowdfunding platform.[31] The background of this rule is that prospective investors should be offered investment opportunities on a neutral basis.[32] This means that CSPs are not allowed to request or receive a certain fee in order to route investors to the crowdfunding project of a specific project owner. The Crowdfunding Regulation, however, does not provide for any further restrictions in respect of the payments that CSPs may request or receive from project owners and investors, other than that such payments should be in accordance with the general duty of care obligations, including in respect of disclosure of costs and charges and prevention of conflicts of interest.

---

[26] Art 7 and 38 Crowdfunding Regulation. See also Chapter 8.
[27] Art 19 Crowdfunding Regulation. See Chapter 12.
[28] Art 10 Crowdfunding Regulation.
[29] Art 25 Crowdfunding Regulation. See Chapter 14.
[30] Art 11(7) Crowdfunding Regulation. See also Recital 24 Crowdfunding Regulation.
[31] Art 3 Crowdfunding Regulation.
[32] Recital 19 Crowdfunding Regulation.

The remuneration rules in the Crowdfunding Regulation are hence less strict than the inducement rules set out in MiFID II.[33] In the Netherlands, an exemption to the inducement ban for investment firms applies to crowdfunding platforms that qualify as an investment firm and receive and transmit orders from retail clients.[34] Taking into account that crowdfunding service providers that have obtained an authorization under the Crowdfunding Regulation are exempt from MiFID II, the inducement ban does not apply either. However, the exemption to the inducement ban may still be relevant for crowdfunding platforms that provide investment services that are not in scope of the Crowdfunding Regulation.

3. Due Diligence of Project Owners

9.16 In addition to the duty of care obligations that CSPs have on the basis of the Crowdfunding Regulation and the restrictions that apply in relation to remuneration structures, CSPs need to undertake at least a minimum level of due diligence in respect of project owners that propose their projects to be funded through their crowdfunding platform. This means that the service provider should obtain evidence that the project owner:

(1) has no criminal record in respect of infringements of national rules in fields of commercial law, insolvency law, financial services law, anti-money laundering law, fraud law, or professional liability obligations; and

(2) is not established in a non-cooperative jurisdiction, as recognized by the relevant Union policy, or in a high-risk third country.[35]

For the project owner, this means that sufficient information must be provided to the service provider to ensure that it can obtain sufficient evidence.

For example, in the Netherlands, we could think of a declaration of no objection (*verklaring omtrent gedrag/van geen bezwaar*) issued by Justis (the Dutch Ministry of Justice and Safety), a check of the public insolvency register and a statement provided by the project owner in this respect. The AFM requests for certain applications a background statement (*antecedentenverklaring*) which may potentially also be used by the service providers to comply with this obligation.[36]

In addition, to protect investors, CSPs should have a policy that ensures that projects on their platforms are selected in a professional, fair, and transparent way.[37] As a result, the CSP can decide not to accept a project owner on its platform if this is not in line with such a policy, although the minimum level of due diligence has been undertaken with good result. CSPs should however always treat project owners in a fair and non-discriminatory way.[38]

---

[33] Arts 24(7), (8), and (9) MiFID II.

[34] Art 168a(1) under (f) Decree on Supervision of Conduct of Business Financial Undertakings AFS (*Besluit Gedragstoezicht financiële ondernemingen Wft*).

[35] The high-risk third countries are defined by the European Commission in delegated acts pursuant to Art 9(2) Fourth AML Directive. At the time of writing this chapter, the most recent delegated act is Commission Delegated Regulation (EU) 2020/855 of 7 May 2020 amending Delegated Regulation (EU) 2016/1675. The list of non-cooperative jurisdictions for tax purposes is adopted by the Council and was published in the Official Journal on 7 October 2020 (2020/C 331/03).

[36] In the Netherlands, insolvencies are listed in a public register: <https://insolventies.rechtspraak.nl>.

[37] Recital 18 Crowdfunding Regulation.

[38] Recital 57 Crowdfunding Regulation.

4. Credit Risk Assessment and Valuation

Pricing is one of the most important aspects to consider before a crowdfunding project is launched. Such pricing can either be determined by the project owner or the CSP. When the CSP determines the price, this results in certain obligations.[39] In order to fulfil these obligations, CSPs will require certain information from the project owners.   **9.17**

The Crowdfunding Regulation obliges the CSP that determines the price of a crowdfunding offer to undertake a reasonable assessment of the credit risk on the basis of clear and effective policies and procedures. For debt instruments/loans, it is specified that the risk will be assessed that the project owner will not pay on the relevant due date(s).[40] The service provider should base the assessment on sufficient information including: **9.18**

(1) where available, audited accounts covering the two latest financial years;

(2) information of which it is aware at the time the credit risk assessment is carried out;

(3) information which has been obtained, where appropriate, from the project owner; and

(4) information which enables the CSP to carry out a reasonable credit risk assessment.

The list is quite generic and open-ended. The European Banking Authority (EBA), however, will develop draft regulatory technical standards (RTS) to specify the information and factors that CSPs should consider when carrying out a credit risk assessment.[41] In the absence of such draft being available at the time of writing this chapter, we can imagine that such information may include information regarding the business plan, information regarding the incorporation and governance of the company, such as a structure chart, shareholders register, articles of association, excerpt of the chamber of commerce, information regarding management and shareholders and group companies of the company, (possible) (current and future) claims, lawsuits and security rights, and compliance documents.

If the CSP determines the price of a crowdfunding offer, it should not only conduct a credit risk assessment before the crowdfunding offer is made but also conduct a valuation of each loan at certain moments in time (including when it is originated and following a default).[42] The CSP therefore has an ongoing obligation to value the loan. The EBA will again develop draft RTS to specify the information and factors that CSPs should consider when conducting a valuation of a loan.[43] We expect this information to include information provided by the project owner.   **9.19**

Lastly, the CSP has to ensure that the price is fair and appropriate, including where an exit is facilitated before the maturity date of the loan, in line with the risk-management framework that the CSP is required to have and use.[44] The EBA will specify factors that a   **9.20**

---

[39] Art 4(4) Crowdfunding Regulation.
[40] For transferable securities, other than bonds or other forms of securitized debt, it is not specified which risks should be assessed. See eg L Hornuf and M Neuenkirch, 'Pricing Shares in Equity Crowdfunding' (2017) 48 Small Bus Econ, 795–811.
[41] Art 19(7) Crowdfunding Regulation.
[42] Art 4(4) under (e) Crowdfunding Regulation.
[43] Art 19(7) Crowdfunding Regulation.
[44] Art 4(4) under (d) and (g) Crowdfunding Regulation.

CSP should take into account when ensuring that the price of a loan it facilitates is fair and appropriate.[45]

IV. No Authorization Requirement for Project Owners?

9.21   The Crowdfunding Regulation explicitly states that Member States should not apply national requirements implementing Article 9(1) of the Capital Requirements Directive (CRD), and should ensure that their national laws do not require an authorization as a credit institution or any other individual authorization, exemption or dispensation for project owners.[46] Although this seems to be a clear instruction to the Member States, we have identified a number of issues that require clarification and questions that we discuss below.

> The current text of Article 1(3) of the Crowdfunding Regulation was introduced by the Council at first reading and approved by the European Parliament at second reading. In the original proposal from the European Commission, no statement was included in relation to the regulatory position of the project owner. The European Parliament introduced at first reading Article 2(2a), that stated that 'National laws on licence requirements relating to project owners or investors shall not prevent those project owners or investors from using crowdfunding services provided by crowdfunding service providers pursuant to, and authorised by, this Regulation'.

1. Exemption from Authorization Requirement for Credit Institutions

9.22   First, it is unclear to us how the instruction to the Member States relates to the European framework for credit institutions set out in CRR/CRD. The Crowdfunding Regulation

---

[45] Art 19(7) Crowdfunding Regulation. Some interesting research has been done on the factors that make a crowdfunding project a success. Cai, Polzin, and Stam, for example, focus on the project owners' social capital, being one of the main determinants of crowdfunding success. Unlike offline investment in which trust and reputation are built through interpersonal interactions, crowdfunding, which is by definition online, makes it difficult for founders to build relationships with potential investors. This makes it interesting to see how social capital affects crowdfunding performance (W Cai, F Polzin, and E Stam (2019) 'Crowdfunding and Social Capital: A Systemic Literature Review', USE Research Institute Working Paper Series 19-05). In addition, Zhou and others focused on the project descriptions as a determinant for the success of a crowdfunding project (M Zhou and others, 'Project Description and Crowdfunding Success: An Exploratory Study (2018) 20 Information Systems Frontiers 259–74).

[46] Recital 9 Crowdfunding Regulation, Art 1(3) under (a) Crowdfunding Regulation. The above seems to imply that next to the authorization requirement as a credit institution, also any other, national prohibitions to attract (repayable) funds from the public should not apply if the funds are attracted via a crowdfunding platform within the meaning of the Crowdfunding Regulation. Art 3:5 AFS contains the prohibition to attract, obtain or have redeemable funds in the Netherlands from the public. This prohibition does not apply if this is the result of an offer of securities in accordance with the provisions of the Prospectus Regulation. This also includes offers that are made under an exemption from the prospectus obligation. In the Netherlands, currently such an exemption exists for project owners attracting funds via a crowdfunding platform (Art 24b Exemption Regulation AFS (*Vrijstellingsregeling Wft*)). Certain criteria need to be met in order for the exemption to apply, including that the project owner will not provide credit (since it could qualify as a credit institution in that situation), a limitation of EUR 2.5 million (instead of EUR 5 million) and a crowdfunding platform which obtained an exemption on the basis of Art 4:3 AFS (instead of a crowdfunding platform with a licence on the basis of the Crowdfunding Regulation). Taking into account that the Crowdfunding Regulation introduces an exemption from the prospectus requirement under different criteria, the Dutch exemption needs to be amended. Project owners acting in accordance with this new exemption, will also be exempt from the prohibition to attract repayable funds from the public. Reference is also made to ELM van Kranenburg and DAJM Melchers, 'De toekomstige Europese Verordening voor Crowdfundingdienstverleners (Deel II)' (2020) 12 Tijdschrift voor financieel recht 587, 588.

does not provide for an amendment of CRR/CRD to exclude project owners from the scope thereof. The question therefore is, how this instruction sets aside the applicability of CRR/CRD, in case the project owner qualifies as a credit institution, within the meaning of Article 4 of the CRR.[47] Such qualification is triggered when a project owner attracts repayable funds from the public—through the crowdfunding—and grants credit for its own account. Although we believe that the Crowdfunding Regulation intends to exclude project owners from the authorization requirement on the basis of Article 8 CRD, it seems wise also to change the CRR (by excluding project owners from the definition of credit institution) or to change the CRD (by including an exemption to the authorization requirement for project owners).

> Article 1(3) of the Crowdfunding Regulation further complicates the matter by stating that, if the project owner is authorized as a credit institution in accordance with Article 8 of the CRD, Article 1(3) of the Crowdfunding Regulation does not apply. We understand this to cover the situation where the project owner already qualifies as a credit institution, because of activities other than raising funds for crowdfunding projects.

2. Exemption from the Prohibition to Take Deposits and Other Repayable Funds

In addition, Article 1(3) of the Crowdfunding Regulation states that Member States should **9.23** not apply national requirements implementing Article 9(1) of the CRD, which contains the prohibition for persons that are not credit institutions to carry out the business of taking deposits or other repayable funds from the public. Again, this raises questions. Does the prohibition not apply? Or should Member States only not apply the national requirements? And if they do not apply the national requirements, can they be faced with the reproach that they do not apply Article 9(1) of the CRD correctly? Another question would be why the European legislator did not make use of Article 9(2) of the CRD. In accordance therewith, cases expressly covered by national or Union law are exempt from the prohibition, provided that those activities are subject to regulations and controls intended to protect depositors and investors. In our view, it would have been possible to argue that the fact that the project owner raises funds through the services of a CSP that is authorized under the Crowdfunding Regulation would provide such regulations and controls.

3. Project Owners that Accept Funds through Loans or the Issuance of Debt Securities

The Crowdfunding Regulation also creates uncertainty as to the question whether the in- **9.24** struction to the Member States applies to *all* project owners, or only the project owners that accept funds through loans. Although reference is made in Recital 9 of the Crowdfunding Regulation to project owners that 'accept funds for the purposes of offering crowdfunding

---

[47] See also Art 9(4) CRD in that respect, that specifically prohibits Member States to exempt credit institution from the application of CRD and CRR.

projects', Article 1 of the Crowdfunding Regulation indicates that this only relates to project owners that 'in respect of loans facilitated by the crowdfunding service provider accept funds from investors'. Article 1, therefore, seems to entail that it is still allowed (or maybe it is even necessary) to require a licence or other authorization, if a project owner attracts funds through the issuance of transferable securities, including bonds.[48] This would however, in our view, result in an arbitrary distinction between project owners that attract funds through loans or debt securities. It would therefore be logical, in our view, that the instruction to the Member States also applies when project owners issue bonds or other debt securities on a crowdfunding platform.

4. Project Owners that Accept Funds through the Issuance of Equity Securities

9.25   Although there is uncertainty in respect of debt securities, it seems to be clear that project owners that attract funds through the issuance of equity securities are out of scope of the instruction to the Member States as mentioned in Section IV.4. This means that the Crowdfunding Regulation does not prevent Member States from requiring any individual authorization, exemption, or dispensation for project owners that attract funds through the issuance of equity securities. Such project owners could, for example, depending on their activities, require an authorization or registration as (the manager of) an alternative investment fund (AIF) or an undertaking for the collective investment in transferable securities (UCITS), based on the applicable national implementation of the Alternative Investment Fund Managers Directive (AIFMD) or UCITS Directive. This situation, though, should be rare, since funding attracted through crowdfunding will generally have a general commercial purpose, as a result of which no qualification as (the manager of) an AIF or UCITS applies.[49]

> If the project owner requires an authorization as (the manager of) an AIF or UCITS, one should be aware of the requirement to publish a prospectus and key investor information under the AIFMD or UCITS Directive, as this is not explicitly excluded in the Crowdfunding Regulation.[50] Therefore, although the basic principle is that only the Crowdfunding Regulation information requirements apply to project owners, this could be different in case the qualification as (the manager of) an AIF or UCITS applies.

---

[48] Bonds can both fit within the definition of transferable securities as well as the definition of loan. 'Loan' means an agreement whereby an investor makes available to a project owner an agreed amount of money for an agreed period of time and whereby the project owner assumes an unconditional obligation to repay that amount to the investor, together with the accrued interest, in accordance with the instalment payment schedule.

[49] ESMA, Guidelines on key concepts of the AIFMD, 24 May 2013.

[50] Art 23 AIFMD and Art 68 and 78 UCITS Directive. The Crowdfunding Regulation does provide for exemptions from the prospectus requirement under the Prospectus Regulation and the requirement to publish a key information document for PRIIPs under the PRIIPS Regulation. See also sections V.3.A and V.3.B. Art 45 Crowdfunding Regulation obliges the European Commission to present a report with an assessment of the functioning of the market for CSPs and the impact of the Crowdfunding Regulation in relation to other European Union law including the AIFMD. The UCITS Directive is not explicitly mentioned.

V. Main Obligations of the Project Owner under the Crowdfunding Regulation

1. Information Obligations

The (potential) investors on a crowdfunding platform will need to receive sufficient infor- **9.26** mation to make an informed decision regarding their investment. In this respect, several information obligations apply to the CSPs. The project owner will need to provide relevant information to the CSPs to ensure that they can comply with their obligations. This is an important requirement since the project owner will not be able to launch its project if the service provider cannot comply with its obligations.

The project owner should prepare the relevant (pre)contractual information, including the **9.27** key investment information sheet (KIIS). This document should be drawn up by the project owner, since the project owner is in the best position to provide the information required to be included therein.[51] The project owner will be responsible for the information in the KIIS, and this should also be made explicitly clear therein. Those responsible for the KIIS should be clearly identified in the key investment information sheet by, in the case of natural persons, their names and functions or, in the case of legal persons, their names and registered offices, as well as declarations by them that, to the best of their knowledge, the information contained in the KIIS is in accordance with the facts and that the KIIS makes no omission likely to affect its import.[52] However, since the CSPs are responsible for providing the KIIS to prospective investors, it is the CSPs that should ensure that the KIIS is clear, correct, and complete.[53]

The CSP is allowed to present more information than required in the KIIS drawn up by the **9.28** project owner. Such information should, however, be complementary and consistent with the other information provided in the KIIS.[54] It seems obvious that the additional information should be coordinated and agreed with the project owner, to make sure that the information is correct and in accordance with his or her representations.

The KIIS should reflect the specific features of lending-based and investment-based crowd- **9.29** funding. The KIIS should also take into account, where available, the specific features and risks associated with project owners, and should focus on material information about the project owners, the investors' rights and fees, and the type of transferable securities, admitted instruments for crowdfunding purposes, and loans offered.[55]

The information to be included in the KIIS is standard and is included in Annex I to the **9.30** Crowdfunding Regulation.[56] Further, a disclaimer and risk warning should be stated directly underneath the title of the KIIS with the following text:

---

[51] Art 23 Crowdfunding Regulation.
[52] Art 23(9) Crowdfunding Regulation. This responsibility clause is similar to the responsibility clause included in the Prospectus Regulation (see Art 11 Prospectus Regulation).
[53] Art 23(9) and Recital 51 Crowdfunding Regulation.
[54] Recital 52 Crowdfunding Regulation.
[55] Reference is also made to Recital 53 Crowdfunding Regulation.
[56] See also ESMA, Consultation Paper Draft technical standards under the ECSP Regulation, 26 February 2021, ESMA/35-36-2201, 29–32.

This crowdfunding offer has been neither verified nor approved by competent authorities or the European Securities and Markets Authority (ESMA). The appropriateness of your experience and knowledge have not necessarily been assessed before you were granted access to this investment. By making this investment, you assume full risk of taking this investment, including the risk of partial or entire loss of the money invested.

Investment in this crowdfunding project entails risks, including the risk of partial or entire loss of the money invested. Your investment is not covered by the deposit guarantee schemes established in accordance with Directive 2014/49/EU of the European Parliament and of the Council. Nor is your investment covered by the investor compensation schemes established in accordance with Directive 97/9/EC of the European Parliament and of the Council. You may not receive any return on your investment. This is not a savings product and we advise you not to invest more than 10 % of your net worth in crowdfunding projects. You may not be able to sell the investment instruments when you wish. If you are able to sell them, you may nonetheless incur losses.[57]

The KIIS should be drafted in at least one of the official languages of the Member State whose competent authorities granted the authorization to the CSP or in another language accepted by those authorities. The languages accepted will be made available on the ESMA website.[58]

9.31   The obligation to provide the document to the (potential) investors is not on the project owner but on the crowdfunding service provider.[59] The document should be provided on a durable carrier.

9.32   As already stated, it is required for the CSPs to make sure that the KIIS is clear, correct, and complete. In complying with this requirement the service provider is, of course, dependent on the information provided by the project owner.[60] If the CSP identifies an omission, mistake, or inaccuracy in the KIIS which could have a material impact on the expected return of the investment, it should signal such an omission, mistake, or inaccuracy promptly to the project owner. It is the responsibility of the project owner to complete or correct the information included in the KIIS. If the project owner does not comply with this obligation, the service provider should, under certain conditions, suspend or even cancel the crowdfunding offer.[61] It is therefore very important for the project owner to ensure that the KIIS is correct and complete. The project owner is required to inform the service provider about any changes in the information included in the KIIS during the term of the offer. The KIIS should be kept updated during the term of the offer.[62]

9.33   By contrast, if a CSP provides individual portfolio management of loans, the information obligations for the service provider and the project owner are different. In that situation, a KIIS should be provided at a platform level.[63] This KIIS should include the information provided in Parts H (fees, information, and legal redress) and I (information on individual portfolio management of loans to be provided by CSPs) of Annex I to the Crowdfunding

---

[57]   Art 23(6) Crowdfunding Regulation.
[58]   Art 23(2) Crowdfunding Regulation.
[59]   Art 23 Crowdfunding Regulation.
[60]   Reference is also made to Recital 51 Crowdfunding Regulation.
[61]   Art 23 Crowdfunding Regulation. Reference is also made to Recital 53 Crowdfunding Regulation.
[62]   Art 23(8) Crowdfunding Regulation.
[63]   Art 24 Crowdfunding Regulation.

Regulation. The KIIS does not have to include information about the project owner(s) and the crowdfunding project (Part A of Annex I to the Crowdfunding Regulation). The responsibility for such a KIIS lies exclusively with the CSP. The project owner has no role in that respect.

2. The Crowdfunding Offer

A project owner can launch a 'crowdfunding project' on a crowdfunding platform. A crowd- **9.34**
funding project is defined as a business activity or activities for which a project owner seeks funding through the 'crowdfunding offer'.[64] The crowdfunding offer is any communication by a CSP, in any form, and by any means, presenting sufficient information on the terms of the offer and the crowdfunding project being offered, so as to enable an investor to invest in the crowdfunding project.[65]

The potential interested investors will be provided with the relevant information by the CSP. **9.35**
Once they have expressed their interest in a specific crowdfunding project, it is relevant for the project owner that the non-sophisticated investors[66] have a reflection period of four calendar days. The investor is informed about this reflection period by the CSP.[67]

For the project owner, the crowdfunding offer shall remain binding as of the moment that **9.36**
the crowdfunding offer is published on the crowdfunding platform, until the earlier of the following dates:

(1) the expiry date of the crowdfunding offer announced by the crowdfunding service provider at the time of listing the crowdfunding offer; or

(2) the date when the target funding goal is reached or, in the case of a funding range, when the maximum target funding goal is reached.[68]

To avoid being bound by an offer that the project owner is no longer interested in, it seems appropriate for the project owner to keep the offer period relatively short, in combination with an option to extend the offer period (to make sure that the period can be extended if the target funding goal is not reached yet).

3. Concurrence with Other EU Directives and Regulations

A. The Prospectus Obligation
If a project owner issues securities to the public in the EU, a prospectus requirement ap- **9.37**
plies, in principle, on the basis of the Prospectus Regulation.[69] However, the Crowdfunding Regulation introduces an exemption from the prospectus requirement when the offer of securities (a) is from a crowdfunding service provider that is authorized under the Crowdfunding Regulation and (b) does not exceed the threshold of EUR 5 million

---

[64] Art 2(1) under (h) and (l) Crowdfunding Regulation.
[65] Art 2(1) under (f) Crowdfunding Regulation.
[66] The difference between sophisticated and non-sophisticated investors is discussed in Chapter 12.
[67] Arts 19 and 22 Crowdfunding Regulation.
[68] Art 22 Crowdfunding Regulation.
[69] Art 3 Prospectus Regulation.

calculated over a period of twelve months. This exemption is included in Article 1(4) under (k) of the Prospectus Regulation.[70]

Offer from a CSP that is authorized under the Crowdfunding Regulation

9.38   Although the text refers to an offer of securities to the public 'from a crowdfunding service provider', the provision should be understood as exempting the relevant crowdfunding offer of the project owner via the crowdfunding platform.[71]

Threshold of EUR 5 million calculated over a period of twelve months

9.39   Article 3 of the Prospectus Regulation allows Member States to decide to exempt offers of securities to the public from the obligation to publish a prospectus, provided that the total consideration of each such offer in the EU is less than a monetary amount calculated over a period of twelve months which shall not exceed EUR 8 million. In implementing this Member State option, most Member States have however opted to use a threshold of EUR 5 million. This is the reason that the threshold is set at EUR 5 million in the Crowdfunding Regulation.[72]

> Article 49 of the Crowdfunding Regulation provides for a temporary derogation for a period of twenty-four months from 10 November 2021, where in a Member State the threshold of total consideration for the publication of a prospectus in accordance with the Prospectus Regulation is below EUR 5 million. In that case, the Crowdfunding Regulation shall apply in that Member State only to crowdfunding offers with a total consideration up to the amount of that threshold.

The threshold should be calculated over a period of twelve months as the sum of:

(1)   the total consideration of offers of transferable securities and admitted instruments for crowdfunding purposes and amounts raised by means of loans through a crowdfunding platform by a particular project owner; and

(2)   the total consideration of offers to the public of transferable securities made by the project owner referred to in point (1) in its capacity as an offeror pursuant to the exemption under Article 1(3), or Article 3(2), of the Prospectus Regulation.[73]

Interestingly, the calculation of the threshold should not only take into account the total consideration of offers of transferable securities and admitted instruments for crowdfunding purposes but also the amounts raised by means of loans, although no prospectus requirement applies for raising funds by means of loans. In addition, if the project owner raises funds through the issuance of transferable securities under another exemption of the Prospectus Regulation, this should also be taken into account in the calculation. No

---

[70]   The Crowdfunding Regulation amends the Prospectus Regulation (Art 46 Crowdfunding Regulation). See also ESMA, Consultation Paper Draft technical standards under the ECSP Regulation, 26 February 2021, ESMA/35-36-2201, 29–30.

[71]   See also Recital 67 Crowdfunding Regulation. If this is different, the exemption would not be effective in practice. See also ELM Kranenburg and DAJM Melchers, 'De toekomstige Europese Verordening voor Crowdfundingdienstverleners (Deel I)' (2020) 11 Tijdschrift voor Financieel Recht 4.

[72]   Recital 16 Crowdfunding Regulation.

[73]   Art 46 in combination with Art 1(2) under (c) Crowdfunding Regulation. See also ELM Kranenburg and DAJM Melchers, 'De toekomstige Europese Verordening voor Crowdfundingdienstverleners (Deel I)' (2020)11 Tijdschrift voor financieel recht 3–5.

distinction is made between offers of different types of securities, such as bonds or shares. It would therefore not be possible for the project owner to combine several offers of different financial instruments to obtain funds above the EUR 5 million amount. In addition, the threshold cannot be circumvented through an offer through several different crowdfunding platforms.

> For completeness' sake, the threshold only applies if the project owner wants to make use of the services of a CSP that is regulated under the Crowdfunding Regulation. If the project owner wants to raise funds above the threshold of EUR 5 million it could still make use of a crowdfunding platform that has, for example, a MiFID II authorization. In addition, it would also still be possible for the project owner to attract funds above the threshold of EUR 5 million through the services of a CSP that is regulated under the Crowdfunding Regulation, if these funds are not considered to be attracted from *the public*. In the absence of a further clarification of this term at EU level, in the Netherlands, funds attracted from 'professional market parties' or funds attracted 'within a restricted circle' are not considered to be attracted from the public.[74]

The Crowdfunding Regulation does not provide any further guidance as to the period of twelve months that should be used for the calculation of the EUR 5 million amount. If this threshold is surpassed, the project owner can no longer make use of the exemption and is therefore subject to the prospectus requirement, unless it can make use of another exemption (which is not included in the threshold calculation). As an additional consequence, the services provided by the CSP to such project owner are no longer covered by its authorization. Surpassing the threshold, thus, is relevant not only for prospectus obligations, but also for the CSP. The service provider, therefore, should check whether the project owner stays below the threshold, taking into account the restrictions of its authorization.

B. PRIIPS

If the key investment information sheet is provided in accordance with the Crowdfunding **9.40** Regulation, the project owner shall be considered to have satisfied the obligation to draw up a key information document on the basis of the Packaged Retail Investment and Insurance-based Products (PRIIPS) Regulation.[75] The obligation to draw up a key information document on the basis of the PRIIPS Regulation applies to PRIIP manufacturers before a PRIIP is made available to retail investors. This means that this exemption is relevant for project owners to the extent that they would qualify as PRIIPS manufacturers and make available PRIIPs to retail investors (the crowd). This would for example be the case if the project owner qualifies as (the manager of) an AIF or UCITS, albeit that an exemption applies until 31 December 2021 when an authorization has been obtained on the basis of (the national implementation of) the UCITS Directive, or, in relation to AIFs, the AIFMD when a Member State applies the rules on the key information document, as laid down in the UCITS Directive to AIFs.[76]

---

[74] DCB, Definition of a bank, 1 April 2017, <http://www.dnb.nl> accessed 24 February 2021.
[75] Art 23(15) Crowdfunding Regulation. See also ESMA, Consultation Paper Draft technical standards under the ECSP Regulation, 26 February 2021, ESMA/35-36-2201, 29.
[76] Art 32 PRIIPS Regulation. See critically on the exemption to draw up a key information document ELM Kranenburg and DAJM Melchers, 'De toekomstige Europese Verordening voor Crowdfundingdienstverleners (Deel II)' (2020) 12 Tijdschrift voor financieel recht 589.

VI. Protection of the Project Owner: The Missing Piece?

9.41   Although we recognize that the position of the project owner has been improved under the Crowdfunding Regulation, as there is a clearer regulatory environment to obtain funds in the EU through a crowdfunding platform, we also have some concerns, which we discuss below.

1. Multi-Layered Relationship between Project Owner and Crowdfunding Service Provider

9.42   First, the relationship between the CSP and the project owner can be considered multi-layered. On the one hand, the CSP provides a service to the project owner and, as such, has a duty of care towards it. On the other hand, the CSP and the project owner depend on each other in fulfilling their respective obligations towards the investors. As discussed in sections III and V.1, for instance, the CSP is responsible for ensuring that the project owners that propose crowdfunding offers on its platform are of sufficiently good repute, and that the information provided on the crowdfunding offer is complete, correct, and clear. In fulfilling such obligations, the CSP is dependent on the project owners and the information provided by them. Conversely, the project owner is dependent on the CSP in actually providing the information to the (potential) investors. If the CSP does not (fully) comply with its obligations towards the investors, while the project owner has provided all required information in this respect, this could result in problematic (liability) situations. In the end, the investor enters into a direct contract with the project owner and the investor needs to have received the required information to make an informed investment decision. The complexity of the relationship between the CSP and the project owner is not reflected in the Crowdfunding Regulation. Moreover, the focus of the Crowdfunding Regulation seems to be on the protection of the investors. In our view, it would have benefitted the new framework if the relationship between the CSP and the project owner had received some more thought, also taking into account that the regulation aims to ensure a European market for crowdfunding without unnecessary obstacles.

2. Civil Liability Aspects of Crowdfunding

9.43   This brings us to another topic, namely the civil liability aspects of crowdfunding.[77] Although the provisions on the KIIS in the Crowdfunding Regulation resemble the provisions on the prospectus in the Prospectus Regulation, there are also some differences.

9.44   Pursuant to Article 23(9) of the Crowdfunding Regulation, Member States have to ensure the responsibility of at least the project owner or its administrative, management, or supervisory bodies for the information given in a KIIS.[78] Those responsible should be clearly

---

[77] These could particularly be relevant when the crowdfunding service provider ceases to exist while the contractual relationship by and between the project owner and the investors is still there.

[78] This is different when the relevant crowdfunding service provider provides individual portfolio management of loans. See subsection V.1.

identified in the KIIS and should declare that, to the best of their knowledge, the information contained in the KIIS is in accordance with the facts, and that the KIIS makes no omission likely to affect its import. Pursuant to Article 11 of the Prospectus Regulation, Member States have to ensure that responsibility for the information given in a prospectus, and any supplement thereto, attaches to at least the issuer or its administrative, management, or supervisory bodies, the offeror, the person asking for the admission to trading on a regulated market, or the guarantor, as the case may be. Also, those responsible for the prospectus, and any supplement thereto, should be clearly identified in the prospectus, and a similar declaration should be included. The Crowdfunding Regulation and the Prospectus Regulation therefore differ in the parties responsible for the information given, as the Crowdfunding Regulation requests to ensure such responsibility only for the project owner and not for the CSP, notwithstanding the fact that the CSP is responsible for the completeness, correctness, and clarity of the information contained in the KIIS.[79]

Both under the Crowdfunding Regulation and the Prospectus Regulation, Member States **9.45** have to ensure that their laws, regulations, and administrative provisions on civil liability apply to natural and legal persons responsible for the information given in a KIIS and prospectus, respectively.[80] Prospectus liability is a topic that has been extensively covered in literature.[81] It will be interesting to see how this doctrine develops in respect of liability for the information in the KIIS.

3. Issues Requiring Clarity in Respect of Exemption from Authorization and Prospectus Requirements

Although the Crowdfunding Regulation provides that national law should not require an **9.46** authorization as a credit institution for the project owner and introduces an exemption to the prospectus requirement, the text of the relevant articles still invokes questions and leads to uncertainty, as highlighted in section IV and subsection V.3.A. As a result, project owners may still be dependent on the interpretation and implementation thereof by the different Member States, and/or they need to obtain legal advice to ensure that their crowdfunding offer is made in compliance with the framework set out in the Crowdfunding Regulation.

4. Dependence on National Regimes Due to Restrictive Scope of Crowdfunding Regulation

Furthermore, because of the restrictive scope of the Crowdfunding Regulation, project **9.47** owners should be aware of the fact that only certain crowdfunding projects can be facilitated through the services of CSPs that are authorized on the basis of the Crowdfunding Regulation. We refer to section II. For crowdfunding projects that are outside the scope of the Crowdfunding Regulation, they are still dependent on the national regimes of the different Member States.

---

[79] Recital 51 and Art 23(11) Crowdfunding Regulation.
[80] Art 23(10) Crowdfunding Regulation. Art 11(2) Prospectus Regulation.
[81] See eg D Busch, G Ferrarini, and JP Franx, *Prospectus Regulation and Prospectus Liability* (OUP 2020).

5. No Differentiation between Sophisticated and Non-Sophisticated Project Owners

9.48 Lastly, where the Crowdfunding Regulation differentiates between sophisticated and non-sophisticated investors in the level of protection, such a difference is not made between sophisticated and non-sophisticated project owners. In our view, this is a missed opportunity, taking into account that project owners come in many different sizes and shapes. It is not only investors who take risks by investing in crowdfunding projects. Along similar lines, the project owners take risks by receiving funds. As discussed above, they are responsible for the information provided to the investors, they enter into a contractual relationship with the investors on the basis of which they have to comply with certain obligations, *inter alia*, in respect of repayment and/or dividend/interest payment, and they need to be aware of the regulatory environment in which they operate and which may still be challenging. In a future version of the Crowdfunding Regulation, the due diligence that CSPs have to conduct on the basis of Article 5 of the Crowdfunding Regulation may be extended in respect of non-sophisticated project owners, with a check conducted on whether they understand what accompanies starting a crowdfunding project. In addition, one might consider making the CSP also responsible for the information provided in the KIIS, in case the project owner is a non-sophisticated project owner.

VII. Conclusion

9.49 In this chapter we discussed the regulatory position and obligations of a project owner. This topic has not been rigorously examined for quite some time, possibly because of the assumption that regulating the position of service providers would be sufficient. As a result, it was not always clear whether project owners require certain authorizations, and if not, whether any other regulatory obligations apply. The Crowdfunding Regulation brings some more clarity for the position of the project owner as it takes as a starting point that Member States should ensure that national law does not require an authorization for project owners and that an issuance of securities via a regulated CSP does not require an approved prospectus. However, as we have discussed in this chapter, there are still some issues that are not resolved.

9.50 In addition, under the Crowdfunding Regulation, project owners need to be aware of certain regulatory obligations when raising funds, most importantly in relation to the information provision towards investors. The introduction of the KIIS provides for more clarity and uniformity within the EU in this respect. This standardization hopefully results in lower compliance costs for the project owner while creating better possibilities to obtain the required funds by broadening the geographical area in which investors can be approached.

9.51 Since civil liability is a matter of national law and the project owner depends on the CSP for the fulfilment of several of its obligations in relation to a crowdfunding offer, certain uncertainties and (liability) risks will remain for the project owner. Especially for non-sophisticated project owners, it may be beneficial to see how their position can be further improved, for example by including more checks in the due diligence by the CSP and by making the CSP also responsible—and liable—for the information provision.

Overall, we consider the Crowdfunding Regulation to be an improvement for the project **9.52** owner. However, in our view, a subsequent version could benefit from more clarity in respect of the regulatory position of the project owner, and more attention to the risks that project owners have to deal with, including suitable protection, in order to increase the functioning of the internal market of crowdfunding services.

10

Crowdfunding and Intellectual Property Protection

Christopher A Cotropia

I. Introduction

Crowdfunding and intellectual property law can facilitate both innovation and new business ventures. Crowdfunding performs these tasks by allowing multiple individuals to make small investments or contributions to fund the development and ultimate commercialization of a given project, such as in the case of reward-based crowdfunding discussed in Chapter 15. Intellectual property (IP) law grants exclusivity over certain ideas or expressions to allow their creators to recoup their creation costs and coordinate implementing and distributing the creation. Both crowdfunding and IP law are modern tools of innovation. While they share a common goal—promoting innovation—crowdfunding and IP law also interact at a more mechanical level when it comes to the crowdfunding campaign itself. **10.01**

First, IP can, in certain circumstances, help projects avoid unauthorized copiers of crowd-funding campaigns.[1] By its nature, crowdfunding is a public endeavour. Most crowd-funding platforms, especially in reward-based crowdfunding, are accessible by everyone and they even encourage public engagement with the project owner. In turn, projects are incentivized to disclose not only the particulars of their ideas but also the development schedule and pricing structure. Crowdfunding even discloses the level of market interest **10.02**

---

[1] BJ Cowden and SL Young, 'The Copycat Conundrum: The Double-Edge Sword of Crowdfunding' (2020) 63 Business Horizons 541.

for a given project. Furthermore, all this information becomes public when the project is in its infancy, often a long time before the project will ever hit the market. These factors make crowdfunding campaigns uniquely susceptible to copiers. Individuals can copy the public information, find their own manufacturers, and beat the project owner to the market. This is particularly possible when the project is (a) idea-focused, with actual implementation being relatively easy, and (b) a long way from going to market.

10.03   As this chapter will explain, for these kinds of campaigns with high copying exposure, IP protection may provide the project with its only hope of deterring, or at least seeking legal redress from, copiers. Different IP regimes fit better with different types of crowdfunding campaigns. The comparison of the costs of obtaining certain IP protections and the resulting benefits of such protection are discussed.

10.04   Second, while such IP protections may help against copiers, recent studies indicate that the protections are not well received by the crowdfunding community. Traditionally, IP protection sends positive signals to investors and buyers, indicating quality and market exclusivity. However, empirical data from both the equity-[2] and reward-based[3] crowdfunding areas indicates that a type of IP—patents—do not correlate with crowdfunding success. In fact, two studies find that publicizing patents correlated with crowdfunding failure. The only potential bright spot is that some backers view pending patents—application for patents that have yet to be granted—as a positive feature of a crowdfunding campaign. The details of these studies, and possible explanations of their results, are explained in this chapter.

10.05   From these two contrasting issues regarding IP in crowdfunding, an interesting and complex picture emerges. The need for IP protection is real, given the risk of copying that the early, extensive, and often very public disclosure crowdfunding entails. However, research indicates that IP protection signals, particularly via issued patents, are not as positively received as they are in other investing situations. This means the crowdfunding campaign needs to be nuanced in its IP strategy. Campaigns need to obtain the necessary IP protection to ward off potential copiers. But campaigns also need to be careful not to over-publicizing such protections, particularly issued patents, or at least to place them in the proper context as to not push funders away.

II. Crowdfunding and Intellectual Property as
Innovation Facilitators

10.06   Crowdfunding and IP law are both meant to help inventors and other early-stage entrepreneurs take their creations to market. IP protection and crowdfunding are vehicles via which innovations can secure funding and, in turn, commercialization. The specifics as to how each of these innovation facilitators operates are detailed below.

---

[2] GKC Ahlers and others, 'Signaling in Equity Crowdfunding' (2015) 39 Entrepreneurship Theory and Practice 95.
[3] CA Cotropia, 'Patents as Signals of Quality in Crowdfunding' (2021) 2021 Illinois University Law Review 193; A Meoili, F Munari, and J James Bort, 'The Patent Paradox in Crowdfunding: An Empirical Analysis of Kickstarter Data' (2019) 28 Industrial and Corporate Change 1321.

1. Crowdfunding as Innovation Accelerator

Crowdfunding allows multiple individuals to make small contributions to fund a particular **10.07** project and help it get to market. Crowdfunding can take many forms, as illustrated in Chapter 1, but is essentially an online request for money to support a project, often in its early stages.[4] These projects can range from new technological innovations to books or even board games. The funding provided can be in the form of equity in the project, a reward for providing funding, a loan, or a simple donation. The reward for many crowdfunding campaigns is the subject of the campaign itself—the product or service (essentially 'preselling', as explained in Chapter 15). Reward-based crowdfunding is the most prevalent currently, with Kickstarter and Indiegogo being popular crowdfunding sites.[5] A crowdfunding campaign is defined by a goal and how contributors can move the campaign closer to the defined goal. Even in reward-based crowdfunding, supporters view themselves as 'investors', believing they are 'part' of the project and their contribution, however small, was important to bringing the product or service to market.[6]

Crowdfunding, just like venture capital investing, is a mechanism to facilitate the commer- **10.08** cialization of a particular project.[7] The funding for the campaign itself fosters innovation. Resources obtained via crowdfunding are used to advance research, develop, and/or produce the subjects of the campaign. In this way, crowdfunding acts as an alternative to other funding mechanisms for start-ups such as venture capital funding. This is the case even with reward-based crowdfunding because even though contributors to such campaigns are not receiving equity in the project, they are still funding the project by pre-purchasing.

Crowdfunding can also further innovation by acting as a marketing tool—creating a buzz **10.09** around a product or service in its early stages.[8] Crowdfunding sites provide a platform for the inventor to communicate the advantages of their product or service and gain media attention. Engagement with the online community creates interest in the project, allows creators to respond and adapt the project to community feedback, and, particularly in the case of reward-based crowdfunding, enlist initial customers.

2. Intellectual Property as an Innovation Facilitator

IP is another tool to promote innovations. IP incentivizes the creation of new ideas and **10.10** facilitates the commercialization of these ideas.[9] The general theory is that the exclusivity granted by IP protection incentivizes inventors and artists to devote the time, and take the

---

[4] M Cholakova and B Clarysse, 'Does the Possibility to Make Equity Investments in Crowd-funding Projects Crowd Out Reward-Based Investments?' (2015) 39 Entrepreneurship Theory and Practice 145, 147–48.

[5] E Mollick, 'The Dynamics of Crowdfunding: An Exploratory Study' (2014) 29 Journal of Business Venturing 1, 2.

[6] P Belleflamme, T Lambert, and A Schwienbacher, 'Crowdfunding: Tapping the Right Crowd' (2014) 29 Journal of Business Venturing 585, 586.

[7] AK Agrawal, C Catalini, and A Goldfarb, 'Some Simple Economics of Crowdfunding' (2014) 14 Innovation Policy and Economics 63.

[8] EM Gerber, J Hui, and P-Y Kuo, 'Crowdfunding: Why People Are Motivated to Post and Fund Projects on Crowdfunding Platforms' (2012) *Proceedings of The International Workshop on Design, Influence, And Social Technologies: Techniques, Impacts and Ethics.*

[9] WM Landes and RA Posner, *The Economic Structure of Intellectual Property Law* (Belknap 2003).

risk, to create new and useful ideas and expressions for society.[10] The resulting exclusivity over their creation, due to IP protection, allows the innovator to control the creation's price. This price control allows the creator to enjoy returns not only to cover their costs but make it worth their while to expend the opportunity costs in coming up with the underlying idea.

10.11   IP law is also seen as facilitating commercialization of the idea or expression because exclusivity attracts investment and removes coordination barriers that may inhibit efficient and fast commercialization.[11] Exclusivity also provides a means by which distributors can guarantee returns. IP protection can also signal to investors and buyers that the covered innovation is both high-quality and it enjoys exclusive market space and thus a high likelihood of a return on any investments.

10.12   These general theories of IP protection apply to the various specific areas of IP law. Utility patents are tasked with incentivizing and bringing to market functional innovations: things with social utility.[12] In contrast, design patents (also known as industrial design protections in some countries) provide exclusivity over the ornamental, instead of functional, aspects of a given innovation for a limited time.[13] Both types of patents use exclusivity to incentivize creation and enable commercialization. These patents are also meant to act as signals of quality and efficient organization.

10.13   Copyrights, in contrast, create incentives by granting exclusivity for a limited time over original expressive works.[14] Copyright also incentivizes distribution of the expression for the same reason: the ability to control price via exclusivity and not worry about competitors free-riding at marginal cost. Copyrights additionally protect the author's moral rights in the underlying work.[15] Copyright ensures the author can control attribution and modification of the expression to protect their personhood.

10.14   Trade secrets create incentives to innovate by providing additional protections against those who break promises not to disclose secret information, or who use improper means to obtain such information.[16] This protection is only for information that is not generally known, and thus exclusivity is warranted to promote such scarce intangibles. Trade secret protection facilitates the information transfers needed to coordinate commercialization and further innovation.

10.15   Trademarks, while considered IP in most jurisdiction, are granted not to incentivize the creation and investment in the marks themselves but to promote fair competition and encourage investment in the marked product or service.[17] By granting exclusivity over a mark—a source identifier for a good or service—the company selling that good or service is willing to make the necessary investment to improve its quality and in turn improve the

---

[10] MA Lemley, 'Ex Ante Versus Ex Post Justifications for Intellectual Property' (2004) 71 University of Chicago Law Review 129.

[11] EW Kitch, 'The Nature and Function of the Patent System' (1977) 20 Journal of Law Economics 265.

[12] CA Cotropia, 'What Is the "Invention"?' (2012) 53 William and Mary Law Review 1855.

[13] E Lee, M Mckenna, and DL Schwartz, *The Law of Design: Design Patents, Trademarks, & Copyright, Problems, Cases, and Materials* (West Academic Publishing 2017).

[14] S Balganesh, 'Foreseeability and Copyright Incentives' (2009) 122 Harvard Law Review 1569.

[15] G Dworkin, 'The Moral Right of the Author: Moral Rights and the Common Law Countries' (1994) 19 Columbia-VLA Journal of Law and the Arts 229.

[16] M Risch, 'Why Do We Have Trade Secrets?' (2007) 11 Marquette Intellectual Property Law Review 1.

[17] MP McKenna, 'A Consumer Decision-Making Theory of Trademark Law' (2012) 98 Virginia Law Review 67.

goodwill in the branded product or service. Trademark law ensures that others cannot trade on the mark holder's goodwill. There are some theories of trademark law, particularly those focused on famous marks, that view the mark itself as the target of incentives.

III. Copying Exposure in Crowdfunding and Potential Intellectual Property Solutions

Crowdfunding, by definition, involves disclosing details of the project to the public. This disclosure involves not only details of the project but also the level of interest in the project, and even pricing information. The disclosure also typically takes place early in the development cycle, where the time to market is still distant. This early, robust, and very public disclosure, before a clear path to commercialization is set, can leave the innovator exposed to others who may copy the valuable disclosed information and, in turn, beat the project to market. This 'copycat' concern in the crowdfunding context is very real and is explored in detail in a recent article by Cowden and Young.[18] Their insights on the copy-rich environment created by crowdfunding are explored next.   **10.16**

Luckily, as explained by Cowden and Young, IP can provide some protections against such copying, leading to deterrence, or, at the very least, legal action against such copiers. The extent to which IP law can assist is detailed below. Notably, copying concerns, and the various areas of IP law's ability to address such concerns, vary depending on the type of project, whether the value of the project sits in the idea or the mechanics of implementation, and how quickly the project can be brought to market once the campaign ends.   **10.17**

1. Crowdfunding and Public Disclosure

The power of crowdfunding is its ability to harness the interest, and in turn the resources, of the public.[19] The Internet's ability to reach everyone, provide them with videos, images, and text, and facilitate interaction amongst them all makes crowdfunding possible. These factors also make crowdfunding a very public and information-rich vehicle by which to obtain funding.   **10.18**

Compared to traditional innovation funding, crowdfunding by definition discloses the project to many more people.[20] What is more, the disclosure can be to those who have no interest in investing at all, whereas typical investment vehicles such as venture capital involve disclosure only to those who show genuine interest. Typical investing involves one-on-one connections between the innovator and possible investor, with the investor taking the time to hear the pitch and interact with the innovator. In crowdfunding, the 'pitch' is typically available for all to see, posted on a public website, and can be digested by others, even non-investors, with little effort. The more successful a crowdfunding campaign is in   **10.19**

---

[18] Cowden and Young (n 1) 541.
[19] P Belleflamme, T Lambart, and A Schwienbacher, 'Crowdfunding: Tapping the Right Crowd' (2014) 29 Journal of Business Venturing 585.
[20] P Belleflamme, N Omarani, and M Peitz, 'The Economics of Crowdfunding Platforms' (2015) 33 Information Economics and Policy 11.

terms of investment, the more publicized such campaigns become on the crowdfunding platform.[21] Often, the more backers a campaign gets, the more likely it will be highlighted on the home page of the crowdfunding website or 'endorsed' by the website's curators. This attracts even more attention to the campaign and discloses the information to more people. Essentially, crowdfunding's disclosure is, in many cases, global and costs less to consume, while traditional funding is local, personal, and cost-intensive.

10.20   The public level of disclosure does vary by crowdfunding platform. As Cowden and Young explain in their research, some crowdfunding platforms are very public.[22] Kickstarter, for example, allows crowdfunding campaigns to be viewed by anyone, even those without accounts on the site. In contrast, some equity crowdfunding sites require registration prior to viewing any of the campaigns, and the Crowdfunding Regulation demands an assessment of suitability before granting access to the offers, as illustrated in Chapter 12. Some platforms may also act as gatekeepers to disclosure, with some high-level, general disclosures being initially available and detailed ones being disclosed only to those who show interest. This next level of disclosure can also require permission from the campaign, meaning the disclosure takes places on a potential investor-by-investor basis, more closely mimicking traditional investing.

10.21   Crowdfunding also prompts the disclosure of more information compared to traditional investing. First, the culture of crowdfunding is one of openness and transparency.[23] Successful crowdfunding campaigns provide extensive information. Cowden and Young explain that crowdfunding campaigns are pushed to disclose the 'product, state of the business, and their vision for the future'.[24] Even the specific schedule to completion and project launch dates are communicated on crowdfunding platforms. Second, campaigns often respond to specific inquiries regarding the project, and these responses are public. In contrast, an individual, traditional investor's question and the response are rarely heard by others. Third, crowdfunding also discloses the level of interest in the campaign.[25] The number of backers, the level of investment, and the overall level of engagement with a campaign is often available for everyone to see. This provides information not only about the campaign itself but about the potential market and consumer base. This real-time market information is not available in traditional investing.

10.22   Finally, crowdfunding often prompts earlier public disclosure of projects compared to traditional investing.[26] Crowdfunding attracts projects in their nascent stages because this is when many, particularly smaller projects, cannot attract traditional investing and often turn to crowdfunding. This early public disclosure is also part of the crowdfunding culture, with backers being able to influence the project at its early stages and shape the final product or service and become truly 'invested' in the project.

---

[21]   Ahlers and others (n 2).

[22]   Cowden and Young (n 1) 547–49.

[23]   M Hossain and GO Oparaocha, 'Crowdfunding: Motive, Definitions, Typology and Ethical Challenges' (2017) 7 Entrepreneurship Research Journal 1.

[24]   Cowden and Young (n 1) 543.

[25]   D Zvilichovsky, S Danziger, and Y Steinhart, 'Making-The-Product-Happen: A Driver of Crowdfunding Participation' (2018) 41 Journal of Interactive Marketing 81.

[26]   MG Colombo, C Franzoni, and C Rossi-Lamastra, 'Internal Social Capital and the Attraction of Early Contributions in Crowdfunding' (2015) 39 Entrepreneurship Theory and Practice 75.

2. Limits to Trade Secret Protection and Self-Help in Crowdfunding

Trade secrets are valuable information not generally known by others that a company takes   **10.23**
reasonable efforts to maintain secret. These efforts to keep the information secret often
succeed, by themselves, in keeping the information from leaking to potential competitors.
Trade secret law, however, adds an additional layer of protection, giving the trade secret
owner the right to sue those who breach confidentiality promises or engage in improper
means to obtain the trade secret. Trade secret protection is thus a mixture of self-help—the
efforts to maintain secrecy—combined with legal support when competitors breach duties
of confidence or engage in corporate espionage.[27]

Early-stage innovators rely heavily on trade secrets to keep their product or service design   **10.24**
from being copied before they reach the market.[28] Such entrepreneurs require potential investors, external manufacturers, and independent contractors to sign non-disclosure agreements, promising to keep information confidential and use it only for limited purposes.
Entrepreneurs also limit the distribution of such valuable information, furthering its trade
secrecy, and often mark it as confidential.

Then, once the innovator is ready to go to market, the secrecy, and its accompanying pro-   **10.25**
tection, is extinguished, but the innovator now has a head start over others in the market
who did not have access to this information.[29] This head start creates a first mover advantage, particularly for an innovative product or service the consumer has yet to experience.
As a consequence, even though would-be competitors can copy the now public innovation,
the innovator is already way ahead with a fully working product or service and now loyal
customers.

In the crowdfunding context, this typical trade secrecy and resulting first-mover advantage   **10.26**
is at risk because of the very public nature of the crowdfunding campaign. Unless the crowdfunding platform limits information distribution dramatically and, in turn, forces potential
funders to sign non-disclosure agreements,[30] crowdfunding will eliminate trade secret protection for any information provided via the platform. The amount of unprotectable information can be vast, given that the culture in crowdfunding is to over-disclose.[31]

These disclosure concerns become even greater when crowdfunding takes place early in   **10.27**
the development of project. The longer it takes a campaign to get to market, the less of a
first-mover advantage is enjoyed by the project owner, if information about the project is
freely available to potential competitors.[32] This long time to commercialization increases
the necessity of trade secrecy to gain a true first-mover advantage. To put it another way, the
more time potential competitors have to catch-up (through the use of public information)

---

[27] MA Lemley, 'The Surprising Virtues of Treating Trade Secrets as IP Rights' (2008) 61 Stanford Law
Review 311.
[28] DS Levine and T Sichelman, 'Why Do Startups Use Trade Secrets?' (2018) 94 Notre Dame Law Review 751.
[29] F Castellaneta, R Conti, and A Kacperczyk, 'Money Secrets: How Does Trade Secret Legal Protection Affect
Firm Market Value? Evidence from the Uniform Trade Secret Act' (2017) 38 Strategic Management Journal 834.
[30] Cowden and Young (n 1) 547–48.
[31] ibid 543.
[32] ibid 545–46.

before the project goes to market, the less first-mover advantage a crowdfunding campaign can enjoy.

10.28   The rich public disclosure combined with no trade secrecy protection makes crowdfunding campaigns ripe for copiers. As Cowden and Young describe, such copying has happened where crowdfunding campaigns were beaten to market by copiers who took the public information and were quicker to find manufacturers and get the product to consumers.[33] This is why, in the traditional investment context, early-stage innovators rely heavily on limited disclosure and trade secret law. Such behaviour reduces the number of instances for copying and leaves open trade secret misappropriation enforcement for those who misuse the information that was disclosed. Such self-help (keeping the information secret) and trade secret enforcement (suing those who misappropriate the secret information) are often just not available on crowdfunding platforms.

10.29   The copying risk is not the same for all crowdfunding campaigns. Two major factors contribute to the campaign's copying exposure: (a) the extent to which the project's complexity and value are idea- versus implementation-centred, and (b) how close the campaign is to market when seeking crowdfunding. Essentially, the more idea-focused a campaign is and the further it is from market, the more susceptible to copying.

10.30   Innovations require both an idea and implementation of that idea.[34] The idea is the general concept behind the project, often thought of as the 'invention'. This is the functional specification of product—what it is supposed to do and how, generally, will it do it. In contrast, implementation comprises the steps needed to manufacture the product efficiently and consistently so that the idea can actually become a product and reach the consumer's hands. All innovations need both but they vary as to where the complexity, and thus value in the solution, sits. The value of the project predominantly sits either in the idea or the implementation. In order to be copied, a competitor needs both.

10.31   Crowdfunding campaigns often disclose much of the idea but rarely all of the specifics of implementation. For example, a campaign will go into depth about the various functionalities of the product and how, in general, the product will perform them. But that campaign may not detail specific suppliers, manufacturing processes, or component costs. Thus, if the project's value rests in the idea, copiers will gain access to these ideas via the public campaign. Since implementation is the easier part of the project's innovation process, the lack of access to this information does not inhibit successful copying.[35] In contrast, an implementation-centred project is less likely to disclose this valuable information in its campaign, and copiers will have difficulties successfully competing with the project by only copying the idea. Cowen and Young discuss this in terms of how easy is it for the copier to imitate the project based on the crowdfunding information.[36] Such imitation is easier when the 'hard part' is the idea, and implementation is easy, compared to when the difficulty comes in actually implementing the idea—making the product or performing the service.

[33] ibid 542.

[34] R Chandy and others, 'From Invention to Innovation: Conversion Ability in Product Development' (2006) 43 Journal of Marketing Research 494.

[35] A Schwienbacher, 'Entrepreneurial Risk-Taking in Crowdfunding Campaigns' (2017) 51 Small Business Economics 843.

[36] Cowden and Young (n 1) 545.

Table 10.1 Crowdfunding Campaign's Copying Exposure

		Time to Market	
		None to Little	Large
Idea v. Implementation	Idea Focused	Medium exposure	Most exposure
	Implementation Focused	Least exposure	Medium exposure

The other factor to consider in a campaign's exposure to copying is the time to market. **10.32**
Cowen and Young detail this factor in their research, noting that the quicker a campaign
can get to market when it ends, the less exposed it is to copiers.[37] Even though information
is copied, if the runway to market is short enough, the copier obtains no advantage. In fact,
in most cases, the copier remains at a disadvantage because, despite the copying, the original innovator has a natural advantage given their familiarity with the project. However,
when there is a long time between the end of the campaign and reaching the market, the
copier has time to catch up and possibly surpass the innovator. This long time to market
gives the copier space to use the copied information fully and remove any advantages of the
original innovator.[38]

The interaction between these two factors—idea versus implementation and time to **10.33**
market—are set out in Table 10.1.

The biggest exposure to copying lies in idea-focused campaigns, where crowdfunding **10.34**
discloses the most valuable information about an innovation that will take a long time to
get to market. Those campaigns that are ideas-driven but entail a short time to market, or
implementation-driven but entail a long time to market, have medium copying exposure.
Campaigns that are implementation-complex and will get to market quickly have the least
to worry about.

3. Possible Intellectual Property Solutions to Address Copying Concerns

Given the huge funding benefits of crowdfunding, but the real copying risks, the question is **10.35**
what is a crowdfunding campaign to do? As Cowen and Young recognize, IP law may have
an answer for some campaigns.[39] Entrepreneurs need first to recognize what regime of IP
law will protect the valuable aspects of the project. Different IP regimes provide better for
protection for different types of projects. Second, once the proper area of IP law is identified, perfecting protectability and understanding the scope of such protection is critical.
There are possible solutions to the copying exposure presented by crowdfunding but the solutions vary in cost, benefits, and availability. Understanding all of this will help campaigns
navigate copying threats.

---

[37] ibid 545–46.
[38] ibid.
[39] Cowden and Young (n 1) 547–49.

10.36   There is an important initial point all campaigns must consider: while this chapter discusses the protection of the IP being created by the campaign, crowdfunding campaigns also risk being liable because they use others' IP protection without permission.[40] This chapter does not explore this issue, but many projects should vet their material for the IP infringement issues it may present. For example, campaigns involving fan-fiction of existing works (where fans write new stories including popular fictional characters) or including pre-existing source code, even under an open-source licence, should carefully review such usage, to determine permissibility of the copying.[41]

A. Technology-focused Projects

10.37   Technology-focused project campaigns are those seeking funding and support for products and/or services with technology at their core. The value of these products or services derives from their functionality—the results they achieve and/or how they achieve it. This functionality can take the form of a new electronics or mechanical apparatus or may be embodied in the project's software code. Two types of IP protection are well suited for such technology-focused projects: utility patents and copyright.

Utility patents

10.38   Patents, specifically utility patents, are meant to protect the ideas behind functional products and methods.[42] Patents are government-issued documents granting an inventor exclusivity over a new, not obvious (ie it includes an inventive step), and useful invention. The inventor, in order to obtain a patent, must describe the invention and its use, and detail its scope in one or more patent 'claims'—single sentences at the end of the patent document, defining the metes and bounds of the patented invention.[43] Patent protection begins once the relevant patent office examines the patent application and determines that the patent claims are not only new (having never been done before) but also not obvious (representing a significant technological advance). The process of applying and getting a patent is long, taking roughly two-and-a-half years in the US, and relatively expensive, with patent office and attorney fees running close to USD 20,000.[44]

10.39   While difficult to reach, overcoming this high bar grants the inventor a wide scope of protection.[45] An issued patent excludes everyone, even independent inventors who knew nothing about the inventor's work and were simply second to develop a similar device or method. The patent system rewards the first-to-file patent exclusivity for limited period of time, typically twenty years from the filing date.

10.40   Utility patents are uniquely situated to address the copying concerns of crowdfunding for technology-focused projects. A major purpose of patent protection is to facilitate the inventor's public disclosure of an idea without them being afraid of others copying it without permission.[46] If a crowdfunding campaign files for patent and is eventually awarded this,

---

[40] N Wells, 'The Risks of Crowdfunding' (2013) 60 Risk Management 26.
[41] G Roberts and M Nowotarski, 'The IP Issues of Crowdfunding' (2013) 229 Managing Intellectual Property 36.
[42] R Merges and J Duffy, *Patent Law and Policy: Cases and Materials* (Carolina Academic Press 2017).
[43] ibid.
[44] JS Masur, 'Costly Screen and Patent Examination' (2010) 2 Journal of Legislation Analysis 687.
[45] Merges and Duffy (n 42).
[46] ibid.

the campaigners can enforce the patent against anyone who copies the idea claimed by that patent, even if the idea is disclosed in the campaign itself. The biggest initial issue with patent protection is its cost. Furthermore, as will be detailed below, communicating the issuance of a patent may have a negative effect on the campaign's success because of the signals patents send in the crowdfunding context. But the presence of a patent, or even a pending patent, could deter would-be copiers and provides remedies against those who do copy. At least applying for a utility patent (or filing a provisional patent application if available in the relevant jurisdiction)[47] is a good first step in preparing for possible copiers of technology-focused crowdfunding campaigns.

Copyrights

Copyright law protects the computer code, both in its binary and source code form, used by various technologies.[48] And given the rise and importance of software to most current technologies, copyright protection is a quick, low-cost way to get narrow protection over original code that may be the target of copying in the crowdfunding context.   **10.41**

Copyright law provides exclusivity for authors who create original expression that constitutes some modicum of creativity.[49] This standard of creativity is very low, and a work can be original even if it merely compiles and arranges previous works—making copyright easy to obtain. In the software context, this means that copyright protection could apply to a compilation of computer code. The code does not need to be registered to get protection; the computer code merely needs to be 'fixed'—saved on some digital media or written down—for protection to begin. Copyright protection is, thus, automatic in the sense that, for example, if the computer code is disclosed in the crowdfunding campaign, the fixation of the code on the webpage starts the creator's copyright protection.   **10.42**

While easy to get, copyrights provide vary narrow protection.[50] Once there is a protectable copyright, others must obtain permission to make copies of that computer code—regardless of the form copied (from the executable to the human-readable source code)—or make derivative works from the code via modifications and changes. Copyright law does not, however, protect against copying the underlying idea in the code—the general structure and function.[51] In addition, copyright law will not provide exclusivity over copying of non-original portions of the code. For example, if a crowdfunding campaign has source code that is an original compilation of open-source code, copyright law does not grant exclusivity over the individual, unoriginal source code components used in the project. Finally, unlike in patent law, copyright law does not grant protection against independent creators. As the name suggests, copyright law protects against copying.   **10.43**

Copyright law is an efficient, low-cost IP protection against those who copy the project's source code in full. The protection attaches immediately once the code is disclosed, costing the campaign nothing to gain protection. The protection is 'thin' in that it would only   **10.44**

---

[47]   RA Migliorini, 'Twelve Years Later: Provisional Patent Application Filing Revisited' (2007) 89 Journal of the Patent and Trademark Office Society 437.
[48]   JC Fromer and CJ Sprigman, *Copyright Law: Cases and Materials* (2020).
[49]   ibid.
[50]   ibid.
[51]   ibid.

prevent those who make an exact, or near exact, copy of the complete source code. Using copyright to go after copiers who take small snippets of code, while not always unsuccessful, will prove more difficult.

B. Design-focused Projects

10.45   Design-focused campaigns are those whose projects entail new and innovative product designs. The value of the project is in the product's ornamental features, not its functionality. The project is less focused on the underlying technology, but more on the look and feel of a product. Design innovations are commonly the focus of crowdfunding.

Design patents/industrial design

10.46   Design patents, or industrial design protections as they are known in some jurisdictions, are meant to protect the ornamental features of an object.[52] Design patents are similar to utility patents in that they must be applied for, are evaluated by a patent office for protectability, and include a definition of the scope of protection. In the US, a design patent 'claim' is typically a series of drawings depicting the invented ornamental features. Design patents protect ornamental aspects of the product, not their functional ones. Design patents typically issue much faster than utility patents and carry lower fees and attorney costs.[53]

10.47   Similar to utility patents, once issued, design patents exclude others from using the claimed ornamental design. Like utility patents, design patents protect not only against copiers but also independent creators.[54] Given their relatively low cost, design patent protection is an efficient way to ward off potential design project copiers. But, as with utility patents, there is the signalling conundrum that patents present, which will be discussed further below.

Copyright

10.48   Copyright law can also protect aspects of three-dimensional designs. The protection is limited to the expressive elements of these 'useful articles'—those features that are original and contain some modicum of creativity.[55] Copyright law protects these parts that are conceptually separatable from the utilitarian aspects of the design. This line is fuzzy, with a recent Supreme Court decision in the US arguably expanding the designs that can be copyrighted in the US.[56] In contrast to design patents, copyright can exist as long as the design is original to the author, even if it is not actually novel or not obvious. And as noted in the early copyright discussion, the protection begins once the design is fixed.

10.49   Copyright protection over designs, while lasting longer than design patents and being easier to obtain, provides narrower protection. Again, as the name connotes, copyright protects only against copying of the design, not independent creation. In addition, the scope of protection is limited to copies of the actual fixed design or derivatives thereof.

---

[52] DL Schwartz and X Giroud, 'An Empirical Study of Design Patent Litigation' (2020) 72 Alabama Law Review 417.

[53] ibid.

[54] ibid.

[55] Fromer and Sprigman (n 48).

[56] *Star Athletica v. Varsity Brands* (2017) 137 S. Ct. 1002.

The benefit of copyright for design-based crowdfunding campaigns is the immediacy and low cost to obtain protection, without the need for a registration or examination. While protection is narrowly tailored to exact, or substantially similar, copying, this is the very problem presented by crowdfunding. Copyright, thus, is a good tool to both deter and react against design copiers. **10.50**

C. Art-focused Projects

Art-focused projects are quite common on crowdfunding platforms, particularly reward-based platforms. These campaigns may be comic books, art collections, or even novels. Crowdfunding has even been used to fund, or at least partially fund, television shows and movies. **10.51**

Copyright

Art-focused projects fit well under copyright law.[57] The drawings and prose, even if disclosed in the campaign, can get copyright protection. As long as the campaign contains original art, or a compilation of art, copyright protection applies upon fixation. The scope of protection will not reach every variation of the art-focused campaign, nor the underlying idea and themes. However, copyright protection will provide remedies against copiers, even if they make small variations. **10.52**

Trade secret

While the public nature of crowdfunding prevents trade secret protection for most campaigns, art-focused projects, by their very nature, may disclose less of the valuable and important aspects of the project. Supporters of a campaign, while wanting to know the general themes or artistic style, typically do not want to know the specifics of the project. The campaign may disclose sample passages or drawings but the very purpose of the campaign is gaining funding to complete the project—the plot, dialogue, and/or comic drawings. The valuable parts of the project are simply not publicly disclosed. And thus, trade secret protection—keeping such information secret until commercial release after the crowdfunding campaign is over—is a viable option to prevent potential copiers. **10.53**

D. All Campaigns—Trademarks

All campaigns, regardless of their specific subject matter, may be able to use trademark protection to maintain an advantage over copiers. Typically, start-ups do not enjoy reputational advantages because not only is the product or service new to the consumer but the source of that product or service is new as well. Thus, consumers do not associate, and therefore do not value, a particular brand for that product or service. In such situations, trademark protection—exclusivity over a word or design associated with a specific product or service—provides little competitive advantage in the marketplace.[58] Essentially, reputation is often irrelevant with a new product provided by a new company. **10.54**

Crowdfunding, however, can create a relationship between the product or services' source and potential customer even before the product or service hits the market.[59] The **10.55**

---

[57] Fromer and Sprigman (n 48).
[58] MP McKenna, 'Trademark Use and the Problem of Source' (2009) 2009 University of Illinois Law Review 773.
[59] B Beebe, *Trademark Law: An Open-Source Casebook* (2020).

crowdfunding platform, and in particular the direct interactions between creator and consumer, can develop the brand value that trademark exclusivity captures. Funders, having watched a project developed on a crowdfunding platform, identify with that specific campaign and project owner, not just the type of product or service. Trademarks, which protect source identifiers, may be valuable for campaigns that reach such notoriety.[60] And these may be the very projects copiers seek to target.

10.56   This protection can be perfected in most jurisdictions by registering a distinctive mark with the trademark office.[61] Some jurisdictions require actual use of the trademark on sold products or services before protection is given. These use requirements, in countries like the US, may prove difficult for crowdfunding campaigns that occur before the product or service is available to the public. However, even the United States allows the filing of an 'intent-to-use' (ITU) trademark application that reserves the mark for the campaign, allowing them to get protection once the mark is used in commerce.[62]

IV. Signalling Intellectual Property Protection and Crowdfunding Success

10.57   Given the potential for IP protection to prevent copiers, crowdfunding campaigns are likely to obtain such protection and then publicize it. Campaigns may also communicate IP protection to signal to potential investors and buyers the quality of the underlying project. IP theory supports such a signalling assumption: IP protection is good for innovations, and can help investors get a return on their investment and ensure buyers they are purchasing an innovative product or service.

10.58   However, recent research, focused mainly on communicating patent protection in crowdfunding campaigns, indicates that not all IP signals are positively received by the crowdfunding community. Empirical research detailed below finds that 'patented' projects, at best, do not enjoy more success than those that are not patented and, at worst, actually garner less support from crowdfunders. The only potential bright spot in these studies is that 'patents-pending' campaigns correlated with crowdfunding success in one of three recent studies. All this, detailed below, helps fully inform crowdfunding campaigns about how to publicize, if at all, the IP protection they have acquired.

1. Intellectual Property as a Positive Signal to Investors and Buyers

10.59   IP, as explained above, incentivizes the creation of ideas and facilitates their eventual commercialization. IP protection also provides valuable signals to potential inventors and buyers.[63] For patents, the patent document, not the resulting exclusivity, provides 'signals' to potential investors that a company has the wherewithal to conceive a new and non-obvious

---

[60] S Dresner, *Crowdfunding: A Guide to Raising Capital on the Internet* (Bloomberg 2014).
[61] Beebe (n 59).
[62] WR Davis, 'Intent-to Use Applications for Trademark Registration' (1988) 35 Wayne Law Review 1135.
[63] B Hall and D Harhoff, 'Recent Research on the Economics of Patents' (2012) 4 Annual Review of Economics 541, 552–53; C Long, 'Patent Signals' (2002) 69 University of Chicago Law Review 625, 637.

invention and the discipline to document that knowledge.[64] This 'signalling' theory views the patent as a 'proxy for hard-to-measure capabilities and assets' and increases the chances the inventor, particularly in a start-up company, will attract investment.[65]

The patents' signalling ability is often why start-ups obtain patent protection. Studies **10.60** have found that patents send an important signal to venture capital investors and aid in obtaining later-stage financing. For example, Graham, Merges, Samuleson, and Sichelman surveyed 1,332 early-stage technology companies and found that 'early-stage companies patent . . . often seeking competitive advantage, and the associated goals of preventing technology copying, securing financing, and enhancing reputation'.[66] Graham and Sichelman, looking further at this study, concluded that entrepreneurs patent for 'signalling' reasons, such as 'improv[ing] their chances of securing investment'.[67]

2. Empirical Studies on Intellectual Property Signalling in Crowdfunding

The question is whether IP provides this presumed positive signal in the crowdfunding **10.61** context. As patent theory suggests, and studies outside of crowdfunding confirm, patents provide positive signals, attracting both investors and buyers. Crowdfunding campaigns should see similar results. These are campaigns to seek investment—either directly or via pre-purchasing in the reward-funding context—and patents, presumably, will signal similar positive attributes regarding the campaign and the campaign's directors to these 'investors'.

This inquiry fits within the larger area of research on the characteristics of successful crowd- **10.62** funding campaigns. Much of the current research regarding crowdfunding focuses on 'what determines the likelihood of a crowdfunding campaign achieving its funding goal'.[68] Mollick, for example, found that personal networks, the project's quality, and geography are associated with crowdfunding success.[69] Campaigns that focus on the community, communication, and professionalism are also more successful.[70] The geographic proximity between the campaign and the contributor is also shown to be relevant.[71] The philanthropic nature of the campaign is additionally correlated with success.[72]

---

[64] C Helmers and M Rogers, 'Does Patenting Help High-Tech Start-Ups?' (2011) 40 Research Policy 1016, 1025–26; RJ Mann and TW Sager, 'Patents, Venture Capital, and Software Start-ups' (2007) 36 Research Policy 193, 200.

[65] C Haeussler, D Harhoff, and E Mueller, 'How Patenting Informs VC Investors–the Case of Biotechnology' (2014) 43 Research Policy 1286, 129; R Mann, 'Do Patents Facilitate Financing in the Software Industry' (2005) 83 Texas Law Review 961, 985.

[66] SJH Graham and others, 'High Technology Entrepreneurs and the Patent System: Results of the 2008 Berkeley Patent Survey' (2009) 4 Berkeley Technology Law Journal 1255, 1255.

[67] T Sichelman and SJH Graham, 'Patenting by Entrepreneurs: An Empirical Study' (2010) 17 Michigan Telecommunications and Technology Law Review 111, 165.

[68] MA Stanko and DH Henard, 'Toward a Better Understanding of Crowdfunding, Openness and the Consequences for Innovation' (2017) 46 Research Policy 784, 786.

[69] Mollick (n 5) 2–3.

[70] G Calic and E Mosakowski, 'Kicking Off Social Entrepreneurship: How a Sustainability Orientation Influences Crowdfunding Success' (2016) 53 Journal of Management Studies 738, 740.

[71] M Lin and S Viswanathan, 'Home Bias in Online Investments: An Empirical Study of an Online Crowdfunding Market' (2015) 62 Management Science 1393, 1394.

[72] G Giudici, M Guerini, and C Rossi-Lamastra, 'Reward-based Crowdfunding of Entrepreneurial Projects: The Effect of Local Altruism and Localized Social Capital on Proponents' Success' (2017) 50 Small Business Economics 307.

10.63   Along the same lines, IP protection—specifically patent protection—may lead to crowd-funding success. Further investigation into the impact of communicating patent protection, or even a patent pending, is a great way to test IP signalling in crowdfunding. Patents are particularly salient, given that patenting, as detailed above, is the best way both publicly to disclose aspects of a technology-focused project early and enjoy broad protection against those who may copy or even be the second to develop the project independently.

10.64   There is a growing body of literature that is doing just this: looking to see the signalling implications of patents in the crowdfunding context. The studies, perhaps surprisingly, find that crowdfunding campaigns that communicate that the project is patented enjoy either no net advantage compared to those unpatented campaigns or a negative disadvantage compared to such patent-less campaigns. Only campaigns that identify the project as patent-pending may experience a positive uptick in campaign success.

10.65   Ahlers, Cumming, Günther, and Schweizer examined characteristics of successful equity crowdfunding campaigns.[73] They studied 104 offerings between October 2006 and October 2011 on an equity crowdfunding platform called the Australian Small Scale Offerings Board (ASSOB). Equity crowdfunding is similar to traditional capital raising except that the funding process is an open call and the company seeking funding is typically smaller than companies usually seeking equity investments. Ahlers and colleagues focused on AASOB because equity crowdfunding best modelled typical investment into start-up companies.

10.66   ASSOB allowed potential crowdfunding investors to browse small equity offerings before investing. These offerings included general information about the company and, if a possible crowdfunding investor was interested, offering documents to download. The documents provided more detailed information about the company, including their 'intellectual capital', reporting any granted patents the company owned.[74] Ahlers and co-workers coded this patent information using a dummy variable as either a 1 (possessing one or more patents) and 0 (possessing none).

10.67   The researchers examined whether the presence of patents, and other characteristics, correlated with various successes on the crowdfunding platform. On average, 20% of these companies had a patent, while only 10%, again on average, of the companies with patents were fully funded. In their multivariate tests, Ahlers and colleagues found no statistically significant relationship between the presence of patents and the number of investors, funding amount, or speed of capital allocation. Accordingly, they did 'not find evidence of a relationship between intellectual capital (measured as patents granted), and funding success'.[75] This finding was 'somewhat surprising' given the prior literature indicating a positive relationship.[76]

10.68   Ahlers and colleagues posit that perhaps the mere existence of a patent or its absence is a 'rather crude' way to measure the patent signal because it 'ignores the number of patents and more importantly patent quality'.[77] Thus, they leave open the possibility that patents may still have a positive signal to crowdfunding investors that their study could not measure.

---

73   Ahlers and others (n 2) 968.
74   ibid.
75   ibid 974.
76   ibid.
77   ibid.

Meoli, Munari, and Bort study the signalling role of patents and crowdfunding, but this **10.69** time in the context of a reward-based campaign.[78] These researchers focused on Kickstarter, a crowdfunding website based in the US where users can finance entrepreneurs in exchange for rewards, not equity. These rewards come, most often, in the form of pre-purchases of the subject matter of the Kickstarter campaign, which may be a book, board game, or technological device, or other items or digital goods.

Meoli and colleagues sought to answer the same general question posed by Ahlers and col- **10.70** leagues: does signalling that a technology is patented increase the likelihood of funding success? To do this, they collected Kickstarter campaigns with fundraising goals between USD 5,000 and USD 500,000 and identified campaigns that included words or phrases such as 'patent', 'patented', and 'patent pending'.[79] They found 834 such campaigns and then looked for comparable, non-patent signalling projects using propensity score matching (PSM). This resulted in matches for 711 of the 834 patent identified campaigns, creating a matched dataset of 1,422 campaigns.

Meoli and colleagues found '[t]he estimated treatment effect of the presence of patent lan- **10.71** guage on the probability of success was negative and statistically significant (ATT [average treatment effect] = −0.076, $P < 0.001$). That is, signaling a patent is negatively associated with the success of a crowdfunding campaign, where the rate is around 30% lower.'[80] They observed that terminology like 'patent pending' had the strongest relationship with funding failure, while 'patented' language still exhibited a negative relationship with success, albeit a weaker one.[81]

The study explored a number of explanations for this negative relationship. Meoli and re- **10.72** searchers found evidence that the patent terminology was signalling riskier campaigns with higher technological complexity and thus a lower likelihood of campaign success that may have deterred crowdfunding. This conclusion is based on the finding 'that projects signaling a patent tend to use more intensive language related to radical innovation'.[82] The researchers also observed that patent-identifying campaigns were less 'social[ly] orient[ed] as compared to control projects', meaning that these campaigns did not align with the 'values of openness and altruism infusing the crowdfunding community'.[83] Such a lack of alignment may have further doomed the patented campaigns.

A third study, conducted by the author of this chapter—Cotropia—also examined pa- **10.73** tent signalling in reward-based crowdfunding campaigns.[84] Similar to the study by Meoli and colleagues, Cotropia explored whether mentioning patenting in such campaigns is associated with crowdfunding success. The study had two parts—first observing live crowdfunding campaigns on Kickstarter to determine if patented, or patent-pending, crowdfunding campaigns are more likely to obtain their funding goal as compared to non-patented projects and, second, examining the impact of varying the patent status in a 'mock' crowdfunding campaign on participant's willingness to buy into or invest in that campaign.

---

[78] Meoili and others (n 3).
[79] ibid 1322.
[80] ibid 1334.
[81] ibid.
[82] ibid 1335.
[83] ibid.
[84] Cotropia (n 3).

10.74   The first part of the study collected the universe of Kickstarter campaigns in the Technology category from the website's inception in 2009 to 1 June 2017.[85] The study collected multiple attributes of the 9,184 campaigns in the dataset that had ended, including whether the campaign was successful (fully funded) and the identified patent status of the campaign (patented, patent-pending, and no patent identified).

10.75   The second part of the study was a laboratory experiment using Amazon Mechanical Turk, randomly providing subjects with an image of a 'mock' Kickstarter campaign labelled as 'patented', 'patent-pending', or silent on patenting.[86] There were two mock campaigns—headphones and flip-flops—about which 1,509 respondents answered a series of questions, including how likely the respondents would be to invest in or buy the campaign's product. Respondents are also asked questions about whether they noticed the displayed patent status and about their general understanding and opinions on patents.

10.76   Both parts of the study—looking at live and mock crowdfunding campaigns—made somewhat similar findings to the studies by Ahlers and colleagues and Meoli and team. Patented projects are not more likely to obtain funding in comparison to non-patented projects.[87] However, patent-pending projects—where the campaign reports that patent applications are filed but not yet issued—exhibit statistically significant, positive results.[88] This finding, while counter to that by Meoli and colleagues, is supported in both the live and mock crowdfunding parts of the study.

10.77   In addition to confirming Ahlers and Meoli and their colleagues' general findings that a patented project is not more likely to be funded compared to non-patented ones, the Cotropia study's results regarding patent-pending campaigns suggest that there are situations where patent status can positively influence investment and purchase in the so-labelled project. Cotropia posits that having a patent pending may signal, and provide evidence, that the innovation is both new and can benefit greatly from crowdfunding, while projects already patented may be innovations that are older, less in need of crowdfunding, and potentially may already have failed to secure traditional funding.[89] To put it simply, patent pending is more in line with the spirit of the crowdfunding environment, attracting the public to assist smaller, early-stage projects.

V. Conclusion and Takeaways

10.78   IP protection is important for crowdfunding campaigns. When the right IP protection is chosen, such protection can provide a needed shield against possible copiers. But the extent and context in which the protection is communicated in the campaign is also important. For example, patents that deter copiers but also deter potential crowdfunding backers in the end provide no value for the project owner. Recognizing the trade-offs IP protection presents in the crowdfunding context allows campaigns to be strategic in their usage of IP law to help the project become fully funded, get to market, and succeed.

---

[85] ibid 204–05.
[86] ibid 205–08.
[87] ibid 217.
[88] ibid 218–19.
[89] ibid 224–26.

11

Non-Profit Project Owners

Crowdfunding and Public Interest Litigation in the Digital Age

Sam Gaunt and Andrea Longo[1]

I. Introduction

In December 2018, a crowdfunding campaign was launched on the popular platform **11.01** 'GoFundMe' seeking financial support for a war-crimes reparation case before Dutch courts. The campaign, titled the 'Palestine Justice Campaign', was ran by a group of individuals, scholars, and activists to support the plaintiff's legal costs.[2] In three months, the case had raised over EUR 50,000 from hundreds of individuals.[3] Meanwhile, in September 2019, the European Commission rejected a Citizen Initiative to bring the Union's trade policy in line with international law and fundamental rights obligations.[4] Campaigners responded by filing an appeal to the ECJ, which in turn required funds for legal costs.[5] In one month (between November and December 2019), the campaign raised almost EUR 12,000. These are just two of countless cases across crowdfunding platforms that seek donations for litigation which is being pursed for causes in the public interest. Yet, despite this

---

[1] For the purpose of Italian public examinations, the two authors declare that Section II and subsection 'Dilemmas and opportunities' under Section IV are attributed to Andrea Longo, whilst Section III and subsection 'Regulatory mechanisms: Public or Private?' under Section IV are attributed to Sam Gaunt. Both authors contributed equally to the Introduction and Conclusion.

[2] 'Palestine Justice Campaign' <https://palestinejusticecampaign.wordpress.com/> accessed 7 March 2021.

[3] 'Palestine Justice Campaign' (*gofundme.com*) <https://www.gofundme.com/f/palestine-justice-campaign> accessed 7 March 2021.

[4] 'Ensuring Common Commercial Policy Conformity with EU Treaties and Compliance with International Law' <https://europa.eu/citizens-initiative/initiatives/details/251_en> accessed 7 March 2021.

[5] <https://op.europa.eu/en/publication-detail/-/publication/7755286e-4bfd-11ea-b8b7-01aa75ed71a1>.

growing phenomenon, literature for crowdfunded public interest cases remains limited.[6] While the majority of the chapters in this volume have investigated the regulatory position of project owners that fall within the scope of the Crowdfunding Regulation (namely investment- and loan-based crowdfunding), the present chapter addresses donation-based crowdfunding. Indeed, the Crowdfunding Regulation expressly leaves out charitable crowdfunding from its scope of application. Article 2(1)(a), in particular, restricts the definition of 'crowdfunding service' to the facilitation of granting of loans, or the placing without a firm commitment basis of transferable securities and admitted instruments for crowdfunding purposes, as well as the reception and transmission of client orders in respect of those transferable securities and admitter instruments. Furthermore, Article 2(1)(i) defines an 'investor' as 'any natural or legal person who, through a crowdfunding platform, grants loans or acquires transferable securities or admitted instruments for crowdfunding purposes', thus reinforcing the conclusion that charity-based crowdfunding (where the crowd performs a donation) is excluded from the scope of application of the Crowdfunding Regulation. Nevertheless, donation-based crowdfunding remains the second largest type in the sector, with approximately USD 5.5 billion having been raised globally as of 2020.[7]

11.02   Within the context of donation-based crowdfunding, calls for funds to support litigation have become a common staple on platforms, particularly in certain common law jurisdictions such as the US, Australia, and the UK, where civil litigation is particularly costly.[8] These calls often ask for donations to allow the affected persons or groups to access judicial remedies for a private concern. Yet, a different class of cases has become particularly popular on crowdfunding platforms: public interest litigation (PIL). Also known as 'pressure through law',[9] the PIL phenomenon is the 'use of law and legal techniques as an instrument for obtaining wider collective objectives',[10] thus ultimately benefiting society as a whole. Such calls for donations to PIL differ from individual calls for legal fees as these cases confer a promise of public engagement in litigation offering broader social change.

11.03   The rise in the use of crowdfunding for PIL cases results from the fact that such cases are undeniably expensive. Legal costs are high, running into the hundreds of thousands of euros depending on numerous factors such as, *inter alia*, the nature of the legal question(s) discussed, the number of parties and of counsels involved, and the number of appeals.[11] As a result, it appears that crowdfunding is progressively emerging as a means to ensure access to justice for non-private interest claims. Consequently, this chapter will assess the rising phenomenon of crowdfunding for PIL as a distinct category of donation-based crowdfunding, falling outside of the scope of the Crowdfunding Regulation. Section II will begin

---

[6] J Tomlinson, 'Crowdfunding and the Changing Dynamics of Public Interest Judicial Review' in *Justice in the Digital State* (Bristol University Press 2019) 19 <https://www.jstor.org/stable/j.ctvndv808.8> accessed 7 March 2021; MA Gomez, 'Crowdfunded Justice: On the Potential Benefits and Challenges of Crowdfunding as a Litigation Financing Tool' (2015) 49 University of San Francisco Law Review 307; M Elliot, 'Trial by Social-Media: The Rise of Litigation Crowdfunding' (2016) 84 University of Cincinnati Law Review 529.

[7] 'Crowdfunding Statistics: Facts on the Latest Fundraising Craze' <https://blog.fundly.com/crowdfunding-statistics/> accessed 7 March 2021.

[8] Gomez (n 5).

[9] C Harlow and R Rawlings, *Pressure Through Law* (Routledge 1992).

[10] ibid.

[11] Constitutional Law Group, 'Tom Hickman: Public Law's Disgrace' (*UK Constitutional Law Association*, 9 February 2017) <https://ukconstitutionallaw.org/2017/02/09/tom-hickman-public-laws-disgrace/> accessed 7 March 2021.

by presenting an overview of crowdfunding and PIL. This overview is important for understanding the current use of crowdfunding for such cases, framing the reality of the rising phenomenon. Section III will discuss the challenges and opportunities of this novel form of financing in the context of the distinct stakeholders, namely project owners, funders, and lawyers. Section IV will build upon the challenges and opportunities of crowdfunded PIL, to discuss the future of the phenomenon.

II. Crowdfunding and Public Interest Litigation: Blurring the Public/Private Divide

The idea of collecting small amounts of money from disparate people to channel them into specific projects or otherwise achieve specific purposes is not a new phenomenon. On the contrary, it has existed for long time, especially in relation to humanitarian cooperation or charity projects pursuing altruistic goals.[12] What makes crowdfunding different from traditional donation schemes or other more elaborated fundraising strategies is the combination of two elements: first and foremost, today's availability of the Internet, which transposes all the related activities—from communication to donations—onto a virtually barrier-free space, the web;[13] second, as a direct consequence of the former, the near unlimited geographic outreach that certain campaigns can have,[14] which in turn renders the people supporting the project—the 'crowd'—and their goals exceptionally heterogeneous.[15] In this regard, crowdfunding has been defined as the effort of a private individual or group with natural or legal personality (the project owner), who seeks financing from other numerous private persons (the funders or the crowd), through a private facility (the online platform or service provider[16] on the Internet). It is therefore an exclusively private effort that relies on the public and diffuse nature of the web.[17]

11.04

1. Crowdfunding Models and Non-Profit Projects

A quick glance at crowdfunding platforms shows that people turn to crowdfunding to finance virtually any idea, from music recordings to traditional pastry ventures, from renovation works for bars to pet surgery.[18] Indeed, parallel to the booming of the crowdfunding phenomenon, online platforms also started increasing in number and even competing

11.05

---

[12] A Ordanini and others, 'Crowd-Funding: Transforming Customers into Investors through Innovative Service Platforms' (2011) 22 Journal of Service Management 443, 445.

[13] Elliot (n 5) 531.

[14] AK Agrawal, C Catalini, and A Goldfarb, 'The Geography of Crowdfunding' (National Bureau of Economic Research 2011) w16820, 1 <https://www.nber.org/papers/w16820> accessed 7 March 2021.

[15] E Mollick, 'The Dynamics of Crowdfunding: An Exploratory Study' (2014) 29 Journal of Business Venturing 1, 3.

[16] With regard to online platforms, their primary function is that of connecting the PO's idea to potential supporters around the world. See Gomez (n 5), 311.

[17] A Ordanini, 'Crowd Funding: Customers as Investors' Wall Street Journal (23 March 2009) <https://www.wsj.com/articles/SB123740509983775099> accessed 7 March 2021; see also Mollick (n 14).

[18] See, inter alia, pet-specific platform Waggle, available at <https://waggle.org/> accessed 10 May 2021. For a general overview, see AA Schwartz, 'The Nonfinancial Returns of Crowdfunding' (2014) 34 Review of Banking and Financial Law 565, 574.

amongst each other in order to win project owners' business.[19] In particular, platforms started diversifying their offers, identifying the so-called Keep-It-All (KIA) and the All-Or-Nothing models (AON). In general, KIA models allow for project owners to retain all the funds raised regardless of the initial goal set on the platform, while AON models require project owners to meet their goal before having access to the raised funds.[20] Therefore, it should not come as a surprise that the crowdfunding-related transactions have grown considerably since its emergence.[21]

11.06   Concerning the nature of the idea to be funded, the vast majority of crowdfunded projects can be grouped into two primary categories along the profit- and non-profit-oriented spectrum: that of entrepreneurial ventures and that of socio-humanitarian aid.[22] By contrast, the nature of the funder's return is traditionally identified in the literature by four models:[23] (a) the donation-based model, where the backer pursues a purely altruistic purpose and the funding 'is treated as a donation with no expected returns';[24] (b) the reward-based model, where funding is associated with a usually small non-monetary reward, going from a simple thank-you card to more vibrant opportunities—for example, roles in movies projects[25]—depending on the amount of money pledged;[26] (c) the investment-based model, where funding takes the form of investment into the entrepreneurial venture so that investors assume the risk behind the project in exchange for its shares or debt instruments;[27] and (d) the loan-based model, under which funding a project amounts to lending money for its realization, so that investors are entitled to a rate of return on the lent capital.[28] Whereas the Crowdfunding Regulation only applies to the investment-based and loan-based models, this chapter focuses on crowdfunding for PILs, which lies at the non-profit oriented end of the spectrum and, therefore, best suits the donation-based and reward-based crowdfunding models.[29]

---

[19]   Platforms have even begun performing administrative and fiduciary roles in order to increase entrepreneurs' capacity to attract backers and share the risk with them. See Gomez (n 5) 311.

[20]   See DJ Cumming, G Leboeuf, and A Schwienbacher, 'Crowdfunding Models: Keep-It-All vs. All-Or-Nothing' (2020) 49 Financial Management 331.

[21]   For instance, the volume in Europe—which ranks third in the list of largest global markets for crowdfunding—were estimated to be over USD 18 billion in 2018, with the UK covering more than half of this amount. K Wenzlaff and others, 'Crowdfunding in Europe: Between Fragmentation and Harmonization' in R Shneor, L Zhao, and B-T Flåten (eds), *Advances in Crowdfunding: Research and Practice* (Springer International Publishing 2020) <https://doi.org/10.1007/978-3-030-46309-0_16> accessed 7 March 2021. See also T Ziegler and others, *The Global Alternative Finance Benchmarking Report* (Cambridge Centre for Alternative Finance 2020).

[22]   Schwartz (n 17).

[23]   Elliot (n 5); see also D Cumming and SA Johan, *Crowdfunding: Fundamental Cases, Facts, and Insights* (2020) <https://search.ebscohost.com/login.aspx?direct = true&scope = site&db = nlebk&db = nlabk&AN = 1543570> accessed 7 March 2021. Interestingly for the purpose of this article, Mollick clarifies that, when transferring money into a crowdfunding project, people may pursue extremely heterogeneous goals besides that of obtaining a material or monetary return from it. Mollick (n 14), 3.

[24]   Elliot (n 5), 532.

[25]   'LEAP-COACHING Movie to Inspire 1 Million Lives' (*Indiegogo*) <http://www.indiegogo.com/projects/932 767/fblk> accessed 7 March 2021.

[26]   Mollick (n 14) 3 and Elliot (n 5) 532, See Kickstarter's blog for an overview of non-monetary rewards ideas, available at https://www.kickstarter.com/blog/need-some-reward-ideas-here-are-96-of-them?lang = it.

[27]   N Vulkan, T Åstebro, and M Fernandez Sierra, 'Equity Crowdfunding: A New Phenomena' (2016) 5 Journal of Business Venturing Insights 37. See also, M Kuti, Z Bedő, and D Geiszl, 'Equity-Based Crowdfunding' (2017) 16 Financial and Economic Review 187.

[28]   Mollick (n 14), 3.

[29]   The reward-based model is by far the most popular one. 'Websites such as Kickstarter have been doing reward crowdfunding for the past five years, during which time it has quickly grown into a $1.5 billion market' Schwartz (n 17), 567. See also the World Bank-registered annual increase by 524% over a period of four years, from 2009

2. Public Interest Litigation

Public interest litigations (PILs) can be understood as lawsuits lodged with the aim of   **11.07**
bringing about a long-term change in society through the victory in court.[30] Cases may
be initiated by groups or individuals, however the ultimate objective pursued involves a
broader social change.[31] The notion of 'public interest' is disputed, both at the level of theory
and of practice.[32] Whereas the attention for public interest legal actions and proceedings
grew considerably in the 1960s and 1970s, particularly in the US alongside civil right and
civil liberties groups who sought to protect powerless minorities,[33] the notion of public
interest soon developed into a broader concept so as to embrace more diffuse interests from
larger groups, including conservative ones.[34] Yet, crucially for PIL, the societal change that
is sought through a victory in court is inherently linked to a wider social or political movement. As highlighted by Rosenberg's quantitative study, courts are 'almost never effective
producers of significant social reform', because they are dependent on other political organs
and they lack powers to translate potentially charged judicial decisions effectively into a
broader policy change.[35] This factor, long recognized by social movement and communities' organizers, requires successful PIL, namely cases which are able to bring about the social change sought, to be integrated into the wider social and political cause. Therefore, in
light of the rather broad scope of the concept, throughout this contribution, we adopt an
all-inclusive definition of public interest that goes along with that of community interest: an
interest is *public* when it is as diffuse as to engage a community of people, regardless of this
community being large or small, politically progressive or conservative, largely heterogeneous or almost entirely homogeneous.

Interestingly, PIL is usually launched in the context of public interest campaigns, thus being   **11.08**
just one piece of a broader advocacy strategy.[36] Accordingly, we identify two categories
of PILs, namely *centralized top-down* and *decentralized bottom-up* cases. Both of these
categories pursue an overall public interest goal, this being the defining feature of PILs, yet
they have very different structural elements. Centralized top-down PILs correspond to the
more traditional model of PILs: they are promoted and led by fundamental rights organizations often active within the global human rights movement, and are part of a coordinated
effort to advance a given political campaign. Most importantly, crowdfunding in the context of these PILs is just one of the possible tools for funding, given that such organizations

to 2013: The World Bank, 'Crowdfunding's Potential for the Developing World' <https://www.infodev.org/crowd
funding> accessed 4 October 2021.

[30] Harlow and Rawlings (n 8).
[31] S Cummings and D Rhode, 'Public Interest Litigation: Insights From Theory and Practice' (2009) 36 Fordham
Urban Law Journal 603.
[32] ibid 605; see also SA Scheingold and A Sarat, *Something to Believe In: Politics, Professionalism, and Cause
Lawyering* (Stanford Law and Politics 2004).
[33] BW Heineman, 'In Pursuit of the Public Interest' (1974) 84 Yale Law Journal 182, 182–83.
[34] A Southworth, 'Conservative Lawyers and the Contest over the Meaning of Public Interest Law' (2004) 52
UCLA Law Review 1223.
[35] GN Rosenberg, *The Hollow Hope: Can Courts Bring About Social Change? Second Edition* (2nd edn, University
of Chicago Press 2008). See Cummings and Rhode (n 30).
[36] For a more complete analysis of the dynamics between PILs and the broader political campaigns surrounding
them, see Cummings and Rhode (n 30) 615–19.

usually have access to institutional donation channels.[37] An example of a centralized top-down PILs includes the recent case litigated in Dutch Courts, *Urgenda Foundation v The Netherlands*, where a Dutch foundation brought an administrative action against the State invoking its failure to adopt all necessary measure to respect its own obligations on climate change deriving from the 2015 Paris Agreement.[38]

11.09   By contrast, there is increasing evidence of the emergence of decentralized bottom-up PILs, carried out in a rather informal and horizontal way by people who might not even know each other but who share the fundamental values and principles at the basis of the lawsuit. Contrarily to the top-down model, crowdfunding in the context of bottom-up PILs is what ultimately favours the creation of the decentralized community. Indeed, crowdfunding works as an invaluable communication and aggregating tool: it allows project owners to gather media attention around certain issues, even when particularly anchored to a very local context, thus raising awareness about them at a global scale.[39] In addition, by breaking the geographical barriers and connecting people potentially from all over the world, it links individuals by spreading among them a *feeling of belonging*: they start understanding that they are part of a larger community of people sharing the same values and pursuing the same fundamental idea, that is, the will to bring about a change.[40] In this way, crowdfunding is able to aggregate previously unrelated individuals around a common cause and to empower them through the creation of a decentralized community for social change.[41] Taking it to a further level, crowdfunding (ie the act of donating) becomes a means to express a political view, one's 'ability to send a message through consumption choices'.[42]

11.10   In his work on administrative justice in the digital age, Joe Tomlinson highlights the crucial impact of crowdfunding on justice mechanisms and, in particular, the changing dynamics of PIL in the context of the UK judicial review.[43] Whereas before the rise of crowdfunding, PILs always used to be carried out by the same groups or organizations in what he describes as a *closed* model, since the emergence of this alternative source of funding PILs started diversifying and opening up to a wider range of disciplines and areas, as well as to new actors. Differently from the publicly registered organizations in the closed model, the latter are rather informal groups of people who are not accountable to a board of directors or other similar internal-review mechanisms.[44] In this way, PIL is truly becoming a matter of collective decentralized effort, a more *horizontal* one that escapes the formal procedures and dynamics in favour of a more participatory mechanism.

11.11   A bottom-up decentralized approach to PIL can be seen in the 'Palestine Justice Campaign' and the European Citizens' Initiative (ECI) cases mentioned in the opening of this chapter.

---

[37] For a discussion on the avenues of funding open to traditional PIL actors, see *inter alia* CR Albiston and LB Nielsen, 'Funding the Cause: How Public Interest Law Organizations Fund Their Activities and Why It Matters for Social Change' (2014) 39 Law & Social Inquiry 62.

[38] Dutch Supreme Court (*Hoge Raad*), Case no 19/00135, ECLI:NL:HR:2019:2006. See, *inter alia*, M Meguro, 'State of the Netherlands v. Urgenda Foundation' (2020) 115(4) American Journal of International Law Xyz page.

[39] E Hamman, 'Save the Reef! Civic Crowdfunding and Public Interest Environmental Litigation' (2015) 15 Queensland University of Technology Law Review 159.

[40] Schwartz (n 17) 579.

[41] J Tomlinson, 'Crowdfunding Public Interest Judicial Reviews' [2019] Public Law 166. This makes crowdfunding both interesting but also dangerous as community interests may differ in a decentralized approach.

[42] Schwartz (n 17) 576.

[43] Tomlinson (n 5).

[44] ibid 32–33.

Both of these cases are indicative of the changing dynamics of PILs facilitated through crowdfunding as they allowed for informal collective groups to raise funds to support litigation seeking social change. The Palestine Justice Campaign is an informal group comprising individuals, activists, trade unionists, and scholars who support the plaintiff's effort for the accountability of state officials. The ECI case is led by a similar informal group of individuals, activists, scholars, and academics who aim to bring the EU Common Commercial Policy in line with international law and fundamental rights obligations. Both cases would have been impossible without the support of donation-based crowdfunding.

Yet, while crowdfunding for financing PIL is becoming increasingly common in both cen- **11.12** tralized and decentralized cases, it is important to consider the practice within the broader phenomenon of Third-Party Litigation Funding (TPLF), which consists of individuals financially supporting someone else's lawsuit.[45] Common Law systems have in the past been cautious if not reluctant to endorse such an idea, due to concerns of third-party funding undermining the integrity of justice through usury behaviours[46] and through the so-called maintenance, champerty, and barratry practices.[47] However, more recently, legal systems and courts have started changing their approach in favour of opening up the possibility for a third-party to finance others' litigations.[48] This new trend has coupled with the idea of financing litigation through crowdfunding so that today lawsuits are commonly listed among projects to be funded on crowdfunding platforms that support both profit and non-profit models.[49] The phenomenon of crowdfunding for PILs discussed in the present chapter should not, however, be confused with the so-called Alternative Litigation Financing[50] (ALF), which instead consists of the TPLF phenomenon applied to the investment-based crowdfunding model. ALF has boomed in Common Law systems, especially in the US, where it has developed into a new market characterized by the commodification of legal claims and the emergence of an industry of professional financiers.[51] Investment firms spend large sums of money in third-party's lawsuits as an alternative source of investment so that, in case of victory in court, they can recover the capital invested in the litigation and typically make profits proportionally to their initial investment.[52] PIL, however, escapes this trend of legal claims commodification typical of the ALF phenomenon, and is usually characterized by the lack of backers' monetary interest in the outcome of the litigation and, consequently, the comparatively smaller amount of the contributions.[53] The will for a change is, therefore, the ultimate force driving backers' funding for a PIL, with rather small

---

[45] 'Responsible Private Funding of Litigation—Think Tank' <https://www.europarl.europa.eu/thinktank/en/document.html?reference = EPRS_STU%282021%29662612> accessed 7 March 2021.

[46] Elliot (n 5) 537.

[47] These are litigation finance agreements where the litigation 'financier was an outside party improperly involved in the case'. See ibid 540.

[48] See, *inter alia, Saladini v Righellis*, 687 NE2d 1224 (Mass 1997), where the Massachusetts Supreme Judicial Court has struck down the three common law doctrines; see also *Osprey, Inc. v Cabana Ltd. P'ship*, 532 SE2d 269, 279 (SC 2000), where the South Caroline highest court abolished champerty.

[49] See eg 'How to Pay for a Lawyer With No Money: 3 Resources' (*GoFundMe (NL)*, 24 May 2019) <https://nl.gofundme.com/c/blog/how-to-pay-for-lawyer?lang = en> accessed 7 March 2021.

[50] Gomez (n 5) 312.

[51] M Steinitz, 'Whose Claim Is This Anyway—Third-Party Litigation Funding' (2010) 95 Minnesota Law Review 1268, 1321.

[52] Of course, investors will tend to evaluate their investment carefully, considering both the chances of winning the case and the legal opportunity stemming out of it—ie the long-term impact of a favourable case law. See, *inter alia*, R Perry, 'Crowdfunding Civil Justice' (2018) 59 Boston College Law Review 1357.

[53] Gomez (n 5) 307–08.

contributions coming from a large number of backers who do not have a monetary interest in the case but rather share the project owner's ultimate goal.[54]

11.13   Overall, this section has provided the reader with a general overview on crowdfunding for PILs as defined within the broader phenomenon of third-party litigation funding. Crowdfunding has played a fundamental role as 'matchmaker'[55] and, even beyond that, as empowering tool for the individuals financially contributing to a campaign. Accordingly, it has facilitated the creation of decentralized communities capable of altering the originally vertical and stable nature of the PIL world.[56] However, the increase in participation and democratization of PILs described above is just one of the implications of this trend. As section III will discuss, the impact of crowdfunding on PIL has much more nuanced consequences, which deserve further attention.

III. Crowdfunding for PILs and Access to Justice: Revolutionary or Problematic?

11.14   Section II has highlighted the rise of crowdfunding for PIL. As with any new phenomenon, this novel form of funding presents new opportunities and challenges. First, why is funding such a major consideration for legal action that seeks social change? Civil litigation is expensive. The cost of judicial proceedings often appears as a main factor limiting one's access to traditional judicial remedies, which the average citizen does not readily have the financial capacity to pursue.[57] Civil claims can be lengthy and plaintiffs, in the majority of jurisdictions, must not only bear the costs of legal fees and expenses but also risk having to cover, in whole or in part, the costs of the opposing party.[58] Public interest cases, in this regard, are the 'Rolls Royce' of litigation, requiring specialized expertise over a long period of time. As a result, few can afford them.[59] Due to these high costs, PIL has traditionally been limited to cases which represented values that were supported by formal actors for social change, namely charities and other legal persons (eg civil society organizations), as a result of their greater access to funding inherently required for PIL.[60] Grants, membership payments, donations, and other resources available to these formal groups often provide significant funds to pursue such cases, with these formal actors operating in *consultation* with affected communities when pursuing such litigation.[61]

---

[54]   This is especially in line with the donation-based model of crowdfunding, where contributions are driven by a broad range of motivations, including personal relations between the funders and the Project Owner. See L Zhao and R Shneor, 'Donation Crowdfunding: Principles and Donor Behaviour' in R Shneor, L Zhao, and B-T Flåten (eds), *Advances in Crowdfunding: Research and Practice* (Springer International Publishing 2020) <https://doi.org/10.1007/978-3-030-46309-0_7> accessed 7 March 2021. See also Mollick (n 14), 3.

[55]   Gomez (n 5) 310.

[56]   Tomlinson (n 5).

[57]   For further detail on financial barriers to access to justice see JJ Alvarez Rubio and K Yiannibas, *Human Rights in Business: Removal of Barriers to Access to Justice in the European Union* (Taylor & Francis 2017); J Beqiraj and L McNamara, 'International Access to Justice: Barriers and Solutions' (Bingham Centre for the Rule of Law Report 02/2014, (International Bar Association, October 2014); DL Rhode, 'Whatever Happened to Access to Justice' (2008) 42 Loyola of Los Angeles Law Review 869; JH Gerards and LR Glas, 'Access to Justice in the European Convention on Human Rights System' (2017) 35 Netherlands Quarterly of Human Rights 11.

[58]   Tomlinson (n 40) 170.

[59]   Tomlinson (n 5) 19, quoting Hickman (n 10).

[60]   PE Sitkin and J Kline, 'Financing Public Interest Litigation' (1971) 13 Arizona Law Review 823.

[61]   Albiston and Nielsen (n 36).

However, the rise of crowdfunding has challenged this traditional approach to PIL. **11.15**
Community actors and social movements are now able to directly mobilize legal action
through broad and vast funding networks. As informally organized groups are generally
unable to access traditional sources of funding, individual donations—and crowdfunding
in particular—allows for decentralized communities to pursue PIL. In this sense, it can
be argued that crowdfunding has increased access to justice for those previously unable
to pursue litigation for social issues. The relative inaccessibility of litigation financing has
long stood as a barrier to justice for public interest cases; hence formal, centralized actors
have stepped in to represent community interests.[62] However, crowdfunding breaks the
need for formal actors to be involved in communities' access to the courts. Individuals are
now able to mobilize through collective action to overcome financial barriers, allowing for
under-represented groups to pursue social change through litigation *alongside* grassroots
and community level political actions which, as highlighted previously, are often intrinsic-
ally linked to PIL cases.[63]

However, when groups and communities operating in a decentralized manner pursue PIL **11.16**
directly, certain challenges arise in the relationships among stakeholders. In contrast to
a centralized approach to PIL, where often a single actor raises funds, manages litigation
strategy, and runs public campaigns, decentralized groups involve a range of independent
stakeholders. Community organizers, individuals, activists, interest groups, lawyers, and
funders all play an important role in decentralized models.[64] As a result, a dynamic yet complicated relationship emerges.

In the context of challenges and opportunities presented by crowdfunding for PIL, as both **11.17**
centralized and decentralized actors are relevant to the rising phenomenon, a distinction
among different categories of stakeholders must be sketched. More specifically, crowdfunding campaigns for PIL entail three distinct figures: the project owner, the funders, and
the lawyers. These stakeholders all interact with the crowdfunding campaign and the litigation in their own way, with their own interests and concerns. Furthermore, crowdfunding
platforms also play a key role in the dynamics among these stakeholders, as the following
analysis will show.

1. Project Owners

As discussed previously, the project owner is a natural or legal person seeking funding for **11.18**
PIL.[65] This role may be adopted by non-governmental organizations (NGOs) or other lead
actors in a centralized top-down approach, whilst individuals, groups, or associations may
assume this role in decentralized bottom-up cases. In either case, the main objective of the
project owner is to raise funds for their cause, whether this is by crowdfunding or through
other sources. Traditionally, funding for PIL has been provided for by government grants,

---

[62] ibid.
[63] For a wider discussion on open and closed models of judicial review, see Tomlinson (n 40).
[64] For the role of community organizers in wider movement lawyering see: WP Quigley, 'Reflections of
Community Organizers: Lawyering for Empowerment of Community Organizations' (1994) 21 Ohio Northern
University Law Review 455.
[65] See general discussion in section II; see further Gomez (n 5).

private philanthropic foundations, or concerned wealthy individuals.[66] However, there are certain challenges to these forms of funding. Having governments, private individuals, or foundations finance a case allows such actors to maintain a certain degree of control or influence over the litigation.[67] This may be explicit through the provision of funding, or implicit, with only certain cases which pursue particular strategic interests receiving funding. However, whether explicit or implicit, the project owner must, in some way, meet the agenda, standards, and requirements of traditional funders.[68] As a result, this removes a certain amount of agency from the community that the litigation is trying to support and risks diluting the ability of a case to reflect the needs of impacted persons. This issue has been further highlighted by Stikin and Klein stating that 'the vindication of important legal rights should not depend upon the beneficence of private philanthropy or be subject to the whim of government'.[69] Crowdfunding therefore helps alleviate issues caused by traditional sources of funding. Project owners are able to retain agency over a case by spreading the source of funding over the crowd. In doing so, no single individual is able to impact or influence the strategy of the case, offering the project owner a great degree of freedom over how best to shape the litigation to truly serve the public interest.

11.19   Project owners are also able to capitalize on the potential success of a crowdfunding campaign. By engaging hundreds, possibly thousands of individuals in a case, the project owner is able to amplify the support for the social issue at hand, bringing about wider debate outside the bounds of the courtroom.[70] Indeed, PIL is not simply about the merits of the case, but rather the case's ability to incite social change.[71] Where a case fails to achieve change through litigation, broad exposure and debate sparked by a successful crowdfunding campaign can contribute to the wider social concern. For example, where the Palestine Justice Campaign was unsuccessful in the first instance judgement,[72] the wider awareness raised concerning accountability for international crimes was successful in gathering attention for issues of impunity in the Netherlands, sparking public debate on the broader issues at hand.[73]

11.20   Further opportunities are presented by crowdfunding to the project owner through the ability to raise large amounts of money in a relatively short period of time.[74] With funding

---

[66]   Albiston and Nielsen (n 36); Sitkin and Kline (n 59).

[67]   PE Sitkin and J Kline, 'Financing Public Interest Litigation' (1971) 13 Arizona Law Review 823, 824; see generally Gomez (n 5).

[68]   Albiston and Nielsen (n 36).

[69]   Sitkin and Kline (n 66) 824 825.

[70]   See generally Zhao and Shneor (n 53).

[71]   See generally Rosenberg (n 34).

[72]   *Ziada v Gantz and Others* [2020] District Court of The Hague C-09-554385-HA ZA 18-647 (English).

[73]   Although the litigation for the campaign continues as a central aspect, Dutch media widely covered the case with documentaries and news reports being published resulting in continued debate in the Netherlands regarding impunity. See K Clark, 'Ziada v. Gantz and Eshel: A Frontier Case on the Position of Civilian Victims of War' [2020] Journal of International Criminal Justice <https://doi.org/10.1093/jicj/mqaa060> accessed 7 March 2021; 'Ziada Case—Nuhanovic Foundation' <http://www.nuhanovicfoundation.org/en/ziada-case/> accessed 31 January 2020; C Ryngaert, 'Functional Immunity of Foreign State Officials in Respect of International Crimes before the Hague District Court: A Regressive Interpretation of Progressive International Law' (*EJIL: Talk!*, 2 March 2020) <https://www.ejiltalk.org/functional-immunity-of-foreign-state-officials-in-respect-of-international-crimes-before-the-hague-district-court-a-regressive-interpretation-of-progressive-international-law/> accessed 7 March 2021; L Witschge, 'As Victim of War Crimes, War Criminals Have Impunity' <https://www.aljazeera.com/news/2020/1/29/dutch-court-dismisses-case-against-former-israeli-generals> accessed 7 March 2021.

[74]   Elliot (n 5) 546.

being a key aspect to any form of PIL, the opportunity of being able to connect with large community of individuals instantly allows the project owners to increase their chances of meeting funding needs. However, it is important to stress that crowdfunding offers no guarantee that sufficient funds will be available. Unlike traditional sources of funding, which offer a certain degree of assurance to the amount and time frame of funds, crowdfunding has a high degree of uncertainty.[75] Evidently, a simple review of crowdfunding sites highlights a disproportionate number of unsuccessful campaigns related to the funding of legal costs, compared to a few higher profile successful campaigns.[76] The risks of unstable funding for the project is further complicated by the varying size of the funds needed to litigate a public interest case. In Europe, these costs can range from between a few thousand euros to hundreds of thousands of euros, depending on the cost of litigation in the domestic jurisdiction as well as the length and complexity of a case.[77] In this sense, only a select few cases that seek funds for PIL are successful.

Consequently, as result of the high risk of insufficient funding raised for a case, the question **11.21** arises as to what happens to donations in PIL cases which fail to meet goals and deadlines. Certain platforms adopting the so-called AON models, such as CrowdJustice,[78] address this issue by returning funds to donors when a project does not meet its target funding goal in the first thirty days. However, major platforms adopting KIA models, such as GoFundMe, do not address how funds will be used whereby they are insufficient to support litigation.[79] Although certain KIA donation-based platforms allow for the selection of specific campaigns, they apply a one-size-fits-all policy to how donated funds may be used where goals are not met, that is the project owner retains the money. However, if these funds are insufficient to cover the costs needs for the litigation and a case is not pursued, it would appear that project owners bear a responsibly under the general terms of use of a platform to return donations to funders.[80]

Additional complexities are presented for the management and administration of funds by **11.22** project owners in decentralized campaigns. The individuals and campaigners who are engaged in raising funds on a platform are accountable for the direct management of funds. Furthermore, where no legal entity can be identified to receive the donated funds, these individuals also become the direct recipient of the funds. However, many social movements

---

[75] Gomez (n 5). The present range on crowdfunding platform Indiegogo is between USD 3,000 and USD 10,000, see 'Indiegogo Insight: 87% of Campaigns That Reach Their Goal Exceed It' (*Indiegogo Blog*) <https://go.indiegogo.com/blog/2011/12/indiegogo-insight-87-of-campaigns-which-reach-their-goal-exceed-it.html> accessed 7 March 2021.

[76] See 'How to Pay for a Lawyer With No Money: 3 Resources' (n 48); 'Discover the Latest Equality & Human Rights Cases Crowdfunding on CrowdJustice That Need Your Support!' (*CrowdJustice*) <https://www.crowdjustice.com/cases/equality-human-rights/> accessed 7 March 2021.

[77] For example, the EU Justice Scoreboard shows that the availability of legal aid and the level of court fees have a major impact on the access to justice, in particular for people in poverty. See generally, European Commission, *The 2020 EU Justice Scoreboard,* August 2020, available at https://ec.europa.eu/info/sites/default/files/justice_scoreboard_2020_en.pdf; Hickman (n 10).

[78] 'How it Works' (*Crowdjustice*) <https://www.crowdjustice.com/how-it-works/> accessed 8 May 2021.

[79] Cumming, Leboeuf, and Schwienbacher (n 19).

[80] On the platform GoFundMe, for example, project owners must use the funds for the purpose detailed on the campaign. Funds not used for purpose detailed on the campaign page may be considered fraudulent and result in the project being closed by the platform. GoFundMe reserves the right to refund donations where they believe funds have not been used for their intended purpose, as such, the project owner, using this platform has an obligation to refund donations offered to pursue litigation if not used for this purpose. See generally, 'terms' (*GoFundMe*) <http://www.gofundme.com/terms> accessed 8 May 2021.

are developed on horizontal organizational structures, to ensure community ownership and reduced influence of any single individual. A tension therefore arises between the need for accountability and transparency required by platforms to identify a distinct project owner and legal beneficiary for a campaign, and decentralized crowdfunding efforts which naturally avoid transferring such authority and accountability to any single legal or natural person.

11.23   A final consideration for the project owner is the risk of cases falling foul to the so-called tyranny of the majority, whereby smaller campaigns run by minority communities are underfunded whilst campaigns ran by a majority gain extensive support, resulting in risks for minorities.[81] Although the risk of the tyranny of the majority is reduced by increased connectivity of communities facilitated by the Internet, a particular community's access and/or use of crowdfunding sites must be considered by the project owner pursuing such forms of financing for PIL.

2.   Funders

11.24   Another key stakeholder in the context of crowdfunded PIL is the crowd itself. Funders play an important role in this process as, collectively, they have the ability to define the relative success or failure of a campaign through the contributions they donate. The crowd as a whole holds a significant weight in the litigation process, while the role of the individual funders is limited. This, in many ways, is a strength of crowdfunding as a financing vehicle for PIL. Crowdfunding allows the funder to engage with legal actions which they would be unable to access without being part of a crowd.[82] As a member of the crowd, the funder is able to join wider community efforts, dictating which causes are most important to them, which should receive funding and which should not. As a result, by facilitating individual and community engagement, crowdfunding widens litigation to show, through the provision of funds, what is in the public interest. This not only creates a sense of community belonging centred around social change but, as highlighted by Julie Salasky, the CEO and founder of CrowdJustice, it allows people's 'access to the law no matter how much they contribute'.[83]

11.25   However, the position of the funder in the context of PIL also entails certain challenges. It has been argued that, in donation-based models, 'if funders do not pursue financial gain, their decision to fund will be based more on intuitions and emotions, and less on solid data and cost-benefit analysis'.[84] Indeed, Mollick has highlighted that funders' support for a crowdfunded project, litigation or otherwise, can range from friendly support to a genuine belief in the societal change sought by them, or from expressing political statement to even making a joke.[85] Consequently, due to the funders' lack of personal investment

---

[81]   L Guinier, *Tyranny of the Majority: Fundamental Fairness in Representative Democracy* (Free Press 1995).
[82]   See generally access to justice issues for individuals. Tomlinson (n 40).
[83]   'Meet the Lawyer-Turned-Tech Entrepreneur Trying to Make Justice Available to All' (*Guardian*, 29 August 2019)<http://www.theguardian.com/careers/2019/aug/29/meet-the-lawyer-turned-tech-entrepreneur-trying-to-make-justice-available-to-all> accessed 7 March 2021.
[84]   Perry (n 51) 1384.
[85]   Mollick (n 14) 3. See *inter alia*, Gomez (n 5).

into a case, it is suggested that donation-based litigation funding fuels meritless claims, risking overwhelming courts and increasing frivolous litigation.[86] Although it is possible that donation-based crowdfunding may increase the risk of a meritless claim, as the funders do not base their decision on the financial gain of a case, this is not to say such cases should not be pursued or heard by the court. Regardless of the concern for the risk of a meritless claim, project owners rely on the representation of legal professionals, who in turn have their own interest and legal and/or ethical obligations to avoid submitting frivolous claims. Accordingly, financial barriers to justice alone should not play a role in dictating which cases are meritorious, and which are not; this, simply put, should be the decision of the court. Indeed, there are few limitations on actors who have the financial capacity to pursue meritless cases they believe to be in their interest, Strategic Lawsuits Against Public Participation (SLAPP) suits being a key example;[87] as such, there seems to be little reason to restrict crowdfunded PIL.

Another consideration from the perspective of the funder is their legal exposure if costs are **11.26** granted to the opposing party in case of an unfavourable litigation outcome. Although it is not possible in the present chapter to provide a comprehensive overview of the relevant national legislation detailing the allocations of costs and the cases where litigation funders may be liable, it is however possible to discuss whether serious risks are posed in this respect. As highlighted by Tomlinson in the context of donation-based crowdfunded judicial review cases, it is assumed that funders who do not have a personal interest in the case do not have liability beyond their initial pledge.[88] In other words, as the funder holds no control over the strategy or management of the litigation, nor do they have a material interest in a possible award of damages, they will not be liable for the costs of the opposing party. However, this issue may be complicated, depending on the applicable law concerning the size of donation vis-à-vis the liability of the funder. For example, legislation in the UK stipulates that individuals providing 'more than £3000 to judicial review cases may be liable for further costs risks'.[89] Although this legislation has yet to be put to a test in the UK with respect to crowdfunding, the liability of the funder, particularly as a result of the size of their donation, is an important consideration for the development of crowdfunded PIL in the UK and elsewhere.

3. Lawyers

The final stakeholders to consider are the lawyers. Public interest litigation involves the ne- **11.27** cessary engagement of a legal counsel, instructed on the case. Whilst the lawyers are always not directly involved in the crowdfunding campaign, their role can often intersect with those of the project owner and the funder in a number of ways. The counsel can be involved in supporting and promoting wider campaign efforts, or, in certain cases, they can even be

---

[86] Perry (n 51); Gomez (n 5).

[87] GW Pring and P Canan, *SLAPPs: Getting Sued for Speaking Out* (Temple University Press 1996); 'Time to Take Action against SLAPPs' (*Commissioner for Human Rights*) <https://www.coe.int/en/web/commissioner/blog/-/asset_publisher/xZ32OPEoxOkq/content/time-to-take-action-against-slapps> accessed 7 March 2021.

[88] Tomlinson (n 40) 172.

[89] ibid; Criminal Justice and Courts Act 2015 section 86(3).

the direct recipient of the funds. In this case, there is an obligation to ensure that the funds are used exclusively for the activities detailed in the crowdfunding project. This inherently requires that project owners and lawyers collaborate to ensure that funds are used appropriately and managed correctly.[90] Yet, the involvement of lawyers in PIL crowdfunding extend beyond the obvious financial aspect. Crowdfunding allows for a certain degree of professional freedom to pursue cases without the oversight of a single influential donor. As mentioned previously, having a 'crowd' reduces the need for traditional funding sources, in a way that can benefit not only the freedom of the project owner, but also the lawyer, when developing the litigation strategy.

11.28   However, PIL crowdfunding also poses some challenges for counsels. Through crowdfunding, a case becomes publicly visible. This exposure risks impacting the litigation strategy, with potentially undesirable effects for highly sensitive, politically divisive matters, which are often subject of PIL. In this sense, before placing a case in the public eye through crowdfunding, the lawyer must consider how such an exposure would impact the litigation strategy.[91] Furthermore, crowdfunded PIL may also raise ethical issues. While in most cases the project owner will be the direct client in the matter, crowdfunding adds a further actor to the 'attorney–client relationship', namely the crowd. In this regard, the lawyer must consider the project owners' source of funding, to ensure that the manner in which the funds are raised aligns with their use during the litigation. In other words, the lawyer should not accept funds where the project owner has presented a different strategy or case to the crowd through a particular crowdfunding campaign. Conversely, the lawyer must also ensure that the litigation pursues the interests of the crowd and the project owner to achieve the ultimate goal set forth in the crowdfunding campaign. Deviating from this strategy for professional or other reasons might risk constituting a misuse of funds.

4. Concluding Remarks on the Position of Different Stakeholders in PIL Crowdfunding

11.29   In conclusion, the involvement of different stakeholders in crowdfunded PIL generates both opportunities and challenges. New actors, including community-led groups previously excluded from traditional judicial procedures, are able to gain access to the law. On the other hand, by opening up new opportunities, crowdfunding also subverts the traditional roles, typically adopted in centralized models. PIL crowdfunding affords project owners a wide margin of discretion as to how to pursue their case; yet, in return for such a high degree of agency, the stability of traditional donor funding is lost. The relationship of the project owner to the crowdfunding campaign is also complicated where decentralized and informal groups seek to use platforms which require project owners to be natural or legal persons, which may be difficult to identify in a decentralized setting. With respect

---

[90] In this respect, the lawyers acting as a beneficiary have obligations vis-à-vis the platform when accepting funds from a campaign. Although the lawyer may not have an impact on the overall campaign, they do however, have control over funds. For a platforms generals terms and conditions on beneficiaries see: 'GoFundMe Terms of Service' <https://www.gofundme.com/terms> accessed 7 March 2021.

[91] For instance, the ECI crowdfunding webpage was taken down in order not to jeopardize the legal strategy. See 'Ensuring Common Commercial Policy Conformity with EU Treaties and Compliance with International Law' (n 3).

to the funders, crowdfunding offers the chance for community-led engagement in social interest cases; however, questions of liability for the costs of litigation are still to be comprehensively answered. Finally, whereas the lawyer has increased professional discretion over a case compared to traditional sources of funding, the high exposure of the case through crowdfunding platforms may risk undermining the overall litigation strategy.

IV. Future Prospects

As illustrated above, crowdfunding can enhance community engagement in PIL, thus enabling civil society to facilitate social change from a grassroots level. Furthermore, broadening the ability for community engagement and decreasing the need for formal institutional funding or single wealthy donors has allowed for social movements to retain agency over a case. However, as highlighted by Shneor, Flaten, and Zhang, '[a]s the crowdfunding industry evolves from an introductory stage into a growth stage ... new dilemmas, temptations, and opportunities must be considered carefully by all industry stakeholders'.[92] The future of crowdfunding for PIL therefore adds further levels of complexity that have not been explored by the existing literature.   **11.30**

1. Dilemmas and Opportunities

One of the main considerations for the future of crowdfunded PIL is the ability to raise sufficient funds to cover the overall cost of a case. While, as highlighted previously, traditional sources of funding from formal actors, private foundations, and wealthy individuals have their challenges, they do however, provide financial stability for lengthy and complex cases. Crowdfunding, by contrast, provides no such stability. This uncertainty constitutes one of the major challenges faced by the project owners. The success of the crowdfunding campaign depends on a variety of factors, including the quality of the public campaign, the awareness of the cause, and the number and dimension of stakeholders making up the community interested in the cause. As a result, longer-term litigation planning is hindered by uncertainty as to the available funds for the case. This is a serious risk for the future development of PIL crowdfunding, which directly stifles the project owner's ability to plan strategies, while also affecting indirectly both the funder's feeling of self-empowerment as well as—most importantly—the lawyers' interest to commit to a case where the chances of being remunerated are shaky. Hence, the problems arising from the lack of financial stability in PIL crowdfunding need to be addressed systematically, taking into account *inter alia* the risk of also undermining the effectiveness of the judicial machinery through complex litigations that will ultimately be discontinued for lack of funds.   **11.31**

Another consideration for the future development of donation-based crowdfunding concerns its very nature. As described in section II, crowdfunding is an entirely private effort, addressing certain needs. When such a need qualifies as a 'public' or 'common good' (eg   **11.32**

---

[92] R Shneor, B-T Flåten, and L Zhao, 'The Future of Crowdfunding Research and Practice' in R Shneor, L Zhao, and B-T Flåten (eds), *Advances in Crowdfunding: Research and Practice* (Springer International Publishing 2020) <https://doi.org/10.1007/978-3-030-46309-0_21> accessed 7 March 2021, 500.

health and education services), the idea that a private effort is needed to ensure one's access to that good or service may raise some criticism and concerns, with regard to the State's role in granting the very same good or service. To exemplify this, commentators of crowd-funding have often criticized the trend of replacing State welfare with donation-based crowdfunding, particularly in healthcare, with the platform GoFundMe being referred to as 'America's NHS [National Health service]'.[93] Looking at PIL crowdfunding from this per-spective, and taking into account the considerable flows of money it is able to attract, the phenomenon may end up replacing the State's own duty to guarantee an effective right of access to justice through legal aid. In other words, PIL crowdfunding risks favouring the 'unintentional institutionalisation of public authorities' failures and mismanagements'.[94] Similarly to other sectors where the State appears to be unable to discharge its own obli-gation vis-à-vis individuals' fundamental rights,[95] the State may tend to outsource to pri-vate entities both the concrete burden of granting access to justice in the public interest, and the legal responsibility deriving from its failure to do so. Hence, the opportunities that crowdfunding offers in relation to reducing the distance between citizens and justice should not turn the attention away from the deficits of the State in dealing with access to justice. Whereas crowdfunding should not be amplified as a replacement of inherently public func-tions, the latter should work towards regulating such an instrument with a view to con-solidating its positive effects on society, while retaining its duties vis-à-vis the effective actionability of fundamental rights.

2. Regulatory Mechanisms: Public or Private?

11.33 Therefore, the question arises to what extent donation-based crowdfunding for PIL can and should be regulated. On the one hand, regulation would provide clarity for project owners, funders, and lawyers, ensuring accountability for the use of funds, as well as possibly ad-dressing remaining questions on funder/project owner liability. The right of the funder to reclaim a donation in the event that costs are awarded to the applicant may also be ad-dressed. On the other hand, regulation of a niche and novel field may prove impractical and restrictive, should it fail to account for the practicalities of this form of crowdfunding. It would therefore seem logical to suggest that, rather than specifically regulating donation-based PIL crowdfunded, the two aspects of donation-based crowdfunding and PIL should be addressed individually, respecting their own particular complexities. At regional level, a donation-based crowdfunding regulation would ensure the uniform application of rules protecting cross-border stakeholders, whilst national legislation governing the practice of PIL would ensure that particular considerations, such as funders liability, are addressed.

---

[93] See generally 'We Shouldn't Need GoFundMe to Respond to Catastrophes. We Need a Strong Welfare State.' <https://jacobinmag.com/2020/05/gofundme-crowdfunding-coronavirus-covid-cancer-treatment> accessed 7 March 2021.

[94] R Shneor and S Torjesen, 'Ethical Considerations in Crowdfunding' in R Shneor, L Zhao, and B-T Flåten (eds), *Advances in Crowdfunding: Research and Practice* (Springer International Publishing 2020) <https://doi.org/10.1007/978-3-030-46309-0_8> accessed 7 March 2021, 168.

[95] See for instance the State's obligation to save life at sea laid down in Art 98 of the United Convention on the Law of the Sea as applied to the context of borders management and control policies, whereby numerous private NGOs are tacitly given the burden to coordinate search and rescue (SAR) operations.

Therefore, the question as to how to tackle the challenges of PIL crowdfunding remains. **11.34** In this respect, it would seem beneficial to turn to platforms as the facilitating service providers, who have both the knowledge and capacity to adapt their services to the specific needs of PIL crowdfunding. For instance, the law may establish a platforms' duty to adopt clear guidelines, or even requirements to tackle the accountability and transparency issues mentioned above, whilst the platforms offering a space for crowdfunded PIL would be able to share specific information on funders' rights and liability vis-à-vis the relevant national legislation. In this regard, certain platforms have already begun to address some of the challenges presented by the rise of crowdfunded PIL. For instance, CrowdJustice—which stands out as a platform developed for PIL—directly addresses this issue by ensuring that the lawyer engaged in the case is directly in charge of funds. As such, they assume accountability for the proper use of funds due to their own professional obligations, whilst the project owner bears responsibility to ensure funds are used for the purposes described.[96] However, other donation-based platforms which are not specifically designed for PIL crowdfunding presently do not adopt such a practice. A streamlined effort at the platform level, adapting their services and requirements for particular types of donation-based campaigns, that is PIL, would begin to address challenges presented by this growing industry.

V. Conclusion

This chapter has sketched an outline of the rising phenomenon of crowdfunded PIL. **11.35** Crowdfunding is opening up a traditionally narrow sector to new actors by addressing financing and access to justice issues. In this regard, crowdfunding presents opportunities to reconnect PIL with the very communities such cases seek to help. Yet, as with any new practice, certain challenges also emerge. Project owners, funders, and lawyers must interact whilst facing their own issues and considerations, in the absence of formal regulation or guidelines. As crowdfunded PIL continues to rise, the challenges will become increasingly present in debates on how to ensure that campaigns respect the needs of stakeholders. To overcome these challenges platforms should assume responsibility to ensure their services accommodate the nuances of crowdfunded PIL. However, to ensure a uniform practical application, a certain degree of State guidance or regulation is needed, at least to address certain gaps that remain unanswered with respect to crowdfunded PIL. In the meantime, the practice will continue to develop, with project owners, funders, and lawyers seeking to advance their goals of social change with the assistance of crowdfunding in a digital age.

---

[96] 'Terms of Use' (*CrowdJustice*) <https://www.crowdjustice.com/terms-and-conditions/> accessed 8 May 2021.

PART V
PROTECTING THE CROWD UNDER THE CROWDFUNDING REGULATION AND BEYOND

12

Investor Protection on Crowdfunding Platforms

Joseph Lee

I. Introduction

This chapter discusses the protection of investors on crowdfunding platforms under the **12.01** Crowdfunding Regulation. Although there are many provisions in the regulation that protect investors, this chapter concentrates specifically on those included under the heading of Chapter IV 'Investor protection'. Conflicts of interest,[1] complaints handling,[2] and marketing communications[3] are dealt with in Chapter 8 and in Chapter 14, respectively.

Investor protection is a cornerstone of the sound operation of financial markets and a key **12.02** regulatory objective, upon which many principles have been established.[4] It fosters market

---

[1] Art 8 Crowdfunding Regulation.
[2] Art 7 Crowdfunding Regulation.
[3] Chapter 5 of the Crowdfunding Regulation.
[4] N Moloney and others, *The Oxford Handbook of Financial Regulation* (OUP 2015) 160; D Zetzsche and C Preiner, 'Cross-Border Crowdfunding: Towards a Single Crowdlending and Crowdinvesting Market for Europe' (2018) 19 European Business Organization Law Review 217.

confidence and has become an accepted universal moral principle in financial transactions.[5] It has also become a guiding principle for peer-to-peer crowdfunding service providers (CSPs)[6] which aim to increase access to finance,[7] access to a shared economy,[8] and access to justice[9] when disputes occur. CSPs are important stakeholders, as they intermediate between investors and project owners,[10] between access to finance and access to a growing economy,[11] and between market competition and innovation.[12] Hence, when examining how investors are protected, other performance indicators such as the choices provided by the market (competition) or the role that technology can play in that respect (innovation) should not be overlooked.[13]

12.03   This chapter focuses on how investor protection can contribute to the objectives of crowdfunding and, in particular, how the provisions of the Crowdfunding Regulation serve this purpose. To this end, section II discusses the investor-focused objectives of crowdfunding, and the role that technology can play in realizing these objectives. Section III considers the meaning of investor protection within the scope of the Crowdfunding Regulation, and identifies areas where the current regime might be extended in the future. Section IV discusses the categorization of investors and the relevance thereof for the investor protection. Major provisions pertinent to investor protection are subsequently discussed in sections V–IX, including the information to be provided to clients, default rate disclosure, the entry knowledge test and the simulation of ability to bear loss, the pre-contractual reflection period, and the key investment information sheet. The sections also contain reflections pertinent to the different topics discussed in order to put them in a greater context. Section X concludes.

II. Investor-focused Objectives of Crowdfunding

12.04   Crowdfunding platforms are an innovation in digital finance whose novelty lies in the application of technology to peer-to-peer (P2P) financing. The innovation is not the

---

[5] E Schoen, 'The 2007–2009 Financial Crisis: An Erosion of Ethics: A Case Study' (2017) 146 Journal of Business Ethics 805, 830.

[6] M Goethner and others, 'Protecting Investors in Equity Crowdfunding: An Empirical Analysis of the Small Investor Protection Act' (2021) 162 Technological Forecasting and Social Change 1, 5. DOI: https://doi.org/10.1016/j.techfore.2020.120352.

[7] J Lee, 'Access to Finance for Artificial Intelligence Regulation in the Financial Services Industry' (2020) 21 European Business Organisation Law Review 731, 757; A Taeihagh, 'Crowdsourcing, Sharing Economies and Development' (2017) 33 Journal of Developing Societies 191, 222; S Schwarcz, 'Empowering the Poor: Turning De Facto Rights into Collateralized Credit' (2018) 8 Duke Law School Public Law & Legal Theory Series 2018/38. DOI: http://dx.doi.org/10.2139/ssrn.3167507.

[8] J Wirtz and others, 'Platforms in the Peer-to-Peer Sharing Economy' (2019) 30 Journal of Service Management 452, 483.

[9] Columbia Centre on Sustainable Investment, 'Impacts of the International Investment Regime on Access to Justice' (Roundtable Outcome Document 2018) <https://www.ohchr.org/Documents/Issues/Business/CCSI_UNWGBHR_InternationalInvestmentRegime.pdf> accessed 24 April 2021.

[10] Commission Proposal.

[11] K Stanberry, 'Crowdfunding and the Expansion of Access to Start-up Capital' (2014) 5 International Research Journal of Applied Finance 1382, 1391.

[12] A Miglo, 'Crowdfunding in a Competitive Environment' (2018) 13 Journal of Risk and Financial Management 1, 38.

[13] D Awrey and K Judge, 'Why Financial Regulation Keeps Falling Short' (2020) 61 Boston College Law Review 2295 <https://lawdigitalcommons.bc.edu/bclr/vol61/iss7/2> accessed 24 April 2021.

crowdfunding itself but the way in which technology facilitates P2P transactions.[14] Using this technology allows a broader spectrum of the crowd to interact and may increase returns and enhance value for investors (see subsections II.1 and II.2). In order to achieve this, it is however necessary to close the trust gap between investors and the other participants in crowdfunding (see subsection II.3).

1. Reaching Out to Investors

Technology in the form of social media has played a significant role in connecting people   **12.05**
across geographical boundaries[15] and enabling strangers to interact by matching their interests. It can be used to reach people in every corner of the world who have access to the internet. Traditional 'village crowdfunding' did not have the technological infrastructure to reach a larger spectrum of the population outside the village. As a result, legal innovations such as company law and secured transactions were invented to allow investors and savers to participate in ventures that they could not normally access through their limited monetary and physical capabilities, and to transact with people outside their geographical vicinity or social circle. However, stock exchanges only allow their members to participate in trading activities, and this makes the initial public offering process exclusive to a closed circle of institutional parties.[16] The technological ability to reach anybody through a crowdfunding platform means that such platforms are different in nature from modern stock exchanges.[17]

2. Increasing Returns and Enhancing Value for Investors

Investors look for a return on their investment, and technology can play a role in meeting   **12.06**
their expectations.[18] Although the design of business models and the way returns are made on investments are under human control, technology has already demonstrated its ability to yield higher returns for investors, and it has similar potential in the crowdfunding market. For instance, it can be used to manage individual loan portfolios when rates of return and default need to be precisely indicated.[19] Technology can also be used to match investors' offers in the secondary market, while taking into account the regulatory framework set out in the Markets in Financial Instruments Directive II (MiFID II) for operating trading venues (see Chapter 13).

---

[14] J Lee, 'Embedding Cryptoassets in the Law to Transform the Financial Market: Security Token Offering in the UK' in Ph Maume and others (eds) *Law of Crypto Assets* (Beck/Hart/Nomos 2021) Forthcoming.
[15] J Clark and others, 'Social Network Sites and Well-Being: The Role of Social Connection' (2017) 12 Current Directions in Psychological Science 32, 37. DOI: <https://doi.org/10.1177/0963721417730833>.
[16] B Steil, 'Changes in the Ownership and Governance of Securities Exchanges: Causes and Consequences' (2015) <https://core.ac.uk/download/pdf/6649711.pdf> accessed 24 April 2021.
[17] J Lee, 'Law and Regulation for a Crypto-market: Perpetuation or Innovation?' in I Chiu and G Deipenbrock (eds) *Routledge Handbook on FinTech and Law—Regulatory, Supervisory, Policy and Other Legal Challenges* (Routledge 2021) 356–78.
[18] K Judge, 'Investor-Driven Financial Innovation' (2018) 8 Harvard Business Law Review 296, 438.
[19] H Kim and others, 'Corporate Default Predictions Using Machine Learning: Literature Review' (2020) 12 Sustainability 1, 11. DOI: 10.3390/su12166325.

12.07   In addition, investors increasingly look for something beyond monetary returns. Common value is increasingly seen as a reason for investment, rather than simple maximization of returns. For example, crowdfunding has been used to combat climate change[20] and to support performance art[21] that promotes diversity, and it can be used to raise capital for political causes.[22] Although value-related investment funds are already offered in the financial market, crowdfunding platforms can give more direct access to investors and entrepreneurs to match their values with an investment, without incurring excessive agency costs. This is also what the UK Stewardship Code is aimed at achieving.[23]

3. Closing the Trust Gap between Investors and Other Participants in Crowdfunding

12.08   When crowdfunding is not based on technology, it relies on mutual trust between the participants,[24] such as village neighbours or clients of respected institutions. In traditional village crowdfunding, participants were familiar with the background of both the fundraisers and the contributors. The project seeking funding was often sanctioned by a person of prominence in the village such as a religious leader, a wealthy family, a politically influential clan, or a government official. The church was often the place for fundraising for projects to be carried out for the welfare of people in the parish or for a mission abroad. On a crowdfunding platform, by contrast, such trust needs to be created among participants that are strangers to one another. When members of a social circle know and trust one another, a robust credit assessment or disclosure of information regime is unnecessary. However, this is not the case on a technology-based crowdfunding platform; as a consequence, the technology needs to play a role in closing the trust gap.[25] The trust gap is mentioned in the Impact Assessment that accompanies the Commission Proposal as one of the two main problems in the European market for crowdfunding.[26] Diverging measures of investor protection create unnecessary confusion for retail investors that have to familiarize themselves with different systems. Prospective and current investors demonstrate a lack of trust as they may not receive sufficient information about the returns and risks of the projects. This uncertainty is further increased as the conducted due diligence and presented information are often carried out in different ways. This results in high search costs that defer investors who

---

[20] K von Ritter and D Black-Layne (2013) 'Crowdfunding for Climate Change: A New Source of Finance for Climate Action at the Local Level?' (ECBI Working Paper) <https://unfccc.int/files/cooperation_and_supp ort/financial_mechanism/standing_committee/application/pdf/paper_-_microfinancing_.pdf> accessed 24 April 2021.

[21] B Boeuf and others, 'Financing Creativity: Crowdfunding as a New Approach for Theatre Projects' (2014) 16 International Journal of Arts Management 33, 48.

[22] Crowdfunder, 'Crowdfunding for Political Change on Crowdfunder' (2019) <https://www.crowdfunder. co.uk/general-election/political-change> accessed 27 April 2021.

[23] A Reisberg, 'The UK Stewardship Code: On the Road to Nowhere' (2015) 15 Journal of Corporate Law Studies 217, 253.

[24] K Moysidou and P Hausberg, 'In Crowdfunding We Trust: A Trust-Building Model in Lending Crowdfunding' (2019) 11 Journal of Small Business Management 32, 37. DOI: doi.org/10.1080/00472778.2019.1661682.

[25] R Randy Suryono and others, 'Challenges and Trends of Financial Technology (Fintech): A Systematic Literature Review' (2020) 11 Information 1, 20. DOI: 10.3390/info11120590.

[26] European Commission Staff Working Document, 'Impact Assessment Accompanying the document Proposal for a Regulation of the European Parliament and of the Council on European Crowdfunding Service Providers (ECSP) for Business and Proposal for a Directive of the European Parliament and of the Council amending Directive 2014/65/EU on markets in financial instruments', SWD(2018) 56 final—2018/048 (COD), 19.

would otherwise be willing to invest in other Member States. The issue of trust is also highly applicable in defining the selection criteria used in cases where automatic decisions on investors' money are taken by the platform.[27]

The Crowdfunding Regulation therefore aims to enhance investors' trust by strengthening platforms' integrity and transparency for investors, for what concerns the project, the instruments being intermediated, and the processes performed by the platform. The sector adherence to a common set of standards may promote its reputation and help establish itself as a stable and reliable source of alternative finance. Proper levels of governance requirements, to ensure that management is fit and proper, and adequate internal controls are important steps to achieve the second specific objective.[28] Appropriate levels of information disclosures to ensure that prospective and current investors receive sufficient information about the returns and risks of the projects, together with fitting safeguards to prevent fraudulent activities by the platforms as well as by the project owners (fundraisers), are paramount.[29]   **12.09**

III. Investor Protection and the Scope of the Regulation

The dynamic nature of business models and different interpretations across Member States of existing EU legislation has led to a large variety of regulatory frameworks for CSPs ranging from no regulation to strict application of investor protection rules. As a result, the investor protection frameworks (eg conduct rules and information disclosure) were fragmented across the EU, while the nature of the risk is similar. One of the objectives of the Commission Proposal therefore was to create harmonized, solid, and proportional investor protection rules to cover the activities of CSPs in the EU.[30] In the end, a high level of investor confidence contributes to the growth of crowdfunding services.   **12.10**

The investor protection rules included in the Crowdfunding Regulation are inspired by MiFID II. The general principle that an CSP should act honestly, fairly, and professionally in accordance with the best interests of its clients (Article 3(2) Crowdfunding Regulation) is copied from MiFID II (Article 24(1) MiFID II). Also, the requirements in respect of investor categorization, information to clients and the entry knowledge test are based on the requirements set in MiFID II in that respect, although there are some differences as discussed below in the relevant sections. At the same time, the Crowdfunding Regulation includes some provisions on investor protection that are tailored to the risks that come along with crowdfunding such as the provisions on default rate disclosure, the simulation of the ability to bear loss, investment limits, and the pre-contractual reflection period.   **12.11**

---

[27] ibid 27.

[28] See Chapter 8.

[29] European Commission Staff Working Document, 'Impact Assessment Accompanying the document Proposal for a Regulation of the European Parliament and of the Council on European Crowdfunding Service Providers (ECSP) for Business and Proposal for a Directive of the European Parliament and of the Council amending Directive 2014/65/EU on markets in financial instruments', SWD(2018) 56 final—2018/048 (COD), 31. See Chapter 9 on the safeguards to prevent fraudulent activities.

[30] Commission Proposal, 2, 5, and 8. See also Recital 15 Commission Proposal.

12.12   While (harmonization of) investor protection was a driver for creating the Crowdfunding Regulation, at the same time it also set some restrictions to the scope thereof. First, as discussed in Chapter 3, the Crowdfunding Regulation is not applicable to crowdfunding offers with an overall consideration of more than EUR 5 million over a period of twelve months. The reason is that any issuance above this threshold was considered to warrant the application of more mature and complex regulatory regimes, like MiFID II, or a more mature credit intermediation regime, because of the spillover effects that this greater amount would generate on risks for investor protection and financial market stability.[31] In addition, the exclusion of non-transferable securities from the scope of the Crowdfunding Regulation lies in the structure of the product that should not allow transferability, plus the risks that these products may have in terms of investor protection, by locking in investors with limited exit options.[32]

12.13   Lastly, there are several types of crowdfunding, each giving different investment returns and having a different relationship between project owners and investors. As illustrated in Chapter 1, they fall into four main types: loan-based, investment-based, reward-based, and donation-based crowdfunding.[33] There are also hybrid forms so that, for instance, loan-based crowdfunding includes raising capital through loans and through individual portfolio management of loans,[34] but if the platform facilitates issuance and trading of bonds it is categorized as investment-based crowdfunding. As explained in Chapter 3, the Crowdfunding Regulation only covers the first two types of crowdfunding (loan-based and investment-based), which are similar to the current capital markets. The exclusion of reward- and donation-based crowdfunding from the scope of the Regulation may be a strategic decision to test the market sentiment on crowdfunding. Once the Crowdfunding Regulation has been shown to support the crowdfunding market, reward- and donation-based crowdfunding could be brought under its aegis as well, or a similar regime can be created to support them, based on the lessons learnt. Already, there are examples of how these two types of crowdfunding can increase access to finance and shared economy as well as matching the common values of the parties involved. From an investor protection perspective, it may make sense to further regulate reward and donation-based crowdfunding, taking into account the (financial and moral) contribution that is involved in these types of crowdfunding.

---

[31] European Commission Staff Working Document, 'Impact Assessment Accompanying the document Proposal for a Regulation of the European Parliament and of the Council on European Crowdfunding Service Providers (ECSP) for Business and Proposal for a Directive of the European Parliament and of the Council amending Directive 2014/65/EU on markets in financial instruments', SWD(2018) 56 final—2018/048 (COD), 34.

[32] ibid 35.

[33] M Hossain and G Onyema Oparaocha, 'Crowdfunding: Motives, Definitions, Typology and Ethical Challenges' (2017) 1 Entrepreneurship Research Journal 1, 14. <https://www.degruyter.com/document/doi/10.1515/erj-2015-0045/html> accessed 28 April 2021.

[34] B Yasar, 'The New Investment Landscape: Equity Crowdfunding' (2021) 21 Central Bank Review 1, 16.

IV. Categorization of Investors: Sophisticated and Non-Sophisticated

To ensure adequate protection for different kinds of investors as they participate in crowd-   **12.14**
funding projects while facilitating investment flows, the Crowdfunding Regulation distinguishes between sophisticated and non-sophisticated investors and introduces appropriate
safeguards for each category.[35] This section discusses the definition and treatment of sophisticated and non-sophisticated investors. It also presents some general reflections on
investor categorization and discrimination.

1. Definition of Sophisticated and Non-Sophisticated Investors

The definition of sophisticated investor in Article 2(1)(j) of the Crowdfunding Regulation   **12.15**
encompasses two types of sophisticated investors, as further explained below.

A. *Per se* Sophisticated Investors
First, the definition includes any natural or legal person that qualifies as a professional client   **12.16**
under points (1), (2), (3), or (4) of section I of Annex II to MiFID II (so-called *per se* professional clients under MiFID II). These are hereinafter referred to as *per se* sophisticated
investors. They include entities that are required to be authorized or regulated to operate
in the financial markets, large undertakings meeting certain size requirements on a company basis, national and regional governments, Central Banks, international and supranational institutions, and other institutional investors whose main activity is to invest in
financial instruments. *Per se* sophisticated investors can be qualified as sophisticated under
the Crowdfunding Regulation simply by providing proof of their professional status.[36]

B. Opt-up Sophisticated Investors
Second, Article 2(1)(j) qualifies as sophisticated 'any natural or legal person who has the   **12.17**
approval of the crowdfunding service provider to be treated as a sophisticated investor in
accordance with the criteria and the procedure laid down in Annex II' of the Crowdfunding
Regulation (hereinafter referred to as *opt-up* sophisticated investors). This Annex sets forth
different identification criteria for legal and natural persons (section I) and a procedure
to assess the request to be treated as a sophisticated investor (section II). Investors may be
categorized as sophisticated investors, if they meet the identification criteria, *and* if the procedure set out in section II of Annex II is followed. Under the Crowdfunding Regulation,
legal persons must be regarded as sophisticated when they meet at least one of the following
identification criteria:

(1) own funds of at least EUR 100,000;
(2) net turnover of at least EUR 2 million;
(3) balance sheet of at least EUR 1 million.

---

[35] Recital 42 Crowdfunding Regulation.
[36] Annex II, Part III Crowdfunding Regulation.

Natural persons, instead, must be considered sophisticated under the Crowdfunding Regulation if they meet at least two of the following identification criteria:

(1) personal gross income of at least EUR 60,000 per fiscal year, or a financial instrument portfolio, defined as including cash deposits and financial assets, that exceeds EUR 100,000;

(2) having at least one year of work experience in the financial sector, in a professional position which requires knowledge of the transactions or services envisaged, or having held an executive position for at least twelve months in a legal person that qualifies as a sophisticated investor according to the aforementioned criteria;

(3) having carried out transactions of a significant size on the capital markets at an average frequency of ten per quarter, over the previous four quarters.[37]

CSPs must make available to investors a template, through which investors can request to be treated as sophisticated investors. The template should contain a warning about the consequences of such qualification in terms of reduced investor protection. When making such a request, an investor should not only specify the identification criteria that they meet but also state that they are aware of the consequences of losing the protection reserved to non-sophisticated investors, and that they remain liable for the veracity of the information they provide in the request. The CSP must take 'reasonable steps to ensure that the investor qualifies as a sophisticated investor', and 'implement appropriate written internal policies to categorise investors'. The request should be approved, unless the CSP has 'reasonable doubts' as to the correctness of the information. Once an investor has been approved as sophisticated, the approval will have a duration of two years. *Opt-up* sophisticated investors must keep the CSP informed of any change that may alter their status, and CSPs must inform the investors that they will no longer be treated as sophisticated, if the criteria are no longer fulfilled.[38]

C. Non-Sophisticated Investors

12.18 Non-sophisticated investors are defined in Article 2(1)(k) as investors who are not sophisticated investors.

2. Treatment of Sophisticated and Non-Sophisticated Investors

12.19 The treatment of sophisticated and non-sophisticated investors under the Crowdfunding Regulation differs. The Crowdfunding Regulation has introduced different levels of investor protection safeguards appropriate for each of the categories.

12.20 First, CSPs have to run an entry knowledge test of prospective non-sophisticated investors in order to ascertain their understanding of their investments. They should also explicitly warn prospective non-sophisticated investors that have insufficient knowledge, skills, and experience that the crowdfunding services provided might be inappropriate for them. Given that sophisticated investors are, by definition, aware of the risks associated with investments in crowdfunding projects, there is no merit in applying an entry knowledge test to them.

---

[37] Annex II, Part I Crowdfunding Regulation.
[38] Annex II, Part II Crowdfunding Regulation.

Similarly, CSPs should not be required to issue risk warnings to sophisticated investors.[39] In order to ensure that non-sophisticated investors have read and understood these explicit risk warnings, they should expressly acknowledge the risks that they are taking when they invest in a crowdfunding project. In order to maintain a high level of investor protection and given that an absence of such acknowledgement indicates a potential lack of understanding of the risks involved, CSPs should only accept investments from non-sophisticated investors that have expressly acknowledged that they have received and understood those warnings.[40]

In addition, given the risk associated with crowdfunding projects, non-sophisticated investors should avoid overexposure to them. There is a significant risk of losing large amounts of the initially invested sums or even of experiencing total loss. It is therefore appropriate to set out a maximum amount that non-sophisticated investors can, without further safeguards, invest in an individual project. By way of contrast, sophisticated investors who have the necessary experience, knowledge, or financial capacity, or a combination thereof, should not be limited by such a maximum amount.[41]   **12.21**

Furthermore, non-sophisticated investors receive some additional information compared to sophisticated investors, for example in respect of the application of the investor compensation scheme and the operation of a bulletin board.[42]   **12.22**

Lastly, in order to strengthen the protection for non-sophisticated investors, they have a reflection period during which a prospective non-sophisticated investor can revoke an offer to invest or an expression of interest in a particular crowdfunding offer. That is necessary to avoid a situation where a prospective non-sophisticated investor, by accepting a crowdfunding offer, thereby also accepts an offer to enter into a legally binding contract without any possibility of retraction within an adequate period of time.[43]   **12.23**

3. Comparison with MiFID II

It can be derived from Recital 42 of the Crowdfunding Regulation that the distinction between sophisticated and non-sophisticated investors should build on the distinction between professional clients and retail clients established in MiFID II. However, that distinction should also take into account the characteristics of the crowdfunding market. For that reason, the Crowdfunding Regulation introduced the definitions of sophisticated and non-sophisticated investor which deviate from the definitions used in MiFID II.   **12.24**

First, MiFID II does not contain separate identification criteria in respect of legal persons and natural persons. Instead, Annex II to MiFID II contains the following three identification criteria that have to be assessed by the investment firm in respect of all clients, both legal persons and natural persons, that request to be treated as a professional client. Again, of these three criteria, as a minimum, two have to be satisfied: **12.25**

---

[39] Recital 44 Crowdfunding Regulation.
[40] Recital 45 Crowdfunding Regulation.
[41] Recital 46 Crowdfunding Regulation.
[42] Recital 49 Crowdfunding Regulation. Art 25(3)(d) Crowdfunding Regulation.
[43] Recital 47 Crowdfunding Regulation.

(1)   the client has carried out transactions, in significant size, on the relevant market at an average frequency of ten per quarter over the previous four quarters;

(2)   the size of the client's financial instrument portfolio, defined as including cash deposits and financial instruments exceeds EUR 500,000;

(3)   the client works or has worked in the financial sector for at least one year in a professional position, which requires knowledge of the transactions or services envisaged.

As a result of the differences in identification criteria, it is possible that an investor can request to be treated as a sophisticated investor under the Crowdfunding Regulation while, at the same time, it does not meet the identification criteria under MiFID II. In addition, MiFID II does not contain a maximum duration of the approval for treatment as an *opt-up* sophisticated investor.[44] Another difference is that under MiFID II, *per se* professional clients must be allowed to request non-professional treatment and investment firms may agree to provide a higher level of protection. The Crowdfunding Regulation does not contain a similar provision in respect of *per se* sophisticated investors. As a result, *per se* professional clients that requested for non-professional treatment under MiFID II would still be considered *per se* sophisticated investors under the Crowdfunding Regulation.

4. Reflections on Investor Categorization and Discrimination

12.26   Categorizing investors into sophisticated and non-sophisticated, in order to assess whether a product or service is suitable for them, has long been a way to protect investors against fraud and mis-selling. This *ex ante* approach, which might be seen as paternalistic,[45] has shown how differentiating between investors can serve the legitimate function of promoting investor confidence. However, it can also result in overprotection, leading to discrimination.[46] Any requirement for assessing the suitability of products for particular categories of investors may protect the non-sophisticated, but it risks denying them access to a shared economy, thereby extending the wealth gap in society. Digital technology could remove this disadvantage by informing investors better and by using indicators to assess the risks that they might be exposed to. This approach would not make all investors equally sophisticated but it could help give better access to the non-sophisticated.

12.27   Start-ups have been considered risky investments[47] and have been reserved for venture capital firms.[48] This means that start-ups are experienced at pitching their projects to venture capital firms but they may need to change their approach when making an offer to 'crowds' of people with whom they do not normally deal. The crowds are not necessarily less

---

[44]   See also Recital 42 Crowdfunding Regulation.

[45]   C Sunstein, 'The Storrs Lectures: Behavioural Economics and Paternalism' (2013) 122 Yale Law Journal 1826, 1899.

[46]   The approach would be discriminatory if non-sophisticated investors are denied access to products or services that are only available to people who have the experience, the money and the information that allows them to analyse the risks and benefits of products, and the ability to share or spread any risks further through packaging products, and selling them on the market.

[47]   Jumpstart, 'Risky Business: All Startup Investments Come with Risk, but that doesn't Erase the Need for Storing Founder Fundamentals' (2017) <https://www.jumpstartinc.org/risky-business/> accessed 24 April 2021.

[48]   J Jeong and others, 'The Role of Venture Capital Investment in Startups' Sustainable Growth and Performance: Focusing on Absorptive Capacity and Venture Capitalists' Reputation' (2020) 12 Sustainability 1, 13. DOI: 10.3390/su12083447.

sophisticated in terms of the amount of funds they have to invest or their ability to process information and assess risk, but they lack experience, because they have previously been excluded from the market by the regulatory criteria. The role of technology deployed by the platforms is therefore to increase the level of expertise of the crowds, and to compensate for their lack of experience. There may be a temptation for platform providers to use Big Data and algorithms to increase the efficiency of confirming the level of sophistication of investors,[49] but the aim must always be to remove barriers, so that technology does not result in denying access to a shared economy.

It is not only investors who may be categorized; there is an equivalent variety among projects. More specifically, CSPs may attach a risk score to a project, and only allow certain investors to be involved in high-risk projects. It might also be that certain project owners prefer longer-term commitment, whereas non-sophisticated investors are considered to be more likely to switch among projects. In this case, it is the preference of the project owner that discriminates rather than the riskiness of the project. Categorizing investors can become discriminatory, especially if project owners prefer not to associate their projects with a particular type of investor based on their geography, nationality, social class, gender, or race. This is why CSPs need to respect anti-discrimination laws to prevent discrimination. Technology can play a part by detecting and preventing it. **12.28**

V. Information to Clients

This section discusses the requirements that the Crowdfunding Regulation sets for the information provision to clients. It does not discuss the key investment information sheet (KIIS), as this topic is covered separately in section IX. This section also contains some general reflections on market transparency and market confidence. **12.29**

1. General Requirements

Article 19(1) of the Crowdfunding Regulation contains the general rule that all the information, including marketing communications,[50] that CSPs give to clients[51] about themselves, about the costs, financial risks, and charges related to crowdfunding services or investments, about the crowdfunding project selection criteria, and about the nature of, and risks associated with, their crowdfunding services shall be fair, clear, and not misleading. All this information should be communicated to clients whenever appropriate, at least prior to entering into a crowdfunding transaction. This information will generally be included in the KIIS, as discussed in section IX. CSPs should also inform investors that their services are not covered by the deposit guarantee scheme and that transferable securities or admitted instruments for crowdfunding purposes acquired through their crowdfunding **12.30**

---

[49] Deloitte, 'How can Fintech Facilitate Fund Distribution?' (2016) <https://www2.deloitte.com/content/dam/Deloitte/lu/Documents/technology/lu_how-can-fintech-facilitate-fund-distribution.pdf> accessed 24 April 2021.
[50] See Chapter 14.
[51] Art 2(1)(g) defines 'client' as any prospective or actual investor or project owner to whom a CSP provides, or intends to provide, crowdfunding services.

platform are not covered by the investor compensation scheme.[52] If credit scores or pricing suggestions are given, the provider must make available a description of the method used to calculate them.[53] The European Banking Authority (EBA) will publish draft regulatory technical standards (RTS) that specify the elements, including the format, that are to be included in the description of such method.[54] All the information mentioned above should be available to all clients on a clearly identified and easily accessible section of the website of the crowdfunding platform and in a non-discriminatory manner.[55] Non-sophisticated investors should also be informed of the reflection period (discussed in section VIII). The Crowdfunding Regulation states in that respect that whenever a crowdfunding offer is made, the CSP should provide that information in a prominent place of the medium, including on every mobile application and webpage where such an offer is made.[56] See for a comparison with the requirements on information provision under MiFID II Chapter 14.

2. Reflections on Market Transparency and Market Confidence

12.31 The theory of market transparency to ensure market confidence applies to crowdfunding as well. The burden is on CSPs to ensure that clients are properly informed so that they can make rational choices. CSPs, thus, act not only as a broker for the parties but also as trusted third-party information gatekeepers. This role is pivotal to the platforms' duty to provide critical market infrastructure. There have been cases where social media and search engines have provided platform services without ensuring the accuracy of their information, and this has led to a greater problem than asymmetric information: disinformation.[57] In the financial markets, financial intermediaries safeguard the accuracy, quality and dissemination of information, and CSPs need to play a similar role in order to safeguard investor confidence and also to ensure market safety and, potentially even, democratic values.[58] They need to ensure that project owners and investors are safe and honest players and, to this end, they need to create their own rules to evaluate project owners and investors. On the one hand, they must ensure that the projects are safe for investment,[59] but on the other hand, they must also make sure that investors do not intend to use the platform to launder illegally obtained money, or to manipulate the market in a way that harms the projects.[60]

VI. Default Rate Disclosure

12.32 This section discusses the requirements that the Crowdfunding Regulation sets in respect of default rate disclosure. This section also contains some general reflections on distinction

---

[52] Art 19(2) Crowdfunding Regulation.
[53] Art 19(6) Crowdfunding Regulation.
[54] At the time of writing this chapter, these draft RTS were not available.
[55] Art 19(5) Crowdfunding Regulation.
[56] Art 19(3) Crowdfunding Regulation.
[57] European Commission, 'Tackling Online Disinformation' (2021) <https://digital-strategy.ec.europa.eu/en/policies/online-disinformation> accessed 24 April 2021.
[58] One could think of projects that go against democratic values.
[59] See Chapter 9 on due diligence of project owners.
[60] See on the (lack of) AML obligations of CSPs, Chapter 8.

between different defaults in order to assist investors in appreciating what the consequences are of a default for their investment.

1. General Requirements

Under Article 20 of the Crowdfunding Regulation, CSPs that facilitate the grant of loans must annually disclose the default rates of the crowdfunding projects offered on their platform over at least the preceding thirty-six months. This should be done in a prominent place on the website of the CSP. In addition, within four months of the end of each financial year, they should publish an outcome statement indicating: **12.33**

(1) the expected and actual default rate of all loans facilitated on the platform;
(2) a summary of the assumptions used in determining the expected default rates; and
(3) the actual return achieved if a target rate in relation to individual portfolio management of loans was offered by the provider.[61]

On 26 February 2021, ESMA published draft RTS to specify the methodology for calculating the expected and actual default rates.[62] These draft RTS also introduce a definition of 'default'. According to Article 1 of the draft RTS, a default should be considered to have occurred when either or both of the following have taken place:

(a) the CSP considers that the project owner is unlikely to pay or otherwise fulfil its credit obligations in full, without enforcing any relevant security interest or taking other steps with analogous effect;
(b) the project owner is more than 90 days past due on any material credit obligation.

In order to establish whether the project owner is unlikely to pay, the CSP should at least consider the investor's consent to a distressed restructuring of the credit obligation where this is likely to result in a diminished financial obligation caused by the material forgiveness, or postponement, of principal, interest or, where relevant, fees and the project owner's application for, or placement in, bankruptcy or similar protection where this would avoid or delay repayment of a credit obligation to the investors. In addition, CSPs should disclose the criteria used to identify the materiality thresholds for the purpose of point (b). CSPs have to inform investors without delay in case of default of loan. In order to be able to do that, they also need to have effective processes that allow them to obtain the relevant information in order to identify the occurrence of default of loans offered on their crowdfunding platform without undue delay.[63] The standardization of the calculation of default rates will facilitate the comparison of the performance of CSPs and of loans offered on crowdfunding platforms.[64]

---

[61] Art 20(1)(b) Crowdfunding Regulation.
[62] ESMA, Consultation Paper Draft technical standards under the ECSP Regulation, ESMA/35-36-2201, 26 February 2021, Annex VII Draft RTS pursuant to Art 20(3) of the ECSPR (hereinafter draft RTS on default rates).
[63] Art 1(4) and (5) draft RTS on default rates.
[64] Recital 3 draft RTS on default rates.

2. Reflections on Default Differentiation

12.34   The default rate information on borrowers is a key indicator of their creditworthiness.[65] However, small businesses often have an unhealthy cash flow, which may be the reason why they seek a loan through a crowdfunding platform. While business lenders may understand how borrowers may face cash flow problems, less sophisticated investors may easily be scared off by a default on the part of the borrower, and react less rationally than a business lender would. Although the default rate is important information for investors, platforms can also help investors understand whether a default has been caused by a cyclical issue,[66] by an event not likely to be avoided by diligent borrowers, or simply due to borrowers' carelessness. To this end, CSPs could provide indicators, showing what has contributed to a default rate, so as to differentiate one default from another. This is however currently not required under the Crowdfunding Regulation.

VII. Entry Knowledge Test, Simulation of the Ability to Bear Loss and Investment Limits

12.35   This section discusses the requirements that the Crowdfunding Regulation sets in respect of the entry knowledge test, the simulation of the ability to bear loss and the investment limits. These requirements only apply in respect of non-sophisticated investors, see section IV. This section also compares the entry knowledge test with the appropriateness test under MiFID II, in addition to giving some general reflections.

1. General Requirements

12.36   The requirements in respect of the entry knowledge test, the simulation of the ability to bear loss and the investment limits are included in Article 21 of the Crowdfunding Regulation. In addition, ESMA published draft RTS to specify the entry knowledge test and the simulation of the ability to bear loss for non-sophisticated investors on 26 February 2021.[67]

A. Entry Knowledge Test

12.37   CSPs are required to assess whether and which crowdfunding services offered are appropriate for prospective non-sophisticated investors, before giving them full access to investing in projects on their platform (this assessment is hereinafter referred to as the entry knowledge test). For the purposes of the entry knowledge test, CSPs have to request information about the prospective non-sophisticated investor's experience, investment

---

[65] A Morse (2015) 'Peer-To-Peer Crowdfunding Information and the Potential for Disruption in Consumer Lending' (National Bureau of Economic Research Working Paper Series 20899) <https://www.nber.org/papers/w20899> accessed 27 April 2021.

[66] N Nemoto and others (2019) 'Optimal Regulation of P2P Lending for Small and Medium-Sized Enterprises' (Asian Development Bank Institute Working Paper Series) <https://www.adb.org/sites/default/files/publication/478611/adbi-wp912.pdf> accessed 27 April 2021.

[67] ESMA, Consultation Paper Draft technical standards under the ECSP Regulation, ESMA/35-36-2201, 26 February 2021, Annex VIII Draft RTS pursuant to Art 21(8) of the ECSPR (hereinafter: draft RTS on entry knowledge test).

objectives, financial situation, and basic understanding of risks involved in investing in general and in investing in the types of investments offered on the crowdfunding platform, including information about:

(1) the prospective non-sophisticated investor's past investments in transferable securities or past acquisitions of admitted instruments for crowdfunding purposes or loans, including in early or expansion-stage businesses;

(2) the prospective non-sophisticated investor's understanding of the risks involved in granting loans, investing in transferable securities, or acquiring admitted instruments for crowdfunding purposes through a crowdfunding platform, and professional experience in relation to crowdfunding investments.[68]

CSPs have to review the entry knowledge test every two years after the initial assessment.[69]

12.38 CSPs have to take reasonable steps to ensure that the information collected from non-sophisticated investors is reliable and reflects accurately their knowledge, skills, experience and financial situation, investment objectives, and basic understanding of the risks involved. These steps should at least include raising attention of investors on the importance of providing accurate and up-to-date information, ensuring that the means used to collect information are fit for purpose and appropriately designed and ensuring that the questions used in the process are likely to be understood by non-sophisticated investors and granular enough.[70] Where prospective non-sophisticated investors do not provide the required information or where CSPs consider, on the basis of the information received, that the prospective non-sophisticated investors have insufficient knowledge, skills, or experience, CSPs have to inform those prospective non-sophisticated investors that the services offered on their crowdfunding platforms may be inappropriate for them and issue them a risk warning conform Annex I to the draft RTS on entry knowledge test. That risk warning clearly has to state the risk of losing the entirety of the money invested. Prospective non-sophisticated investors have to expressly acknowledge that they have received and understood the warning issued by the CSP by accepting the text set out in Annex II to the draft RTS on entry knowledge test.[71]

B. Simulation of Ability to Bear Loss

12.39 For the purposes of the entry knowledge test, CSPs should also require prospective non-sophisticated investors to simulate their ability to bear loss, calculated as 10% of their net worth, based on the following information:

(1) regular income and total income, and whether the income is earned on a permanent or temporary basis;

(2) assets, including financial investments and any cash deposits, but excluding personal and investment property and pension funds;

(3) financial commitments, including regular, existing, or future commitments.[72]

---

[68] See also Art 4 draft RTS on entry knowledge test.
[69] Art 21(1)–(3) Crowdfunding Regulation.
[70] Art 1 draft RTS on entry knowledge test.
[71] Art 21(4) Crowdfunding Regulation. See also Art 5(2) draft RTS on entry knowledge test.
[72] See also Arts 7–10 draft RTS on entry knowledge test.

In order to enable investors to simulate their ability to bear loss, CSPs have to make available on their website an online calculation tool. It should, however, not be mandatory for investors to use this tool.[73] The non-sophisticated investors have to acknowledge that they have received the results of the simulation. The simulation should be reviewed by the CSP every year after the initial simulation made.[74]

C. Investment Limits

12.40 Each time before a prospective non-sophisticated investor or non-sophisticated investor accepts an individual crowdfunding offer thereby investing an amount that exceeds the higher of either EUR 1,000 or 5% of that investor's net worth as calculated in respect of the simulation to bear loss, the CSP has to ensure that such investor:

> (1) receives a risk warning conform Annex III to the draft RTS on entry knowledge test;
> (2) provides explicit consent to the crowdfunding service provider; and
> (3) proves to the CSP that the investor understands the investment and its risks.

For the purposes of point (3), the entry knowledge test may be used as proof that the prospective non-sophisticated investor or non-sophisticated investor understands the investment and its risks.[75]

12.41 Investors should not be prevented from investing in a crowdfunding project,[76] even if they exceed the investment limits[77] or show that they do not have sufficient knowledge or the ability to bear the risk. CSPs should however refrain from encouraging the prospective non-sophisticated investor to proceed with the investment.[78]

2. Comparison with MiFID II

12.42 The entry knowledge test can be compared with the appropriateness assessment under MiFID II that applies when investments firms provide investment services other than investment advice or portfolio management (eg receipt and transmission of orders or placement activities).[79] The appropriateness assessment requires investments firms to ask the client or potential client to provide information regarding that person's knowledge and experience in the investment field relevant to the specific type of product or service offered or demanded so as to enable the investment firm to assess whether the investment service or product envisaged is appropriate for the client. Where the investment firm considers, based on this assessment, that the product or service is not appropriate to the client, it should warn the client. There are however some differences between the appropriateness assessment and the entry knowledge test. First, the appropriateness assessment applies to all clients, not only

---

[73] Art 6 draft RTS on entry knowledge test.
[74] Art 21(5) and (6) Crowdfunding Regulation.
[75] Art 21(7) Crowdfunding Regulation.
[76] Art 21(6) second paragraph Crowdfunding Regulation.
[77] See also Recital 46 Crowdfunding Regulation: 'Given the risk associated with crowdfunding projects, non-sophisticated investors should avoid overexposure to them. There is a significant risk of losing large amounts of the initially invested sums or even of experiencing total loss. It is therefore appropriate to set out a maximum amount that non-sophisticated investors can, without further safeguards, invest in an individual project.'
[78] Art 2(2) draft RTS on entry knowledge test.
[79] Art 25(3) MiFID II.

to non-sophisticated investors as is the case under the Crowdfunding Regulation, although the modalities of the appropriateness assessment differ depending on the type of client.[80] Furthermore, MiFID II provides for an exemption to the requirement to conduct the appropriateness test in case of so-called non-complex instruments.[81] Taking into account the nature of these non-complex instruments, it makes sense that a similar exemption is not included in the Crowdfunding Regulation, as these, for example, include certain shares and bonds admitted to trading on a regulated market or a Multilateral Trading Facility (MTF), money-market instruments and shares or units in an Undertaking for the Collective Investment in Transferable Securities (UCITS).[82] In addition, MiFID II does not include the requirement to review the appropriateness assessment every two years. Lastly, the entry knowledge test is more extensive than the appropriateness test under MiFID II as it also includes an assessment of the investment objectives and financial situation of the investor.[83] As such, the entry knowledge test resembles more the suitability assessment that MiFID II requires in respect of portfolio management and investment advice than the appropriateness assessment.[84] This is interesting, taken into account that the crowdfunding services under the Crowdfunding Regulation do not include portfolio management and investment advice. As a result, when an investment firm provides so-called execution only services in respect of Crowdfunding Investments that are outside the scope of the Crowdfunding Regulation (eg because the maximum threshold of EUR 5 million is exceeded), it is required to conduct an appropriateness assessment, unless such Crowdfunding Investments can be considered 'non-complex', in which case no assessment is conducted. When a CSP provides the same services in scope of the Crowdfunding Regulation, it has to conduct an entry knowledge test that resembles more the suitability assessment.

3. Reflections on the Entry Knowledge Test

The entry knowledge test is a way to differentiate between investors for the purpose of protecting them.[85] In essence, it is a good way to test not only investors' knowledge but also to educate them about the potential risks of their investment. This educational purpose is particularly visible when the investor can gain the 'knowledge' by repeating the test set by the CSP so that the outcome of such test would not reveal much about the real investment ability of the investor. When investors select their own products and services on crowdfunding platforms and professional agents are not involved, the entry knowledge test and simulation are intended to warn investors about the risks they are taking before they act. This kind of risk warning is also used in other retail markets, such as when consumers buy

12.43

---

[80] See Art 56 Commission Delegated Regulation (EU) 2017/565.

[81] Art 25(4) MiFID II.

[82] Crowdfunding Investments may however qualify as non-complex instruments under Art 57 Commission Delegated Regulation (EU) 2017/565, although a requirement is that 'there are frequent opportunities to dispose of, redeem, or otherwise realise that instrument at prices that are publicly available to market participants and that are either market prices or prices made available, or validated, by valuation systems independent of the issuer'. The question is whether the bulletin board, as provided for in Art 25 Crowdfunding Regulation, provides such frequent opportunities. See further on secondary trading of Crowdfunding Investments Chapter 13.

[83] See ESMA, MiFID II supervisory briefing Appropriateness test and execution only, 4 April 2019, ESMA35-36-1640, para 11.

[84] Art 25(2) MiFID II and Art 54 Commission Delegated Regulation (EU) 2017/565.

[85] Art 21 Crowdfunding Regulation.

cigarettes. When they design the test questions, CSPs should make sure that they are not so difficult as to prevent investors from engaging in the market.

VIII. Pre-contractual Reflection Period

12.44   This section discusses the requirements that the Crowdfunding Regulation sets in respect of the pre-contractual reflection period. These requirements only apply in respect of non-sophisticated investors, see section IV. This section also contains some general reflections on the impact of such pre-contractual reflection period on the efficiency of the capital raising process and investor protection.

1. General Requirements

12.45   Article 22 of the Crowdfunding Regulation provides that CSPs must allow a pre-contractual reflection period of four calendar days, during which prospective non-sophisticated investors may, at any time, revoke an offer to invest, or an expression of interest in the crowdfunding offer, without giving a reason and without incurring a penalty. These four days run from the moment the offer to invest or an expression of interest by the prospective non-sophisticated investor has been made. During this period, no reason needs to be given if the investors decide to revoke their offer. CSPs must inform investors of this reflection period, and the way in which their offer or expression of interest can be revoked.[86]

12.46   In the case of individual portfolio management of loans, this requirement only applies to the initial investment mandate given by non-sophisticated investors, and not to investments in specific loans made under that mandate.[87]

2. Reflections on the Pre-contractual Reflection Period

12.47   The pre-contractual reflection period is designed to protect investors from over-hasty action, when investments can be made simply by the click of a button.[88] It is important to ensure that investors, especially when they are consumers, can retract investment decisions made in error, through misinformation, or on perceived market pressure, after considered reflection. To this end, the Crowdfunding Regulation requires CSPs to give prospective non-sophisticated investors a reflection period of four calendar days.[89]

12.48   CSPs cannot be expected to read the minds of investors and know whether they have made conscious and rational decisions. For this reason, once the reflection period has elapsed, investors can no longer cancel an investment without legal consequences. This rule serves the purpose of ensuring legal certainty, not only in the interest of the project owner and the

[86] Art 22(6) Crowdfunding Regulation.
[87] Art 22(7) Crowdfunding Regulation.
[88] Art 22 Crowdfunding Regulation.
[89] Art 22(3) Crowdfunding Regulation.

service provider, but also because the contractual commitment of the investor indirectly affects the whole investment community. If somebody decides to withdraw their investment (especially a large amount), other investors or potential investors may question the reason behind such a cancellation and draw negative inferences about the project. The reflection period can also prevent people from making a claim of mistake in contract law,[90] thereby manipulating the market sentiment.[91] Interactive discussion in a chat room[92] on the platform can even prompt committed investors to worry and cause the project fundraising to fail.

Some questions are left unanswered by the Crowdfunding Regulation. First, when an offer or expression of interest is made, should it be made public during the reflection period? This may have a critical impact on the start of a campaign, especially if it is on a 'first-come-first-served' basis. Some apparently impressive projects that have the backing of sophisticated investors can herd the non-sophisticated ones into investing. When a campaign fails to reach a critical momentum at the beginning, it may not impress non-sophisticated investors. Equally, if information is made public about the number and amount of investment offers (and expressions of interest), would the sudden withdrawal by non-sophisticated investors cause a market shock? Further study is needed on the behaviour of investors on crowdfunding platforms, and the subsequent rules designed by ESMA should take account of potential market abuse and irrational investor behaviour. Providers may need to take remedial action to address market failures, such as by publishing information about market dynamics—offers made and cancelled—during the reflection period.   **12.49**

The second question is whether a reflection period needs to be given to sophisticated investors as well, allowing them to withdraw without giving reasons. Further studies may be carried out to observe the dynamics of sophisticated investors during the four-day reflection period[93] in order to decide whether offers to invest should be made public, and whether the reflection period should be lengthened.[94]   **12.50**

The third question is how technology can help minimize the impact of the reflection period on market dynamics. Currently, the Crowdfunding Regulation does not require investors to disclose reasons for their withdrawal. An alternative approach, in the future, would be to require CSPs to publish information about why investors have withdrawn offers to invest or cancelled expressions of interest. Investors, for instance, could be required to state why they have withdrawn, but without the information being immediately disclosed to the investor community; statistics could only be published later, for example after a delay of twelve months. Furthermore, in order to protect investors, providers could anonymize the responses and have systems in place to protect investors' privacy and personal data.   **12.51**

---

[90] D Sheehan, 'Vitiation of Contracts for Mistake and Misrepresentation of Law' (2003) 11 Restitution Law Review 26, 45.

[91] M Meoli and S Vismara, 'Information Manipulation in Equity Crowdfunding Markets' (2021) 67 Journal of Corporate Finance 1, 17.

[92] Swindon, 'How Online Platforms Have Implemented Chat Rooms for Users' (2021) <https://www.swindon24.co.uk/lifestyle/how-online-platforms-have-implemented-chat-rooms-for-users/> accessed 24 April 2021.

[93] P Belleflamme and others (2019) 'Crowdfunding Dynamics' (CESifo Working Paper No 7797). Available at SSRN <https://ssrn.com/abstract = 3468029> accessed 27 April 2021.

[94] See also Art 45(2)(x) Crowdfunding Regulation.

IX. Key Investment Information Sheet

12.52   This section discusses the requirements that the Crowdfunding Regulation sets in respect of the KIIS. This section also contains some general reflections on the role of the CSP as a trusted information gatekeeper and the role that technology can play in that respect.

1. General Requirements

12.53   Article 23 requires CSPs to provide prospective investors with a KIIS that is drawn up by the project owner for each crowdfunding offer. The KIIS must contain:

(1) the information specified in Annex I, including details of the project owner, the main features of the process, the main risks associated with the project, information related to the offer of transferable securities or admitted instruments (where applicable), information on the use of a Special Purpose Vehicle (SPV) (where applicable), investor rights, disclosures related to loans (where applicable), fees, and legal rights;

(2) the disclaimer that the offer has been neither verified nor approved by competent authorities or ESMA; and

(3) a warning of the risk of losing all or some of the money invested.[95]

In addition, those responsible for the KIIS should be clearly identified in the sheet.[96]

12.54   The KIIS is similar but not identical to a prospectus. As already mentioned, it sets out the information to be disclosed to prospective investors, according to the structure set forth in Annex I to the Crowdfunding Regulation. The exact information to be provided depends, *inter alia*, on the type of crowdfunding service that is provided and whether or not an SPV is interposed between the project owner and the investor.

12.55   CSPs act as information gatekeepers[97] and therefore need to have procedures in place through which they can verify the completeness, correctness, and clarity of this information,[98] and to signal any defaults in the KIIS to project owners so that they can complete or correct it. CSPs should suspend an offer if a project owner does not complete and correct the information, and they should inform the investors of any irregularities. If the project owner does not rectify the irregularities, the provider must cancel the offer.[99]

12.56   When CSPs provide individual portfolio management of loans, they need to provide a KIIS to investors at the platform level instead of the KIIS drawn up by the project owner.[100] This KIIS at platform level only includes the information provided in Parts H (fees, information and legal redress) and I (information on individual portfolio management) of Annex I to the Crowdfunding Regulation. In addition, it has to contain the information about the persons responsible for the information given therein and a responsibility statement.[101]

---

[95] Art 23(2) and (5) Crowdfunding Regulation.
[96] Art 23(9) Crowdfunding Regulation. See also Chapter 9.
[97] J Armour and L Enriques, 'The Promise and Perils of Crowdfunding: Between Corporate Finance and Consumer Contracts' (2018) 81 Modern Law Review 51, 84.
[98] Art 11 Crowdfunding Regulation.
[99] Art 23(12) Crowdfunding Regulation.
[100] Art 24(1) Crowdfunding Regulation.
[101] Art 24(1) Crowdfunding Regulation.

Providers must inform investors who have made an offer to invest, or expressed an interest in a crowdfunding offer, about any material change to the information, and must rectify any omissions, mistakes, or inaccuracies in the KIIS if they could have a material impact on the expected return of the individual portfolio management of loans.[102] The KIIS at platform level also has to be fair, clear, and not misleading,[103] and must be updated by the providers throughout the duration of the crowdfunding offer.[104]

In neither of these two types of KIIS do the competent authorities exercise screening control. In other words, the sheets do not need to be pre-approved by the competent authority. However, competent authorities may require an *ex ante* notification of a KIIS drawn up by the project owner.[105] In addition, as previously mentioned, the CSP needs to have procedures in place, by which it verifies the accuracy of the information. For the KIIS provided by a project owner, the provider is thus clearly an information gatekeeper. By contrast, in the case of individual portfolio management of loans, there is no equivalent entity that can verify the information provided by the CSP, so the latter must itself verify the information it provides. There may be a need to require the provider to have a separate and independent department within its institution, to provide the risk management function.   **12.57**

2. Reflections on the Role of the CSP as a Trusted Information Gatekeeper

The Crowdfunding Regulation is grounded on the theory of market transparency, whereby investors should be able to make their own decisions based on disclosed information. The role of the CSP is to act as a trusted information gatekeeper. Furthermore, the provider has a duty to educate non-sophisticated investors about the generic risks of investment on crowdfunding platforms rather than any risks specific to a particular project. In this regard, technology can enhance market transparency by extracting more accurate data for investors,[106] by verifying the accuracy of the information provided by the project owners,[107] by compiling an index based on benchmarks to highlight aspects of projects,[108] by indicating the risks related to the project,[109] and by providing guidance on the price of the investment.[110]   **12.58**

---

[102] Art 24(7) Crowdfunding Regulation.

[103] Art 24(3) Crowdfunding Regulation.

[104] Eversheds Sutherland, 'EU Regulation on European Crowdfunding Service Providers—A New Dawn for Crowdfunding' (2020) <https://www.eversheds-sutherland.com/global/en/what/articles/index.page?Articl eID = en/global/ireland/eu-regulation-on-european-crowdfunding-service-providers_a-new-dawn-for-crowd funding> accessed 24 April 2021.

[105] Art 23(14) Crowdfunding Regulation.

[106] J Podlesny and others, 'The Power of Emerging Technologies: Finding Value through Data' (2020) <https://www.mckinsey.com/business-functions/mckinsey-digital/our-insights/tech-forward/the-power-of-emerging-technologies-finding-value-through-data#> accessed 24 April 2021.

[107] R Klaschka, 'Construction Verification—A Revolution in Accuracy' (2020) <https://www.thenbs.com/knowledge/construction-verification-a-revolution-in-accuracy> accessed 24 April 2021.

[108] Project MI, 'Improving Project Performance through Leadership and Technology' (Paper Presented at PMI Research Conference: New Directions in Project Management 2006) <https://www.pmi.org/learning/library/proj ect-performance-through-leadership-technology-8105> accessed 27 April 2021.

[109] A Nehari Talet, 'Risk Management and Information Technology Projects' (2014) 4 International Journal of Digital Information and Wireless Communications 1, 9.

[110] PwC, 'Beyond Automated Advice: How FinTech is Shaping Asset & Wealth Management' (Global FinTech Survey 2016) <https://www.pwc.com/gx/en/financial-services/pdf/fin-tech-asset-and-wealth-management.pdf> accessed 24 April 2021.

12.59   When ESMA develops the Level 2 regulations, it needs to bear in mind how the regulatory objectives can be achieved through the use of technology.[111] Technology can be used to extract more data from projects, for instance through the digital regulatory reporting system; yet the information generated would need to be further processed to make it useful to investors.[112] What information might be useful to investors would depend on their background, their risk tolerance, and their preferences.[113] While standardized information disclosure can be simple for investors to understand, individuals may want additional information to be disclosed to them. The significant factors are not the quantity or quality of data disclosed through the digital regulatory reporting system[114] but rather the processed information that investors have available to them, as they make their investment decisions. Such processed information would include ratings of the expected default rate, the Environment, Social, and Governance (ESG) rating,[115] and various other indicators. In the context of individual portfolio management of loans, the Crowdfunding Regulation requires providers to disclose how they calculate credit risk, even though it is questionable whether the methodology, and especially its implications, can be properly understood by non-sophisticated investors.

X. Conclusion

12.60   Loan- and investment-based crowdfunding functions on a smaller scale than bank lending and initial public offerings, without the involvement of banks and other intermediaries.[116] The innovation is not in the business model, but in the role of technology as an alternative to professional intermediaries. The question, then, is how technology can assist the CSP in complying with the investor protection rules by acting as an honest broker, an information gatekeeper, a value enhancer, and a social transformer.[117] This chapter discussed how investors are protected under the Crowdfunding Regulation. Such protection is based on the theory of market transparency, whereby investors are enabled to make rational decisions based on available information. Since the profiles of crowdfunding investors are disparate, and it is an aim of crowdfunding to increase participation by non-sophisticated investors,

---

[111] ESMA, Consultation Paper Draft technical standards under the ECSP Regulation, ESMA/35-36-2201, 26 February 2021.

[112] M Samatani, 'UK Digital Regulatory Reporting Pilot Completes Phase Two' (2020) <https://www.regulationasia.com/uk-digital-regulatory-reporting-pilot-completes-phase-two/> accessed 24 February 2021.

[113] F Wang and P De Filippi, 'Self-sovereign Identity in a Globalized World: Credentials-based Identity Systems as a Driver for Economic Inclusion' (2020) 2 Frontiers in Blockchain <https://www.frontiersin.org/articles/10.3389/fbloc.2019.00028/full?field=&id = 496586&journalName = Frontiers_in_Blockchain&utm_campaign = Email_publication&utm_content = T1_11.5e1_author&utm_medium = Email&utm_source = Email_to_authors> accessed 27 April 2021.

[114] J von Solms, 'Integrating Regulatory Technology (RegTech) into the Digital Transformation of a Bank Treasury' (2020) 1 Journal of Banking Regulation 1, 17. DOI: <https://doi.org/10.1057/s41261-020-00134-0>; PA, 'Digital Regulatory Reporting: A Review of Phases 1 and 2 of the Digital Regulatory Reporting Initiative' (2020) <https://www2.paconsulting.com/rs/526-HZE-833/images/DRR-Report-Sept-2020.pdf> accessed 24 April 2021.

[115] E Escrig-Olmedo and others, 'Rating the Raters: Evaluating How ESG Rating Agencies Integrate Sustainability Principles' (2019) 11 Sustainability 1, 16. DOI: 10.3390/SU11030915.

[116] J Lee and G Geidel, 'Mapping an Investor Protection Framework for the Security Token Offering Market: A Comparative Analysis of UK and German Law' (2021) <http://dx.doi.org/10.2139/ssrn.3765581> accessed 28 April 2021.

[117] European Commission, 'Study on the Role of Digitalisation and Innovation in Creating a True Single Market for Retail Financial Services and Insurance' (Final Report of the Centre for European Policy Studies, Luxembourg Institute of Science and Technology, University College Cork, 2016).

more research is needed to achieve access to a shared economy. Although technology already puts crowds of investors in touch with project owners, there is much that technology can do to increase investors' ability to make informed choices. More information does not necessary translate into more informed judgment by investors; therefore, in addition to the information gatekeeping role, CSPs should use technology to help investors digest information and make choices.

13

Secondary Trading of

Crowdfunding Investments

Anne Hakvoort

I. Introduction

The recent credit crisis did not only bring bad things. Crowdfunding was developed as an **13.01** alternative form of financing for small and medium-sized enterprises (SMEs) when banks closed their credit desks. About thirteen years after the bankruptcy of Lehman Brothers, crowdfunding is ready for the next step: a European regulation will be harmonizing the regulatory framework applicable to the operators of crowdfunding platforms. These crowd-funding service providers (CSPs) have, until now, been subjected to the national laws of their home Member State as well as to the national laws of each of the Member States where they offered their services. Due to the crowdfunding regimes not being aligned at a European level, CSPs were confronted with multiple sets of rules and obligations which were not always consistent with each other. The result was a costly and difficult compli-ance puzzle. Only a handful providers took the effort of becoming active in more than one Member State.

Thanks to the Crowdfunding Regulation, this is expected to change soon. One of the fun- **13.02** damental principles of the EU is the free movement of capital. To foster a stronger and more resilient EU, the Commission announced its objective to create a Capital Markets Union (CMU) in 2017. One of the main objectives behind the CMU is that a source of capital for financing SMEs can not only be found in established credit institutions but also in investors and savers. The Crowdfunding Regulation serves this purpose. It creates convergence and removes obstacles to the free movement of capital throughout the EU by offering a CSP the possibility to offer services in other Member States on the basis of its authorization as granted by the national competent authority of its home Member State. This European 'passport' is one of the main benefits of the Crowdfunding Regulation.

13.03   Another big step forward is the acknowledgment of the importance of offering secondary trading options to investors who have invested in a crowdfunding project. Up until now there has not really been a secondary market in crowdfunding investments that were concluded via a crowdfunding platform. It is in the interest of investors to enable the availability of a secondary market for crowdfunding investments, in particular because most of the investors are retail investors. To protect the interests of these investors, the possibility to exit their crowdfunding investments is important. The availability of trading options and a secondary market in crowdfunding investments could also give a boost to the further growth of this form of alternative finance.

13.04   This chapter focuses on the secondary trading option that can be facilitated by a CSP under the Crowdfunding Regulation. A CSP may operate a bulletin board on its platform to enable its clients to advertise their interest to buy or to sell a crowdfunding investment. Before we dive into the relatively technical description of the different manners of trading and trading venues in paragraph three, it is important to get a better understanding of the scope of the Crowdfunding Regulation and how it can be distinguished from the Markets in Financial Instruments Directive II (MiFID II). In the next paragraph, an analysis of the interconnectedness of these frameworks shall be given. After comparing a bulletin board with two regulated trading venues, the multilateral trading facility (MTF) and organized trading facility (OTF) in the subsequent paragraph, the concluding paragraph of this chapter will take a look into the potential future of the secondary crowdfunding market.

II. The Scope of the Crowdfunding Regulation Compared with the MiFID II Framework

13.05   The MiFID II framework[1] provides for an extensive set of rules applicable to undertakings that provide investment services and/or perform investment activities. Annex I to MiFID II lists which services and activities fall within the scope of the MiFID II framework. Important to emphasize is that the MiFID II framework applies to investment services and investment activities relating to financial instruments as defined in MiFID II.[2] Crowdfunding projects can be financed through the issuance of financial instruments as well as by not-transferable loans. Such loans do not qualify as financial instruments. That clarifies why national competent authorities in numerous Member States have subjected operators of investment-based crowdfunding platforms to the MiFID II framework whilst subjecting operators of lending-based crowdfunding platforms to a less burdensome national framework. In

---

[1] With the MiFID II framework, I refer to the full set of European legislation on Level I and Level II applicable to investment firms, including MiFID II, MiFIR, and CRR, recently amended by CRR II which were partially replaced by the Investment Firm Directive and Investment Firm Regulation which apply as of 26 June 2021, as well as the implementing and delegated acts and standards promulgated thereunder.

[2] Financial instruments are the instruments specified in section C of Annex I to MiFID II. These include transferable securities. Pursuant to Art 1(4) MiFID II, parts of MiFID II also apply to structured deposits.

order to take away the legal obstacle formed by MiFID II for operators of investment-based crowdfunding platforms, MiFID II shall be amended by including CSPs in Art 2(1) MiFID II, resulting in MiFID II not to apply to CSPs.[3] In other words: if an undertaking qualifies as a crowdfunding service provider within the meaning of Art 2(1)(e) of the Crowdfunding Regulation, the MiFID II framework shall not apply to such undertaking. Full stop. This is essential for CSPs.

For that reason, it is important that CSPs stay within the boundaries provided for in the **13.06** Crowdfunding Regulation. If they do not, they will be confronted with the MiFID II framework when they offer their services in respect of financial instruments. Upon reading this chapter, one can assess that staying within these boundaries could be relatively difficult as the distinction between the Crowdfunding Regulation and the MiFID II framework is not particularly clear when it comes to secondary trading.

To understand the intended scope, it is essential to elaborate on the terms used, both in the **13.07** Crowdfunding Regulation and in MiFID II.

1. CSP and Crowdfunding Services

A CSP is defined to be 'a legal person who provides crowdfunding services'.[4] Crowdfunding **13.08** services are defined to be 'the matching of business funding interests of investors[5] and project owners[6] through the use of a crowdfunding platform[7] and which consists of any of the following activities:

- the facilitation of granting of loans;[8]
- the placing without a firm commitment basis (as referred to in point (7) of Section A of Annex I to MiFID II) of transferable securities[9] and admitted instruments for

---

[3] Art 1 of Directive (EU) 2020//1504 of the European Parliament and of the Council of 7 October 2020 amending MiFID II.

[4] Art 2(1)(e) of the Crowdfunding Regulation.

[5] An investor is defined in Art 2(1)(i) of the Crowdfunding Regulation as 'any natural or legal person who, through a crowdfunding platform, grants loans or acquires transferable securities or admitted instruments for crowdfunding purposes'. The Crowdfunding Regulation distinguishes non-sophisticated investors from sophisticated investors. Please see Art 2(1)(k) Crowdfunding Regulation and Art 2(1)(j) Crowdfunding Regulation respectively. This is, unfortunately, not fully aligned with the terms 'non-professional client' and 'professional client' respectively as used in MiFID II.

[6] A project owner is defined in Art 2(1)(h) of the Crowdfunding Regulation as 'any natural or legal person who seeks funding through a crowdfunding platform'.

[7] A crowdfunding platform is defined in Art 2(1)(d) of the Crowdfunding Regulation as 'a publicly accessible internet-based information system operated or managed by a crowdfunding service provider'.

[8] A loan is defined in Art 2(1)(b) of the Crowdfunding Regulation as 'an agreement whereby an investor makes available to a project owner an agreed amount of money for an agreed period of time and whereby the project owner assumes an unconditional obligation to repay that amount to the investor, together with the accrued interest, in accordance with the instalment payment schedule'.

[9] Transferable securities are defined in Art 2(1)(m) of the Crowdfunding Regulation as 'transferable securities as defined in point (44) of Article 4(1) of MiFID II'. In MiFID II transferable securities are defined as 'those classes of securities which are negotiable on the capital market, with the exception of instruments of payment, such as: (a) shares in companies and other securities equivalent to shares in companies, partnerships or other entities, and depositary receipts in respect of shares; (b) bonds or other forms of securitised debt, including depositary receipts in respect of such securities; (c) any other securities giving the right to acquire or sell any such transferable securities or giving rise to a cash settlement determined by reference to transferable securities, currencies, interest rates or yields, commodities or other indices or measures'.

crowdfunding purposes[10] issued by project owners or a special purpose vehicle and the reception and transmission of client[11] orders (as referred to in point (1) of Section A of Annex I to MiFID II), in relation to those transferable securities and admitted instruments for crowdfunding purposes.[12]

Crowdfunding services relate to (a) loans, (b) transferable securities, and (c) admitted instruments for crowdfunding purposes[13] (jointly referred to as Crowdfunding Investments). With the aforementioned scope of MiFID II in mind, it is important to note that—other than (non-transferable) loans—transferable securities are considered financial instruments within the meaning of MiFID II. If CSPs were not excluded from the scope of MiFID II, providing crowdfunding services in respect of transferable securities (or any other financial instrument) would result in a CSP to be subjected to the much heavier MiFID II framework.

13.09   The interconnectedness between the Crowdfunding Regulation and MiFID II clearly follows from the last type of crowdfunding service: placing without a firm commitment basis and reception and transmission of client orders. These crowdfunding services are (also) investment services within the meaning of MiFID II. Those operators, that are already authorized as an investment firm within the meaning of MiFID II, shall need to obtain a new authorization under the Crowdfunding Regulation, albeit under a simplified authorization procedure. On the basis of Recital 35 of the Crowdfunding Regulation such operators can decide to combine their current MiFID II authorization with an authorization as CSP under the Crowdfunding Regulation. Naturally, if it is no longer expedient to maintain the MiFID II authorization, such a CSP can choose to only hold an authorization under the Crowdfunding Regulation and have its MiFID II authorization been withdrawn by the national competent authority of its home Member State.

2. Difference between a CSP and an Investment Firm

13.10   In order to safeguard the exempt position under MiFID II for CSPs, they must ensure that they stay within the boundaries of the Crowdfunding Regulation. Due to the fact that both regulatory frameworks partially involve the exact same services (namely providing the services of (a) reception and transmission of client orders in transferable securities[14] and/

---

[10]   Admitted instruments for crowdfunding purposes are defined in Art 2(1)(n) of the Crowdfunding Regulation as 'in respect of each Member State, shares of a private limited liability company that are not subject to restrictions that would effectively prevent them from being transferred, including restrictions to the way in which those shares are offered or advertised to the public'.

[11]   A client is defined in Art 2(1)(g) of the Crowdfunding Regulation as 'any prospective or actual investor or project owner to whom a crowdfunding service provider provides, or intends to provide, crowdfunding services'.

[12]   Art 2(1)(a) of the Crowdfunding Regulation.

[13]   During the law-making process of the Crowdfunding Regulation, the Council added the term 'admitted instruments for crowdfunding purposes' in order to ensure that transferable shares in private limited liability companies would be covered by the Crowdfunding Regulation. This appeared to be needed; despite the relatively clear definition provided in MiFID II, transferable securities do not have the same meaning in each Member State. This also follows from a survey that was conducted to national competent authorities by ESMA in respect of the legal qualification of crypto-assets. See ESMA, Annex 1—Legal qualification of crypto-assets—survey to NCAs, January 2019, ESMA 50-157-1384, part 3, pp 4–11 (ESMA Survey). I will not separately refer to admitted instruments for crowdfunding purposes in this chapter but I deem these to be a form of transferable securities within the meaning of both MiFID II and the Crowdfunding Regulation.

[14]   We note that the MiFID II framework has a broader scope and regulates investment services (and investment activities) in respect of financial instruments. Transferable securities are only one type of financial instruments.

or (b) placing transferable securities without a firm commitment basis), it is essential to understand the differences between a CSP on the one hand and an investment firm on the other hand.

The determining distinguishing element seems to be the use of a crowdfunding platform **13.11** by a CSP since reference is made to the use of a crowdfunding platform in each of the definitions provided in the Crowdfunding Regulation for 'investor', 'project owner', and 'crowdfunding services'. A crowdfunding platform is, however, very broadly defined in the Crowdfunding Regulation as 'a publicly accessible internet-based information system operated or managed by a crowdfunding service provider'. The cross reference to a CSP in the definition of a crowdfunding platform results in an impasse. Combining these defined terms, an undertaking is considered to be a CSP if it provides crowdfunding services, which include, at least partially, two services that are also considered investment services under MiFID II but which fall out of scope of the MiFID II framework if such services are provided through the use of a crowdfunding platform, which in turn is operated by a CSP.

An investment firm can provide the exact same investment services to its clients, for ex- **13.12** ample in the event of an equity or (corporate) bonds offering by a company or Special Purpose Vehicle (SPV) that seeks funding. The only difference appears to be that a CSP can only offer these services through a publicly accessible Internet-based information system that is operated by such a CSP, whilst an investment firm can use other means to bring the opportunity to invest to the attention of its investor base. Would this then also mean that an investment firm, duly authorized in accordance with MiFID II, that wishes to use its website (or another publicly accessible Internet-based information system operated by such firm) to enable its investor base to invest in any such equity or (corporate) bonds offering, all of the sudden needs to obtain an authorization as a CSP under the Crowdfunding Regulation as well? On the basis of the recitals in the Crowdfunding Regulation, it can be derived that this is not intended.[15] It is considered that the *joint* provision of reception and transmission of client orders and the placement of transferable securities without a firm commitment basis is the key feature of crowdfunding services within the meaning of the Crowdfunding Regulation compared to investment services within the meaning of MiFID II. But then again, an investment firm can provide these joint investment services as well. It will become apparent when reading this chapter that the lines between the Crowdfunding Regulation on the one hand and the MiFID II framework on the other hand are wafer-thin.

An investment firm that uses a platform to bring an investment opportunity to the attention **13.13** of its investors base may claim that it does not purport to provide crowdfunding services because the investment opportunity does not qualify as a crowdfunding offer in respect of a crowdfunding project. A crowdfunding project is defined to be 'the business activity or activities for which a project owner seeks funding through the crowdfunding offer'.[16] A crowdfunding offer is defined as 'any communication by a crowdfunding service provider, in any form and by any means, presenting sufficient information on the terms of the

However, for the purpose of comparing investment firms with CSPs, the provision of these investment services in respect of transferable securities are relevant only.

[15] Recital 10 Crowdfunding Regulation.
[16] Art 2(1)(l) of the Crowdfunding Regulation.

offer and the crowdfunding project being offered, so as to enable an investor to invest in the crowdfunding project'.[17] These terms unfortunately do not result in a clear delineated scope of the Crowdfunding Regulation when compared to the MiFID II framework.

13.14   Recital 10 of the Crowdfunding Regulation may be the way out. It could be argued that the scope of the Crowdfunding Regulation should be limited to undertakings aiming to facilitate the funding of business activities of, primarily, start-ups and SMEs, by raising capital from an unrestricted pool of investors who are predominantly natural persons who each contribute relatively small investment amounts through a publicly accessible Internet-based information system. Unfortunately, this consideration did not make it to the body of the Crowdfunding Regulation though. It is questionable whether a mere appeal to the recitals of the Crowdfunding Regulation will be sufficient for an undertaking to claim that it does not fall under the scope of the Crowdfunding Regulation, for example, if it does not open up its platform to 'an unrestricted pool of investors', or not to 'investors who are predominantly natural persons who each contribute relatively small investment amounts'. Time will tell.

3.   Some Further Scoping Questions

13.15   Does the scope of the Crowdfunding Regulation that could be derived from Recital 10 as described above mean that any debt funding via a platform shall only be considered crowdfunding if the loan is split in multiple loan parts and therefore requires a 'syndicate' of lenders 'who are predominantly natural persons'? And what if an undertaking provides intermediation services via a platform in respect of business loans (other than transferable debt securities) granted to the borrower by non-public lenders only? If these non-public lenders are not 'predominantly natural persons', would such an undertaking fall out of scope of the Crowdfunding Regulation? This is relevant to clarify, because this form of intermediation is currently, at least in the Netherlands, not prohibited or subject to a regulatory authorization.[18]

13.16   The Crowdfunding Regulation enables both non-sophisticated investors and sophisticated investors to invest in a crowdfunding offer through a crowdfunding platform. Sophisticated investors include both *per se* professional clients within the meaning of section I of Annex II to MiFID II as well as 'opt-up' non-professional clients who have requested to be treated as a sophisticated investor in accordance with Annex II to the Crowdfunding Regulation.[19] As long as the Commission has not clarified who should be considered to be part of 'the public',

---

[17]   Art 2(1)(f) of the Crowdfunding Regulation.

[18]   From a Dutch law perspective, non-public lenders include professional market parties. A natural person can be considered a professional market party vis-à-vis the borrower if such person provides an amount of at least EUR 100.000 at once to the borrower. EBA has recently requested the Commission to provide for clear definitions on an EU, harmonized, level for material terms that compose the notion of 'credit institution'. One of these key terms is 'the public'. As such, it could well be that the Dutch interpretation is overruled by the Commission in the near future. Please see: Opinion of the European Banking Authority on elements of the definition of credit institution under Art 4(1), point 1, letter (a) of Regulation (EU) No 575/2013 and on aspects of the scope of the authorization, 18 September 2020, EBA/OP/2020/15 (EBA Opinion).

[19]   Art 2(1)(j) Crowdfunding Regulation.

as called upon by the European Banking Authority (EBA),[20] *per se* professional clients (and therefore sophisticated investors) are considered non-public lenders in any event.

On the basis of the Crowdfunding Regulation, it appears that undertakings that inter-   **13.17**
mediate in non-transferable loans provided only by sophisticated investors, including *per se* professional clients within the meaning of MiFID II, to businesses through an internet-based platform fall within the scope of the Crowdfunding Regulation and require an authorization as CSP. The only way out seems to be a reasoning on the basis of Recital 10 of the Crowdfunding Regulation as described above.

The answer to this scoping question is also relevant when determining the consequences   **13.18**
of Art 1(2)(c) of the Crowdfunding Regulation. This provision limits the applicability of the Crowdfunding Regulation to crowdfunding offers of an individual project owner with a total consideration that does not exceed EUR 5 million, calculated in a period of twelve months and taking into account each crowdfunding offer for raising capital in the form of a loan, transferable security, or admitted instrument for crowdfunding purposes as well as each offer of transferable securities made pursuant to an exemption under the Prospectus Regulation without the involvement of a crowdfunding platform. This threshold of EUR 5 million is set in the interest of an effective protection of investors who invest in crowdfunding projects and similar offerings under the exemption regime pursuant to the Prospectus Regulation. But what if a project owner or SPV offers transferable securities to qualified investors only or against a consideration of at least EUR 100.000 per investor?

Under the Prospectus Regulation, any such offering would be exempt from the obligation   **13.19**
to publish an approved prospectus drawn up in accordance with the Prospectus Regulation, also if the total consideration of such offering exceeds EUR 5 million. Does this mean that any such offering cannot be intermediated for through a platform that is operated by a CSP or can this still be serviced by a CSP that also holds an authorization as investment firm in accordance with MiFID II? In my view, it follows from Recital 35 of the Crowdfunding Regulation that the latter interpretation should prevail. Moreover, the Crowdfunding Regulation does not include a prohibition to service crowdfunding offers exceeding the threshold of EUR 5 million. It merely determines that the Crowdfunding Regulation does not apply to any such crowdfunding offer. This means, in my view, that an undertaking that intermediates in any offering exceeding EUR 5 million is subjected to national laws, including the MiFID II framework and the Prospectus Regulation in respect of transferable securities.

These scoping questions primarily relate to market entrance and services in the pri-   **13.20**
mary market. These questions are nevertheless interesting to touch on in this chapter relating to the secondary market as it shows the indistinctness as to the exact scope of the Crowdfunding Regulation. This lack of clarity also becomes apparent when moving to the secondary trading options made available under the Crowdfunding Regulation.

---

[20] See the EBA Opinion.

III. Secondary Trading of Crowdfunding Investments

13.21   The Crowdfunding Regulation allows CSPs to operate a bulletin board on which their clients can advertise their interests in buying and selling their Crowdfunding Investments that were initially offered on the crowdfunding platform operated by such CSP.

13.22   When operating a 'bulletin board' a CSP does not take any role in relation to the transactions that can be executed between two individual investors outside the bulletin board. A bulletin board is no more than a digital place where investors can show their interest to buy or sell Crowdfunding Investments without an ability to interact through the bulletin board. A bulletin board is meant to only enable investors to exchange information necessary to make an offer and to conclude a transaction bilaterally outside the bulletin board. It may not effectively qualify as an MTF or an OTF within the meaning of MiFID II. Operating an MTF and/or an OTF qualifies as an investment activity within the meaning of MiFID II and requires an authorization as investment firm under MiFID II. A mere bulletin board, however, does not trigger this authorization obligation and a CSP can offer its clients secondary trading possibilities on a bulletin board operated by it.

13.23   This is in line with Recital 8 of the Markets in Financial Instruments Regulation (MiFIR) in which it is clarified that 'facilities' on which no genuine trade execution or arranging takes place in 'the system' are not considered an MTF or OTF. In line with guidance of the predecessor of the European Securities and Markets Authority (ESMA), the Committee of European Securities Regulators (CESR),[21] MiFIR lists a number of excluded facilities, amongst which bulletin boards on which 'buying and selling interests' are advertised.[22] But what is a bulletin board and how does it differ from an MTF or OTF? What is 'a facility' or 'a system' as referred to in Recital 8 MiFIR? What are 'buying and selling interests'? In order to have an understanding of the possibilities and limitations for a CSP when offering a bulletin board on its platform, these terms need to be analysed in more detail.

1. Bulletin Board

13.24   In order to get a better understanding of the possibilities, and limitations, of a CSP that operates a bulletin board and that offers its clients a secondary trading option on the crowdfunding platform, it is essential to determine what a bulletin board is. The Crowdfunding Regulation itself does not provide any clarity in this respect, albeit that it does specifically include which characteristics a bulletin board cannot have.[23]

13.25   As referred to above, the term bulletin board was firstly used by CESR in 2002 in a document providing standards for alternative trading systems when compared to regulated markets. CESR distinguished a passive bulletin board from an active bulletin board. CESR

---

[21] CESR, 'Standards for Alternative Trading Systems', July 2002, CESR 02-086b (CESR 2002).

[22] Other examples of excluded facilities that were given by CESR in 2002 are: other entities aggregating or pooling potential buying or selling interests, electronic post-trade confirmation services, or portfolio compression, which reduces non-market risks in existing derivatives portfolios without changing the market risk of the portfolios.

[23] Art 25(2) Crowdfunding Regulation.

considered a passive bulletin board to be a mere advertisement system; investors could only conclude the trade outside the bulletin board. By contrast, an active bulletin board enabled execution within the system. CESR seemed to focus on the ability of execution of a transaction in the system when assessing whether such system would be in scope of the MiFID framework.[24] This is still the point of departure of CESR's successor, ESMA.[25] CESR published its standards in a time prior to MiFID I introducing the term MTF, let alone MiFID II introducing yet another trading venue: the OTF. This guidance given by CESR in 2002 has found its way into formal EU legislation in MiFIR over time.

Nonetheless, a lot has changed since then. Think of the speed of trading nowadays and the   **13.26** rise of high-frequency algorithmic trading. The development and use of trading technology have resulted in many benefits for secondary trading, such as more trading venues and therefore more possibilities to ensure best execution of trades, wider participation, more liquidity, reduction of short-term volatility, and increased competition leading to better pricing. On the other hand, it has also resulted in increased complexity and an incredible growth in trading volume. In order to ensure orderly and fair trading conditions, the obligations applicable to trading venues have changed enormously over time. The current regulatory framework applicable to operators of a regulated market, MTF or OTF, is by no means comparable to the provisions that applied to operators of regulated markets as recently as in 2002. This development and tightening of legislation was needed and welcome. However, one could question whether it is proportional to apply such heavy regulatory framework to a CSP that wishes to enable its clients to trade their Crowdfunding Investments whenever they need or want to. The European legislator seems to agree that the answer to this question is negative: CSPs may offer a secondary trading possibility to their clients through a bulletin board.

The Crowdfunding Regulation emphasizes that such a bulletin board cannot be used to   **13.27** bring together buying and selling interests by means of the protocols or internal operating procedures of the CSP in a way that results in a contract. Additionally, it is emphasized that a bulletin board cannot consist of an internal matching system that executes client orders on a multilateral basis.[26] These limitations directly follow from MiFID II and the defined terms of an MTF and OTF included therein, which will be elaborated on in the next paragraph.

Each type of regulated trading venue within the MiFID II framework, being a regulated   **13.28** market, an MTF, and an OTF, purports a genuine trading platform: the arranging and the execution of trades take place in the multilateral system offered by its operator. A bulletin board on which merely buying and selling interests are advertised without genuine trade execution or arranging taking place in the system offered by the operator of such bulletin board is not considered a genuine trading platform.[27] The term buying and selling interests should be interpreted broadly. MiFIR points out that it includes orders and quotes as well as indications of interest.[28] A bulletin board, or its underlying rules, protocols, or internal

---

[24] CESR 2002, p 5 and p 20.
[25] ESMA, MiFID II review report on the functioning of Organised Trading Facilities, ESMA 70-156-4225, 23 March 2021 (the document itself mistakenly refers to 2020), § 102, p 26 (hereafter referred to as ESMA OTF Report).
[26] Art 25(2) Crowdfunding Regulation.
[27] Recital 8 MiFIR.
[28] Recital 7 MiFIR.

operating procedures, cannot, in any way, match or bring together the buying and selling interests that are listed on the bulletin board. In addition, the operator cannot offer any type of trading system, such as a voice trading system, a request for quote system, a central (limit) order book system, order management system, execution management system, or distributed trading system.[29] ESMA states that a bulletin board only advertises trading interests without facilitating the interaction of those buying and selling interests in any way. ESMA considers that this is the material difference between a bulletin board and the regulated trading venues such as an MTF or OTF.[30]

13.29   A bulletin board can include information on prices, quantities available, and list contact details of the persons who advertise their buying and selling interests on the bulletin board.[31] You can compare it to an electronic/digital advertisement board that can still be found in local supermarkets.

13.30   ESMA ascribes the following characteristics to a bulletin board and recommends including a definition hereof in MiFID II:

- it is an interface that only aggregates and broadcasts buying and selling interests in financial instruments (including financial securities registered in a distributed ledger);
- the system neither allows for the communication or negotiation between advertising parties, including any notification of any potential match between buying and selling interests in the system, nor imposes the mandatory use of tools of affiliated companies; and
- there is no possibility of execution or the bringing together of buying and selling interests in the system.[32]

In other words: the actual arranging, bringing together, matching, negotiating, and execution of the transaction takes place offline, outside the bulletin board, its system, rules, protocols, or internal operating procedures.

13.31   This gives clear guidance as to the possibilities and in particular the limitations for a CSP when operating a bulletin board for Crowdfunding Investments on its platform. However, some questions remain unanswered. For example, according to the above, no communication can take place between investors via the bulletin board nor can the bulletin board automatically create matching notifications. I presume this limitation is intended to relate to pre-transaction notifications to be sent to users of the bulletin board, rather than post-transaction notifications to be sent to the CSP via the bulletin board. After all, CSPs that provide asset safekeeping services should be notified of any transaction for administration purposes.[33]

13.32   In addition, the Crowdfunding Regulation leaves room for the CSP to suggest a reference price for the buying and selling interests. This is more than only aggregating and broadcasting buying and selling interests. However, it follows from Art 25(5) Crowdfunding Regulation that a CSP that operates a bulletin board can have such further involvement.

[29]   ESMA OTF Report, § 84 and § 99–100, p 26.
[30]   ESMA OTF Report, § 107, p 27.
[31]   ESMA OTF Report, § 117, p 29.
[32]   ESMA OTF Report, § 116, p 29.
[33]   Art 25(4) Crowdfunding Regulation.

Can it then also provide other ancillary services, such as template transaction documents to ensure that a transaction in respect of the Crowdfunding Investments is settled in a legally valid and binding manner? Such assistance would, in my view, be pre-eminently a post-matching form of assistance and therefore would not trigger the bulletin board to be changing colours to an MTF or OTF. Taken the presumed involvement of 'predominantly natural persons' in crowdfunding projects, such assistance could be in the interest of investors trading Crowdfunding Investments via a bulletin board. To take it one step further, one could even argue that it is part of the duty of care of a CSP to ensure that any secondary trading via a bulletin board offered on its platform is performed in a fair and orderly manner, which may include a derived obligation, rather than an option, to suggest a reference price as well as to assist in the valid settlement of the transaction. But the Crowdfunding Regulation does not provide any clarity in this respect. Again, time will tell.

Lastly, and most importantly, the Crowdfunding Regulation enables a CSP also to offer a secondary trading opportunity to its clients who invested in loans through the crowdfunding platform. The characteristics that ESMA ascribes to a bulletin board, as referred to above, only relate to financial instruments or financial securities registered in a distributed ledger. This may be based on the fact that regulated trading venues such as an MTF or OTF only relate to financial instruments under the MiFID II framework. Non-transferable loans are not financial instruments (or financial securities registered in a distributed ledger), yet the Crowdfunding Regulations does enable loans to be traded via a bulletin board. Apparently, this trading possibility does not entail a requalification of the loans as transferable debt securities; this issue, however, will be scrutinized in further detail below (see paragraph 13.43 a.f.). This also raises the question whether a CSP, or the bulletin board operated by it, can have a more substantive involvement in the arranging and execution of transactions via the bulletin board if these transactions relate to loans only. Given the limitations included in Art 25(2) of the Crowdfunding Regulation, the answer to this question is likely to be negative. However, one could question whether this limitation is fair when it comes to trading of loans only, assuming these are not considered transferable debt securities. After all, MiFID II would not subject an operator of such a 'trading venue' to an authorization obligation, as long as the trading does not relate to financial instruments. **13.33**

At all times, a CSP needs to prevent itself (or the bulletin board) from crossing the line to an MTF or OTF as this will trigger the MiFID II framework to become applicable. As will follow from the below, this line is rather thin. **13.34**

2. A Multilateral Trading Facility (MTF) and an Organized Trading Facility (OTF)

An MTF is defined as 'a multilateral system, operated by an investment firm ... which brings together multiple third-party buying and selling interests in financial instruments— in the system and in accordance with non-discretionary rules—in a way that results in a contract ...'.[34] **13.35**

---

[34] Art 4(1)(22) MiFID II.

13.36   An OTF is defined as 'a multilateral system which is not a regulated market or an MTF and in which multiple third-party buying and selling interests in bonds, structured finance products, emission allowances or derivatives are able to interact in the system in a way that results in a contract . . '.[35]

A. Multilateral System

13.37   Both types of trading venues are multilateral systems rather than bilateral systems on which an investment firm trades on its own account with its client, such as in case of systematic internalization and matched principal trading. A multilateral system is defined as 'any system or facility in which multiple third-party buying and selling trading interests in financial instruments are able to interact in the system'.[36] From MiFIR it can be derived that the intended scope is very broad. This also follows from Art 1(7) MiFID II.[37] This provision requires all multilateral systems in financial instruments to operate on any of the regulated trading venues (regulated market, MTF, or OTF). This provision is aimed at ensuring that each multilateral system, irrespective of it qualifying as a regulated market, MTF, or OTF, or not, shall be subject to the MiFID II framework as regards such regulated trading venues. Operating a multilateral system is therefore material for determining whether its operator falls within the scope of the MiFID II framework.

13.38   The underlying system could be a mere set of rules determining the functioning thereof. Whether or not it provides for the matching of orders through underlying technology is irrelevant. The same applies to the type of trading protocol; it is explicitly considered that it also includes systems whereby investors are able to trade against quotes they request from multiple providers.[38] Even if there is no trading protocol but only a set of rules in respect of access to trading, admission of financial instruments to trading, rules in respect of trading and reporting rules, such a system can form the basis of a regulated trading venue such as an MTF or OTF if it offers the opportunity to have multiple third-party buying and selling interests to interact.[39] A crowdfunding platform, being a publicly accessible Internet-based information system, as operated by a CSP will be considered 'a system' within the meaning of MiFIR. A CSP shall not be able to change this, as such a system (the platform) is a material part of its business operations and its services. The mere fact of using a system does not result in the MiFID II framework becoming applicable to CSPs. Thankfully, it takes more to draw that conclusion. Only multilateral systems could bring the operator of a bulletin board in the danger zone.

13.39   This means that a bulletin board cannot be a multilateral system. But what should be considered a 'multilateral system'?

13.40   In a preliminary ruling, the European Court of Justice (ECJ) gave some insights on what should be considered a multilateral system when compared to a bilateral system.[40] Although this ruling was provided under MiFID I and related to the definition of a regulated market

---

[35] Art 4(1)(23) MiFID II.

[36] Art 4(1)(19) MiFID II.

[37] ESMA recently proposed to move this provision to MiFIR in order to foster consistency and convergence within the EEA. See ESMA OTF Report, § 36, p 14.

[38] Recital 7 MiFIR.

[39] Recital 7 MiFIR.

[40] C-658/15 *Robeco Hollands Bezit N.V. v AFM* [2017] ECLI:EU:C:2017:870.

rather than an MTF, the ruling, and particularly the underlying opinion of the Advocate General, shed some light in the darkness around the meaning of a multilateral system. The Advocate General upheld a very strict reading of the objectives of the MiFID framework. This resulted in his interpretation of what should be considered a multilateral system to be very broad. He concluded (in my words) that a system that enables investors or their brokers to conclude a transaction in accordance with the rules established by the operator of the system should be considered a multilateral system.[41] Only if the transaction is concluded outside the system could it be a considered a bilateral trading system or over-the-counter (OTC) trading system.[42] The Advocate General also shared his view that price formation is not a relevant factor for determining whether 'buying and selling interests are able to interact in the system'. The Court followed the opinion of the Advocate General.

Recently, ESMA has provided further guidance on the meaning of multilateral systems.[43]   **13.41**
The crux is in the interaction of multiple third-party trading interests in the system. On the basis of Art 20(6) MiFID II, it could be derived that an OTF can operate a system that crosses client orders and a system that arranges transactions where the operator facilitates negotiations so as to bring together two or more potentially compatible trading interests in a transaction. This would both be forms of 'interaction of trading interests in the system'.[44] In line with the aforementioned ruling of the ECJ, ESMA seems to uphold a much lower threshold: exchange of information in respect of material terms of a transaction, such as price and quantity with a view to conclude a transaction between parties via the system, already results in such system falling under the scope of the MIFID II framework, irrespective of such exchange of information resulting in a transaction in the system or not.[45]

How can this be compared to the aforementioned characteristics of a bulletin board (see   **13.42**
paragraph 13.30)? And how to interpret the possibility for a CSP to suggest a reference price, as explicitly included in the Crowdfunding Regulation? Apparently, the mere listing of pricing and quantity information on a bulletin board cannot be deemed to be 'an exchange of information with the view of concluding a transaction'. It appears to me that a 'one way' publication of a buying or selling interest on a bulletin board including pricing and quantity information, directed at any user of the bulletin board and not to one or some individual investors, as well as the publication of a reference price by the CSP, is acceptable, provided that any follow-up negotiation or conclusion of a transaction occurs offline, outside the bulletin board. The exchange of information as referred to by ESMA seems to aim at a one-on-one contact between users of the system with the aim of getting the deal done. As such, electronic messaging or any form of communication through the bulletin board would trigger the conclusion that the system is considered a multilateral system and should comply with the MiFID II framework.[46] A bulletin board can therefore not be compared

---

[41]   C-658/15 *Robeco Hollands Bezit N.V. v AFM* [2017] ECLI:EU:C:2017:870, § 87–89.

[42]   C-658/15 *Robeco Hollands Bezit N.V. v AFM* [2017] ECLI:EU:C:2017:870, § 83–84.

[43]   ESMA OTF Report, part 4.2, p 12 a.f.

[44]   See also ESMA, Questions and Answers on MiFID II and MiFIR market structures topics, ESMA 70-872942901-38, 6 April 2021, § 5.2, Q&A 10, p 45 (ESMA Q&A).

[45]   ESMA OTF Report, § 23, p 12, § 40, p 15. This could be based on the standards given by CESR in 2002 already. CESR considered that any communication system whereby investors contact each other outside the system to negotiate material terms of a transaction will not fall under the scope of—then current—MiFID I. See CESR 2002, §13(d), p 5.

[46]   This is emphasized by EMSA in the ESMA OTF Report, § 117, p 29.

with platforms like eBay or the Dutch Marktplaats.nl because persons can negotiate and conclude a transaction on such platform.

B. The Use of Discretionary Powers

13.43   The next step is to determine whether and how multiple third-party buying and selling interests interact with each other in the multilateral system. On an MTF this must take place on the basis of non-discretionary rules. Non-discretionary rules mean that the operator of an MTF does not have any discretion in respect of the way in which buying and selling interests interact in the system. These rules, protocols, or internal operating procedures of the system, whether or not embodied in technology or computer software, result, on a non-discretionary basis, in a transaction between the buyer and the seller.[47] As such, it is typical for an MTF (or regulated market) that a transaction is the automatic result of the coming together of a buying and selling interest on the basis of the rules, protocols, or internal operating procedures of the system operated by its operator.[48] In other words, the execution of a transaction on an MTF (and regulated market) is the outcome of rules, protocols, or internal operating procedures which the operator cannot influence.

13.44   An OTF deviates from an MTF (and regulated market) in this respect. An operator of an OTF has the obligation to carry out discretion.[49] The discretionary powers of an operator of an OTF enable it (a) to decide on the inclusion and withdrawal of orders in the system ('order discretion') and (b) to influence the matching process of orders in the system subject to best execution obligations and specific instructions (eg within an asset management mandate) ('execution discretion').[50] The access to an OTF should, however, be determined on the basis of non-discretionary rules. This deviating feature of an OTF compared to an MTF makes the boundaries between the Crowdfunding Regulation and the MiFID II framework even thinner. Where an MTF seems to have some sort of matching protocol within its system which automatically, or in any event on a non-discretionary basis, results in the conclusion of a transaction on the MTF upon buying and selling interests interacting, an OTF does not seem to operate in the same manner. Despite multiple third-party buying and selling interests still interacting on the OTF which results in a transaction, the operator of the OTF can steer or influence the matching process prior to such trade being concluded on or via the OTF.

3. From Loans to Transferable Debt Securities

13.45   With reference to the aforementioned scope of MiFID II, it is also important to note that MTFs and OTFs only relate to trading in financial instruments, where OTFs are limited to non-equity financial instruments.[51] As emphasized above, not all Crowdfunding Investments qualify as financial instruments within the meaning of MiFID II. In any event loans do not, provided that such loans do not qualify as transferable debt securities. This

---

[47] Recital 7 MiFIR.
[48] Recital 7 MiFIR.
[49] Art 20(6) MiFID II.
[50] Recital 9 MiFIR. See also ESMA Q&A, §5.2, Q&A 19, p 50, and ESMA OTF Report, § 135, p 33.
[51] Within the meaning of Art 4(1)(15) MiFID II.

raises questions as to the opportunities and limitations for a CSP when operating a bulletin board for loans only.

Taken the fact that the Crowdfunding Regulation, including Art 25 dealing with the pos-   **13.46**
sibility to operate a bulletin board, applies to both loans as well as transferable debt securities, it is interesting to get an understanding what the difference is between these two sorts
of Crowdfunding Investments. Apparently, a loan does not automatically requalify into a
transferable debt security if it can be traded bilaterally after having found a counterparty via
a bulletin board. If this would be the case, Art 25 of the Crowdfunding Regulation would
not (need to) have included 'loans' as well.

A loan is defined to be 'an agreement whereby an investor makes available to a project   **13.47**
owner an agreed amount of money for an agreed period of time and whereby the project
owner assumes an unconditional obligation to repay that amount to the investor, together
with the accrued interest, in accordance with the instalment payment schedule'.[52] Under
the Crowdfunding Regulation, the borrower of a loan shall always be a person acting in the
course of its trade, business or profession.[53] A loan is a form of repayable funds within the
meaning of the Capital Requirements Directive (CRD) IV, as amended by CRD V, and the
Capital Requirements Regulation (CRR), as amended by CRR II. EBA recently called on the
Commission to clarify certain material elements of the notion of 'credit institution'—including in respect of the term 'repayable funds' and the term 'the public'—to establish a
truly level playing field across the European Economic Area.[54]

Transferable securities include debt securities and are defined as   **13.48**

> those classes of securities which are negotiable on the capital market, with the exception
> of instruments of payment, such as (i) shares in companies and other securities equivalent
> to shares in companies, partnerships or other entities, and depositary receipts in respect
> of shares, (ii) bonds or other forms of securitized debt, including depositary receipts in
> respect of such securities, or (iii) any other securities giving the right to acquire or sell any
> such transferable securities or giving rise to a cash settlement determined by reference to
> transferable securities, currencies, interest rates or yields, commodities or other indices or
> measures.[55]

From the definition of transferable security it can be derived that it is negotiable on the cap-   **13.49**
ital market. In order to be negotiable on the capital market, a transferable security needs to
be interchangeable/fungible and therefore standardized in the sense that the same rights
and obligations attach to each class of securities that are negotiated on the capital market.
'Negotiable on the capital market' does not entail that it needs to be listed on a trading
venue. A transferable and fungible debt instrument can be considered a debt security if the
characteristics and nature of the debt instrument do not prevent such debt instrument from
being negotiated on the capital market. As such, a debt security differs from a 'regular loan'

---

[52] Art 2(1)(b) Crowdfunding Regulation.
[53] This follows from Art 1(2)(a) Crowdfunding Regulation in which is it clarified that the Crowdfunding Regulation does not apply to project owners who qualify as consumers within the meaning of Art 3(a) of the Consumer Credit Directive. Consumer is defined therein as 'a natural person who, in transactions covered by this Directive, is acting for purposes which are outside his trade, business or profession'.
[54] See EBA Opinion as referred to in n 18.
[55] Art 4(1)(44) MiFID II.

on the basis of three elements: it is (a) transferable, (b) interchangeable/fungible, and (c) its characteristics and nature do not preclude it from being negotiated on the capital market.

13.50   A lending-based crowdfunding platform would usually entail numerous small investments by multiple investors who each provide a loan or jointly provide one aggregated loan to a project owner. Each investor will have the same rights and obligations vis-à-vis the project owner under the loan facilitated via the crowdfunding platform pro rata to their investment in the loan. Their loans or loan parts are therefore interchangeable/fungible.

13.51   Under the Crowdfunding Regulation, loans are explicitly included in Art 25 which describes the possibility for a CSP to operate a bulletin board. Investors can advertise their selling or buying interest in respect of a loan or loan parts on the bulletin board. This means that the loans facilitated through the crowdfunding platform cannot include restrictions on transferability. If the transfer of the loan or loan parts would be restricted, it would not make sense to advertise a buying or selling interest in respect of such a loan or loan part. This results in these loans or loan parts to be considered transferable.

13.52   The material question that is left is whether these loans or loan parts can be considered to be negotiable on the capital market. This seems to be the only distinctive element between a transferable crowdfunded loan and a transferable debt security. There is, however, no consensus in the EU as to the meaning of this element. There is no harmonized definition of 'capital market' included in European legislation, nor on a national level.[56] It is generally considered a place where buying and selling interests meet. Does this mean that a bulletin board, by nature, cannot be deemed a capital market since the buying and selling interests cannot meet (or interact) on the bulletin board? If this conclusion can be validly upheld, could it then be argued that crowdfunded loans are not negotiable on the capital market and therefore will not requalify to a transferable debt security as long as the only secondary trading option for these crowdfunded loans is via a bulletin board?

13.53   This could be a game changer, at least from a Dutch law perspective. This third characteristic of a transferable security—'negotiable on the capital market'—was always considered to be satisfied relatively easily under Dutch law. The Dutch law interpretation is that if the category instruments similar to the loans or loan parts are generally negotiated on the capital market, such loans or loan parts shall be deemed to be negotiable on the capital market as well. It is considered not decisive whether there is a market available for the particular instruments, but rather that the instruments, considering their characteristics, *could* be negotiated on the capital market.[57] In the Policy on Tradability (*Beleidsregel Verhandelbaarheid*), the Dutch Authority for the Financial Markets (the AFM) concludes that if an instrument is transferred on a periodic basis, it will be deemed to be negotiable and as such a transferable security. The AFM has further clarified that it takes an economic approach when qualifying instruments tradable or not. The AFM considers that all arrangements where the economic interest of a standardized instrument can or will be transferred—directly or indirectly—to a third party, are considered tradable instruments. The AFM regards the transferability of the beneficial ownership/economic value of an instrument as the decisive factor for determining whether an instrument is tradable or not. Moreover, the AFM believes that only in

---

[56]   ESMA Survey, § 22–23, p 7.
[57]   This view seems to be shared in other Member States as well. See ESMA Survey, §20, p 6.

the event that an instrument ceases to exist in a formal legal sense without being replaced by another (economically similar) instrument, the original instrument could be considered not tradable.[58]

This Dutch law interpretation may need to be revisited. Apparently, a loan provided via a **13.54** crowdfunding platform does not automatically requalify to a transferable debt security in the event that the CSP operates a bulletin board and offers its clients a secondary trading option in respect of those crowdfunded loans outside the bulletin board.

4. What Can a CSP Do When Operating a Bulletin Board?

Not much. That is the short, but presumably valid answer. A CSP can merely enable its **13.55** clients to publish an electronic advertisement on the digital bulletin board in respect of a crowdfunding project that was financed through the crowdfunding platform operated by the CSP earlier.

Upon operating a bulletin board, Art 25 of the Crowdfunding Regulation subjects the CSP **13.56** to some requirements, mainly focused on ensuring that investors are able to make their investment decision on a well-informed basis.

If the CSP plays it safely, it (or the system) does not become involved in any way in respect of **13.57** any advertisements published on the bulletin board other than suggesting a reference price. The Crowdfunding Regulation explicitly accepts a CSP to suggest a reference price for any buying and selling interests in respect of Crowdfunding Investments that are advertised on the bulletin board.[59] I encourage CSPs to offer this service to their clients, in particular in respect of crowdfunding projects that are primarily financed by non-sophisticated investors. These investors will benefit from an objective third party suggesting a reference price and substantiating how it came to such reference price. How would such investors otherwise know what the appropriate market value of such Crowdfunding Investment is at that moment if no such market may be offered on a bulletin board? One of the most important principles in economics is the interaction of supply and demand as the basis for price formation. As described above, one of the main characteristics of a multilateral trading venue is that buying and selling interests interact or are brought together in the system. Despite the view of the Advocate General (as followed by the ECJ in the *Robeco* matter) that price formation is not relevant for assessing whether buying and selling interests interact in a system,[60] which in my opinion fails to convince, price formation seems to be the undeniable consequence of such interaction. With this main economic principle in mind, it is regrettable that CSPs are not allowed to let the market do its job by enabling this interaction in the system without its operator being confronted with the heavy MiFID II framework.

---

[58] AFM, Policy on Tradability, p 8; AFM, Feedback Statement on Policy on Tradability, p 5. We note that the AFM explicitly rejected the argument made in the consultation conducted in respect of the Policy on Tradability that the interpretation of the AFM is broader than intended under (the then current) MiFID and the then current Prospectus Directive. The AFM considered its interpretation as laid down in the Policy to be in line with the intentions of both the Dutch and the European legislators. A recent decision of the Dutch Trade and Industry Appeals Tribunal backs this broad interpretation of the AFM (ECLI:NL:CBB:2017:409).

[59] Art 25(5) Crowdfunding Regulation.

[60] C-658/15 *Robeco Hollands Bezit N.V. v AFM* [2017] ECLI:EU:C:2017:870, § 83–84.

13.58   Since the bulletin board cannot in any way bring clients together in the system, and as such neither the rules, protocols, or internal operating procedures underlying the bulletin board can have that effect, clients should include their contact details in the advertisement that they publish on the bulletin board. However, in my view, a CSP should be able to service its clients in a very limited way by, for example, safeguarding a client's privacy by offering the possibility to publish an advertisement under a unique client or advertisement number and the CSP only providing the personal contact details of the person having published the advertisement to other clients who request these details when they are interested in the advertisement. In my modest view, this cannot be deemed the exchange of information in respect of material terms of a transaction which would make the bulletin board a multilateral system according to ESMA.[61]

13.59   In the same line of thought, and taking into account the duty of care that a CSP has towards its clients, in my view a CSP should be able to publish template transaction documents on the crowdfunding platform which the clients can use if they have, bilaterally amongst themselves and outside the platform or bulletin board, agreed on a trade in respect of Crowdfunding Investments. Taken that crowdfunding investors are 'predominantly natural persons'[62] who, presumably, do not conclude transactions such as contract takeovers, assignments, or security transfers on a daily basis, the CSP should be able to offer template transaction documents that comply with local law requirements to safeguard a valid and legally binding transaction between its two clients. In addition, where the involvement of a civil law notary or a similar third party is required pursuant to local law, I do not see any regulatory issue with the CSP listing contact details of one or more of such professionals on the platform with the aim of assisting its clients. Any such assistance to settle a bilaterally agreed transaction in Crowdfunding Investments outside the bulletin board would also have a cost benefit for the clients of the CSP. Lower transaction costs stimulate secondary trading, which is beneficial to the investors as well as the further growth of the crowdfunding market.

13.60   From a costs perspective, it is regrettable that it is not allowed to execute the transaction on the bulletin board automatically without the CSP becoming subjected to the MiFID II framework for operating a multilateral trading venue. Where third party professionals need to become involved, such as a civil law notary, to transfer the Crowdfunding Investment by the seller to the purchaser validly, it is doubtful whether a secondary market in those Crowdfunding Investments will actually arise. As crowdfunding typically involves relatively small investments, the transaction costs will possibly not outweigh the benefits of trading. In this respect, CSPs should take into account the local law requirements for validly transferring a Crowdfunding Investment when structuring their services. By way of example, from a Dutch law perspective, it may be more client-friendly to have an intermediate foundation administration office issue depositary receipts to investors, with these depositary receipts being linked to shares held by such foundation in the capital of the project owner, rather than having a project owner issuing shares to the investors directly. The issuance and each transfer of shares in a Dutch capital company requires a notarial deed. By

---

[61] See n 45.
[62] Recital 10 Crowdfunding Regulation.

placing a foundation administration office in between the project owner and the investors, the terms and conditions that apply to the depositary receipts can determine that a transfer can take place by means of a private deed rather than a notarial deed. Another benefit of this structure is that the project owner is not confronted with many new shareholders but rather with one new shareholder (the foundation administration office) that represents the interests of the depositary receipt holders (the investors).

The requirements when operating a multilateral trading venue in accordance with the **13.61** MiFID II framework are so far beyond the regulatory framework applicable to a CSP that it is essential for CSPs that they do not, mistakenly, cross the line and would be deemed to operate an MTF or OTF rather than a mere passive bulletin board. It should prevent the system to become a genuine trading platform if it does not consciously aim to 'jump to the other side'.

5. Or Is There a Workaround?

The limitations for a CSP naturally also offer chances to other market parties. In light of **13.62** the G20 commitments and one of the objectives of MiFID II to move trading to organized, multilateral regulated venues 'in order to increase market transparency, add more quality to the price discovery process, increase investor protection and access to liquidity',[63] operators of already regulated trading venues may decide to include a market segment for Crowdfunding Investments.

CSPs could cooperate with such regulated trading venues. A particular interesting point **13.63** is that the role of a CSP could in the event of such a cooperation possibly become much bigger. The system operated by the CSP may even enable the pre-arranging of transactions in Crowdfunding Investments between clients of the CSP, as long as the actual execution of the transaction takes place on the regulated trading venue. ESMA considers such (multilateral) 'arranging system' an outsourced service by a regulated trading venue on which the pre-arranged transaction is executed.[64] Apparently, ESMA holds the view that a 'arranging system operator' is not considered to be an operator of a multilateral trading system if the actual execution of the transaction takes place on a regulated trading venue on the basis of an outsourcing agreement between the arranging system operator and the operator of the regulated trading venue. Whether this is a commercially viable option to consider for CSPs is questionable, as well as whether this view will be followed by national competent authorities. Again, time will tell.

---

[63] ESMA OTF Report, §15, p 11.

[64] In this way, it is ensured that the MiFID II framework is still applicable, albeit not directly on the 'arranging system operator' but rather via the operator of the trading venue that outsources the arrangement to such other person. Please see: ESMA OTF Report, § 103–105, p 26–27. ESMA emphasizes that it does not work the other way around as the fundamental characteristic of a trading venue is to execute transactions. See in this respect also ESMA Q&A, § 5.1, Q&A 7, p 41.

IV. Full Regulation: Just a Matter of Time?

13.64   As mentioned in the introductory paragraph of this chapter, the Crowdfunding Regulation will presumably stimulate the further growth of the European crowdfunding market. This form of alternative finance is by no means in its infancy anymore; the global market size as per 2019 is expected to triple to approximately USD 40 billion by 2026.[65] Although this is still a fraction compared to the size of the global capital markets, the expected continuing exponential growth of crowdfunding could be taken as a forerunner of further regulation yet to come. Generally, the adage applies that the bigger the market, the higher the risks, the more regulation is developed. Regulation always lags behind the developments and innovation. This was also explicitly brought to the attention of the Commission by trading venues, expressing their concerns about the rise of alternative platforms in which trading interests are matched on a bilateral basis rather than a multilateral basis. The regulated trading venues claim that these alternative platforms cause competitive distortions because the operators do not comply with the MiFID II framework. On the basis of the analysis in this chapter, matching of trading interests in a system would result in such system to qualify as a multilateral system and as such would result in the operator of such a system falling under the scope of the MiFID II framework. A recent consultation document on the review of the MiFID II framework considers whether the MiFID II framework should 'take a more functional approach and define the operation of a trading facility in broader terms than the current definition of trading venues or multilateral system as to encompass these systems and ensure fair treatment for market players'.[66]

13.65   With this recently conducted consultation in mind, it would not be surprising if the bulletin board option in the Crowdfunding Regulation would only be a temporary means of boosting secondary trading in Crowdfunding Investments, and over time CSPs would be required to move trading in Crowdfunding Investments to regulated multilateral trading venues.

13.66   However, CSPs should not be discouraged, and should start with the first step: open up secondary trading in Crowdfunding Investments by operating a bulletin board, and protect clients' interests by enabling them to exit their investment when they want or need to in an orderly and informed manner against fair value.

---

[65] <https://www.statista.com/statistics/1078273/global-crowdfunding-market-size/>.
[66] Public consultation on the review of the MiFID II/MiFIR regulatory framework, part VI (Multilateral systems), 17 February 2020, p 82.

14

Marketing Communications and the Digital Single Market

Catalina Goanta, Marije Louisse, and Pietro Ortolani

I. Introduction

Chapter V of the Crowdfunding Regulation sets forth rules for the marketing communications of crowdfunding service providers (CSPs). The chapter consists of two provisions (Articles 27 and 28), which are applicable not only to the CSPs' advertisement aimed at investors, but also to communications of CSPs towards project owners. Indeed, Article 2(1)(o) defines marketing communications as 'any information or communication from a crowdfunding service provider to a prospective investor or prospective project owner about the services of the crowdfunding service provider, other than investor disclosures required under this Regulation'. The chapter, thus, has a broad scope of application, and pursues at least three goals. **14.01**

The first goal is the protection of the clients. Article 27 builds upon the CSP's general obligation under Article 19(1) to provide 'fair, clear and not misleading' information to clients. According to Recital 57, the purpose of this obligation is to ensure the fair and non-discriminatory treatment of clients, without distinction between investors and project owners. For this reason, Articles 27 and 28 are not included in the 'Investor Protection' chapter of the Regulation, despite their unquestionable role in the protection of prospective or actual investors, alongside project owners. **14.02**

14.03   The second goal is legal certainty. Importantly, the Crowdfunding Regulation addresses certain specific aspects of marketing communications by CSPs but does not set forth a comprehensive harmonized regime. As a result, there will be differences between Member States in respect of the laws, regulations, and administrative provisions that apply to any aspects of marketing communications by CSPs that are not governed by the Regulation. Thus, whenever a CSP provides services in a Member State other than the one where it is established, it has to be aware that its marketing communications may be subject to different requirements. In order to foster legal certainty, Article 28 requires the competent authorities of the Member States to publish national provisions online concerning CSP marketing communications, and to provide a summary thereof to the European Securities and Markets Authority (ESMA).[1] Through these requirements, the Crowdfunding Regulation aims to avoid that uncertainty as to the national legal framework will deter CSPs from providing their services on a cross-border basis.

14.04   The third goal is to monitor the enforcement of the national frameworks applicable to marketing communications. In the absence of complete harmonization in this area, the risk cannot be ruled out that certain competent authorities will proactively enforce their national laws, regulations, and administrative provisions, while other authorities will refrain from taking enforcement actions. Such an uneven enforcement would prevent the development of a level playing field for crowdfunding services in the EU. For this reason, Article 28 requires the competent authorities to periodically report to ESMA on the enforcement actions they have taken.

14.05   The remainder of this chapter proceeds as follows. Section II illustrates the requirements set forth by Article 27 in respect of marketing communications. Section III, in turn, focuses on Article 28, illustrating the role of the competent authorities and ESMA in the publication of national provisions on marketing communications, and on the monitoring of enforcement actions in this area. Finally, section IV presents some conclusions.

II.   Requirements Regarding Marketing Communications

14.06   This section illustrates the origin of the provision and draws a comparison with the Markets in Financial Instruments Directive II (MiFID II), since the latter served as a 'source of inspiration' for the provision (subsection II.1). Subsequently, the requirement of the identifiability of marketing communications is scrutinized, and a parallel is drawn with the analogous rules existing in the EU consumer acquis with reference to advertisement towards consumers (subsection II.2). Subsection II.3, in turn, analyses the requirement of identifiability in cases where the CSP outsources services to a third party. Subsequently, this part of the chapter discusses the obligation to provide fair, clear and not misleading information (subsection II.4), the language requirements in case of cross-border communication (subsection II.5), the prohibition of disproportionate targeting (subsection II.6), and the role of competent authorities in overseeing compliance with the national legal framework applicable to marketing communications (subsection II.7).

---

[1]   Recital 58 of the Crowdfunding Regulation, with reference to Art 28.

1. Origin of the Provision—Comparison with MiFID II

Articles 19 and 27 of the Crowdfunding Regulation contain the requirements regarding marketing communications for CSPs. Article 27(1) requires that that all marketing communications about the services of CSPs, including those outsourced to third parties, are clearly identifiable as such (see subsections II.2 and II.3). In addition, Article 19 states that all information, including marketing communications, from CSPs to clients about themselves, about the costs, financial risks, and charges related to crowdfunding services or investments, about the crowdfunding project selection criteria, and about the nature of, and risks associated with, their crowdfunding services should be fair, clear, and not misleading. Article 27(2) second paragraph repeats this requirement. According to Article 27(2) second paragraph, the information contained in a marketing communication must be fair, clear, and not misleading, and must be consistent with the information contained in the key investment information sheet (KIIS), if the KIIS is already available, or with the information required to be in the KIIS, if the KIIS is not yet available (see subsection II.4). It seems that the duplication is a consequence of the rigorous changes that the Commission's proposal was subject to in the first reading of the European Parliament. In the Commission's proposal, there was no provision similar to Article 27(2) second paragraph.   **14.07**

The marketing requirements in the Crowdfunding Regulation are similar to the marketing requirements set out in MiFID II. Article 24(3) MiFID II requires that all information, including marketing communications, addressed by the investment firm to clients or potential clients shall be fair, clear, and not misleading and that marketing communications shall be clearly identifiable as such. The only difference is in the term 'client'. In MiFID II, client is defined as 'any natural or legal person to whom an investment firm provides investment or ancillary services'.[2] As such, this term includes only the investors in crowdfunding projects, as these are the persons to whom the investment services are provided. This is only different where placement activities are conducted, since in that case, the project owners would (also) be considered the clients (issuer clients) under MiFID II.[3] By contract, the term 'client', as used in Article 19 of the Crowdfunding Regulation includes both the investors and the project owners, independent of the type of crowdfunding service that is provided. As a result, the marketing requirements for CSPs that operate under a MiFID II authorization (eg because the crowdfunding offers that can be put on their platform exceed the threshold of EUR 5 million) differ slightly in scope, compared to the marketing requirements that apply for CSPs under the Crowdfunding Regulation. In addition, the requirement in respect of the disproportionate targeting does not have an equal in MiFID II. In addition, whilst MiFID II includes more specific requirements in respect of marketing besides the general identifiability requirement and the 'fair, clear and not misleading' requirement (as further discussed in subsection II.4), the Crowdfunding Regulation remains silent in that respect.   **14.08**

---

[2] Art 4(1)(9) MiFID II.
[3] See Recital 59 Commission Delegated Regulation (EU) 2017/565 of 25 April 2016 supplementing Directive 2014/65/EU of the European Parliament and of the Council as regards organisational requirements and operating conditions for investment firms and defined terms for the purposes of that Directive (MiFID II Delegated Regulation).

2. Identifiability of Marketing Communications: A Comparison with the EU Consumer Acquis

14.09   Article 27(1) requires that marketing communications by CSPs are clearly identifiable as such. This provision, together with the aforementioned obligation to present 'fair, clear and not misleading' information, creates a regime that is seemingly comparable with the rules governing advertisement in the EU consumer acquis, and more specifically with the Unfair Commercial Practices Directive (UCPD).[4] In the EU consumer acquis, information duties are seen as a tool for consumer empowerment that ought to lessen the informational asymmetry between two contracting parties with disproportionate bargaining power.[5] According to Recital 14 of the UCPD, the Directive 'sets out a limited number of key items of information which the consumer needs to make an informed transactional decision'. In doing so, the UCPD pursues two interrelated goals which have been traditionally interpreted as procedural fairness (ensuring freedom of choice and an informed choice), and substantive fairness (ensuring a just bargain between consumer and trader).[6] As an illustration, in defining misleading actions, Article 6(1) UCPD refers to a number of elements which, when reflecting false information or untruthful presentations, can render a commercial practice unfair. Such elements include the main characteristics of the product (point b), the price or the calculation of the price (point d), the nature, attributes and rights of the trader or his agent (point f), or the consumer's rights (point g). With specific reference to the identifiability of advertisement, the UCPD sets forth an absolute presumption that a trader engages in an unfair commercial practice when 'using editorial content in the media to promote a product where [the] trader has paid for the promotion without making that clear in the content or by images or sounds clearly identifiable by the consumer (advertorial)'.[7] Hence, the Crowdfunding Regulation and UCPD are similar, inasmuch as they prevent respectively CSPs and traders from advertising their products or services without allowing the recipients of the communications to identify them as advertisement.

14.10   The requirement that advertisement is identifiable as such is a traditional limitation on the private freedoms enjoyed by commercial actors in markets around the world.[8] In the past decades, there has been a steady global trend in helping audiences recognize different types of speech and interests behind advertising (eg ad disclosures) in order to protect consumers from a situation in which asymmetrical information may manipulate their decision-making processes to the detriment of their interests. However, the proliferation of advertising on the Internet has complicated this consumer protection mission. New business models

---

[4] Directive 2005/29/EC concerning unfair business-to-consumer commercial practices in the internal market and amending Council Directive 84/450/EEC, Directives 97/7/EC, 98/27/EC and 2002/65/EC and Regulation (EC) No 2006/2004 (Unfair Commercial Practices Directive) [2005] OJ L 149.

[5] See for instance C Busch, 'Implementing Personalized Law: Personalized Disclosures in Consumer Law and Data Privacy Law' (2019) 86 University of Chicago Law Review 309; R Van Loo, 'Rise of the Digital Regulator' (2017) 66 Duke Law Journal 1267.

[6] A Giordano Ciancio, 'The Unfair Commercial Practices Directive and the UK Consumer Protection from Unfair Trading Regulations: A Possible Conceptual Convergence of General, Flexible European Standards and English Law Concepts Relevant to Fairness in the EU Context of Consumer Protection' (2008) <https://ssrn.com/abstract = 1099309>.

[7] Annex I(11) UCPD.

[8] D Lowenstein, 'Too Much Puff: Persuasion, Paternalism, and Commercial Speech' (1988) 56(4) University of Cincinnati Law Review 1205; A Tananbaum, '"New and Improved": Procedural Safeguards for Distinguishing Commercial from Noncommercial Speech' (1988) 88(8) Columbia Law Review 1821–48.

for digital advertisement have emerged, based *inter alia* on the social media communications by popular users, known as 'influencers' (influencer marketing).[9] Because it is hard to situate these new developments within the traditional landscape of advertising, the regulatory work done so far on revealing the commercial interests behind product placement, native advertising, or content marketing suffered an enforcement setback.[10] On social media, it may be practically difficult to distinguish between 'user-generated content', created and uploaded by a normal user, and 'monetization' undertaken by influencers who post content to promote certain goods or services, and earn revenue in doing so.[11] The underlying danger is that consumers will no longer be able to distinguish between ads and non-ads. The question thus arises whether and to what extent this type of concern applies to marketing communications by CSPs as well. Inasmuch as the boundaries of identifiability become blurry, Article 27(1) of the Crowdfunding Regulation may be difficult to enforce in practice.

To gain practical insights into how crowdfunding services are advertised on social media, **14.11** Facebook's Ad Library was consulted.[12] According to Facebook, 'the ad library provides advertising transparency by offering a comprehensive, searchable collection of all ads currently running from across Facebook apps and services, including Instagram'.[13] The US ad archive was consulted for examples of companies that buy advertising from Facebook,[14] with the goal of promoting their commercial message to particular demographics.[15] In addition, a brief search was conducted on TikTok potentially to reveal other stakeholders.[16] This exercise does not aim to provide a comprehensive overview of the landscape of actors involved in the marketing of crowdfunding services covered by the Crowdfunding Regulation but it can reveal important insights for a critical analysis of Article 27. On Facebook, crowdfunding-related advertisement is purchased not only by CSPs but also by project owners and consultancy companies. On TikTok, another category of advertising stakeholder is emerging: the *investment influencer*. With growing numbers of followers, investment influencers make content that promotes investments (including crowdfunding) to their followers. In this context, the boundaries between personal opinions and advertisement are often porous. While this evidence is anecdotal and further empirical investigation would be necessary to map the current reality of crowdfunding-related marketing communications, it seems that identifiability may become elusive in practice for crowdfunding-related advertisement. From this point of view, the enforcement of Article 27(1) of the Crowdfunding Regulation faces challenges that are similar to the ones faced by consumer law in general.

---

[9] C Goanta and S Ranchordás, *The Regulation of Social Media Influencers* (Edward Elgar 2020).
[10] AJ Campbell, 'Rethinking Children's Advertising Policies for the Digital Age' (2016) 29(1) Loyola Consumer Law Review 1.
[11] A Tsesis, 'Marketplace of Ideas, Privacy, and the Digital Audience' (2019) 94(4) Notre Dame Law Review 1585–630.
[12] Facebook Ad Library <https://www.facebook.com/ads/library>.
[13] ibid.
[14] The US version of the Facebook Ad Archive is the most comprehensive, as for other jurisdictions only a specific array of advertisements is visible (eg housing, employment). It is important to keep in mind that the results are thus focused on ads bought by US companies.
[15] The search string used on Facebook was 'crowdfunding investment'.
[16] The search string used on TikTok was the same as for Facebook.

3. Outsourcing to Third Parties

14.12   Pursuant to Article 27(1) of the Crowdfunding Regulation, the CSPs' obligation to ensure that marketing communications are identifiable as such applies not only when the CSP itself provides services to investors and/or project owners, but also when such services are 'outsourced to third parties'. When outsourcing, thus, the CSP has a duty to cooperate with and supervise the third party, to preserve identifiability.

14.13   When dealing with third parties, identifiability may be hard to monitor for the CSP. As already mentioned, the current reality of crowdfunding-related advertisement seems to be characterized by new business models, especially on social media, which blur the boundaries of what constitutes a 'marketing communication'. This development raises some delicate questions. First of all, the CSP may find it harder to ensure compliance with Article 27(1) when services are outsourced to third parties. Furthermore, these new advertisement models are shrouded in regulatory uncertainty, and different Member States may subject them to additional media or consumer law obligations. When outsourcing, thus, CSPs may need to consider different national regimes.

14.14   In case of outsourcing, the Crowdfunding Regulation does not extend the obligation to ensure identifiability to the third party. Therefore, the question whether the third party may be liable, if it fails to ensure identifiability, must be answered with exclusive reference to the applicable national law and/or contractual arrangements between the CSP and third party. The third party may, for instance, be liable in contract towards the CSP, whenever the outsourcing contract between CSP and a third party includes an obligation on the latter to ensure identifiability. In other cases, the third party may be liable in tort, depending on the applicable law and on the facts of the case.

14.15   Interestingly, in the near future, the Crowdfunding Regulation may interact with the Digital Services Act (DSA),[17] a draft Regulation that (if adopted) would update the e-commerce Directive,[18] and set forth a comprehensive regime for digital services in Europe. Pursuant to Article 24 of the DSA proposal, online platforms that display advertisement would have the obligation to 'ensure that the recipients of the service can identify, for each specific advertisement displayed to each individual recipient, in a clear and unambiguous manner and in real time … that the information displayed is an advertisement'. Thus, as a result of the interplay between the Crowdfunding Regulation and the DSA, when a CSP outsources services to a third party that will in turn advertise the services through social media, EU law will impose an obligation to ensure identifiability on the CSP (pursuant to Article 27 of the Crowdfunding Regulation) and on the social media platform (pursuant to Article 24 of the DSA, if adopted). By contrast, EU law would not directly impose such an obligation on the third party, and on any other links in the 'advertisement supply chain'. The question arises whether such a piecemeal approach is the best strategy to ensure the identifiability of marketing communications, especially in light of the aforementioned regulatory fragmentation

---

[17] European Commission, 'Proposal for a Regulation on a Single Market For Digital Services (Digital Services Act)' COM(2020) 825 final (European Commission, December 2020) <https://eur-lex.europa.eu/legal-content/EN/TXT/PDF/?uri = CELEX:52020PC0825&from = en>.

[18] Directive 2000/31/EC of the European Parliament and of the Council of 8 June 2000 on certain legal aspects of information society services, in particular electronic commerce, in the Internal Market.

and uncertainty concerning certain types of advertisement. This issue is particularly relevant, considering that CSPs form part of an evolving digital ecosystem that comprises numerous other stakeholders and 'third parties'.

4. Fair, Clear, and Not Misleading Content

Article 27(2) of the Crowdfunding Regulation requires that the information contained **14.16** in a marketing communication be 'fair, clear and not misleading'. As already mentioned, the rule is modelled after Article 24(3) MiFID II. However, despite the identical wording, the context of the two provisions is different. Articles 44 and 46 of the MiFID II Delegated Regulation set out a number of conditions that marketing communications must fulfil. As a result, the general notions of 'fair, clear and not misleading' information in MiFID II should not be read in isolation but interpreted in the light of the more specific rules on the provision of information to clients and potential clients.[19] These rules, as a whole, are meant to curb behavioural exploitation of investors.[20] By contrast, in Articles 19 and 27 of the Crowdfunding Regulation, the obligation to provide 'fair, clear and not misleading' information is not complemented by an equally detailed framework of obligations for the CSP. Thus, the Crowdfunding Regulation seems to place greater importance on the general notions of 'fair, clear and not misleading', which are the touchstone against which the CSP's compliance with marketing communications requirements should be tested. On the other hand, the absence of a frame of reference makes it difficult to assess compliance with Article 27(2) in practice, given the generality of the formulation.

Furthermore, Article 27(2) requires that the information contained in marketing commu- **14.17** nications is 'consistent with the information contained in the key investment information sheet'. Interestingly, however, the provision acknowledges the possibility that the marketing communication will be undertaken at a moment when the KIIS is not yet available. In this case, the marketing communication should be consistent with 'the information required to be in the key investment information sheet'. The CSP, therefore, will need to draft the marketing communication while already having in mind the contents of the future KIIS.

Importantly, even though the Crowdfunding Regulation requires consistency between the **14.18** KIIS and any marketing communication, the latter cannot merely replicate the former. In fact, pursuant to Article 23(7), the KIIS must be 'clearly distinguishable' from marketing communications. The same holds true for the KIIS at platform level, under Article 24(3).

---

[19] See Recital 61 MiFID II Delegated Regulation. See also Arts 36 and 37 MiFID II Delegated Regulation that contain additional organizational requirements in relation to marketing communications. The Crowdfunding Regulation does not impose similar organizational requirements.
[20] M Brenncke, 'The Legal Framework for Financial Advertising: Curbing Behavioural Exploitation' (2018) 19 European Business Organization Law Review 853.

5. Cross-border Dissemination of Marketing Communications and Translation

14.19   Article 27(3) requires that marketing communications be made in one or more official languages of the Member State in which the marketing communications are disseminated. Hence, when CSPs disseminate their marketing communications in more than one Member State, they may be required to translate their communications for each of those Member States. However, communications may also be made in a language accepted by the competent authority of the relevant Member State.

6. Disproportionate Targeting

14.20   Article 27(2) of the Crowdfunding Regulation states that, prior to the closure of raising funds for a project, no marketing communication shall disproportionately target planned, pending, or current individual crowdfunding projects or offers. The original wording of Article 27(2) in the Commission Proposal was different. It required that no marketing communication should comprise marketing of individual planned or pending crowdfunding projects or offers. Marketing communications could only indicate where and in which language clients could obtain information about individual projects or offers. The final wording of Article 27(2) of the Crowdfunding Regulation, by contrast, allows marketing of individual crowdfunding projects or offers as long as this does not disproportionately target such projects or offers. The final wording is therefore less strict than the wording that was proposed by the Commission. However, it is also less clear as there is no further guidance available as to what 'disproportionate' means. The question arises, for instance, whether it would be unlawful to highlight new crowdfunding projects on the homepage of the crowdfunding platform to inform investors about new investing opportunities. Taking into account the broad definition of marketing communication, this could be the case, although such an outcome could potentially not be in the interest of the investors. As such, we would welcome more guidance on this provision.

7. Role of Competent Authorities in Overseeing Compliance

14.21   The marketing communications of CSPs are governed by different laws, regulations, and administrative provisions in different Member States. Under Article 27(4) of the Crowdfunding Regulation, the competent authorities oversee compliance with these rules, and enforce them. However, Article 27(5) sets an important limitation: the competent authorities cannot impose an obligation on the CSPs to notify their marketing communications in advance, nor can they subject the CSPs' marketing communications to *ex ante* approval. The Regulation, hence, strikes a balance between the enforcement of the national legal framework applicable to marketing communications, and the need to ensure that such a framework will not make it excessively burdensome for CSPs to promote their services in all Member States where they operate. For completeness' sake, we note that CSPs need to include a description of their marketing strategy in their application for an authorization.

In accordance with the Annex to the draft regulatory technical standards (RTS) on the authorization process published by ESMA on 26 February 2021,[21] this description should include the languages of the marketing communications, and an identification of the Member States where advertisements will be most visible in media and expected frequency. As such, there is still some type of *ex ante* supervision on marketing, although not on the level of individual marketing communications.

III. Publication of National Provisions

Article 28 of the Crowdfunding Regulation pursues two interrelated goals. First, it aims to **14.22** 'provide more legal certainty'[22] for CSPs operating across the EU, by ensuring electronic access to the national laws, regulations, and administrative provisions applicable to marketing communications in different Member States. As already mentioned, regulatory divergences in this respect may deter CSPs from advertising their services in Member States other than the one in which they are established. Thus, ease of access to the different national framework is instrumental to facilitating market access. It remains to be seen whether Article 28 will be sufficient to ensure legal certainty in practice, or whether further harmonization of the law applicable to marketing communications will be necessary in the future. Pursuant to Article 45(2)(n) of the Crowdfunding Regulation, the 2023 Commission's report on the application of the Regulation should assess, *inter alia*, 'the effects that national laws, regulations and administrative provisions governing marketing communications of crowdfunding service providers have on the freedom to provide services, competition and investor protection'.

In addition, Article 28 aims to monitor the enforcement of these national regimes by the **14.23** competent authorities. There are certain risks inherent in the fact that different competent authorities are entrusted with the task of enforcing different frameworks on marketing communications. If the level of enforcement is uneven across the EU, this could result in uneven market access, with some Member States adopting a strict approach towards marketing communications while others maintain a 'hands off' stance. Such a divergence may also distort competition, favouring CSPs that operate in more 'liberal' Member States. In order to minimize these risks, the competent authorities must periodically report to ESMA on the enforcement actions they have taken, the outcomes, and the techniques to deal with non-compliance. This rule does not ensure an even level of enforcement *per se* but does at least allow for scrutiny.

1. Role of Competent Authorities in the Publication of National Provisions

The competent authorities designated pursuant to Article 29 of the Crowdfunding **14.24** Regulation are responsible for the publication of national laws, regulations, and

---

[21] ESMA, Consultation Paper; Draft technical standards under the ECSP Regulation, ESMA/35-36-2201, 26 February 2021, Annex VI Draft RTS pursuant to Article 12(16) of the ECSPR.
[22] Recital 58, Crowdfunding Regulation.

administrative provisions on marketing communications. In particular, under Article 28(1), they have a duty to publish these provisions on their website and keep them up-to-date. However, this duty only extends to those provisions that the competent authorities are responsible for overseeing compliance with and enforcement vis-à-vis CSPs. As a consequence, the website of the competent authorities may be practically insufficient for a CSP to gain a comprehensive picture of the national regime applicable to its marketing communications in a given Member State. By way of example, there may be national provisions of media or consumer law, which apply to the CSPs' marketing communications, but which are not enforced by the competent authority designated under Article 29. In light of this, Article 28(4) sets forth an additional provision: if the competent authorities are not responsible for overseeing compliance with certain laws, regulations and administrative provisions, they must publish on their website 'contact information', indicating where it should be possible to retrieve the relevant information. Furthermore, under Article 28(7), the competent authorities act as 'single points of contact responsible for providing information on marketing rules in their respective Member States'.

14.25   Apart from the publication of information on their own website, the competent authorities also have some notification duties towards ESMA. First of all, under Article 28(2), the competent authorities must notify ESMA of the laws, regulations and administrative provisions for which they oversee compliance. Secondly, they must provide ESMA with a summary of those provisions, 'in a language customary in the sphere of international finance'. Thirdly, pursuant to Article 28(4), they must notify ESMA of any change in the aforementioned provisions and update the summary 'without delay'.

2.   Role of ESMA in the Publication of National Provisions

14.26   ESMA has two main tasks with respect to the publication of national provisions on marketing communications. First, it streamlines the competent authorities' notifications under Article 28, drafting the relevant technical standards. Second, it facilitates access to the information provided by the competent authorities.

14.27   As far as standardization is concerned, ESMA published the draft implementing technical standards (ITS) on 26 February 2021.[23] Pursuant to Article 28(5), ESMA shall submit the draft ITS to the Commission by 10 November 2021, and the Commission has the power to adopt the ITS. The draft ITS set forth two different templates, depending on whether the competent authority's communication concerns the national laws, regulations, and administrative provisions (as per Article 28(2)), or changes in the information concerning those provisions (as per Article 28(3)). In case of a notification under Article 28(2), the ITS requires the competent authority to provide information on the type of national measure,[24] its official title, the translation of the official title in a language customary in the sphere of international finance, the date of entry into application, a hyperlink to an official website containing the full text of the instrument, and a summary of the notified instrument in a

---

[23] ESMA, 'Consultation Paper: Draft technical standards under the ECSP Regulation', ESMA35-36-2201, 26 February 2021.
[24] The competent authority must choose between law, regulation, and administrative procedure.

language customary in the sphere of international finance.[25] In addition, the template contains an optional space, where the competent authority can provide any additional information, if necessary. If a competent authority makes a notification involving multiple national measures, the aforementioned information must be provided separately for each measure.

In case of a notification under Article 28(3), the information to be provided according to **14.28** the draft ITS is similar but not identical. Once again, the competent authority is required to indicate the type of national measure, its official title, and translation thereof. In addition, however, the competent authority must indicate the dates of both adoption and entry into application of the notified instrument, which changes the information initially provided under Article 28(2). Furthermore, the template requires the provision of a hyperlink to the full text of the instrument. As for the provision of a summary in a language customary in the sphere of international finance, the ITS specifies that the competent authority should provide a summary of the instrument, 'as updated further to the changes notified' under Article 28(3).[26] The summary should therefore be of the entire amended instrument, and not only of the changes that have been made to it. Furthermore, the competent authority has the option to provide any additional information.

As for the goal of facilitating access to information, Article 28(6) requires ESMA to publish **14.29** on its website the summaries provided by the competent authorities, as well as the hyperlinks to the websites of the competent authorities. The aforementioned ITS should ensure that the information is presented consistently and clearly for all Member States. However, ESMA does not control the accuracy of the information notified by the competent authorities and cannot be held liable for the information provided in the summaries, pursuant to Article 28(6).

3. Competent Authorities Reporting to ESMA on Enforcement Actions

As already mentioned, Article 28 aims at facilitating the monitoring of the enforcement **14.30** actions undertaken by the competent authorities with respect to the national provisions on marketing communications. More specifically, Article 28(8) requires the competent authorities to report to ESMA regularly, and at least annually, on the enforcement actions taken during the previous year on the basis of their national provisions on marketing communications, with specific reference to:

(1) the total number of enforcement actions taken by type of misconduct;
(2) the outcome of these actions, including both the types of penalties imposed on CSPs, and the remedies provided by them; and
(3) examples of how the national authorities have dealt with the CSPs' failure to comply with the national provisions on marketing communications.

The information provided by the competent authorities under Article 28(8) can be useful not only to assess whether major discrepancies exist in the level of enforcement of national provisions across the EU but also to identify best practices as to how to react to

---

[25] ESMA, 'Consultation Paper' (n 23) 157.
[26] ibid 163.

non-compliance. By sharing this type of information with ESMA, the competent authorities may learn from each other and progressively develop a uniform approach to enforcement of their national provisions on marketing communications. However, should such a uniform approach fail to emerge, the question would arise whether the regulatory divergences in the field of marketing communications constitute an obstacle against the provision of crowdfunding services. As already mentioned, the Commission will be required to assess this issue in its report in 2023.[27]

14.31   In our view, the fact that the Crowdfunding Regulation contains this specific provision with regard to enforcement of marketing requirements underlines the importance that the European law-makers attach to sound marketing of crowdfunding projects.

IV. Conclusions

14.32   This chapter has presented a general overview of Chapter V of the Crowdfunding Regulation. While not setting forth a comprehensive regime for the marketing communications of CSPs, the Crowdfunding Regulation sets forth some important provisions in this respect. The requirement of identifiability of marketing communications draws direct inspiration from MiFID II and is comparable to similar requirements in the EU consumer acquis, and in particular in the UCPD. In practice, however, the emergence of new forms of advertisement and new media may make it increasingly difficult to distinguish between undisclosed advertisement and social media 'content'.

14.33   The requirement to provide 'fair, clear and not misleading' information also draws inspiration from MiFID II. However, the Crowdfunding Regulation does not contain any specific requirements detailing this general requirement, similar to the specific requirements included in the MiFID II Delegated Regulation. As a consequence, it remains to be seen whether Article 27 of the Crowdfunding Regulation will provide the necessary legal certainty in practice, despite the general wording of the provision. In any event, we do not expect any further harmonization of marketing requirements between the Member States to be achieved solely based on this general provision.

14.34   Chapter V of the Crowdfunding Regulation also aims at providing CSPs legal certainty and ease of access to the national provisions on marketing communications. The ITS published by ESMA should provide guidance as to how the information should be streamlined.

14.35   Finally, the competent authorities must report to ESMA on their enforcement actions in the field of marketing communications. It will be interesting to see if this reporting is an incentive for competent authorities to intensify their supervision on marketing communications, despite the competition between Member States to attract financial technology companies. In case of uneven levels of enforcement, further harmonization of the law applicable to the CSPs' marketing communications may prove necessary.

---

[27]   Art 45(2)(n), Crowdfunding Regulation.

15

Reward-based Crowdfunding, the Digital Single Market, and EU Consumer Law

Margarita Amaxopoulou and Mateja Durovic

I. Introduction

Every day, reward-based crowdfunding (RBC) backs a range of ideas—extraordinary or pe- **15.01** culiar, inspiring or remarkable, but each with the promise to make our lives easier or better in some way. RBC campaigns help small and medium-sized enterprises (SMEs) or even solo start-ups not only with financial support from the 'crowd' but also with marketing tools, as well as useful insights and information to realize their dreams and sell their innovative products.[1] This 'crowd' is often thought of as an amorphous mass of people and limited attention has been paid to the position of its members from a consumer protection law perspective;[2] however, individuals supporting an RBC-based project have legal rights that they should be able to rely on when things do not unfold as expected. While the Crowdfunding Regulation applies across the EU from 10 November 2021, it excludes RBC from its scope. Hence, the question arises: does the current consumer acquis adequately address the challenges raised by RBC, or should it be modernized to do so? In that regard, will the EU New

---

[1] See Recital 4, Regulation (EU) 2020/1503 of the European Parliament and of the Council of 7 October 2020 on European crowdfunding service providers for business and amending Regulation (EU) 2017/1129 and Directive (EU) 2019/1937 [2020] OJ L347/1.

[2] See, as an exception, J Biemans, 'Rewards-Based Crowdfunding and EU Consumer Rights' (2020) 28 ERPL 51, 67.

Deal for Consumers,[3] including the 'Omnibus Directive' 2019/2161[4] that is aimed to adapt consumer protection landscape to the digital market, contribute effectively to the legal protection of the crowd in instances of RBC?

15.02 This chapter examines the consumer protection law dimensions of RBC in the light of the EU legal framework on consumer protection, focusing foremost on the unfair commercial practices[5] and unfair contract terms regimes.[6] According to our analysis, RBC gives rise to novel legal puzzles that could cause complications concerning the applicability of the current consumer acquis. In spite of these complications, we maintain that the current acquis provides in principle a salient source of legal protection for the crowd, particularly once the reforms introduced by the 'Omnibus Directive' take effect in the year 2022. As a matter of fact, this Directive imposes strict requirements for platforms hosting RBC campaigns, heightening their responsibilities to protect consumer rights and potentially raising compliance costs.

15.03 That being said, we argue that the novel character of RBC stretches the conceptual boundaries of central consumer law provisions, giving rise to interpretative issues that may cause uncertainty as to the rights of the 'crowd' and the obligations of both platforms and project owners. In the case of unfair commercial practices, this is demonstrated, for example, by reference to the need to ensure that platforms will not be engaging in unfair actions or omissions against members of the crowd, in spite of certain practical difficulties to establish what might be perceived as misleading compared to conventional transactions. In the case of unfair contract terms, this is reflected in the difficulties for both consumers and project owners to establish what should be seen as satisfying the custom-based standard of good faith and the context-specific assessment of significant imbalance in the parties' rights and obligations. On the one hand, these difficulties may put crowd members at a disadvantage compared to project owners, threatening the practical assertion of their rights to redress as consumers. On the other hand, they may impose undue regulatory constraints on the innovative action of small-scale entrepreneurs and SMEs, assuming that they fit the conventional profile of a trader operating in a well-established marketplace. Bringing our arguments about the two frameworks together, we conclude by offering suggestions that will allow RBC to flourish but without sacrificing the legal protection granted to consumers backing original projects. We suggest that there is nonetheless further scope to modernize the legal treatment of RBC via EU consumer law by ensuring that the responsibilities are fairly distributed between platforms and project owners. Further regulatory guidance by EU policymakers will be needed to achieve this.

15.04 To substantiate this argument, we begin with an introduction to RBC (section II), before addressing the general applicability of the EU consumer protection acquis (section III). Then, we assess the challenges raised by RBC in the light of the Unfair Commercial

---

[3] European Commission, 'Review of EU consumer law—New Deal for Consumers' (11 April 2018) <https://ec.europa.eu/info/law/law-topic/consumers/review-eu-consumer-law-new-deal-consumers_en> accessed 12 April 2020. All links hereinafter were accessed on the same date.

[4] Directive (EU) 2019/2161 of the European Parliament and of the Council of 27 November 2019 amending Council Directive 93/13/EEC and Directives 98/6/EC, 2005/29/EC and 2011/83/EU of the European Parliament and of the Council as regards the better enforcement and modernisation of Union consumer protection rules [2019] OJ L328/7.

[5] Directive 2005/29/EC of the European Parliament and of the Council of 11 May 2005 concerning unfair business-to-consumer commercial practices [2005] OJ L149/22 'Unfair Commercial Practices Directive' (UCPD).

[6] Council Directive 93/13/EEC of 5 April 1993 on unfair terms in consumer contracts [1993] OJ L95/29 'Unfair Contract Terms Directive' (UCTD).

Practices Directive (UCPD) (section IV), followed by an examination of such challenges in the context of the Unfair Contract Terms Directive (UCTD) (section V). In doing so, we also consider the changes brought by the EU New Deal for Consumers. We conclude with suggestions for further modernization of the existing EU consumer law framework for the purposes of regulating RBC (section VI).

II. A Brief Overview of Reward-based Crowdfunding

RBC is an alternative source of funding for project owners (typically SMEs or individual entrepreneurs),[7] enabling them to finance small-scale projects.[8] Whereas a business may seek to raise funds directly via a campaign promoted on their own website ('direct crowd-funding'), most often, SMEs use a crowdfunding platform ('indirect crowdfunding' via, for example, Kickstarter or Indiegogo) to advertise a novel product or service that they seek, but are still unable, to launch.[9] The reasons for this inability may vary. For instance, the product may be in its early stages and need further financial support for the creation of the first prototype; in other cases, the first prototype may be already created, but there are additional costs for the manufacturing process or the scalability of the production.[10] Where crowdfunding platforms are used, RBC involves the following relational triangle: **15.05**

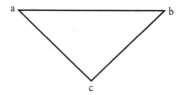

(a)   the **project owner**, initiating a project to be financially supported by RBC;
(b)   the '**crowd**', **giving money to back the project**;
(c)   the **platform that hosts this interaction** between the project owner and the crowd.

An RBC campaign typically consists of two elements: a 'call' and a 'promise'. First, the project owner calls for people to 'back' their project with a small amount of money. The project owner provides compelling reasons why one should support the project, explaining the problem that the project solves and why it is the best option existing in the market to date. Second, they promise that if this project gains the support it needs to bring the product or service into life, then the backers of the project will be given a 'reward', that is, a product or a service in exchange for their support.[11] This 'reward' in RBC is not a monetary incentive.[12] While it can take many forms depending on the contribution level, the following are the

---

[7] Problems may arise where individual entrepreneurs offering RBC are seeking to make a profit, but are not acting as a business, see below at subsection III.2.A. The terms 'SME', 'business', and 'entrepreneur' may be used interchangeably in this chapter to refer to project owners in the context of RBC campaigns.

[8] G Gabison, 'Understanding Crowdfunding and its Regulations' (2015) Joint Research Centre Science and Policy Report 26992, 20.

[9] A Tomczak and A Brem, 'A Conceptualized Investment Model of Crowdfunding' in R Harrison (ed), *Crowdfunding and Entrepreneurial Finance* (Routledge 2016) 53, 60–61.

[10] D Lavinsky, 'Funding fathers' (Smart Business, 17 August 2010) <http://www.sbnonline.com/article/fund ing-fathers-the-birth-of-business-crowdfunding-is-providing-new-ways-to-get-money/>.

[11] *Gabison* (n 8) 3.

[12] A Parhankangas, C Mason, and H Landström, 'Crowdfunding: An Introduction' in H Landström, A Parhankangas, and C Mason (eds), *Handbook of Research on Crowdfunding* (Edward Elgar 2019) 4.

most common 'rewards': (a) the very product or service that the business will create if their RBC campaign is successful at a discounted, 'early-bird' price (pre-order/pre-selling); (b) a different product or kind of service that the business can provide to the supporters; (c) some form of personal acknowledgement.[13]

15.06   To offer a particular hypothetical example: the start-up e-sports company 'Brain Gain' intends to develop a novel competitive video game that breaks new ground in the gaming industry by cultivating skillsets that are applicable to real-world employment for its players. The company pitches the game on Kickstarter.com and asks people to financially back their initiative in order to achieve their target of EUR 100,000. In return, Brain Gain promises that, once the game is created and ready to be released onto the market, the backers will receive a 50% discount on its market price. Martin, a passionate player of competitive video games, is excited by the project and would certainly want to purchase the game if it were available on the market. Enticed by the discount offered, he 'pledges' EUR 50 to the campaign. It is important to note that Martin will not pay this amount of EUR 50 immediately; for now, he only provides his bank account details. Only if the project 'tilts',[14] that is if the required amount of money that should be raised for the project by a particular set deadline is actually reached, will the pledged sums be debited from backers' bank accounts. Thus, it is the decision of several people to pledge in aggregation that constitutes the necessary prerequisite for the RBC campaign to be successful. Once the condition to raise EUR 100,000 is satisfied, Martin will be obliged to pay his pledge of EUR 50, and Brain Gain to provide the promised reward in the future. What happens, however, if Brain Gain receives Martin's money, but then the start-up reneges on its obligation? Does EU consumer law regulate the relationship between the two parties?

III. Applicability of the EU Consumer Protection Law Acquis to RBC

15.07   In purchasing the game at the discounted price, Martin and Brain Gain would conclude a standard sales contract, a type of contract for which European consumer law provides a range of rights and obligations—such as guarantee rights, information obligations, and withdrawal rights—subject, however, to particular requirements.[15] However, it is far from straightforward that all consumer rights can be asserted in the context of RBC, as this may depend, for example, on the classification of the contract under domestic law.[16] Even though RBC is excluded from the Crowdfunding Regulation's scope, the European

---

[13] E Mollick, 'The Dynamics of Crowdfunding: An Exploratory Study' (2014) 29 Journal of Business Venturing 1, 3; See also Johannes Wick, 'Pre-purchase Crowdfunding: ein atypischer Kaufvertrag außerhalb der Verbraucherrechterichtlinie' (2018) 2 Vebraucher und Recht 49 (unofficial translation: J Wick, Pre-purchase Crowdfunding: An Atypical Form of Sales Contracts outside the Consumer Rights Directive' (2018) 2 Consumers and the Law at A); *Biemans* (n 2) 57.

[14] *Biemans* (n 2) 57.

[15] Directive 1999/44/EC of the European Parliament and of the Council of 25 May 1999 on certain aspects of the sale of consumer goods and associated guarantees [1999] OJ L 171/12, though from 1 January 2022 Directive (EU) 2019/770 of the European Parliament and of the Council of 20 May 2019 on certain aspects concerning contracts for the supply of digital content and digital services [2019] OJ L 136/1 (guarantee rights); Directive 2011/83/EU of the European Parliament and of the Council of 25 October 2011 on consumer rights [2011] OJ L304/64 (information obligations and withdrawal rights).

[16] *Biemans* (n 2) 61. See also below at subsection IV.2.

Commission has stressed that 'EU consumer protection legislation already applies to reward-based crowdfunding with strict rules to safeguard consumers'.[17] In order to provide an explanation of this affirmation, we must clarify when consumer protection legislative frameworks apply, and why RBC meets these applicability requirements.

1. Who Is Who: 'Consumers' versus 'Traders'

Generally, EU consumer protection legislation applies when one party qualifies as a 'consumer' and the other party (or parties) as a 'trader'; certain directives or individual provisions may also require a particular type of contract (eg consumer credit contract) or contractual situation (eg distance selling contract). Despite an initial focus on the need to establish coherence in European consumer law,[18] there is no unified and overarching notion of who is a 'consumer' or a 'trader'; each individual directive on particular consumer rights has its own definition of these terms. In other words, the notions of 'consumer' and 'trader' are constructed in a way that fits the context of the applicable directive.[19] There is thus always a need to establish the applicability of a particular Directive by reference to its own definitions and scope of the concepts defined therein. However, regardless of the diversified wording found in EU Directives regarding the 'consumer' and 'trader' definitions, the legislation does contain a number of common characteristics for each: the 'consumer' is understood as (a) a natural person, (b) acting for purposes outside of their profession, while the 'trader' as (a) a natural or legal person who is (b) acting for purposes relating to his trade, business, craft, or profession. These elements are found in both focus areas of the present chapter, namely the UCPD and the UCTD,[20] two Directives of general, horizontal scope of application. The word 'acting' in the 'trader' and 'consumer' definitions in the majority of the EU consumer protection directives is particularly crucial for RBC as it is purposefully broad enough to encompass situations not initially foreseen by the EU legislator. Does this mean, however, that the definitions apply smoothly in the case of RBC?   **15.08**

2. The Parties in RBC: Backers, Project Owners, and Crowdfunding Platforms

In RBC, the 'crowd' members who are 'backing' a particular project, in principle, qualify as 'consumers'. They typically are natural persons 'acting' for purposes outside of their trade, business, craft, or profession. This 'acting' may consists of, for example, clicking through an RBC campaign's website, 'pledging' a certain amount of money in the campaign, paying it when the project 'tilts' in exchange for the reward they will be getting. Most often, the   **15.09**

---

[17] European Commission, 'Proposal for a Regulation of the European Parliament and of the Council on European Crowdfunding Service Providers (ECSP) for Business' COM(2018) 113 final, 2.

[18] European Commission, 'A More Coherent European Contract Law—An Action Plan' COM(2003) 68 final [31], [50], [73]; European Commission, 'Green paper on the review of the consumer acquis' COM(2006) 744 final, 11.

[19] For a detailed table with all the 'consumer' and 'trader' definitions in the consumer law acquis see W Schoenmaekers, 'The Notion "Consumer" in European Private Law' Master in Law Dissertation (2014) University of Ghent 70–78.

[20] (n 6). Note that the English version of the UCTD uses 'seller or supplier' rather than 'trader'. The French and German language versions of the Directive do not use equivalent terms, using the more general terms *professionnel* and *Gewerbetreibender*, respectively.

backers' actions relate to purposes that lie outside of their business or profession. Backers support an RBC campaign for 'what they will get out of it' in their personal lives,[21] for example because they will feel genuinely joyful, excited, or satisfied if they acquire and use the innovative product/service that is set as a reward in an RBC campaign in their everyday life.

15.10 The picture, however, gets a bit blurrier on the 'trader' side. The project owners typically fall under the definition of the 'trader', only if, as natural or legal persons, they are 'acting'—for example, advertising the product/service under development, promising to offer it at a certain price in the future in exchange of the financial support they are getting from the project 'backers', for purposes *relating to their trade, business, craft, or profession*. The commercial purpose of their activity is a very important element of the 'trader' definition and, in RBC, it is not always a given. As a culture of innovation becomes more and more widespread in our days,[22] some project owners may be individual inventors, who have an extraordinary project idea and want to 'make it happen' by utilizing every means possible.[23] These individual inventors may often differ significantly from corporate and business actors operating in well-established and conventional marketplaces; they may not have deep experience and knowledge in the related field, and may even have another profession. Hence, RBC project owners may be less or more experienced, work full- or part-time on their project, be more or less knowledgeable in their field, as well as more or less strategic about their business plan and strategy for making profits.[24]

15.11 The assessment becomes even more complex due to the fact that project owners may not be considered as 'traders', in spite of the alleged presence of one of those factors (having knowledge and experience for the product/service, organizational capacities, working full-time or part-time, gaining profit, etc), or despite the fact that they claim such a characterization for themselves.[25] For example, the circumstances that a project owner aspires to generate profit by developing a product or service through an online RBC campaign, and then selling its product, does not suffice for his/her characterization as a 'trader'.[26] A case-by-case approach is needed, with a holistic assessment of all those factors in each case, to decide whether a project owner in RBC is just an individual inventor, or whether the campaign is indeed conducted in the context of the project owner's business, and in order to support his/her commercial activity.[27] Not unexpectedly, consumers backing RBC campaigns may

---

[21] *Biemans* (n 2) 57.

[22] M Lounsbury and others, 'Culture, Innovation and Entrepreneurship' (2019) 21(1) Innovation: Organization and Management 1, 2.

[23] For motivations see also *Parhankangas, Mason and Landström* (n 12).

[24] Questions therefore arise whether an individual inventor meets the elements of the definition of 'trader'. In Case C-105/17 *Kamenova* ECLI:EU:C:2018:808 the ECJ refers in para 38 to a series of factors which may determine whether the definition of 'trader' is satisfied, among them are 'whether the sale on the online platform was carried out in an organised manner, whether that sale was intended to generate profit, whether the seller had technical information and expertise relating to the products which she offered for sale which the consumer did not necessarily have, with the result that she was placed in a more advantageous position than the consumer, whether the seller had a legal status which enabled her to engage in commercial activities and to what extent the online sale was connected to the seller's commercial or professional activity'. See also European Commission, 'Guidance on the implementation/application of Directive 2005/29/EC on unfair commercial practices' SWD(2016) 163 final, 2.1.

[25] The ECJ has clarified that 'the criteria ... are neither exhaustive nor exclusive, with the result that, in principle, compliance with one or more of those criteria does not, in itself, establish the classification to be used in relation to an online seller with regard to the concept of "trader"', see *Kamenova*, ibid, para 39.

[26] ibid.

[27] ibid 37.

not have a clear picture of the other person's legal status, and thus may not know which legal rights they would have, were something to go wrong.

EU regulators have taken some positive steps towards providing more clarity in this dir-   **15.12** ection. Under the New Deal for consumers, the recently introduced 'Omnibus Directive' provides that consumers must be clearly informed in online marketplaces on whether they are dealing with a trader or not.[28] This information disclosure requirement contributes to enhanced transparency for consumers in online environments such as RBC. How crowdfunding platforms will operationalize this information requirement will become apparent in 2022, once the EU Member States will have transposed the Directive into their national legal orders and begin to apply their newly created national legal provisions.[29]

The 'Omnibus Directive' may ultimately make a key contribution to solving the challenge   **15.13** concerning the classification of project owners as traders, yet another problem relates to the legal status of the platform hosting the RBC campaign. Does the crowdfunding platform fall within the scope of the 'trader' definition? The answer lies in another context-specific assessment: the platform that brings together project owners and backers will typically be a legal entity that qualifies as a 'trader' if it 'acts' for purposes relating to their trade and business.[30] This is most often the case when, for example, the crowdfunding platform charges project owners with a commission for its 'hosting service', that is, providing the online environment for the interaction between the project owner and the project backers. It will also qualify as a 'trader' if it provides extra paid services, such as 'premium' access to particular services (eg offering project owners the option to engage with a closed community of very generous and particularly active backers), or if it makes revenue from advertising in its environment. It is difficult to envisage a platform that does not engage in any kind of commercial activity, either through charging its users, or through generating revenue via advertising. Hence, in most cases, platforms will qualify as traders.

As it will be further elaborated in the end of the subsection IV.2 below, whenever the pro-   **15.14** ject owner is a trader, his/her relationship with the platform will be a business-to-business (B2B) relationship and the UCPD and UCTD will not apply. With regard to the platform's relationship with the crowd, the former also offers services to the latter, as it does with the project owners (eg matchmaking, offering access to exclusive crowd communities, etc). In this case, however, these services are directed to individuals that do not act for purposes relating to their trade, business, or profession, but act as consumers instead. Thus, in the context of this supply of services from the platform to the backers, the relationship between these two actors is a B2C relationship, and the above-mentioned Directives apply.

---

[28] Directive (EU) 2019/2161 (n 4) Recital 26, introducing Art 6a (Additional specific information requirements for contracts concluded on online marketplaces) to Directive 2011/83/EU.
[29] ibid Art 7.
[30] European Commission, 'Guidance on the Implementation/ Application of Directive 2005/29/EC on Unfair Commercial Practices' SWD (2016) 163 final (25 May 2016) 5.2.2 <https://eur-lex.europa.eu/legal-content/EN/TXT/?uri = CELEX:52016SC0163>.

IV. The Unfair Commercial Practices Directive in RBC:
Protective Thresholds and Interpretative Challenges

15.15   Assuming that the RBC actors match the 'profile' of a 'consumer' or a 'trader', there is still one important step to be taken to establish the applicability of the UCPD[31] and UCTD.[32] The Directives' definitions clearly state that the instruments refer to consumers and traders acting 'in commercial practices covered by this Directive'[33] and 'in contracts covered by this Directive',[34] respectively. Does RBC meet these criteria? The following sections answer this question by separately delving into the two instruments' applicability criteria, before elaborating on further challenges raised by their application to RBC. In principle, the UCPD applies to RBC campaigns, yet there are particular difficulties concerning the compliance of small companies with the framework, and a lack of clarity with regard to the precise expectations vis-à-vis the crowdfunding platform, leading to uncertainty for the realization of consumer claims. While the 'New Deal for Consumers' has taken some positive steps to modernize the consumer law acquis and render it more suitable for the digital economy,[35] certain challenges still remain. We start by referring to the scope of the UCPD with regard to RBC, before elaborating on the particular consequences of its application.

1. Background

15.16   To provide some background, the Directive was adopted in 2005 to enhance consumer confidence and create a level playing field for businesses of different sizes in cross-border trade.[36] The Directive's three main pillars are an exhaustive list of unfair commercial practices that are unequivocally outlawed,[37] a general clause prohibiting unfair commercial practices,[38] as well as specific clauses on misleading and aggressive practices.[39] The Directive is currently under amendment in the context of the 'New Deal for Consumers' initiative, with the introduction of the new 'Omnibus Directive'.[40] The modernized rules require the establishment of private redress mechanisms for the damage suffered by consumers involved in unfair commercial practices, as well as transparency in online marketplaces.

---

[31] UCPD (n 6).
[32] UCTD (n 6).
[33] UCPD (n 5) Art 2(a).
[34] UCTD (n 6) Art 2(b).
[35] (n 3).
[36] UCPD (n 6) Recitals 3 and 4 UCPD; see also European Commission, 'Proposal for a Directive of the European Parliament and of the Council concerning unfair business-to-consumer commercial practices in the internal market' COM(2003) 356 final 3–6. On Directive, see M Durovic, *European Law on Unfair Commercial Practices and Contract Law* (Hart Publishing 2016).
[37] ibid Annex I.
[38] ibid Art 5.
[39] ibid Arts 6, 7, 8–9.
[40] Directive (EU) 2019/2161 (n 4) Art 3.

2. Scope and Application to RBC

Does the scope of the UCPD raise specific complications for its application to RBC cam- **15.17**
paigns? The protection of consumers' interests that are *not* of an economic nature lie beyond the scope of UCPD; the latter does not preclude EU Member States to establish trade
restrictive measures for health, safety, or environmental reasons, to protect 'human dignity',
or to introduce measures relating to 'taste and decency'.[41] Thus, RBC campaigns involving
particular content such as pictures and videos showing nudity, or violent and antisocial behaviour, may be subject to national frameworks that are not covered by the UCPD. The same
applies to RBC campaigns involving a manufacturing process that is particularly harmful
for the environment, or if the offered reward involves risks for consumers' health and safety;
the protection of these interests falls outside of the scope of the UCPD.

Coming closer to the provisions of the Directive, the UCPD covers 'business-to-con- **15.18**
sumer (B2C) commercial practices ... before, during and after a commercial transaction
in relation to a product'.[42] The wide definition of these practices includes 'any act, omission,
course of conduct or representation, commercial communication ... by a trader, directly
connected with the promotion, sale or supply of a product to consumers'.[43] Where project
owners or online platforms qualify as 'traders' within the meaning of Article 2(b) UCPD, do
all *their* various actions *and* omissions in the context of an RBC campaign also fall under the
UCPD's umbrella?

Importantly, for the UCPD to apply, these actions and omissions must be commercial **15.19**
in nature,[44] that is, '*directly* connected with the *promotion, sale or supply* of a *product* to
consumers' (emphasis added).[45] A more careful look at these elements unravels the legal
puzzles arising in the context of the RBC. Under the recently amended UCPD, the term
'product' refers to 'any good or service including immovable property, digital service and
digital content, as well as rights and obligations'.[46] It is important to highlight that, in RBC,
we may have two different 'products': the product or service under development (by the
project owner) that lies at the heart of the crowdfunding campaign may not be the same
as the offered reward. For example, the product or service under development may be an
innovative electric motorbike, but the offered reward may be a (traditional) bike-repair service, or an acknowledgement and commemoration of the backer's name on a photograph
of the innovative bike. Both will qualify as 'products' pursuant to the UCPD; the *obligation*
itself to provide the small-value reward (eg the commemoration on the photograph or a
T-shirt printed with the campaign's logo, etc) is considered to be a 'product' under UCPD.

---

[41] See *European Commission, 'Guidance'* (n 30) 1.2.1.
[42] UCPD (n 6) Art 3(1).
[43] UCPD (n 6) Art 2(d). See also Case C-540/08 *Mediaprint Zeitungs- und Zeitschriftenverlag* ECLI:EU:C:2010:660, para 17; see also Joined cases C-261/07 *VTB-VAB Belgium NV* and C-299/07 *Galatea BVBA* ECLI:EU:C:2009:244, para 49.
[44] *Kamenova* (n 24) para 41; Case C-632/16 *Dyson* ECLI:EU:C:2018:599, para 30; Case C-391/12 *RLvS* ECLI:EU:C:2013:669, para 37.
[45] UCPD (n 6) Art 2(d). Case C-540/08 *Mediaprint Zeitungs- und Zeitschriftenverlag* ECLI:EU:C:2010:660, para 17; see also Joined cases C-261/07 *VTB-VAB Belgium NV* and C-299/07 *Galatea BVBA* ECLI:EU:C:2009:244, para 49.
[46] Directive (EU) 2019/2161 (n 4) Art 3(1)(a).

15.20   However, do we have a *promotion, sale, or supply* of these 'products' as defined in UCPD, Article 2(c) in the case of RBC? With regard to *promotion*, the assessment will depend on the means–ends relationship between certain commercial practices and the advertisement of the product/service under development. Only those actions that aim to promote the product will fall under this ambit, for example, a preview video highlighting the product/service's competitive advantages against existing solutions. Conversely, actions that are of a different nature (eg a call to the crowd to sign a petition in favour of animal rights in the context of an RBC campaign to fund an eco-friendly motor bicycle) fall outside of the scope of the Directive. The term *sale* is conventionally associated with goods, while the term *supply* is associated with services (and now also with digital content). If this product is the same as the reward (eg the reward is the eco-friendly motor bike itself, at 40% of its commercial price), then project owners aim at its 'pre-selling'; this means that their acts and omissions in the RBC campaign will be connected with the sale of the good or the supply of the service. When the reward is something else, for example, a decorative badge commemorating the backer's support in the campaign, then the question arises whether the project owners' acts and omissions in the context of the RBC campaign are (directly) connected with the presale of the badge. In this respect, there is an interplay between the UCPD and the Consumer Rights Directive, as the latter defines 'sales' and 'services' contracts.[47]

15.21   Biemans has drawn an important distinction when analysing the applicability of Consumer Rights Directive in RBC: if consumers support the crowdfunding campaign by paying an amount of money and are just rewarded with an item (eg a badge or a photograph) which, in terms of its value, has no relationship with the payment made, then this most probably qualifies as a *donation* and not as a sale (if it is a product) or supply (if it is a service) of the set reward.[48] This means that, in that case and for UCPD purposes, project owners' actions and omissions cannot be connected with the reward's sale or supply in their strict sense. In such cases, (where a campaign's reward is something different than the campaign's product and small in value), it is rather questionable whether a 'supply' of a 'product' exists under the UCPD. Further guidance is needed from EU regulators in this regard, to clarify whether acts or omissions associated with such small-value rewards are to be seen as donations or charitable acts, as opposed to a sale of goods or provision of services falling under the EU consumer law acquis.

15.22   Lastly, the commercial practices of project owners in an RBC campaign need to be *directly* connected with the promotion, sale, or supply of a product. The EU Commission, in its guidance document regarding the application of the UCPD, has clarified that 'it is difficult to define a limit for when a commercial practice would no longer be 'directly connected' to the promotion of a product'.[49] However, it is apparent in the document that this connection requirement is not constructed in an overly restrictive way. In RBC, when the 'product' under creation/development also constitutes the reward (eg at a discounted/early

---

[47]   Consumer Rights Directive, Art 2 Nos 5 and 6. Sales contract as defined in Art 2 No 5 is any contract under which the trader transfers or undertakes to transfer the ownership of goods to the consumer and the consumer pays or undertakes to pay the price thereof, including any contract having as its object both goods and services and 2(6) services contract means any contract other than a sales contract under which the trader supplies or undertakes to supply a service to the consumer and the consumer pays or undertakes to pay the price thereof.

[48]   *Biemans* (n 2) 61.

[49]   See *European Commission, 'Guidance'* (n 30) 2.2.

bird price), the affirmation of the required direct connection is straightforward: commercial practices of project owners—for example, presenting and advertising the innovative product/service—are *directly* connected with the promotion, sale or, supply of this very product/service under development. In cases, however, where the product or service under development is something different than the reward, does this differentiation disrupt the direct connection required by UCPD? The answer is that project owners' commercial practices will in most cases be directly connected with a product's promotion, sale, or supply. Actions and omissions revolving around the differentiated reward (eg making backers click through the 'pledging' website with colourful blinking signals, or providing the payment mechanism for the selected reward) will be *directly* connected with at least the promotion, if not the sale or the supply, of the main 'product' reward itself.

Assuming that these hurdles are overcome for the project owners, an additional concern **15.23** arises about the intermediary platform hosting the RBC campaign. Does the crowdfunding platform also engage in B2C commercial practices that fall under the scope of the UCPD? As mentioned in the previous section, platforms will typically qualify as 'traders' as they are acting for purposes relating to their trade and business. As far as their relationships with the platform are concerned, backers will qualify as 'consumers' within the meaning of Article 2(a) UCPD, so that the B2C criterion will in principle be met. However, with regard to the platform's relationship with project owners, we need to distinguish between two cases. When the project owners are only individual inventors acting outside of their trade or business, then indeed their relationship with the platform is a B2C relationship, and the platform is liable towards them as it is for the crowdfunding backers. More specifically, the platform in that case acts as the 'trader' that supplies the service of online hosting to the project owners. As already stated in a previous section, when project owners use the platform services for purposes relating to their business, their relationship with the platform is a B2B relationship, and the UCPD will not apply. This relationship, however, is not left unregulated. Other legal instruments come into play, most notably the P2B (Platform to Business) Regulation, which addresses transparency and fairness issues arising in the relationship between businesses (project owners, in the case of RBC) and actors providing online intermediation (crowdfunding platforms, in the case of RBC).[50]

3. Implications of the Application of the UCPD to RBC

Having presented these challenges about the scope of the UCPD, we now move to the con- **15.24** sequences of applying the UCPD to RBC campaigns. Project owners that are 'traders' and engage in B2C commercial practices shall not conduct any of the practices exclusively listed and prohibited in Annex I of the UCPD. When engaging in the promotion, sale, or supply of a product to consumers, they shall refrain from misleading actions, omissions or aggressive practices as defined in Articles 6, 7, and 8 UCPD, respectively. Lastly, they shall act with a degree of a professional diligence as required by the general clause prohibiting unfair commercial practices in Article 5(2) UCPD. These legal obligations may carry significant

[50] Regulation (EU) 2019/1150 of the European Parliament and of the Council of 20 June 2019 on promoting fairness and transparency for business users of online intermediation services OJ L 186/57.

compliance costs that are borne more easily by established large businesses than by SMEs. Since the consumer protection acquis supplements the EU competition regulatory regime and the goal for the internal market enhancement through the creation of a level playing field for traders, this factor shall be taken into serious consideration. The legal requirements for project owners engaging in RBC should be clarified with further guidance and presented in an accessible way.

15.25   Traders aside, our main focus here remains the implications for the legal protection of the consumer 'crowd'. The practical enforcement of consumers' rights may be threatened by the difficulties in applying the UCPD to platforms, with reference to the nature and extent of their obligations under the Directive. Insofar as the crowdfunding platform qualifies as a 'trader' engaging in B2C commercial practices, it is subject to the same obligations listed above for project owners. In other words, legal obligations arise when the crowdfunding platform offers matchmaking services and other (premium) services to its consumers (ie to the backers in RBC, or to project owners that will not qualify as traders). More specifically, traders are required, whenever engaging in the promotion, sale, or supply of a product, to refrain from misleading their consumers by either action or omission[51] and 'act with a degree of professional diligence',[52] 'commensurate to its specific field of activity'.[53] Compared to established online marketplaces selling widely known products (eg Amazon), however, crowdfunding platforms may face two serious difficulties: the lack of capacity and resources to gain certain information about the products advertised under their auspices, and the originality of the advertised products which may (often) not have been created at the time of launching an RBC campaign.

15.26   How does the current EU consumer law envisage the responsibility of RBC platforms in that regard? While not, strictly speaking, a UCPD matter, an important distinction that should be made to assess platforms' capacity to fulfil their obligations in this context relates to whether platforms play an 'active' or a 'passive' role in online commerce. The ECJ has concluded that platforms play an 'active' role when they provide 'assistance which entails, in particular, optimising the presentation of the offers for sale in question or promoting them'.[54] On the other hand, platforms play a 'passive' role when they have limited capacity to have 'knowledge of or control of the data stored',[55] and to shape, for example, the content of the presentations created on their website due to the originality of their users' content. Crowdfunding platforms, depending on their functions, may fall under the first or the second category. A platform will play an 'active' role if, for example, it intervenes in the content of an RBC campaign, or prioritizes some RBC campaign over another by showing it first in the search results. In the rare case that the crowdfunding platform does not have control over the stored data associated with project owners' campaigns, it would be closer to the 'passive' end of the spectrum.

---

[51]   UCPD (n 6) Arts 6(1)(f), 7(2).

[52]   ibid Arts 5(2) and 2(h).

[53]   *European Commission, 'Guidance'* (n 30) 5.2.2.

[54]   Case C-324/09 *L'Oréal* ECLI:EU:C:2011:474, para 123–124.

[55]   ibid. See also recital 42 of Directive 2000/31/EC of the European Parliament and of the Council of 8 June 2000 on certain legal aspects of information society services, in particular electronic commerce, in the Internal Market ('e-Commerce Directive') [2000] OJ L 178/1.

Crowdfunding platforms, either in an 'active' or 'passive' position, are considered to be **15.27**
'traders' if they meet the requirements of Article 2(b) UCPD;[56] in this case, 'they are required to act with a degree of professional diligence'.[57] Nonetheless, the characterization of
whether the platform plays an 'active' or 'passive' role is important with regard to the interpretation of the meaning of 'professional diligence' under the general assessment of (un)
fairness pursuant to Article 5(2)(a) UCPD, which is assessed when a breach of Articles 6
or 7 cannot be substantiated.[58] According to Article 5(2) UCPD, a commercial practice is
unfair if '(a) it is contrary to the requirements of professional diligence, and (b) it materially
distorts or is likely to materially distort the economic behaviour with regard to the product
of the average consumer whom it reaches or to whom it is addressed'. Failing to demonstrate
'professional diligence' may, thus, result in 'misleading omission' claims (Article 7 UCPD)
against a crowdfunding platform, if the latter does not inform potential backers about certain aspects of an RBC campaign. What kind of aspects might these be?

Professional diligence as defined in Article 2(h) UCPD refers to 'the standard of special **15.28**
skill and care which a trader may reasonably be expected to exercise towards consumers,
commensurate with honest market practice and/or the general principle of good faith in
the trader's field of activity'. It reflects notions of 'honest market practices' or 'good faith' already existing in EU Member States.[59] While 'professional diligence' has been further elaborated in established trade sectors in different EU jurisdictions,[60] its boundaries are much
less established with respect to crowdfunding platforms.[61] The extent of this 'special skill
and care' that the platform is required to demonstrate in RBC is thus unclear. The European
Commission in its guidance has noted that 'platforms which are considered "traders",
should take appropriate measures which—without amounting to a general obligation to
monitor or carry out fact-finding (see e-Commerce Directive,[62] Article 15(1))—enable
relevant third party traders to comply with EU consumer and marketing law requirements, and users to clearly understand with whom they are possibly concluding contracts'.[63]
Importantly, this aspect of 'professional diligence' duties has been incorporated into the
New Deal for Consumers, as now the 'Omnibus Directive' requires that platforms clearly
indicate whether the project backers will be concluding a contract with a trader, or another
private individual.[64] However, it is questionable how platforms can effectively design their

---

[56] *European Commission, 'Guidance'* (n 30) 5.2.2.

[57] ibid.

[58] Case C-435/11 *CHS Tour Services* ECLI:EU:C:2013:574, para 45: 'having regard both to the wording and to
the structure of Articles 5 and 6(1) [UCPD], and to its general scheme, a commercial practice must be regarded
as "misleading" within the meaning of the second of those provisions if the criteria set out there are satisfied,
and it is not necessary to determine whether the condition of that practice's being contrary to the requirements
of professional diligence, laid down in Art 5(2)(a) [UCPD], is also met'. Confirmed in Case C-388/13 *UPC*
ECLI:EU:C:2015:225, paras 61–63.

[59] *European Commission, 'Guidance'* (n 30) 3.2.

[60] See eg the Decision no DKK 6/2014 of The Urząd Ochrony Konkurencji i Konsumentów (Polish Office of
Competition and Consumer Protection) which acted against a trader providing satellite television services on the
grounds that it had not shown 'professional diligence'.

[61] This is also problematic with respect to project owners. In RBC, the campaigns may be devoted to the development of a good/or a service that is truly innovative, and the whole process may be more experimental than
expected. In such 'innovation stories' it is very unlikely for the project owner to have a long history engaging in the
development or sale/supply of this good/service.

[62] Directive 2000/31/EC of the European Parliament and of the Council of 8 June 2000 on certain legal aspects
of information society services, in particular electronic commerce, in the Internal Market ('Directive on electronic
commerce') OJ L 178.

[63] *European Commission, 'Guidance'* (n 30) 5.2.2.

[64] Directive (EU) 2019/2161 (n 4).

systems so as to enable project owners to inform consumers in a way that will not result in misleading actions or omissions in the absence of a fact-finding obligation. In many cases, the project owners' original products/services will be first of their kind and thus new to the public eye, resulting in uncertainty as to what kind of information is needed to achieve clarity for consumers. To what lengths should platforms go to investigate whether certain RBC campaigns are delivering on their promises? How will it be established that innovative and novel products that have not yet been created will correspond to the expectations of the backers? All these, and many similar questions will need to be considered by 'professionally diligent' platforms, and tackling them might require a significant investment in resources.

15.29   Considering the rise in compliance costs engendered by such difficulties for platforms, questions arise about the practical and effective realization of consumer rights, and whether the recently introduced 'Omnibus Directive' will really enhance the protection of these rights.[65] More specifically, this Directive brings a fundamental change to the consumer law acquis regarding the enforcement of the UCPD. From 2022 onwards, there will be a mandatory private redress mechanism for consumers who have suffered from unfair commercial practices. In other words, consumers who have suffered harm from unfair or misleading actions and omissions shall now have 'proportionate and effective remedies including compensation for damage suffered … and where relevant a price reduction or the termination of the contract'.[66] In RBC, backers may seek redress from project owners or online platforms (when they qualify as 'traders') that have engaged in B2C unfair commercial practices harming the backer. Under the new provisions, Member States 'shall lay down the rules on penalties' which means that, they could impose fines up to (at least) 4% of the trader's annual turnover (or up to EUR 2 million when turnover information is not known).[67] This framework implements a stricter regime towards all traders; this may be particularly onerous for platforms, which could find themselves in the crossfire between backers and project owners, considering the above-mentioned uncertainties about the requirement of 'professional diligence' in this context. This lack of balance threatens to create practical difficulties for consumers bringing their claims for redress forward, potentially limiting their options to seek redress against individual project owners without a stable and reliable economic infrastructure. The next section grapples with challenges arising for the protection of the 'crowd' in RBC in the context of the UCTD.

V. Unfair Contract Terms Directive: 'Good Faith' in the Brave New World of RBC

1. Background

15.30   The UCTD[68] is one of the most important Directives in the consumer protection acquis, currently under amendment after the introduction of the 'Modernization Directive'.[69] To

---

[65] Directive (EU) 2019/2161 (n 4).
[66] Directive (EU) 2019/2161 (n 4) inserting a new article to UCPD, Art 11(a) para 1.
[67] ibid Art 3, replacing UCTD art 13.
[68] UCTD (n 6).
[69] Directive (EU) 2019/2161 (n 4) Art 1.

provide some background, the UCTD, when created in 1993, was one of the first brave steps of the EU towards the establishment of not only a homogenous consumer law framework, but also a 'European approach to fairness'.[70] This is because at the heart of the Directive lies the general unfairness clause whereby the assessment is made on whether a contractual term is unfair. The Directive constitutes a regulatory intervention on the freedom of contract; it disrupts the general principle of *pacta sunt servanda* to empower consumers who find themselves trapped in contractual arrangements involving unfair contract terms. The rationale behind this protection is that, in the majority of consumer contracts, the contractual parties do not hold the same amount of information and level of knowledge about the subject matter of the transaction, nor do they have the same level of bargaining power. When this power is abused by the trader, who typically holds a great amount of information about the product or service provided, this asymmetry justifies regulatory intervention in order to protect the consumer as the weaker party. While this seems to be introducing 'an insurance-like, welfarist approach to consumer protection',[71] there are certain limitations in scope.

2. Scope and Application to RBC1

The UCTD, while covering all economic sectors, *only* applies to consumer contracts, that is, between a 'seller or supplier' and a 'consumer' (B2C),[72] and *only* to the contractual terms which have *not* been individually negotiated. Moreover, 'contractual terms which reflect mandatory statutory or regulatory provisions and provisions or principles of international conventions' are not subject to the Directive.[73] With regard to the parties' legal status in spite of the different wording on 'seller or supplier' vis-à-vis 'trader' in the UCPD, the respective definitions overlap.[74] Regarding the terms that could fall under the unfairness assessment, the UCTD clarifies that terms are considered as not individually negotiated if they are drafted in advance and the consumer has therefore not been able to influence their substance.[75] In other words, this refers to standard and pre-formulated contract terms, very often found in 'take-it-or-leave-it' contracts.   **15.31**

Such contracts are, arguably justifiably, the standard practice adopted in the context of RBC. Standard terms and conditions allow for more efficiency in commercial transactions, especially where the terms are to be used for a vast number of transactions. They enormously simplify the tasks of internal administration within a business unit, the status of the transaction, orderly fulfilment, orderly planning, etc. In case of the RBC, there are potentially thousands of consumers who would like to contribute to the funding, and thus standard contracts are a justified approach for the project owners and the platforms. That being said,   **15.32**

---

[70] G Howells, C Twigg-Flesner, and T Wilhelmsson, *Rethinking EU Consumer Law* (Routledge 2018) 129.

[71] ibid 131.

[72] According to UCTD Art 2(c)a 'seller or supplier' is 'any natural or legal person who ... is acting for purposes relating to his trade, business or profession, whether publicly owned or privately owned' while 'consumer' is 'any natural person who ... is acting for purposes which are outside his trade, business or profession'. See also Case C-290/16 *Air Berlin* ECLI:EU:C:2017:523, para 44.

[73] UCTD (n 6) Art 1(2).

[74] UCPD (n 6) Art 2(b).

[75] UCTD (n 6) Art 3(2). According to the same article and section, the burden of proof that a term has been individually negotiated lies on the seller or supplier who makes that claim.

it is certainly the case that the risks for consumer rights that are applicable in this type of contracts are also present in RBC. Such contracts effectively remove the bargaining process between the parties or reduce it to a very thin and superficial exercise, rendering freedom of contract a theoretical construct rather than a tangible reflection of transactional realities. Since RBC contracts concluded are not individually negotiated, they include standard terms and conditions offered by the one party and agreed and signed upon by the other. These contracts are 'adhesion contracts', meaning that their terms and conditions are previously set up and cannot be erased, modified, or added.

15.33   Furthermore, in terms of applicability of the UCTD to RBC, the B2C relationship is a necessary prerequisite. When this element is affirmed, the contract will fall within the scope of the Directive. As discussed above, this will most often be the case for contracts concluded between the project owner and the backers, as well as for the contracts between the crowdfunding platform and the backers, but not between the crowdfunding platform and the project owner.[76] The latter typically acts for purposes relating to their trade, business, or profession and thus qualifies as a 'seller or supplier' under the UCTD. This means that in their relationship with the platform, the project owner will not enjoy the protection offered by UCTD; rather, as already mentioned in subsection IV.2, this relationship will be regulated by other legal instruments, such as the P2B Regulation.[77] In other words, the UCTD mainly protects the members of the crowd in RBC as backers. This is consistent with the broader rationale of the UCTD, particularly considering that the informational and bargaining power asymmetry is truly inherent in RBC, due to the originality of the product/ service under creation. The project owner has a deep knowledge about their product's attributes and characteristics, as they are not only an actor promoting or selling the product but they conceived the very idea of it in the first place. Along similar lines, the crowdfunding platform has much greater knowledge about the service it provides, that is, the hosting of the RBC campaign, than what the consumer understands when agreeing to use their service online.

15.34   As may have already become apparent from the present discussion, unlike the unfair commercial practices framework (which applies independently of whether there is a contract between the trader and the consumer), the UCTD requires a given contract, as it focuses on the validity of the contract's terms. If a particular contract term is considered to be unfair, then this term is not binding on the consumer.[78] How should we assess the fairness or unfairness of a term set by the project owner or the platform in the context of RBC? The next section addresses this question, by outlining the main legal obligations that these actors hold and identifying certain practical difficulties with regard to the assertion of the backers' rights.

---

[76] With the caveat of the project owner acting for purposes not relating to their trade, trade, business, or profession (B2C relationship between the platform and the project owner), see subsection IV.2.

[77] (n 50).

[78] UCTD (n 6) Art 6(1).

3. Implications of Application of the UCTD to RBC

The UCTD provides two main toolkits for the assessment of contractual terms. First, it pro- **15.35**
vides a non-exhaustive list of indicative value, with consumer contract terms that may be regarded as unfair.[79] According to the examples of this list, in the RBC context, a term would
be unfair if it excluded the project owner's liability for the personal injury incurred by the
backer, resulting from an act or omission of the project owner.[80] Another example would
be a term that enables the project owner to alter the terms of their contract with the backer
'unilaterally without a valid reason which is specified in the contract'.[81] However, due to the
indicative nature of this list, contract terms 'should not automatically be considered unfair'
when they reflect an example mentioned in the Annex; rather, 'their unfairness still has to
be assessed in the light of the general criteria defined in Articles 3(1) and 4 of the UCTD'.[82]
Nevertheless, the European Court of Justice (ECJ) has emphasized that the list constitutes
an important element in the assessment of the unfairness of the contract terms, having particular weight in the overall assessment.[83]

The criteria of Articles 3 and 4 of the UCTD constitute the second toolkit of the Directive **15.36**
and its main power, as they contain and specify the general unfairness clause. According to
the latter, a standard contract term is unfair[84] 'if contrary to the requirement of good faith,
it causes a significant imbalance in the parties' rights and obligations arising under the contract, to the detriment of the consumer'.[85] In order to unveil the practical difficulties that
arise in the context of RBC, we shall take a careful look at the 'good faith' requirement of
this provision. With regard to the first element of the clause, that is, the good faith principle,
the Recitals of the UCTD clarify that 'the requirement of good faith may be satisfied by the
seller or supplier where he deals *fairly* and *equitably* with the other party whose legitimate
interests he has to take into account' (emphasis added).[86] The ECJ has explained that 'fairly
and equitably' is assessed by reference to whether the seller or supplier could reasonably
assume that the consumer would have agreed to such a term in individual contract negotiations,[87] if they had the chance to individually negotiate the term. As the previous analysis
of the UCPD has indicated, however, this requirement may prove to be complicated for the
novel landscape of RBC. Assessing whether a particular business practice is 'fair' and 'equitable', as well as whether 'reasonable' assumptions can be made about consumers agreeing
to it if negotiated independently, requires rich knowledge about the subject matter, and experience of previous practices in the relevant sector. In the case of RBC, some practices may
easily yield the conclusion that they are not conducted in good faith. For example, a project

---

[79] UCTD (n 6) Art 3(3) and Annex.

[80] ibid Annex 1(a).

[81] ibid Annex 1(j).

[82] Commission notice, 'Guidance on the interpretations and application of Council Directive 93/13/EEC on unfair terms in consumer contracts' OJ C323/4 (27 September 2019) 3.4.7 <https://eur-lex.europa.eu/legal-content/
EN/TXT/?uri = uriserv:OJ.C_.2019.323.01.0004.01.ENG>.

[83] Case C-472/10 *Invitel* ECLI:EU:C:2012:242, para 26.

[84] Albeit with the exception of the terms that are not subject to the unfairness test, ie the terms that relate the
definition of the main subject matter of the contract or the adequacy of the price and remuneration, on the one
hand, as against the services or goods supplies in exchange, on the other as specified in UCTD Art 4 (2).

[85] UCTD (n 6) Art 3(1).

[86] UCTD (n 6) Recital 16.

[87] C-415/11 *Mohamed Aziz v Caixa d'Estalvis de Catalunya, Tarragona i Manresa (Catalunyacaixa)*
ECLI:EU:C:2013:164, paras 68 69.

owner would not act in good faith, if a term stipulated that the backers will receive their pre-selling discount as a reward *only if* they reiterate their support to the project within ten hours of the project's successful 'tilting'. That being said, the very conception of this example is indicative of the relative infancy of RBC as a commercial phenomenon. Many other cases may prove to be hard ones, giving rise to contested and diverging interpretations as to what is 'fair', 'reasonable' and 'equitable'. Guidance by EU policymakers is needed to help all parties of the RBC triangle navigate these difficulties, until RBC becomes much more established and well-understood.

15.37   Further, the UCTD also involves transparency requirements for the contractual terms that have not been individually negotiated.[88] More specifically, the Directive requires contractual terms to be drafted in plain and intelligible language.[89] According to this requirement, contractual terms should not be hidden; they should be communicated to the consumer in a direct and appropriate manner (eg avoiding confusing small print).[90] Hence, a contractual term can be declared unfair simply because its presentation is unclear.[91] In the context of RBC, where the consumer is provided with the terms of the contract in e-forms, these terms have to be presented in a manner that is plain and clear, with appropriate fonts and colours so that the terms 'are given the prominence they deserve'.[92] In addition, the contract terms must be comprehensible to the consumer. This means that, in RBC contracts, terms must not be presented in an overly complex manner (using overly technical terms) so the consumer is able to understand their true meaning, without requiring specialist legal knowledge.[93] This is in line with the approach that considers information as a privileged instrument for consumer protection. However, this transparency requirement concerns not only the linguistic aspects and the formal presentation of the term but it requires, in addition, that the real consequences of the term should also be economically understandable to the consumer.[94] In other words, the contractual term must not only be 'formally and grammatically intelligible' to the consumer, but the latter should be 'in a position to evaluate ... the economic consequences for him which derive from it'.[95] Do the transparency requirements match the realities of RBC in practice, when it comes to consumers' understanding of the contractual terms?

15.38   There are certain limits as to the extent to which backers will be substantively understanding all the terms of an RBC campaign. Even in more conventional and established marketplaces, the truth is that there are salient doubts as to consumers' actual engagement with standardized terms and conditions. Furthermore, there are certain 'transaction costs', for example, investing considerable amounts of time or paying for legal advice, which make it less likely that consumers will have an informed opinion about the substance of the terms.[96] This means that project owners and crowdfunding platforms shall take appropriate steps to

---

[88]   UCTD (n 6) Arts 4(2) and 5.

[89]   ibid.

[90]   *Commission notice* (n 82) 3.3.1. See also Case C-191/15 *Verein für Konsumenteninformation v Amazon*, point 2 of the operative part and paras 65–71.

[91]   ibid.

[92]   *Commission notice*, ibid.

[93]   ibid 3.3.1, 3.4.6.

[94]   Case C-186/16 *Andriciuc* ECLI:EU:C:2017:703 paras 44 and 45.

[95]   C-26/13 *Árpád Kásler, Hajnalka Káslerné Rábai v OTP Jelzálogbank Zrt* ECLI:EU: C:2014:282 paras 71–72; C-96/14 *Jean-Claude Van Hove v CNP Assurances SA* ECLI:EU:C:2015:262 para 40.

[96]   *Howells, Twigg-Flesner and Wilhelmsson* (n 70) 99, 131.

make sure consumers comprehend what they are signing for. For example, the web environment shall be structured in such a way that the consumer must pass through many steps (eg consent boxes) that would include separately—in big font and plain terms—the key elements of the contract as well as the economic consequences of the transaction (rather than a single tick box for a long contract not clearly visible and comprehensible to the consumer). This web 'infrastructure' would be a practical step to 'operationalize' transparency requirements in the environment of the crowdfunding platform.

A major step towards the modernization of the unfair contract terms framework is introduced by the 'Omnibus Directive'. The amended UCTD will provide that 'Member States shall lay down the rules on penalties' in the case of unfair contract terms 'and shall take all measures necessary to ensure that they are implemented', emphasizing that these penalties must be 'effective, proportionate and dissuasive'.[97] Most importantly, the Omnibus Directive provides the UCTD with stronger 'teeth': for widespread infringements that affect consumers in several EU Member States, national authorities will be able to impose fines up to 4% of the seller's or supplier's annual turnover.[98] This is particularly relevant for crowdfunding platforms, as their operation involves a large number of consumers in multiple EU Member States. The new penalties frameworks shall be considered along with the principle that, in case of unclear or ambiguous contract terms, the most favourable interpretation for the consumer prevails,[99] and Member State courts have an *ex efficio* obligation to always assess the fairness of contract terms on their own motion.[100] This provides good reasons to believe that there will be satisfactory protection against unfair contract terms drafted by 'traders' involved in RBC campaigns.   **15.39**

VI. Conclusion

With the consumer law acquis undergoing its ambitious modernization reform, it is evident that EU lawmakers have not stood still in the face of increasing digitalization of the marketplace. While novel market phenomena such as RBC redefine the relationships between consumers and businesses and stretch the boundaries of well-established consumer law concepts, we have shown that the existing consumer law acquis, in the light of its forthcoming modernization, will provide a satisfactory level of protection for the 'crowd' of consumers seeking to experiment with the brave new world of RBC. Backers may not be the archetypical consumers, as envisaged by the acquis, and project owners or platforms may not be necessarily resembling the businesses that operate in conventional and established marketplaces. This, it has been shown, does not mean that the EU consumer protection directives, with the UCPD and UCTD being prominent examples, will not apply to RBC campaigns and regulate the relationship between the parties with a view to enhancing the legal protection of the 'crowd'. Regardless of this finding, scholars and practitioners may have been right in feeling concerned about the exclusion of RBC from the forthcoming EU Crowdfunding Regulation. As our analysis has demonstrated, there are certain implications   **15.40**

---

[97] Directive (EU) 2019/2161 (n 4) Art 1.
[98] ibid Art 4.
[99] UCTD (n 6) Art 5 and Recital 20.
[100] Case C-243/08 *Pannon GSM* ECLI:EU:C:2009:350 para 35.

of applying the consumer law acquis to RBC that may create complications and uncertainties for all parties of the RBC triangle. These may discourage parties to participate in RBC, hindering the policy-making efforts to further foster a more widespread innovation culture within the EU, and harness the innovation potential of crowds and small businesses.

15.41   Looking forward, the idiosyncrasies of law-making at the EU level call for a certain amount of pragmatism. In lieu of expecting another EU legal instrument that will provide the necessary clarity, it would be more realistic to issue a call for much-needed regulatory guidance from the consumer protection authorities, both in Brussels and at a domestic level. As our analysis has shown, the challenges lying ahead for the application of the EU consumer law to RBC campaigns relate much more to interpretative latitude and lack of authoritative precedents than to fundamental or textual limitations of the legal provisions. The regulatory aims of consumer protection (that is, above all, the protection of consumers who find themselves in relationships characterized by information and power asymmetries, but also the maintenance of a level playing field between businesses) confirm the importance of providing more clarity on such legal challenges as the ones fleshed out in the present chapter.

PART VI

MANAGING, PREVENTING, AND RESOLVING CROWDFUNDING-RELATED DISPUTES

16

Civil and Commercial Jurisdiction in Crowdfunding-Related Litigation

Pietro Ortolani

I. Introduction

As the European crowdfunding market develops, disputes will unavoidably arise between **16.01** investors on the one side, and project owners and crowdfunding service providers (CSPs) on the other. Since one of the goals of the Crowdfunding Regulation is to 'foster cross-border crowdfunding services and to facilitate the exercise of the freedom to provide and receive such services in the internal market', many of these disputes will be cross-border in nature.[1] As a consequence, the question of jurisdiction unavoidably arises: which Member State courts (hereinafter, MSCs) will be competent to hear these cases, and on the basis of which rules? The Crowdfunding Regulation does not set forth any specific rule for the allocation of jurisdiction over crowdfunding-related disputes. In the absence of a specialized regime, it is necessary to look at the Brussels I*bis* Regulation, which regulates the allocation of civil and commercial jurisdiction among MSCs.[2] This chapter assesses which of the provisions in the Brussels I*bis* Regulation may be invoked to establish jurisdiction in crowdfunding-related cases. Some of the observations included in the chapter may also be relevant for the establishment of jurisdiction under the 2007 Lugano Convention,[3] whose

---

[1] Recital 7 Crowdfunding Regulation.
[2] Regulation (EU) No 1215/2012 of the European Parliament and of the Council of 12 December 2012 on jurisdiction and the recognition and enforcement of judgments in civil and commercial matters.
[3] Convention on jurisdiction and the recognition and enforcement of judgments in civil and commercial matters, OJ L 339, 21.12.2007.

relevance for crowdfunding in the near future depends, among other things, on whether the UK will access the Lugano regime.[4]

16.02 In most crowdfunding-related disputes, the claim will be brought by an investor, against the CSP or the project owner. The relevance of different heads of jurisdiction must be evaluated separately in the two scenarios, depending on a number of factors, including the nature of the claim. To this end, the remainder of this chapter proceeds as follows. Section II will expound on the importance of jurisdiction in crowdfunding-related disputes. Section III will discuss the application of the Brussels I*bis* Regulation to the case where an investor brings a claim against a CSP. In turn, section IV will analyse the scenario where the investor brings a claim against a project owner. Section V, in turn, will consider the role of private autonomy. The parties to a crowdfunding-related dispute may seek to limit the uncertainty arising out of the multiple jurisdictional criteria of the Brussels regime, by entering into either a choice-of-court or an arbitration agreement. It is therefore necessary to discuss the limits within which such private ordering solutions are possible. Finally, section VI will present some conclusions.

II. Role of Jurisdiction in Crowdfunding-Related Disputes: Why Does It Matter

16.03 The parties to a cross-border crowdfunding case are likely to have diverging preferences and strategic reasons for action concerning jurisdiction. For instance, they may have a predilection for the courts of their own place of residence or establishment. As a consequence, the parties to a cross-border crowdfunding-related dispute are likely to put forth diverging interpretations of the jurisdictional criteria (often referred to as 'heads of jurisdiction') of the Brussels I*bis* Regulation, in an attempt to persuade the seized MSC to retain or decline jurisdiction. In order to understand why jurisdiction is likely to be an important battlefield in disputes between investors on the one hand, and CSPs and/or project owners on the other, it is necessary to summarize in brief the general features of the Brussels I*bis* Regulation.

16.04 The Brussels I*bis* Regulation is governed by the principle of mutual trust, which puts all MSCs on an equal footing (under the supervision of the European Court of Justice (ECJ)), implicitly forcing national courts to assume that all competent MSCs are functionally equivalent and equally well-equipped to deal with a given dispute.[5] The reality of European civil and commercial litigation is not a level playing field: civil procedure remains largely unharmonized, and the parties to a crowdfunding-related dispute may have a host of reasons to prefer a certain MSC over the others. Apart from the aforementioned preference for a party's 'home court', MSCs differ from each other in a number of important ways. Predictability, technical expertise of the judges, and familiarity with the technicalities of crowdfunding-related disputes are likely to be key concerns for the parties. In practice, and

---

[4] At the time of writing, it is unclear whether the United Kingdom will accede to the 2007 Lugano Convention, but the European Commission published a negative assessment, concluding that the UK's application to accede should be refused: European Commission, 'Assessment on the application of the United Kingdom of Great Britain and Northern Ireland to accede to the 2007 Lugano Convention', COM(2021) 222 final, 4.5.2021.

[5] Case C-116/02, *Erich Gasser GmbH v MISAT Srl*, ECLI:EU:C:2003:657, para 72; Case C-185/07, *Allianz SpA and Generali Assicurazioni Generali SpA v West Tankers Inc*, ECLI:EU:C:2009:69, para 29.

despite the theoretical assumption of functional equivalence among MSCs, different national courts may deal with complex issues concerning the application of the Crowdfunding Regulation (as well as other instruments of EU and national law) in different ways, and with different levels of sophistication and expertise. A related but distinct set of concerns revolves around the different degree of judicial independence of different MSCs, which has already threatened to undermine the principle of mutual trust (albeit more visibly in the field of judicial cooperation in criminal matters).[6]

Speed is likely to be another crucial concern for the litigants: MSCs notoriously differ in terms of duration of proceedings.[7] On the one hand, the investor/claimant will often try to establish jurisdiction before a MSC that will ensure swift proceedings, issuing an enforceable title (ideally, with *res judicata* effects) within a reasonable time. Recalcitrant respondents, on the other hand, may attempt to establish jurisdiction in a Member State where court proceedings are slow in an attempt to hinder claims against them. This attempt is often pursued through the filing of a negative declaratory action (often referred to as 'torpedo action'). By way of example, when faced with the imminent threat of a breach of contract claim, a party may decide to file a claim for declaratory relief in the court of his/her preference, requesting that court to declare that the contract has not in fact been breached and, thus, the other party's claim is unfounded. According to the ECJ's established case law,[8] such a negative declaratory claim must be deemed to have the same cause of action as a claim by the other party to enforce the contract. As a result, the *lis pendens* mechanism of Article 29 of the Brussels I*bis* Regulation is applicable, and the court first seized in time will retain jurisdiction, to the exclusion of all other Member State courts that may have had jurisdiction under the Regulation. The risk of a 'rush to the courts', where a party files a negative declaratory action for the main purpose of establishing jurisdiction in a forum that is unfavourable to the counterparty, is increased by the case law of the ECJ, according to which the merely chronological criterion of Article 29 cannot be derogated from, even in cases where a 'bad faith claimant' initiates litigation in a court whose proceedings are 'excessively long'.[9]   **16.05**

This line of case law has been developed by the ECJ before the adoption of the Brussels I*bis* Regulation, with reference to the 1968 Brussels Convention[10] and the old Brussels I Regulation.[11] On the one hand, the general architecture of the Brussels regime has remained unaltered, so that the case law concerning the old instruments is generally still good law with respect to the Brussels I*bis* Regulation as well. On the other hand, however, the EU law-maker has sought partially to resolve the problem of torpedo actions, with exclusive reference to the case where the action is brought in violation of an exclusive choice-of-court agreement concluded between the parties. If the parties have concluded such an agreement, the general first-come-first-served *lis pendens* rule will not apply, and the court selected by   **16.06**

---

[6] Joined Cases C-404/15 and C-659/15 PPU, *Pál Aranyosi and Robert Căldăraru v Generalstaatsanwaltschaft Bremen*, ECLI:EU:C:2016:198.

[7] European Commission, 'EU Justice Scoreboard 2020' <https://ec.europa.eu/info/sites/default/files/justice_scoreboard_2020_en.pdf> accessed 14 May 2021, 9.

[8] Case 144/86, *Gubisch Maschinenfabrik KG v Giulio Palumbo*, ECLI:EU:C:1987:528.

[9] Case C-116/02, *Erich Gasser GmbH v MISAT Srl*, ECLI:EU:C:2003:657.

[10] 1968 Brussels Convention on jurisdiction and the enforcement of judgments in civil and commercial matters, OJ L 299, 31.12.1972.

[11] Council Regulation (EC) No 44/2001 of 22 December 2000 on jurisdiction and the recognition and enforcement of judgments in civil and commercial matters.

the parties in the choice-of-court agreement will not be bound to stay proceedings, even when it is not seized first.[12] For the purposes of this chapter, therefore, it will be important to assess to what extent the parties to a crowdfunding-related dispute are free to derogate from the jurisdictional rules of the Brussels regime by entering into an exclusive jurisdiction agreement; the chapter will address this problem in section VI.

16.07   A further reason why the parties to a crowdfunding-related dispute may prefer a particular national court over another is related to another fundamental principle of European civil and commercial litigation: the so-called procedural autonomy of the Member States.[13] While the Brussels I*bis* Regulation (and its predecessors) sets forth a harmonized regime for the allocation of jurisdiction and the recognition and enforcement of judgments, the content of the civil procedure rules applicable before each court is still largely[14] determined by the legislators of each Member State. As a result, a particular national civil procedure system may offer the parties a certain type of procedure, which is suitable for crowdfunding-related disputes and would not be available before a different national authority. The most obvious example, in this respect, is collective redress: while the new Collective Redress Directive[15] will bring about more harmonization in this area, there are still significant differences among Member States as to what extent collective redress procedures are available. The relevance of collective redress procedures for crowdfunding will be scrutinized in Chapter 17. In this chapter, by contrast, the analysis mainly focuses on the allocation of jurisdiction in 'bilateral' disputes, with one claimant (an investor) and one respondent (a CSP, or a project owner). Needless to say, the conclusions reached in this group do not necessarily apply to litigations involving a group of claimants. A particularly relevant example is Article 18 of the Brussels I*bis* Regulation (which will be discussed in detail in section III.1), whereby a consumer may bring a case in the 'courts for the place where the consumer is domiciled'. The ECJ has clarified that if the case is brought by a consumer who asserts not only his own claims but also 'claims assigned by other consumers domiciled in the same Member State, in other Member States or in non-member countries', Article 18 does not apply.[16]

16.08   As previously mentioned, this chapter considers two different litigation scenarios. In the first scenario, an investor brings a claim against a CSP. The claim will typically revolve around the provision of certain crowdfunding-related services, such as the provision of the key investment information sheet (KIIS) and the verification of the completeness, correctness, and clarity of the information contained therein.[17] In other cases, the dispute may

---

[12] Art 31(2) Brussels I*bis* Regulation.

[13] A Wallerman, 'Towards an EU Law Doctrine on the Exercise of Discretion in National Courts? The Member States' Self-Imposed Limits on National Procedural Autonomy' (2016) 53(2) Common Market Law Review 339; DU Galetta, *Procedural Autonomy of EU Member States: Paradise Lost?: A Study on the 'Functionalized Procedural Competence' of EU Member States* (Springer 2010).

[14] The EU law-maker has introduced certain harmonized procedures, thus departing from the traditional approach whereby European civil procedure would mainly focus on the allocation of jurisdiction, and on the recognition and enforcement of judgments. The first example, in this respect, is the European Small Claims Procedure: see Regulation (EC) No 861/2007 of the European Parliament and of the Council of 11 July 2007 establishing a European Small Claims Procedure. However, the available empirical evidence suggests that this instrument of uniform European procedure is not widely used in practice: X Kramer and A Ontanu, 'The Functioning of the European Small Claims Procedure in the Netherlands: Normative and Empirical Reflections' (2013) 3 Nederlands Internationaal Privaatrecht 319.

[15] Directive (EU) 2020/1828 of the European Parliament and of the Council of 25 November 2020 on representative actions for the protection of the collective interests of consumers and repealing Directive 2009/22/EC.

[16] Case C-498/18, *Maximilian Schrems v Facebook Ireland Limited*.

[17] Art 23 Crowdfunding Regulation.

concern, for example, the reception and transmission of the investor's orders in relation to those instruments,[18] or the individual portfolio management of loans.[19]

In the second scenario, an investor brings a claim against a project owner. The claim may   **16.09**
concern *inter alia* the project owner's failure to comply with the terms and conditions of the crowdfunding offer, the inclusion of misleading or inaccurate information in the KIIS, or the omission of key information in the same document.[20]

III. Investor versus Crowdfunding Service Provider: Overview and General Jurisdiction

The Brussels I*bis* Regulation allocates jurisdiction on the basis of multiple criteria. The   **16.10**
question whether and to what extent these criteria can be invoked by the investor/claimant to establish jurisdiction must be answered separately, in the two scenarios described above, and depending on the circumstances of the case. This section focuses on the scenario where an investor brings a claim against a CSP.

The Brussels I*bis* Regulation enshrines the *actor sequitur forum rei* principle in the so-called   **16.11**
general head of jurisdiction of Article 4(1), according to which 'persons domiciled in a Member State shall, whatever their nationality, be sued in the courts of that Member State'. Pursuant to Articles 3(1) and 12(1) of the Crowdfunding Regulation, CSPs are always established in a Member State. As a consequence, an investor may certainly seize the courts of the Member State where the CSP is established, on the basis of Article 4(1) of the Brussels I*bis* Regulation. This, however, may not be the most desirable choice for the claimant, from a practical and/or strategic point of view. Therefore, claimants may often attempt to establish jurisdiction elsewhere, relying on a different jurisdictional ground.

1. Consumer Jurisdiction

Since claimants often prefer litigating in their 'home court', it is necessary to consider   **16.12**
whether and to what extent an investor/claimant may be able to seize the courts of his/her own place of domicile, on the basis of Article 18(1) of the Brussels I*bis* Regulation. The provision at hand can only be used by consumers, as defined in Article 17(1) of the Brussels I*bis* Regulation. Article 17 sets forth three conditions which a claimant must comply with, to qualify as a consumer:[21]

(1) The dispute must relate to a contract;
(2) The contract must be concluded 'by a person, the consumer, for a purpose which can be regarded as being outside his trade or profession';

---

[18] Art 2(1)(a)(ii) Crowdfunding Regulation.
[19] Art 6 Crowdfunding Regulation.
[20] Art 23(10) of the Crowdfunding Regulation expressly requires the Member States to ensure the applicability of 'laws, regulations and administrative provisions on civil liability' to the last two hypotheses.
[21] Cases C-297/14, *Hobohm*, ECLI:EU:C:2015:844, para 24; C-375/13, *Harald Kolassa v Barclays Bank plc*, ECLI:EU:C:2015:37, para 23; C-419/11, *Česká spořitelna, a.s. v Gerald Feichter*, ECLI:EU:C:2013:165, para 30.

(3) The contract falls within one of three categories listed by Article 17(1). While the first two categories are not relevant to the case of disputes with CSPs, the third prong of the provision requires that the contract be 'concluded with a person who pursues commercial or professional activities in the Member State of the consumer's domicile or, by any means, directs such activities to that Member State or to several States including that Member State, and the contract falls within the scope of such activities'.

As for the first requirement, the case law of the ECJ clarifies that Article 18(1) can only be invoked if privity of contract exists between claimant and respondent, and the dispute relates to that contract.[22] As for disputes between investors and CSPs, it is certain that the parties are bound by a contractual relationship, and that disputes would relate to such contract when they concern, for example, the placement of securities to the investor, the reception or transmission of orders from the investor, or individual portfolio management of loans.

16.13   As for the second requirement, a claimant can only qualify as a consumer if he/she is a natural person.[23] Therefore, all legal persons qualifying as investors under Article 2(1)(i) of the Crowdfunding Regulation are barred from relying on Article 18(1) of the Brussels I*bis* Regulation to establish jurisdiction in their home court, irrespective of their level of sophistication. Since crowdfunding is increasingly attracting capital not only from retail but also from professional investors, this requirement may prove to be a significant bottleneck for certain categories of claimants.

16.14   Being a natural person is a necessary but, obviously, not sufficient requirement for a claimant to qualify as a consumer for jurisdictional purposes. In addition, the claimant must conclude the contract 'for a purpose which can be regarded as being outside his trade or profession'. In this respect, the question arises whether the qualification of an investor as 'sophisticated' or 'non-sophisticated' for the purposes of the Crowdfunding Regulation should have any bearing on the qualification of the same party as a consumer for jurisdictional purposes. This differentiation 'build(s) on the distinction between professional clients and retail clients established in Directive 2014/65/EU' (Markets in Financial Instruments Directive II (MiFID II)).[24] Therefore, the question should be answered by looking at the ECJ case law concerning the relationship between the MiFID qualification of an investor as a 'retail client' and the qualification of the same investor as a consumer for jurisdictional purposes. This issue has been recently addressed by the ECJ in *Petruchová*.[25] In that case, a Czech resident (Petruchová) brought an action against a Cypriot brokerage company (FIBO). The contract between Petruchová and FIBO contained an exclusive choice-of-court clause in favour of Cyprus courts; nevertheless, claimant argued that she could disregard the clause and seize the court of her place of domicile (pursuant to respectively Articles 19 and 18 of the Brussels I*bis* Regulation) because she should be regarded as a consumer

---

[22] Case C-45/13, *Andreas Kainz v Pantherwerke AG*, ECLI:EU:C:2014:7.

[23] Cases C-89/91, *Shearson Lehman Hutton, Inc. v TVB Treuhandgesellschaft für Vermögensverwaltung und Beteiligungen*, ECLI:EU:C:1993:15, paras 20–22; C-269/95, *Francesco Benincasa v Dentalkit Srl*, ECLI:EU:C:1997:337, para 35; C-27/02, *Petra Engler v Janus Versand GmbH*, ECLI:EU:C:2005:33, para 34; *Česká spořitelna* (n 21) para 32.

[24] Recital 42 Crowdfunding Regulation.

[25] Case C-208/18, *Jana Petruchová v FIBO Group Holdings Limited*, ECLI:EU:C:2019:825.

within the meaning of Article 17 of the Regulation.[26] The first important indication offered by the ECJ is that the qualification of a party as a 'consumer' for the purposes of Article 17 requires a reference to 'the position of that person in a given contract, in relation to the nature and purpose of the contract, and not to the subjective situation of that person.'[27] In other words, a person concluding a contract for use outside his/her professional activity can qualify as a consumer, irrespective of his/her level of knowledge, expertise, or economic resources.[28] This objective (rather than subjective) criterion, in and of itself, militates against the relevance of the qualification of an investor as 'sophisticated' or 'non-sophisticated', since Annex II to the Crowdfunding Regulation links the identification of sophisticated investors to subjective (rather than objective) criteria, such as the 'awareness of the risks associated with investing in capital markets', the investor's economic resources or the number of transactions that the investor enters into.[29] In *Petruchová*, the ECJ then proceeds to observe how a client can qualify as 'retail' for MiFID purposes, even when it is a legal person.[30] This is incompatible with the Brussels I definition of consumer which, as already mentioned, can only apply to natural persons. The ECJ, thus, concludes that it is always jurisdictionally irrelevant whether the claimant is a retail client under MiFID, even when he/she is a natural person. The ECJ's line of reasoning can be applied the Crowdfunding Regulation too: according to Annex II, legal persons can qualify as non-sophisticated investors. Therefore, the notion of 'non-sophisticated investor' under the Crowdfunding Regulation is essentially unrelated to the notion of 'consumer' under the Brussels I*bis* Regulation. The fact that a natural person qualifies as non-sophisticated under the Crowdfunding Regulation has no bearing on whether he/she should qualify as a consumer for jurisdictional purposes.

Furthermore, in *Petruchová*, the ECJ highlights another reason why the qualification of the claimant as a 'retail client' is irrelevant for jurisdictional purposes. According to the Court, the Brussels I*bis* Regulation and MiFID II pursue two different objectives. On the one hand, the qualification of 'consumer' in the Brussels I*bis* Regulation protects the weaker contractual party at the jurisdictional stage. On the other hand, the qualification of 'retail client' in MiFID II ensures that the client will be provided with adequate investment information.[31] The same divergence of rationales exists with respect to the Crowdfunding Regulation: the purpose of Articles 17–19 of the Brussels I*bis* Regulation remains the same irrespective of the type of investment performed by the claimant, and the Crowdfunding Regulation (similarly to MiFID II) ensures that non-sophisticated investors be adequately informed about their investments. At first sight, it may be objected that the Crowdfunding Regulation and the Brussels I*bis* Regulation are ultimately similar in purpose, since the former also aims to protect weaker contractual parties by setting forth a protective regime for non-sophisticated investors. However, according to the ECJ, the fact that the subject matter of the litigation is governed by substantive EU law which contains protective provisions in favour

16.15

---

[26] For a description of the situations where claimants that qualify as consumers are allowed to disregard a choice-of-court agreement see below, subsection V.1.

[27] *Schrems* (n 16) para 29.

[28] Cases C-110/14, *Horaţiu Ovidiu Costea v SC Volksbank România SA*, ECLI:EU:C:2015:538, para 21; *Schrems* (n 16) para 39; C-774/19, *AB and BB v Personal Exchange*, EU:C:2020:1015, para 38.

[29] Case C-500/18, *AU v Reliantco Investments LTD and Reliantco Investments LTD Limassol Sucursala Bucureşti*, paras 53–54.

[30] *Petruchová* (n 25) para 71.

[31] ibid para 75.

of a certain party is not determinative of whether that party can rely on the head of jurisdiction of Article 18 of the Brussels I*bis* Regulation, when bringing a claim.[32] In other words, according to the ECJ, the purpose of protecting a party at the jurisdictional stage (through procedural EU law) cannot be conflated with the protection of the same party at the merits stage (through substantive EU law).

16.16   The question arises whether this conclusion would change, *de lege ferenda*, if the Crowdfunding Regulation were to include a provision in respect of the provision of information to non-sophisticated investors on jurisdiction and dispute settlement. If this were the case, and depending on the contents of such hypothetical provision, it could be argued that the Crowdfunding Regulation and the Brussels I*bis* Regulation both pursue the objective of protecting the weaker contractual party at the jurisdictional stage. As a consequence, the qualification of a natural person as a non-sophisticated investor under the Crowdfunding Regulation may become relevant to his/her qualification as a consumer under the Brussels I*bis* Regulation. To date, however, the Crowdfunding Regulation includes no such provision, so that *Petruchová* applies, and the qualification of the claimant as a non-sophisticated investor remains irrelevant.

16.17   In light of the above, it can be concluded that the qualification of a claimant as a 'non-sophisticated investor' is irrelevant to his/her ability to invoke Articles 17–19 of the Brussels I*bis* Regulation. This, of course, does not entail that the two categories do not overlap; to the contrary, a 'non-sophisticated investor' will often be able to invoke the head of jurisdiction of Article 18, or to disregard a choice-of-court agreement which does not comply with Article 19 of the Brussels I*bis* Regulation. To this end, however, the claimant should not rely on his/her qualification as a 'non-sophisticated investor' for the purposes of the Crowdfunding Regulation but rather should demonstrate that the nature and purpose of the contract falls outside of his/her trade or profession. To this end, it should not matter whether the claimant is a sophisticated investor with in-depth knowledge of the crowdfunding market, or whether his/her decision to enter into a contract with the CSP was based on an extensive awareness of the nature of this market, and the consequences of the decision to invest. A case in point here is *Emrek*,[33] where the ECJ held that a claimant can rely on consumer jurisdiction, even when it concluded a contract out of his own initiative, without any causal link between the conclusion of the contract and 'the means employed to direct the commercial or professional activity to the Member State of the consumer's domicile'. In other words, it may be possible for a claimant to voluntarily engage in crowdfunding, concluding a contract with a CSP while having an extensive understanding of the crowdfunding market and the risk associated with it,[34] and at the same time qualify as a consumer for jurisdictional purposes, as long as his/her trade or profession is not related to crowdfunding investments.

16.18   As for the third and last requirement of Article 17, there is no doubt that CSPs pursue 'commercial or professional activities'. Article 17, however, also requires that those activities be

---

[32] *Kainz* (n 22) para 31.
[33] Case C-218/12, *Lokman Emrek v Vlado Sabranovic*, ECLI:EU:C:2013:666; see also joined cases C-585/08 and C-144/09, *Peter Pammer v Reederei Karl Schlüter GmbH & Co. KG and Hotel Alpenhof GesmbH v Oliver Heller*, ECLI:EU:C:2010:740.
[34] Case C-774/19, *AB v BB*, ECLI:EU:C:2020:1015, para 40.

pursued 'in the Member State of the consumer's domicile' or be, 'by any means', directed 'to that Member State or to several States including that Member State, and the contract falls within the scope of such activities'. The rationale of such requirement is ensuring predictability for the professional/respondent, who can expect to be sued in those Member States where he/she pursued or directed his/her professional activities. In the case of CSPs, the question whether this requirement is fulfilled depends on whether and to what extent the respondent provided cross-border services. As already mentioned, one of the purposes of the Crowdfunding Regulation is precisely the creation of a 'Union-wide crowdfunding market', overcoming the situation whereby regulatory fragmentation discourages CSPs from providing services outside of the Member State in which they are established.[35] To this end, CSPs are allowed to provide services on a cross-border basis, without necessarily having a physical presence in the territory of the Member State(s) other than the one where they are authorized.[36] The question then is whether the Member State where the claimant is domiciled is included in the list of jurisdictions in which the CSP has notified its intention to provide services, which is publicly available in the register of CSPs pursuant to Article 14(2)(e) of the Crowdfunding Regulation. If that is the case, the CSP should be deemed to direct its activities to the Member State where the claimant is domiciled.

It should incidentally be noted that the interplay between Article 18(1)(a) of the **16.19** Crowdfunding Regulation and Article 17 of the Brussels I*bis* Regulation may have the undesired effect of undermining, rather than fostering, the cross-border provision of crowdfunding services. More specifically, by mentioning a certain Member State in the list of jurisdictions where the CSP intends to provide services (as set forth in Article 18(1)(a) of the Crowdfunding Regulation), the CSP assumes the risk of being sued in that Member State by a claimant fulfilling the requirements of Article 17 of the Brussels I*bis* Regulation. This, in turn, may induce the CSP to exclude certain Member States from the list in situations where the risk of litigation in that jurisdiction (in light of all of the factors mentioned in section II, such as the average duration of court proceedings) outweighs the forecasted revenues associated with the provision of services towards that Member State.

2. Contractual Jurisdiction

Apart from the general head of jurisdiction of Article 4, the Brussels I*bis* Regulation also **16.20** enshrines some so-called specific heads of jurisdiction, in Article 7. If the claimant's action falls within one of the categories listed in Article 7, the defendant may be sued in a certain court other than the one of the place where he/she is domiciled. Article 7, therefore, may allow a claimant to seize a court other than the defendant's 'home court'. This option may be particularly attractive for claimants that do not qualify as consumers and cannot, as already illustrated, establish jurisdiction in the place where they are domiciled under Article 18 of the Brussels I*bis* Regulation.

Article 7(1) of the Brussels I*bis* Regulation concerns 'matters related to a contract'. An **16.21** investor may be able to establish jurisdiction on the basis of this provision when his/her

---

[35] Recital 6 Crowdfunding Regulation.
[36] Art 12(12) Crowdfunding Regulation.

claim against the CSP arises out of or in connection with the provision of crowdfunding services. To mention some examples, the dispute may concern an alleged failure to discharge the informational duties under Article 19 of the Crowdfunding Regulation. In other cases, the CSP may have failed to disclose the default rate of loans under Article 20 of the Crowdfunding Regulation. In yet other cases, the CSP may have granted full access to non-sophisticated investors[37] without first assessing whether and what services are appropriate, as required by Article 21 of the Crowdfunding Regulation. Pursuant to Article 7(1) of the Brussels I*bis* Regulation, jurisdiction lies with 'the courts for the place of performance of the obligation in question'. For contracts for the provision of services, Article 7(1) specifies that this is the place where, 'under the contract, the services were provided or should have been provided'. This will be the Member State where the CSP provided crowdfunding services, which will often coincide with the jurisdiction where the investor is habitually resident. As already mentioned, this may not be the place where the CSP is established but one of the Member States where the CSP has notified its intention to provide services under Article 18 of the Crowdfunding Regulation. In any event, the claimant will need to prove the territorial link between the Member State of the seized court and the specific service(s) which the CSP provided or should have provided, which forms part of the cause of action in the litigation. Therefore, the circumstance that a certain Member State has been indicated by the CSP for the purposes of Article 18(1)(a) of the Crowdfunding Regulation should never be *per se* sufficient to establish jurisdiction in the courts of that Member State under Article 7(1) of the Brussels I*bis* Regulation, in the absence of any concrete territorial link between that State and the facts of the case.

16.22 In order to establish contractual jurisdiction on the basis of Article 7(1), the circumstance that the CSP does not have a branch, agency, or other establishment in the place where the services are provided should be irrelevant. In this respect, Article 12(12) of the Crowdfunding Regulation prevents Member States (other than the Member State of establishment) from requiring a CSP to establish a physical presence in their territory. However, if the CSP does have such a branch, agency, or other establishment, the claimant can then establish jurisdiction on the basis of Article 7(5) of the Brussels I*bis* Regulation, in the place where the branch, agency, or other establishment is situated.

3. Tortious Jurisdiction

16.23 Most causes of action against a CSP will be contractual in nature. For this reason, the relevance of tortious jurisdiction in the first scenario is limited. However, it is worth noting that, under Article 7(2) of the Brussels I*bis* Regulation, in matters relating to 'tort, delict or quasi-delict', jurisdiction lies with the MSCs of the 'place where the harmful event occurred or may occur'. Section IV, concerning the situation where the investor brings a claim against the project owner, will provide an overview of where the 'harmful event' should be deemed to occur, according to the case law of the ECJ. Importantly, however, the practical relevance of this assessment is mainly limited to the second scenario, where the investor

---

[37] As mentioned above, a non-sophisticated investor may not qualify as a consumer for the purposes of the Brussels I*bis* Regulation, and may therefore be unable to establish jurisdiction at its own place of domicile, on the basis of Article 18.

initiates litigation against the project owner, and the cause of action is more likely to be non-contractual than in the first scenario.

IV. Investor versus Project Owner

From a jurisdictional point of view, the first crucial difference between the first scenario **16.24** (investor versus CSP) and the second one (investor versus project owner) is that project owners (unlike CSPs) are not necessarily established in an EU Member State. Article 5(2) (b) of the Crowdfunding Regulation only requires CSPs to obtain evidence 'that the project owner is not established in a non-cooperative jurisdiction, as recognised by the relevant Union policy, or in a high-risk third country pursuant to Article 9(2) of Directive (EU) 2015/849'. It is, therefore, possible for a project owner established in a third State to seek funding through a crowdfunding platform. If the project owner is established in a third State, many of the jurisdictional rules of the Brussels I*bis* Regulation (such as the general head of jurisdiction of Article 4, or the specific heads of jurisdiction of Article 7) will not be applicable. As a result, the claimant/investor may need to establish jurisdiction pursuant to the non-harmonised jurisdictional rules of the forum. This chapter cannot provide an overview of the national rules of jurisdiction that would apply, in settings where the Brussels I*bis* Regulation is not applicable. However, subsection IV.1 will highlight an important exception: in cases where the investor qualifies as a consumer within the meaning of Article 17 of the Brussels I*bis* Regulation, it may be possible to establish jurisdiction on the basis of Article 18, irrespective of the fact that the defendant is not domiciled in an EU Member State.

Conversely, in cases where the project owner is domiciled in an EU Member State, the in- **16.25** vestor/claimant will be able to establish jurisdiction pursuant to Article 4(1) of the Brussels I*bis* Regulation, in the Member State where the project owner is domiciled, according to the aforementioned *actor sequitur forum rei* rule. This, however, may not be the best strategic choice for the claimant for the reasons already pointed out above with reference to the first scenario. Therefore, it is necessary to determine to what extent the investor may be able to establish jurisdiction in the courts of another Member State, relying on a jurisdictional rule other than the one of Article 4(1).

1. Consumer Jurisdiction

As already mentioned, consumer jurisdiction can be invoked by a claimant against a re- **16.26** spondent, irrespective of whether the latter is domiciled in an EU Member State or not. This is an exception to the general rule whereby the Brussels I*bis* Regulation is only applicable if the respondent is domiciled in a Member State, and constitutes an important innovation of the recast Regulation, as compared with the 1968 Brussels Convention and with the old Brussels I Regulation.[38] According to Recital 14 of the Brussels I*bis* Regulation, 'in order

---

[38] P Mankowski and P Nielsen, 'Introduction to Articles 17–19' in U Magnus and P Mankowski (eds), *European Commentaries in Private International Law: Brussels Ibis Regulation* (Otto Schmidt 2016) 442, 447.

to ensure the protection of consumers … certain rules of jurisdiction … should apply regardless of the defendant's domicile'. Accordingly, Article 18 allows a consumer to bring a claim against a professional in the courts of the Member State where he/she is domiciled, 'regardless of the domicile of the other party'. In order to be able to invoke this head of jurisdiction, however, the three conditions already listed above with reference to Article 17 of the Brussels Ibis Regulation must be met.

16.27   As for the first condition, the dispute must 'relate to a contract'. This requires, first of all, privity between claimant and respondent. As a result, it should not be possible to establish jurisdiction successfully on the basis of Article 18 if the claimant has bought loans, transferable securities or admitted instruments on the secondary market, for instance from another investor that advertised the availability of those loans, securities, or instruments through a bulletin board, as provided for by Article 25 of the Crowdfunding Regulation. In this respect, the case law of the ECJ offers some clear indications: *Kolassa*, in particular, clarified that consumer jurisdiction can only be established if a direct contractual link exists between issuer and subscriber.[39] For jurisdictional purposes, it is irrelevant whether a chain of contracts (such as, for instance, one or more secondary market transactions) resulted in the transfer of 'certain rights and obligations of the professional' to the consumer/claimant.[40]

16.28   The fact that the claimant has acquired the loans, securities, or admitted instruments on the primary market is necessary but not sufficient to meet the first prong of the test of Article 17. In addition, the dispute must 'relate' to the contract, that is it must be contractual in nature. Examples of such a contractual nature refer to cases where the project owner failed to repay a loan, or to comply with the terms and conditions of the relevant security. In other cases, however, the action brought by an investor against the project owner should be qualified as tortious: examples include the case where the investor has suffered damages as a result of the provision of misleading or inaccurate information in the KIIS, or of an omission of key information therein.[41] The question then arises whether a consumer can establish jurisdiction under Article 18, even if the action is tortious in nature. The question should generally be answered in the negative, given the wording of Article 18, as well as the ECJ case law clarifying how the applicability of a protective substantive regime of tortious liability does not *per se* trigger the applicability of the protective head of jurisdiction of Article 18.[42] However, the ECJ has acknowledged the existence of an exception to such general rule. According to the ECJ, Article 18 can be successfully invoked if the cause of action is tortious, but the action is 'so closely connected' to a contract 'as to be indissociable'.[43] The ECJ has held in *Reliantco* that such an indissociable connection exists in the case of *culpa in contrahendo*, where the professional (in this case, the project owner) failed 'to comply with pre-contractual obligations vis-à-vis the other, consumer, party'.[44] This, however, would generally require a direct communication between the project owner and the investor, where the former made misleading representations, thus inducing the latter to enter into a contract. Conversely, in case of standard communications to the market (such as the KIIS),

---

[39]   C-375/13, *Harald Kolassa v Barclays Bank plc*, ECLI:EU:C:2015:37, para 30.
[40]   ibid.
[41]   Art 23(10) Crowdfunding Regulation.
[42]   *Kainz* (n 22) para 31.
[43]   Case C-96/00, *Rudolf Gabriel*, ECLI:EU:C:2002:436, paras 56–57.
[44]   *Reliantco* (n 29) paras 68–70.

the provision of misleading, inaccurate, or incomplete information should normally not be construed as 'indissociable' from the conclusion of a contract, thus preventing the claimant from establishing jurisdiction on the basis of Article 18 of the Brussels I*bis* Regulation.

As for the second requirement of Article 17, the claimant must qualify as a consumer. This **16.29** means, as already illustrated in section III.1 above, that the claimant must be a natural person, and the contract must be concluded for a purpose which can be regarded as being outside of the claimant's trade or profession. In the case of crowdfunding, this calls for different analyses, depending on the nature of the crowdfunding offer. In the case of loans, the question will be whether the granting of loans forms part of the claimant's trade or profession. As mentioned with reference to the first scenario, this should be assessed on the basis of objective criteria, and not subjective ones (such as the investor's knowledge of the crowdfunding loan market). As for shares, shareholders should generally not be regarded as consumers.[45] By contrast, for securities other than shares, it may be possible to establish jurisdiction on the basis of Article 18, provided that all other requirements are met.

As for the third requirement, the project owner must pursue 'commercial or professional ac- **16.30** tivities'. In order to determine whether this requirement is met, we must first of all take into account Article 1(2)(a) of the Crowdfunding Regulation. According to this provision, as illustrated in Chapter 5 of this book, the Regulation does not apply to 'crowdfunding services that are provided to project owners that are consumers, as defined in point (a) of Article 3 of Directive 2008/48/EC'.[46] If the crowdfunding service falls within the exception of Article 1(2)(a) of the Crowdfunding Regulation, therefore, jurisdiction over disputes between an investor and the project owner cannot be established under Article 18 of the Brussels I*bis* Regulation. Conversely, in cases where the Crowdfunding Regulation is applicable, the project owner should generally be deemed to pursue commercial or professional activities.

2. Tortious Jurisdiction

When an investor brings a claim against a project owner, the cause of action will often be **16.31** non-contractual in nature. In particular, this holds true when the case is based on the provision of allegedly misleading, incorrect, or incomplete information in the KIIS. With reference to prospectus liability, the ECJ has clarified that investor claims should be qualified as non-contractual for jurisdictional purposes.[47] Commentators have correctly pointed out that this qualification is consistent with the approach of most national legal systems, which qualify prospectus liability claims as non-contractual.[48] Furthermore, this qualification is in line with the fact that a prospectus is not individually addressed to the claimant but to the market as a whole.[49] The same reasoning applies to the KIIS: if the project owner fails to provide transparent and accurate information in accordance with the model provided in

---

[45] M Gargantini, 'Prospectus Liability: Competent Courts of Jurisdiction and Applicable Law' in D Busch, G Ferrarini, and JP Franx, *Prospectus Regulation and Prospectus Liability* (OUP 2020) 441, 459–60.

[46] The provision defines a consumer as 'a natural person who, in transactions covered by this Directive, is acting for purposes which are outside his trade, business or profession'.

[47] Case C-168/02, *Rudolf Kronhofer v Marianne Maier and Others*, ECLI:EU:C:2004:364.

[48] Gargantini (n 45) 446.

[49] ibid.

Annex I to the Crowdfunding Regulation, the project owner will be liable in tort, and not in contract, towards the investors. Therefore, a claimant may establish jurisdiction on the basis of Article 7(2) of the Brussels I*bis* Regulation, which, as illustrated above, confers jurisdiction upon the MSC of the 'place where the harmful event occurred or may occur'. The case law of the ECJ, however, raises numerous doubts as to how this rule should be applied in practice, in situations where the 'harmful event' is a financial loss suffered by an investor.

16.32   A first layer of uncertainty concerns the notion of 'place'. A literal interpretation of Article 7(2) would *prima facie* suggest that this should be the place where the damage materializes. However, the ECJ adopted a different approach, which practically splits this head of jurisdiction into two alternative territorial criteria. More specifically, according to the ECJ, the harmful event is deemed to take place both in the place where the damage occurs, and in the place where the events giving rise to that damage took place.[50] The latter criterion will often refer to the place where the project owner is established, so that reliance on Article 7(2) would result in no practical advantage for the claimant, as compared with Article 4 of the Brussels I*bis* Regulation. The former criterion, instead, may help the claimant establish jurisdiction in a Member State other than the one where the project owner is established. In practice, however, the case law of the ECJ on these matters leaves many questions unanswered.

16.33   In *Kronhofer*, the ECJ was confronted with the question whether a claimant may establish jurisdiction in the place where he/she is domiciled, or where his/her 'assets are concentrated', on the basis of Article 7(2) of the Brussels I*bis* Regulation. The underlying reasoning, here, is that if the investor suffers a financial loss as a result of an investment, that loss will be suffered in the place where the investor is domiciled and holds the majority of his/her assets. The ECJ held that these circumstances are, in and of themselves, insufficient to establish jurisdiction under Article 7(2), as this would generate legal uncertainty, making it difficult for the defendant to foresee the forum where litigation may be commenced.[51] However, in subsequent judgments, the ECJ has qualified this finding, ultimately blurring the boundaries of Article 7(2).

16.34   In *Kolassa*, the ECJ specified that, in cases where the damage 'occurred directly in the applicant's bank account', the Member State where the bank is established should be considered as the place where the harmful event occurred. As a result, the claimant would be able to establish jurisdiction in the place where he/she holds a bank account, on the basis of Article 7(2). As noted by Gargantini, however, the ECJ falls short of clarifying the relevant notion of 'account', which could in principle refer either to a securities account where financial instruments are registered, or a bank account from which the investor draws money to perform the investment.[52]

16.35   After *Kolassa*, the ECJ qualified its findings concerning the relevance of the location of the claimant's bank account, in *Universal Music*.[53] According to this judgment (which does not concern harm suffered by investors) the Court stated that the location of the injured party's

---

[50]   Case 21-76, *Handelskwekerij G. J. Bier BV v Mines de potasse d'Alsace SA*, ECLI:EU:C:1976:166.
[51]   *Kronhofer* (n 47) para 20.
[52]   Gargantini (n 45) 447.
[53]   Case C-12/15, *Universal Music International Holding BV v Michael Tétreault Schilling and Others*, ECLI:EU:C:2016:449, paras 36–39. See also the AG Opinion in the same case, ECLI:EU:C:2016:161, paras 44–45.

bank account is not sufficient, in and of itself, to establish jurisdiction under Article 7(2). To the contrary, further factual circumstances must be present. With specific reference to prospectus liability, the ECJ has clarified what those circumstances could be, in *Löber*.[54] In this case, the claimant was a non-professional investor, claiming compensation from the issuer of a financial instrument. The ECJ held that the location of a bank account should not be considered in isolation, when assessing jurisdiction under Article 7(2),[55] but should rather be evaluated together with other connecting factors. Among these further factors, the ECJ mentions the notification of the prospectus to the supervisory authority of the Member State where the investor/claimant is domiciled, and the place where the investor/claimant signed the investment contract.[56] These factors may be relevant for crowdfunding-related disputes as well. While the KIIS is not subject to verification or approval by competent authorities,[57] it must be made available (in cross-border settings) 'in at least one of the official languages of [the Member State where the claimant/investor is domiciled] or in a language accepted by the competent authorities of that Member State'.[58] This circumstance, together with the location of the claimant/investor's bank account, may be invoked to establish jurisdiction in the Member State where he/she is domiciled. Sufficient predictability for the project owner/respondent would be guaranteed by the fact that the CSP has mentioned the Member State where the investor is domiciled in its notification concerning the cross-border provision of services,[59] so that the project owner will be able to anticipate that the CSP will provide services in that jurisdiction. Similarly to what has been highlighted with reference to CSPs, the ultimate result of the interplay between the Crowdfunding Regulation and the Brussels I*bis* Regulation may in some cases be the discouragement, rather than the promotion, of a pan-European crowdfunding market. More specifically, project owners may prefer to rely on CSPs that do not provide cross-border services in order to minimize the risk of being hit with tortious claims from investors that could be able to establish jurisdiction in their place of residence under Article 7(2) of the Brussels I*bis* Regulation. On the other hand, of course, the cross-border operation of a CSP allows project owners to seek funding in more than one Member State. In conclusion, thus, project owners will need to balance the prospect of cross-border fund-seeking with the risk of foreign litigation.

3. Contractual Jurisdiction

As already illustrated, the 'specific' contractual head of jurisdiction of Article 7(1) is an al-   **16.36**
ternative to the 'general' head of jurisdiction of Article 4 and can only be invoked against defendants domiciled in a Member State. Article 7 may be an attractive alternative to Article 4,

---

[54] *Helga Löber v Barclays Bank PLC*, Case C-304/17, ECLI:EU:C:2018:701; see also AG Opinion, ECLI:EU:C:2018:310, in particular paras 68–81. M Gargantini, 'Capital markets and the market for judicial decisions: in search of consistency' (2016) MPI Luxembourg Working Paper Series 18; M Lehmann, 'Prospectus Liability and Private International Law—Assessing the Landscape after the ECJ Kolassa Ruling (Case C-375/13)' (2016) Journal of Private International Law 318; A Andra Cotiga, 'C.J.U.E., 28 janvier 2015, Harald Kolassa c. Barclays Bank PLC, Aff. C-375-13' (2015) Revue internationale des services financiers 40.

[55] *Löber* (n 54) para 30; see also AG Opinion in Case C-709/19, *Vereniging van Effectenbezitters v BP plc*, ECLI:EU:C:2020:1056, para 46.

[56] *Löber* (n 54) para 33.

[57] Art 23(6)(b) Crowdfunding Regulation.

[58] Art 23(3) Crowdfunding Regulation.

[59] Art 18 Crowdfunding Regulation.

for claimants that do not meet the requirements necessary to establish consumer jurisdiction under Article 18 of the Brussels I*bis* Regulation, when the cause of action is contractual in nature.

16.37 Article 7(1) is only applicable in 'matters relating to contract'. An investor/claimant, therefore, will only be able to use this provision if he/she has purchased the loans, transferable securities or admitted instruments on the primary market. Furthermore, the litigation must concern the project owner/defendant's failure to perform its contractual obligations. As illustrated in the previous subsection, KIIS liability cases are normally unlikely to meet this requirement, given their probable tortious nature. In order to determine whether the case relates to 'a contract' within the meaning of Article 7(1), it will be necessary to consider the nature of the claim, and the type of crowdfunding it relates to. For instance, with respect to loans, a failure to comply with the loan's terms and conditions may trigger a contractual claim. Along similar lines, for securities other than shares, a claim will be contractual if it concerns the project owner's failure to comply with its obligations under the terms of the relevant security.

16.38 In the case of shares, some types of shareholder disputes are covered by the exclusive head of jurisdiction of Article 24(2): in proceedings concerning the 'validity of the constitution, the nullity or the dissolution of companies ... or the validity of the decisions of their organs', jurisdiction will lie with 'the courts of the Member State in which the company ... has its seat', to the exclusion of all other courts. By contrast, other types of intra-corporate disputes should be qualified as contractual, so that Article 7(1) can be used to establish jurisdiction. More specifically, the ECJ has qualified corporate charters as contracts,[60] so that claims arising out of corporate charters should fall within the scope of application of the provision at hand.

16.39 Article 7(1) provides that, in 'matters relating to a contract', 'the courts for the place of performance of the obligation in question' may be seized. Article 7(1)(b) contains a definition of the place of performance, for contracts for the sale of goods and for the provision of services. However, the contractual relationship between investor and project owner should typically not fall within either of these categories; more specifically, the sale on the primary market of loans, securities or admitted instruments should generally not be regarded as a sale of goods, since the primary market transaction concerns immaterial rights, rather than the instruments that may serve the purpose of representing those rights.

16.40 In practice, the investor's contractual claim against the project owner will often concern the payment of a sum of money, for example in repayment of a loan or in compliance with the terms of a debt security. In these cases, the KIIS should contain sufficient information to identify the place of performance. More specifically, under lit. (f) of part G of Annex I to the Crowdfunding Regulation, the KIIS should contain information on 'the servicing of the loan, including in situations where the project owner does not meet its obligations'. Along similar lines, if the contractual dispute concerns the custody and delivery of transferable securities or admitted instruments, the KIIS should contain the relevant information, pursuant to lit. (e) of Part D of Annex I.

---

[60] Case C-214/89, *Powell Duffryn plc v Wolfgang Petereit*, ECLI:EU:C:1992:115; Case C-34-82, *Martin Peters Bauunternehmung GmbH v Zuid Nederlandse Aannemers Vereniging*, ECLI:EU:C:1983:87.

V. Private Ordering Solutions

According to the analysis carried out so far, jurisdiction in crowdfunding-related dis-   **16.41**
putes under the Brussels I*bis* Regulation is likely to be distributed among multiple MSCs.
As a consequence, CSPs and project owners may often be unable to foresee where an investor may start litigation against them. As already mentioned, the interplay between the
Crowdfunding Regulation and the Brussels I*bis* Regulation may ultimately bring about
the unintended effect of discouraging (rather than promoting) the cross-border provision
of crowdfunding services. In light of this, it is necessary to evaluate to what extent CSPs
and project owners may increase legal certainty by concentrating dispute resolution in a
single forum, through the use of choice-of-court or arbitration agreements. At first sight,
the use of such agreements seems to be particularly attractive for CSPs since, as illustrated
above in section III.2, disputes between investors and CSPs are often contractual in nature.
Therefore, the insertion of a choice-of-court or arbitration clause in the contract between
CSP and investor may apparently seem like a viable option. However, in practice, the effects
of such techniques will often prove limited, as the following subsections will explain.

1. Choice-of-court Agreements

Pursuant to Article 25 of the Brussels I*bis* Regulation, the parties have the possibility (re-   **16.42**
gardless of their domicile) to agree 'that a court or the courts of a Member State are to have
jurisdiction to settle any disputes which have arisen or which may arise in connection with
a particular legal relationship'. A choice-of-court agreement can generate two effects. On
the one hand, the parties can confer jurisdiction upon a MSC that would not have had jurisdiction to hear the case, in the absence of an agreement. On the other hand, if the choice-
of-court agreement is exclusive, it also excludes the jurisdiction of the non-chosen MSCs
that would have been competent to hear the case in the absence of an agreement. Article 25
stipulates that choice-of-court agreements are exclusive (ie they exclude the jurisdiction of
non-chosen MSCs), 'unless the parties agreed otherwise'. As explained in section II above,
an additional advantage of exclusive choice-of-court agreement is the derogation from the
lis pendens mechanism of Article 29, so that the chosen court will not have to stay the proceedings, even when it is not the court first seized.[61]

Despite this apparently favourable regime, the possibility to use choice-of-court agree-   **16.43**
ments in the context of crowdfunding is limited in practice, because of Article 19 of the
Brussels I*bis* Regulation. This provision concerns choice-of-court agreements concluded by
consumers, and it is therefore applicable in the same situations described above, in subsections III.1 (with references to contracts concluded by investors/consumers with CSPs) and
IV.1 (with reference to contracts concluded by investors/consumers with project owners).
Whenever the investor qualifies as a consumer for jurisdictional purposes, any choice-of-
court agreement concluded with a CSP or a project owner will only be valid in one of the
following three situations:

---

[61] Art 31 Brussels I*bis* Regulation.

(1) the choice-of-court agreement is entered into after the dispute has arisen;

(2) the choice-of court agreement allows the consumer to bring proceedings in courts other than those that consumers are able to seize under the Brussels I*bis* Regulation; or

(3) the consumer and the counterparty are both domiciled or habitually resident in the same Member State at the time of conclusion of the contract, and the choice-of-court agreement confers jurisdiction on the courts of that Member State, provided that such an agreement is not contrary to the law of that Member State.

None of these situations corresponds to the typical scenario where an investor may enter into a choice-of-court agreement with a CSP or a project owner. As for the first situation, it is unlikely that an investor/consumer will enter into a choice-of-court agreement after the dispute has arisen, especially considering that, in the absence of such agreement, it will be possible for the investor/consumer to seize the courts for the place where she is domiciled, pursuant to Article 18(1) of the Brussels I*bis* Regulation. The second situation, in turn, contemplates a choice-of-court agreement that would bring about a further fragmentation of jurisdiction, by allowing the consumer/investor to start litigation in other MSCs, in addition to those that already have jurisdiction in the absence of an agreement. Needless to say, this would run counter to the CSP's or project owner's purpose to concentrate all litigation in a single forum, excluding the jurisdiction of all other MSCs. As for the third situation, it is not applicable in most cases of cross-border crowdfunding, in which the CSP or the project owner are not established in the same Member State where the consumer is domiciled or habitually resident.

16.44 In light of this, an investor who qualifies as a consumer will normally be able to disregard the existence of a choice-of-court agreement in the contract with the CSP or project owner and commence litigation before the MSC of the place where he/she is domiciled, pursuant to Article 18 of the Brussels I*bis* Regulation.[62] The practical relevance of choice-of-court agreements is therefore mainly limited to situations where the investor does not qualify as a consumer. As already mentioned in subsections III.1 and IV.1 above, the qualification of an investor as 'sophisticated' for the purposes of the Crowdfunding Regulation is not relevant to the qualification of the same investor as a 'consumer' for jurisdictional purposes.

2. Arbitration Agreements

16.45 Arbitration is excluded from the scope of application of the Brussels I*bis* Regulation.[63] When the parties enter into an arbitration agreement they exclude the applicability of the Regulation altogether. This option may at first sight appear attractive in the context of crowdfunding, given the uncertainty surrounding the allocation of jurisdiction in crowdfunding-related disputes, and the difficulties connected with choice-of-court agreements, especially when the investor/claimant is a consumer. Furthermore, arbitral awards rely on a friendly regime for recognition and enforcement, set forth by the 1958 New York Convention on the Recognition and Enforcement of Foreign Arbitral Awards. For this reason, CSPs providing

---

[62] *Petruchová* (n 25) para 28.
[63] Art 1(2)(d) Brussels I*bis* Regulation.

cross-border services may be tempted to insert an arbitration clause in the standard agreements they conclude with investors. In practice, however, EU law limits the viability of this solution as well. Similarly to what happens with choice-of-court agreements, the parties' autonomy to enter into an agreement to arbitrate is limited, where the investor is a consumer. These limitations may derive from both domestic and EU law.

From the point of view of domestic law, in some national legal systems, consumer disputes **16.46** are altogether not arbitrable, and any arbitration agreement will be regarded as null and void.[64] In theory, the parties may select a seat of arbitration where consumer disputes are deemed to be arbitrable. In practice, however, the resulting arbitral award may not be enforceable in the jurisdiction where the award debtor is located if that jurisdiction does not allow for the arbitrability of consumer disputes. More specifically, under Article V(2)(a) of the New York Convention, a State may refuse to recognize and enforce an arbitral award if '(t)he subject matter of the difference is not capable of settlement by arbitration under the law of that country'. A CSP therefore may prevail in an arbitration against an investor/consumer, only to find out later that the award cannot produce legal effects in the State where the consumer is domiciled (and, hence, where recognition and enforcement may be needed).

From the point of view of EU law, although Article 19 of the Brussels I*bis* Regulation does **16.47** not apply with respect to arbitration agreements, the EU consumer acquis does impose some significant limitations. First of all, Article 10(1) of the Alternative Dispute Resolution (ADR) Directive[65] requires Member States to 'ensure that an agreement between a consumer and a trader to submit complaints to an ADR entity is not binding on the consumer if it was concluded before the dispute has materialised and if it has the effect of depriving the consumer of his right to bring an action before the courts for the settlement of the dispute'. This provision seems to refer to arbitration, as arbitration agreements typically exclude the jurisdiction of the national courts that would have had jurisdiction in the absence of an agreement.[66] Furthermore, Article 10(2) of the ADR Directive requires Member States to 'ensure that in ADR procedures which aim at resolving the dispute by imposing a solution' (such as arbitration), 'the solution imposed may be binding on the parties only if they were informed of its binding nature in advance and specifically accepted this'. If taken at face value, the ADR Directive rules out the possibility of an exclusive arbitration agreement concluded by a consumer before any dispute has arisen. The directive, however, has been described as a 'paper tiger' in practice,[67] as it only applies to ADR entities that have been officially accredited for the purposes of the directive, and such accreditation is not mandatory.[68] Therefore, a CSP or a project owner may theoretically enter into an arbitration agreement with an investor/consumer, selecting an arbitral institution that is not accredited

---

[64] I Bantekas, 'Arbitrability in Finance and Banking' in L Mistelis and S Brekoulakis (eds), *Arbitrability: International and Comparative Perspectives* (Kluwer 2009) 293.

[65] Directive 2013/11/EU of the European Parliament and of the Council of 21 May 2013 on alternative dispute resolution for consumer disputes and amending Regulation (EC) No 2006/2004 and Directive 2009/22/EC.

[66] Art II(3) New York Convention ensures the enforceability of such agreements, by requiring the courts of the contracting states to refer the disputing parties to arbitration, whenever the subject-matter of the litigation is covered by an arbitration agreement that is not null and void, inoperable, or incapable or being performed, and one of the parties objects to the jurisdiction of the chosen court.

[67] M Knigge and C Pavillon, 'The Legality Requirement of the ADR Directive: Just Another Paper Tiger?' (2016) 4 EuCML 155.

[68] See Arts 19 and 20, ADR Directive.

for the purposes of the ADR Directive. In practice, however, the Unfair Contract Terms Directive (UCTD) curtails this possibility.

16.48 The UCTD sets forth a protective regime for consumers, requiring Member States to ensure that unfair contract terms will not be binding on consumers.[69] Article 3(1) UCTD defines an unfair contract term as a 'contractual term which has not been individually negotiated' and, 'contrary to the requirement of good faith, it causes a significant imbalance in the parties' rights and obligations arising under the contract, to the detriment of the consumer'. The UCTD also includes an Annex, enumerating terms that 'may be regarded as unfair'.[70] Point (q) of this list, in particular, refers to terms 'excluding or hindering the consumer's right to take legal action or exercise any other legal remedy, particularly by requiring the consumer to take disputes exclusively to arbitration not covered by legal provisions'. To be sure, not all arbitration clauses included in consumer contracts must automatically be regarded as unfair, as the list is merely indicative and the UCTD entrusts MSCs with the task of assessing whether a particular term is unfair in each specific case. Nevertheless, there is a significant risk that if a CSP or a project owner inserts an arbitration agreement in a contract with an investor/consumer, the latter may be able to escape the effects of such agreements and seize the competent court under the Brussels I*bis* Regulation. According to the ECJ, even if the consumer/investor does not plead the invalidity of the agreement to arbitrate during the arbitral proceedings, such invalidity may be declared by the MSC competent for the annulment of the resulting arbitral award. In other words, not only may it be possible for an investor/consumer to ignore the agreement to arbitrate and commence court litigation; in addition, even if the counterparty commences arbitration and the investor/consumer does not raise any objections as to the unfairness of the arbitration agreement, the latter may be voided after the end of the arbitration, in the context of a setting aside action introduced by the investor/consumer against the arbitral award.[71] The ECJ thus derogates from the general rule, prevailing in most national legal systems,[72] whereby a disputant appearing before an arbitral tribunal without raising jurisdictional objections loses the right to plead the invalidity of the arbitration clause at a later stage. The ECJ has also applied the same rationale to a case where the invalidity of the arbitration agreement is pleaded neither in the context of arbitration proceedings nor in court proceedings for the annulment of the resulting award, but only in proceedings for the enforcement of the award.[73] This line of case law resonates with a broader standpoint of the ECJ, whereby MSCs must be able to assess the unfairness of a contract term *ex officio*.[74]

16.49 In light of this, the EU consumer acquis largely prevents CSPs and project owners from excluding the application of the Brussels I*bis* Regulation by means of an agreement to arbitrate, whenever the investor qualifies as a consumer (as defined by Article 2 UCTD).

---

[69] Art 6(1) UCTD.

[70] Art 3(3) UCTD.

[71] Case C-168/05, *Elisa María Mostaza Claro v Centro Móvil Milenium SL*, ECLI:EU:C:2006:675.

[72] This tendency is reflected in Art 7(5) Option I of the 2006 UNCITRAL Model Law on International Commercial Arbitration.

[73] Case C-168/15, *Milena Tomášová v Slovenská republika—Ministerstvo spravodlivosti SR and Pohotovosť s.r.o.*, ECLI:EU:C:2016:602, para 32.

[74] Case C-240/98, *Océano Grupo Editorial SA v Roció Murciano Quintero (C-240/98) and Salvat Editores SA v José M. Sánchez Alcón Prades*, ECLI:EU:C:2000:346; Case C-473/00, *Cofidis SA v Jean-Louis Fredout*; ECLI:EU:C:2002:705; Case C-243/08, *Pannon GSM Zrt. v Erzsébet Sustikné Győrfi*, ECLI:EU:C:2009:350.

Therefore, similarly to choice-of-court agreements, arbitration agreements only constitute a viable option in cases where the investor does not qualify as a consumer.

VI. Conclusion

This chapter has analysed the jurisdictional aspects of crowdfunding-related disputes in the EU, with specific attention to cases concerning the Crowdfunding Regulation. A distinction has been drawn between situations where the investor/claimant commences court proceedings against a CSP, and situations where the respondent is a project owner.   **16.50**

In the first scenario, the respondent is always established in a Member State, so that Article 4(1) of the Brussels I*bis* Regulation will be applicable, and the investor/claimant will be able to sue the CSP in the Member State where the latter is established. As an alternative to the general *actor sequitur forum rei* rule, the investor/claimant may be able to establish jurisdiction under Article 18 of the Brussels I*bis* Regulation and commence litigation in the Member State where he/she is domiciled, provided that the requirements of Article 17 are met. In cases where the investor/claimant does not qualify as a consumer, it may be possible to establish jurisdiction under Article 7 of the Brussels I*bis* Regulation, relying on different territorial criteria, depending on whether the cause of action is contractual or tortious.   **16.51**

In situations where the respondent is the project owner, reliance on Article 4 of the Brussels I*bis* Regulation is contingent on whether the project owner is established in a Member State. If that is the case, jurisdiction may also be established on the basis of Article 7. In practice, the tortious head of jurisdiction of Article 7(2) will often be relevant, whenever the litigation concerns the provision of misleading of incorrect information in the KIIS, or the omission of information, given the typically tortious nature of this type of claim. By contrast, reliance on Article 18 will be possible irrespective of where the project owner is domiciled, as long as the requirements of Article 17 are met. According to the ECJ, the requirement of contractual privity of Article 17(1) is not met, if the claimant/investor has acquired instruments issued by the defendant/project owner on the secondary market.   **16.52**

Given the overlap of different jurisdictional criteria in the Brussels I*bis* Regulation, and the resulting unpredictability, the question arises whether CSPs and project owners may enhance legal certainty by way of private autonomy. In theory, this goal may be pursued either through an exclusive choice-of-court agreement, or by excluding the applicability of the Brussels I*bis* Regulation altogether, through an arbitration agreement. Both techniques, however, are not practically viable whenever the investor is a consumer, due to the provisions of EU law aimed at protecting consumers, as interpreted by the ECJ. In light of this, the insertion of an exclusive head of jurisdiction in the Crowdfunding Regulation may have been a sounder regulatory choice, limiting the overlap of multiple fora and ensuring predictability for all actors involved in crowdfunding. To date, however, the EU law-maker has not adopted this approach, and the jurisdictional aspects of crowdfunding-related litigation must be assessed through a delicate coordination between the Crowdfunding Regulation and the Brussels I*bis* Regulation.   **16.53**

17

Collective Redress in Crowdfunding

Tomas Arons

I. Introduction

As the European crowdfunding market grows in volume, disputes will unavoidably arise be- **17.01**
tween investors, on the one hand, and project owners or CSPs, on the other hand. Investors,
for instance, may claim compensation from the project owner, because of misleading, inaccurate, or missing information in the key investment information sheet. As mentioned in
Chapter 9, pursuant to Article 23(9) of the Crowdfunding Regulation, Member States must
'ensure the responsibility of at least the project owner or its administrative, management or
supervisory bodies for the information given in a key investment information sheet [KIIS]'.
In other situations, as illustrated in Chapter 16, investors may bring a tortious claim under
the applicable national law against the CSP, claiming damages for an alleged failure to verify
the completeness, correctness, and clarity of the information contained in the key investment information sheet, as required by Article 23(11) of the Crowdfunding Regulation. In
yet other cases, investors may bring a claim against the CSP concerning, for example, the
individual portfolio management of loans under Article 6 of the Crowdfunding Regulation,
or the provision of full access to the platform without a prior assessment of appropriateness,
as mandated by Article 21 of the Crowdfunding Regulation.

The examples mentioned above are, in many respects, disparate: some of them relate to **17.02**
tortious causes of action, while other ones are contractual in nature. Furthermore, in some
cases (such as the liability of the project owner for the information contained in the KIIS)
the Crowdfunding Regulation partially harmonizes the content of the applicable national
law, requiring the Member States to ensure the responsibility of the project owner, while in
other scenarios the viability of the action depends largely on the contents of national law.

Nevertheless, one distinctive feature links many of these litigation scenarios: these cases will often involve a high number of claimants. For this reason, investors may choose not to litigate individually but to collectively seek redress against the project owner or crowd-funding service provider (CSP). The losses suffered by different members of the crowd are similar, and easier to quantify than, for example, bodily harm. Moreover, the assessment whether the information provided was misleading is abstract, relying on the notion of the 'average investor' as a touchstone.[1] In fact, most collective proceedings in the last decades have been initiated by investors suffering investment losses as a result of alleged corporate mismanagement or misinformation. These losses normally consist in the decrease in value of equity participations or bonds. The advantage of collective proceedings is that similar questions of law and fact are presented and dealt with by the court in a single procedure. Not only the disputants but also the court system benefits from this efficiency gain.

17.03   In collective proceedings, associations or foundations will typically act as claimants, repre-senting a constituency of investors that allegedly suffered the same type of harm, and taking decisions with (legal) consequences for the individual members of this group. The interests of the group members, thus, need to be adequately protected. It is therefore important to analyse whether and to what extent the procedural law of different EU Member States af-fords the possibility of collective redress, and how the interests of the group (in this case, crowdfunding investors) are safeguarded within these procedures. To this end, this chapter will scrutinize collective redress under EU, French, German, and Dutch law, and its rele-vance for crowdfunding dispute resolution. Section II will discuss the recently adopted EU Directive on representative actions.[2] Subsequently, sections III, IV, and V will discuss col-lective redress in French, German, and Dutch law. Finally, section VI will present some conclusions.

II. Directive on Representative Actions for the Protection of the Collective Interests of Consumers

17.04   On 24 November 2020, the European Parliament adopted the Directive on representative actions for the protection of the collective interests of consumers. This Directive must be implemented in the various national laws of the Member States by 25 December 2022.[3] This instrument aims to ensure that in all Member States at least one effective and efficient pro-cedural mechanism for representative actions for injunctive measures and for redress meas-ures is available to consumers.[4] It explicitly does not seek to replace or harmonize existing

---

[1] *World Online/VEB* [27 November 2009] Dutch Supreme Court, ECLI:NL:HR:2009:BH2162, JOR 2010/43 annotated by K Frielink; Ondernemingsrecht 2010/21 annotated by H Vletter-van Dort, *NJ* 2014/201 anno-tated by E Du Perron, AA20100336, annotated by G Raaijmakers [4.10.3]; *De Treek/Dexia* [5 June 2009] Dutch Supreme Court, ECLI:NL:HR:2009:BH2815, JOR 2009, 199 annotated by K Lieverse; *AA* 2010, 188 annotated by W van Boom and S Lindenbergh [4.5.3]. In both cases the 305a-organization based its claim on the regula-tion of Misleading or Comparative Advertising in the Dutch Civil Code (Art 6:194–6.195 BW) which in its cur-rent reading is only applicable to professional investors. Consumer can base their claim on regulation of Unfair Commercial Practices (Art 6:193a up to and including Art 6:193j BW).
[2] Directive (EU) 2020/1828 of the European Parliament and of the Council of 25 November 2020 on represen-tative actions for the protection of the collective interests of consumers and repealing Directive 2009/22/EC [2020] OJ L 409/1.
[3] ibid art 24.
[4] ibid Recital 7.

national procedural mechanisms for collective redress.[5] Only certain aspects of collective redress are harmonized.[6]

First of all, its scope is limited to consumer to business (C2B) claims concerning infringe-   **17.05** ments of the EU consumer acquis, that is, the corpus of EU legislation on consumer protection (Annex I of Directive). Therefore, although the Crowdfunding Regulation is not expressly included in Annex I at the time of writing, the Directive is relevant to the phenomenon of crowdfunding litigation, inasmuch as the dispute concerns the alleged violation of the EU consumer acquis (eg allegedly unfair contract terms).[7] Member States have to ensure that entities, in particular consumer organizations (including those that represent members from more than one Member State), are eligible to be designated as qualified entities for the purpose of bringing domestic representative actions, cross-border representative actions, or both. A representative action is an action for the protection of the collective interests of consumers that is brought by a qualified entity as claimant on behalf of consumers to seek an injunctive measure (declaratory relief),[8] a redress measure, or both.[9] A domestic representative action is brought by a qualified entity in the Member State in which the qualified entity was designated.[10] Conversely, a cross-border representative action is brought by a qualified entity in a Member State other than that in which the qualified entity was designated.[11] The designated entities must operate on a not-for-profit basis.[12]

As far as third-party funding is concerned, the Directive provides for the following re-   **17.06** quirements. A conflict of interest between the third-party funder and the qualified entity that poses a risk of abusive litigation must be prevented.[13] The qualified entity has to provide thereto that it is independent and not influenced by persons other than consumers, in particular by traders, who have an economic interest in any representative action, including in the event of funding by third parties. To that end, it has to establish procedures to prevent such influence, as well as to prevent conflicts of interest between itself, its funding providers and the interests of consumers.[14] Importantly, the Committee on Legal Affairs of the European Parliament submitted on 17 June 2021 a recommendation to the Commission to adopt a Proposal Directive on Responsible private funding of litigation.[15] This Recommendation seeks to introduce a regulatory regime addressing key issues relevant to third party litigation funding, including transparency, fairness, and proportionality so as to ensure that the interests of claimants are protected by establishing a fiduciary relationship between claimants and litigation funders.[16] Furthermore, under the Directive,

---

[5] ibid Recital 11.
[6] ibid Recital 12.
[7] For an overview of the relevance of the consumer acquis in crowdfunding see Chapter 5.
[8] Directive (EU) 2020/1828 of the European Parliament and of the Council of 25 November 2020 on representative actions for the protection of the collective interests of consumers and repealing Directive 2009/22/EC [2020] OJ L 409/1 Art 6. This declaratory relief may consist of a court order to cease a business practice and a declaratory ruling that the business practice infringes on protected consumer rights.
[9] ibid Art 3(5).
[10] ibid Art 3(6).
[11] ibid Art 3(7).
[12] ibid Art 4(3)(c).
[13] ibid Art 10 and Recital 52.
[14] ibid Art 4(3)(e) and Recital 25, Preamble.
[15] Draft Report with recommendations to the Commission on Responsible private funding of litigation (2020/2130(INL)), PE680.934. On 16 July 2021, this Committee on Legal Affairs submitted Amendments to this Draft Report, PE695.342.
[16] ibid pp 4–5.

Member States have to ensure that the decisions of qualified entities in the context of a representative action, including decisions on settlement, are not unduly influenced by a third party in a manner that would be detrimental to the collective interests of the consumers concerned by the representative action.[17] Representative actions may not be brought against a defendant that is a competitor of the funding provider, or against a defendant on which the funding provider is dependent.[18] Courts must be empowered to assess compliance, in cases where any justified doubts arise in this respect. To that end, qualified entities must disclose to the court a financial overview that lists sources of funds used to support the representative action.[19] Courts must have the authority to take appropriate measures, such as requiring the qualified entity to refuse or make changes in respect of the relevant funding and, if necessary, rejecting the legal standing of the qualified entity in a specific representative action. If the legal standing of the qualified entity is rejected in a specific representative action, that rejection shall not affect the rights of the consumers concerned by that representative action.[20]

III. French Collective Redress Model: *Action de Groupe*

17.07 After lengthy debate in the French Parliament, a collective action procedure was introduced in 2014 in French civil law. This collective action (*action de groupe*) was enacted in the Consumer Code (*Code de la consommation*, hereinafter 'C. consomm.').[21]

17.08 Chapter III of Title II of book IV C. consomm. (Articles L423-1 to L423-26) is titled *action de groupe*. Because of the constitutionally protected right to individual access to court,[22] the *action de groupe* is based on the opt-in model. In other words, the court judgment will bind not all members of the group in whose interest the collective action is brought, but only those that explicitly made themselves known. However, the French legislator has explicitly set forth that the individual group members do not have to be known to the litigating parties nor the courts at the start of the collective action. It is up to the court to define the interested or affected group, and rule upon the defendant's liability towards this group.[23] The French collective action has few formal requirements and regulations.[24] Much is left to judicial autonomy.

---

[17] Directive (EU) 2020/1828 (n 8) Art 10(2)(a).
[18] ibid Art 10(2)(b).
[19] ibid Art 10(3).
[20] ibid Art 10(4).
[21] Loi no 2014-344 du 17 mars 2014 relative à la consommation. After endorsement by the Constitutional Council (*Conseil consitutionnel*) in its judgment of 12 March 2014, ECLI:FR:CC:2014:2014.690.DC, JORF 2014/65, no 2, 18 mars 2014, p 5450, the law was proclaimed by presidential order, JORF 2014/65, 18 mars 2014, no 2, p 5400.
[22] Judgment of the *Conseil Constitutionnel*, 25 July 1989, ECLI:FR:CC:1989:89.257.DC, JORF 1989, 28 juillet 1989, p.9503; referred to in the following parliamentary document: Sénat, No 809, 24 July 2013, Rapport fait au nom de la commission des affaires économiques (1) sur le projet de loi, adopté par l'Assemblée nationale. relatif à la consommation, M Bourquin and A Fauconnier, pp 34–35.
[23] Assemblée nationale, No 1156, 13 juin 2013, Rapport fait au nom de la commission des affaires économiques sur le projet de loi relative à la consommation, R Hammadi and A Le Loch, p 60.
[24] M Bacache, 'Action de groupe et responsabilité civile' [2014] *Revue trimestrielle de droit civil*, 450; E Claudel, 'Action de groupe et autres dispositions concurrence de la loi consommation: un dispositif singulier' [2014] *Revue trimestrielle de droit commercial*, 339; N Molfessis, 'L'exorbitance de l'action de groupe à la française' [2014] Recueil Dalloz 947.

On the basis of Article L423-1 C. consomm., associations officially recognized by the **17.09** French government (*associations agréés*) may act in the common interest of consumers by filing claims, in order to obtain compensation for the individual damages suffered by consumers. The consumers need to have suffered damages in an identical or similar situation. The group's defining common ground (*cause commune*) lays in a violation of the (pre-)[25] contractual legal obligations by (a) person(s) trading in a professional or business capacity (*professionel*)[26] in the context of the sale of a good or service, or in losses incurred as a result of violations of (EU) competition law.[27] In the parliamentary debate it was made clear by the Minister that 'sale of a good or service' must be interpreted so as to encompass pure economic losses incurred by consumer-investors as a result of financial services provided to them or securities and financial products offered to them. The Ministry mentioned the example of a violation of information, advisory, or warning duties by banks or professional service providers.[28]

The *action de groupe* consists of three stages. At the first stage, the court rules on the admis- **17.10** sibility of the association and its claim, as well as the liability of the defendant for its alleged behaviour towards the consumers specifically mentioned as examples by the association in its writ of summons.[29] In its ruling, the court also need to address: (a) a class description and selection criteria; (b) the reimbursable loss items for each (category of) consumer(s); (c) the (individual or categorical) compensation; and (d) the compensation evaluation criteria.[30]

Once this ruling is no longer appealable, the court will order the manner in which it shall **17.11** be made public.[31] The court determines the opt-in period (two to six months) in which the individual members of the group have to register at the defendant or at the association.[32] By law, the association has a mandate to act in the interest of the consumers who opt-in.[33] If the identity and number of the consumers involved in the harmful event are known from the start, and the amount of damages is identical, the court may immediately order the defendant to directly pay the compensation to these consumers.[34]

---

[25] Ministerial reaction to Amendment CE345 of T Benoit. This amendment restricted the scope to contractual obligations. It was rejected by the French Parliament. Assemblée nationale, No 1574, 21 novembre 2013, Rapport fait au nom de la commission des affaires économiques sur le projet de loi, modifié par le Sénat, relatif à la consommation (No 1357), R Hammadi and A Le Loch, p.40.

[26] At the request of the French Senate the possibility was introduced that consumer associations can claim against multiple defendants in one procedure for identical or similar matters. See Sénat, No 282, 15 janvier 2014, Rapport fait au nom de la commission des affaires économiques (I) dur le projet de loi, adopté pas l'Assemblée nationale, relatif à la consommation, M Bourquin and A Fauconnier.

[27] C. consomm., Art L423-1. Please note that the Act of 18 November 2016 (*Loi de modernisation de la justice du 21ᵉ siècle*), Art 85, the material scope has be broadened to include actions for the protection against harms to (a) discrimination; (b) environment; (c) health; (d) personal data. Furthermore, this Act also introduced an identical collective procedure before the administrative court (Chapter X–XII of Title VII of Book VII Code de justice administrative).

[28] Ministerial reaction to Amendement CE31 of D Abad, Assemblée nationale, No 1574, 21 novembre 2013, Rapport fait au nom de la commission des affaires économiques sur le projet de loi, modifié par le Sénat, relatif à la consommation (n° 1357), R Hammadi and A Le Loch, p 42.

[29] C. consomm., Art L423-4.

[30] C. consomm., Art L423-1.

[31] C. consomm., Art L423-8.

[32] C. consomm., Art L423-5.

[33] C. consomm., Art L623-5.

[34] C. consomm., Art L423-10 '*Procédure d'action de groupe simplifiée*'.

17.12   At the second stage, the court will determine which type of losses will be compensated either for each individual consumer, or for defined categories of consumers. In the same ruling, it will also establish the method to calculate the damages to be awarded either individually or categorically.

17.13   The third stage centres on the compensation schemes execution. In principle, the French legislator assumes that the defendant will, in accordance with the stage one ruling, pay the compensation due to the individual consumers.[35] Should there be any conflict as to how the compensation should be carried out, the court will issue a single ruling on all outstanding compensation claims.[36] The individual claimants will be represented by the association involved in the proceedings.[37]

17.14   In sum, if the litigating association and defendant do not settle, the court will give a ruling at the second stage, determining how the individual members of the group must be compensated. It can provide for a calculation mechanism of damages to be awarded on an individual basis, or per category. This ruling is quite similar to the one the Dutch courts give under the new collective action proceedings (*Wet Afwikkeling Massaschade in Collectieve Actie*, WAMCA), which will discussed below in section V. Unlike Dutch law, however, French law specifically provides how courts have to solve problems concerning the execution of the judgment (third stage).

17.15   The litigating parties may, at any stage before and during the court proceedings, conclude an out-of-court settlement. This settlement needs court approval in order to bind the group. The court will assess whether the settlement is in the interest of the consumers affected. The settlement has only binding effect on those consumers that opt in during the term set by the court in its approval ruling.[38] Thus, unlike the Dutch proceedings, the French collective proceedings does not provide for an opt-out settlement model where all group members are bound by the settlement unless they explicitly refuse it.

IV. German Collective Redress Model

1. Capital Markets Model Case (KapMuG) Proceedings

17.16   Collective proceedings were introduced in German law in 2005 with the Capital Markets Model Case Proceedings Act (*Kapitalanleger-Musterverfahrensgesetz*, KapMuG).[39] One of the major driving forces behind the KapMuG was the *Deutsche Telekom* case.

17.17   In 2000, Deutsche Telekom, the state (mobile) phone operator, was privatized by issuing shares on the Frankfurt Stock Exchange. In order to inform potential investors a prospectus was published. The initial issuing price was set at EUR 66.50 per share. Soon after floating,

---

[35]   C. consomm., Art L423-3.

[36]   C. consomm., Art L423-12.

[37]   C. consomm., Art L423-9 and Art L623-5. The legal costs of the association will be borne by the defendant (C. consomm., Art L423-8).

[38]   C. consomm., Art L423-16.

[39]   BGBl. I 2005, S. 2437. This Act has been replaced by the entry into force of KapMuG-ReformG (*Gesetz zur Reform des Kapitalanleger-Musterverfahrensgesetzes und zur Änderung anderer Vorschriften*), BGBl. I 2012, S. 2182.

the share price fell considerably. Many investors suffering losses initiated individual court proceedings against Deutsche Telekom, claiming damages for the losses incurred as a result of allegedly misleading statements in the prospectus.

In order to alleviate the German courts from the burden to deal with a vast number of iden-   **17.18** tical individual claims against the same defendant, the KapMuG was introduced.[40] Without the KapMuG, traditional *res judicata* rules would prevent a court judgment from binding the members of a group that are not a formal parties to the proceedings.[41]

In KapMuG proceedings (*Musterverfahren*), Higher Regional Courts (*Oberlandesgericht*)   **17.19** rule with binding effect on factual and legal issues that these claims have in common. The use of this method of collective redress in mass claims is limited to damage claims for losses suffered as a result of misleading information disseminated on public capital markets.[42]

A district court (*Landgericht*) may at the request of (one of the) litigating parties initiate   **17.20** a collective procedure.[43] A precondition is that the individual dispute needs to be solved by answering questions of law and/or fact that it has in common with other claims. If the *Landgericht* rules that there is sufficient ground to establish that its decision in the pending case depends on establishing an element of liability or an answer to a legal question that is common to more court proceedings,[44] it stays proceedings and makes a public an- nouncement in the KapMuG register of the electronic version of the German State Gazette (*Bundesanzeiger*).[45] In the case that, within six months of registration, at least nine requests to initiate model case proceedings have been made in cases concerning similar claims, the *Oberlandesgericht* selects one of the claimants as the model case claimant.[46] In the model case proceedings, the *Oberlandesgericht* rules with binding effect on the common factual and legal issues.

During the model case procedure before the *Oberlandesgericht*, other cases concerning   **17.21** claims in which one of these common factual and/or legal issues also arise are stayed *ex officio* until the *Oberlandesgericht* has given its model case ruling (*Musterentscheid*).[47] This ruling is binding in the sense that the *Landgerichte* have to apply this ruling in their deci- sions on the pending claims.[48] The individual circumstances of each claimant will be dealt with by the *Landgerichte* when they resume the pending proceedings after the model case

---

[40] German scholars were not convinced that this Act would solve the problem of overburdening the courts as long as all claimants would, as third parties to the model case proceedings, have the right to participate in those proceedings. According to them, the only practical solution would be to introduce an opt-out procedure which happened in the KapMuG Reform Act 2012. See J Jahn, 'Der Telekom-Prozess: Stresstest für das Kapitalanleger-Musterverfahrensgesetz' [2005] ZIP 29, 1317. In practice, these problems seem to be overcome quite efficiently by the use of electronic means. See the KapMuG evaluation: A Halfmeier, P Rott, and E Fees, *Kollektiver Rechtsschutz im Kapitalmarktrecht: Evaluation des Kapitalanleger-Musterverfahrensgesetzes* (Banking & Finance aktuell, Band 40 Frankfurt School 2010) 30, 54–55. In particular, the uniform provision of evidence and the enhancement of legal certainty by the factual binding effect of early decisions by the German Court of Justice are regarded advantageous.

[41] A Stadler, 'Group Actions as a Remedy to Enforce Consumer Interests' in F Cafaggi and H-W Micklitz (eds), *New Frontiers of Consumer Protection: The Interplay Between Private and Public Enforcement* (Intersentia 2009) 313.

[42] KapMuG, § 1.

[43] KapMuG, § 2(1). The Landgericht may not ex officio start the KapMuG proceedings.

[44] KapMuG, § 3(1).

[45] KapMuG, § 3(2).

[46] KapMuG § 6(1) and § 9(2).

[47] KapMuG, § 8.

[48] KapMuG, § 22.

ruling. Issues of fault on the part of the claimant, and of causation, which are not common to all claimants, remain to be decided by the lower courts when they rule upon the claim for damages.

17.22   An example is again the *Deutsche Telekom* case. On 21 October 2014 the German Supreme Court (*Bundesgerichtshof*, BGH) upheld the *Oberlandesgericht*'s KapMuG decision that the prospectus was indeed misleading.[49] The BGH also ruled that individual circumstances (such as causation) cannot be decided in model case proceedings. The questions need to be addressed by the *Landgericht* in the individual cases.

17.23   One of the basic features of the KapMuG is the opt-in character. Only similar claims against the common defendant(s) brought before the *Landgericht* are subject to the binding effect of the *Musterentscheid*. Furthermore, only in regard of claims brought before the courts, or registered at the OLG,[50] is the limitation period of the claim interrupted.[51] The KapMuG's material scope is limited to claims for damages related to corporate misinformation in a prospectus, violation of disclosure duties by listed companies,[52] and contractual claims regarding the offer and sale of securities.[53]

17.24   On 1 November 2012 the KapMuG Reform Act entered into force.[54] This Reform Act introduced the possibility for the model case parties to settle their dispute during the proceedings and have the *Oberlandesgerichte* declare the settlement agreement binding for all pending cases. The individual claimants may opt out of the binding effect of the settlement and continue the stayed proceedings against the defendant in the individual proceedings before the *Landgericht*.[55]

2. Model Declaratory Proceedings (*Musterfeststellungsverfahren*)

17.25   In July 2018, the German legislator adopted the model declaratory proceedings (*Musterfest stellungsverfahren*) in book 6 of the German Code of Civil Procedure (*Zivilprozessordnung*, ZPO).[56] Qualified consumer associations may file a collective declaratory claim regarding questions of law and fact common to claims of consumers against a business or company.[57]

---

[49] BGH, 21.10.2014, Az. XI ZB 12/12.

[50] KapMuG, § 10(2).

[51] F Reuschle, § 77, in P Derleder, K-O Knops, and H G Bamberger (eds), *Deutsches und europäisches Bank- und Kapitalmarktrecht* (Springer 2017) 1416.

[52] KapMuG, § 2(2)(3) as modified by Act of 30 June 2016 (§ 16 van Erstes Gesetz zur Novellierung von Finanzmarktvorschriften auf Grund europäischer Rechtsakte (1. FiMANoG) vom 30 Juni 2016 (BGBl. I S. 1514)). Violations by listed companies of their duty to disclose inside information to the public as required by the EU Market Abuse Regulation (Regulation (EU) No 596/2014 of the European Parliament and of the Council of 16 April 2014 on market abuse (market abuse regulation) and repealing Directive 2003/6/EC of the European Parliament and of the Council and Commission Directives 2003/124/EC, 2003/125/EC and 2004/72/EC [2014] OJ L173/1, Art 17) are brought under the material scope of the KapMuG.

[53] KapMuG, § 1(1).

[54] BGBl.I S.2182.

[55] KapMuG, § 23(3).

[56] BGBl.I S.1151.

[57] ZPO, § 606(1). Qualified consumer associations include non-German associations registered for at least four years at the European Commission on the basis of art. 4 of Directive 2009/22/EC of the European Parliament and of the Council of 23 April 2009 on injunctions for the protection of consumers' interests (Codified version) [2009] OJ L110/30, see ZPO, § 606(2).

The writ of summons must detail at least ten consumer claims.[58] The issue may concern the (non-)existence of a legal relationship between a consumer and a business.[59] In the case that at least fifty such claims are filed at the court registry (*Klageregister*)[60] within two months of registering the collective declaratory claim, the model declaratory proceedings will start.[61] If individual consumers brought claims to court in individual proceedings concerning the same matter before the collective declaratory proceedings were initiated, these consumers may register their claim on the basis of § 607 ZPO, and their individual proceedings are stayed.[62]

The declaratory judgment (*Musterfeststellungsurteil*) is published at the court registry.[63] If a   **17.26**
declaratory judgment can no longer be appealed,[64] it is binding on all registered consumers and the defendant.[65] If the consumer has withdrawn his registration before this judgment, the latter has no binding effect.[66]

A settlement concluded between the association and the defendant needs court approval.[67]   **17.27**
Upon approval, it has binding effect on the consumer claims registered.[68] Every consumer has the right to opt out of this settlement within one month after being notified of the court approval of the settlement.[69]

The structure of these model declaratory proceedings is similar to the Dutch collective   **17.28**
proceedings when declaratory relief is sought by the claimant organization (see paragraph 7). An important difference is that not all associations may file such a claim. Access to the *Musterfeststellungsverfahren* is restricted to officially recognized consumer associations. Like the KapMuG, it is an opt-in model. The binding effect of the declaratory judgment is limited to consumer claims registered.

V. Dutch Collective Redress Models

Given the prominence of the Netherlands as a crowdfunding market, Dutch courts seem to   **17.29**
be in a promising position as a forum for the resolution of crowdfunding-related disputes. For this reason, this section will present an in-depth case-study of the Dutch collective action scheme, which could be potentially used by crowdfunding investors in the future.[70]

The Dutch collective action was first codified in 1994 in the Dutch Civil Code in Article   **17.30**
3:305a BW. This legislation has been thoroughly renewed as at 1 January 2020. Under the

---

[58] ZPO, § 606(2)(2).
[59] ZPO, § 606(1).
[60] ZPO, § 607.
[61] ZPO, § 606(3).
[62] ZPO, § 613(2).
[63] ZPO, § 612(1).
[64] ZPO, § 614.
[65] ZPO, § 613(1).
[66] ZPO, § 613(1) last sentence.
[67] ZPO, § 613(3).
[68] ZPO, § 611(1).
[69] ZPO, § 611(4).
[70] It should incidentally be noted that Dutch law also allows collective action for public interest, non-commercial litigation. This facet of the phenomenon, however, is not directly linked to the resolution of disputes between investors, project owners, and CSPs, and will therefore not be discussed in this chapter.

new regime, as subsection V.3 will illustrate in detail, it is possible to collectively claim damages, so that the court will order a collective damage schedule, in cases where the parties fail to reach a collective settlement. The defendant will be obliged to perform this judicially ordered damage schedule by paying accordingly to the victims.

17.31   Collective redress in the Netherlands has many different legal structures. The legal person representing the class may:

- claim on the basis of agency or proxy (agency model);
- bundle individual claims transferred to it by assignment (assignment model); or
- bring a claim in its own name, in the interest of their constituency (305a-collective model).

In the agency model, the claim vehicle[71] is the formal party to these proceedings, and the individual victims are the material party; in the other two models (assignment model and collective model) the claiming entity is the formal as well as the material party to the proceedings.[72] When acting on a mandate from an undisclosed principal, the formal party to the proceedings acts in its own name on behalf of the represented principal (in this case, the individual victims). The latter are the material parties to the proceedings.

17.32   The first two models (agency model and assignment model) amount to bundling individual claims. Even though these claims are dealt with in a single procedure, the individual relationships between the alleged tortfeasor and his victims are central. In the 305a- or 'collective' model, this is different. The organization claims in his own right (a collective claim), in the interest of other parties. In a 305a-model, legal action and claims instigated by the organization must serve the protection of similar interests of other persons. On the basis of Article 3:305a of the Dutch Civil Code (*Burgerlijk Wetboek*, or BW) a foundation or association (often referred to as a '305a-organization') with full legal capacity may institute a legal action for the protection of similar interests of other persons, provided that it represents these interests in accordance with its articles of association and these interests are adequately safeguarded.[73] The 305a-organization does not have a cause of action if the case only benefits its own members or constituency; all victims suffering losses as a result of the event must benefit.[74] As a necessary condition for such a collective claim, the court must be able to judge this claim in a sufficiently abstract manner, without involving the individual circumstances of the members of the group of persons whose interests are protected.

17.33   As will be discussed in the next paragraphs, these different models each have their own judicial review framework to assess admissibility. Especially the obligation to furnish facts and give evidence for each individual claim, the service of a list of represented persons to the defendants, and the assessment of third-party funding differs per model. Some organizations

---

[71] Unlike in the 305a-model no formal restriction to certain types of legal persons is applicable in the agency model and assignment model. In principle, every (legal) person may instigate an action on the basis of agency or because of the claim has been assigned to that party by the original claimant. In practice, collective action proceedings of any kind are instigated by foundations.

[72] See on the difference between formal and material parties to proceedings J Biemans, *Rechtsgevolgen van stille cessie* (Kluwer 2011) para 3.5.2.1.

[73] Until 1 January 2020 it was prohibited to claim damages in a collective action (former Art 3:305a(3) BW).

[74] *Stichting GIN schade/IDM Financieringen BV* [25 April 2018] Amsterdam District Court, ECLI:NL:RBAMS:2018:2693 [4.6]; *NAM/Christelijke Woningstichting Patrimonium Groningen* [23 January 2018] Arnhem-Leeuwarden Court of Appeal, ECLI:NL:GHARL:2018:618 [6.2–6.8].

have their own funds or receive (government) subsidies to bring a collective claim; typically, they will choose the 305a-model. Conversely, *ad hoc* foundations are dependent on commercial litigation funders. These foundations will only act on behalf of their own clients and more often opt for an agency or assignment model.

1. Safeguard Assessment

To safeguard the interests of the organization's constituency, the court will check if the legal   **17.34**
person is sufficiently representative, both in view of its constituency and the value of the claims represented.

Claims brought by a 305a-organization are inadmissible if the action is not sufficiently in   **17.35**
the interest of the constituency. The test involves issues of corporate governance, appropriateness, and effectiveness of mechanisms for participation or representation in decision-making by persons whose interests are the subject of the legal action, and sufficiency of resources to bear the costs of instituting a legal action, which ensures that the legal person has sufficient control over the legal action. Furthermore, the court can prevent 305a-organizations and their affiliated litigation funders from using the collective redress mechanisms mainly to enlarge their commercial litigation business.[75] In order to be able to assess whether the interests are properly safeguarded, the interests (including the possible commercial ones of third-party litigation funders) involved in the collective proceedings have to be known. The 305a-organization has to show how many persons it represents and must demonstrate that it fulfils certain organizational requirements.[76]

This test safeguards the interests of all parties involved on the claimant side, including the   **17.36**
305a-organizations itself. If the collective proceedings are financed by a third party, the conditions set in the finance agreement are subject of judicial scrutiny as well.[77] In particular, the control and decision-making powers of this funder and the fee conditions are tested. The judiciary, as well as the Dutch legislator, recognize the useful function of third-party funding in collective litigation.[78]

Such a judicial scrutiny of third-party financing has not (yet) occurred in collective pro-   **17.37**
ceedings involving a foundation or any other (legal) person demanding damages for claims assigned to it. Unlike in the agency model, the claiming party is in this case the formal as well as the material party in the proceedings.

In some situations, another third party is involved in the collective proceedings. The foun-   **17.38**
dation agrees to claim on behalf of the victims, in exchange for a success fee. The victims

---

[75] Parliamentary Papers I 2012/13, 33126, C, pp 1–2.

[76] See Parliamentary Papers II 2011/12, 33126, 3, pp 12–13.

[77] Parliamentary Papers II 2017/18, 34608, 6, p 25.

[78] *Stichting Petrobras Compensation Foundation/Petrobras* [29 January 2020] Rotterdam District Court ECLI:NL:RBROT:2020:614, *JOR* 2020 /119 annotated by T Arons, *Ondernemingsrecht* 2020/49 annotated by L van Bochove [5.15]; *Stichting Union des Victimes des déchets toxiques Côte d'Ivoire/Trafigura Beheer BV* [14 April 2020] Amsterdam Court of Appeal ECLI:NL:GHAMS:2020:1157, *Ondernemingsrecht* 2020/117 annotated by T Arons [2.13] and [3.28]; *PAL/Aegon* [4 February 2020] The Hague Court of Appeal, ECLI:NL:GHDHA:2020:102, JOR 2020/116 annotated by T Arons [19]; *VEB/Steinhoff* [26 September 2018] Amsterdam District Court, ECLI:NL:RBAMS:2018:6840, JOR 2019/121 annotated by F Kroes [4.21].

agree that the foundation can outsource this task of bringing a claim to a third party, the subagent. In most cases, this will be a company or other commercial organization.

17.39   The judiciary seeks to establish an equitable balance between all parties involved in collective redress. If the claimant organization opts to pursue collective proceedings under Article 3:305a BW, its claim has to be sufficiently collective so as to enable the court to deal with it without regard of any individual circumstances (abstractness of the claim). To this end, the claim has to be structured in an 'abstract' fashion, so as to enable scrutiny of multiple individual positions within a single procedure. Furthermore, the organization has to comply with the organizational and governance requirements, and any agreements with clients and/or funders will be subject to judicial review.

2. Collective Proceedings: Declaratory Relief

17.40   Collective proceedings based on the alleged violation of information duties (such as the ones relating to the key investment information sheet) are structured as follows. A 305a-organization instigates a claim for declaratory judgment that the project owner or CSP acted tortiously towards the group of clients or investors, thus causing financial losses. As already mentioned, the claim has to be capable of being dealt with in a 'bundled' way. The court will abstract from any individual circumstances, and rule on the legal relationship between the defendant and the constituency as a group.

17.41   If the court rules that the defendant (eg the project owner, or the CSP) acted tortiously towards the group of investors, and this judgment is no longer subject to appeal, the defendant and the claimant organization will seek a settlement out of court. A settlement concerns either the constituency of the 305a-organization (partial settlement) or the entire group of persons equally affected by the same tortious behaviour and suffering similar losses (worldwide settlement). In the latter case, the 305a-organization and the defendant may jointly request the Amsterdam Court of Appeal to declare the settlement binding upon the entire group, except for those who opted out of it within the time limit set by the Court of Appeal.

3. Collective Damage Claims

17.42   Alongside the possibility to seek declaratory relief through a collective action, the Dutch lawmaker has introduced a new collective action regime, as of 1 January 2020. The most notable innovation of the WAMCA is the possibility for 305a-organizations to claim damages collectively, rather than only seeking a declaratory judgment and then seeking an out-of-court settlement.

A. Stages in the New Collective Action Regime
17.43   The new Dutch collective action procedure consists of the following steps:

(1) *Invitation to consult the defendant:*[79] The 305a-organization is under a duty to make sufficient efforts to achieve its claims by entering into consultations with the defendant. In any case, a time limit of two weeks after receipt by the defendant of a

---

[79]   BW, Art 3:305a(3)(c).

request for consultation, stating the alleged claim against the defendant, is sufficient for this purpose.

(2) *Writ of summons:*[80] The writ of summons must contain the following: (a) a description of the event or events to which the collective claim relates; (b) a description of the persons whose interests the collective claim aims to protect; (c) a description of the extent to which the questions of fact and of law to be answered are shared; (d) a description of the way in which the cause of action requirements of Article 3:305a BW are met; (e) information that enables the court to appoint an exclusive representative for this collective claim, in the event that other collective claims for the same event are instituted.

(3) *Registration and time limit:* A 305a-organization submits the writ of summons at the central register for class actions.[81] Thereafter, a time limit of three months starts; the court may extend this time limit with a maximum of three months.[82] Other 305a-organizations wishing to instigate a collective claim for the same event or events as those concerned in the first submitted claim involving similar questions of fact and of law have to submit their writs of summons within the time limit of three months.[83]

(4) *Admissibility test:* The court will test each registered 305a-organization on the following: (a) whether the organization fulfils its admissibility conditions under Article 3:305a BW; (b) whether the organization has been able to show that its collective claim is a more efficient and more effective way instead of dealing with the individual claims; and (c) whether it is summarily apparent that the collective damage claim is unfounded.[84] At this stage, the defendant can limit its defences to the aforementioned issues.

(5) *Appointment of the exclusive representative/limitation of group and claim:* The court appoints the exclusive representative for this collective claim.[85] It can also appoint more than one exclusive representative, if the respective constituencies are too dissimilar to be represented by a single party. Furthermore, the court will also determine (a) the exact content of the collective claim and (b) the group of persons in whose interest the exclusive representative will act.[86]

(6) *Individual opt-out (minimum one month):* Individual members of the group have a possibility to opt out from this collective action within a one-month period after the appointment of the exclusive representative and the determination of the exact content of the collective claim and the group.[87]

(7) *Negotiating a settlement:* If the claimant organization and the defendant reach a collective settlement in the sense of Article 7:907(2) BW, a second opt-out possibility exists.[88] In case the parties do not reach a settlement, the exclusive representative

---

[80] The conditions for the write of summons can be found in Art 1018c(1) of the Dutch Code of Civil Procedure.

[81] <https://www.rechtspraak.nl/Registers/centraal-register-voor-collectieve-vorderingen>.

[82] Dutch Code of Civil Procedure, Art 1018c(3); other organization may register at the court on the basis of Art 1018d Dutch Code of Civil Procedure.

[83] Dutch Code of Civil Procedure, art 1019d(2).

[84] Parliamentary Papers II 2016/17, 34608, 3, p 46. The purpose of Art 1018(5)(c) Dutch Code of Civil Procedure is to enable the court to dismiss, in exceptional circumstances, unfounded claims before the stage at which the substantive claim is being heard.

[85] Dutch Code of Civil Procedure, Art 1018e(1).

[86] Dutch Code of Civil Procedure, Art 1018e(2).

[87] Dutch Code of Civil Procedure, Art 1018f.

[88] Dutch Code of Civil Procedure, Art 1018h(5) and Art 1018f(1).

may add to the grounds of the claim. The defendant may of course also add to its defences.[89]

(8) *Substantive hearing*: The court may order the parties to submit their settlement proposals.[90]

(9) *Judgment*: The court will determine the collective damage scheme.[91]

(10) *Announcement*: The members of each constituency of the 305a-organizations will be informed about the aforementioned judgment.[92] On the basis of Article 1018j(1) Dutch Code of Civil Procedure, the defendant has to make this announcement, unless otherwise decided by the court. In addition to this, an announcement of the judgment shall be made as soon as possible in one or more newspapers designated by the court. This announcement shall give a brief description of the collective claim settlement, in particular as to the way in which compensation can be obtained from the defendant or how the collective claim settlement can otherwise be invoked and, if the collective claim settlement so determines, the time limit within which a claim to such settlement should be made.

In most collective settlement agreements, a newly instituted foundation ('settlement foundation') will be involved. The victims entitled to compensation will file their claim with this foundation, on the basis of the judicial decision on the collective damage scheme. In case of disputes between these claimants and the settlement foundation, the scheme will provide for alternative dispute settlement. The WAMCA does not provide for any judicial involvement with the execution of the damage scheme.

B. Extra Requirements for all 305a-organizations

17.44 The WAMCA imposes extra requirements for all 305a-organizations. Nevertheless, the court may declare a legal person to have a cause of action without these requirements having to be satisfied, where the legal action is instituted with a non-commercial objective and a very limited financial interest, or where the nature of the claim of the legal person or of the persons whose interests the legal action aims to protect, gives reason thereto. In those cases, the legal action cannot result in monetary compensation.[93]

17.45 On pain of inadmissibility of the claim, 305a-organizations have to be sufficiently representative, both in view of its constituency, and the value of the claims represented. Furthermore, 305a-organizations need to fulfil the following requirements of having (a) a supervisory body; (b) appropriate and effective mechanisms for participation or representation in decision-making by persons whose interests are the subject of the legal action; (c) sufficient resources to bear the costs of instituting a legal action, which ensures sufficient control over the legal action; (d) a publicly accessible Internet page, on which important information concerning governance and financing arrangements is available; and (e) sufficient experience and expertise to commence and conduct the legal action.[94]

---

[89] Dutch Code of Civil Procedure, Art 1018g.
[90] Dutch Code of Civil Procedure, Art 1018i(1).
[91] Dutch Code of Civil Procedure, Art 1018i(2).
[92] Dutch Code of Civil Procedure, Art 1018j.
[93] BW, Art 3:305a(6).
[94] BW, Art 3:305a(2).

The requirement that the 305a-organization has to have sufficient control over the legal ac-   **17.46**
tion is a reaction by the legislator to developments in the mass litigation funding market.[95]
The legislator deems it important to stress that the 305a-organization is entitled to determine—after consulting its constituency, but not its funder—the procedural strategy of the
collective claim proceedings.[96] The 305a-organization decides on any settlement presented
by the defendant and chooses whether judicial decisions are appealed.[97] The court tests *ex
officio* the degree of influence and control the funder has on the basis of the financing arrangement with the 305a-organization.

The legislator recognizes the positive aspects of litigation funding in collective redress pro-   **17.47**
ceedings, in terms of enhancement of access to justice for victims. However, the legislator
seeks to prevent any excessive litigation. Furthermore, it deems that an excessive fee for the
funder would lead to a situation where compensation for victims becomes secondary.[98] It
is left to the courts to determine the right balance;[99] the aforementioned admissibility requirement provides the competent court with the tools to test whether the third-party litigation funder submits excessive costs and/or is not transparent about its cost structure. In
case the court gets signals of abusive commercial behaviour, it may appoint another 305a-
organization as exclusive representative, in order to redress this situation.[100] The court may
order the submission of the financing arrangement with the funder, so as to perform the
admissibility test.

A 305a-organization shall only have a cause of action if its directors involved in the forma-   **17.48**
tion of the legal person and their successors do not have a profit motive that is achieved directly or indirectly through the legal person.[101]

C. Connection with the Jurisdiction of Dutch Courts

The new Dutch collective redress procedure is limited to cases that have a sufficiently close   **17.49**
connection to the jurisdiction of the Dutch courts. This requirement is fulfilled when:

(1) the 305a-organization person makes it sufficiently plausible that the majority of the
persons whose interests the legal action aims to protect have their habitual residence
in the Netherlands; or
(2) the party against whom the legal action is instituted is domiciled in the Netherlands,
and additional circumstances suggest that there is a sufficiently close connection to
the jurisdiction of the Dutch courts; and
(3) the event or events to which the legal action relates took place in the Netherlands.[102]

---

[95] BW, Art 3:305a(2)(c). See Parliamentary Papers II 2017/18, 34608, 10.
[96] Parliamentary Papers II 2017/18, 34608, 6, 11, 26; Parliamentary Papers II 2017/18, 34608, 9, 2; 9; 10.
[97] See I Tillema, 'Exclusieve en concurrerende belangenbehartigers: balanceren op glad ijs?' (2018) Ars
Aequi 0476.
[98] Parliamentary Papers II 2016/17, 34608, 3, 11. The courts has been lenient so far. Success fees between 9
and 20 per cent have been judged no unreasonable. See *VEB/Steinhoff* [26 September 2018] Amsterdam District
Court, ECLI:NL:RBAMS:2018:6840 [4.21] and *PAL/Aegon* [4 February 2020] The Hague Court of Appeal,
ECLI:NL:GHDHA:2020:102 [27].
[99] *Stichting Petrobras Compensation Foundation/*Petrobras [29 January 2020] Rotterdam District Court,
ECLI:NL:RBROT:2020:614 [5.15].
[100] Parliamentary Papers II 2017/18, 34608, 6, p 25.
[101] BW, Art 3:305a(3)(a).
[102] BW, Art 3:305a(3)(b).

D. Opt-out Structure

17.50   As already mentioned, the WAMCA collective action is an opt-out scheme. The parties that wish not to be bound by it may submit a written declaration to this effect to the court registry. This declaration must be submitted within one month after the appointment of the exclusive representative.[103] If the number of opt-outs no longer justifies the continuation of the collective action, the court may order the end of this procedure.[104] As already mentioned, a second opt-out possibility exists, after the claimant organization and the defendant have reached a collective settlement agreement during the procedure.[105]

4. Binding Collective Settlements

17.51   The Dutch legislator expects the parties in collective damage proceedings to often reach a settlement agreement, so that the court will not issue a damage scheme. In order to facilitate collective settlements, the legislator adopted in 2005 the *Wet collectieve afwikkeling massaschade* (WCAM). Under this law, the 305a-organization and the defendant can have their settlement agreement declared binding on the entire group, so as to achieve finality of litigation for all similar claims.

17.52   The Amsterdam Court of Appeal has the exclusive jurisdiction to rule on such a request.[106] The individual members of the group may submit an opt-out declaration to the person designated in the WCAM settlement agreement.[107]

17.53   The court may decline the request on a limited number of grounds.[108] One of these grounds is the reasonableness of the compensation. The court should play an active role,[109] assessing reasonableness in light of the volume of losses, the ease and promptness with which compensation may be obtained, and the possible causes of the loss. The court, however marginally, will need to evaluate liability, and the legal relationship between the defendant and its alleged victims.[110] The court will take into account the costs and expected degree of litigation success, should the case be heard by a court in adversarial proceedings.

---

[103] Dutch Code of Civil Procedure, Art 1018f.
[104] Dutch Code of Civil Procedure, Art 1018f (1) last sentence.
[105] Dutch Code of Civil Procedure, Art 1018h(5) and Art 1018f(1).
[106] Dutch Code of Civil Procedure, Art 1013(3).
[107] BW, Art 7:908(2) and Art 7:907(2)(f).
[108] BW, Art 7:907(3).
[109] Parliamentary Papers I 2004/05, 29414, C, p 6.
[110] Parliamentary Papers II 2003/04, 29414, 3, p 13.

The Amsterdam Court of Appeal has so far declared eight WCAM settlement agree-   **17.54**
ments binding, specifically *Des*,[111] *Dexia* (Duisenberg settlement),[112] *Vie d'Or*,[113] *Shell*,[114]
Vedior,[115] *Converium*,[116] *DSB*,[117] and *Fortis*.[118]

5. Claimcode 2019

The Claimcode 2019 is a self-regulatory instrument made by parties involved in collective   **17.55**
redress in the Netherlands. In legal practice, there has been uncertainty as to the status of
the predecessor of this instrument, the Claimcode 2011. In case law, it has been established
that the Claimcode has an indirect legal basis.[119]

The Claimcode 2019 is applicable to associations and foundations instigating or involved in   **17.56**
collective proceedings on the basis of Article 3:305a BW, or in collective settlement agreements, or submitting a WCAM request. While an exhaustive overview of the principles
enshrined in the Claimcode falls beyond the scope of this chapter, it is important to highlight that this instrument sets forth a number of important principles for organizations engaging in collective redress procedures in the Netherlands. The Claimcode requires *inter
alia* transparency as to the governance structure of the organizations, the safeguard of the
interests that the organization is supposed to pursue, transparency as to the role of third-
party funders, avoidance of conflict of interests, as well as other provisions aimed to ensure
that the organization operates in line with its stated purposes.

VI. Conclusion

The comparative analysis carried out in this chapter demonstrates that the European land-   **17.57**
scape of collective redress is far from being harmonized. Under the collective action regimes set forth in the law of some EU Member States (such as the French *action de groupe*

---

[111] *DES settlement* [1 June 2006] Amsterdam Court of Appeal, ECLI:NL:GHAMS:2006:AX6440-.
[112] *Duisenberg settlement* [25 January 2007] Amsterdam Court of Appeal, ECLI:NL:GHAMS:2007:AZ7033, *JOR* 2007/71 annotated by Leijten.
[113] *Vie d'Or settlement* [29 April 2009] Amsterdam Court of Appeal, ECLI:NL:GHAMS:2009:BI2717, *JOR* 2009/ 196 annotated by Leijten in *JOR* 2009/197, *NJF* 2009/247.
[114] *Shell* settlement [29 May 2009] Amsterdam Court of Appeal, ECLI:NL:GHAMS:2009:BI5744, *JOR* 2009/197 annotated by Leijten.
[115] *Vedior settlement* [15 July 2009] Amsterdam Court of Appeal, ECLI:NL:GHAMS:2009:BJ2691, *JOR* 2009/ 325 annotated by Pijls, *Ondernemingsrecht* 2009/162 annotated by De Jong ().
[116] *Converium settlement* [17 January 2012] Amsterdam Court of Appeal, ECLI:NL:GHAMS:2012:BV1026, *JOR* 2012/51 annotated by De Jong.
[117] *DSB settlement* [4 November 2014] Amsterdam Court of Appeal, ECLI:NL:GHAMS:2014:4560, *JOR* 2015/ 10 annotated by Tzankova.
[118] *Fortis settlement* [13 July 2018] Amsterdam Court of Appeal, ECLI:NL:GHAMS:2018:2422.
[119] See J van Mourik and E Bauw, *De Claimcode van 2011 tot 2019* (BJu 2019) 52.

and the Dutch WAMCA), organizations may bring a collective action, claiming compensation for losses incurred by crowdfunding investors. Under other national regimes (such as the German KapMuG), it is up to the individual investors to initiate a claim for damages; however, if multiple similar cases are brought, model case proceedings can be started. It remains to be seen whether this lack of harmonization at the procedural level will hinder the uniform enforcement of the Crowdfunding Regulation across the EU. As already mentioned, crowdfunding-related cases are often well-suited for collective dispute resolution. Yet, depending on which national courts will have jurisdiction to hear the case (as illustrated in Chapter 16), the availability and distinctive character of collective procedures may vary drastically.

17.58   A further layer of problems concerns the tension between the collective nature of these proceedings (where available), and the 'bilateral' assumptions implicitly underlying the substantive law invoked by the claimants. This tension is particularly visible in the case of the calculation of damages. In a collective procedure such as the Dutch WAMCA or the French *action de groupe*, the court is expected to calculate the damages for the whole group of affected crowdfunding investors, whenever the litigating parties fail to reach a collective settlement agreement. However, the 'traditional' rules on liability and damage valuation are not designed for this purpose, since the lawmaker originally envisaged their application in a two-party litigation, rather than in a mass case.[120] Thus, when the proceedings involve an abstract of a group of persons (eg a group of crowdfunding investors) vis-à-vis the liable party (eg the project owner, or the CSP),[121] the calculation of damages may raise questions that cannot be resolved by reference to 'traditional' liability laws. It will be interesting to see how national courts (eg in the Netherlands and France) will deal with this inherent tension, when establishing a collective damage scheme. Crowdfunding-related disputes may be one of the sectors where the question arises in the future.

17.59   Finally, this chapter has illustrated how some collective redress procedures (such as the Dutch WAMCA) require the appointment of an exclusive representative, which will represent the interests of all constituencies of all representative organizations. In a crowdfunding-related case, such an exclusive representative would play a pivotal role in the enforcement of the Crowdfunding Regulation. In practice, however, this role entails responsibilities that may deter the relevant organization from agreeing to perform this task. For this reason, it remains to be seen whether the requirements set forth by national law for the exclusive representative in a collective procedure may end up hindering the use of these procedures as an enforcement tool for the Crowdfunding Regulation.

---

[120] Dutch Code of Civil Procedure, Art 1018i(2). Neither the French Civil Code nor the Consumer Code provides for any special provision of substantive liability law for collective actions.

[121] See T Hartlief, 'Massaschaderecht in ontwikkeling' [2019] Tijdschrijft voor Privaatrecht 464–65; M Klein Meuleman, 'Schadeberekening in collectieve acties' and Ronny de Jong, 'Regressieanalyse in het (massa) schadevergoedingsrecht' in M Hebly and others (eds), *Schaalvergroting in het privaatrecht* (BJu 2019) 145.

Index